D1075025

Ford:

THE DUST AND
THE GLORY

A RACING HISTORY
VOLUME 1 (1901–1967)

THE DUST AND
THE GLORY

A RACING HISTORY
VOLUME 1 (1901–1967)

LEO LEVINE

INTERNATIONAL ®

Society of Automotive Engineers, Inc.
Warrendale, Pa.

Library of Congress Cataloging-in-Publication Data

Levine, Leo.
Ford, the dust and the glory: a racing history / Leo Levine.
  p. cm.
Vol. 1 was originally published: New York : Macmillan, 1968.
Includes bibliographical references and index.
Contents: v. 1. 1901-1967
ISBN 0-7680-0663-5
  1. Ford Motor Company. 2. Automobile racing--History.
3. Ford automobile--History. I. Title.

GV1029.15 .L49 2001
796.72--dc21   00-059522

Society of Automotive Engineers, Inc.
400 Commonwealth Drive
Warrendale, PA 15096-0001 U.S.A.
Phone: (724)776-4841
Fax: (724)776-5760
E-mail: publications@sae.org
http://www.sae.org

ISBN 0-7680-0663-5

SAE Order No. R-292

DEDICATION

For S.R., S.A. and N.R.

And for Rem, Lump, Cisco,
Ak, Honker, Termite,
Ralph, Dan, Shel and Greasy,
who were so much a part of it.

AUTHOR'S NOTE

IT IS NOT THE SPORT ITSELF, but the hyper-organization and the ceaseless recording of the facts *and* the trivia, that have made baseball this country's alleged national game. That is the trouble with automobile racing: Although more Americans pay to watch it than any other non-parimutuel sport, nobody ever really organized it, and few persons ever wrote it down. What follows is an attempt to record some of it—some of the facts, and some of the people.

It is told from the standpoint of the Ford Motor Company, because no other major American manufacturer has been so involved with the sport. In many respects, the competition history of Ford parallels the progress of auto racing in this country. Ford may be a profit-oriented concern, but racing is a sport. During the planning, building and development of the cars it is a business, regardless of whether the constructor is a great industrial enterprise or some backyard mechanic. The word money is mentioned perhaps more than any other, because you can't build cars without it and you always build to the limit of your budget, if not beyond. But once the starting flag drops, it is a sport, pure and simple. There are some who are in it only for the money. They are seldom winners. It is akin to the difference between a racing driver and the driver of a racing car.

Following is a list of persons who were of aid in the research for this book, and their help is greatly appreciated. In addition, I would like to express my particular thanks to six persons:

Ken Purdy, the outstanding American writer on automotive subjects, who was a constant source of advice and encouragement.

Chris Economaki, the editor of *National Speed Sport News,* who devoted much time to reading the manuscript for accuracy.

Federico Kirbus, the auto editor of *La Prensa*, in Buenos Aires, who did all the South American research.

Al Bloemker, the public relations director of the Indianapolis Motor Speedway, who was helpful not only for his research assistance, but for the material in his two books, *500 Miles to Go,* and *Gentlemen, Start Your Engines.*

Griff Borgeson, the leading racing historian in the United States, who provided a mine of information in his book, *The Golden Age of the American Racing Car.*

And my wife, who did a lot of typing and put up with an enormous amount of nail-biting and other forms of procrastination.

Hartsdale, N.Y.
February, 1968

LEO LEVINE

ACKNOWLEDGMENTS

Bob Anderson • Mario Andretti • Zora Arkus-Duntov • Klaus Arning • Chris Baldwin • Henry Banks • Chuck Barnes • Dean Batchelor • Gary Beard • Jack Beckley • Leo Beebe • Logan Bentley • Bill Benton • Owen Bombard • Bob Bondurant • Eric Broadley • Ray Brock • Bill Burnett • Jep Cadou, Jr. • Harry Calton • Ken Caskey • Austin Clark • Barney Clark • Jimmy Clark* • Don Coleman • Harley Copp • John Cowley • Chuck Daigh • Don Davidson • Dave Davis • George DeAngelis • Howard DeHart • Bradley Dennis • Pete DePaolo • Dick Dolan • Mark Donohue • Al Dowd • Maurice Dreyfus • Rene Dreyfus • Danny Eames • Joe Eastman • Hank Edmunds • Joe Epton • Al Esper • Dave Evans • Norm Faustyn • Bill Fleming • Fonty Flock • Jim Foster • Chuck Foulger • Jack Fox • A. J. Foyt • W. C. France • W.H.G. France • Don Frey • John Gager • Frank Gardner • Don Garlits • Bill Gay • Ray Geddes • Richie Ginther • Ken Gooding • Leo Goossen •Charlie Gray • Bob Greenberg • Hank Gregorich • Dan Gurney • Jim Hall • Bob Harnar • Jack Hart • Ed Hayes • Walter Hayes • Fran Hernandez • Howard Hill • Phil Hill • John Holman • Randy Holman • Zona Holman • Lindsey Hopkins • Vern Houle • Ron Householder • Bill Humphrey • Jim Hunter • Lee Iacocca • Joe Ihnacik • Bill Innes • Trant Jarman • Danny Jones • Parnelli Jones • Benny Kahn • Connie Kalitta • Dick Kimball • Karl Kizer • Al Krause • Frank Kulick • Joe Lane • Houston Lawing • Robert G. Layton • Hank Lennox • Lujie Lesovsky • Joe Linman • Joe Littlejohn • Fred Lorenzen • Karl Ludvigsen • Roy Lunn • Joe MacKay • Walter Mackenzie • Joe Macura • Alan Mann • Johnny Mantz • Scott Matchan • Denise McCluggage • Roger McCluskey • Bruce McLaren • Henry McLemore* • George Merwin • Al Michaelian • Ken Miles* • Ak Miller • John Millis • Wayne Mills • Bob Montgomery • Ralph Moody • Bud Moore • Chase Morsey • Albert Moseley • Alfred Moss • Stirling Moss • Chuck Mountain • Max Muhleman • Charlie Mulcahy • Moon Mullins • Bob Myers • Duke Nalon • John Oliveau • Cotton Owens • Raymond Parks • Wally Parks • Jacque Passino • Homer Perry • Sam Petok • Bob Pope • Paul Preuss • George Rand • Phil Remington • Al Rominsky • Peter Revson • Doris Roberts • Monty Roberts • Lloyd Ruby • Dick Ruddell • Troy Ruttman • Bob Sall • Hank Schoolfield • Skip Scott • Gus Scussel • Win Sears • Edouard Seidler • Carroll Shelby • Carroll Smith • Jim Smith • Steve Smith • Bill Speedie • Jim Stickford • Bill Stroppe • Don Sullivan • Al Swenson • Gene Tarnowsky • Bob Tasca • George Taylor • Henry Todd • Al Turner • Curtis Turner • Bill Tuthill • Dick Van der Feen • C. W. Van Ranst • Bud Volberding • Red Vogt • Don Wahrman • John Wanderer • Rodger Ward • Gayle Warnock • T. Taylor Warren • Ed Winfield • Pete Wiseman • John Wyer • Frank Wylie • Brock Yates • Smokey Yunick • Frank Zimmerman

*Deceased.

CONTENTS

Part I. (1901–1913)
Henry Goes Racing
Sales Promotion, World Records and Prosperity

Part II. (1918–1941)
From the Backyard to the Brickyard
After Paper Routes ... Hot Rods and the Mojave Desert

Part III. (1940–1959)

Stocks Are Up!

Darlington and Daytona Become Important

Part IV. (The 1960s)

Advance to the Rear

**Ford Broadens Outlook: Lotus and the 500, Cobras,
Rallies and Dragsters**

Part V. (The 1960s)
Grapes Instead of Wrath
Victories and Records at Le Mans

Part 1

(1901–1913)

Henry Goes Racing

Sales Promotion, World Records, and Prosperity

1

THE BEGINNING

IN THE FALL OF 1901 the auto industry was in its infancy and Henry Ford was approaching middle age. He was 38, and although his reputation as a mechanic was a good one in local circles, he was still far from his dream of becoming an automobile manufacturer. In his youth he was a farmer in Dearborn; he repaired watches and machinery in his spare time, operated a sawmill, fixed engines and thought about his own horseless carriage. By Christmas of 1893 he had built his first internal combustion engine, and in 1896 he constructed his first car. In 1899, after further experiments on his own, he became superintendent of the Detroit Automobile Company.

By January of 1901 they were out of business and all Henry had left were his plans, plus a somewhat wider circle of acquaintances. But fulfillment demanded money, and after the first failure money would be forthcoming only when Ford could prove his ideas were better than anyone else's. So in the spring of the year he turned to racing, the quickest and most public way of showing which product was best. The success of what eventually turned into the Ford Motor Company, and its growth into the second largest automaker, with more than 365,000 employees and factories throughout the world, stems from this decision.

Henry won his race and got his money.

In those times practically every competitive event brought with it real technical improvements to the cars that participated, and every victory could be measured by an increase in sales, if the winning make were one produced in series. The leading families had taken to the automobile, and with their approval this new machine became The Thing To Own. At the turn of the century it was a question of keeping up with the Vanderbilts and the Whitneys rather than with the Joneses.

The most practical way to find out what other constructors were doing was to look at pictures. In addition Ford traveled to New York and Buffalo and saw for himself what was happening in other cities. What he then came up with was one of the earliest examples of a favorable power-to-weight ratio. This first machine (not the famous Quadricycle of 1896) had a two-cylinder opposed engine with a 7-inch bore, a 7-inch stroke and what they estimated to be 26 horsepower out of 540 cubic inches. The car weighed approximately 1,600 pounds, and although no weights of the competition are available, photographs show Ford's vehicle was obviously lighter and lower. More than 60 years later the company bearing his name showed you could still use a relatively low-revving, relatively low specific-output engine in a race car and win with it, if you made the engine big enough.

Although it was the furthest thing from anyone's mind when Ford finished 1-2-3 at Le Mans in 1966, the 427-cubic-inch V8s they used—modified production engines designed for durability—were direct descendants of Henry's conception.

The day was October 10, 1901 and the place was Grosse Pointe, today an exclusive residential area but then the location of the Detroit Driving Club's one-mile oval. There were to be four races, with the feature scheduled for 25 miles and paying $1,000 to the winner, plus a cut-glass bowl. Even before the race, the money, plus the bowl, were considered the property of Alexander Winton, a Scottish immigrant who was building cars in Cleveland and who was the best driver of the season. He was an odds-on choice to win and his sales manager, in an attempt at a little personal public relations, had gone to the length of getting together with the promoters before the trophy was purchased. He wanted to make sure it was something the boss would like.

Ford's entry was probably the principal work of Oliver Barthel, an engineer who was with him in the early days as the leading technical man of the tiny organization. For that matter Barthel also had a hand in the construction of the 999 and the Arrow, the latter (in all except detail work) being the twin of the 999. But there is also little doubt that Ford was the instigator, the moving force, behind the projects. Without his basic idea it would not have happened. Barthel built well enough to win—that much is obvious; but he may also have built the world's fastest automobile. In July of 1901, while testing, he claimed to have reached 72 mph on a road outside Detroit. There was no official timing to support this claim, but it is interesting to note the record at the time was only 65.79 mph, set by Belgian Camille Jenatzy in an electric car, the famous "Jamais Contente," in 1899. The next time Henry took one of his vehicles out to see how fast it would go, he made sure there were stopwatches present—and newspapermen.

Because the first three events on the card took longer than expected, the Grosse Pointe feature was cut from 25 miles to 10. Then, because of mechanical troubles, one of the three entrants withdrew and only Winton and Ford were left. Winton had set a local record earlier in the day, and he was expected to have little trouble with this mechanic turned race driver. Ford first took a two-lap warm-up run with Tom Cooper, a well-known professional bike rider of the day, as the passenger. According to news paper accounts Cooper did this in order to give advice on the condition of the track and on how to drive fast. Henry was more of a neophyte at this business than everyone thought. To the crowd, the sight of this almost unknown, inexperienced mechanic challenging the great Winton was an amusing one.

(Top) Henry Ford and Otto Barthel seated in Ford's first racing car, late summer 1901. (Inset) The cut-glass bowl, complete with cups, offered as a prize for Ford's first—and last— race. (Bottom) Ford, in the foreground, passes Alexander Winton at Grosse Pointe.

Winton took the lead at the start and after three miles was more than 300 yards in front, with Ford faster on the straights but having to shut off in the turns, despite riding mechanic Spider Huff leaning out of the car to help balance the machine. Then Ford started to cut down on Winton's lead, and as smoke started to pour from the Winton exhausts, Ford moved in front on the eighth lap. Winton managed to finish, but Ford won in 13:23.8—an average of 44.8 mph.

Henry had barely gotten out of the car when he announced his retirement, saying "Once is enough." He had proven himself right in two respects: His vehicle was fast, and more persons had learned the name Henry Ford in a shorter time than ever before.

It was the great step, not only from a promotional standpoint, but also from one of personal finances. Although Ford wasn't exactly destitute the $1,000 came in handy, as letters written by his wife show they were far from prosperity. In December, although still excited over the victory, Clara Ford realized the situation could be better. A letter of hers is one of the only personal reminiscences remaining:

> Henry has been covering himself with glory and dust.... I wish you could have seen him. Also heard the cheering when he passed Winton. The people went wild. One man threw his hat up and when it came down he stamped on it, he was so excited. Another man had to hit his wife on the head to keep her from going off the handle. She stood up in her seat ... screamed, 'I'd bet $50 on a Ford if I had it.' Enough of this automobile talk. We are keeping house again and are very glad to be alone. We have a very nice cozy little house. We did not build on account of Henry building the racer, he could not see to anything else. So we will have to put up with rented homes for a while longer.

From Henry's comments after the race it is obvious he saw his limitations and figured building cars was better than driving them. He was right: Clara didn't have to live in a rented house for too long.

When they finally moved into Fairlane, the famous Ford mansion, in 1915, one of the first pieces set into place was the 1901 trophy. It had a spot on a table in the main entrance hall, and as the years went past, less and less attention was paid to it. By the time Ford died in 1947 its significance was forgotten. Even his grandchildren didn't know, and when they went through the house picking out what they wanted to keep, no one chose the innocuous piece. It wound up being sold to the Parke-Bernet Galleries in New York, and was shipped along with thousands of other items, listed, as were many of the minor pieces, under the anonymity of "One lot ... bowls."

Months later, when Ford officials realized what they had lost, a man was dispatched to locate the bowl. But by then it was gone to a private customer. Today the only race trophy Henry Ford ever won holds apples, or oranges—if it is still in one piece.

The fame, the money and the cut-glass bowl were not the only important results of that October day. Cooper, who later went into partnership with Ford and who was the principal financier of the 999 and the Arrow, ran in an exhibition bicycle race between two of the automobile events. His opponent was Berna Eli Oldfield, the immortal Barney, the man who did more to popularize auto racing the early days than anyone else. Ford and Oldfield had their first meeting that afternoon.

Although in later years Oldfield was to drive such famous cars as the Winton Bullet, the Peerless Green Dragon, the Blitzen Benz and Harry Miller's Golden Submarine, Ford's car was the first. It was with 999—and with the duplicate Arrow—that Barney became famous, and it was with 999 that his name is most firmly linked. This was the first car he drove; he won his first race in it, set his first record in it and built his reputation behind its four enormous, gas-gulping, bellowing cylinders.

Years later, when both were old men, Ford is alleged to have said to Oldfield, "You made me and I made you."

Barney laughed and replied, "I did a damn sight better for you than you did for me."

In the winter of 1902 Ford was disenchanted with his latest group, this one known as the Henry Ford Company, and as the cold months dragged on he toyed with the idea of becoming a race promoter. Henri Fournier, a famous French driver of the time, had just set a record on New York's Coney Island Boulevard. His mark for the mile, set November 16, 1901, was 69.5 mph, and Ford thought he could build a car to run against Fournier's, and they could barnstorm around the country. A letter to his brother said:

> If I can bring Mr. Fournier into line there is a barrel of money in this business. It was his proposition and I don't see why he won't fall in line. If he don't I will challenge him untill [sic] I am black in the face … my company will kick about me following racing but they will get the advertising and I expect to make $ where I can't make ¢ at manufacturing.

Ford finally left the Henry Ford Company in March, 1902, to go racing. He took with him the incomplete plans for the race car and $900, and he got the firm to take his name off the letterhead. What happened to Henry Ford is common knowledge. The company went through various phases and eventually became the Cadillac Division of General Motors.

Ford, Cooper and a small staff started building their cars in May. The one called 999 was named after a New York Central locomotive that set what should have been the land speed record of the time during a run of the Empire State Express from New York to the Chicago World's Fair of 1893. It was clocked at 112.5 mph near Grimesville, N.Y., and this, in effect, meant all drivers of autos, through Arthur MacDonald in 1905, were being somewhat narrow-minded when they claimed the record for themselves. Fred Marriott was the man who finally beat the locomotive variety of 999 with a 1906 run of 127.66 mph at Ormond Beach, Fla., in the Stanley Steamer.

(Top) Ford, Spider Huff and the 1901 race car, with Huff crouching in his accustomed position. (Inset) Four decades later—Ford with a replica of his first winner with a young mechanic taking the place of the long-departed Huff. (Bottom) An artist's impression of Ford and Huff during their great day at Grosse Pointe.

What were 999 and Arrow like? *The Automobile,* one of the leading publications of the time, described it best in August of 1903, when Oldfield was driving one of the cars at the Empire City race track in Yonkers, N.Y. (now Yonkers Raceway):

"Technically, the 'Red Devil'. . . is an automobile, practically it is an engine on four wheels, a machine in which brute strength and a disregard for nearly all the essentials of modern automobile construction are embodied."

If the 1901 race car was the first hot rod, then these were the first slingshot rails, in best hot-rod tradition. While other constructors took the trouble to at least put a hood over the engine, Ford did not bother. These primitive monsters, with their enormous, coughing four-cylinder engines tucked in between wooden rails, were perhaps the most stripped-down competition cars of all time.

They were not the best race cars, they were not the most sophisticated race cars, they were not even very good race cars. But they had three things going for them:

The first was Oldfield's courage and remarkable touch in driving them on oval tracks.

The second was their creator's display of nerve the day he bounced one of them across a frozen lake to capture the land speed record. Although his mark lasted less than three weeks, the legend of 999 had gotten a good running start—and it wasn't even 999 that set the record. It was the other car, the Arrow.

And they were fast.

The in-line engines, an en-bloc casting, had a bore of 7¼ inches and a stroke of 7 inches, giving a total displacement of 1155.3 cubic inches. There was no valve cover, and the huge crankshaft also rode in the open, meaning whoever drove would be covered with oil in short order. There was not even a steering wheel, steering being managed by a two-handed tiller. This was an iron bar, pivoting in the middle, and Henry felt it was useful in more ways than one. The system was questioned by Walter Baker, creator of the Baker Torpedo, an electric car which had run slightly better than 70 mph the year before on Staten Island.

"When the machine is making high speed," Ford told him, "and for any reason the operator cannot tell at the instant, because of the dust or other reasons, whether he is going perfectly straight, he can look at this steering handle. If it is set straight across the machine he is all right and running straight."

Henry didn't say what to do if the handle was not straight and the driver couldn't see.

There are no accurate records of the early history of the cars, but one thing is clear: when Henry took one on its first test run in September, it was a flop and Ford unloaded the two vehicles on Cooper. The latter took them to Toledo, Ohio, and there he and Huff worked to make them raceworthy while Oldfield came in from Salt Lake City. "He had never driven a motor car before," Ford said years afterward, "but he liked the idea of trying it. He said he would try anything once."

At the end of October the cars were back in Detroit, the 999 painted yellow, the Arrow painted red. Oldfield showed up, and they towed the car to Grosse Pointe. The car was pulled to the race site by horses, which thus became the first race vehicle transporter, pulling what would eventually replace them as the primary means of transportation.

Barney got in the driver's seat, Huff crouched behind him after a few words of instruction, and they went for a ride. When they came in Huff said, "Take her out again, you can get more speed out of her than Cooper or I." A racing driver was born.

Getting more speed out of "her" was a problem. Behind the giant, grease-spewing engine was a 230-pound flywheel, connected to the driveshaft by means of a wooden-block clutch. At the other end of the shaft there was no differential, merely a stone-age crown wheel and pinion arrangement to send the power to the rear wheels; it was lubricated with grinding compound. There were no universal joints anywhere in the setup, all of it being bolted to the wooden frame, and to make things even more interesting there was no rear suspension. The driver's feet were only a few inches from the exposed flywheel, and it was a rather grim proposition. It would seem the reason Oldfield went so fast right from the start was that he didn't know enough about the potential dangers to let them worry him.

This race, held October 25, 1902, was another five-miler, and Winton was again the leader of the opposition. Barney won easily, with his giant rail emitting a low-pitched roar that scarcely let up as he slid through the corners. Winton was the only driver who could even stay close, and when his car started to misfire he dropped out after four miles. That was the second time Winton's mechanical misfortunes helped Ford on the road to success.

Oldfield's time was 5:28.0, a record for a five-mile race on a one-mile closed course. Before he was through with the car, he would become the first man to lap a one-mile oval in less than a minute, and would become known from one end of the country to the other.

The vehicle that Oldfield drove that autumn day at Grosse Pointe was the one daubed yellow and dubbed 999. It later turned out to be the slower of the two, and the probable reason for this was the difference in the intake manifolds. The 999's manifold had several right angle turns, that of the Arrow had only gentle bends, making it easier for the fuel and air to reach the cylinders. This is the easiest way to identify them in photos.

Later Oldfield drove the other car, but the terminology got mixed up. At times it was called the "Red Devil," and Barney played the role by wearing a red vest, and at times it was called 999. But it was really the Arrow.

Where did he drive it? In 1903, once the snow left the ground, he and Cooper were on tour. He set a one-lap record at Empire City in Yonkers at the beginning of June, then toward the end of the month finally got below the magic minute at the Indianapolis Fairgrounds. A few weeks later, in Columbus, Ohio, he set one-mile, five-mile and 10-mile records in the car (by now called the "Red Devil" almost all the time), then chopped his record to 55.8 seconds at Yonkers in August. Cooper was in the hospital at this stage, but Barney, complete with his inimitable style, was swinging. They would wheel the car out on the track, fuss with the engine to impress the farmers lining the rail and then put on an exhibition run. The timekeepers (paid by Oldfield) would announce some stupendous clocking, and the county fair crowds would gasp in amazement. Then would come the race, Barney in one car, Cooper or Harley Cunningham in the other.

Barney won, of course. Sometimes, if they were running the thing in three heats, he would lose the second one to give the rubes an extra thrill. Racing has never seen another showman like him, and it has seen few faster drivers. In 1903 he gave Ford its first single-seat national championship, and its last until Mario Andretti won the USAC title in 1965.

But Barney was also a businessman, and when Winton came up with a faster car late that summer, Oldfield left Cooper. There is no accurate record of how many races he drove with 999/Arrow—the number was around 20. But that was enough. It made the legend almost complete, and Henry himself wrote the final chapter.

While Oldfield and Cooper were busy barnstorming, Ford was occupied with the company that was to give him eventual domination of the industry. It was incorporated June 16, 1903—although work went on before that date—and now he was building a four-cylinder model. Clara Ford was just as happy to see him sticking to business and keeping away from racing and Cooper. "He (Cooper) thinks too much of lowdown women to suit me," she wrote her brother.

Then Henry got his vehicle back in pieces. With Oldfield gone, the cars arrived at Milwaukee in September for the first series of races ever to be held at the Wisconsin Fairgrounds. Huff, who seems to have been employed by the cars rather than Ford or Cooper, was to drive one, and Frank Day was the pilot of the other. Day, 23, was the central figure in a melodrama that soon turned into a tragedy. The son of a wealthy insurance company official from Columbus, Ohio, he was driving against his parents' wishes, and this was his first major event. In most Hollywood scripts of this type Our Hero goes on to win the race and is then kissed by his beaming mother. When Day took the track on September 12 for a five-mile exhibition run in the Arrow he never made it past the fourth lap, going out of control and through the fence. Day, thrown off his high perch, was killed instantly, putting an end to the races. Day's body was returned to his parents; the remains of the Arrow were shipped back to Detroit.

2

THE ICE, GARIBALDI AND A MUSKRAT DINNER

BY THE FALL OF 1903 the Ford Motor Company was a going concern, but the idea of providing mass transportation had not taken hold. Ford's financial backers were convinced a more expensive vehicle would sell best, and the $2,000 Model B was then under development. Equipped with a four-cylinder, 318-cubic-inch engine, the vehicle had little to distinguish it from dozens of other makes.

Sales promotion was in order, but doing something notable with the Model B was a problem, as it was not a notable car. So Ford looked for another four-cylinder engine instead, and rescued Cooper's Arrow from the Detroit yards of the Pere Marquette Railroad, where it went after Milwaukee. Ford had his eye on the land speed record, which then stood at 77.13 mph, set by a French Mors in 1902. His limited talents as an oval-track driver, plus the car's limited roadholding ability when attempting to negotiate curves, dictated the straightaway attempt. But there was no smooth, flat straight in the area, at least not in the fall. They waited for the winter, when the ice on nearby Lake St. Clair would be thick enough.

The car was made ready, with numerous minor modifications and additions, and in early January it was taken to New Baltimore, Mich., which fronted on the Anchor Bay area of the lake. They stored the vehicle in the New Baltimore power-house when they weren't using it, and the entire party (including wife Clara, son Edsel and the ever-present Huff) stayed at a hotel on the lakefront. The hotel obviously had a piece of the action, as is shown by the billboards it scattered throughout Detroit.

By this time local newspapers were referring to the car as the "new" 999. Eventually the adjective was dropped, and through this the confusion arose as to which car did what. From a publicity standpoint, the myth-cum-legend was a much better one if Oldfield's first mount was also the land speed record vehicle, and this is the way it has come down through the years. Unfortunately, this was not the case.

In one of the early tests on the ice the flywheel tore loose and Ford was lucky to escape with his life. It is not clear when this manhole-cover-like affair spun free, but

(Top) Barney Oldfield at speed with the 999, photo believed to have been taken at Columbus, Ohio, in 1903. (Bottom) The Big Three, early-day version: Oldfield at the wheel, Ford and the 999 in the winter of 1903.

(Inset) Advertising racing successes is nothing new. Soon after Ford set his record, the accessory suppliers were buying space in the journals of the day. (Bottom) The team to beat: Oldfield and the 999, equipped at this stage of its life with an overhead camshaft (Columbus, Ohio, 1903).

*(Top) Ready to go: Ford with Huff hanging over the engine, at the start of their epic
journey on the ice of Lake St. Clair. (Bottom) Stopping for adjustments on the
cinder-strewn surface. It was all Huff could do to pry himself loose.*

A Wild Mile *by* Henry Ford

39 2-5 Seconds

On January 12, 1904, Henry Ford, Manager of the Ford Motor Company, Detroit, Mich., drove a mile on the ice of St. Clair Lake at the terrific speed of 91 1-3 miles an hour. Mr. Ford used in this drive the famous "999" Ford racer, equipped with

G&J TIRES

This record is official, having been sanctioned and officially timed. It replaces as the world's fastest mile for any class of machine the record of M. Angieres (46 seconds) made on the Dourdan course in France.

G & J TIRE COMPANY *Indianapolis, Ind.*

(Top) One of the few times Ford drove the original car was during an exhibition run at Grosse Pointe in 1903. At right is Harry Harkness in a Simplex. (Middle) More sponsors get on the bandwagon. (Bottom) One last time—Ford and the 999 on the proving grounds at Dearborn years later.

it could well have been on the day Ford was advertised to run. Henry was there on January 9, but the timers were not. There was still the deal with the hotel, however, so he went out and ran for the few hundred persons who had assembled. Eventually it was announced he achieved the advertised 36 seconds flat (100 mph), and the spectators went home satisfied—and cold. Then the AAA timers arrived, and on January 12 they went for the record. All the previous marks, held by Europeans, were set over a flying kilometer and the equivalent mile average had been worked out mathematically. The AAA, working with American measurements, put its timers one mile apart, three at one end and three at the other. There weren't enough watches on hand to station another three men at the end of the measured kilometer. The total length of the course was not four miles, as intended, but only three, scraped free of snow by local farmers and with at least part of it sprinkled with cinders. The first two miles were for getting up to speed, the time trap was the third mile, and then Henry was on his own. No one had worried about the run-out area.

The ride was a wild one, but it wasn't lonely. Huff, who was along during Ford's only race and who also taught Oldfield how to drive the monster, once again hung on to the side of the machine despite the high speeds and near-zero temperatures. That he managed to secure a foothold is unbelievable, but somehow he did, and he also operated the throttle. The ice was so bumpy, they found, Henry's foot kept bouncing off the gas pedal. Huff, it would seem, should be given credit for at least half the record.

When the time came to make their try they fired it up and took off, the wheels spinning as the lumbering machine fought for traction, then the loud blast of the engine leveled off as the car grew smaller in the distance. The noise echoed over the lake as they roared ahead, bumping up and down, slipping from side to side, without goggles, with only a rudimentary windshield, flying along into history.

At least two times Ford and Huff nicked the snowbanks on the sides of the course, kicking up clouds of white spray and narrowly averting tragedy. Then, after crossing the finish line, the situation became even more critical as they attempted to slow down. With only one primitive mechanical brake on the rear axle this was practically impossible, and they were headed right for the schooner "Garibaldi," which was locked in the ice. At the last moment Ford managed to spin out of the way and the world's fastest car wound up in a snowbank, still on its wheels.

The time was 39.4 seconds, the average speed was 91.37 mph. For the first time an American car held the record, beating not only the Mors mark but also Frenchman Arthur Duray's record of 84.73 mph (set in a Gobron-Brillie), about which Henry knew nothing.

Years later, Ford still remembered the run. "The ice seemed smooth enough," he said, "so smooth that if I had called off the trial we should have secured an immense amount of the wrong kind of advertising, but instead of being smooth, the ice was seamed with fissures which I knew were going to mean trouble the moment I got up speed. But there was nothing to do but go through with the trial, so

I let the old Arrow out. At every fissure the car leaped into the air. I never knew how it was coming down. When I wasn't in the air I was skidding, but somehow I stayed top side up and on the course."

Ford and Huff were white-faced when it was over, due partly to the cold and partly to their experience. But that was done now, and the party assembled at the Hotel Chesterfield for a victory dinner which featured muskrat as the main dish. Henry liked it; most of the others did not.

Ford's mark was certified by the AAA on January 21, after some discussion over whether the land speed record could be set on water, frozen or not. He was in New York during the AAA meeting, as the car was a feature of one of the company's Madison Square Garden auto show exhibits. While Ford went to New York, Oldfield headed for Ormond Beach, intent on breaking the record held by his ex-employer, and others dreamed of wilder stunts. One man approached Oldsmobile with a scheme to drive to the North Pole. At the time Admiral Peary had yet to arrive there on foot.

The Detroit *Journal*, reporting on the record run, had some interesting opinions. "The machine ... is more famous than its driver," the Journal said, and added "Ford is a mechanic and began to design automobiles several years ago, when the craze for them began. He is now the head of the Ford Motor Company...."

Later on, the machines were still better known than their maker, but better known is a relative term; the entire motorized world knew about Fords; only 99 percent knew about Henry.

Both the Arrow and 999, still Cooper's property at the time of the Lake St. Clair episode, were sold to W.H. (Billy) Pickens, one of the famous promoters of the early 1900s who staged a series of exhibition runs with them. Then, as the cars became outmoded, Pickens switched to promoting a group of 24-hour races in the East, and the Arrow and 999 were abandoned.

The Arrow eventually disappeared, but 999, or rather the wreck of it, was discovered in a West Coast junkyard around 1911. Oldfield heard of it; he took one look at the mess and decided against buying it. Dana Burke of Santa Monica, Calif., purchased what was left and started the restoration, then sold it to W.L. (Billy) Hughson, the first Ford Dealer in San Francisco. Hughson completed the car, and eventually it found its way to the Ford Museum in Dearborn, where today it occupies a place of honor.

But it is not exactly the car Hughson had. When the 999 arrived it had a new type of radiator on it. By the time it was put on display, it was equipped with the radiator that was on the wrecked Arrow when it arrived at the factory in 1903. This radiator was not used for the record run, and obviously had been stored someplace. Henry hadn't forgotten where it was.

<u>**3**</u>

THE BEACH—WAY BACK WHEN

NO ONE KNOWS for sure who first got the idea of racing on the hard-packed sands of Florida's northeast coast. It may have been J.F. Hathaway of Stanley Steamer fame, or it may have been a group of local citizens who were looking to attract more winter business.

Whoever it was, if he were to return he would find the beach an outmoded antique, with its only tire tracks made by the cars of tourists going from Ormond Beach at the northern end of the famous strip to Daytona, slightly farther south. Now they have the speedway in Daytona, where stock cars roar around a high-banked oval at nearly 200 mph; the elements of the genteel life of the early 1900s, when John D. Rockefeller had his winter home in Ormond, have been replaced by the garish modern architecture of a motel row which stretches from Ormond to Daytona. But they still come to see the cars.

The first vehicles to compete on the beach were R.E. Olds' Pirate and Winton's Bullet, with their designers as drivers. They took part in a test in mid-April, 1902, and found the beach to be suitable for racing. They also found it politic to announce they had achieved the same speed (57 mph), thus helping both in the sales promotion department.

The 1903 meet at Ormond was a considerable success, attracting numerous socialites as well as drivers; then in late January of 1904 Vanderbilt, the fabulous "Willie K," who later donated the Vanderbilt Trophy for America's premier auto race, set his record of 92.3 mph, and the beach became famous.

The beach made many reputations and killed several seekers of same, but one man for whom it never did anything was Henry Ford. He was there three times in the early days without success. It wasn't until Milt Marion won the famous beach race of 1936 that a Ford did something noteworthy in Ormond or Daytona.

When Vanderbilt set his record Ford and his wife were on hand watching Henry's new-found distinction as the world's fastest man taken over by one, who was also

(Top) Ford behind the wheel of his Model K race car, taken at either Cape May or Atlantic City, N.J., in 1905. (Middle) Ford, with goggles, waits while mechanics work on the Model K. Man standing at right is Frank Kulick. (Bottom) The day the record was broken—William K. Vanderbilt and his Mercedes, at right in photo, ready to race the Ross steamer at Ormond in late January 1904.

(Top) Barney Oldfield and the Winton Bullet at Ormond Beach, Fla., circa 1904.
(Middle) Ransom E. Olds and his Pirate, one of the first cars on the beach in 1903.
(Bottom) Bob Burman and his Blitzen Benz after setting a land speed record
of 141.732 mph at Ormond in 1911.

close to being the world's richest. After Vanderbilt's feat Ford wired Pickens in an effort to bring the 999-Arrow to Ormond to reclaim the record; an announcement was made February 1, saying the car was being shipped from Philadelphia and that Ed Hausman, a veteran bicycle rider from New Haven, Conn., would do the driving in an effort to return the record to a "professional."

By the time the car and Hausman arrived, everyone else had gone home. So on the 26th of the month Hausman and 999 raced against Oldfield and the Winton Bullet in Savannah, Ga., in an attempt to make expense money.

The next year Henry brought his newest creation, the six-cylinder Model K, to Florida. This was the most unsuccessful of all his competition cars, and it started an undistinguished career by breaking its crankshaft while being warmed up in the Ormond Beach Garage (which still stands on East Granada Avenue and is now used as the equipment house for a golf club). Henry lived in a tent behind the garage, and when he found he hadn't brought enough money along, he subsisted on a diet of cheese and crackers while waiting for funds to arrive and watched the world record go even higher. The crank, which he had ordered turned from a solid steel billet, had been welded together instead. It cracked at a weld.

This time it was Scotsman Arthur MacDonald, driving a Napier, who boosted the land speed record to 104.65 mph. H.L. Bowden, a Boston millionaire, actually went faster in a twin-engined Mercedes, clocking 109.75 mph in his ingenious creation. He had a 60-horsepower Mercedes and a Daimler boat that used the same engine, so he stretched the car's chassis and put the second engine alongside the first. But then he was disqualified, in one of those remarkable decisions by automotive ruling bodies which have hampered the sport ever since its beginnings: His car was 400 pounds too heavy, and therefore was not eligible for the record. Too *heavy?* This decision by the AAA, plus the general incompetence with which the meet was run, almost spelled the end of speed week. Vanderbilt, for one, resigned his honorary AAA job and left for Palm Beach before the races were over. Ford left when the money arrived.

In the late summer of 1905 he found more beaches where they were running races—at Cape May and Atlantic City, N.J.—and again the six cylinder went out to prove itself. At Cape May, where the course was not nearly as fast as in Florida, an 80-horsepower Darracq driven by A.L. Campbell clocked fastest time in the flying mile, 38 seconds flat. A 120-horsepower Fiat, driven by a young Swiss mechanic with the name of Louis Chevrolet, was second in 39.4, then came Walter Christie and his front-wheel drive Christie in 39.8, then Ford in 40.0.

Christie became famous for his work with tanks; Chevrolet and his two brothers became famous as race drivers and race car builders. Louis made another notable contribution to Ford's destiny, although scarcely a positive one. In 1911, with the backing of W.C. Durant, he designed the first passenger car that bore his name. Although Louis unwisely sold out to Durant three years later, the car stuck around little longer.

Even when he wasn't directly involved, Ford attended many races. Here he is (second from left) at the Grand Prize of the U.S., held in Savannah, Ga., in 1908. The driver is Frenchman Rene Hanriot; the car a Benz.

After Cape May came Atlantic City at the beginning of September, and this time it was Christie who beat Ford in a head-to-head match. About the only notable item to come out of Atlantic City was the race committee waiving Ford's $25 entry fee when he said he didn't have it. (At that time the company had already paid several hundred thousand dollars in dividends).

They took the car back to Ormond for January speed week of 1906, and this time they went in style. In addition to Ford, James Couzens and Horace Dodge made the trip, and Frank Kulick, the rising young driver who was one of the Ford Motor Company's five original employees, went along to run the improved (they hoped) six-cylinder, which now produced 100 horsepower instead of its original 60.

Things were truly international by this time, and also very social. Vincenzo Lancia, the great Italian driver, was the top Fiat pilot, and Victor Hemery, the star Frenchman, was leading the Darracq team. Private railroad cars were numerous, and Henry M. Flagler's Ormond Beach Hotel was overflowing. The clerk of the course failed to inform Kulick when his first day's heat was to be run, so he missed it. In the one-mile straightaway event the best he could do was 40.0, while Louis Chevrolet hit 30.6 with a Darracq. In the 30-mile race for American touring, cars, Kulick got stuck in the soft sand after he spun out. To make things worse, the world record was boosted to 127.66 mph by Fred Marriott and the Stanley Steamer. This so alarmed the builders of conventional automobiles (cries of "freak" and the like lasted for days) that speed week took a long time recovering.

Never again did they have such mass gatherings at Ormond. From then on the beach was used for individual record attempts, which culminated with Malcolm Campbell's 276 mph in 1935. After that they went to Bonneville, which afforded a better opportunity for record breaking. But even at the beginning, beach adherents knew the sand wasn't the ultimate answer. After the 1905 speed week, a group of Ormond citizens had a meeting to discuss the possibility of building a three-mile track *near* the beach, on which races could be held when the sand wasn't in good shape, or when the tide was in.

Thirty years later an unemployed mechanic from Washington, D.C., ran out of money in Daytona and decided to make it his home. Later on he not only gave the area back its speed week, but he built the world's fastest race course inland from the ocean. Had William Henry Getty France known about the Ormond meeting, he might have made it three miles per lap; as it is, the Daytona International Speedway measures 2.5.

But all that came later. In the meantime Ford went back to Detroit and to building, cars. The Model T was only a year away. One legend has it that during his first trip to Ormond, Ford became interested in vanadium steel, when he found some while poking around in the wreckage of a French car. So maybe Ormond was important after all.

4

24 HOURS—THE FIRST TIME

LE MANS was not the birthplace of 24-hour racing. It started in the United States, and in the decade before World War I there were dozens staged in this country—eight of them, in fact, on the one-mile dirt track at Brighton Beach, in what is now one of the more crowded sections of Brooklyn.

They started as outright sales promotion efforts for one make or another, with the first endurance run being the 1,000-mile effort (in 29 hours and 53 minutes) by Packard at Grosse Pointe in 1904. The first real 24-hour event was held at Columbus, Ohio, in July, 1905, in which a Pope-Toledo covered 828.5 miles; then ex-Oldfield manager Pickens took over in 1907 and turned them into carnivals for the spectators and commercial propositions for himself. He was the first to realize you could dress up the track with banners bearing the names of auto and auto-accessory companies, and also the first to understand that the fans were just as interested in watching the repairs as they were in the race itself. Pickens moved the pits right out front, and shone spotlights on them at night.

Of all the various early-day endurance races, held from Brooklyn and the Bronx to such widely scattered spots as Birmingham, Ala., and St. Paul, Minn., there was one race that differed from the rest. It was held at the Detroit Fairgrounds' one-mile oval in June of 1907, and it was the only outstanding performance of the six-cylinder Ford. The rules allowed you to switch not only the drivers, but the car itself. In the end, Ford's having spare cars on hand was what won the race—although this fact was conveniently omitted from the advertisements that followed. The Detroit *News* greeted the race with great enthusiasm and ran several learned articles on the subject, prophesying—not very accurately—"This event sounded the death knell of the professional daredevil pilots of modern juggernauts." Seeing how the race was for stock touring cars, they figured stripped-down single seaters of the type exemplified by 999 were on the wane. Had the writer been present 50 years later he would have been surprised.

Whoever the press agent was, he did quite a job; in the days preceding the race the various drivers got considerable exposure in the local papers. There was Eddie (Cannon) Bald, "the famous Buffalo ex-champion cyclist"; there was Ralph Mongini, referred to as "The terrible Italian, one of the greatest and most daring drivers the Old World has sent to America"; and there were such others as C.A. Coey, "The young Chicago millionaire enthusiast," and Kid McCoy, "The ex-pugilist and social lion of East Orange, N.J." The term "social lion" was probably a reference to McCoy's being well on the way to a total of eight marriages.

There were 12 teams entered and nine showed up, including a Ford Model K six-cylinder with 40 (they said) horsepower. Kulick and Bert Lorimer were the drivers. Lorimer, a tester at the factory, wasn't scheduled to drive, but someone whose name has become lost in antiquity didn't make it, so Lorimer got the job. This happened on Friday evening, before the start. By the time readers were able to peruse Sunday morning's paper, the neophyte racer was being hailed as "One of the greatest automobile drivers in the world.... He out-Oldfielded Barney Oldfield ... and strangely enough for such a speed maniac, he avoided accident [sic] which might cripple the Ford's chances just as skillfully as he drove." Even then, papers were confused over what the driver was trying to accomplish, and were already assuming the nonsense of the death wish.

Ford's competition came from the following: a 50-horsepower Pope Toledo, a 60-horsepower Thomas Flyer, a 30-horsepower Wayne, a 24-horsepower Buick and a Stevens Duryea with the same output and a 40-horsepower American. Ford also had two more entries, these being 15-horsepower runabouts.

The big event was preceded by a 10-mile race for the "Detroit runabout championship," and a 50-miler for "the middle-distance championship of Michigan." Then, at 10 p.m., with the track partially lit by a series of gas lamps, and with a bright moon helping, the long grind started. The Pope Toledo set a hot pace from the outset, despite questionable visibility, while the Ford lay back and was soon in the company of the Thomas Flyer, in which Coey was aiming for a solo run of at least 1,000 miles.

Lorimer relieved Kulick at the wheel—in fact with a brand new car—at the end of the fourth hour, with his team 18 miles behind the Pope-Toledo. With an almost constant flame roaring out of his exhaust, he shot past the flickering gas lamps and between 3 and 4 a.m. averaged 55 mph, cutting the Pope-Toledo's lead to nine miles as he rode high on the slightly banked turns. This brought the number one driver back to work in the Pope-Toledo, and by 8 a.m., after 10 hours of the event, the margin was back to 12 miles. Then both Lorimer and Kulick increased the pace, and just before noon, after 14 hours, the two cars were even. Now Kulick moved in front, and the erstwhile leader ducked into the pits to change drivers. The Pope Toledo soon caught the Ford again, and with Kulick riding high, his pursuer attempted to pass on the inside of a turn.

There are two stories concerning what happened. (There are *always* two stories). The Pope-Toledo version is that a tire blew at this instant. The Ford version is that the other car tried to run Kulick into the wall, and when Kulick would not back off, his challenger spun through the fence.

The driver wasn't hurt and the relief car took the track immediately—but now there was no relief car. The team had brought only two vehicles, and one of them was wrecked. The remaining car was a slow one and consistently lost ground. A call to the factory in Toledo brought a substitute up in a hurry, but by then the Ford had a 36-mile lead and the race was all but over. Kulick and Lorimer, alternating on at least two cars, covered 1,135 miles for an average speed of 47.29 mph. The Ford runabouts finished fifth (798 miles) and seventh (728 miles).

Coey, attempting to cover 1,000 miles, wound up at 990 after also encountering relief-vehicle problems. His first mount developed a water leak and he was forced to drive much of the way in a standard touring model. (Even then there was a difference between a stock car and a "stock" car.) Coey was so punch-drunk when it was all over that he didn't see the checkered flag and drove two extra laps, stopping only when his crew jumped onto the track and waved him down. When Coey climbed out, he collapsed.

Ford was quick to publicize this one, not only after the event but during it, which must be some sort of all-time standard for an advertising manager's courage. In Saturday afternoon's paper, with a Ford in the lead, the company advised everyone of this fact and wound up with the following hard-sell haymaker: "To prove it is an ordinary touring car we will sell it—at list price, $2,800—to the first one who speaks for it. We make five every day just as good."

On Sunday, after the affair was over, Ford repeated the offer, this time in the following manner: "We'll sell it for $2,800 to the first applicant and keep it in repair gratis for two years."

And at the bottom there was a slogan—"Watch the Fords go by."

5

MR. GUGGENHEIM'S IDEA

IT WAS 1909 and Robert Guggenheim, not yet 30 years old, had a mining fortune and the time to enjoy it. The Alaska-Yukon-Pacific Exposition was to open June 1 in Seattle, and Guggenheim was interested in promoting it. And since no car had ever driven from New York to this corner of the U.S., what better than an automobile race from coast to coast?

The transcontinental record was 15 days, 2 hours, and 15 minutes, set by a Franklin in 1906 from New York to San Francisco. No one was willing to predict how long it would take to traverse the wilds of Wyoming, Idaho, and Washington that would be encountered on this newest test.

Today it is no problem to make the trip by car, in air-conditioned comfort. Without pushing it can be done in seven days, and some drivers have done it in three. In 1956, as a latter-day Ford promotional stunt, Danny Eames and Chuck Daigh made it from New York to Los Angeles in 47 hours, and since then that record has been lowered. In 1909 there were those who thought Seattle was unattainable by automobile, and as a result the event generated a great deal of interest. The race, with various cash prizes and a trophy, which must rank as one of the great examples of Edwardian high camp, received wide publicity. President William Howard Taft, who was to open the exposition by pressing a golden telegraph key in the White House, would start the race with this same movement of his finger; Western Union had connected the Washington-Seattle line with another reaching to New York. When Taft hit the key, New York Mayor George McClellan was to fire a gold-plated pistol that would get the cars under way.

Now all Guggenheim had to do was wait for the entries to arrive. There were more than 200 automakers in the U.S. in 1909, and it was reasonable to expect many of them would jump at the chance for some national publicity. But the first list of "probables" to appear included only 35 makes, and this number dwindled rapidly to 14. Some didn't like racing, others didn't like the rules—especially the lack of speed limits through the already "crowded" eastern section of the country. Still another drawback, and the most important one, was opposition to the event from the

Association of Licensed Automobile Manufacturers—that group of automakers, 83 strong at this juncture, who were paying tribute to the Selden Patent. The famous Selden Patent suit, with Henry Ford as the primary opposition, was at its height in 1909, and since Ford welcomed the race with open arms, that automatically meant many others would stay home. In an effort to attract as many entries as possible, the rules were changed. The principal ones read as follows:

I. Each entrant, on leaving New York, will be provided with a passport containing the names and the locations of the checking stations along the route. The checking official at these stations will vise [sic] these passports which must be turned in to the committee at Seattle, while the crew must also sign a prepared card which they will mail to the referee.

II. Any member of the crew of a contesting car who shall have ridden in that car continuously from New York may drive. Each competitor may have as many members in the crew as he may desire. No competitor can, however, add members to this crew after the start.

III. There will be no observers on the cars. The technical committee of the Automobile Club of America will stamp each car before departure as follows: the side members of the frame, front and rear axles, engine base and cylinders, transmission case and steering gear. Contestants will be allowed to replace, without penalization, any of these parts except the frame, twice during the contest, but such reserved parts must be stamped by the committee before the contest and one set must be held at Chicago and the other set at Cheyenne, Wyo. These parts will be in charge of a member of the committee, and may when desired, be secured ONLY from either one of these two places. The winning car must bear the stamps on arrival at Seattle. All other parts can be changed at will.

(Note: Several manufacturers claimed the changing of basic parts would take the race out of the endurance category, and Henry Ford was the first to rise to the challenge. The *Ford Times,* in those days the official voice of the company, answered these critics with the following thoroughly impractical but nevertheless impressive blast: "All right; cut out the repairs and replacements. Ford will stay in even if they prohibit tire replacements or spark plug renewals." As a result, on April 18 Rule III was changed to eliminate the phrase beginning, "Contestants will be allowed to replace ..." and ending "... one of these two places." The changing of any major part was now prohibited.)

XIII. No contestant can carry on his car, or use at any point during the race, wheels equipped with flanges suitable for traveling on railroad tracks. Checkers will be instructed to particularly look for violations of this rule.

Later a 14th rule was added, providing for a pace car (a six-cylinder Model K Ford) to lead the entries from New York to St. Louis and decreeing no car could

(Top) The way west—and east again: The route of the 1909 Ocean-to-Ocean race, with the lighter line indicating the return trip of the winners. (Bottom) At the start in New York; Ford No. 1 with Frank Kulick and advertising manager H.B. Harper.

(Top) Coming into Cleveland: Kulick and Harper at right, Bert Scott and Jimmy Smith at left, with a Model T sent out by the local dealer acting as escort. (Bottom) Scott and Smith and a little overheating trouble in front of their Cleveland hotel.

leave any of the designated east-of-the-Mississippi cities until 12 hours after arrival. The time schedule for the early part of the race:

	MILES	LEAVE	ARRIVE	DATE
New York to Poughkeepsie	73	1 p.m.	6 p.m.	June 1
Poughkeepsie to Syracuse	207	6 a.m.	7 p.m.	June 2
Syracuse to Buffalo	150	7 a.m.	5 p.m.	June 3
Buffalo to Toledo	296	5 a.m.	8 p.m.	June 4
Toledo to Chicago	244	8 a.m.	9 p.m.	June 5
Chicago to St. Louis	283	9 a.m.	Midnight	June 6

It was wide open from St. Louis to Seattle. There were 19 checkpoints where teams had to have their passports stamped, but that was all. How they got from place to place and whether or not they slept or ate was their own business.

The race finally drew an entry of six cars. Only five made it to the starting line.

Ford, in another effort to drum up business, offered to bet any amount of money on the race, "between your car and his," as the *Ford Times* said, "to be run under the original ocean-to-ocean rules or under the new ones. Take your pick." One individual offered to bet Ford $100 the Stearns would win, but that was all. The other manufacturers remained silent. As events turned out, it was a good thing Ford didn't take him up on it. The Stearns was the car that never made the start. It finally got under way five days later, then broke down in Tarrytown, N.Y.—24 miles from City Hall. If nothing else the crew at least had the good sense to quit early.

The two Fords entered were 20-horsepower Model Ts, stripped from their normal 1,200 pounds to somewhere between 900 and 950. They were completely open and had only the front two seats, meaning there was no place for one man to sleep while the other drove. If you were in it, you were awake. Frank Kulick and advertising manager *Ford Times* Editor H.B. Harper drove one car, and Bert Scott and Jimmy Smith were in the other. The opposition was as follows:

A six-cylinder, 48-horsepower Acme, weighing 3,500 pounds and with a four-man crew.

A four-cylinder, 45-horsepower Shawmut, weighing 4,500 pounds and with a three-man crew.

A four-cylinder, 50-horsepower Itala, the only foreigner in the group. It weighed 4,000 pounds and had a three-man crew,

In order to help contestants through the West, a pathfinder car with four men was sent out from New York on March 20. They took more than 1,000 photographs and wound up with hundreds of pages of notes explaining how to get from one town to the next, how the roads were, what places to avoid, etc., including the mileage between more than 350 towns and cities. Then the pathfinder (a Thomas Flyer of the type that won the New York-Paris race of 1908) broke down in the Snoqualmie Pass through Washington's Cascade Mountains. Loaded on a freight car, it finally arrived

Somewhere in Colorado, the eventual Winner stops, Scott gets out to take a
photograph, and the travel-weary Smith doesn't even turn.

in Seattle May 25—six days before the start in New York. As a result very little of the information got back to the competing cars; they were once again on their own—except for the Fords. They had two advantages: the dealer network, which had been built up over the past six years, and considerable advance planning. The dealers were told to help their cars in any way they could, and Henry also used a bit of psychological warfare:

"Mr. Ford has personally authorized a reward," the *Ford Times* of June 1, 1909 said, "of $1,000 to any man who furnishes information that will convict any entrant of riding on the rails, using flanged or special wheels or being carried any part of the distance on any sort of a railroad car.

"He also desires and has so instructed all dealers that the police officials in the towns through which Ford cars pass meet our cars outside of town and riding with us pilot us through the town so as to guarantee compliance with official requirements. Any dealer who has not received this request is asked to consider this notice as Mr. Ford's invitation to him and act accordingly."

The trip from New York to St. Louis was covered more or less without incident until the last leg, when steady rains and muddy roads slowed everyone on the way through Illinois. The two Fords got in almost seven hours late, and the Shawmut, which was to be the main competition, arrived two hours after them. There was no 12-hour stop required in St. Louis, but the crews realized this was probably the last place they would get any real rest. They all went to bed.

When they left St. Louis that evening it started to rain again, and it rained for a week—all the way across Missouri, Kansas and Colorado and clear up to Cheyenne, they were in the mud in their open cars, crawling across the Great Plains. Tiny mechanical dots on the face of the continent, they knew only which way was west as they struggled toward the Rocky Mountains, heading for Seattle across what even 60 years ago was almost trackless territory. Hardly any of them, as Jimmy Smith said years later, knew where the competition was. They just kept driving and repairing, with the end of the rainbow at Seattle seeming more like a cruel joke than an attainable goal.

The roads, not much when in good condition, were now so bad the drivers found they could make better time going cross-country. Then, outside Williamstown, Kan., on June 8, Scott and Smith decided to push on while Kulick and Harper holed up for the night. Within a few miles the eventual winners skidded down an embankment into a stream. They were already so wet the dunking didn't make much difference, but they had to wait until morning for Ford Number 1 to come along and pull them out. Then they saw the front axle was bent, and this was a part that couldn't be replaced. "We found we were right near a railroad," Smith said, "so we got the section gang there and straightened the axle again. We got back in and away we went. We didn't know where we were—that is, know where the others were."

The Itala was now far behind. That unfortunate had tried to cross the Missouri River on the Union Pacific trestle near Glasgow, Mo., and had been bumped by a freight train, bending an axle and puncturing the gas tank. From there to Kansas

Mud, mud, and then more mud: (Top) Scott and Smith somewhere in Colorado, and before that (middle) in Kansas, and in Kansas again (bottom).

City, where repairs could be made, the front seat passenger sat with a can of fuel in his lap, nursing the gas through a tube leading to the carburetor. The Shawmut took the lead, with two accidents dropping the Acme behind, and the pacemaker, John Gerrie, arrived back in New York on June 12. Either the Acme or the Shawmut would win, Gerrie said. *The New York Times,* repeating Gerrie's pronouncements, predicted one of the Fords would win because of a better power-to-weight ratio.

As Gerrie arrived in New York, the Fords moved into the lead just east of Denver when the Shawmut got trapped in quicksand. But then Henry's boys mired themselves in Sand Creek, a few miles west of the Shawmut. As they were running together at the time, the Fords found it relatively easy to extricate themselves. They ripped the roof off an abandoned pigpen they saw nearby and working waist-deep in water, got the cars across by lifting the rear wheels, pushing the planks underneath, driving a few inches, then repeating the process.

From Cheyenne westward the race started in earnest, as the drivers began to sense that they could actually make it to Seattle, and that they had better make it there first. Kulick, who had stopped in Denver to overhaul his car, left Cheyenne four hours after the other Ford and the Shawmut. From Cheyenne to Laramie, Kulick raced a Union Pacific mail train and actually beat it into town by five minutes!

Then a bit of foresight—and a bit of bribery, the opposition later claimed—put the Fords out front. The wagon bridge across the Platte River at Fort Fred Steele had been washed out by recent rains, but the Union Pacific trestle was still intact. The Ford men in Cheyenne had been advised of this and they wired ahead, requesting permission to use the trestle. It was granted, and when Ford number two came up it went across. Right behind it, having made up a six-hour deficit from the time he left Denver, was Kulick. They bumped their way across the wooden structure with the muddy waters boiling below, clearly visible through the ties. The Shawmut had to sit and wait for permission to cross, which was in itself an adventure; the ties were from 15 to 18 inches apart. The bumping and jouncing were vicious, and Ford number one limped into Rawlins, Wyo., with a broken wheel. Then, just west of Rawlins, Scott and Smith went into a ditch, broke their front axle again, and had to be towed back to town for a repair job.

Now the lead went back and forth. The two Ford mishaps put the Shawmut five hours in front; then it ran into trouble at Point of Rocks, Wyo., and the Fords were ahead again. On June 16 the Shawmut regained the lead as the cars struggled through the mountains and forests of southwestern Wyoming, where an occasional Indian would stand at the side of the trail, watching curiously and ready to run if these mechanical apparitions turned on him. As the three cars limped into Opal, Wyo., a thunderstorm drove them for cover. The crews, making a gentleman's agreement at least in part motivated by their exhausted state, decided to sleep until dawn. Shortly thereafter the two Fords decided to split up; from here on it would be every man for himself, with no stopping to help the other team. The durability of the Shawmut was beginning to worry them.

Kulick put on the pressure, and as they crawled along the horse trails on the rims of Nugget Canyon and Bancroft Canyon, with hundreds of feet of air next to their outside wheels, he opened up a lead. At American Falls, Ida., the Kulick-Harper Ford was 12 hours ahead of its teammate and even farther in front of the Shawmut, which had been delayed by a broken ball race. They were so far ahead, in fact, they were also beating the timetable Ford set up for them. The guide scheduled to point the way from American Falls to Twin Falls was not there. Rather than wait, they listened to the first person who told them he knew the way.

He didn't. They lost 24 hours and were now 12 hours astern.

On June 21, with the leading Ford crossing the Columbia River west of Wallula, Wash., the Shawmut and Ford number one were about 14 hours behind, but Scott and Smith still weren't out of the woods. While refueling at Prosser, Wash., that evening, the grandfather of all filling station attendants pulled a trick which has been repeated many times since, but usually in less critical circumstances. He let some gas slosh over the car. At that moment, someone threw a firecracker at the car and suddenly it was in flames. Several onlookers beat out the fire, and Scott and Smith continued. Prosser was also the downfall of the number one Ford, which was ahead of the Shawmut at this point. Again, it was guide trouble. The man who was to show Kulick and Harper the way to Prosser got lost in what is known as the Horse Heaven region of the state. To find their way out they had to travel over bumpy railroad ties for eight miles, including through a tunnel a half-mile in length. To make sure he wouldn't encounter a train, Kulick forced the errant guide to walk through first and wave a flag at the other end.

At Lake Keechelus, Wash., the ferryboat operator didn't want to transport the lead car until the others caught up with them. Scott and Smith thought otherwise, and got the sheriff to intervene. Their crossing cost the Shawmut about four hours as it had to wait an uncommonly long time for the boatman to reappear. Later on, suspicions that the leaders had bribed the ferryboat operator took some of the luster off the victory.

From the lake Scott and Smith headed into Snoqualmie, last obstacle on the way to Seattle and a rugged, rock-filled gorge that still had five feet of snow at some points. "At that time of the year," Smith said, "there was ice on top of the snow. We rode along the pass until we got pretty nearly over it, and then we broke through the snow. We could hear fellows pounding in the distance; they were working on a railroad across there. So we got the section gang and they helped shovel us out."

On the way down the western slope, now only 90 miles from their goal, Scott and Smith were met by Henry himself, who had driven up with his Denver and Seattle branch managers. At the fairgrounds gate in Seattle, with a crowd of 15,000 watching, Guggenheim stood with his stopwatch poised. When he clicked it on June 23, the Model T had covered the New York to Seattle distance of 4,106 miles in 22 days and 55 minutes—an average of 7.75 mph.

The Shawmut finished second, 17 hours behind the Ford, while Kulick and Harper came in June 25. They also had trouble in the Snoqualmie, striking a boulder hidden by the snow. They were forced to spend seven hours on the roof of the Cascades Range, installing a new axle and knocking the dents out of the transmission case. They knew the axle would disqualify them, but after coming this far they were in no mood to quit. The Acme arrived June 29, while the Itala came in on a freight car. It had given up in Cheyenne.

The Great Race was over, but Scott and Smith had some more driving to do. Ford asked them if they would take the car back to Detroit and after five days rest and a complete overhaul of the vehicle they headed south, then east, on a sales promotion tour.

And while Scott and Smith continued their Odyssey, the advertising drums started to beat. The punch line in one of the classic hard-sell ads of the time was typical:

"A duplicate of the winner with a five-passenger touring car body costs you $850. No other car was entered that cost less than five times as much. The winner was a stock car. Any Model T could do as well. It's the one reliable car that does not require a $10,000 income to buy, a $5,000 bank account to run and a college course in engineering to keep in order. Better get in line if you want August delivery."

Would that things were so simple today.

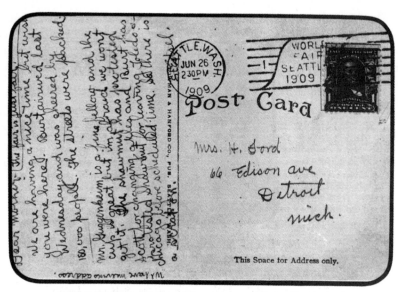

Edsel Ford was there, too: a postcard to his mother.

At the finish line in Seattle: Scott behind the wheel, Smith on his right,
Guggenheim at left and Ford (in derby and white tie) on the right.

There was, however, a slight catch. Five months later it was discovered that the winning Ford had managed to change its engine en route, and disqualification was the result. From a sales-promotion standpoint it didn't make much difference: The story of the race had already had its impact on Ford sales.

Henry's reaction to getting caught was not recorded.

6

FRANK KULICK

PINE LAKE, MICHIGAN, lies to the west of Telegraph Road, between Pontiac and Dearborn. Some of the higher-priced talent in the auto industry lives here, and as a result certain neighborhoods are relatively exclusive. One of these is Interlaken Drive, a road whose entrance is guarded by a sign that says "private," which winds past several lovely homes on its way to the most valuable property in the area, directly on the water. There, in the midst of vice-presidents' row, sometimes you can spot an old man working on the lawn of his tree-shaded house. He limps as he walks, because 60 years ago he and his car took a 70-mile-an-hour trip through the fence at the Michigan State Fairgrounds, and since then his right leg has been shorter.

The car he was driving that day was a racing version of the six-cylinder Model K, a vehicle that was forgotten as it disappeared under the avalanche of the Model T. Its pilot has also been forgotten. His neighbors know his name is Frank Kulick, but they would be surprised to learn he was one of the five original employees of the Ford Motor Company, and he was Ford's number one factory racing driver for a decade.

It's not that Kulick is destitute; he is financially well off, and spends the colder months at his other home in Florida. He is one of the few survivors of the early days of American auto racing, and it is a pity so few know he is still around. His name is not Oldfield or DePalma, or Bruce-Brown, or Burman, Tetzlaff or Vanderbilt, so no one remembers him. He drove the smaller cars, while the newspapers of the day paid most of their attention to the pilots of the bigger machines. But in his own class, in his own time, Kulick was practically unbeatable.

He worked for the Northern Automobile Company at first ("And it was a damn good car, too; I remember one year at the Detroit show it was the only one they allowed to run inside the building, it was so quiet"). Then one day Ford came over to Northern to borrow a car, and Kulick was the youngster who picked it out for him. Soon afterward he hired Frank. Like any young man of the time, and especially one working for an automaker, Kulick was interested in speed, and even made the journey

More Victories for Kulick

And His Ford T Racer at Brighton Beach, Coney Island
August 13th

HAVE you noticed what Kulick and the Ford races are doing on eastern tracks against cars twice the T size and power? One thing at least, Frank is making them all sit up and take notice that the Ford is in a class by itself when it comes to power and durability. Some of our dealers are already beginning to notice the effects of the grand showing made by the Ford car in Philadelphia and New York. Numerous inquiries are coming to our Eastern dealers as a direct result of these races, and many of them claim "that racing is one of the best advertising stunts that can be pulled off by Ford."

(*Continued on page 23*)

Kulick beating Palmer-Singer in the stretch at the end of second mile.

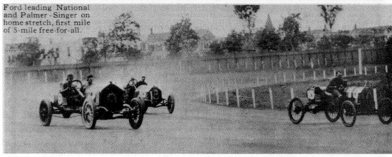

Ford leading National and Palmer-Singer on home stretch, first mile of 5-mile free-for-all.

Palmer-Singer trying to pass Kulick 4th mile— it was no go.

(Top) Ford in a long-wheelbase version of the six-cylinder race car, the one most notable for taking Kulick through the fence. (Bottom) The tire companies advertise again, this time after Kulick's victory at Empire City.

up to Lake St. Clair to watch his boss set the record with the Arrow. The next spring, as he was driving Ford out to the farm in Dearborn, Henry said, "I'm going to build you a racing car."

Kulick doesn't remember exactly where his career started, but he thinks it was at Grosse Pointe. The first recorded mention of his name was on August 20, 1904, in Buffalo, N.Y., when he came in second in a short race with the Ford that was to be his first regular mount—a low-slung, lightweight affair with two Model A (the *first* Model A) two-cylinder engines hooked together, giving him a flat four-cylinder that preceded Dr. Porsche's air-cooled Volkswagen version by almost three decades.

A week later, after winning a five-mile event at Grosse Pointe for cars weighing less than 1,432 pounds, he came in second to Oldfield in the feature handicap, a five-mile event in which Kulick was given a three-eighths of a mile head start. The rest of that fall was a busy one for Kulick, whose primitive chain-drive machine had no transmission and only the most rudimentary way of changing ratios. ("When I got to a heavy track," he says, "I would change sprockets on the rear axle.")

On September 10 he was at Narragansett Park, near Providence, R.I., winning a five-miler; two days later, at the Dutchess County Fair in Poughkeepsie, N.Y., he won again. On October 5, at the Chicago A.C.'s one-mile track he not only won his class, but also won the five-mile feature, which was open to all. In both events he defeated a former race promoter from Indianapolis who would later build the Indianapolis Motor Speedway, and then go on to something even bigger; the runner-up was Carl Fisher, progenitor of the Florida land boom. They were so closely matched in their first two meetings, with Fisher driving a Premier, that the promoters wound up the day with a head-to-head, best-of-three confrontation. Kulick won the first heat, lost the second and just managed to nip Fisher in the third.

It was on Election Day of that year, 1904, that Kulick made his reputation as a first-line driver and also gave careful observers another look at what a favorable power-to-weight ratio could achieve.

Kulick and his tiny vehicle, called by some the "Baby Limited," were at Empire City in Yonkers, with the car by this time so light it was eligible for the 881-pound class. Frank was to run the feature, pitting his 20 horsepower against the 90-horsepower Fiat of Paul Sartori and the 60-horsepower Renault of Maurice Bernin, the outstanding eastern pilots of the day.

Sartori lost a wheel right after the start, putting him out and leaving Kulick running behind the big Renault. On the second lap he ducked inside Bernin on a corner, and the race was his; the Renault had it on the straights, but the Ford was faster in the corners. En route to the victory, Kulick's little car, which on October 29 at Empire City achieved the distinction of being the first to navigate a one-mile dirt track in less than a minute, wound up with a five-mile record as well—4:48.4, an average of 62.4 mph. In the doing, he lowered the one-mile record several times.

The next two years were spent mostly in development work on the six-cylinder, the car that failed in Florida and Jersey, the car that (with help from similar ones) won the 24-hour race, and the car that finally took Kulick through the fence.

Kulick was trying to get under 50 seconds for a mile on an oval track when it happened in October of 1907, and he says a rear wheel collapsed. He blames it on Ford, saying, "The old man wouldn't let me have a differential, and the strain was such that it broke the wheels."

The onlookers rushed to the wreck, and they were surprised to find Kulick still alive, even though his kneecap was fractured, his leg was broken in two places and he appeared to be suffering from internal injuries. While the others wondered what to do, Ford had someone take a saw, cut off the top of a nearby touring car and stretch a board across it so they had a makeshift ambulance. Kulick wore a brace for two years and has limped ever since.

That was the end of the Model K race car, and also the beginning of Henry's aversion to anything with that number of cylinders. He was so shaken by the near death of his driver that he said he would build no more race cars until the rules were changed. Right after it happened he was quoted as saying, "I'll bury the car where it lies. As far as I'm concerned it can remain on the refuse heap where it landed. I was afraid of something of this sort, but didn't have the courage to forego trying for the record ... the Ford Company will build no more racing cars until a more sane method of classification is adopted. My idea would be to limit the power of the motor by setting a limit on the piston displacement. This should be not over 250 cubic inches." This started a personal and later corporate dissatisfaction with the rules that several times was to take the factory's colors out of racing. The closing part of Ford's complaint:

"There must be a change in conditions if motor racing is to continue. At present track racing is more cruel than the gladiatorial contests of ancient Rome. We must get back to contests that will prove something to the motoring world." In the years since Henry said it others from all branches of the sport have repeated his complaint. Yet it grew bigger almost regardless of the rules. There were always men ready to drive, and others ready to build cars for them.

Kulick didn't get back to full-time racing until 1910, when Ford weakened enough to permit further participation. There is little doubt the decision to return was influenced at least in part by the opening of the Indianapolis Motor Speedway in 1909. It was the biggest enclosed race course the world had ever seen, and everyone with an ounce of sales promotion sense was figuring ways to take advantage of it.

In 1909, when the announcement of the track was made (artists' drawings of the time showed a full-fledged road course inside the 2.5-mile Speedway), Ford said he would rebuild what would be known as a six-cylinder 999 and that it would be driven by Kulick. But this never came to pass.

Kulick, driving a stripped and reworked Model T, raced an iceboat on Lake St. Clair in February of 1910 in what was a publicity stunt more than anything else,

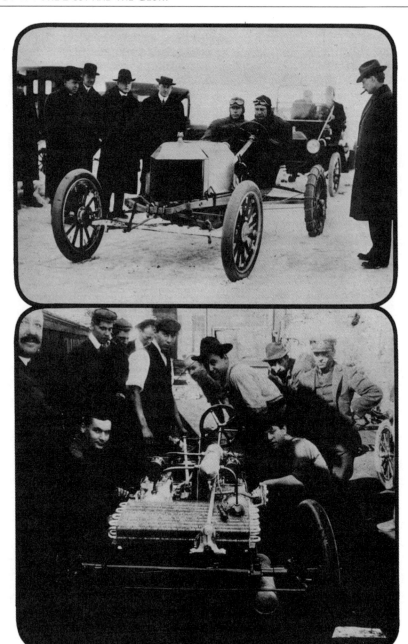

(Top) Kulick and his co-driver before their run at Lake St. Clair in 1912.
(Bottom) Mechanics working on Kulick's first race car, 1904.

Kulick and his Model T pose with the defeated iceboat: Lake St. Clair, 1910.

as the car scarcely needed a push in the direction of prospective customers. Kulick won, of course, and then when the weather got warmer he went racing on the dirt. In August he came in third in a six-hour event at Point Breeze, near Philadelphia, and also picked up three firsts in an afternoon at Brighton Beach, one of the three main tracks in the New York area. In September he won twice at Syracuse, N.Y., and then in 1911 went racing in earnest.

In February, at the Mardi Gras meeting in New Orleans, he registered five firsts and two seconds, despite having the lowest advertised horsepower of any car entered. In June he won Chicago's Algonquin Hillclimb, setting a record; won at Hawthorne, outside Chicago, then went north to Milwaukee to score three firsts in two days. In the Elgin road races, where Kulick had failed the technical inspection the year before (too light, they said), he finished second in the light-car class.

Later in 1911 he went to Syracuse to race Bob Burman's famous Blitzen Benz, the world's fastest car in a straight line, but again they wouldn't let him run for the records: too light. So they went back to Detroit, where Kulick's boss had more influence with the officials.

They got together at the Detroit Fairgrounds on September 26, with 8,000 in the stands and Henry leaning over the rail. Kulick, driving another stripped T, won two preliminary races, then went back to what served as the paddock and took out his record car, the one with the prow-shaped radiator that now graces the Ford Museum in Dearborn.

It looked vaguely like a Model T, then again it didn't. One thing was certain: The four-cylinder engine under the hood was not that of the Tin Lizzie, but a considerably stronger power plant. From what Ocean-to-Ocean winner Jimmy Smith said of the experimental department's activities, there were numerous special blocks, camshafts, etc., lying around, and it is certain someone made good use of them.

After one warm-up lap Kulick came by the timing stand flat out, his hand raised just as they do today at Indianapolis when a driver wants to make a qualifying run. Once around and the clocks read 50 seconds flat, a new mark according to the Detroit journals of the day (which considered anything local and good a "world" record). Ford, watching from the infield rail, looked upset but stayed where he was as Burman went out with the German car. His best performance was 51.4 and the tiny Ford was the winner.

Then Henry marched over to Kulick, digging in his pants pocket as he went through the circle of officials who were congratulating his pilot. "Here, Frank, take this," he said, shoving something into his hand. "You're going too fast."

Ford was obviously happy that he had won, but he was also frightened after having watched his car in terrifying slides through the loose dirt. He remembered Kulick sliding through a corner and then through the fence a few years before.

The "this" he handed Kulick was a $1,000 bill. "I'll give you that to quit racing," Ford added, and Kulick, somewhat abashed now, pocketed the money. The

Detroit *News,* reporting on the incident the next day, said the amount was "enough … for another house and lot. This fellow owns about a block of Highland Park property, which he won racing."

Ford then withdrew whatever entries he had in the remaining races of the day, shaking up the AAA officials. They threatened to suspend Kulick as a consequence, although no reason was given in the journals which relate the incident. "If he's disqualified," Ford said, "it's all the better."

But he was finally prevailed upon to let Kulick into a 10-mile event for 231–300 cubic-inch cars (the stock Model T was 177 cubic inches) for the sake of the crowd. But his final instructions to Kulick were in keeping with his emotional state of the moment. "Don't win," Henry said.

By this he obviously meant go slow, but Kulick found another method. He took an early lead against the same group of cars he had already beaten easily. Then, to finish as directed, he slowed on the backstretch and zigzagged back and forth, to the delight of the crowd and the annoyance of his boss.

In the winter of 1912, seeking to drum up some off-season publicity, Ford sent Kulick up to Lake St. Clair with the Burman-beating car. The vehicle, by now named 999 II, twice topped 100 mph. On the first run, with a riding mechanic, Kulick averaged 103.4 mph. On the return trip, riding solo, he averaged 107.8 mph.

"Kulick's time will undoubtedly stand for some time as the new world's record for the straightaway mile," the *Ford Times* crowed proudly, not bothering to mention that Burman had done 141 at Daytona the previous year. "At times," the report continued, "the slightest raise [*sic*] in the ice would send the machine into the air and it sped on with all four wheels spinning in the air. A small crowd of enthusiastic spectators viewed the record-breaking performance ... and although nearly frozen by a cold, piercing wind sweeping across the barren expanse of ice, expressed their enthusiasm ... by giving three rousing cheers that echoed and re-echoed across the silent bareness of the big lake."

That summer Kulick won the Algonquin Hillclimb again, this event notable for the fact that it had a flying start, and then he was entered in the light-car class of the Vanderbilt Cup race at Milwaukee. After a few practice laps, Kulick packed up and went home, saying the course was too dangerous. Years later, he still remembered the Milwaukee circuit. "It was too narrow," he said. "Try to pass someone at 60, and you'd have to go off the road and into a ditch and then come out onto the road again." The AAA threatened him with loss of his license, but he headed back to Dearborn. Then David Bruce-Brown, a standout driver of the day, was killed in the next practice session. During the race Ralph DePalma went off the road while trying to pass eventual winner Caleb Bragg, and there were various other accidents. After these graphic examples of what Kulick saw in his first reconnaissance laps, no action was taken against Ford's driver.

The Vanderbilt Cup was still America's premier race, but the Indianapolis "500" was getting bigger and bigger. The 1912 running was the second one, and Henry Ford had seen both of them. For the 1913 renewal he attempted to enter the prow-shaped car Kulick had used so successfully, equipped with the hotted-up version of the four-cylinder or a revived edition of the six-cylinder. From what Ford had observed at the first two races, he was convinced his light car could beat the elephantine creations of the day, even on a high-speed circuit such as Indianapolis.

"They told him he'd have to add 1,000 pounds to the car to make the minimum weight limit," Kulick recalls, "and old Hank told 'em 'We're building race cars, not trucks,' and that was the end of that."

Kulick worked for the company for another 15 years until he finally ran afoul of the notorious Harry Bennett in the late 1920s. Then he was out. Today he walks in the garden under the shade trees, long divorced from the dusty tracks and the rickety race cars. A lot of it has grown dim now, but he remembers some of the little things. Like the day in Syracuse when Teddy Roosevelt called him over to the grandstand and shook his hand.

It was a long time ago.

7

THE END OF IT—FOR A WHILE

HENRY FORD and his company got out of racing in 1913 for numerous reasons. Some were practical, some were personal. All of them were obvious. On the pragmatic side he was at this time involved in the technological explosion that made his company the biggest industrial undertaking the world had ever seen, and his day-to-day dealings with production and expansion demanded all of his personal attention. Another reason was his car's competitive capabilities were not in keeping with the size of his company's reputation—not, that is, if he intended to send them against the world's best. The Model T was a small, light, tough car. With better roads and better race tracks, it was not competitive with the big-engined, specialized race vehicles of the day—and Ford was not going to look bad by matching it against the more advanced designs.

Cars such as the Peugeot, at the time of its introduction in 1911 the most advanced vehicle of its day, were vastly superior to the Ford for competition work. (The Peugeot designers were even bold enough to try a desmodromic valve system.) So were the Mercedes, the Fiat, the Locomobile, the National and many others. The big races in the United States (Indianapolis, the Vanderbilt Cup, the U.S. Grand Prix and Elgin) were being won by these. It was a case of build something to compete with them or get out. Since Ford was already number one from the standpoint of series production, he chose the latter course. In the 1920s the Millers and the Duesenbergs kept Ford away—and by this time numerous speed-equipment manufacturers had put the Model T back in the racing business on their own.

Before he left racing Ford several times expressed dissatisfaction with the rules, at least partially because he was trying to influence their authors to alter them in his favor. A factory statement of October 1, 1909, not only displays this attitude, but is surprisingly, in certain cases, a valid argument today:

Doubtless many of the Ford dealers have been questioned and criticized because Ford cars have not taken part in the racing events of recent months.

Aside from the fact that Mr. Ford's decision to keep out of racing originated at the time of the accident to Frank Kulick and a consequent lack of desire to subject other men to similar risk ... there are the reasons presented by the rules under which racing is now conducted.

The contest rules of the American Automobile Association, under which rules all sanctioned racing is now held, under the heading of "Classification," designates six classes A to F.... Practically all racing is planned for Class A or Class B, the requirements of which classes are:

Class A–Open to any car which complies with the definition "stock car" and governed by the following price classification:

Class 1	$4,001 and over
Class 2	$3,001 to $4,000
Class 3	$2,001 to $3,000
Class 4	$1,251 to $2,000
Class 5	$851 to $1,250
Class 6	$850 and under

Class B–Open to the chassis of any car which is eligible under Class A, but with the exemptions provided by the definition of a "stock chassis," and under the following table of piston displacements and minimum weights:

Class 1	451–600 cu. in.	2,400 lbs.
Class 2	301–450 cu. in.	2,100 lbs.
Class 3	231–300 cu. in.	1,800 lbs.
Class 4	161–230 cu. in.	1,500 lbs.
Class 5	160 and under	1,200 lbs.

No car shall compete in any class above that which its weight entitles it [*sic*].

Now then under these rules, let us suppose a Ford car should enter a "stock car" race—that's a Class A race. It may be a hillclimb, a reliability run, a 24-hour race, or a road contest. The Model T selling at $850 could only compete with other cars at $850, or less. After we had beaten all the one and two-lungers and other low-priced cars, what good would the victory do us?

The Model T Ford is not a competitor of other cars selling at the same price, its [*sic*] the active competitor of cars at a considerably higher price and should be allowed to compete with them in races as in sales.

A Ford car cannot enter a Class B or stock chassis race, for while its piston displacement puts it in Class 4, its weight prohibits its entry. That's a rule made by heavy car manufacturers to insure heavy cars making a showing. It bars competition from light cars.

A classification which recognizes only piston displacement is the only fair and above-board racing classification. Price is a matter of profit, cost of production, size of output and similar conditions absolutely divorced from racing. Weight is a matter of design. It's the idea of the builder, just as size of wheels, length of wheelbase and a hundred other features are the ideas of the individual designer. In these ideas he may be wrong, if he is, competition will prove it. If the Ford car were too light, open competition with heavy cars would quickly prove it.

The war cry of "open competition" was to be used again more than a half-century later, but that is another story. The business of weight limits, as already seen, also kept Ford out of Indianapolis; from a sheer technical standpoint, that soured him more than anything else. The next time racing organizations tried to keep Fords out through minimum weights—in 1964, and also at Indianapolis—it didn't work.

From a strictly commercial standpoint, Ford didn't want to be associated with the numerous fatalities that accompanied auto racing in those times; in his position, the resultant publicity would have been far more damaging than success would have been helpful. His car was the leader in the great movement for better roads and highways, and racing was no longer needed as a sales promotion tool. So he turned his back on the sport he had used perhaps more effectively than anyone else. The bell tolled in the May 2, 1913, issue of *Ford Times*. It rang at the end of an innocuous report describing the victory of a Ford in a race that ran from Latrobe to Bedford, Pa., and return, a distance of 113 miles, with each car occupied by four persons. The story—and the racing program—closed with the following:

The first Indianapolis 500, photo supposedly taken by Ford.

Automobiles weren't the only things produced in Dearborn: Some pre-World War I sheet music sponsored by the company.

"But it should be remembered that the Ford's racing qualities are subordinated to its qualities of comfort and all-round serviceability. It is primarily a car for all people, and is not intended for the speed specialist."

Henry got out. But he had started something that would not be stopped.

Part 2

(1918–1941)

From the Backyard to the Brickyard

After Paper Routes ...
Hot Rods and the
Mojave Desert

8

FRONTY, RAJO AND THE REST

THE WAR WAS OVER, and one of the roars of the 1920s was the readily identifiable blast out of the straight-pipe exhaust of a hot Model T. It was the time of Jack Dempsey and Babe Ruth, of Charles Lindbergh and Al Capone, of Bobby Jones and Bix Beiderbecke, and it was also the time of thousands of dusty racetracks, on which the youth of a generation attempted to duplicate the feats of Barney Oldfield and Ralph DePalma.

Some of them made it, some made it big—men like Wilbur Shaw, who won the Indianapolis "500" three times before he retired. Some of them got killed, as did Frank Lockhart, the bright young hero of his day, who, like Icarus, died trying to reach the sun. Shaw started in a Model T rebuilt with his own hands, and so did Lockhart and thousands of others. It was the poor man's race car of its time—in fact of all time.

What the Model T needed to become a race car was more power, and for more power it needed better breathing—overhead valves. It wasn't long after its introduction that someone came up with a cylinder-head conversion, and even before World War I they were being used in races. C.D. Noonan, of Paris, Ill., was the first to advertise an overhead-valve setup, and in 1915 or 1916 Craig Hunt of Indianapolis, with race driver Bill Hunt as the mainspring in the organization, came up with a single overhead cam, 16-valve (four per cylinder) design. It was so primitive that it was delivered with a straight camshaft and loose cam lobes. The owner could then locate the lobes to produce whatever timing suited his needs. Robert M. Roof of Anderson, Ind., who later joined Laurel Motors, came up with his own 16-valve head at about the time the United States entered World War I, and after the war, came the two most successful additions to the Model T block. One was the Rajo, built by ex-racing, driver Joe Jagersberger in Racine, Wis., and the other was the immortal Frontenac, built by the Chevrolet brothers in Indianapolis. Before the famous Fronty was through—and there may be a few still running someplace, for all anyone knows—it had given its name to the car as well, and Fronty-Ford was the appellation for all the racing Model Ts, almost regardless of what type of head was used. The Chevrolet brothers built the heads to raise capital for more sophisticated designs, and they built racing heads to publicize the ones intended for passenger cars. Without knowing it, they created a legend.

Model T's were racing before 1914, but the postwar boom was what really got them going. It began, of course, with the kids, those who were mechanics and perhaps had $10 left over at the end of the month and an old Model T on which to spend it. One month you couldn't buy anything, and the next month, when you had $20, you could get the "underslinging" parts from Craig-Hunt for $20 and lower the car a few inches. Later, Morton and Brett dropped the price to $10. In 1922 an eight-valve Roof head (complete with intake and exhaust manifolds, plugs and wires) cost $65. Wheel discs, to hide the spokes and help them support the rim, cost $10 a set, and if you could come up with $150 you could buy a Morton and Brett single-seater racing body, the *ne plus ultra* of the day. In the 20 years the Model T was being built, accessory manufacturers managed to produce more than 5,000 different items for the car, and a good many of them were in the speed equipment category.

So over perhaps a two-year period, the kid mechanic would build up his racing car and then he'd find a place to try it. And he'd either get better and go on with it, as did Shaw, Lockhart, Mauri Rose, Dutch Baumann and others, or he'd quit. The hotted-up Model T did more to create a racing element in the United States than did anything else. It provided the cars for the myriad of dirt tracks, the young drivers provided the sport with a proliferation of new names, and the ones that quit driving gave auto racing a hard core of fans, especially in the Middle West and California. Even Edsel Ford had a stripped-down Model T, but his was a little fancier than most. His father had it built at the factory.

It was a primitive time, of cut-and-try backyard engineering, of probing for answers. In the 1920s, when tetraethyl lead first came into use, GM genius Charles H. (Boss) Kettering had found that 12 cc per gallon worked well. So Leon Duray, one of the great drivers of the time, promptly went to 20 cc. Adjustments from one circuit to another also took forms that seem laughable today: The 16-valve Fronty-Ford, for example, was fine on banked dirt tracks of a half-mile in length, but had too much horsepower for flat half-mile circuits. So instead of changing anything on the chassis, car owners merely substituted an eight-valve head when they got to the flat courses. Starting in 1925, with the advent of balloon tires (5¼ inches wide), they could keep the 16-valvers on all the time. Later, they got an eight-valve head that turned out more horsepower.

On either form of dirt half mile, banked or flat, the Frontys were too much for even the supercharged Millers to handle. The sophisticated machinery may have been all right for Indianapolis, but down in the bullrings the Ford was king. Remember, the price tag on a 7,500 rpm Miller was $15,000; the cost of a ready-to-race Ford from Fronty was $2,700 with a 16-valve, double overhead cam engine that might wind to 5,000. Everyone had a track, and everyone was a promoter. The AAA ran the board tracks, but the dust-filled pits of the Middle West were on their own. There was no publicity to speak of, no billboards or anything like that, but the word

The Model T in sportive clothing: (Top and bottom) mid-1920s runabouts, their engines equipped with Frontenac cylinder heads.

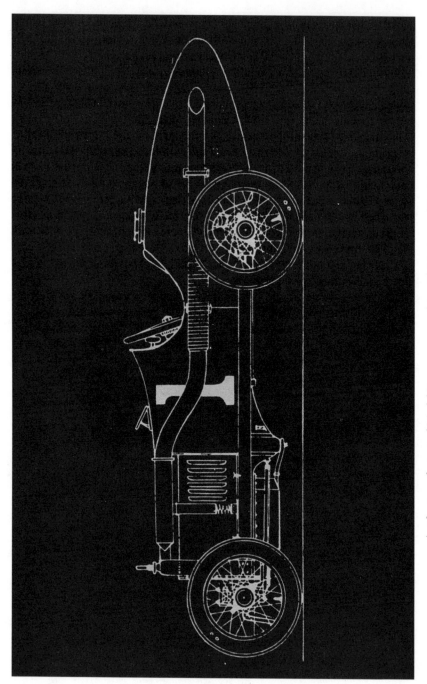

A side view of a typical Model T race car, complete with Morton and Brett body.

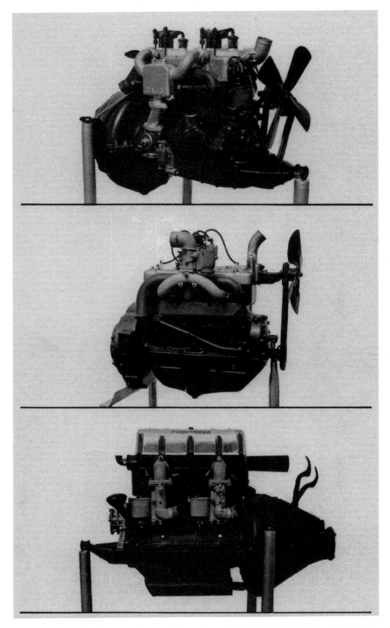

The cylinder-head designers were in their glory: (Top) 1926 Model T with Rajo head, Bosch distributor, Winfield carburetor. (Middle) 1930 Model A with Winfield head, Mallory distributor, Winfield carburetor and manifold. (Bottom) 1925 Model T with Frontenac head, oiler and water pump, Bosch twin-spark magneto and twin Zenith carburetors.

*More conversions: (Top) 1918 Model T with Roof head, Atwater-Kent distributor,
Zenith carburetor and Universal water pump. (Middle) 1930 Model A with
Miller-Schofield head, Wico magneto, Winfield carburetor and manifold.
(Bottom) 1912 Model T with 1923 Waukesha-Ricardo head, Winfield carburetor
and manifold, Splitdorf magneto, Eskimo water pump.*

would get around there was a race on Sunday, and the crowd would gather. If the drivers split $250 that was a lot.

The high-speed, high-banked boards were not for the Model T's. The Millers and the Duesenbergs won those races. The Fords just didn't have the horsepower. They were good down where it was tough, where the tracks were dirty and bumpy, on the small-town circuits which changed the racing tradition of America. In earlier days it had a distinct society patina; now it became the province of the mechanic.

There were no records to speak of; only the AAA kept books, and they looked down on the outlaw activity. To the AAA these drivers might just as well have been bootleggers (who made good use of Fronty heads to outrun the revenue agents). Many of these men went on to make their names at Indianapolis, others were tough only on the dirt and as a consequence never achieved the fame of their contemporaries.

One of the outstanding performances of those early days was Noel Bullock's surprising win in the Pike's Peak Hillclimb of 1922. Bullock, who made the 12-mile trip in 19:50.8, was a Nebraska flight instructor who spent six years building his car. He would race it, then take it home and fix something, race it again, then bring it home and improve it some more. In the six years before 1922 he won 74 events on half-mile and mile tracks, so he was scarcely a novice. But the sight of his dilapidated vehicle lining up against sleek Mercers, Packards and Judsons was almost laughable, until he got to the top of the mountain. Bullock, whose car weighed 975 pounds ready to run, used a Rajo head and had a rather shabby looking homemade hood over the engine. He never got around to ordering from Morton and Brett.

Of all the drivers who piloted Fronty-Fords, perhaps none was more successful than Baumann, who stayed on the Midwestern dirt while Shaw and others went on to Indianapolis and the West Coast. In 1928, for example, driving a 16-valve DOHC Fronty, Baumann drove in 52 races and won 43 of them.

Before that the veteran Baumann was one of Shaw's teachers when the Hoosier kid from Shelbyville was working for Bill Hunt in Indianapolis at $12.50 a week, cleaning out the garage and acting as general errand boy in 1920. When Hunt went out of business, young Wilbur had already started work on his own car in the second-floor loft of the building, scraping and welding on a rusted and cracked Model T frame. Shaw took all his savings and sunk them in the car. When the vehicle was finished, Wilbur found to his dismay that it was too bulky to get out of the room. So he and his friends knocked out a wall and lowered the prize package to the ground. That weekend Shaw took his gem to the Hoosier Motor Speedway, a half-mile dirt track on the outskirts of Indianapolis—and was promptly sent home as inexperienced. Two weeks later, determined to drive it, Shaw went to Lafayette, Ind., where Hunt was on hand and tried to caution the youngster. But Wilbur wanted to drive, and Hunt qualified the car for him so he wouldn't have to start back in the pack. Hunt put the Model T on the outside of the front row alongside Ralph Ormsby, one of the hotshots of the 1920s. Shaw was the first car through the first turn and by the time he got to the backstretch he was running flat out. The only trouble was he didn't know enough to lift for the next turn and he went through the fence, wrecking his cherished car a few seconds after it made its racing debut.

But Wilbur got another Model T, and then another; eventually people were lining up to give him cars.

Frank Lockhart was probably the most single-minded driver the sport has ever known. From his childhood in Dayton, Ohio, through his formative years in Southern California, he only lived for one thing—the automobile. His attitude toward life in general was to ignore it, unless it was that particular facet that concerned his getting into a racing car. When he was 16, someone gave him a rusty Model T chassis. It was six miles from his house, so every day Frank and his brother made the trip by foot and carried another piece of it home. One of the local speed shops which Lockhart haunted gave him a junked Model T engine, and he got that home, too, and rebuilt it on the kitchen floor. When the car was ready he took it to Ascot and other local tracks, and he won most of the time. The money he made went back into the car. There was none for anything else, and his mother took in sewing to make ends meet.

When he needed racing tires and had no money, he went to his mother. She reminded him of their financial situation. He told her to borrow on the house or on the furniture, and she did. He got his tires. The Model T kept on winning, although before races Lockhart was so tense be would vomit. Once the flag dropped, he was fine. In 1926, when he was 23, Lockhart went to Indianapolis for the first time; he wanted to see the "500." In the days preceding the race he got a ride in a Miller and went faster than the car's regular driver. The day before the race another driver got sick and Lockhart was given his place. He led for practically the entire distance, and when the event was called at 400 miles because of rain, the kid fresh out of a Model T was two laps in front of the field. It was a Horatio Alger story in the best tradition, and Lockhart became a popular hero ranked with Dempsey and the rest.

After that he won nearly everything. But he wanted something bigger and better than mere races. He wanted the land speed record, and designed his own car for the attempt. At Daytona Beach in late February of 1928 be crashed his Blackhawk Special into the surf at better than 220 mph. But he lived, and they repaired the car. On April 25 he tried again. This time a tire blew out, and he went to his death. The record at the time was 203.79 mph. Lockhart was far above it when the end came.

Lockhart died quickly, the Model T died hard. In 1947, 20 years after Ford stopped making them, Al Miller took Nile McKinney's 1923 Model T race car, complete with a single overhead cam, Fronty head, a billet crank, tubular rods and drysump lubrication, and ran it 120 mph at El Mirage dry lake. And a little while after that Kenny Palmer took the same car and won a race with it on the old Gardena track's dirt half-mile. McKinney still has the vehicle.

Henry not only put America on wheels; he put it behind the wheel of a race car.

(Top) The Model T racers made it into the movies, too: Wallace Reid and his mount in the 1921 Paramount picture "Across the Continent." Reid was a registered driver with the AAA contest board. (Bottom) Howdy Wilcox 11 and his Fronty-Ford at Winchester, Ind., in 1933.

(Top) He also started with a Model T—Frank Lockhart and his Indianapolis-winning Miller Special, 1926. (Bottom) The front page of the Chevrolet brothers' 1925 catalog.

9

A LOST GEAR, A CRACKED FRAME

THE CIRCUIT of the Sarthe was well known to Americans in the 1920s. Here, just outside the city of Le Mans, was where Jimmy Murphy and his Duesenberg won the Grand Prix of France in 1921—the first-ever major victory for an American car and driver in Europe. Another 45 years were to pass before a second Yankee auto won a big one on that side of the Atlantic. It would also take 45 years before an American car won again at Le Mans, by then the site of the world's most famous endurance race.

The 24 Hours of Le Mans, first run in 1923, was not to be won by an American car until 1966, when Fords finished 1-2-3 and shattered all speed records on the famous old course. But the distinction of being first was reserved for Ford by luck. In later years the incident was to be forgotten by practically everyone, but as long ago as 1928 a Stutz discovered being in the lead after 22½ hours was no guarantee of victory.

A French-built Montier Special, with a Model T-based engine, competed in the inaugural event, placing 14th before it disappeared into obscurity and yellowed newspaper clippings. There was a factory-sponsored Chrysler entered in the 1925 race, and in 1926 an Overland and a Willys-Knight were on hand. None of these did anything of note, and then in 1928 Stutz came in with a 4.9-liter straight-eight Blackhawk, and Chrysler returned in force with a quartet of 4.1-liter cars. Their main opposition was the three-car Bentley team, victors of the year before, and the Stutz soon surprised the Englishmen; they hadn't known an American vehicle could corner so well and still run that fast in a straight line.

One of the Bentleys was forced to drop back early in the race, and two of the Chryslers went out, leaving the Stutz and one Bentley fighting for the lead, with another Bentley and the remaining Chryslers astern. Then, soon after midnight, one of the Bentleys came in with a cracked frame and was withdrawn. What worried W.O. Bentley most was not the loss of the car, but the cause of the retirement. "It had not been a freak fault but metal fatigue," he said, "and it would only be a matter of time before the same thing happened to Babe [Woolf Barnato, chairman of the company and one of the drivers of the other car]." So the Bentley remained in second place, while the Stutz rolled on in the lead with W. O. crossing his fingers, afraid to send his runner-up car after the Stutz, just hoping it would be able to finish ahead of the pursuing Chryslers.

At 2:30 p.m., running comfortably about two miles in front of the Bentley, Stutz pilot Edouard Brisson stripped a gear and was forced to slow down. The Bentley took the lead, but that was not the end of it.

With four laps to go, the Bentley came limping past the pits at 70 mph, Barnato giving the thumbs-down signal to the crew, who saw the hood had slipped back. The frame had cracked, and they knew it had torn the hose between the radiator and the engine block. There was no more water.

Somehow or other the Bentley made it to four o'clock, the Stutz on its heels, and the Chryslers running third and fourth. If the gear had held up a little while longer—or if the Bentley's frame had cracked a half hour earlier ... Kipling had something to say about that.

At left: (Top) The first one—Jimmy Murphy and his Duesenberg winning the French Grand Prix at Le Mans, 1921. (Bottom) Close behind: The Stutz trails the eventual winning Bentley, driven here by Chairman of the Board Woolf (Babe) Barnato. Above: (Top) The Start: Tim Birkin leads Frank Clement with two white Chryslers close behind. (Bottom) At Pontlieu corner (not a part of the modern circuit), the Stutz harries a Bentley.

Jimmy Murphy, the first American to win at both Le Mans and Indianapolis.

10

FRONTY'S HEAD AND STIRLING'S FATHER

THE 1920s were the great days of American race car construction. Harry Miller, the Duesenberg brothers and the rest were turning out new and better engines every year, and as the economy went up so did auto racing. Through this period the only way Ford got into the act was through the back door and in the minor leagues of the dirt tracks.

The greatest contributors to the success of the Fords were the Chevrolet brothers and their chief designer, ex-Ford man C.W. Van Ranst. In 1920 and 1921 they were the kingpins of race car construction, having won the Indianapolis 500 both years and with different engines. In 1920 Gaston Chevrolet won the race with a 3.0-liter four-cylinder car dubbed the Monroe due to financial backing from the automaker of that name, but actually nothing more than one of the brothers' own Frontenacs. The next year Van Ranst came up with a 3.0-liter straight eight, and Tommy Milton drove it to victory.

While he was working on the design of the eight, Van Ranst had an idea, and in 1920 he talked Louis Chevrolet into taking a crack at it. It was financially just as profitable, Van Ranst reasoned, to run cheap equipment on the dirt tracks as it was to run expensive, sophisticated stuff at Indianapolis and on the high-banked boards. So why not take a Model T with the underslung suspension and a Morton and Brett body and put a decent engine in it? The Roof-Laurel heads weren't very reliable, and Van Ranst felt he could easily make a cylinder head conversion for the Model T that would be better.

When the work was done on the prototype Van Ranst looked around for a car on which to test it, and the nearest one was the Model T belonging to Skinny Clemons, the shop welder. Later Clemons became a star dirt track driver, a car owner and Wilbur Shaw's mechanic, but right now he was staggered that Van Ranst would even approach him with this jewel.

"If it's any good," Van Ranst told him, "we'll give it to you."

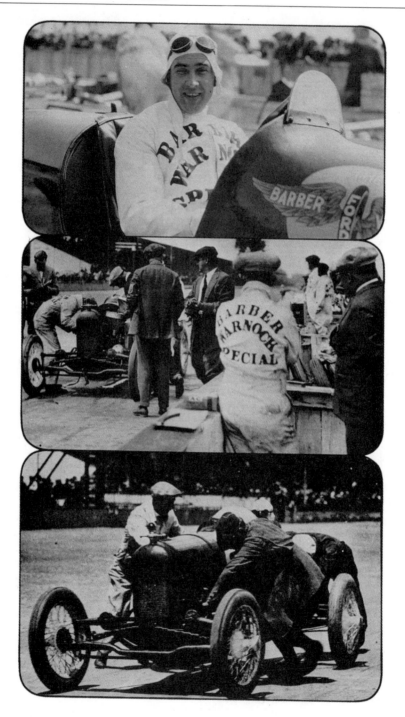

At left: (Top) Alfred Moss in his 1924 Barber-Warnock Special. (Middle) In the pits, 1924.
Man in middle wiping his hands is Arthur Chevrolet. (Bottom) Under way again—
Chevrolet and the mechanics push one of the Barber-Warnocks back into the race.
Above: (Top) Moss (28) and Fred Harder (27) at speed during the 1924 event.
(Bottom) Bill Hunt, the other man on the three-car team.

Wilbur Shaw was one of the great ones at the Brickyard. At the height of his fame, in 1941 (above, top), he drove a Maserati. Long before he ever got to the Speedway (bottom) he drove a Fronty-Ford on the dirt for Skinny Clemons and (right, bottom) for Roscoe Dunning. At right: (Top) Industry comes to Indianapolis. From left, Gar Wood, Harvey Firestone, Ford, Oldfield and Dr. Boyd Gardner. (Middle) Ford posing in one of the 1924 Model T-based cars. Oldfield is directly behind him, with the inimitable cigar.

About all Clemons could say was "wow," and they torqued the head down and took off in the little sedan that was used for hauling parts, Louis Chevrolet driving and Van Ranst hanging on. As soon as they got the speeding Model T into the countryside, they ran off the paved roads and onto the dirt ones; a pile of gravel in the middle of the road was their undoing and they got upside down in a hurry, sliding on the roof of the car for such a distance that the top was ground down through the wooden slats.

They rolled out the door and Louis looked at Van Ranst. "It's fast enough for a race car," Chevrolet said. They got it turned right side up again and drove back to their shop on West 10th Street in Indianapolis, where Clemons' somewhat battered vehicle was returned.

The head was an immediate success. It revolutionized dirt-track racing, and when the Frontenac Motor Corporation was involved in its financial catastrophe of 1922, it was the only thing that kept the brothers going. At peak production, more than 60 a day were leaving the plant, and more than 10,000 of them were built. In 1922, with the Indianapolis displacement maximum at 183 cubic inches (3.0 liters), the Chevrolet brothers entered a Fronty Ford for Glenn Howard, and John Curtner entered his own car for the initial appearance of the make in the "500." They were using the Model R head, a pushrod operated setup with two valves per cylinder, a single carburetor and a three-port exhaust system. Howard qualified his car at 83.90 mph, Curtner got the 27th (and last) starting spot without qualifying. He spent most of the pre-race period repairing the vehicle after it had been wrecked.

Both ran like clockwork in the race, but it was obvious they were no match for Jimmy Murphy's Murphy Special, the 1921 Le Mans-winning Duesenberg now powered by a Miller engine. When Murphy completed his 200 laps, Howard had covered 162. Curtner's car, incidentally, turned a 92 mph lap at the 1⅛-mile board track in Uniontown, Pa., in June of the same year.

In 1923, with the displacement limit cut to 122 inches (2.0 liters), Art Chevrolet prepared a Fronty for Barber-Warnock, the local Ford dealer, and the result of their efforts was fifth place—the best showing any Ford-powered machine made at the Speedway until Jimmy Clark and Colin Chapman came along in 1963. The Barber-Warnock Special was driven by L.L. Corum, who was to share the seat of the winner the next year, and it was equipped with the prototype of the Frontenac S-R head. This one had two carburetors, the compression raised from the previous 85 pounds to 100 pounds, and had two spark plugs per cylinder. Corum qualified the car at 86.92 mph, and in the race it ran perfectly, stopping only for gas and winding up with an average of 82.58 mph to winner Milton's (Miller) 90.95. Corum drove the entire race himself, a rarity in those days, and finished in front of various Mercedes and Bugattis.

Corum was far behind Milton at the finish, but he was the favorite of the crowd, many of whom were Ford owners, and he got one of the biggest hands of the day when he was finally flagged off the track.

The dealer was so happy that the next year he entered three cars. And curiously, Henry Ford accepted the position of referee for the 1924 race. A regular at the Speedway ever since the first 500-miler in 1911, this time Ford not only acted in an official capacity, but also took out a $10,000 life insurance policy for each driver. The three Barber-Warnock cars were to be driven by Bill Hunt (Shaw's friend), Fred Harder and by a young Englishman who was attending dental school in Indianapolis. The reputation of the race, at this time scarcely more than 10 years old, had carried across the ocean, and if there was one thing Alfred Moss wanted to do, it was drive in the "500." He had some experience in minor British events and he intended to become a dentist, so he decided the best way to fulfill both ambitions was to go to school in Indiana and look for a ride at the same time. He got one for the 1924 race, and it was the third Ford. Two of the cars had the S-R eight-valve Fronty head that Corum used in 1923, carrying a 6.75 to 1 compression ratio and developing 65 horsepower at 3,700 rpm. The other, to be driven by Harder, had the new D-O head, complete with double overhead cams, 16 valves, a 7.5 to 1 compression ratio and 80 horsepower at an undisclosed rpm figure. (The Duesenbergs were producing about 120 horsepower.)

An average of at least 85 mph for the 10 qualifying laps was necessary, and both Moss (85.27) and Hunt (85.04) made it. Harder, whose new engine was having teething troubles, could do no better than 82.77 but got in anyway, being the sole occupant of the eighth and last row of the grid as only 22 cars were on hand. Whether Harder made it to help fill out the field or as a gesture to the referee from Dearborn is something that is not recorded and Moss doesn't remember, even though he can recall numerous other minor details (all chassis bolts were welded in place, for example, and as a result the lightweight cars withstood the pounding of the bricks much better than did the others). The closest the Fords came to the winning Duesenberg of Corum and Joe Boyer was at the start; Corum's car was in the seventh row, alongside those of Moss and Hunt. After that they were simply overmatched; although the Fords went fast enough to have placed in the top 10 the year before, technical progress had left them behind. The Duesenberg brothers had unlocked the secret of the supercharger, and the blown Duesy shared by Corum and Boyer averaged 98.23 mph for the distance—almost 4 mph better than the old mark set by a 3.0 liter. Hunt was flagged off after 191 laps, Moss covered 177 despite a few long pit stops, and Harder did 176. Their places were 14th, 16th and 17th, and again, no Ford driver had to be relieved. Parenthetically, Moss got another ride as a relief driver the following year, then went back to Britain armed with a diploma and a Frontenac distributorship. He remained a great racing enthusiast even in later years, and the spirit of competition was something he instilled in both his son and daughter, first with horses, when they were young, then later in cars. Stirling, his son, never drove at Indianapolis, although he drove—and won—almost everyplace else.

That was the end of it for a while; the true race cars were just too fast for the hot rods on the high-speed tracks. Art Chevrolet prepared the Skelly Special, another

Daytona Beach Florida February 1928.

At left: (Top) Shaw in his RED Special again. (Middle) Chet Miller and mechanic Jimmy Brock before the 1930 race, during which they borrowed a front spring from a spectator's car. (Bottom) Fred Harder and his Barber Warnock Special, 1924. Above: Lockhart's last car—the Blackhawk Special, with the photo erroneously captioned as being taken at Daytona Beach, where he died. The shot was made in Indianapolis.

Fronty-Ford, which ran in 1925 and went out early with transmission trouble, and in the same year the Green Engineering Works of Dayton actually entered a flathead Ford which didn't make the field. When the engine size was reduced to 91.5 cubic inches (1.5 liters) the next year, the day of the Fronty-Ford was practically over. Only one more attempt was made—as expected, by the Chevrolet brothers. The car was a front-wheel drive creation called the Hamlin Special, with the bore and stroke dimensions achieved by sleeving the block and installing a short-stroke crank. The engine was turned around in the frame and a Roots-type supercharger was driven off the nose of the crankshaft. It was good for 6,000 rpm, and the wail of the engine was spectacular, if nothing else. But the car, driven by Jack McCarver, lasted only 22 laps before a rod bearing failed.

The next time a Ford appeared at the Speedway was in 1930, when the Depression forced the management to take up the 366 cubic inch "stock block" formula. A few of the Frontys returned, and Chet Miller, later an Indianapolis great but then a raw rookie, got his first ride in one. His qualifying speed was a remarkable 97.360 mph in the 176-inch car, and he finished 13th, being flagged off with 160 laps after being delayed by a 41-minute pit stop that must have been one of the funniest in Speedway history. Miller, who had set out to average 100 mph, came in after 92 laps for a carburetor adjustment, and the technical committee discovered a broken front spring. They refused to let him continue until the spring was replaced, and there was no spare in the pits.

Miller and his mechanics ran into the infield, found a stock Model T with no owner around, removed the spring and put it on the race car. After the race they took the spring, put it back on the street car, and left before the owner arrived. Miller's average—without the stop—was 96 mph.

In 1931 Gene Haustein brought another Fronty Ford to the Speedway, this one equipped with a Model A engine bored to 218.5 cubic inches and sponsored by the Fronty Sales Company. He qualified at 108.395, then went out after 116 laps when he lost a wheel. Charles Moran Jr.—later to be the founder-president of the Automobile Competitions Committee of the United States, but then just a youngster—entered a Model A Ford to see if he could make the field, just as he did the year before with a stock DuPont covered by a racing body. The first time he lasted 22 laps before leaning it against the wall. With the Ford he never got to the starting line. And there was one more Ford, the Tucker Tappet Special, a late entry that barely made it to the track in time. It was the 10th fastest in the field of 40, qualifying at 111.321 mph, but it started on the last row of the grid and its pilot, Francis Quinn, had one of the shortest careers of any Indianapolis contestant. He lasted for three laps before an axle broke. It was his only appearance at the Speedway; the car collected $250.

The flathead V8 made its Indianapolis debut in 1933, with C.O. Warnock, the hometown Ford dealer, again trying his luck. The car was the slowest of all that attempted to qualify and didn't make the field—scarcely an auspicious beginning for the next engine that was to capture the youth of the country. In 1934 there were two more of them, semi-stock entries with flathead V8s. One was the Bohn-a-Lite Special, driven by Chet Miller which crashed on the 11th lap to finish 33d. Another was driven by Charles Crawford for 110 laps and 16th place.

The Fords weren't doing well, but the stock cars were. The country was in the depths of the Depression, and the powerful Millers and Duesenbergs were getting older. Since the Speedway changed the formula to allow stock block engines one or more had always placed well, and most of these were Studebakers. Russ Snowberger was eighth with a Studebaker engine in 1930, fifth in 1931, and Cliff Bergere placed third with another Studebaker in 1932. The next year Stubby Stubblefield was fifth with a Buick, and Studebakers filled the sixth through 12th places. It was obviously time for someone who was smart to take advantage of the rules.

Who was clever enough to do it?

Preston Tucker *knew* he was.

*L.L. Corum
and the fifth-place car
of the 1923 "500."*

11

Henry Todd Takes a Trip

AT THE CONCLUSION of the 1935 Indianapolis "500" only 12 cars were given the checkered flag, the rest of the field having succumbed to mechanical attrition or accidents. All the finishers were powered by engines bearing the name of Harry Miller; but the four cars he entered in the race, much less the 10 he brought to the Speedway, were gone long before the American classic was finished.

Miller's quartet, the remnants of the 10 he built for the event, were Fords. They represented the first official return to competition by the Ford Motor Company since before World War I.

They were the cause of a major rift between Henry Ford and his son Edsel.

Their failure kept Ford away from auto racing for another 17 years.

They were one of the last racing creations of Harry Armenius Miller, a genius of the sport and a tragic story unto himself. His last try at the Speedway, just before the war, was with a rear-engined car and many considered this the ultimate heresy.

And oddly enough his Fords were the direct ancestors of the Novis, those powerful, supercharged cars that in a quarter of a century were not beaten by anyone but themselves.

Projects of this type have a peculiar nature. In the world of big business people approach corporate citadels many times a day, each with an idea they are positive will make millions for them and for their financiers. Most of them never get inside the gates, figuratively speaking. Either their idea is no good (or too nebulous), or they don't have any contacts, or their approach is not clever enough. Preston Tucker was not handicapped by any of these problems. The magnetic, dapper promoter, who made his biggest splash after World War II with his scheme to establish another auto manufacturing company, had the idea, the contacts and the ability to sell almost anything. His idea, even when viewed in the objective light of history, was a good one. The project just ran out of time. Tucker, a familiar figure at Indianapolis in the early 1930s, formulated his plans after the 1934 race. The stock-block cars, despite their obvious backyard engineering, had been doing well in the "500." So the thing to do was take a production model and do a really sophisticated job of converting it. Tucker first rounded up Miller, who was in his financial decline and ready to work for anyone. The chance to collaborate on another racing car sold him in a moment, and from his vast supply of ideas he rapidly laid out the basic specifications. As soon as Tucker had Miller involved, they set up Miller-Tucker, Inc., and headed in two directions at once in the fall of 1934.

Miller went out looking for drivers, and with his name and his reputation they were easy to find. Pete DePaolo, who was seriously injured at Barcelona in the Spanish Grand Prix that year, agreed to lead the team, and Miller busily added others to his lineup. Drive a new Harry Miller car? Getting pilots for the creations of the genius was like selling dollar bills for 50 cents. Cliff Bergere was signed early and so was Ted Horn, at that time a promising rookie from California. The word was out, and the grapevine of the racing fraternity was alive.

While Miller lined up drivers and drew his plans, Tucker went about the business of selling the project to Ford. He'd worked for the company at one time and knew Edsel would be more amenable than Henry, so he spoke to the younger man. In the final analysis this is where the plan broke down; corporations do not move as quickly as promoters, and the time they took to make up their minds—and for Edsel to convince his father—eventually doomed the cars to failure. It simply took too long. Although much had been talked about, things did not start to move until Tucker sent the following telegram to W.C. Cowling, the general sales manager, on January 3, 1935:

"Relative to pending deal Ford V eight race cars or Miller Specials visualize Movietone news reels taken at Speedway Mr. Ford Mr. Miller world's leading race drivers even Barney Oldfield and Eddie Rickenbacker inspecting race cars then the V-eights coming in 1st and 2nd to clinch their performance superiority it would be real news interesting stories pictures spreading all over the world creating great dealer salesman enthusiasm stop This would be Miller's eighth consecutive win and this with the famous Ford V eight engine giving to entire performance records in this country stop Surely Miller's ability on race cars is supreme our sincerity absolute stop We will assume all responsibility. Preston Tucker"

The reply was not as enthusiastic, but more to the point:

"So far have not made progress realize its possibilities hope to get final decision next week. W.C. Cowling"

By the end of the month things had seemingly been worked out, and Tucker sent a letter to John R. Davis, then the assistant general sales manager, giving him a detailed outline of the costs. The letter is one of the great examples of over-optimism, even when it is remembered that costs in 1935 were considerably less than they are in the 1960s. (The cash price of the project—according to Tucker's January projection—was little more than the present list price of a Ford Indianapolis engine.)

The first engine and the last one: (Top) The modified flathead Ford V8 originally installed in Harry Miller's chassis, complete with the ill-conceived steering box at left. (Bottom) The supercharged Novi, shown here in its initial container; it was inserted into the Miller chassis in the spring of 1941. With the car are, from left, designer Leo Goossen, Fred Offenhauser and Bud Winfield.

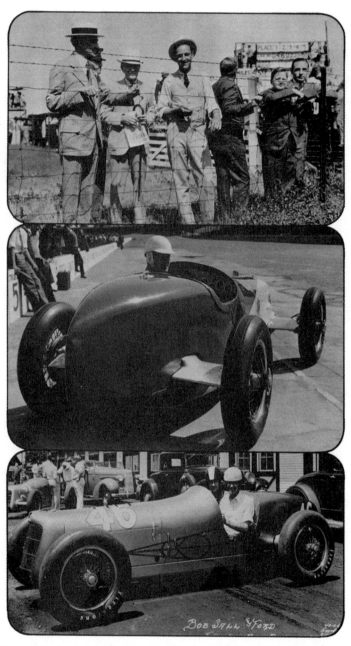

(Top) Preston Tucker in his shirt sleeves with, from left, Henry Ford, Harvey Firestone, Henry Ford II (back turned), Benson and Edsel Ford at Indianapolis in the early 1930s. (Middle) Cliff Bergere ready to go, 1935. (Bottom) Bob Sall and his late-arriving car.

The cars and their designer: (Top) Driver George Bailey with one of the Miller-Fords, and (Bottom) Bailey again, posing with Miller (white hat). The company also supplied cars for the officials.

January 21st, 1935

Mr. J.R. Davis,
Ford Motor Co.
Dearborn, Mich.

Dear Sir:

Approximate cost estimated on ten race cars using Ford V-8 engines and as many Ford parts as possible.

The following parts to be furnished by you:

12 V-8 engines with starters
12 sets ring gears, pinions, and differential units
12 oil and heat indicators
12 sets brakes

Below are the parts we must make up:

Chassis

Front end assembly	
Rear end assembly	
Brakes	$7,500.00
Transmissions and universal joints	
20 special carburetors and manifolding	
Frames, cross members and fittings	1,500.00
Wheels, inner hubs, wing nuts, ball bearings	2,000.00

Bodies

Tails	
Hoods and pans	
Cowls	3,500.00
Radiator shells	
Tires	
Upholstery and trim	6,500.00
Labor and incidental expenses	
Detail drawings	1,500.00
Patterns	1,500.00

Tanks

Gas, 15 gal. Balloon	
Oil	1,000.00
Radiator cores and assembly	
	$25,000.00

We agree to complete the ten cars by May 10, 1935, and will then enter them in the Indianapolis 500-mile race. We will select five of this country's best drivers and five good drivers. Mr. Miller and I will assume all responsibility and expense, team management, handling pit crews, timing, etc.

It is our sincere belief that these cars will finish 1-2-3, making this Mr. Miller's eighth consecutive win in this international classic.

(signed) Preston Tucker

Now the project was ready to go and Ford bowed out for legal reasons, turning the operation over to N.W. Ayer, its advertising agency at the time.

On paper Ayer would be the one dealing with Miller-Tucker, Inc. The only thing Ford had to do—or so the company thought—was approve the expenditure. The manner in which it was handled is seen in an intracompany communication of February 4, 1935 from T.W. Skinner of the sales department to B.J. Craig, the corporate secretary:

"We discussed with you the other day a plan for the handling of the expense in connection with the building of 10 racing cars which Messrs. Miller & Tucker are undertaking for the Indianapolis races.

"It is our understanding that Mr. Edsel Ford has approved using $25,000 of the dealer advertising and sales promotion fund to assist in the development of these cars. We would appreciate your authority to handle this expense through the Dearborn branch dealer fund. As soon as the work has been completed all branches will be billed their proportionate share of the expense."

On February 7, 1935, Ayer was given the go-ahead. Then, later in the month, Ayer and Miller-Tucker got together on paper. Tucker had a reputation for being a great promoter of the dollar, and a look at the contract proves this. In addition to this $25,000, they came up with another $50,000. And $75,000 in the Depression-ridden thirties was a lot of money.

But time was running out. The machinery, equipment, etc., that Tucker borrowed from Ford for the workshop in Detroit didn't arrive until March 12. That left little more than two months in which to build 10 cars, test them, take out the inevitable bugs, get them qualified for the race—and win it. This was patently impossible. That they got 10 cars built and to the Speedway by May 26 (the date the last one arrived) was in itself miraculous.

Even more amazing was Tucker, from whom ideas flowed in a never-ending stream. On March 26, while Miller and his crew were working day and night to build the cars, Tucker was propositioning Ford for still another deal: after he and Miller had won the "500," Tucker wanted to set the land speed record in a car sponsored by the company.

While Miller worked and Tucker promoted, the word got around, and Ford dealers throughout the country were getting excited over the Indianapolis project. They each had a share in the cars through their participation in the dealer advertising fund, and they knew victory would be a big help to sales; between the Depression and General Motors, Ford dealers were having a rough time. Years later Leo Goossen, the great engineer who has had a hand in most of this country's racing engines over the past four decades, remembered it. "All the Ford agencies said 'With Henry Ford

The changing faces: From their original 1935 configuration (left-hand page, bottom and middle photos), the Miller-Fords got new body shapes and, in some cases, new engines. At top on left page is Herb Ardinger in one of the first Offenhauser-equipped cars which placed sixth in the 1938 race. On the right-hand page, from the top: the Granatelli brothers'

1947 car, in which Pete Romcevich placed 112th; Cliff Bergere in the Offy-powered third-place finisher of 1939, and Ralph Hepburn in the first Novi, which placed fourth in the 1941 race. The middle car on the left-hand page was driven by Ted Horn with Bo Huckman as mechanic: the men in the bottom photo are not identifiable.

and Harry Miller, how can we lose?'" Then Leo smiled sadly and shrugged his shoulders. As an engineer, and especially as an ex-Harry Miller engineer, he knew racing cars were not built overnight.

Eventually, with the help of a crash program at Ford's River Rouge plant, the cars were built, and they were beautiful. The ultimate in streamlining at the time, everything was enclosed in the smooth, low-slung body. Even the exhaust pipes were built into the steel floor, and this was the Achilles' heel. They were the first front-wheel-drive cars with four-wheel independent suspension ever seen at the Speedway, and Miller had even constructed winglike duraluminum castings which functioned as fairings for the area between the body and the wheels. The exhausts were flexible metal tubes where they left the manifolds, these running under the engine to where they joined with a rectangular pipe 12 inches wide and 1½ inches deep which ran to the rear of the car, with the entire pipe being enclosed in a special spot provided for in the chassis. The steering box was located right alongside the exhaust system, where it was soon to absorb all the heat of a hard-running engine. This would result in the grease being cooked out of the box, and in the eventual distortion of the gears.

The engine was basically stock Ford flathead V8, turned around in the chassis for purposes of front-wheel drive, with 9.5/1 compression ratio, some of the cars with four single-choke carburetors, some with two double chokers. A racing camshaft was used, as were light alloy cylinder heads, and the entire setup produced about 150 horsepower at 5,000 rpm. There were no rev counters in the cars, which had 160 mph speedometers instead—leading observers to believe the advertising agency had done a little more than just provide the money. In an effort to make the cars as slim as possible, Miller had offset the riding mechanic's seat several inches behind that of the driver, and had provided a hole in the bodywork through which the mechanic could stick his left arm, thus getting it out of the driver's way.

When the first one was delivered to the track May 12, practice had been under way for almost two weeks and the Ford drivers were itchy. Then team captain DePaolo was scheduled to drive the new arrival in a demonstration run for a large group of dealers who were invited to the Speedway May 15 to see their new baby.

"I looked at the car and the engine looked beautiful," DePaolo says, "but it had a new arrangement for the steering gear, with various rods, and there was one connection where they had this little gear, and I said, 'What's that,' and Miller said, 'It's the steering box,' and I said, 'It looks like an oil pump to me, Harry, how you going to keep it lubricated?' He said, 'Don't worry, you just drive it,' and I said, 'It doesn't look good to me.' So I drove it around for a couple of laps, and then when I stepped on it going out of the second turn, I couldn't straighten this thing, out. It was heading for the inside. So I came back in and told Harry I wouldn't drive the car. So we tried everything—grease, soap, lard, trying to fix it. I told him that car wasn't safe, and he asked me to at least drive it for the dealers some more."

So DePaolo got out of the car and so did Bergere, leaving Ted Horn, Johnny Seymour, Dave Evans, George Barringer, Bob Sall, Billy Winn, George Bailey, the veteran Lora Corum (who drove a Barber-Warnock in 1923), Wes Crawford and Johnny Rae. Suddenly the stars were gone. Other Fords were also having difficulty. There were five of them entered, in mostly stock condition, and a day or two after DePaolo hung it up, a Ford from Chicago also pulled out. The story reporting this fact called the vehicle's rookie pilot Duke Nolan. In a few years, the fact that the "a" and the "o" were transposed would be common knowledge, as Nalon went on to a long career at Indianapolis. None of the five made it.

In Detroit they were frantically putting cars together, and in Dearborn they were working day and night to get engines ready. All details of the contract were forgotten now—everyone knew there were Fords in the race, and the object was to get the best possible engines into them. Henry Ford was angry, and Edsel Ford crossed his fingers. All available men were thrown into the job of engine building. Don Sullivan, who as a young engineer had helped with the design work on the flathead and the V8-60 in the fall of 1931, had come up with the intake manifold design for the race cars, and they were cast and rushed to the engine assembly room. (Years later Sullivan was responsible for the high performance versions of the 289-inch V8 that was so successful in the mid-1960s, plus a host of other engine improvements.)

Bill Speedie, one of the company's best mechanics, had some hot flatheads installed in a few speedboats across the Detroit River in Canada, and he was contacted and told to rush them to Indianapolis. When he got there, Speedie and *de facto* Ford chief engineer Laurence Sheldrick spent the entire pre-race period installing engines, and worked Horn's pit during the event itself.

Henry Todd, one of the top mechanics on Henry Ford's personal staff, remembered that three weeks before the race there were no engines. "We started to build those engines," Todd says, "and I couldn't begin to say how many vendors we had in here—pistons, bearings, everything. Then we began to work on the engines and in the first week I had eight hours' sleep. Clocks didn't mean much in those days. At the end of the week P.E. Martin asked me, 'How are you standing it?' and I said I'd been home twice and had four hours' sleep each time. He said, 'You're doing better than I am—I haven't even been home once.' As soon as an engine was ready—we didn't even test them—it was put into a coupe and taken right to Indianapolis."

Todd also remembered the visits. "Both Fords were around every day during those last weeks—and you could sense that Mr. [Henry] Ford didn't like it. By the time of the race he was so mad that he wouldn't even go."

At the track the drivers were still cooling their heels and getting nervous, especially those who were making their debut at the big circuit. One of these was Sall, a slim, bespectacled youngster from Ridgewood, N.J., who had cut his racing teeth on a Fronty-Ford in the late 1920s and who was the terror of the eastern dirt tracks in the early 1930s. A close friend of Horn and Winn, they had recommended him for a seat, and Tucker signed him. Early in May Sall packed a suitcase and headed west. Now, with the month almost over, he was still without a race car. What made it worse was the knowledge that the cars could be pretty good—if they would ever arrive and get the steering problem solved.

"The cars themselves were way ahead of anything that had been seen at the Speedway," Sall says, "and with the lack of real power we could just stand on them all the way around. If we had a comparable engine to any of the better engines that were there—in that automobile, I think we could have run off and hid from them. In that day, the car was far ahead in design ... you could even say it was the forerunner of the roadster, it was so low."

Qualifying opened May 19 and Rex Mays won the pole position with an average of 120.736 for his 10 laps, during which drivers were restricted to 2½ gallons of fuel (for the race itself they were limited to 42½ gallons). The Fords—those that were there—did not line up to qualify, and it was not until May 27 that the first two made the field—Horn at an average of 113.213, Seymour with a speed of 112.696. The panic in the Ford plants, garages and points between continued. Then Bailey made it with 109-plus, and on the final day Sall qualified. His car, the last to arrive, had shown up only two days earlier.

Sall had perhaps 10 laps of practice before he went out to qualify. "We never had the opportunity to run long enough in practice to see if the steering *would* lock up," he says, "and there wasn't any time to experiment with the rear-end ratios; you just ran what they'd put in the car." While Sall was getting his vehicle ready, Todd was drawing a breath of relief back in Dearborn. At least his job was done and now he could go home and get some sleep, or so he thought. He was called in by Henry Ford and told he was to go to the Speedway.

"Here's a box seat ticket," Ford said. "I don't even want to see the race. You go down and watch it and tell me what you think about it." Then, as Ford turned to go he added, "and don't forget—we're going to work Friday." Todd found a friend with a car and they left for Indianapolis, arriving at 8 a.m. after driving all night.

Sall's was the first Ford to drop out. "The car was overheating and it was also steering real hard, so I came in to get some water, and as I was sitting in the pits a technical inspector came over and tried to turn the steering wheel and he couldn't. Then I tried it and I couldn't either; it had locked up so bad that when we tried to get it out of the pits we had to jack it up to get it back to the garage. I think it was probably bad enough out on the race track, where a little air was getting in there to cool it off, but when you stopped, it seized permanently." Sall lasted 22 laps, Bailey 65, Seymour 71, and Horn 145. All of them, with the possible exception of Seymour, went out with the same malady, and Seymour's—if it was not the steering box—was located right next to it in the front-drive housing and was also caused by the heat from the exhaust.

It was an ignominious end to a project that began with great hopes and little time. It was also a mediocre start for Horn: He was to enter the "500" nine more times and never finish lower than fourth. The cars were confiscated by Henry Ford, despite the contract that said they were the property of Miller-Tucker, Inc., and stored in one of the back rooms of the Highland Park plant. Speedie remembers, "If you wanted to look at them you kind of had to sneak around through the back door and make sure nobody caught you." What methods Ford used to reclaim the cars from Miller and Tucker are not known, but there are documents dated later that summer in which all right and title to the vehicles was turned over to the Ford Motor Company.

The cars were locked up for more than two years. Then, sometime in late 1937, certain friends of the company were able to buy them. Lou Fageol, the bus manufacturer, and Lew Welch, the spare parts supplier, are assumed to have purchased most of them. Welch was from nearby Novi, Mich., which got its name from being the sixth stop on the Detroit-Lansing toll road, and then having the Roman numerals tacked on the abbreviation for "number." He was not only a parts manufacturer for Ford in Michigan, but he rebuilt Ford engines in California. And, more important, he was friendly with Ray Dahlinger, one of Henry Ford's cronies. Welch saw that Miller's idea was good, that the steering troubles could be cured, and that a more powerful engine was needed.

He installed a four-cylinder Offenhauser in place of the Ford and in 1938 Herb Ardinger drove the car, now dubbed the Offenhauser Special, into sixth place. The next year Cliff Bergere took third with the same vehicle. In 1940 Ralph Hepburn had the car and the steering again gave trouble, freezing on the 47th lap and sending Hepburn into a spin. By this time Welch saw that still more power was needed, so he went to Fred Offenhauser and ordered a 3.0-liter supercharged V8. Offenhauser got Leo Goossen to do the design work on the engine, for which such basic items as bore, stroke, bearing size, etc., were specified by Bud Winfield, Welch's chief mechanic. Goossen started work on the drawings late that summer, and by spring the engine was ready for installation in the old Ford chassis.

For that reason Goossen designed it with the left-hand cylinder block offset forward, just like the flathead Ford, and the engine was also designed to mate up (and it still will) with a Ford bell housing. In its debut at the Speedway, with the veteran Hepburn again driving, the Novi took fourth place, the Miller chassis proving itself despite dealing with 300 more horsepower than its creator had dreamed of having. By the time the war ended the Ford chassis was long gone, but the Novi remained. Through the years it was used and abused, refined in design, and reduced to the instrument of a sales promotion campaign. Like the 1935 race cars from which it stemmed, it never lived up to its promise.

Several of the other cars also returned to Indianapolis. In 1940 George Robson drove one equipped with an Offenhauser engine, lasting 57 laps. Louie Tomei finished 11th in the same car in 1941, and a similar vehicle entered by Fageol left the scene after 13 laps with Mel Hansen driving. In 1946 Shorty Cantlon was able to run 28 laps in a Miller-Ford-Offy, and Paul Russo's Twin-Coach Special (a Fageol conception) used two Miller drive units originally built for Ford—one for each of its

Offenhauser midget engines. The same year Andy Granatelli, a Chicago speed shop owner, showed up with what was known as the Grancor V8 Special. Granatelli, who years later became the STP additive king, had barnstormed the car through the Midwest, with practically the only worthwhile alteration being installation of a fresh Mercury engine which also sported a pair of Granatelli's heads (observers said they bore a remarkable resemblance to those made by Vic Edelbrock on the West Coast).

Danny Kladis drove the car for the 52 laps it lasted that year. In 1947 Henry Banks, now the USAC director of competition, took another (equipped with an Offenhauser engine) around the big Speedway for 38 laps, and Pete Romcevich finished 11th in another of Granatelli's Miller-Ford Mercurys. That was the end of it, as far as participation in the race was concerned. Several were back for qualifying in 1948 and 1950, but none were fast enough. Chris Economaki, the editor of *National Speed Sport News,* recalls seeing Red Byron trying to qualify one of the cars at Langhorne in the early 1950s—one of the few times anyone ever attempted to race a front-drive vehicle on the dirt. But that was a long way from Indianapolis, and even farther from Dearborn.

Time, which Harry Miller had run out of in 1935, had finally caught up with his creations.

The Grancor V8 Special made its last appearance in 1948, with Andy Granatelli as the pilot. He crashed during qualifying. More than a decade later Andy was back—this time as the head of STP.

12

THE DUTCHMEN AND
THE ROMANIANS

THE SOPHISTICATED PRECINCTS of European motorsports received a rude shock in the 1930s. It was the arrival of the flathead Ford, which managed to show its exhaust pipes to a lot of higher-priced machinery in most of the long-distance rallies of the time and especially at Monte Carlo.

Rallying, in its major league form, consists of something on the order of three days and two or three nights of nonstop, high-speed driving on the worst roads imaginable, roads that can effectively destroy an automobile in that span of time and make the crews—even the successful ones—hollow-eyed zombies who keep going mainly on their nerves. Today, with the great number of cars crowding European roads, the time of the long-distance rally is drawing to a close (it never arrived in this country). But back in the 1930s they were real adventures, and the *grande dame* was the Rally Monte Carlo.

Europe's drivers were itching for a chance to do something in the winter and the Monte gave it to them. There was a great deal of romanticism attached to the events, with such starting points as Athens, Tallinn, Berlin, Stavanger, Lisbon. Umea, and even John O'Groats, at the northern tip of Scotland. In those days, with the routes across the Balkans little more than unmarked tracks, many of the crews that chose Athens for the start carried guns. In severe winters wolves would come down out of the mountains and roam the roads in Yugoslavia.

The various routes—you got bonus points for choosing the longest, most difficult one—would all lead toward Monaco, and if you reached every checkpoint on time, at Monte Carlo there was an eliminating test to decide the winner. In years of heavy snow the road section of the rally usually whittled the entry down to a few unpenalized cars; in warmer years, the high-speed gymkhana at the end was the decisive item despite more than 2,000 arduous miles.

In 1936 there were 26 Fords entered and 16 of them finished, with the top ones being first, fourth, sixth and ninth. A trio of Romanians with the music-hall names of

Both Fords? (Top) A Romanian army colonel's special-bodied car that ran in the 1937 Monte, complete with detachable skis for the front wheels and tanklike treads for the rears. Only one set of the rear wheels was actually driven; the others served merely as something on which to hang the treads (the extra set was also easily demountable). (Bottom) The 1938 Monte Carlo winners: Dutchmen Bud Bakker Schut and Klaas Barendrecht.

*Disqualified (top and middle): 1936 winner P.G. Cristea's 1937 entry.
Although special bodies and engine modifications were permitted, the rear wheels
were not supposed to project beyond the fenders. (Bottom) The "tank tread" car
without the accoutrements, at speed in the 1937 final test.*

(Top) Englishman Gerry Burgess in a Ford Zephyr during the 1954 Monte. (Bottom) 1953 winners Maurice Gatsonides (left) and co-driver Peter Worledge with the Zephyr.

Zamfirescu, Constantinescu and Cristea won the event, with the parents of Harry Schell, the postwar grand prix driver, second in a Delahaye.

Cristea, who drove a special-bodied Ford convertible with only the most primitive top, had practiced the gymkhana section of the event more than 400 times in Bucharest, and had fitted his car with a locked rear end in order to gain precious seconds. How he ever got the locked rear through the snows to Monte Carlo is best left to the imagination. Bud Bakker Schut, the Javanese Dutchman who was fourth, had also practiced assiduously, and had even installed a gimmick to help him get around the hairpins in the maneuvering test: A steel cable ran from his steering arm to the rear-wheel brake levers so that he could lock one of the drums while turning the steering wheel (they allowed that kind of modification in those days). Bakker Schut, who was second after the first run through the course, knew he had to establish a large margin over the Romanians the next time through, and he gave it everything. Unfortunately everything was a bit much; his skid around a pylon was so violent that he spun out and was forced to back up before continuing.

Except for a similar error, there was a Romanian Army colonel who might have won the whole thing in his Ford, which was one of the most interesting cars ever seen in the rally. He had the standard flathead V8 and chassis, but on top of this was a light alloy body, and hung on to the sides was an ingenious arrangement designed to carry him through deep snows. There were skis to be fitted on the front tires, and the two spare wheels could be mounted on hubs which placed them in front of the normal driving wheels. A tanklike tread was then fitted over the two wheels, and the Ford would chug through almost anything.

In 1937 Rene Le Begue, the French racing driver, won in a Talbot and Cristea was seventh. Then in 1938 Bakker Schut won as Fords had the greatest success any one make has ever enjoyed in this ancient event. There were 26 Fords (25 of them V8s) at the start: 19 of them won cups of one sort or another, and Fords placed 1-4-5-6-7-14-15 in the general classification. Le Begue, who arrived at the start with a case of champagne in his car, made it close again and was disqualified on another technicality after an improper run through the gymkhana course. Second place went to Jean Trevoux in a Hotchkiss, Trevoux being the man who was to eventually win the rally four times and also perform so impressively with both a Delahaye and a Packard in the later Mexican road races. One of Trevoux's quartet of victories came in the 1951 Monte Carlo, an event which drew such American makes (privately entered) as Plymouth, Pontiac, DeSoto, Graham-Paige, Kaiser, Hudson, Chevrolet, Dodge, Buick, Mercury, Studebaker—and a 1947 Ford convertible from Portugal. This car, which had 30,000 miles on it when the rally started, and which was a veteran of minor Portuguese events, went off without any fanfare, either for itself or its three-man crew—Manuel Palma, the Comte de Real and the Marquis de Fronteira.

Once, they came within an ace of not making it. Lost in the fog, they decided to follow the car in front of them. When he went off the road, they almost did the same.

That year there was a high-speed test around the Monaco grand prix circuit to decide the final classification, and the flathead beat a lot of highly favored equipment to finish in the runner-up spot. Palma, who runs one of the bigger garages in Lisbon, still has the car.

But rallies, from a factory standpoint, were of little interest to Dearborn. A little over a decade later, when Monte Carlo and the rest became attractive to Americans, the rocky walls of mountain roads leading to the Riviera would echo to the roar of another Ford V8—a bigger, more powerful one which produced even faster times and even better slides. In the meantime the make had to content itself with a victory by a British Ford Zephyr in 1953, with Dutch ace Maurice Gatsonides doing the driving. A young Englishman, Stirling Moss, was sixth that year in a Sunbeam. Rallies are a peculiar sport.

13

RENAISSANCE

THE FIRST WORLD WAR served to kill most of the road racing in this country, with oval-track promoters and unsympathetic city officials taking care of what was left. When the Elgin series succumbed after its 1920 running, that was about it; the Vanderbilt Cup, United States Grand Prix, the Cactus Derby and others stopped before or during the war.

From August 28, 1920, when Ralph DePalma won at Elgin in a Ballot, until August 26, 1933, when Fred Frame won on the same circuit in a Ford V8 roadster, there was no major road race held in the United States. In addition to the aforementioned reasons, there was one other: There was no car that was light enough, in possession of the other road-racing qualities and also cheap enough. The introduction in 1932 of the flathead V8 cured this, and a good argument can be made for the Ford being as instrumental as anything else in forming the basis for American sports car racing as it is known today. It was all-conquering in those road races which attracted the oval track type of driver; Ford V8 power was the little-mentioned mainstay of the Automobile Racing Club of America, and other Fords were the kingpins of the Florida promotions that led to the eventual formation of NASCAR.

The Elgin race, plus several others that followed it, were called stock car events, yet the equipment was a curious blend of stock and racing which came out looking more like a sports car than anything else. Fenders were removed from the roadsters and so were windshields, and when 1932 Indianapolis winner Frame crossed the finish line at Elgin, he led a parade of Fords that filled the first seven places in the 203-mile event for the Weidenhoff Trophy. Frame's average for the event, limited to cars of 231 cubic inches displacement, was 80.22 mph on the same 8¼-mile course which DePalma covered at a speed of 79 mph (for 251 miles) in the previous running.

The lack of spectator safeguards put an end to the Elgin series after one attempt at revival, and from there the scene moved to Mines Field. Now the site of Los Angeles airport, part of what is now LAX was the scene of stock-car racing with Ford convertibles from 1932 until 1936. This was the first American circuit to use

FRED FRAME—*famous racing driver,
Winner of Indianapolis Speedway Classic,
1932. Winner of Elgin Stock Car Race,
1933. Holder of twenty-one national and
international world's straightaway records.*

Here's what a Famous Racing Driver says about

The NEW FORD V·8

"I PICKED a Ford V-8 for the 1933 Stock Car Race at Elgin and I thought it was a great car when it brought me home in front. It takes a lot of automobile to average 80.22 miles an hour for 200 miles over a course like that.

"When I heard that the 1934 Ford V-8 was even better than the 1933 job I was just a little doubtful. It just didn't seem possible, but I thought I'd find out.

"I could see it was better-looking, but I wasn't much interested in that. The thing a racing driver looks at is the engine. How does it sound? How is it built? How fast will it go? How does it stack-up on gas and oil?

"So I took it out on the road and opened it up. It held the road like a veteran and the way that speedometer touched the top numbers was something to talk about. If I'd had that car in the Elgin race I'd have averaged closer to 90 than 80.

"You can put me down as saying this New Ford V-8 is going to go places in 1934. It's a sweet job all the way through and that new dual carburetion system is going to save you a lot of money on gasoline."

Fred Frame winning 1933 Elgin Road Race in Ford V-8

THE OUTSTANDING VALUE FOR 1934

ELEVEN BODY TYPES

$515 up

*(F. O. B. Detroit, plus freight,
delivery and tax. Bumpers and
spare tire extra. Convenient terms
through Authorized Ford Finance
Plans of Universal Credit Co.)*

Meet Fred Frame and see his winning Ford V-8 at the Ford Exhibit, Los Angeles Automobile Show, Feb. 3 to 11

Road racing between the two world wars saw a variety of equipment being used. (Top) Fred Frame and Ford after the 1933 Elgin race. (Middle) John C. "Smudge" Draper at Alexandria Bay, N.Y., in 1937 with a Bugatti powered by a Model A engine. (Bottom) An MG leads the pack down the main street of Alexandria Bay in the 1938 race.

(Top) Former Briarcliff novice Joel Thorne at Indianapolis in 1938. One of his mechanics, here sitting in the center, was a young man from Florida—Bill France. (Bottom) The start at Montauk, N.Y., 1940. At left in the front row is Lemuel Ladd and the Old Gray Mare. At right is eventual winner George Rand and his Maserati.

Two of the entries in the 1934 Mines Field race,
Shorty Cantlon (top) and Swede Smith (bottom).

(Top) A French Amilcar equipped with a Model B four-cylinder, driven at Alexandria Bay in 1940 by Dick Wharton. (Middle) A typical MG conversion of the late 1940s, with a Ford V8-60 taking the place of the original engine. (Bottom) Under way at Montauk, 1940, with the Old Gray Mare about to lap an Alfa Romeo driven by Wharton.

parts of airport runways, and this is where Stubby Stubblefield won the Gilmore Gold Cup on February 24, 1934. Of the 26 entries, 22 were Fords, and they occupied the first 10 places in the results. Such name drivers as Al Gordon, Pete DePaolo, Lou Meyer, Rex Mays and Ted Horn finished second through sixth, and the crowd of 60,000 saw a change from the usual round-and-round proceedings. The Mines Field event was probably the first airport race ever held in this country. From there, with enthusiasm high, the party proceeded to Ascot Legion Speedway, which scheduled a 150-miler called the American Targa Florio for March 21. The 1½-mile course utilized most of the half-mile oval track, then ran off into the hills for the rest of the distance. The promoters, never having seen the famous Sicilian road circuit after which they named their event, went at it with a vengeance; there was one hill with a 25-degree grade and another of 28 degrees, making it more suitable for mountain goats than cars.

Horn, after dueling with Meyer most of the way, finally finished second after a loose brake rod slowed him with two laps to go, but he had made his name. This was his first outstanding performance, and it was to lead to an Indianapolis invitation for 1935. The race itself was such a success that it was never run again. Not only did 22,000 spectators pay at the gate, but thousands more were able to sneak in through the hills. The sight of so many party crashers prompted the promoters to go back to their oval track—with everyone paying to watch. From this point on, AAA-style road racing with big-name drivers went downhill. A few weeks later Meyer won a 250-miler for the sports-stockers at the Oakland, Calif., one-mile oval, and then it was back to the minor leagues for roadsters. The only other time big-name AAA talent appeared en masse at a road race was in the Mercedes and Auto Union-dominated Roosevelt Field events of 1936 and 1937, and they were far beyond the capabilities of any Ford.

While road racing again disappeared on the West Coast, in the East it was revived by an informal group of wealthy young enthusiasts who eventually turned out to be the fathers of the Sports Car Club of America, and therefore the predecessors of present-day United States road racing.

The club was started by the three Collier brothers, Miles, Sam and Barron, Jr., on their Pocantico Hills estate near Briarcliff, N.Y. (where as teen-agers they held informal events on the driveways and service roads surrounding the family mansion). From there it grew in 1934 to a miniature circuit of between five-eighths and three-quarters of a mile (with 11 turns!) which was built on some of the family's nearby property. It was at one of these races, in June of the year, that the club got its badge. A young illustrator who worked for the boys' father was at an event and made some sketches which he hung on the walls of his office. The kids liked the drawings so much they prevailed upon him to design an emblem for them, which took the form of a head-on view of an Auburn Speedster. The illustrator was William E. Mitchell, today the General Motors vice president of design, which is a long way from the Sleepy Hollow Ring in Westchester County.

Fords started to come into the picture then, as Model B engines and others of four-cylinder configuration were installed in foreign chassis when the original power plants gave up the ghost. There was a Model B in an Amilcar and there was another Ford in a Lancia Lambda, for example. In 1935 Sidney Shurcliff won at Marston's Mills, on Cape Cod, with a stock flathead roadster in which he installed a suitcase full of stones on the passenger seat to keep himself from sliding across.

The ARCA had a visitor at its Briarcliff race that year, the second of two run on a 3.3-mile circuit of public roads in the area. He was a tall, skinny youngster from New Rochelle, down at the lower end of the county, and he came with a hot Ford roadster that was the quickest car in the race. His name was Joel Thorne, and he was interested in anything that would go fast—be it cars, boats or airplanes. The winter before, he and John Oliveau entered the car in the Monte Carlo Rally and wound up getting stuck in seven feet of snow somewhere near Ljubliana, in Yugoslavia. It was a good one, and it should have been; it had a factory-prepared engine. Oliveau, who is now technical consultant to the Automobile Competition Committee of the United States, remembers how they obtained it:

"We'd gotten the name of Laurence Sheldrick through some people we'd known from boat racing, so we got into Joel's mother's Lincoln and drove out to Detroit. When we told Sheldrick what we were up to, be made a few calls and crooked his finger in the right direction and then they told us to drive the Lincoln around to a certain loading door. When we got there they put the engine in the trunk."

The engine was a duplicate of the one Frame used to win the 1933 Elgin race, and Oliveau is reasonably sure Frame's power plant came from the same source. At the time, Oliveau says, "Anyone who could get hold of Mr. Ford or one of his intimates and tell them what he wanted the engine for—well, a gleam would come into his (Ford's) eyes and he would *do* things; he was still a racing fan." Thorne led for most of the race, but too many excursions up escape roads dropped him to second and he gave up autos for the time being, preferring to stick with his boats. The next time Thorne got close to an automobile race was in 1937, when at the age of 22 he entered five cars at Indianapolis, including one for himself. When he was told to go home and get more experience, he attempted to buy the entire field, creating one of the better legends of the Speedway.

One of the most venerable and most successful cars of the ARCA period was the Old Gray Mare, a creation of John Rueter and Lemuel Ladd which first Rueter, and then in its later years, Ladd drove. It started life with a Model T engine, later went to a Model A, and Ladd eventually stuffed a flathead V8 between its frame rails. Before it was eventually outclassed by the Maseratis and Alfa Romeos that members bought in the late 1930s, it was probably the fastest car in the club, and at one time or another set records at the Mount Washington hill climb (Rueter and Ladd, in different years), had fastest lap at the Memphis Cotton Carnival and at Alexandria Bav, N.Y. (both Rueter), and won races at Alexandria Bay, and Montauk Point, N.Y. (both Ladd). It won more events than any other ARCA car, including the factory-sponsored Willys team. It was a long way from those days to the 190 mph Lolas and McLarens of today, but the genealogy is easy to trace.

After the war, when the Old Gray Mare was resurrected from its place of storage, there were other, faster Ford-powered cars that led to the rebirth of road racing, first in the East and a few years later on the West Coast. At Watkins Glen, N.Y., in 1949, Miles Collier won with a Brooklands Riley equipped with a flathead Ford. The next year at Palm Beach Shores, Fla., George Huntoon drove a Duesenberg-Ford to victory. John Fitch, later the first American to get a top-class ride with a famous European team (Mercedes-Benz, in 1952 and 1955), had two specials equipped with V8-60s, and won another race at Linden Airport in New Jersey with a Le Mans Lagonda equipped with hotted-up flathead. In California, where road racing started in 1950, the winner of the first event was powered by a flathead V8, and MG TCs with a bellyful of V8-60 were a common sight. One of the most successful sports cars of that era was a special built by Frank Kurtis, then the top man among Indianapolis car builders. It was equipped with a three-carburetor flathead and driven by Bill Stroppe, who in later years became a vital part of the Dearborn performance effort.

It went that way until better engines were made available and until the Europeans started to move in. First there were the Cadillac-Allards, and although they could barely get around a corner, they were hell in a straight line, and the Fords started to run second, and then third. When the first Ferraris started showing up, and then the C-type and D-type Jaguars, it was all over for American iron. Then someone discovered a new V8 built by Chevrolet, and the cycle started again. By now it was not only the social thing to do, but it was also showing signs of becoming major league. In a few more years it would be that, with more people in the pits than there were spectators at Pocantico Hills.

Bill Stroppe and his Mercury-powered Kurtis winning at the Phoenix road races in May 1953.

14

THE BEACH AGAIN

EVEN AFTER FRANK LOCKHART was killed at Daytona, others continued to use the narrow strip of sand for record runs. The absolute limit had not been reached, they felt, at the time of his death in 1928, but eventually Malcolm Campbell found it. He achieved 276 mph in 1935 and said that was enough, future record seekers would have to find another site.

Ab Jenkins, the mayor of Salt Lake City, was the man who discovered it in his own state. The name of the place was Bonneville, and when Campbell took his car there and did 301 mph in the fall of 1935, the Florida beach was finished. For 1936, in an effort to maintain Daytona's reputation as the birthplace of speed, the city fathers decided to stage a stock car race that would use the beach and a road that ran parallel to it. The word soon got around, and among those interested was Bill France, a young local mechanic.

Forced to leave high school in Washington, D.C., when his father took sick, France worked at various jobs and eventually wound up as a gas station attendant. By 1929 he had built a Model T race car in his spare time, and now he took it to the half-mile dirt track at Pikesville, Md. France was ready to challenge the world in his little canvas-bodied car with a 16-valve Roof head. Bill had been to the board track at Laurel, Md., to see the hotshots run, and he knew if he had a car he could do the same.

"It was probably the most unsanctioned race there ever was," France says. "We had no entry blanks or anything else ... I had broken a valve early in the day (in one of the first races), and there was another fellow there who had a Fronty head, and he said, 'You can borrow the head off my car,' so I worked for about an hour with him, changing the cylinder heads; the carburetor was on the opposite side and the accelerator linkage wouldn't hook up, so we just wired it wide open, and I got the car started. We had a magneto shorting button on the steering wheel, so when I got into the corners I'd just push the button, and I drove the race with the car wide open ... well anyway, while we were working on it the promoter was announcing, 'Come on drivers, get your cars out on the line, this is the main event, $500 first place money,' and so forth. I finished third or fourth in it and got $12. So I asked him after the race, 'Hey, you're talking about all this prize money, where is it?' and he said, 'Aw, we just said that for the benefit of the spectators—we're not paying that kind of money.'

"This was my introduction to auto racing."

In 1934 France decided if he was to work on automobiles for a living, he might as well do it where the weather was warm, so he loaded his wife Anne and year-old son Billy into the car and they headed south, with $25 in his pocket and another $75 in the bank. When they got to Brunswick, Ga., the car broke down and Bill had to fix it. When they reached Daytona the money ran out so they settled there. Bill hadn't raced since 1932, when his mother became ill and asked him to stop, and he was not to drive again until 1935, after her death. In the meantime he worked at service stations, and when there wasn't enough to eat he'd go out in the evening and shoot rabbits, or go fishing. France still knows some good fishing holes around Daytona which few others have found.

Then came 1936 and the beach race. The AAA sanctioned it and was to run it as a handicap event with some of the most involved rules ever seen: A car's handicap was based on its qualifying time, and if you bettered your best qualifying lap during the race itself, you would be called into the pits for a warning. The third time you did it, disqualification would result.

Wild Bill Cummings, the 1934 Indy winner, was the fastest in his supercharged Auburn and the slowest man in the field was Sam Collier, he and ARCA companion Langdon Quimby having come down from New York with a pair of Willys. Collier was to be given a half hour head start over Cummings in the 78-lap, 250-mile event on a 3.2-mile course. The race drew a good field, and even an international one. Bob Sall, the 1933 eastern AAA king, walked down the Edgewater, N.J., assembly line with his Ford, making sure everything was screwed together properly, then climbed in and drove to Daytona in 19 hours, which is pushing even in this day of interstate highways. What Sall's ride was like can only be imagined—Sall only smiles about it, because as it turned out, the preparations were all for naught. He wrecked in practice.

Major Goldie Gardner, the British record-breaking star, wound up driving United Press columnist Henry McLemore's Lincoln, and there were Fords for such as Doc MacKenzie, the 1935 eastern AAA champion; Wild Sam Purvis and Hick Jenkins from Jacksonville, and a Dodge for midget ace Bill Schindler. Also in Fords were Milt Marion of St. Albans, L.I., and France, who managed to scare up a sponsor five days before the race. Marion's vehicle was actually a sales promotion car sponsored by Permatex, the sealant manufacturer. The engine was put together without any gaskets except for the cylinder head and was advertised as such, with Marion responsible for driving the car from coast to coast and showing it off whenever and wherever possible. What Milt neglected to tell Permatex President C.A. Benoit was that his first stop would be Daytona.

Sir Malcolm Campbell and "Bluebird" at speed on the beach.

Stock-car drivers, mid-1930s vintage: (Top) Bill France and (Bottom) Bob Sall, who drove from Edgewater, N.J., to Daytona only to crash in practice before the 1936 race.

The race wound up along the lines of Peter Ustinov's famous presentation of the Grand Prix of Gibraltar—it never finished, as the tide came in before they were able to complete the required distance. The winner in the event, which saw practically every car pulled out of the sand by a wrecking crew, was Marion with 75 laps. He gave Permatex an even better deal than they had bargained for. Tommy Elmore was second (74 laps), Ben Shaw third (71), Purvis fourth (70) and France fifth (63).

The race drew between 20 and 30,000 fans, and they saw a good show for their money—those that paid. So many sneaked in the city lost several thousand dollars on the promotion and decided they could not afford it the next year (with a little help from outraged churchmen, who thought the race cars were despoiling the Sabbath).

Then the Elks Club took it over, and they didn't make any money either, so when 1938 rolled around, promotion of the race passed into the hands of Charlie Reese, a local restaurant and nightclub owner. Reese took France in as a partner, and a career was born. They paid a $600 purse and split $200 in profits that year, and for the 1939 race France made the first of the decisions that was to stamp him as the promotional genius of auto racing. Benny Kahn, now the sports editor of the Daytona Beach News-Journal, but then just a kid reporter, remembers it:

"Bill and his wife Anne and I were sitting around, and Bill said he was going to up the ticket price from 50 cents to a dollar, and we told him he was crazy. Well, we got outvoted, one to two, and he was right."

"It was my education in race economics," France says. "You have to charge the right price in order to make any money." They got the same number of spectators as the year before, but when it was all over France and Reese came out of it with $1,000 apiece. "It was the first time I'd ever held $1,000 in my hand," France recalls.

Those were the wildcat days of auto racing in the Southland, and France worked at his gas station during the week and if he could find a race somewhere on the weekend, he'd drive. Finding a race could be a problem, and there were times when Bill would go all the way to Fort Wayne, Ind., or Williams Grove or Langhorne, Pa., to run his stock car. On some of the longer trips, Kahn would go along to drive the tow car through states where towing wasn't allowed. France had been Benny's hero ever since a night in the mid-1930s when Bill rescued him.

"I'd been making like a race driver on Atlantic Avenue and the cops had hauled me in," Kahn says, "and when they told me the fine was $25 I was really stuck, so I called France. He got down there in nothing flat and gave the cops a check and we walked away. When we got outside, I started to thank him, and Bill just said, 'Let's not waste any time—I've got to raise $25 real quick, because I haven't got a nickel in the bank to cover that check!'"

France continued his education at the various tracks. Once, at Williams Grove, he found that although his Ford might be considered stock in the Southeast, the Pennsylvania interpretation of the word was something else. So he worked all night to make the necessary modifications—and won the race. Another time, at Langhorne,

Plowing along: The inaugural race found the soft sand presenting more problems for the cars than did anything else. In top photo, Wild Bill Cummings' supercharged Auburn leads three others through the north turn, while at the bottom a group of Fords braves the fast-disintegrating surface.
At right, a few years later, the Daytona cars found the going considerably easier—and there were a lot more of them (circa 1939).

he thought he'd won, but the officials said he was second and placed Henry Banks, now the USAC competitions director but then one of the better AAA pilots, on top. Bill learned what it was to be an outlaw driver trying to crack the big leagues. Banks hasn't beaten France since, although NASCAR and USAC have had their share of jurisdictional disagreements.

In Florida the beach races continued, with France as promoter and driver too, and his gas station at the corner of Halifax and Main grew to be a meeting point for the out-of-town drivers. Sometimes they'd all gather at Red Vogt's garage in Atlanta, all those Georgia and Carolina drivers who were heading for the beach, and they'd bet more money on who'd get to France's place first than there would be in the entire purse after they arrived. Most of them were bootleggers in order to earn a living, and the Daytona races were more a diversion than anything else. Later on, France showed them racing was more profitable than running whiskey.

He held races on the beach through 1941, and all of them were outlaw, or unsanctioned, as was practically everything in the Southeast. The AAA was an Indianapolis-oriented group, and their attitude was to ignore it, so pickings for stock car drivers were slim. France began to see a solution, and it was an imposing dream that formed in the mind of the Daytona gas station owner.

During the war, when racing was shut down, he thought about it some more and Kahn, who was in the Navy, used to get letters from Bill. "He had this everlasting notion of it being a 'wildcat' sport," Benny says, "and when he'd write, he'd always talk about how he thought he could make some sense out of it."

France got his next lesson in 1945, when the war was over and he rented the dirt track at the Charlotte, N.C., fairgrounds for a race. Bill went downtown to visit the local sports editors, and when he talked to Wilton Garrison of the Charlotte *Observer* he met his next obstacle.

"What kind of a race is this going to be?" Garrison asked.

"It's a 100-mile national championship race," France told him.

Garrison wanted to know who was going to drive in it, and France mentioned Buddy Shuman, Roy Hall and some others, and Garrison said "I can't call it a national championship race—you don't have a national championship."

"What do you have to do to have a national championship?" France asked.

"You have to have point standings, you have to have some records. Why don't you go to the AAA and get them to sanction your races and keep points on them? Then we could call it a championship event."

France went to the AAA in the spring of 1946 and they weren't interested in stock cars. It was too minor league. "We're only interested in big races," France was told. So he decided to form his own organization. That year Bill had something called the National Championship circuit and ran it himself. He promoted about a race a month, and Anne kept the records and the point standings, and Bill had someone take care of his Daytona garage. By the time of the 1947 Daytona races, the arguments over what was stock and what was not stock were getting worse. When the cars went into the impound area in the county barns that year, things were getting involved.

One driver, it was discovered, had a 1934 Ford with a 1939 engine and a 1935 flywheel. They finally disqualified him, ruling the flywheel should have been of 1934 or 1939 vintage but not from a third year. Then there was the case of the valve springs. One car was found with red valve springs instead of the standard green, and it was thrown out. The driver sent his wife home for his pistol, and it got touchy for a few minutes.

France laughs when he thinks about it. "It wasn't until years later," he says, "that we found out the color only identified where the spring was made, and had nothing to do with its strength."

Then there was Smokey Purser, another of the old gang, who insisted his car was all right. He got so agitated he yelled "On my dead mother's grave, I swear I'm legal!"

Joe Littlejohn, the veteran Spartanburg, S.C., promoter, who was also a driver in those days, was not impressed. "You sonofabitch, I *know* your mother—she's living! Let's look under that hood!"

Those were interesting times.

But France's dream of getting everyone under a common roof was taking shape, and other independent promoters showed interest in joining him. In December of 1947 they had a meeting at the Streamline Hotel in Daytona, and out of it came NASCAR—the National Association for Stock Car Auto Racing.

France is one of the great talkers of all time, especially when he is trying to convince someone to think the way he does. His speech to the group assembled in the penthouse of the Streamline on that occasion has to be the most persuasive ever made to a group of racing men, people who are traditionally trying to protect their interests of the moment with little thought for the future. By the time France was through, the entire group was ready to embark upon the great adventure along with him. Some of the things he said 20 years ago are still true today. He missed on a few other minor items, but when viewed from an over-all standpoint, it is remarkable how he called the turn. Some excerpts:

"Nothing stands still in this world; things get better or worse, bigger or smaller.... An average man in a fast automobile can still win races if he's just a reasonably good driver.... A dirt track is more than necessary to make a stock car race a good show Stock car races not held on dirt are nowhere near as impressive.... Stock car racing has distinct possibilities for Sunday races. This would allow race-minded boys who work all week, and who don't have enough money to afford a regular racing car, to be in competition with the rich guy.... They can show their stuff and maybe win something, and still not make it a full-time job."

"We don't know how big this can all be if it's handled properly, and neither does anybody else here."

"I believe it was the night of Labor Day, 1939, we had a discussion after a race here at the beach as to what was stock and what was not stock. I'll bet you there's not a man in the U.S., and I don't care if he's been with Ford and been there for 20 years, or with Buick or any other company, who could come down here and say such a car is stock and such and such is not; these drivers will find something wrong with every stock car in the business.... We want to eliminate after-the-race arguments, and we need the same rules everyplace."

"I believe stock car racing can become a nationally recognized sport ... right here within our group, in my mind, rests the outcome of stock car racing in this country. We have the opportunity to set it up on a big scale ... we are all interested in one thing—improving present conditions. The answer lies in our group."

NASCAR was formed then and there. They set up an office in Daytona, with Bill Tuthill to run it, and in 1948 and for half of 1949 they ran older, modified cars, as there weren't enough new models available for racing. On June 19, 1949, at Charlotte, the first NASCAR Grand National event was held on a three-quarter-mile dirt track. It was won by Jim Roper of Great Bend, Kan., of all places, driving a Lincoln. Roper was given first after the original winner, Glen Dunaway of Charlotte, driving a Ford, was disqualified for illegal modifications. Dunaway's disqualification provoked a $10,000 court suit by his car owner. In a milestone decision, the court ruled—and therefore established the precedent—that the sanctioning body could legally enforce its rules; NASCAR was on its way.

France now sits in a large private office with a picture window that leads to a terrace and gives him a view, when he turns around in his leather swivel chair, of the giant Daytona International Speedway. The chair has his name embossed on it, and when it is vacant the letters stand out clearly.

Even if they weren't there, it is doubtful anyone would have difficulty determining its owner. Seldom has there been a chair with such little need for identification.

15

Los Galvez

WHEN AUTOMOBILE RACING BEGAN in 1894, and for almost a decade thereafter, events were staged on open roads, from one city to another. As the cars grew faster, race organizers increased the distances between the starting and finishing points, until by 1903 the premier event of the season was scheduled to run from Paris to Madrid. When they reached Bordeaux the race was stopped; by that time the carnage included dozens of spectators and several drivers and spelled the end of such competition in Europe. In America what little town-to-town activity there was centered around Phoenix, where the Arizona State Fair served as the finishing point for the Los Angeles–Phoenix and El Paso–Phoenix races which were terminated by World War I. The last hurrah came almost four decades later in the form of Mexico's Carrera Panamericana of 1950–1954, but that was more of an anomaly, a throwback, than anything else.

Throughout the world tests of speed are held in the relatively antiseptic confines of closed circuits, ranging from the walled-in ovals of the United States to such curiosum as Germany's Nürburgring, which is 14 miles of twisting asphalt designed and built as a road racing circuit. Even in Sicily, where once a year they close 45 miles of public thoroughfare to renew the competition for the Targa Florio, the principle is still the same: They are going round and round, covering the same course numerous times in order to accumulate enough distance.

Except in Argentina.

South of the equator, in that vast land which stretches 2,500 miles from Cape Horn to the jungles near Brazil and the mountain passes on the Bolivian border, they still race in the grand manner. The name of the game in Argentina is Turismo Carretera, and to play you need something like a 1939 Ford coupe equipped with hotted-up V8, vestigial fenders, two or even three shocks per wheel and a 60-gallon gas tank.

The season consists, for the most part, of one or two-day events over a course of anywhere from 300 to 1,000 miles—and then there is the Gran Premio, which makes the rest seem insignificant. All of it is on open roads. Some is on pavement, some on dirt, some on straights so long they vanish over the horizon of the pampas, and some of it twists and turns through mountain passes higher than the birds can fly, for 3,000 miles at a crack. But that is today; a few decades ago, when it was done properly, the races were even longer.

Take 1940, for instance. A total of 110 cars started in Buenos Aires and that night the first leg of 850 miles wound up in Tucuman, in the foothills of the Catamarcan Precordillera. From there it was into the mountains, struggling over 15,000-foot passes into Bolivia, through La Paz, and then westward into Peru and up to Lima. When they got there the remaining cars turned around and raced back to Buenos Aires, a distance of 5,900 miles for the round trip. The winner, driving a Chevrolet and breaking a six-year Ford monopoly of the race, was a young mechanic from Balcarce, 250 miles south of the capitol. His name was Juan Manuel Fangio and he had gotten to the big time the season before, when the people of his hometown chipped in to buy him a car. In later years he was to win five world championships and be the greatest driver in history. But his toughest competition came in the dusty heat of the pampas and among the soaring peaks of the Andes, from a pair of flat-head Fords driven by two brothers named Galvez.

They were from Buenos Aires and their father owned a small garage. Oscar started to drive first, in the Gran Premio of 1938. By the end of the year brother Juan was acting as co-driver, and some friends were helping as members of their crew. It was the start of a quarter-century of domination of the sport, in which Oscar and Juan were not only the fastest, but to which they also brought more innovations, advancements and popularity than anyone else. Even before World War II they were the first to install oversize radiators and cure the Ford's chronic overheating problems. They were the first in South America to install roll bars and use helmets, after a 1940 crash sent them 600 feet down a cliff, seriously injuring Oscar and giving him his nickname *Aguilucho*, or "Little Eagle." They were also the first to work out an intelligence system through which their service crews could inform them of the state of the race, but curiously enough always refused to make use of strip maps on which every corner could be noted, trusting instead to their intuition and experience. Even in detail work they were the leaders: Los Galvez were the first to install thermos bottles in the space behind the seats, then run hoses forward so they could sip cooling water while roaring across the plains in 100-degree heat.

They could drive, they could organize, and they were also the best mechanically. Oscar could assemble a Ford carburetor blindfolded, for instance, and Juan once changed all his rods and pistons in less than 45 minutes—during a race. As insurance for emergencies of this type, Galvez service vehicles were identical to the race cars and always carried complete sets of already run-in spares. They even found a quicker way to refuel, using the dangerous method of taking on five-gallon cans through a window, then speeding off again while the co-driver opened the top of the gas tank and split open the cans on spikes projecting from the bottom.

When he started, Juan Manuel Fangio (top) drove single-seater race cars he built himself out of Ford parts. He switched to Chevrolet only when the local Ford dealer didn't have a car for him to buy. (Bottom) The victor of the first real Turismo Carretera race—Angel LoValvo after the 1937 event, being carried away on the shoulders of his fans.

(Top) Far ahead: Oscar Galvez storming along the Bolivian Altiplano during the 1948 running of "La Caracas." (Bottom) The Galvez brothers, from left: Juan, Oscar and Roberto. At right: Oscar (left) and Juan before the start of the 1938 Gran Premio.

Eventually others learned the Galvez' tricks, but by then the brothers had something better.

From the time the war ended and racing resumed in 1947, through 1961, the brothers won 14 of the 15 Argentine national championships, Juan taking nine and Oscar five. Of the 18 ultra-long-distance races held in Argentina from 1939 through 1961 the brothers won 11, with Oscar getting six and Juan five (including three in a row for the latter in 1949–1951). Juan was also second four times and Oscar was the runner-up once. Their battles with Fangio consisted of 17 meetings: Fangio won eight, Oscar four and Juan one, with the remaining four being taken by outside, "disinterested" parties. In the six Grandes Premios, in which the brothers faced the world champion, Oscar and Juan took two apiece, Fangio won one, and the other went to someone else. Fangio gave up Turismo Carretera competition in 1949, claiming the difference in driving styles hurt him when he returned to Formula I racing. The Galvez brothers stayed with it, and although they were almost unknown outside of South America, in that part of the world they grew to be legends.

Oddly, the first Argentine auto race of any sort was held not on the open road, but on a horse track in Buenos Aires in 1901. The town-to-town variety took over in 1910, with the forerunner of the Grandes Premios being run from Buenos Aires to Cordoba, about 475 miles. There were seven entries, including a Model T, and the winner took 30 hours and 42 minutes, driving most of the way in a rainstorm. The Model T was involved in a crash with one of the other competing cars—which is somewhat ludicrous considering there were no more than seven motorized vehicles strung out along the route—but nevertheless finished fourth, in 67 hours. The name Gran Premio Nacional was used for the first time in 1916, and through the 1920s it was run over distances varying from 450 to 900 miles, and on courses usually laid out between Moron, Rosario and Cordoba, with open two-seaters based on Studebaker, Hudson, Hupmobile and Reo chassis being dominant. The four-cylinder Fords, running without the overhead valve conversions so common in the United States, never really got into the act until 1933, when the race was run in a southerly direction for the first time.

When they headed out of Buenos Aires that year the weather was good, and of the 28 starters, 20 wound up in Bahia Blanca, 515 miles away, with Ernesto Blanco's Reo averaging 74 mph to win the leg. On the way back the following morning, steady rains turned the dirt roads into mudholes and one by one the remaining cars started to drop out. Back in the Buenos Aires suburb where the finish line was located, anxious officials waited for the cars, but none came. Finally they extended the maximum time allowed by two hours and still no cars appeared. Then, with 13 minutes left before midnight, a mud-covered Model A struggled out of the darkness. It was Roberto Lozano, a rookie in his first big race. He was the only man to make it, and his average for the return leg, run over the same course, was 40 mph slower than that of the southbound winner.

Criticism of the officials for not postponing the event, plus the death of 1928 champion Domingo Bucci in a minor race soon afterward, led to a prohibition of racing in Buenos Aires Province the next year, so the Gran Premio was moved to roads in the northern part of' the country for 1934 before returning to the capitol in 1935. In that year, more as a move to circumvent local laws against racing on public roads than for any other reason, the Gran Premio first took its present form. Organized in six stages, the event was run as a rally from Buenos Aires to the Chilean border. Then, once inside the other country, it was continued as a race until the roads led back to Argentina, where the rally resumed until Buenos Aires was reached. As a consequence, and to help the drivers in coping with extra-long distances and night driving, the open two-seaters began to be replaced by hardtops. Since the flathead Ford V8 had just been introduced in South America, coupes with this engine were naturals.

In 1936 the event became even more of a race, including a full-blast ascent and descent of the Andes crossing to Chile. A Ford lost it on the last leg, but by 1937 it was 100 percent race again, the Fords were dominant and practically wiped out a Plymouth factory team which bad been active in Argentina for several seasons. In 1938 they held two races, one of 3,900 miles in the southern part of the country and one of 4,600 in the north. The second of these was won by a Ford and Ricardo Risatti, who was driving to raise money to send his invalid wife to the shrine at Lourdes. It was one of the great human interest stories connected with the history of the event, and through men like Risatti the race grew even more in stature.

And while the major race was becoming more important, in the minor leagues, on dusty roads, on shorter circuits outside of small towns in the hinterlands and on informal drag strips around Buenos Aires, the three great names of the sport were moving up. In Balcarce, where Fangio was working in a Ford garage, he was putting together two-seater roadsters in his spare time, and by the summer of 1939 he had driven in perhaps a dozen events with indifferent success. But to the onlookers his talents were obvious, just as was the next step: get Juan Manuel a car he could drive in the Gran Premio. A committee was formed to raise the money by popular subscription, and the whole town began to contribute. The wealthier gave as much as 500 pesos, and there were even children who contributed one peso. Two benefits were run at a local movie house and finally the sum was raised and the great moment arrived. The car could now be purchased. There was no question as to what kind. A Ford was the only thing to have.

But when the committee got to the Balcarce dealership, they found there was no car available, nor would it be possible to get one in time for the race. So they went to the General Motors showroom instead, where they came upon a new Chevy coupe awaiting its owner. When the dealer found the car was wanted for the Gran Premio he said they could have it, but there was still doubt. Fangio stood there eyeing the car. Then he looked at the committee.

"Andará esto?" ("Will that thing go?") he asked. But there was no way out, so they bought it, and in the bargain started an Argentine battle between Ford and Chevy that has continued to this day and is considerably hotter than any Giant-Dodger

baseball series ever was. On one side were the "Fordistas" and on the other the "Chevroletistas," and the war was on from the first time Fangio and the Galvez brothers entered the same race. The almost laughably insignificant lack of having one car in one dealership at the right moment was not only to give Ford a stern competitor for the next three decades, but was also to give GM the benefit of having the five-time world champion indelibly associated with products of its manufacture.

The Galvez boys began working for their father as mechanics, and by 1929, when Oscar was 16 and Juan 13, they had gotten their hands on an old Model T. From there the road led to a Model A and by 1935 to their first flathead. That was the car Oscar started taking to the clandestine drag races, and then to his first Gran Premio in 1938. The next year, with his brother acting as co-driver, Oscar won two major events. The original Gran Premio was stopped after two stages due to torrential rains, and Oscar was declared the winner as he was the leader after 850 completed miles. Of the 119 cars that started the second leg of that one, only 41 managed to finish; the Galvez brothers' average of 20 mph gave them victory by 50 minutes. When things dried out nine days later, they continued the competition under another name and over a course of 2,700 miles; Oscar won again, although Fangio took the toughest leg of the event. Fangio's performance in the earlier stages had attracted the notice of the GM team, which had taken him under its wing and put mechanics to work on the car. *"Ahora voy en coche"* ("Now I'm driving a *car*") was the telegram he sent home, and a few days later he won his first leg. In 1940, when they raced to Lima and back, it was Fangio's turn, and he also won the national championship that year and the next.

When everything got going again in 1947, Oscar won the first big one, which ran from Buenos Aires to Santiago, Chile, then north through the Andes to Tucuman and back to Buenos Aires. But those 3,200 miles were only a warm-up for the 1948 race, known as "La Caracas."

It was by far the longest race held in modern times, and in its conception dwarfed anything that has happened before or since: Starting in Buenos Aires, and in 14 stages, the route led to Caracas, Venezuela, 6,000 miles distant. The start was to be October 20, the finish November 8. After that was done the cars were to be driven to Lima and from there, starting December 2 and finishing December 11, they would have a second race back to Buenos Aires—another 3,200 miles. From the time they rolled off the starting platform in the center of Buenos Aires it was almost all Galvez, with Juan by now running in competition with his brother instead of riding in the copilot's seat. On the first leg of over 1,000 miles from the capitol to Salta, Oscar finished first in less than 14 hours, averaging 76 mph on dirt roads with a prewar vehicle. It was incredible, this tiny fenderless Ford coupe roaring along, an enormous rooster tail of dust hanging in the stillness behind it, charging through the treacherous *vados* (dips in the road) made when the floods came out of the mountains in the spring, charging toward the northland. (The veteran Clemente Biondetti, who won Italy's famous Mille Miglia the same year in a far faster Ferrari and on

Latter-day Fords: Oscar Cabalen and his modified Falcon in the 1966 Gran Prenno, starting the climb up the Andean Precordillera near Bariloche.
(Bottom) The Emiliozzi brothers, driver Dante and co-pilot Torcuato, take to the air after hitting a bump at high speed in their TC special.

much better roads, was half a mile per hour slower.) Oscar, pursued closely by Fangio and his brother, showed the way into Bolivia, then Juan won the stage into La Paz, the capitol. Fangio took the mountainous section leading into Peru, but from then on the Galvez brothers outran everyone. The 650-mile leg to Lima was won by Oscar for his fourth victory of the event, and when they got there, the drivers found a revolution in progress. Rather than take the usual day's rest between legs they decided to continue almost immediately, leaving at midnight. During the following stage, with the drivers tired and the cars badly in need of maintenance, Fangio went off a cliff in the middle of the night, killing his co-driver and suffering serious injuries himself. From then on there was no real opposition for the brothers; they won one leg after another as the race wound through Ecuador and Colombia and into Venezuela. On the eve of the last stage, a relative sprint of about 400 miles, Oscar was 2½ hours in front of Chevrolet driver Domingo Marimon. From there to Caracas the Galvez brothers should have cruised, taking it easy with their over-all positions now unassailable. But Juan had other ideas. He wanted the bonus given to the fastest man on the final stage. Eventually, almost inevitably, he went off the road about 150 miles from the finish line, and when Oscar came along Juan asked for help. Oscar tried to tow his brother back onto the road, but he was unable to do so, and in the process managed to damage his crankshaft. He was forced to leave and then a few miles down the road his crank snapped.

A competing car driven by a friend came along and Galvez was able to get a push from him, rolling along in this manner until they were able to find a spectator willing to undertake the job. For mile after mile, being pushed up hills and rolling down them, Oscar bumped his way toward Caracas, until his helper left him two kilometers from the finish line and he coasted downhill the rest of the way. Oscar was still well ahead of the others on total time for the race, but could a man with a broken engine, who had been pushed for 150 miles, possibly be declared the winner? To make it all the more involved, there was no question that Oscar had been the class of the field. Finally, the auto club came to a decision: Oscar was to be considered "unclassified," rather than disqualified. He really hadn't done anything wrong, they said—but they didn't feel they could give him first-place money. The race went to Marimon and Juan finished third, after having lost four hours getting back on the road.

When they returned to Lima for the second part of the event, it was all Galvez. Oscar won the first three stages, Juan the last two, and Oscar took the race, to be greeted as a national hero when he returned to Buenos Aires. The fact that several years later someone found the brothers had used the new Mercury long-stroke crank, giving them 239 inches of displacement against 221 for the other Fords, did little to diminish their popularity. There was no rule against it, and Los Galvez had merely been smart enough to get the cranks first.

After the 1949 season the field belonged to the Galvez brothers. There were always others coming up, but Juan and Oscar were the kingpins and the Fords were the cars to drive. The reign of the brothers lasted another dozen years and so did the flathead V8, by now only a memory in other parts of the world but still the hottest thing for Argentine racing. But the only thing that remains constant is change itself, and slowly the circuits, the rules and the cars underwent a metamorphosis. It became more and more difficult to close 500 or 600 miles of road for a one-day race, so starting in the late 1950s they began to hold events over circuits from 40 to 75 miles in length, with several laps being run over the same piece of road. In the last two or three years it has become difficult to close even this much, so circuits have dropped to 10, 20 or 30 miles; only the Gran Premio itself has clung to the old ways.

At the beginning, as long as a standard American car was used, there was no limit to the engine modifications allowed. Finally, as speeds rose, in 1952 the limit of a single carburetor was imposed. But they still went faster, so the next year they went back to unlimited modifications. In 1956 they decided (some say with the help of Chevrolet interests) to limit engine displacement to 4.0 liters (244 cubic inches), with no restrictions on carburetion. This gave the Chevy six, especially the newest one with seven main bearings, an excellent chance against the tired old flathead. For a while Ford tried to combat this with the six-cylinder, 170-inch Falcon engine, and of late they have gone to the 292-inch Y-block V8 popular in the United States during the mid-1950s. But since the displacement must be reduced by narrowing the bore (destroking is not allowed), they are still at a disadvantage. With the import restrictions of the 1950s, American-built cars became increasingly difficult to get, and for a while it looked as if the class would become extinct. But in the last few years more and more vehicles produced by Argentina's growing domestic auto industry, including Falcons, Dodge Darts, Plymouth Valiants and Chevy IIs (called Chevy 6) have been used. And slowly, the Chevy has become dominant. In 1962 Chevy-engined coupes won six of the 21 races, and the next year they took five of the 18. In 1964 Chevrolet displaced Ford for the first time since the 1940s; Chevy engines took 12 of the 24 events, Fords took nine (all by Dante Emiliozzi, the mechanical wizard who had an overhead valve conversion for his flathead by 1953 and who was the successor to the Galvez brothers) and Dodge slant sixes won three. At least part of the reason for the Chevrolet resurgence was the persons now driving the cars—but the basic reason for better drivers switching brands was the same as in any other part of the world: They thought the other make stood a better chance. Among the Chevy standouts were Carlos Pairetti, who won the Gran Premio in 1963 and 1966, and Juan Manuel Bordeu, Fangio's protege, who won the 1964 Gran Premio and the 1966 season championship—the first for a Chevrolet pilot since Fangio, himself in 1941.

There has even been a class for standard cars the past 10 years, with the height of excitement in the long-distance race for these lasting from 1961 through 1964, when Mercedes-Benz came down and took the event four years in a row. They were fast, but not as fast as the TCs, which now averaged 130 and better on the faster circuits. In 1966 Oscar Cabalen won the standard grand prix with a Mustang, but in general things in Argentina have gotten quiet. Bordeu, son of a wealthy family and a successful rancher in his own right, is typical of the younger driver, who has a squad of mechanics to do his work for him.

Juan Galvez was killed in the first race of the 1963 season, attempting to catch Emiliozzi's faster car. Oscar retired the next year after a crash and now manages the Ford team. Fangio is the Mercedes dealer in Buenos Aires, and the younger men do the racing when they aren't busy playing golf or polo.

And when anyone wants to go to Caracas, they take a plane.

At the start, in this case of the "Triangulo del Oeste," one of the many smaller Argentine races. Car in photo is driven by Angel Tomas Rienzi, the first man to win a TC event with Ford's 292-inch V8.

16

THE LAKES AND THE KIDS

THE GEOGRAPHICAL BACKBONE of the Western Hemisphere is that great range of mountains which extends from the Chukchi Sea north of Alaska to Tierra del Fuego, at the southern tip of Argentina. It goes by different names in different places, such as the Brooks Range, the Mackenzies, the Rockies, the Sierra Nevadas, the Sierra Madres and the Cordillera, and finally, for several thousand miles before they drop into the sea at Cape Horn, they are known as the Andes.

In this enormous system of peaks and valleys, which reaches halfway around the globe, there are such various geological curiosities as the salt lakes in Utah and Argentina and the Mojave Desert, that high plateau at the southern end of the Sierra Nevada range. The scientific reasons for it being formed, and the story of the several million years it took to reach its modern-day configuration, are of no importance to the automotive world. The big thing, the great coincidence, is that it happened to be located at this spot on the earth's surface. This physical phenomena, combined with the settling of Southern California and the growth of the Los Angeles area, provided American racing with its greatest single stimulus.

Here was the automobile, at the beginning of its mass-production stage and still primitive in both design and execution. Here was Southern California, already well settled, yet with many open areas and also with a climate conducive to year-round automobilism. Slightly more than 100 miles away were the dry lakes of the Mojave— the only reasonably accessible place in the civilized world where a youngster could take his car and run at top speed with relatively little danger. When looked at in the light of history, the hot-rod movement and the birth of what Detroit now calls the Youth Market could not have happened anyplace else.

There was performance activity in many other areas of the United States, and the Midwestern speed equipment makers, led by the Chevrolet brothers and their Frontenac cylinder head, were for a time the kingpins of the industry. But there was something *about* Southern California, and in time those who didn't live there managed to migrate to the area. Harry Miller, for example, did his best work in Los Angeles, and so has Leo Goossen. In recent years, the beginning of May sees what amounts to almost a mass exodus from Southern California to Indianapolis for the "500"; Indiana may be where the cars are run, but California is the place where they are made.

From a Ford standpoint, almost every segment of the company's far-flung racing effort of the mid-1960s had key personnel who could trace their lineage back to the dry lakes: In stock car racing there were John Holman and Bill Stroppe, both disciples of Clay Smith; in the Le Mans effort Shelby-American mechanical genius Phil Remington was a former hot-rodder, and a quick one; Fran Hernandez, at Lincoln-Mercury and later at Ford, was one of the very best of the lakes engine builders. Danny Jones, Ford's liaison man on the Indianapolis engine program, was the son of Clay Smith's partner and grew up in their shop. And there are hundreds of others, before you even get around to mentioning the drivers themselves. From the standpoint of the pilots, more of them have come out of this Southern California milieu than from anyplace else: Dan Gurney, Phil Hill, Richie Ginther, Parnelli Jones, Ken Miles, Troy Ruttman, Sam Hanks, Jim Rathmann, Rex Mays, Fred Frame, Frank Lockhart, Ernie Triplett, Louis Meyer, etc., ad infinitum. Some of them were born elsewhere and some of them never saw the lakes, preferring to stick with oval tracks and road circuits. But the lakes were the catalyst that put the men and the machines together, for there you could run them, and there was where the lessons were learned.

The biggest and by far the best was Muroc, which was about 10 miles wide, 22 miles long, and with a level surface so good you could lay rubber on it. Today it is the home of Edwards Air Force Base and is the landing field for the forerunners of America's rocket ships, as the hot-rodders have become a thing of the past: They've gone to Bonneville and to the quarter-mile drag strips, they've gone to Indianapolis and Le Mans, and to a thousand other places.

But this is where it started.

The lakes were the physical facility that was needed, and the intellectual stimulus came in great part from Ed Winfield, who can be considered the father of hot-rodding and its first prodigy. As a child in La Canada, outside of Los Angeles, he was enamored of the automobile almost as soon as he knew what one was. ("Before I was old enough to go to school, automobiles were starting to come into vogue, and when you'd hear one you'd run up to Foothill Boulevard and watch it. On Sundays we'd spend the whole day there watching them go by.") Winfield sent away for car catalogs, too, and before long he had an enormous collection—the literature from which he first learned what made cars run, and why. As an 11-year-old he stripped a Model T, reworked its engine and got it up to 60 mph. The next year he left school; his father had died when he was five, and now it was time to go to work. Winfield was soon drawing pictures of his own engines and working in a nearby garage. The place to go, he knew, was the YMCA technical school on Hope Street, near Wilshire Boulevard, but there was no money. Instead, he talked them into letting him ferry spare parts on his bicycle in lieu of tuition.

The early days at the dry lakes: (Top) Duke Hallock and his Cragar equipped Model A
Ford at Muroc in 1936. (Bottom) Time trials at Muroc, vintage 1939.

Different styles, different builders. At left: (Top) Pete Clark ran this belly-panned roadster at Muroc in the 1930s fitted with a Model A engine; he went on to become a well-known Indianapolis mechanic. (Middle) Jack McAfee's track car, equipped with Model B engine with double overhead cam Hal cylinder head, at the 1948 Hot Rod show in Los Angeles. (Bottom) Earl Evans' lakester at El Mirage in 1948, equipped with a 296-inch Mercury flathead. The World War II aircraft belly tank was the basic body for many cars of this era. Above: (Top) One of the best lakes engine builders, Fran Hernandez (without helmet), at El Mirage, 1950. (Bottom) Harold Daigh and his Mercury-engined roadster at El Mirage in the fall of 1948.

First days at Bonneville (left-hand page): At top, Jim Lindsley, who achieved 137.5 mph
on the Salt Flats in 1949, driving what started life as a flathead V8 in a 1932 Ford.
(Middle) Compared to today, the first Bonneville meet drew a small crowd of entries.
(Bottom) One of the mainstays of hot-rodding and later of the Ford performance effort—
Phil Remington at El Mirage in 1946, in his Mercury-engined roadster.
Above: (Top) Before he built his empire, Hot Rod publisher Robert E. Petersen took
his own photos, as he was doing here at Bonneville in 1949. (Bottom) Push start
at El Mirage, 1948.

Cover Boys: (Top)
Ed Hulse, who graced
the first page
of the first *Hot Rod*
in January 1948,
and Ed Iskenderian,
who made the June 1948 cover
and who today
is the West Coast's
biggest cam grinder.

Ed Iskenderian in his T Roadster JUNE, 1948

By the time he was 14, in 1915, Winfield was working for the La Canada Ford dealer, and he was also setting up a Model T for a wealthy resident whose chauffeur wanted to race it. Somehow the owner had gotten hold of an oddball 16-valve cylinder head which used the original eight valves on the side for exhausts, and an overhead cam with a new set of eight valves for intakes. Winfield made the cams and lifters himself, using a lathe as a milling machine ("It was good for more than 80, too, but I figured it would never be as good as my L-head"). The flathead, the original ineffi-cient configuration, was the subject of most of Winfield's early experiments, and it was through the Model T that Winfield became the first of the great California cam grinders. When he started driving himself in 1921, his Model T (still with the old flathead) soon became the quickest thing on the Coast, and in the six years he com-peted, only Babe Stapp, whose machine had an up-to-date Fronty setup, could even come close to him. When he retired in 1927 to devote his time to engineering, Winfield was already a legend on the West Coast, and the kids who hotted up their cars looked on him as the oracle. If you had a Winfield head, or cam, or carburetor, better yet all three, you had the hot setup and you were ready for the lakes.

Winfield himself never went to the Mojave ("Don't know what they look like— never went because it wouldn't have been worth anything to anyone. If it were worth something for ads, then I would have done it"), but his cams and his carbs made the trip, and so did the ideas that emanated from his shop in Glendale. The shy, retiring Winfield stayed home, probed the secrets of engines and built them. Through the thirties, and then after the war, he was still the man to see, but others were copying his designs and as a result he became more and more inaccessible. Then he moved to San Francisco, and most of grinding work was done on a subcon-tract basis. Today he lives in a big home in Las Vegas, but there is still a shop out back, complete with grinding equipment. When the new supercharged Offy was being built for Indianapolis, they came to Winfield for the camshaft design. There were a few persons who hadn't forgotten.

While Winfield was making a reputation for himself as a race driver, the dry lakes were considered so far from Los Angeles that a trip there was more an adven-ture than anything else, and few youngsters undertook it alone. In the summer, temperatures at the lakes would go over 115 at midday, and in the winter they were covered with a thin sheet of water perhaps six inches deep as the melting snows ran down from the surrounding mountains. The water was a good thing, though; it served to refinish the surface, leveling it once more and preparing it for the next season.

The first famous driver to make an appearance at Muroc was Tommy Milton, who ran 151.3 mph there with a 3.0-liter Miller in the spring of 1924. Three years later Frank Lockhart drove his 1.5-liter supercharged Miller 164 mph at Muroc, and from then on the kids started coming in bunches. At the beginning it was practically all Model T, and at the end it was practically all flathead V8, and throughout the decade that Muroc was available and popular the activity there was dominated by Ford. Had anyone in Dearborn taken note, they would have realized that this was the youth market, and that it was a market owned by Ford. It was typical of the state of the company and of any other Detroit automaker at the time: Nobody noticed what these wild-eyed kids were doing in Southern California. By the time the youth market was discovered (and indeed, given its proper name) it was almost too late.

What Ford had with the Model T, Model A and Model B and the flathead V8 was there, among other reasons because Ford made strong engines with decent horsepower potential, and speed equipment for them was easy to find. In 1947, for example, 97 percent of all cars running in SCTA lakes meets were Ford powered. When Chrysler came along with its hemispherical combustion chamber V8 in 1951, and Chevrolet introduced its lightweight, high-revving V8 in the fall of 1954, Ford's position in this market was given a body blow from which it has never recovered. This is the primary reason for the present performance campaign. But all-out factory efforts weren't even dreamed of back in the late 1920s. The lakes were there, the Model Ts were there, and the kids in Los Angeles who were interested in this sort of thing couldn't wait for the summer weekends and the trips to Muroc. One of them was a tall, skinny youngster from Jordan High School, who became interested in cars when he saw the school shop teacher rebuilding a Model T as a class project. The next thing he knew he was hooked, and from that day on his world has revolved around the automobile. Eventually he became the editor of *Hot Rod* magazine and founder and president of the National Hot Rod Association, but in the late 1920s Wally Parks was just another one of the kids who heard about the lakes via the grapevine.

Crenshaw Boulevard was a big, wide-open space then, and so were Manchester, Sepulveda and Avalon, and if a kid wanted to run fast, all he had to do was get there in the early morning hours and put his foot down. For most of the kids that was enough, as the point of having a hot rod was mostly to motor around the streets and the drive-ins showing off, expressing oneself, with the articulation coming out of the exhaust pipe. But for some the ultimate goal was to make the thing really go, and for this the lakes were the thing.

"I went up as a passenger with some friends of mine," Parks recalls, "in a hopped-up Model T that made it about halfway up Mint Canyon Road and then gave up. But we'd made up our minds we were going to go and see this thing, and we ended up by hitch-hiking in, getting several rides across the desert. When we finally got there it was quite a spectacle, because in the first place you had to travel over rutted dirt roads, and then you broke out into the loose sagebrush and alkali, and then all of a sudden there it was out in front of you. The first time you saw it was quite an experience—like looking at the moon."

The trips were made at night, with the kids leaving Los Angeles between 10 p.m. and midnight. They would work on the cars until the last possible minute, and then, after getting together enough money for gas (a buck apiece), they would meet with several other cars at a drive-in and go up in an informal caravan. As they crossed the San Gabriel mountain range other lights could be seen in the distance, and when they stopped for coffee in Lancaster or Palmdale they would meet more kids, and from there to Muroc—across wasteland now, with no paved roads—there would be a literal string of headlights, with pauses every so often when they stopped to help a buddy who got stuck in the deeper ruts or in the sand. When they got there, the kids would grab a few hours' sleep, either in the back of a pickup truck or on the ground, curled up in a sleeping bag, waiting for the sun to come over the mountains to the east.

It was a wild scene, those late 1920s, early 1930s nights at Muroc: groups of kids, many with their girlfriends, huddled together on the flat floor of the lakes' while almost everywhere you could hear the raucous noises of engines being revved up as their owners sought an extra few horses with 11th-hour tuning. And in the background, out on the vast expanse of the lake bed, some of the wilder ones, with a couple of beers under their belt, were already racing around in the night. Every so often you could hear the sharp rap of two engines heading toward each other and see their headlights. Then suddenly there would be a crash, the peculiar echoless sound of cars on the lakes would cease, and the lights would go out. The next morning some of the contestants would drop a blanket over the bodies. On the way back to Los Angeles they would stop at the coroner's office in Lancaster to tell him he had business at Muroc, 50 miles out in the desert.

The meets themselves were run in the early morning, before the sun got too hot and boiled the water out of the cars, and at the beginning they were staged en masse. After cars had made solo runs to establish classes (by speed only), a group assembled at the start and took off behind a pace car. When the pacemaker felt they were lined up well enough, he dropped the flag and away they went. Parks' first competitive test at Muroc was in one of these mechanical cavalry charges:

"I had a nice ride in qualifying, then I came back in the heat race, and not being one of the first ones out, the experience that I had was sitting back in this tremendous dust cloud in the middle of the pack and wondering if it was more dangerous to back off and try to get or to stay on it and hope I wouldn't run into somebody; I finally decided on the latter course and stayed in there and managed to make it down to the other end without getting hurt. But it was a kind of terrifying feeling, and I decided right then and there that the only way to go to Muroc and race was to be out in front where you could see.

"It was quite a sensation to sit there knowing there were cars running at high speeds all around you and not being able to see any of them; but the kids went anyway, because everybody *knew* that essentially nothing could happen to them."

By noon it was all over, and the dog-tired kids headed home, preserving what water they had to pour into their radiators. Many were practically snowblind from the experience, and the kids and the cars were both covered by the fine, talcum-powder-like dust that was sprayed over everything, but that was OK too—when they got home, they wouldn't wash their cars for days; the dust was the way everyone in Los Angeles could tell they had been to the lakes.

Among those who participated in the 1930s activity was a youngster from the Santa Fe Springs area, Ak Miller. He got his start because of his older brothers, and when he was nine or ten years old, Ak was "all eyes and hands, helping 'em." Those were the pioneer days of the sport, and the speed equipment business was in its infancy. If you wanted something, Miller says, "you couldn't buy it; you had to make it. I remember intake manifolds, for instance—welding, brazing all of those things up, and then setting multiple carburetors on them—we tried updrafts, sidedrafts, you name it."

"Then there were the oil pumps ... we used to get Jewett oil pumps, for instance, and mount them on the front end of an old Chevy four. Then we'd put spray bars in the pan to hurl some oil at the rods, and maybe drill a hole to try and keep 'em in there. For pistons, we went to a guy who made sand-cast pistons for us; all you had to do was give him a general dimension and he'd cast a big ingot—and it weighed like an ingot, too—and then you'd drill a hole in it and cut some grooves, and you'd cut what you wanted off the top for compression. It was a crazy era!"

Miller's parents wouldn't let him go to the lakes at first; they said he was too young. Finally, in 1935, he got his first trip: "My brother had a 1927 Chevy roadster and when he got on the line he was really quivering and shaking.... It was cold, of course, since it was about six in the morning ... and he was just so nervous he didn't want to drive it, and I said 'Hey, you want me to drive?' and he said, 'Yeah, you drive,' so I hopped in and put a cloth helmet on, which was about all I had to keep my ears warm, and went through there and got 94 mile an hour."

As the junior member of the family Ak drew the assignment of steering the race car (sans windshield), which the Miller brothers would tow on the end of a rope; his career almost ended with this assignment when one night, heading through a mountain pass, Ak's brother pulled out to pass a truck, and Ak was so sleepy and frozen in the race car that be never turned the steering wheel. Fortunately the truck was an old-fashioned high bed model; the car went right under it and the next thing the teenager knew he was sitting there looking up at the truck bed, with the big wheels on either side of him. How he missed hitting them, he never knew.

The free-lance days at the lakes, in which the wild desire for self expression overruled everything else, started coming to a close as early as the spring of 1931, when the Gilmore Oil Company sponsored a meet at Muroc which was supervised, more or less, by George Wight, the owner of a tiny speed shop in Los Angeles which has since grown into the giant Bell Auto Parts. Ike Trone, running a Model A equipped with a Riley cylinder head, ran 105 mph in that one and a year later, in the summer of 1932, Joe Mozetti boosted the mark to 118.43 in his Frontenac-equipped Model T. They used Frontys and Rajos and then later, for the Model A, the big things were the Miller-Schofield head (designed by Leo Goossen and later known as the Cragar) and the four-port Riley, and soon everyone had some little thing of his own to use for experimentation. If you had an idea, you became your own engineer.

Hot-rodders, postwar style: (Top) Don Francisco, in car, and Bill Burke with the Burke-Francisco belly tank streamliner that hit 164.83 mph at Bonneville in 1949. (Middle) Mike Magill and his V8-60 roadster, good for use on either oval track or lake bed. (Bottom) More chrome: designed for the streets and the drive-ins— Frank Rose and his roadster.

Carryovers: (Top) Lou Baney, a dry lakes driver who later became a Ford dealer and sponsor of mid-1960s drag racing star Don Prudhomme. (Bottom) Hernandez, who went from the lakes through almost every phase of automotive competition to a key post with the Ford Motor Company.

Engines, hot-rod version: (Top) 1939 Flathead V8 with Offenhauser heads and manifolds and twin Stromberg 97 carburetors. (Middle) 1931 Model A with Cragar head, Wilco magneto, Winfield carburetor and manifold. (Bottom) 1938 flathead with overhead valve Ardun heads designed by Zora Arkus-Duntov, later to become "Mr. Corvette"; Ardun manifolds and Stromberg 97 carburetor.

"The development work," Parks says, "was generally a sort of shoestring project by someone who had an idea or a little money, or maybe he'd find a sponsor with some money, or who had access to a machine shop. Most of it was done the hard way; somebody would go out and make a set of patterns and they were usually fairly crude, by today's standards, and they'd go over to one of the foundries and get the thing cast up and then do their own machine work. A lot of the parts and equipment were even adapted from other makes and models. It was all pretty makeshift and backyard, but a lot of it worked very well." The art-cum-science of cam grinding, with Winfield as the West Coast Messiah, was soon taken up by race driver Pierre Bertrand (with Clay Smith as his clean-up boy in the Long Beach shop). Miller used several Bertrand cams, and he recalls one in particular:

"I remember I bought a Chevy four cam from Bertrand for 10 bucks, and this thing was so spindly it looked like a three-eighths bolt with some knots in it. It was sitting outside the door wrapped in some newspaper, so I took a look at it, and the thing looked sort of crooked, so I said 'Hey Pete, this thing looks like it's bent.' Well, he took it and looked at it and said 'Yes, it is,' so he rapped it on the cement sidewalk and straightened it for me while I was watching. Then he said 'Put it in the block, the bearings will hold it straight and you won't have any trouble.' The things were really primitive by today's standards, but they would lift the valves up higher and hold 'em open a little longer, and that was the point of the thing.

"Automotive education in general was primitive back then. We knew the general concept, naturally, of compression, cam, and carburetion, but when it came to really technically applying it, I didn't, at that time, run into any fellows who were really well versed … much of it was rumor and hearsay. Somebody would tell you, 'Man, this guy's got a Bertrand cam and that thing really winds out. So you'd run down and get a Bertrand cam, and you were going to wind out—you hoped."

As the 1930s progressed, two important changes were made in the world of the California hot-rodder: the first was the development of the flathead V8, and the second was the threat of police interference. Henry's V8, the world's first mass-produced, cheap engine of this configuration, at first found little welcome among the kids, and for good reason, as Parks recalls:

"No one felt that it represented any serious competition, because they already had overhead valve Model T and Model A equipment, and Rileys and the Cragars were running quite well, and no one anticipated that this heavy flathead would do very much. Like anything else, they didn't become popular or be considered seriously until someone stuffed one into something and really went fast with it. I think the first person in Southern California to make an impact with one was Johnny Junkin, who was one of the pioneer hot-rodders in the Los Angeles area. He had a little Model T, a real lightweight thing, and he showed up one day with a flathead V8 in it and proceeded to run off from everything there was. Overnight he created a demand for them, and from then, of course, it was just a short time before development started on manifolds, cams and heads and the V8 became dominant."

The police were another matter. The wild goings-on at the lakes had attracted the attention of the California Highway Patrol, and the street racing in Los Angeles and other towns had drawn the notice of the local constabularies. Control was needed, and the upshot was the forming of the Southern California Timing Association (SCTA) in 1937. At the beginning it had five clubs; in the periods immediately before and after World War II it had as many as 25, and the SCTA also formed the model for Russetta, the Western Timing Association, and several other organizations of this type. Order was on the way.

By December of 1938 the SCTA even had a newspaper, a mimeographed sheet that can be considered the father of *Hot Rod* magazine, and in that first issue it was noted that 1938 champion Ernie McAfee had been fastest qualifier at the last lakes meet with a one-way average of 137.4 mph and that "no traffic citations were given to SCTA members during the weekend of the Oct. 2 races. We feel quite proud of the manner in which the members conducted themselves both going and returning.... It is necessary that we all cooperate with the rules of the association and the ... Highway Patrol ... has been a great help to us ... in keeping the crowd orderly."

Among the big names of the immediate prewar era were McAfee, Eddie Meyer, Vic Edelbrock, Karl Orr, Stu Hilborn, Mel Leighton, Yam Oka, Manny Ayulo, Phil Remington, Chuck Potvin, Sandy Belond, Frank Coon, Paul Schiefer, Jack McAfee, the Spaulding brothers, Bobby Strahlmann and many others, including Bob Rufi, who started the streamliner trend. Rufi may not have been the first SCTA driver to experiment with a streamlined body, but he was the first successful one, and his tiny rear-engined (Chevrolet) vehicle clocked a two-way average of 140 mph as early as 1940. His mark was to stand through the war, which shut down all SCTA activity at the end of 1942 and stopped the runs at Muroc long before that. The place belonged to the government, and when the Army took it over in 1940, the hot-rodders had to stage their meets at Harper, Rosamond and later at El Mirage. Then the lakes went back to the jackrabbits and the occasional gila monster, while Sergeant Parks busied himself hotting up a jeep in the Philippines, Miller lugged a radio and a rifle through the Battle of the Bulge, and hundreds of other hot-rodders did the same. Some, including SCTA founder Art Tilton, never came back. Tilton was killed in a plane crash.

When the rest of them did come home, the sport was bigger than ever. There was more money around, and a whole new car-crazy generation had grown up in the years when the others were off fighting. You could drive from Newport in the south through to the San Fernando Valley in the north, and on the way you were guaranteed to see at least 50 roadsters without fenders, humping along with small tires in the front and big ones in the back, with all sorts of sounds coming out of the loudest legal (and oftentimes illegal) exhaust pipes. At the traffic lights you could see them shudder due to the wild cams that were designed for anything but idling speeds, and the kid behind the wheel would sit there seemingly oblivious to the stares of those around him.

Today you can walk into almost any dealership and buy something that will outperform the postwar roadsters, and the best streamliner time at the lakes is only a poor top speed for a quarter-mile dragster, but in its own era the roadster was king, and the kids paid homage. Speed equipment designed specifically for the hot-rodder was easily available, and whether or not you wanted to use the stuff for racing, you went and bought it and bolted it on; if it wasn't for go, then it was for show at the drive-ins.

There was a distinct difference, it should be noted, between the participants and the enthusiasts. Those who actually took part in the lakes competitions and the like—or at least those who were the most successful—were, in the main, returning veterans who had gained additional maturity in the armed forces. In their late 20s and mid-30s, these were the men who not only ran on the lakes, but who formed the basis for Southern California's giant speed equipment business. The things they built to make their competition cars go faster were the items they later made for sale to the younger generation. They were the spearhead of the movement, and because of them there were still lines of cars heading up to the lakes on Saturday nights. When you got there, preparation for running was simple: Off came the windshield, the carburetors were replaced by a pair set up for alcohol, the fuel supply was switched from the gas tank to the one holding methanol, and you got in line. At Newhall, Calif., where there was a small dirt track running strictly outlaw races, a similar procedure was taking place, and this was the spawning ground of Troy Ruttman, Manny Ayulo and the Rathmann brothers, Dick and Jim. Other kids, not wanting to make the long trips, indulged in street racing, which served to put the rap on the entire movement and gave the name "hot rod" a bad connotation.

Then there were others, who started to experiment in more exotic fields. Among them was Dean Batchelor, a young Army Air Corps veteran who was studying industrial design and spending his spare time building up a street roadster. Batchelor was one of the few persons on the West Coast whose tastes were catholic enough for him to be interested in what the rest of the world was doing with speed, and he was a constant reader of two British motoring weeklies, *The Motor* and *The Autocar*. When John Cobb ran 394 mph in 1947, both magazines were filled with the technical details of the feat, and when Batchelor read about it, an idea started to form. He started talking with Alex Xydias, a friend of his who owned a speed shop and ran one of the typical postwar belly-tank streamliners, and by the fall of 1948 Batchelor had sold his roadster, Xydias had stripped his belly tank and they were embarked on a new project, a streamliner of modern design. When Parks and *Hot Rod* publisher Bob Petersen got Bonneville opened for the kids in 1949, they were ready with their creation, the So-Cal Special. It had the frame and the running gear (by now considerably revised) from Xydias' belly tank, it had a body designed by Batchelor, and it had been set up to take either the V8-60 engine owned by Xydias or a bigger flathead V8 loaned to the boys by Vic Edelbrock. The latter even sent Fran Hernandez, then the shop foreman and chief machinist, to make sure the engine ran properly.

The car posted fastest time of the meet with a 193 mph clocking, and the next year it came back—again with an Edelbrock engine and again with Hernandez in attendance—to record 210 mph, the fastest two-way speed ever achieved by an American-built automobile, although few realized it at the time. When Parks was first dickering for the rights to use the Salt Flats, Art Pillsbury, the boss of the AAA's record-sanctioning activities, informed him that the Class C record was 219.5 mph, and since most of his hot rod engines were in this class, they would look rather puny when compared to the efforts of the sophisticated Europeans. And here, suddenly, were Batchelor and Xydias knocking on the door. Batchelor went on to become editorial director of *Road and Track* and *Car Life*, Xydias is an editor for Petersen Publications, which has grown into the largest automotive publishing house in the world. Pillsbury, who passed away in 1966, lived to see another hot-rodder, Craig Breedlove, become the first human being to surpass 600 mph on land.

Two years after Batchelor and Xydias had done so well with the So-Cal Special, the first international record fell to a hot-rodder, and to a Ford. It was the Hill-Davis City of Burbank streamliner, designed by Batchelor, built by George Hill and Bill Davis, and with an engine built by Don Clark and Clem Tebow. It had a 1946 truck block with a Mercury crankshaft, an overhead valve conversion and a home-built fuel injection system. Although only 248 cubic inches in displacement, well below the class limit of 305 cubic inches, the car recorded an average of 229.774 for the flying mile—10 mph faster than the supercharged Auto Unions managed before the war. And it was done by a bunch of kids in greasy T-shirts.

While the most adventurous of the rodders were making the yearly trip to the salt, the more practical among them were seeking something else as an outlet. With the demise of Muroc much of the enchantment of the lakes was gone, and Bonneville was a once-a-year thing and 700 miles away. The street racing would only bring trouble, so it was only natural that a drag-racing course was discovered. The first of these was on a back road at the Santa Barbara airport in Goleta, Calif., where the Santa Barbara Acceleration Association started running in 1948, and from there it spread over the country. Goleta, it is believed, was the place where in 1949 nitromethane was first used in drag racing, and the man who put the pop in his tank was Hernandez. He used it in a flathead Ford V8 that had been bored and stroked to 296 cubic inches, and he won. About a year later Edelbrock was able to introduce nitro kits. The man Hernandez beat that day at Goleta was Tom Cobb, who was running a supercharged Ford flathead and who went on to be one of the pioneers of blown engines in the hot rod frame of reference.

Two years later, at Santa Ana, Calif., where the first commercially successful drag strip was being operated, the motorcycles were proving themselves faster than the cars. Then Dick Kraft, a veteran lakes driver, took his roadster and stripped it of everything in an attempt to achieve a more favorable power-to-weight ratio. Kraft still didn't beat the motorcycles, but he started a trend; his flathead Ford roadster, in its stripped down form, became the daddy of all dragsters. There was also a Mercury flathead in the drag car a kid by the name of Don Garlits built in Florida, and there was another Merc in the rail that Calvin Rice drove to the first National Hot Rod Association championship in 1955, but the day of the engine was past, and the lack of a Ford-built successor marked what must be viewed as a major, and very costly, mistake.

(Top) One of the busier strips in the early days—Paradise Valley, Calif. (Bottom) The first NHRA Nationals top eliminator, Calvin Rice, the 1955 winner. At right: The Bob Estes-sponsored Hill-Davis Mercury-engined streamliner seen at Bonneville before its 1953 runs.

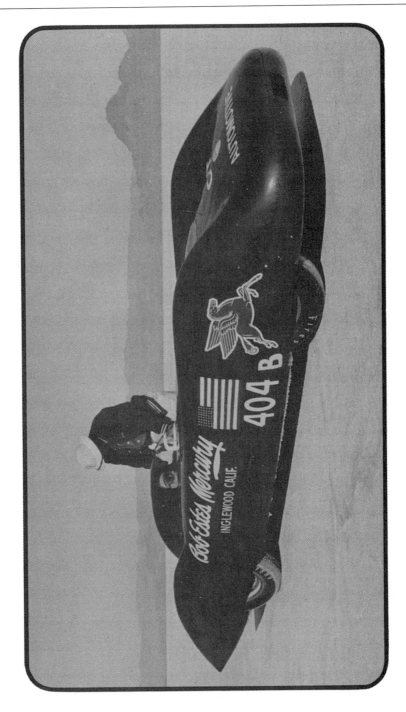

Part 3

(1940–1959)

STOCKS

ARE

UP!

**DARLINGTON AND DAYTONA
BECOME IMPORTANT**

17

VIVA CARRERA

THEY HELD the Mexican road race from 1950 through 1954 and it is a pity they stopped, because the Carrera Panamericana was one of the great automotive contests. It was an open-road affair in the classic, point-to-point manner, it was the only major event in which sports cars and stock cars could be compared on the same course at the same time, and it was the race in which European and American drivers got their first good look at each other.

It was also the event that marked the return of the Ford Motor Company to factory-sponsored competition, and it gave Dearborn a taste of what could be done if your car came home first: Lincolns dominated the sedan section of the race for three years before increasing problems of crowd control and a mounting budget brought a halt to the activity. From the point of view of the American public, the race received little more press than did an average professional golf tournament and it is too bad, because the flavor and the grandeur of the 2,000-mile dash across Mexico were something everyone should have known about. The long straights, with the cars roaring across the plains under a burning sun, the tortuous climbs through the mountains, the crowds lining the roads near every village, even the buzzards circling overhead; they were all part of it.

Ask someone who was there and watch their eyes light up and watch them smile. Those were great days, back when they raced across Mexico. Ask Chuck Stevenson or Johnny Mantz, ask Phil Hill or Juan Manuel Fangio, ask Ak Miller, Troy Ruttman, Bill Stroppe, John Holman, or Piero Taruffi or Karl Kling. Or you could even ask Curtis Turner; he was there too.

They'll tell you.

The story of the Carrera starts in many places, ranging from President Miguel Aleman's office in Mexico City to the Lincoln-Mercury Division in Dearborn, but the best place of all was Pierre Bertrand's garage in Long Beach, Calif., in the late 1930s, where two young hot-rodders used to hang around and absorb all they could.

Bertrand was one of the first of the great cam grinders, one of the first men to change the characteristics of an engine by changing the breathing. Clay Smith was his disciple, in later years taking over Bertrand's equipment when the older man died shortly before the war. But right then they were both kids, Stroppe with his Model T with Fronty head, Smith with his four-cylinder Chevrolet with Oldsmobile head, and they were carrying on an animated discussion over whose car was better.

Finally Bertrand had heard enough. "Goddamit, you guys are talking about a Ford and a Chevy and I'll take a horse and beat you both! Next Sunday we'll settle this thing; Stroppe, you run your Ford, and Smith, you run your Chevy and I'll race a horse."

By the weekend the word had spread and a large number of the local kids were assembled at the Seal Beach airstrip where the great event was to be held. Bertrand had rounded up a retired race horse, and the two youngsters were beginning to have second thoughts about the whole thing. "It was the thrill of our lives," Stroppe says. "They put the horse between the cars at first, and it was sort of nervous, so they put it off to the left of the cars. Then somebody dropped the flag and that goddamn horse took off and left us just sitting there. All we could see was the ass of that horse in front of us." When the horse neared the finish line it stepped in a small ditch and lost its footing momentarily, enabling Smith to beat Bertrand; Stroppe came in third. Bertrand had taught both of them they still had a few things to learn—about cars, and about the starting capabilities of equine competition.

After the war—Stroppe was in the Navy, Smith's asthma kept him out of service—they set up side-by-side Quonset huts in Long Beach and their lives became wrapped around racing. Smith was grinding cams and preparing engines, Stroppe was working days at Art Hall's Lincoln-Mercury dealership and nights in his hut, on a midget racer, or a speedboat, or anything else that would run fast. Stroppe drove them, too, sometimes with great success, sometimes winding up on his head. Money was tight, and if you didn't win you didn't eat. Danny Jones grew up around the huts, helping whenever and wherever he could. One day he and Stroppe set sail for San Diego, where there was a midget race that evening. "We had 28 cents between us," Jones says, "so we bought a quart of milk and a package of cookies and we went. We won the race, too, and it was a good thing."

Stroppe and Smith had a hydroplane which was cleaning up on the West Coast with Bill as the driver, and the boat eventually got them together with Ford. The craft had a radically reworked Ford flathead six in it, and Hall, who was having difficulty obtaining enough new cars in the immediate postwar period, had an idea. The Henry Ford memorial powerboat regatta was coming up in Detroit, and if a boat he sponsored did well, it might help. Smith and Stroppe headed east.

It wasn't even close, Stroppe winning by more than two minutes, and Ford engineers in the crowd wanted to talk to the pair. So after an all-night drive to Muscatine, Iowa, and another win there the next day, they sold the boat on the spot and flew back to Detroit. The engineers were curious about the modifications to the engine,

(Top) Younger days in Southern California—Bill Stroppe and his flathead coupe.
(Bottom) Lewis Hawkins stops for repairs during the 1950 race, a mile high outside Tuxtla.

At right: (Top) Bill France, left, and Curtis Turner, their Nash and a cactus, Mexico, 1950.
(Bottom) Chuck Daigh, left, and Walt Faulkner, one of Lincoln's most reliable teams.

and Smith described how he had altered the combustion chambers, changed the breathing and done a complete revise on the bottom-end lubrication. Then one of them asked Smith what rpm he used and Clay told him 5,000.

The engineer blanched. "But that engine is critical at 4,500," he said. Smith smiled. "We go past 4,500 so fast it doesn't get a chance to do any damage." The engineers never got over it. Hall got his extra cars.

Early in 1950, when Stroppe and Smith were taking care of Johnny Mantz' cars, which were owned by J.C. Agajanian, Mantz came up with the idea of entering the first Mexican road race. Money, naturally, was a consideration, and they didn't have any, so they wound up with Mantz giving Stroppe his personal Lincoln to make over into a stock racing machine. They promoted $500 from Bob Estes, the Inglewood, Calif., Mercury dealer, and another $500 from the bread salesman who had Stroppe's home on his delivery route. He was Les Viland, and years later he was to become the king of all the Mobil Economy Run drivers. Back then he helped Mantz and Stroppe, not only with money, but with his mechanical talents.

When the first race was held in May of 1950, shortly after the Mexicali section of the Pan-American Highway had been completed, it was a far cry from the major event into which it would grow. They ran from north to south, and instead of ending it at Tuxtla Gutierrez (the starting point for the next four Carreras) the route wound up at El Ocotal, a jungle hamlet on the Guatemalan border which required an additional 171 miles of driving, 107 of that on twisting dirt and gravel roads.

The entry list, too, was an unusual one. Italian stars Piero Taruffi and Felice Bonetto entered Alfa Romeos, four-time Monte Carlo Rally winner Jean Trevoux came with a Delahaye, and there was a strange conglomeration of American pilots. They ranged from such well-known drivers as Mantz and Joel Thorne, the millionaire playboy who had a Cadillac for this one, to a small group of elderly tourists who were treating the event as little more than a chance to cross Mexico without worrying about oncoming traffic. There were even several all-female crews, and then there was Mrs. H.R. Lammons of Jacksonville, Tex., whose Buick had as a sponsor "Hi-A Brassieres by Marja," and proclaimed this fact in large letters on both sides of the vehicle. Buried somewhere in the pack was a group of southern drivers from NASCAR, who were little known at the time and who came along just to see what this road racing was all about. They were used to driving stockers, they figured, so this might be a good opportunity to win some money; first place was to pay $17,400, so they were right. The southerners were led by Bill France, and he took along a young and unknown (outside the South) Curtis Turner in his six-cylinder Nash, a car that was given little chance against the hot Olds 88s and Cadillacs, or against Mantz's Lincoln.

There were 123 starters and 52 finishers, and it was more a race of attrition than anything else. With little experience at this sort of thing, most of the cars were not backed up by the type of organization needed for a long-distance event, and it cost them dearly. Tires, too, were found wanting in quality, and rubber trouble hit almost everybody. About the only car which ran the entire 2,178-mile route free of tire and mechanical difficulties was the 1950 Olds of Hershel McGriff, a youngster from Portland, Ore., who wound up beating Tom Deal, the Cadillac dealer in El Paso, Tex., by one minute and 16 seconds with a come-from-behind performance on the last leg. McGriff, who averaged 78.4 mph for the race, almost didn't make it. About 1,000 yards from the finish his car ran over some rocks which ripped a hole in both the oil pan and the gas tank. When he got the checkered flag, McGriff could not have gone another mile. Mantz, who had Stroppe as his co-driver and chief mechanic, was the hard-luck driver of the first Mexican road race, just as he was to be several times in the future.

Never lower than fourth through any of the first six legs and 12 minutes in front on total time, Mantz lost his rear brakes in the mountains between Puebla and Oaxaca, and got sick at the same time. They stopped the car, and Stroppe managed to make a quick repair that permitted them to run on their front brakes only, but there was little he could do about Mantz, who had that popular Mexican malady sometimes known as the Turistas, the Aztec Two-Step, or Montezuma's Revenge.

After their impromptu pit stop Stroppe decided to drive, but after a few miles of sitting next to his mechanic Mantz figured he wasn't *that* sick and took over again. They finally pulled into Oaxaca with the 69th fastest time of the 75 cars to complete the leg, and while Mantz went to bed, Stroppe got down in the mud to fix the brakes. When he finished, around midnight, he went back to the hotel and found Mantz had taken a turn for the worse. "I went looking for a doctor," Stroppe recalls, "and I wound up at the police station and they went out with me to get one. They finally picked this guy up in one of the local saloons and he was drunk, but they took him home and he got his kit and came over.

"Then he took out a hypodermic that looked big enough for a horse, and when Mantz took one look at that he just fainted dead away. The doctor was so drunk be could barely stick the thing in Johnny's arm, but he seemed to know what was the matter with him; at least the next morning, when I woke up and looked over at Mantz, expecting to find him dead or something, there he was, sitting up and feeling fine."

That day Mantz took off in pursuit of a hopeless cause. He won the next leg, 335 miles from Oaxaca to Tuxtla through the mountains, and moved back to fourth in the over-all standings. On the last day Mantz was trying to move up from fourth place and make up the 28 minutes he was behind. For half the 171 miles Mantz and Stroppe were roaring along in great style, pulling farther and farther ahead of the field they were certain, and then, below them, Mantz spied the gleaming white road stretching across a valley. "Got 'er made now," he yelled to Stroppe, and they tore ahead. This last 90 miles was the only stretch Mantz and Viland hadn't driven during their spring scouting trip, but they weren't worried about it; someone had told them the road was all gravel from here to the finish, and that meant no trouble. When they got to the white road, they found it wasn't gravel but crushed rock, with each piece as big as a man's fist. In a moment, they had blown all four tires. They stopped, changed them, and got going again at a slower pace. Before they reached the finish they had blown three more, and went limping across the line on the rims—which were wrapped around the brake drums. They wound up ninth, but if nothing else Mantz and Stroppe had taken a good look at the race, and when they came back two years later this reconnaissance trip was to stand them in good stead.

France and Turner, who were in third place after the fourth leg, were later slowed by tire and wheel trouble and go to Tuxtla in 20th place, with little chance of salvaging anything the last day. Then they found that Roy Pat Connor of Corsicana, Tex., was sick. Connor, who was also driving a Nash, had made an unspectacular trip of it, but it had also been a trouble-free ride and his car was in sixth place, 33 minutes out of first. Was it worth a try? It was, and the next morning Turner was behind the wheel of Connor's Nash as they took the starter's flag, with four minutes between cars because of the horrible condition of the roads ahead.

What went on between Tuxtla and El Ocotal was seen by no one except a few stray goats, Indians and soldiers standing by the side of the road. Had there been any way to film it, the resultant footage would have made one of the great racing movies. Here was Turner in an underpowered, ill-handling car, starting in eighth place, 32 minutes behind the first car to depart. Taruffi, the great Italian mountain king, was four minutes in front of him in a nimble 2.5-liter Alfa sedan, the best car in the field for the mountain work ahead. Turner not only passed Taruffi but went on to pass all the other cars that had started first, before being sidelined by a flat tire. He changed the flat, then roared off in pursuit of the few who had repassed, catching all except Taruffi, whom he had in his sights when they got to the finish line. Curtis Turner later became a legend in the wild southeastern world of stock car driving, but it is doubtful if he, or anyone else, ever put on a greater performance behind the wheel of an automobile.

Turner beat Taruffi in elapsed time for the leg by three minutes and 25 seconds and had worked his way up to third place over-all. But he was disqualified for the switch in cars, and his performance on that hot, dusty day in the mountains near Guatemala is accorded only the barest mention in the official records.

McGriff, who finished first, never hit the headlines again. Today he drives stock cars in France's West Coast NASCAR races. Deal, who was second, went back to his Cadillac agency. Al Rogers, the Pike's Peak hillclimb veteran, was third and Taruffi was fourth. France wound up with the radiator of his Nash hung on a rock—one of the few times France has been hung up on anything. And then there was the lady with the brassiere ads on the sides of her car. She married her driver in Mexico City. They didn't make it to the finish.

The next year, the Carrera Panamericana was the race of Ruttman and Smith.

Their used-car-lot Mercury did not win the race; it came in fourth, behind the Ferraris (sports cars were admitted for the first time) of Taruffi and Alberto Ascari, and behind the powerful Chrysler Saratoga of Bill Sterling, the El Paso driver who led for a good portion of the 1950 race. Ruttman was 20 minutes astern of Taruffi, 13 behind Ascari and a little over four minutes back of Sterling. For Ruttman, the race was another chapter in the tragic story of one of the great natural driving talents. For Smith, it was the beginning of a period in which he left his stamp on the Mexican classic as did no other man; cars for which he was responsible dominated the stock-vehicle category of the remaining three races, and people who worked for him carried away what they learned about the art of long-distance race preparation. John Holman, for example, carried it all the way to victory in the Tour de France of 1964 and to Le Mans in 1966 and 1967. And for Ford in general and the Lincoln Mercury Division in particular, Smith's use of the tiny Mercury with the flathead engine was the awakening of corporate interest in the Mexican road race.

Fran Hernandez, now one of Ford's most important performance administrators and a veteran of the California dry lakes and dirt-track days, remembers when Ruttman first came up through the hard-fought roadster races on the West Coast. He got going in the old Ashcan Derbys, where he and his father shared the wheel of a jalopy that was part Model A Ford, part Chevrolet and part Model T. From there, when he was 16, he went to Carrell Speedway in Gardena on a night when Mantz was hurt and Stroppe needed a driver. From the beginning he was a star. "The roadsters were getting pretty professional then," Hernandez recalls, "and we had Jack McGrath, and Manuel Ayulo and a lot of guys who could really go; then all of a sudden here comes this tall, skinny kid, about as big around as my pinky, and he just ran off and left them."

Ruttman was supposed to drive in the 1950 Mexican race, but couldn't make it and Bud Sennett drove Troy's car into fifth place. When Ruttman heard about this he thought he could do better the next year, and he and Smith got together. The best car, Smith said, would be a Chrysler Saratoga with the new hemispherical combustion chambers, so they went to Ruppert Motors in Pomona to try and talk the Rupperts into entering a car. It didn't work; the Rupperts weren't about to turn loose a high-priced automobile for a scheme that would surely result in a wreck. But Ruttman and Smith kept right on talking, and finally the Rupperts relented a bit. They had a used car lot over on Figueroa Street, and if Ruttman and Smith went there, they would find a 1948 Mercury they could have.

"When I first saw it," Ruttman says, "I thought 'What a sled,' but we towed it back to Long Beach, stripped it down to the frame rails and started to put it back together."

While Smith and Stroppe and others worked on the car, Ruttman went out and promoted the pieces they needed. Exhaust headers, distributor, cylinder heads, intake manifold, fuel pump—almost everything. They had to buy their tires, 19 of them, and it took most of the money they had left. Smith put the car together in the manner

The winners of the sports-car category: (Above, top) 1952 champion Karl Kling and his Mercedes 300SL. (Bottom) Juan Manuel Fangio in his Lancia, 1953.

Some of America's first steps toward a road-racing car. (Top) Duane Carter pushes his crippled Lincoln-engined Kurtis, 1954. (Bottom) Ak Miller's famous Caballo de Hierro, which placed eighth in 1953. Doug Harrison was the co-driver; the crew consisted of, from left, Hot Rod *staffers Ray Brock and Racer Brown, Clem Tebow and Pete Coltrin.*

that gave him his reputation. Griff Borgeson called him "The man who talked to engines." NHRA president Wally Parks, no mean operator with a wrench himself, says, "You got the feeling Clay could just walk up to an engine and lay his hands on it, and the thing would start to run."

Ruttman drove the race and Smith drove it with him, occupying the copilot's seat and giving Troy instructions every mile of the way. Clay had a manual spark control on his side of the cockpit to adjust the timing for the mountainous sections, and also had a rev counter and a vacuum gauge mounted where he could see them. Ruttman handled the brakes, the gas pedal and the steering wheel, and Smith took care of everything else, including the horn.

When they arrived at Tuxtla for the start, the Ruttman-Smith used car special attracted little attention, but by the time the convoy roared into Mexico City three legs later they were in front and the wires carried the story of the California kid who was leading the world's best. His Mercury was ahead of the Ferraris of Taruffi and Ascari, ahead of the hopped-up Packard of Jean Trevoux—ahead of everyone. It was too much to expect Ruttman to keep his edge through the high-speed stages that lay ahead, and slowly he dropped back as the faster Ferraris moved up. In Parral, Taruffi was four minutes in front of Troy and Ascari was third, 6½ minutes behind. At Chihuahua he fell to third behind Ascari and on the final and fastest leg, Sterling finally got by to take third on the strength of a vast horsepower superiority. Few people knew Ruttman drove most of the race with a severe case of diarrhea caused by the Mexican water, and was wrapped in a diaper made out of a bath towel.

For Ruttman it was one of the first headline performances in an amazing career. The next year, with Smith and Stroppe in the pits of his J.C. Agajanian-owned car, Ruttman became the youngest man ever to win the Indianapolis "500," doing so at the age of 22. The world was his oyster, and this big, good-looking kid had everything he wanted. When the wealthy Agajanian suggested he keep Troy's share of the Indianapolis purse and invest it for him, Ruttman demanded the money immediately.

Later that season Ruttman broke his arm in a sprint car race at Cedar Rapids, Iowa, and when it didn't heal properly he was laid up for some time, and he started drinking. It got to the point where Troy couldn't leave the stuff alone and he bounced from one ride to another, carrying the bad rap with him. Years later he drove stock cars for Mercury; sometimes they'd have to sober him up the morning of the race, and during the event itself he'd get so sick he would vomit in the car—and keep on driving. Ruttman eventually joined Alcoholics Anonymous and got away from the whiskey, but he was on his way out as a driver. At Trenton in the spring of 1964, he was bumped by Chuck Hulse and his car flipped end for end several times—but he walked away from it. At Indianapolis that year he started in the same row as Eddie Sachs and Ronnie Duman. When he came out of the fourth turn on the first lap, he saw Dave MacDonald hit the inside wall and "I figured he'd bounce back like a golf ball; so I kept my car headed where it was and I just made it through. Sachs was to my right and he didn't."

Troy quit in the fall of that year, and now he runs a small go-kart shop on Ford Road in Dearborn Heights, almost literally in the shadow of Ford. He doesn't see many races, but a year or two ago he bumped into Agajanian, who in the meantime had kept Parnelli Jones' share of the 1963 Indy purse and made him a wealthy man by investing it. "How much," Troy asked Aggie, "would I be worth now if I'd have let you invest the prize money back in 1952?" Agajanian didn't have the heart to give him an answer.

Ruttman's success in Mexico, and Stroppe's experience with Mantz the year before, got Smith to thinking about mounting a full-scale attack. Clay was by now a successful and widely known operator, with his cams considered the best in the business, his engines likewise, and his activities for Agajanian also contributing to his reputation. But with it all, Smith and Stroppe were far short of the necessary cash. All they could do was dream about it, and plan what they could do *if* they had the backing. A manufacturer's blessing was needed.

The obvious automaker was Lincoln-Mercury, as Smith and Stroppe had their best contacts there. In addition Lincoln was coming up with a good engine for the 1953 model year, and it had impressed the West Coast pair when they first saw it in February of 1952. As it happened, Smith and Stroppe got their break the day Ruttman won at Indianapolis.

Benson Ford, at that time general manager of the Lincoln-Mercury Division, and John Millis, his public relations man, were in attendance at the Speedway, and during the closing stages of the event, with Bill Vukovich on the way to a convincing victory, they stopped by Ruttman's pit. Between signals to their driver, who was in second place, Smith and Stroppe told Ford about their Mexico plans. Then, suddenly, the loudspeaker came forth with the news that Vukovich had hit the wall, and Agajanian and the crew leaped into the air. Smith whirled on them. "Shut up, you sons of bitches; he may be hurt or he may be dead—don't cheer now!"

Properly abashed, they waited a moment or two for the announcement of Vuky's welfare. Nothing Smith was to say or do in his later discussions impressed Benson Ford as much as that one spur-of-the-moment remark. It took almost two months for the final decision. On the part of Lincoln Mercury there were several items to be considered before sponsoring a racing team:

1. Should a prestige car such as a Lincoln be entered in a race?
2. Will we be starting a snowball which can't be stopped?
3. Are we using good judgment in entering such an important event with no previous experience to guide us?

By July 30 the decision was made, and the Ford Motor Company was embarked on its first official return to competition since the Indianapolis venture of 1935. The three Smith cars were to be entered in the names of California dealers, but in the over-all picture that was of little importance; everyone knew whose cars they were. It was a big step, as it was the first time in the modern era any major American manufacturer had seen fit to enter a competitive speed event, and an international one at that. On one count, however, the planners greatly underestimated the impact of what they were doing. Would it snowball? Yes it would, and before long this comparative snowflake was to turn into an avalanche with dimensions of which no one dreamed. The Mexican road race participation was the progenitor of all Ford competition since that date—and if not literally, at least it served to set the psychological stage.

Although mechanical changes are usually slow-moving affairs in auto companies, this time everything proceeded at the highest rate of speed. A 1952 Lincoln with a 1953 engine was available in Denver, and on August 6 Stroppe picked it up; they made some changes and took it to Bonneville for testing. Due to its half-1952, half-1953 configuration, the vehicle was not eligible for any AAA stock car records, but it beat many of these marks just the same and word got out Lincoln had something hot. Private entrants started asking for cars, and eventually, instead of the three vehicles that were scheduled, seven were built.

The next problem was to make the cars "stock," and this word has its own special meaning in the world of racing. Smith and Stroppe had come up with dozens of modifications necessary to make the cars raceworthy, and under the rules of the event most of these had to be listed in the catalog as optional extras. So between the time of the Bonneville test and the production of the cars, these parts had to be designed, ordered, delivered and installed. It was, for the engineering staff, just as tough a race as the actual one a few months later. For the engine they found a suitable camshaft which was already in use in a Ford truck, and also took the truck's mechanical valve lifters to replace the standard hydraulic setup. A three-blade cooling fan from the Ford six-cylinder engine was substituted for the standard Lincoln fan, and on the rest of the vehicle there were such new items as shot-peened steering arms and spindles, induction-hardened rear axles, heavy duty sway bars and heavy duty springs and shock absorbers. Then every piece was made to fit—and to perform in the same manner.

Even the building of the cars was a problem, as in order to get them to Smith on time they had to be produced before the regular 1953 run of vehicles came off the assembly line. Smith and Stroppe got their three cars on October 22, less than a month before the start of the race. By working day and night they managed to get them ready, got the rest of their armada set, and headed for Tuxtla Gutierrez, several thousand miles away.

The team had the following lineup: Chuck Stevenson, the 1952 AAA national champion, drove the first car (as a substitute for the injured Ruttman) with Smith as his co-driver. Mantz and Stroppe were in the second car, while the third was handled by West Coast star Walt Faulkner with Chuck Daigh as his co-pilot. With them was a small army, including cooks, doctors and factory engineers, and a large supply of spare parts under the care of John Holman, who was to drive his own personal race every night to keep the parts truck ahead of the competing cars. He was in charge of the logistics of the operation, and his talents in this area thus first became noticed by people at Ford. There was one other item with the team that was Smith's idea, and had been developed by him during Mobil Economy runs several years earlier. This was a strip map, a long sheet stretched over two rollers which had a mile-by-mile description of the course on it, complete with landmarks denoting particular corners, recommended gears and cornering speeds—the entire race on a piece of paper. It was the co-driver's job to hold this and to keep the driver informed of what was next.

Now it was up to Holman and his spare-parts crew to get the cars to the starting line on time. Holman, who had left his trucking business to help out, had everything loaded on an old transporter powered by a Ford six-cylinder which was never designed to carry the amount of material they heaped onto it. In addition, they had a small sleeping trailer for the drivers that was towed by a sedan delivery truck, and they both set sail from Long Beach, driving practically nonstop to Mexico City. In order to save time, when a change of driver was needed the sedan delivery would pull alongside the transporter, the next driver would hop from the trailer to the rig on which the Lincolns were perched, then clamber over the cars and the equipment and into the cab.

Once, when they got off the main highway and onto the rutted roads of a town, Daigh was driving the sedan delivery and he never backed off, causing the occupants of the trailer to be bounced around like ping-pong balls, breaking a gallon jar of mustard and generally creating havoc in the tiny room. Somehow, they made it into Mexico City, where Ford's Mexican representative greeted them. He was so enthusiastic he gave Holman a brand-new truck and insisted on providing three men to act as security guards. Holman told him they only had enough food and supplies for Smith's crew.

"Don't worry," he said, "they have money and they'll take care of themselves." So when Holman left Mexico City and headed south, he had three Mexicans, all named Francisco, hanging on to the transporter, and a letter from President Miguel Aleman in his pocket in case he needed it. The letter came in handy right away, as the next border between two Mexican states was controlled by a rough-looking bunch, complete with rifles, who wanted to inspect everything. They took a long look at Aleman's letter, then finally let the caravan through. They were little more than bandits, and one of the Franciscos told him they were lucky to have gotten away. The next night, while rolling through the brush country to the south, Holman's headlights suddenly picked up a large tree which had fallen—or been dragged—across the road. He took one look and made up his mind in a hurry. He put his foot down and steered for the vulnerable part of the tree, the end with the branches on it. A crash, much noise, and they were through, "load, guts, feathers, and all," as Holman says. When they stopped a few hours down the road to refuel, Mexican driver Paco Ibarra happened to catch up with the caravan and was asked if he'd had trouble with the tree.

When Ibarra passed through, the tree had disappeared.

Tuxtla Gutierrez was charming, with minor earthquakes every morning, bird droppings in the rooms, meals cooked over open fires and the resumption of the

Umberto Maglioli, one of the stars of the 1953 race, came back in 1954 to shatter all records in his 4.9-liter Ferrari.

Umberto Maglioli (top), and Ray Crawford (bottom),
the 1954 stock car winner, at the finish in Juarez.

sickness that hit Mantz in 1950 and Ruttman in 1951. But Tuxtla also had its good point: It was the start.

As opposition the Lincolns had 1951 winner Taruffi in an Oldsmobile, Marshall Teague in a hot Hudson Hornet, and various Chryslers, the best driven by Royal Russell, Speed McFee and Dave Evans. If they cared to look for an over-all victory, the sports car class had three factory-entered Mercedes 300SLs and there were various Ferraris, led by the 4.1-liter "Mexico" models of Ascari and Luigi Villoresi.

They had nothing to fear from the stock cars. Smith's organization put his Lincolns in 1-2-3 order at the finish. En route they had been challenged, but at the end it was all theirs. After Faulkner won the first leg from Tuxtla to Oaxaca, Russell and his Chrysler captured the second from Oaxaca to Puebla and Tommy Drisdale in another Chrysler was second. But the Lincolns were within a few minutes, and even when Taruffi put on an amazing performance in winning the Puebla-Mexico City portion of the race, it didn't worry the Lincoln team: Taruffi had lost 40 minutes on the first leg and would never regain it. From Mexico City north to the American border it was all Lincoln, as the roads got straighter and speeds went higher. First Bob Korf, in a privately entered Lincoln, then Mantz, then Duane Carter (another private entry), then Stevenson and then Mantz again—they swept the final legs of the race and Lincolns roared across the finish line in the first four places.

Mantz was only 31 seconds behind Stevenson at the finish, and Stevenson's time was good enough to give him seventh place in the sports car class. Oddly, Mantz was the only factory-sponsored Lincoln driver who had to make an unscheduled stop for tires. He and Stroppe took 3½ minutes to do this the one time it was necessary, and had Mantz not run into the unexpected trouble, he would have been the victor. Faulkner was another four minutes back, then came Korf, five minutes behind him. He had lost practically all of this on one leg, between Leon and Durango. Chrysler finished fifth and sixth, Teague was seventh and Taruffi 11th. To win would have been marvelous, but to come in first through fourth was almost too good to believe. Lincoln-Mercury officials were ecstatic and so were the dealers, as floor traffic shot up all over the country.

Smith's car had little trouble, aside from the usual close calls that occur in any long-distance, open-road event. Stevenson's air cleaner started to rotate on the carburetor at one point, locking the secondary throttle partly open, so he drove the rest of that leg on his ignition key. The brakes, which could have been a weak point, held up well, thanks in part to Smith's device for cooling the rear ones: He employed two heater fans in the cockpit which blew cold air over the drums and at the same time kept the drivers' compartment free of fumes. When Stevenson lost one fan for part of a leg, examination that night showed one brake lining was down to the rivets. Mantz also had his brakes done over during the race, while Faulkner went the whole way on the same set. The GM Hydramatic transmissions, which were standard equipment on 1953 Lincolns, also performed flawlessly.

The winners were given a lot more grief by an entrant running one of their own vehicles than by anyone else: The creator of trouble in Lincoln's new-found paradise was Carl Kiekhaefer's car (Korf was the driver), which was one of the pre-production models supplied to private entrants. It was lacking certain late modifications made by Smith and Stroppe, and when Kiekhaefer found out about these, he raised a scream that could be heard all the way to Dearborn. Kiekhaefer started quietly, however, at the postrace technical inspection. Everyone was standing around congratulating each other, and Smith had just given Kiekhaefer a cigar when a member of the committee approached him. He was apologetic about it, but he told Smith his Lincolns were being protested, and Smith asked by whom.

The Mexican looked somewhat embarrassed, and answered "Mr. Kiekhaefer."

Smith took a long look at Kiekhaefer, then reached across and yanked his cigar out of the outboard tycoon's breast pocket. It was the start of an enmity toward Ford that stuck with Kiekhaefer for years. To this day he will not use Ford blocks in his marine engine conversions. He was complaining primarily about two things: One was the fact that Smith's Lincolns had the heat riser passage to the carburetor blocked off, while he had been told this modification would remove his car from the stock category. The other was the condition of the intake manifolds and cylinder head ports, which had been matched.

Smith went down and took a look at Kiekhaefer's Lincoln and saw it wasn't much different from his. It became apparent Kiekhaefer was hoping all four would be disqualified, as a Chrysler he had sponsored finished fifth. Smith's parting shot to Kiekhaefer was "As long, as you're going to use Chrysler valve springs in that Lincoln, you ought to at least tell your mechanic to put them in right-side up." Eventually all the protests were thrown out, the Mexicans realizing they had a lot more to learn about what was stock and what was not, and Lincoln-Mercury took out additional insurance in the form of a service bulletin that read:

"It is recommended that ... the cylinder head ports and intake manifold be matched and finished, including sand blasting or polishing as necessary to reduce turbulence. It is also recommended that the intake manifold gaskets be used which have been produced with a heat riser hole omitted to alter the amount of manifold temperature for all types of operations and various altitudes." So now it was legal, even if after the fact. But Kiekhaefer never forgot.

The 1952 race was important not only because Lincoln sponsored a factory team, but for two other reasons: it was the start of automakers preparing special parts for racing and listing them in the catalog, and it was the only confrontation between Smith and Alfred Neubauer, the legendary chief of the Mercedes-Benz team, whose 300SL prototypes finished first and second in the sports category that year with Karl Kling and Hermann Lang. Mercedes and Lincoln weren't racing each other, being in different classes, but Neubauer had long ago developed a reputation for being without peer when it came to race preparation. Smith's operation was every bit as good.

If 1952 was good, the next year was even better. Not only was the team loaded with experience and buoyed by the success of the previous season, but Stevenson, Mantz, Faulkner, Jack McGrath and Bill Vukovich drove nearly 10,000 miles in practice, rechecking their charts, testing modifications to the cars and in general making sure they knew every curve on the 2,000-mile route. During the weeks of practice Mantz, Faulkner and Stevenson would ride in the same car, with one driving and the other two making notes. Since there was no speed limit, and they were attempting to duplicate race conditions, whoever was behind the wheel would go as fast as possible, and after each corner would call his estimate of the speed to the others. It would be "60," or "90" or "flat out," and when the two who were riding didn't agree with the driver on what he felt was a full speed curve, they would write "flat out—JLS," or "flat out—JLM," or "flat out—JLF." In each case the initials stood for "just lost Stevenson," or Mantz, or Faulkner.

There were 22 Lincolns at the start, with the factory team being backed up by such as Ray Crawford, who had his car prepared by Smith and Stroppe, and also Duane Carter, Rodger Ward and even Argentina's Oscar Galvez, who led a large group of his countrymen north for the race. (Import duties on automobiles were very high in Argentina, but through some governmental dispensation, anyone who bought a car and drove it in the Mexican road race could bring it home and pay very little duty. Many Argentines took advantage of this, and most of them drove rather cautiously in order to preserve the vehicle for more mundane duties at home. Some even quit at Oaxaca and drove straight to the port of Veracruz.) Not only the other Lincolns but also the various Chryslers and Cadillacs rarely managed to come close to Smith's team.

On the first leg, 330 miles from Tuxtla to Oaxaca, Stevenson, Faulkner, McGrath and Mantz finished in that order at the head of their class. Four days later, when they sped across the finish line at Juarez, the order was still the same. Stevenson and Smith were 1:03 ahead of Faulkner and Daigh, McGrath and Ron Ferguson were another 32 seconds behind, and Mantz and Stroppe were 23 seconds astern of McGrath—and less than two minutes behind Stevenson. It was one of the great displays of team strength in the history of auto racing, with these four cars occupying the top four spots in six of the eight legs. Only Crawford's Lincoln, which placed second on the third leg, and Frank Mundy's Kiekhaefer Chrysler, which finished second on the second leg, managed to intrude. On an over-all basis the Chrysler that finished fifth was 48 minutes behind Mantz. As he had been in previous races, Mantz was again the hard-luck pilot of a team that drove to orders: on the first day he was slowed by fan-belt trouble and he was the only member of the group to suffer a blowout. As a result he finished that leg seven minutes behind the leader. There was no way he could make up the deficit before they got to Juarez.

Those were high times for the Lincoln team, and although the large, heavy touring cars were ostensibly no match for the sports racing models that won the fastest category of the race, on an over-all basis Stevenson's time would have given him seventh place in the sports-car class. That division was taken by Juan Manuel Fangio, who at the time had won only one of his five world championships. He led a three-car sweep by the Lancia team in this event. Taruffi was second and young Italian Eugenio Castellotti was third, but all of them knew they had been in a race: Umberto Maglioli, driving a Ferrari, had hounded them throughout. Two minutes behind Fangio after four legs, Maglioli's original car then succumbed to mechanical failure. He proceeded to take over the wheel of another Ferrari which was far behind on aggregate time, and with this allegedly slower car he won the last three stages. There was no one capable of offering such opposition to the Lincoln team. Despite this, they were 44 minutes faster than the year before.

Then came 1954, and the world of auto racing was Smith's own private oyster. Cars he prepared were winning everywhere, his cams were the hottest thing on the speed-equipment market, and he was looking forward to taking it easier. At DuQuoin, Ill., for the AAA championship race on Labor Day, his asthma had been bothering him, and he was ready to quit. Clay called Stroppe in Long Beach the evening before the race.

"Bill, this is my last dirt race," he said. "I'm so fed up that from now on we're going strictly Ford and Indianapolis."

The next day Smith and Agajanian were standing in the pits when Stevenson and another car hit each other. The other car went out of control and came spinning toward them. Agajanian leaped to safety. Smith, weakened by his asthma, could not get out of the way in time.

When Stevenson, who was driving for Smith, came into the pits and saw what had happened, he threw his helmet into a nearby lake and didn't participate in another single-seater event for several years.

It was a crushing blow to many, and those who worked with Smith have never forgotten him. John Holman:

"We used to work for him as a labor of love—just to be around a guy as great as Clay ... I liked him, and that's the reason I went to work for him. He was probably the greatest man I've known in racing. That's a strong statement, but I don't think it's just my imagination because you'll find many other people with the same opinion."

Without Smith it was a dispirited crew, now led by Stroppe and aided by Don Francisco, that got ready for the 1954 race. They ran into bearing trouble during the assembly of the engines, and this cost valuable time. Then, when they reached the start, they got another bad break, one which hit them harder than any of the others.

At Tuxtla there was a large concrete tank from which all competitors obtained their fuel. Through most of the year it was filled with the low-octane stuff they used for farm tractors and the few local automobiles. When the race came, a tank truck from Mexico City was dispatched to fill it up with a better grade. That year they did not empty the concrete tank completely before the refill, and as a result the fuel the race cars took on was a mixture of good and bad—meaning mediocre. It was too much for the Lincolns' high-compression engines to take, and they had a problem.

The team was carrying little bottles of tetraethyl lead which they could dump in the gas tank to boost the octane, but they had been warned there would be a fuel check at the end of each leg, and there was much discussion over whether or not to take the chance. Some did and some didn't. As a result, both Mantz and Stevenson retired on the first leg with burned pistons, and McGrath also ran off the road during this stage. Six Lincolns, including the private entries, went out the first day.

On the next day Vukovich went off the road in one of the more spectacular accidents of the race. Vern Houle was Vuky's co-driver, and legend has it that when the car was sailing through the air, Vuky said "It's your turn to drive now," but Houle says this is exaggerated. When the car finally stopped rolling the door was torn off on Houle's side and there was dust in the air as they unhooked their safety belts, Houle with a few broken ribs, Vukovich with a minor neck injury. Then the dust settled a bit and Houle looked out. All he could see was air—and the ground, several hundred feet below. They had landed on a ledge.

Houle turned to Vukovich. "Better hook it up again, the sonofabitch is going to go some more."

They sat there for a moment, and when the car seemed stable enough, they crawled out through the place where the windshield had been and clambered up to the road and hitched rides into Mexico City. Houle was picked up by Giovanni Bracco, the Mille Miglia winner who had trouble with his Ferrari a little while earlier. It was fixed now, and Houle was taken on an even faster ride than he'd had with Vukovich, Bracco giving him a good fright every time he wanted a cigarette. He would merely indicate that Houle was to take the wheel and would reach into his pockets for a cigarette and his lighter, never taking his foot off the gas.

And Bracco was a chain smoker.

Benson Ford was in Mexico City waiting for the cars, and when they arrived he found that instead of an Armada, only Faulkner and Crawford, the Southern California grocery magnate, were left out of the original group. Crawford's car was one prepared by Stroppe and bought by Crawford (the price was $10,000 for the vehicle and service throughout the race). From Mexico City to Juarez, across the river from El Paso, Crawford and Faulkner were to be hounded by an army of the other big stock cars, all eager to finally knock off the Lincoln team. By the time they got to Chihuahua, Stroppe was good and worried, and not about the condition of the cars.

The veteran Faulkner was running a close second to Crawford at this point, and Stroppe knew Walt wanted to win. What he was afraid of was that Faulkner might want to win at any cost, and in so doing, might throw the whole team—and Stroppe's company—right out the window. He was afraid Walt might put a wheel under Crawford in a corner, or something like that, so that night Stroppe sat them both down in the motel and started to talk.

Some of the mainstays: (Top) Bill Vukovich, left, and Vern Houle. (Middle) Hard-luck Johnny Mantz and Bill Stroppe. (Bottom) Ray Crawford and Rick Iglesias, the only private Lincoln team to come home a winner.

"Ray," Stroppe said, "you're leading this race and Faulkner's right on your bumper. Now are we going to blow this race by you two fighting it out and trying to run each other off the road, or what?"

Faulkner never gave Stroppe or Crawford a chance to say anything else.

"Don't worry, Stroppe. If I can pass him and leave him plenty of room I will— but that's the only way."

The next day they ran from Chihuahua to Juarez and both of them took it easy. Keith Andrews won the leg in a Cadillac, but first and second for the race went to Crawford and Faulkner. The sports cars were faster than the previous year, and Crawford's time was slightly over that of Stevenson in 1953, so at the end he was a full three hours behind over-all winner Maglioli in his 4.9-liter Ferrari. But it made little difference; they weren't running against Maglioli in the first place. On an over-all basis, Crawford was ninth.

There was the usual post-race technical inspection, and this year the flap was about the automatic transmissions. Houle had rigged them so they downshifted at higher speeds, and then they even changed the speedometer drive so this fact wouldn't be apparent to any inspector who took the car out for a ride. But they got through that OK, even though assistant technical inspector Fran Hernandez had to get out of town in a hurry. Hernandez, who was working for the Mexican Government during the race, was also on Stroppe's payroll, and someone found out about it.

Then, suddenly, it was all over. The race had become too unwieldy, and crowd control was almost impossible. Rather than risk anything the government brought the classic to an end, just five years after it had started. It was one of the great chapters in auto racing history, and one of the shortest.

Meanwhile another type of stock car racing was about to blossom. Just a few weeks before this event was run in November, 1954, Chevrolet had introduced a new V8 engine.

18

COOLING OFF THE HOT ONE

WHEN THE FORD MOTOR COMPANY EMBARKED on its first struggling steps as an automobile manufacturer, its sales promotion-cum-racing activities were undertaken on the initiative of its founder, owner and even chief mechanic. But when Ford went back to racing in a big way in 1955, the corporation did so only because it was forced to by another manufacturer.

The situation was a peculiar one. Here was the company, just beginning to realize it was losing the youth market and still struggling to survive the corporate near-catastrophe of the immediate postwar period. Its flathead V8, that good and reliable workhorse of two decades, was outmoded; when it was replaced with an overhead valve engine of the same configuration, the new powerplant was—relatively speaking—not as good. It was not, for example, as good as the high-revving, free-breathing V8s which now propelled Oldsmobiles and Cadillacs. But Ford went along with it anyway, being at this time more interested in bringing order to its own house than it was in mounting any aggressive campaign to recapture a market it hardly knew was gone.

On the other side of the fence was Chevrolet, GM's biggest division, following in the path of the other General Motors brand names by bringing out an engine of V8 pattern—and in Chevy's case its first V8 since the post-World War I era. Even at Chevrolet, where the hierarchy included several racing-minded persons, there was no one who dreamed this new engine, which started life with a displacement of 265 cubic inches and 162 advertised horsepower, would be so successful. More than a dozen years later the same basic design, by now stretched to 360 cubic inches and highly developed by various independent tuners, could be made to produce 500 reliable horsepower and was the logical replacement, with the youth of America, for Ford's flathead.

The most laughable—and to a few the most irritating—feature of the whole Ford-Chevy stock car encounter was that neither had the best vehicle. This distinction belonged to Chrysler, whose expensive 300 series was far and away the fastest thing on the tracks in 1955 and 1956. The catch here was that Chrysler was not competing. Its colors were being carried by Carl Kiekhaefer, the dynamic, auto-cratic and irascible manufacturer of Mercury outboard engines. Kiekhaefer's team went racing on a scale that no private entry has attempted before or since, and his cars won NASCAR Grand National championships both years. But whenever a Chrysler won there was little publicity. Whenever a Ford or a Chevy won, the drums started to beat again and the national newspaper ads were loud in their announce-ments of this latest victory. Kiekhaefer quit after the 1956 season, having been practically forced out of it by the factories. But before he left he proved one impor-tant thing. It doesn't make any difference how many races you win unless you tell someone about it.

The stage on which Ford and Chevy fought it out was also a most unusual one. These giant corporations, which think nothing of spending $50,000 for a press pre-sentation in some exotic setting, complete with string music, cocktails and muted lights, were now spending millions to bump heads on a bunch of dusty, rutted dirt tracks carved out of pine forests in the economically weakest section of the United States—the Southeast. They had to go south, because that's where the action was; it was the home of NASCAR, the brainchild of Bill France. He tied together a lot of itinerant promoters, part-time bootleggers and sometime race drivers, added a group of shade-tree mechanics, shook the whole conglomeration carefully and came up with the best opportunity the manufacturers ever had to show that one make of pas-senger car was faster than another.

If the stock car tracks of the mid-1950s looked shabby compared to the superspeedways of a decade later, they were still a vast improvement over their beginnings in the period preceding World War II.

Auto racing had never been as strong in the Southeast as it had, say, in the Middle or Far West, and one of the many reasons for this was the long-term eco-nomic depression that hit the South after the Civil War. Aside from the Daytona Beach races, the first major stock car event to be held in this region was staged at Lakewood Speedway in Atlanta in 1938 and was put on by Ralph Hankinson, the legendary promoter of the 1930s. When Hankinson wondered out loud if they could get together enough stockers for a suitable field, mechanic Red Vogt laughed. "Hell," he said, "we've got enough bootleggers and numbers runners right here in Atlanta to make a good field even if we don't get anyone else." The race was held, and it was found spectators would pay just as much money to see stock cars as they would to watch more sophisticated single seaters.

Atlanta, not the Carolinas or for that matter Daytona, was the birthplace of stock car racing. One of the reasons for this was the density of population, another was the presence of the one-mile dirt oval at Lakewood, one of the few big tracks in the Southeast. In addition there was single-seater racing at Lakewood; this enabled the track to draw driving talent not only from the immediate locality, but also from the Midwest. Most of the Lakewood races were for sprint cars, and then there were "Skeeters," a sort of bastardized monoposto halfway between present-day sprinters

(Top) Buddy Shuman, the man who started it and never lived to see the real results of his handiwork. (Bottom) At Daytona, the first turn of the first lap was often disastrous. Photo taken during a 1955 sportsman race.

and super-modifieds, with the heritage of both thoroughbred and standard-bred apparent at first glance. Among the drivers of these was Louis G. (Buddy) Shuman, who was running a Hudson-engined sprinter out of Charlotte, N.C., and it was through men like Shuman that the message of Atlanta and the innovations developed by Vogt, the king of the area's race car mechanics, spread through the Southland. When Shuman and the others went home after an event, they took what they learned back with them.

There they were, scattered all over, some of them were mechanics during the week and race drivers on Sunday, others were bootleggers who could use their hotted-up cars for business as well as competition (there was no more social stigma attached to running whiskey in the South than there was to getting a traffic ticket in New York or Los Angeles). They had little or no organization and little or no idea of what could be made out of all this until France came along to show them. He gave shape and substance to the picture, and at his first Grand National event there were 14,000 spectators—more than had ever seen a stock car race before.

Daytona, Lakewood, Hankinson, France—they were all major influences in the development of stock car racing. But none of them was the basic one, the key that established the proper climate and attitude. That was something entirely different. It was a religious belief, one that held man should not partake of alcohol. As a result of this, great areas of the Southeast were dry. Because they were, an enormous illicit liquor business sprang up, with the bulk of it being brewed in thousands of back-woods stills, then taken to the larger cities for distribution and resale. Soon a whole new set of folkways and folklore grew up around the trade. Words like moonshine and revenooer (regardless of what Webster says) became a part of the language, tall tales were told of the exploits involved in getting the goods to market, and even taller ones were told about the men who ran the business.

One of the most interesting personalities, and one of the more important men in the development of stock car racing, came out of the hill country of Georgia in the early 1930s. When he got to Atlanta, the red clay barely off his shoes, he could neither read nor write. Up in the mountains this lack of education had caused certain difficulties in his coterie of bootleggers; none of them possessed these skills, so they had an old woman who kept their books. Eventually the day came when one thought another was cheating. Since he couldn't interpret the woman's columns of figures, he simply took his suspicions to be fact and murdered the man he suspected.

The one who moved to the city eventually learned to read and write, being taught to do so in the Federal Penitentiary at Chillicothe, Ohio. He later referred to his time there as "going to college," and it stood him in good stead. He was to become the man to see in the Southeast, the number one bootlegger and numbers banker in Atlanta. Now the others worked for him, and if they happened to be picked up, he would either buy the hauling car back at the next sheriff's auction or provide them with a new one.

The Federal men suspected where the whiskey was being made, and they suspected where it was being sold. But they *knew* how it got from one place to the other. So the most vulnerable link in the chain was the transport, and this was the point the revenuers hit the hardest. The little Ford coupes, loaded down with 150 gallons of bootleg whiskey (that added more than 1,000 pounds to the load), were at a disadvantage when it came to outrunning the Federals, so the solution became simple: Hop up the cars, get faster drivers. The mechanical modification process spawned what was later to be the first group of stock car mechanics and they were led by Vogt, whose Atlanta garage turned out as many cars intended for hauling White Lightning as it did vehicles built for racing. Although hotter engines (some ordered complete from the California speed shops) and heavier springs were the stock-in-trade improvements, sometimes things were more sophisticated. There was the time the whiskey agents started shooting into radiators, which usually resulted in the car coming to a halt with a cooked engine a few miles down the road. The radiators were soon mounted in the trunk, and it took the Federals a few months before they caught on to this trick.

The whiskey went one way and sometimes, on the return trips, the cars would go with small safes jammed full of money. Our entrepreneur had to bide the cash in the hills, because the receipts he collected were not the type you deposited in an Atlanta bank. Then, one day in the late 1930s, he went to a single-seater race at Lakewood and was standing by the fence, watching the mechanics. He wanted to walk inside the garage area but was stopped by the guard.

"What do I have to do to get in there?" he asked.

"You have to be a driver, a mechanic or a car owner," he was told.

He moved a few paces down the fence, called to one of the men, and bought his car on the spot.

Then he walked past the guard.

He soon became one of the first sponsors to put real money into the sport, with his flathead Ford coupes running—and winning—as far north as Fort Wayne, Ind., and Langhorne, Pa. And when they weren't in races, many of the cars were used for hauling.

It was a free and easy world in those early days of stock car racing, and despite the well-worked-over vehicles of the bootleggers, anyone with a good-running coupe stood a decent chance to win—as long as it was a Ford. The flathead V8 was the most powerful and most durable engine in the low-price class, the car had the best power-to-weight ratio, and it hardly ever entered anyone's head to use a different make.

How easy was it? In 1940 Alvin Hawkins bought a 1939 Ford coupe on a used-car lot in Detroit, then drove it back to Spartanburg, S.C. They changed the oil and the plugs, greased the car and gave it a good general tune-up, and a youngster by the name of Joe Epton towed it to Daytona. Hawkins sat the car on the pole for the big race, clocking the fastest time in the measured mile straightaway runs which were used for qualifying. Stock was really stock.

The story also has an aftermath. Hawkins, with little experience as a race driver, decided he didn't want to pilot the car in the main event and turned it over to Fonty Flock. Fonty was leading the first lap when Roy Hall rammed him in the

Esses, putting the car into the palmettos and Flock into the hospital for six months.

Before he was through as a driver, this member of the fabulous Flocks visited the hospital 40 times. He and his brothers, Carl, Tim and Bob, plus his sister, Ethyl, composed the biggest family ever to compete at one time in any form of auto racing, and they were just a small part of the colorful gang that populated the prewar stock car scene. There were Skimp Hersey, and Sam Purvis from Florida, Red Byron was the big star in the Atlanta area, there was Joe Littlejohn from Spartanburg, there was Roy Hall, who at times drove with "The Bootlegger" painted on the side of his car, and there was Buddy Shuman and Red Singleton, and dozens of others. Fonty Flock was 17 when he started, and hid his activities from his parents by driving under the name of Wild Bill Dawson. Since he was driving out of Dawsonville, Ga., it sounded even better, and then he added a trim little moustache, the same as that sported by his idol, Indianapolis hero Ted Horn. Fonty piled up more than 200 victories before he finally retired in 1957, and he made little more money out of them all than the winner of the Daytona "500" picked up in the 1960s. In 1941, when Fonty won the big Labor Day race in Atlanta, he collected $166.

But you didn't need much money. Littlejohn made his first trip from Spartanburg to Daytona in 1938, having heard there was racing going on. When he arrived and inquired where one registered he was told the guy at the filling station was running it. The guy turned out to be France. That night Littlejohn got himself involved in a poker game with some strangers and lost his meager stake. Penniless, he made his way for the next few days by selling some turnip greens he'd brought south in the back of his stock car. Littlejohn learned his lessons in more ways than one. After seeing what France had achieved, Joe went back to Spartanburg and sponsored his initial event on Armistice Day of 1939, with France the first driver to sign.

At Daytona the races resembled Roman holidays. The nature of the four-mile course, which had one straightaway and both turns on the sand and the start-finish straight on the paved highway, prevented anyone from practicing; the constant stream of cars would churn up the sand. So they qualified via the flying mile method, and on the day of the race there were usually well over 100 cars lined up on the road. When they got to the first turn there was almost invariably an epic accident that involved at least a dozen cars and usually more. The resultant carnage left the turn looking like a junkyard, but the crowds loved it. The beach was also the scene of numerous innovations by the smarter mechanics, with one of the more involved ideas being to fill the windshield washer with nitromethane or some other illegal fuel, then run the line from the washer tank to the carburetor just before the start, when the technical inspectors weren't watching. If the pistons would take it, the nitro guaranteed you a hell of a lead before the volatile fluid ran out and you were forced to run on gasoline alone. There was even the guy, some oldtimers maintain, who came with two identical cars, putting one at the starting line and hiding the second on the other side of the course. When the flag dropped, his starting-line

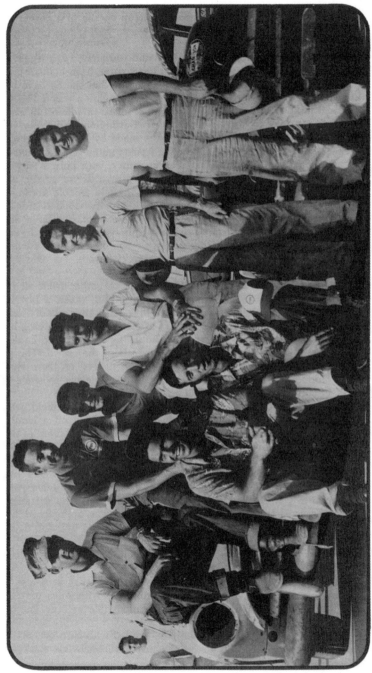

Some of the good old boys, plus a few outsiders: (From left, front row) Ralph Liguori and Don Thomas. (Back row) Speedy Thompson, Herb Thomas, Bob Welborn, Buck Baker, Hershel McGriff and Slick Smith.

henchman drove off into the pileup on the first corner and the originator of the idea streaked up the beach, half a lap in front of the field.

Aside from the founding of NASCAR in the winter of 1947–1948, the biggest boost the sport received in the Southeast came from a small group of South Carolina businessmen, who in 1950 built what should have been the most colossal white elephant in history. Their creation was a 1¼-mile (lengthened in 1953 to 1⅜ miles) paved track in the middle of the South Carolina cotton and tobacco country near Darlington, which is near nothing. The proposal to build the track was made by Harold Brasington and was jokingly accepted one night during a poker game. Then, incredibly, it was built. Far from any large population center, with only a two-lane state highway running by it and only one entry road to the infield, after the Darlington dreamers got their oval built they had trouble finding an organization to sanction a race. It was the first major asphalt track in the Southeast, and all, including NASCAR, were hesitant over a stock car's chances to last 500 high-speed miles on this type of surface. In addition Darlington, with a population of perhaps 6,000, had no hotel facilities of which to speak. It should have been a dismal failure. Yet slowly, interest grew.

The day before the event the faithful started to gather from all over the Southland; they'd banked the fire under the still, taken a last look at the crops, another at the creeks to make sure they weren't rising, and headed for Darlington. By late Sunday afternoon there were long lines of traffic outside the speedway, tying up Route 151. The police came to the promoters and told them to do something about the crowd. The promoters replied they couldn't very well sell them tickets, as there was a state law forbidding racing events—or the sale of tickets to such—on Sundays. Finally the track and the police got together.

The track agreed to let the fans (and their cars) into the infield, where they could stay overnight. In the morning they would set off a bomb to wake everyone up, shoo them back outside, sell them tickets, then let them back in again. By midnight the lines outside were much longer than before, and it was clear the plan was headed for disaster. When the bomb went off just before sunrise it created havoc, with lines of cars inside trying to get out, other lines outside trying to get in, and ticket takers working like mad to collect what money they could. High in the grandstand watching the maelstrom below was France, who was approached by a fan who had slept in his car all night. He had recognized Bill, and figured he could help him.

"Mr. France, can you tell me where I could find a drugstore open right now?"

Bill eyed the rising sun and explained to the man that at 6 a.m. on Labor Day, a few miles removed from Darlington, with lines of traffic blocking the road back to the town, it was impossible to even get to a drugstore, much less find one open.

Then, curious, he asked the man what he wanted with a drugstore.

"Well, it's my wife," he was told. "She just gave birth last week, and she's havin' all kinds of trouble, and I got to find a breast pump for her."

France thought about it a moment, then said, "Well, Buddy, why don't you help her out yourself?"

"Mr. France," the answer came, "I been helping her out all night, and it makes me sick!"

That's how the Southern "500" was born. They almost tore the gates down to get in. More than 30,000 of them made it, and right from the beginning the race was a success. The bonanza of Darlington, which at that time was a dateline unknown to even the most experienced Associated Press staffer, eventually led to the building of the super speedways at Daytona, Charlotte, Atlanta and Rockingham, N.C., and helped bring Detroit money to the South.

In that first year the prospect of running a 500-mile race for stock cars was an awesome one. The running gear on the vehicles was fairly close to production configuration, and there were some who were sure not a car would last the distance. Among these was Red Byron, the fastest qualifier and a heavy favorite in his new Cadillac. As he sat on the starting line, he reiterated his conviction. "There won't be one of these cars finish," he said, "not a damn one."

Not only did Byron finish, but he probably would have won had racing tires been available. The finances of the times, plus the minimal interest of the tire companies, led to an almost complete absence of anything but regular passenger rubber. Byron wound up changing 22 of these during the race and others among the 75 starters exceeded even that number.

The winner was Johnny Mantz, the hard-luck driver of the Mexican road race that year, who wheeled a six-cylinder Plymouth home at the respectable speed of 76.26 mph in a little over 6½ hours. Mantz was far from the fastest in this maiden voyage over 500 miles, but his car gave him absolutely no trouble, and while the others headed for the pits every few laps, Mantz kept churning around in the steamy summer heat.

Mantz's route from California to South Carolina was an interesting one, because in those times single-seater pilots driving under AAA sanction were as far removed from NASCAR and the Southeast as the earth is from the outer planets. While in Mexico, Mantz and co-driver Stroppe met France and Curtis Turner and became friendly with the Southern pair—in fact France and Turner fed their new-found friends for a good deal of the distance, as their Nash had foresightedly been loaded with provisions before they left El Paso. Later in the year France invited Mantz to the Southern "500," and Johnny headed east. Bill had lined him up with a ride in an Olds 88, and that was considered the hottest car at the time.

In order to be eligible for the "500" drivers had to participate in at least two other NASCAR races, so Mantz geared up a Lincoln for an event in South Carolina; then he and Hubert Westmoreland took the latter's Olds to Dayton, Ohio. Late in the race, while Mantz was running near the front of the pack, he blew a tire and smacked the wall, bending the car slightly and ending up stalled in the middle of the banking. In a moment another car rammed him from behind, demolishing the Olds and wiping out all the hours Westmoreland had spent preparing the car for Darlington. Mantz went back to Darlington anyway, and as the cars were circling the track in practice, he had an idea. Mantz turned to France, Turner and Alvin Hawkins, who were standing with him.

"You know what can win this race?" Mantz said. "A goddamn Plymouth can win it." He had been watching the constant tire-changing in the pits and suddenly realized that the race would be won not by speed, but by the car that kept its tires in one piece. The Plymouth, a gutless wonder but also extremely light, would be the answer. France, Turner and Hawkins got together and bought one for Mantz, and he took the hubcaps off and qualified the car in showroom condition. From there he drove north to Winston-Salem, N.C., where he set up the car for the race by installing such items as heavy-duty shock absorbers. He never took the engine apart, satisfying himself with a good general tune-up. Mantz's aces in the hole were not under the hood, they were on the wheels: As an AAA driver he had good contacts in Akron, and procured several sets of racing tires. These were to be the only examples of real racing rubber in the event, and as further insurance Mantz organized a set of pneumatic lug wrenches so the few tire changes he made would be done with all possible speed.

Mantz spent the night before the event at Myrtle Beach, a resort some 50 miles away, where he attended a party that got wilder as the night grew older. It didn't break up until dawn, and Johnny was right there at the finish. He dived into the ocean to refresh himself, drove to Darlington, ate several aspirin tablets for breakfast and climbed into his machine. When the 75 cars roared off, Mantz was deep in the middle of the pack with no idea of how fast he or his car could go. He spent the first few laps checking the stopwatch he carried with him, trying to find a reasonable pace. Then he settled down and started to run.

During the race, Turner recalls, "I was driving an Olds 88 and I lapped Johnny about every 15 laps, or so it seemed. Then I'd blow a tire and have to go back to the pits, and Mantz kept right on running." There were a lot of other hot dogs in the same boat as Turner, and slowly Mantz moved up on them. By the 48th of the 400 laps he was in front, and he never lost the lead. Westmoreland and his friends were acting as Mantz' pit crew, and the pneumatic wrenches gave them a big edge over the other mechanics. Mantz made only three tire changes, and at the finish was comfortably in front of the pack. After the race Mantz took his winnings, bought himself a new car and vanished into the sunset. His defection from the AAA ranks cost him a $2,500 fine, but it had been worth it.

As Darlington grew and the sport prospered, new heroes came into prominence and old ones faded away. Some of them, like Skimp Hersey, died in flaming pools of gasoline. Others simply quit when they found the new standard of professionalism demanded they become full-time drivers. And whenever one did, the crowd and the promoters found another man to take his place—with a single, notable exception.

This was Curtis Turner, and he was the Babe Ruth and Paul Bunyan of stock car racing, all rolled up into one.

From the northern fringe of the stock car cosmos in the Shenandoah Mountains of Virginia, Turner became a legend in his own time. The only man to successfully make the transition from the dirt tracks to the 180-mph speeds of the mid-1960s Daytona, Curtis could outdrive and outdrink anyone else on the circuit, and when he wasn't driving or drinking or chasing women he was bound to be involved in some million-dollar timber deal—or maybe a two-million dollar timber deal—or maybe ...

That's the trouble with Curtis Turner. He is too big to define accurately. There was, and is, just too much of him, and perhaps the primary reason he is sometimes known as "the living legend" is that observers of the genus have trouble separating the fact from the fancy. Curtis was born just outside the little town of Floyd, which has a population of about 1,000, and according to Turner he hauled his first load of moonshine whiskey when he was 9 years old. He was driving it down the narrow dirt road that led from the still back in the woods to the family farm when he encountered a postman going the other way. This was the youngster's first involvement with another vehicle heading in the opposite direction on the same stretch of road, and he didn't know on which side he was supposed to pass. As a result, Curtis ran the postman up the bank.

And when Turner tells this story, he does so with a straight face.

That was his start in the liquor-hauling business. He began his career as a lumberman a few years later, at 14, holding down one end of a cross-cut saw for 15¢ an hour and working a 10-hour day. According to one version of the legend, by the time he was 20 he was running three sawmills, plus all the logging equipment necessary to keep them going, plus a truck line that included eight tractor-trailers and five lumber haulers.

And in his spare time he hauled whiskey in a Ford coupe, complete with heavy springs and shock absorbers and with a McCulloch supercharger under the hood. That was the Ford that gave him his basic training as a racing driver, outrunning the Federal agents through the mountain country of his native state. One cop, Curtis says, "ran me 39 times, but he never came close. In these days there was this rule that if they didn't catch you on the road you were safe, and I used to talk with that ol' trooper and he'd say 'I'm gonna catch you if it's the last thing I do, Curtis.' Later that old boy committed suicide, and some people say it was because he could never catch me. I don't know about that, but 39 times sure is a lot."

Ironically, the only time Curtis was caught he was running sugar back into the hills during the war, having traded white lightning for the then rationed sweet stuff at the Little Creek, Va., naval base. The only way they caught him was to post a guard around his daddy's place back in Floyd, and there are many who feel the Federals used a method that wasn't quite cricket. After all, if you could make it back home, you were supposed to be let go. The judge, who was wise in the ways of the mountain men, fined him $1,000 and gave him a two-year suspended sentence.

Turner's beginnings as a racing driver came after he was discharged from the Navy in the summer of 1946. Curtis heard some of the boys who hauled liquor during the week were running their cars on Sundays at Mt. Airy, N.C., and he went down for a look. The race was rained out, but Turner got out on the track anyway, broadsliding his way around in the slippery red earth just for the hell of it. When he pulled off the empty track, heading for home, Curtis found a small crowd had remained to watch. They had passed the hat, and he came away with $22. A week later he was back and they had a race. Curtis finished last, his car being reasonably stock and the others having extensive chassis modifications. The next few days at Floyd were spent in beefing up the suspension. On the following Sunday he took it to Marion, Va., where he started at the back again. He won easily, and the legend acquired another chapter.

Within a few years Curtis was the king of the stock car drivers. He didn't win the most races, and he never owned the Grand National title, but every time Turner took the track with a competitive automobile the crowd knew who would be the fastest. Not the Flocks, not Herb Thomas or Speedy Thompson, or Lee Petty or Joe Weatherly, or even Fireball Roberts: it was Turner, whose flamboyant broadsliding style on the dirt tracks was an art unto itself.

Someplace or other during his midnight rides over the mountain roads of Virginia, Curtis had picked up the knack of getting his car practically at right angles to the direction of flight, and keeping it there almost indefinitely as he bombed his way through the hills. Now he applied this same technique to the half-mile dirt ovals that were the backbone of NASCAR. The sight of Turner on the dirt, or on the sands of Daytona, applying full opposite lock, his right foot planted firmly on the gas pedal, with his vehicle defying all laws of centrifugal force and tire adhesion, was one never to be fogotten.

There was the time at Mount Airy when Curtis smashed through the board fence twice—once when he spun out, the second time when he rejoined the race by the most direct route. There was another time (nobody seems to remember just where) that Curtis spun and wound up facing the oncoming traffic. Rather than wait for them to go by he simply slammed the car into reverse and drove a lap backwards. Then, when most of the pack had passed, he spun around again and proceeded in the proper manner.

Then there was the time, but there were thousands of times, and anyone who has ever spent more than five minutes with Turner has at least five stories to tell about the big soft-voiced man who came flying into the nearest cornfield, drove the race, then flew off again, heading for another party. Ask the rent-a-car people. There are some places where they still won't give him a vehicle. They suspect the last one they loaned him was run in a race when he couldn't find a proper mount.

Sometimes the cars weren't strong enough for the driver, and at other times the partying or the timber business got into the act a bit too strongly, but when everything was right, he was unbeatable.

Turner and his competitors were a tough bunch, and they ran in hard circumstances. The unpaved tracks, the tiny purses—none of it was very glamorous or lucrative. But it was a way of life, and slowly but surely France was getting his drivers more money, and in the South at least, more space in the papers.

He tried to make NASCAR a nationwide organization, and every year or so the drivers would make a northern tour through Pennsylvania and New York, or perhaps

Illinois and Ohio, and they would draw fans. But they never got the crowds like they did down South, and the distances they had to travel to were unbelievable.

One weekend in 1953, for example, there was a race scheduled on the evening of July 3 in Rochester, N.Y., and one the next night in Spartanburg, S.C., about 800 miles away and in an era when the interstate highway network was unknown. Spartanburg promoter Littlejohn arranged to have some of the drivers flown down for his race. But there were others who either couldn't afford planes, or who only had one race car. Among these was Lee Petty, who loaded his car on the trailer after the race at Rochester, and headed south with only his wife for company. His son Richard was still too small to make the trips.

Sometime in the middle of the night, after Petty had slept an hour or so, his wife woke him up as they were careening down a mountain and told him the brakes had faded. So he took over and drove the rest of the way into Spartanburg. Then he went out and won the race.

That was the day Tim Flock and Herb Thomas flew down to Spartanburg, and being the first ones there, found a convenient car in the infield and crawled under it, hoping to catch a few hours' sleep in the shade before the race. The owner returned a while later, and not being in the habit of checking under his vehicle to see who was in residence, started to drive away. He ran over a part of Flock's head.

Flock came back to win the Grand National championship in 1955, just as he had done in 1952. The first year Tim won, his brother Fonty was the one who captured the Southern "500." When Fonty climbed out of his car at the conclusion of the race, he was wearing Bermuda shorts.

That's how it was, back when.

In December of 1953, at the same time NASCAR was getting its feet on the ground, one of the newest engineers at General Motors was busy writing a memo. He bore the rather colorful and often mispronounced name of Zora Arkus-Duntov, he spoke excellent English with a heavy Russian accent, and at the time he was one of the few professionally trained engineers in the American auto industry who understood anything about racing. He was educated in Berlin and spent his early professional years working in Europe, he had been the man behind the Ardun heads and camshafts for the flathead Fords, and he had also been a class winner at Le Mans while driving for Porsche. He knew the business from both ends, and as soon as he went with GM in May and saw the new Chevrolet engine, he realized its possibilities. His memo of early December, addressed to Maurice Olley, then the Chevrolet director of engineering research and development, was an outline of how to take the youth market away from Ford. The way to do it was to make use of this engine, and to make good speed equipment available for it at a reasonable price. Whether or not Duntov's memo was followed—or whether anyone in the company is still aware of its existence—is not known. Whatever the case, it is interesting that the actions of General Motors since that date have paralleled the course Duntov recommended.

At left, two of the greatest—and most durable—drivers in NASCAR, with the photos taken in their prime: Lee Petty (top, left) and Curtis Turner, with the latter also standing by his famous Wild Hog at Daytona, 1956. Also on the beach, and at an early age, was Fireball Roberts (above, top). Others got their start in a different part of the country: John Holman (bottom) worked as a mechanic on Lou Fageol's race cars as a teen-ager in Los Angeles during the mid-1930s.

The Beach—prewar flatheads were the mainstays of the modified races.

The second step in Detroit's going racing took place in the late summer of 1954, when Arthur B. (Barney) Clark went to work for Campbell-Ewald, Chevrolet's advertising agency. When he arrived, Clark was most impressed by two things: the first was the fact that few persons in the agency really knew or cared anything about automobiles *per se*, and the second was the new V8 engine. As a longtime car buff Barney was excited over the engine, and felt it could be raced successfully and through this medium would boost Chevy sales. His feelings were confirmed at the end of February, 1955, when he spotted an item in the Detroit *Free Press* which related the result of the flying mile trials at Daytona, now open to all comers even if they didn't want to compete in the circuit races.

Jack Tapscott of Deland, just west of Daytona, had been clocked at 112.113 mph in a 1955 Chevy. Now Tapscott, who was a highway patrolman, didn't even win his class, losing by a fraction of a mile to a DeSoto, but that made little difference. "In those days you just didn't buy a low-priced car that could top 100," Clark says. As soon as he got into the office he called Jim Wangers, another of the few fans in the place, and found that Wangers had been trying to call him: He'd also seen the item.

That was the start of it. "You can't put your finger on one particular guy who was specifically responsible," Clark says, but the fact remains he was in the right place at the right time to crystallize a lot of seemingly unrelated items. The proposal was made, racing-minded Ed Cole, then the chief engineer of the Chevrolet Division, backed it, and things started to roll, including money for an advertising campaign and engines and even complete cars for the "proper" persons.

On March 15 of that year, at the first NASCAR short-track race of the season at Fayetteville, N.C., Herb Thomas showed up with a Chevy and won. The newspaper advertisements followed almost immediately, and the rest of Detroit was shocked. They had never seen anything like this before. It was all right to show a picture of a car with a pretty girl alongside and intimate that if you bought the car your sex appeal would increase to the point where you could have the girl as well; that had been the party line for years. But this, this advertising *racing*, well, it seemed not quite *de rigeur*. But it worked. Two weeks later, at Greenwood, S.C., Fonty Flock won a Grand National 100-miler in another Chevy, and the newspapers and radio stations were quick to remind the country of this latest triumph. Interestingly, Flock's win was only one of two the Chevys were able to record in the 45 Grand National races held that year, as the Chryslers took 27 (18 by Tim Flock) and the Oldsmobiles won 10, but the type of race made little or no difference to Campbell-Ewald. A victory was a victory, and the details of the event were of no importance for an ad campaign. One time, when short-track star Jimmy Reed beat some over-age (and poorly driven) Jaguars and other foreign cars on a quarter-mile oval, Campbell-Ewald was ready with an ad that made it appear as if their baby, always referred to as "The Hot One," had beaten Europe's best.

The Chevrolet dealers, especially those in the South, loved it. When their car won a race on Sunday, it had a measurable effect on Monday traffic in the showrooms, and they yelled for more. The fact that the country's largest automaker was now bucking their product with a V8-engined model had been the first big shock for Ford. When Chevy started racing this car, it became too much to bear. Something had to be done, and incentive for the move came from several directions.

From the top the word came down, and by midsummer Robert McNamara, then general manager of the Ford Division, was talking the situation over with engineers Hans Matthias, Harley Copp and Bill Burnett. It became obvious that a full-blown effort was needed, and as McNamara, Matthias and Copp sat around one evening discussing it, McNamara turned to Copp and said, "Harley, how would you recommend we do this?"

"Get it outside the company," said Copp.

McNamara wanted to know who could head the operation, and Copp, then chief engineer of the Continental and perhaps the only Ford executive who was a racing buff, suggested former Indianapolis winner Pete DePaolo as the best symbol for the company. So Copp called DePaolo and discussions were started, discussions that in a few months led to the major effort.

At the same time, in Charlotte, Bill Benton was getting worked up over the situation. The field service manager for Ford's Charlotte District, Benton had been raised there and had watched races on the dirt track at nearby Salisbury as far back as 1937 and 1938. He was a low man on the corporate totem pole, but he was one of those in a position to see first hand what Chevy's campaign was doing, and he had the guts and intelligence to do something about it. As far back as 1951, when the dealers in the Carolinas started asking for action, Benton had done his bit in a *sub rosa* fashion, helping individual dealers outfit a few cars for races.

Now the complaints grew into a storm. "Our dealers kept giving us the business," Benton said." "'We've owned this market for years,' they told us; 'We've had the V8 all of our lives—and now you're letting Chevy do *this* to us.'"

In early summer Benton sent a wire over the signature of district manager Jack Snyder to Carl Doman, then the Ford Division national service manager. Boiled down, it said: We need help. We need it for Darlington. A few weeks later Benton, who had only been to Dearborn once before in his corporate career, flew up to explain what he wanted. To make sure they would understand the technical needs as well as the marketing problems, he took with him Shuman, the Charlotte expert at building race cars and one of the brighter lights on the NASCAR circuit. Buddy, complete with loud sport shirt and country way of talking, was something the cloistered Ford engineers had never encountered before. Then, when he started to explain just what had to be done to a stock chassis to make it raceworthy, he left them nonplussed and skeptical.

"The engineers thought he was nuts," Benton recalled. "You just didn't *do* things like that to cars."

But you did do things like that to cars if you wanted them to run fast on oval tracks, and Buddy knew it. What he did not realize at the time was that the engineers'

*Joe Weatherly (above, top), the clown prince of NASCAR, at Daytona in 1956.
(Bottom) Action in Daytona's south turn, the mid-1950s. At right: (Top) Lee Petty in his
Plymouth and Tim Flock in a Hudson, sideways on the dirt of the Carolinas. Ralph Moody,
who finished third in the 1956 beach race, did so only after rolling to avoid Petty, who was
unable to see through his sand-blasted windshield and who came roaring back on the
course after wandering out into the Atlantic (middle and bottom).*

ego, bolstered by university degrees and healthy salaries, refused to let them accept some back-country hick telling them their cars were no good. Slowly, Buddy and Benton, each working from a different approach, got the engineers to thinking their way. Finally, as the meeting drew to a close, Burnett turned to Benton.

"I recognize what you want," he said. "I realize what you're trying to do in counteracting Chevrolet. But we don't have enough time to test and put together two cars with the proper equipment for this race."

"The decision is yours," Burnett said. "Would you rather go down just to let everyone know you're there, or would you rather stay out until the February races at Daytona?"

So it was all put on the shoulders of a young Ford field man with about as much power to make a corporate decision as he had to fly to the moon. Benton didn't hesitate.

"We'll go," he said. That's how Ford got into stock car racing. It was Benton's personal opinion that Ford would be better off with *any* sort of representation, regardless of the performance, and as it turned out later, he was right.

The cars were built in the Ford experimental garage and transported to Charlotte, where they arrived a few weeks before the race and were put into the service area of Schwam Motors, which was the entrant for the race. Charlie Schwam, a showman by nature, had them painted a vivid purple, had cartoons of pigs painted on and nicknamed them "Schwam's Wild Hogs." The name alone was worth a good deal of ink in the southern papers.

Not only were the cars a fortuitous circumstance for Ford, but so were their drivers. Through a series of coincidences, not through any special planning, Turner and his buddy Joe Weatherly, two of the very best, were signed for the race. They were talked into it by a longtime fan who was a friend of Weatherly's and a salesman for Schwam. He talked to Weatherly, Joe talked to Turner, and that was that. Later, when Ford was in with both feet, negotiations were more complicated. With one driver, they even had to pay his back income tax.

A few engineers came to Charlotte with the cars to supervise the race preparation, and they were having their problems. They had diplomas, but they didn't understand how to get ready for 500 miles of racing, and the situation got sticky. Work went on almost around the clock, and in the early hours of the morning the cars would leave Charlotte and drive down to Darlington, some three hours distant, for secret sunrise practice sessions.

Finally Benton called in Shuman, and Buddy took charge. Working almost without sleep for the last week before the race, he got the cars in shape. He worked himself, he cajoled Schwam's mechanics, and he talked the Ford engineers into letting him do what he wanted.

If that wasn't enough, after Weatherly qualified at 109.006 mph, Shuman found Turner couldn't get his machine over 106. That was too much for Buddy, who had put his heart into the effort. "Jesus Christ, Pops," he exploded, "if you can't get the damn thing going let me show you how."

With that Shuman climbed into the car and qualified it at 109.054, to the eternal embarrassment of Turner.

Neither car, despite the commotion they caused among the fans, could be considered a favorite. Fireball Roberts was on the pole with a Buick he had qualified at 110.682, and Tim Flock had set a new record of 112.041 in one of Kiekhaefer's Chryslers, the reason he wasn't up front being that he qualified the second day.

When the 75 cars got under way Turner soon charged forward, and the fans who had come to see a Chevy show were watching Fords running out front. For Benton, in the pits, that was his race car out there, and he drove every lap with Turner. Next to him was Shuman, the man obsessed with victory, and he too was riding with Turner in everything but his person. Then the front suspension let go and Curtis crashed. He was out of it. Weatherly, not far behind, took the lead.

Little Joe led from lap 180 through lap 278 (there are 364 in all), when he pitted for fuel and tires and let Herb Thomas into the lead with his Chevrolet. Thomas, who won at Darlington in 1951 and 1954 and lost the 1953 race when he broke a crankshaft with eight miles to go, proved to be no opposition for Weatherly, who regained the lead on lap 304. Joe and the Purple Hog soon moved more than a lap in front, charging through the hot afternoon sun, well ahead of Thomas and the rest of the pack. In the pits Shuman paced back and forth in his baggy pants, chain smoking and nervously checking his stopwatch to see how his driver was doing.

Then, on the 325th lap, it happened. Going into the second turn Weatherly's front suspension collapsed, just as Turner's had earlier. He rammed the wall, then slid slowly into the infield. His race was run.

Someone told Shuman. He looked at the man for a moment, then shrugged his shoulders and walked away, wanting to be by himself for a moment.

Soon Weatherly came in, walking across the infield. He went to Shuman and said, "I'm sorry as hell, Buddy," apologizing not for the mechanical failure of the car, but for his being a part of the machine that had let Buddy down.

Shuman looked at Joe. There really was nothing to say.

Thomas won that race, Chevys also finished 2-4-7-8-9-10, and Chevrolet's ad agency blared forth with more claims of super performance. But Benton wasn't sorry, once he recovered from the initial disappointment. "When it was all over," he says, "I was more than ever convinced that we had done the right thing. We'd given the fans a kind of excitement they'd never experienced before." Although Benton was not at that time aware of the over-all picture of Ford and competition, he had nevertheless played an important part in it.

Ford officials soon found they were not only involved with an entirely new form of sales promotion and image building, but they were also dealing with a totally unfamiliar type of person. They discovered most of this through their relationship with Shuman. Since Buddy was hired as a regular employee of the Ford Motor Company, the industrial relations division ran a background check on him. It wasn't long before a somewhat shaken individual in the personnel department called Burnett's office.

Shuman not only had a police record for bootlegging, he said, but he had also done time on a chain gang for other, more severe crimes. Did engineering know this? Burnett cut him off in a hurry. "As far as I know, he's doing a good job for us, we're getting along fine with him, and we don't intend to throw him out."

Later, some people were to find that when Buddy was on the chain gang, some influential friends managed to arrange a pardon. Buddy turned it down. "When I get out of here," he said, "I don't want anything hanging over my head."

It was a different world, a brawling, hard-drinking, high-living world unto itself, with codes of honor, as Detroit soon discovered, considerably more stringent than those in economically healthier parts of the nation. At the beginning there were many problems of communication to overcome. The shade-tree mechanics and the diploma engineers many times refused to accept one another. But when they finally did, the cars went faster than ever before.

Soon after Darlington Ford signed a contract with DePaolo, who had set up DePaolo Engineering, Inc., as the outside organization that would run the company's racing activities. DePaolo would own everything, make the contracts with the drivers and bill Ford. For any major American automobile manufacturer to go racing, three things are needed: a good basic product, which is the responsibility of the automaker; a good planning-liaison-race preparation organization, which is partly inside the factory and partly outside; and good drivers, who can make even a mediocre race car competitive.

At the outset there were serious deficiencies in the Ford setup. The basic product, from which the racing stock car must be developed, was not as good as the Chevrolet. To complicate matters, at Chevy engineering there were people who knew the racing business, were very much interested in it, and who had the full and complete support of the general manager of the division. As a consequence Chevrolet incorporated right into its basic engineering anything it felt would be beneficial to racing. It was years before Ford did this. At Ford there was no community of interest among engineering, the Ford Division and central staff. At General Motors not only did the autonomy of the divisions make a united front possible for Chevy, but they had a powerful supporter up higher in Harley Earl, the vice president in charge of styling.

On the second level, the planning-liaison-race preparation setup was not what it might have been. Engineering did not pick the right persons to run it, and DePaolo, although one of the finer public relations types in the racing business, did not have the administrative background to operate a large program of this nature. At the beginning, the only thing Ford had going for it was the drivers; they were the best.

Lincoln-Mercury was in better shape at the outset. The division had been carrying on a working relationship with Smith and Stroppe since 1952, and even though Smith was killed in the early fall of 1954, the organization was still there and so was a contract that ran through June 30, 1955. By April Mercury was already eyeing the AAA stock car circuit where Inglewood, Calif., dealer Bob Estes had been successful with several entries the previous year. Stroppe was in possession of a few cars on which he had run extensive high speed tests for the division in early April. They were Mexican road race prototypes, and when that event was canceled the cars were parked in Long Beach. When his contract was renewed July 1, Stroppe was practically ready to go. On July 17 at Milwaukee the first Mercurys made their factory-backed debut, with Jack McGrath and Walt Faulkner doing the driving. Faulkner got third, behind Norm Nelson driving one of Kiekhaefer's Chryslers and Marshall Teague in a Chevy, as the Wisconsin Fairgrounds track ran its first race on a paved surface. On August 21 McGrath ran second to Tony Bettenhausen in another of Kiekhaefer's cars, and four days later McGrath was second again, this time to Teague. After being that close for three straight races victory was almost inevitable, and it finally came at Milwaukee on September 18: McGrath won the 200-miler in Stroppe's Mercury. The race itself was one of the very last run under the AAA sanction, as that organization had announced on August 4 it was giving up its duties as the holder of the international auto sporting power in the United States. The next year's races on the erstwhile AAA circuit would be held under the banner of the new United States Auto Club; the names of the drivers and most of the officials would be the same.

But neither the AAA nor USAC had a stock car circuit that approached the magnitude of NASCAR's. The Southeast was the place, and the Southeast was the Ford Division's prime target. The business of setting up for the 1956 season went on through the fall of 1955, with DePaolo establishing his headquarters in Long Beach next door to Stroppe (the new group also had the benefit of considerable help from Stroppe at the outset, in the matters of both personnel and advice). This location was almost 3,000 miles removed from the scene of battle in NASCAR, and 2,000 miles from USAC's midsummer Big Apple. To run things from that distance was impossible, even though Shuman was turned over to DePaolo to be his man in the Carolinas.

Just how far DePaolo's infant team had to go was shown on October 9 at West Memphis, Ark., the first race for DePaolo Engineering. DePaolo flew in from the West Coast along with veteran hot-rodders Don Francisco, his new operations manager, and Chuck Daigh, who came over from Stroppe's organization to be shop foreman. Stevenson and Mantz were DePaolo's drivers, and Shuman brought Turner and Weatherly in from Charlotte. There were four cars—all built in Dearborn—and there were 300 miles to go on a 1½-mile, high-banked clay track.

When Shuman, Daigh and Francisco saw what the engineers wanted to do, they were aghast. Unfamiliar with dirt-track racing, they wanted to use an air filter that would have given the rocks and the dirt on the track easy access to the innards of the engine. The racers complained. The engineers insisted. DePaolo sided with the engineers. Inevitably, the cars dropped out, one by one, some of them with rocks as big as jellybeans inside the cylinders, with valves bent and pistons broken. Francisco soon quit in disgust. To make things worse, the race was won by Speedy Thompson in a Kiekhaefer-owned Ford, and when Ford's advertising agency publicized this fact, Kiekhaefer threatened to sue. Later in October Kiekhaefer rubbed it in again when 1956 Grand National champion Buck Baker drove one of his Fords to victory at North Wilkesboro, N.C.

A few weeks after West Memphis, on November 13, there was a race at Hickory, N.C., and Shuman brought the Turner and Weatherly cars. The night before, as he turned in, Buddy decided to have one more cigarette before putting out the light. He fell asleep, and the ashes ignited the bedclothes. In a short time Shuman was asphyxiated.

After the funeral, needing someone in the Southeast, DePaolo contacted Vogt, who was then with the Fish Carburetor Company in Daytona. They came to terms and on December 1 Red headed for Charlotte, where he thought he would start preparing cars. But there were delays. First there was the problem of finding a suitable garage, and the lack of communication between East and West made this a difficult job. It got so bad Vogt threatened to hang a sign from a tree in an empty lot, the sign saying "Ford Racing Hq." He never did, but the sign was painted and ready. Money was not plentiful either, with DePaolo keeping most of it for his Long Beach setup, and Vogt was constantly trying to pry some more out of California. Somehow, between Long Beach and Charlotte, they got four cars built (two sedans, two convertibles) and shipped them to Daytona for the February races. They rented space at Vogt's old hangout, Fish Carburetor, and started to install the late-arriving equipment from Dearborn Steel Tubing, their outside supplier. At the same time they hired Fireball Roberts for the team and DePaolo's men started work building a third convertible for him, putting the shop on a round-the-clock basis. Then Speedy Thompson, just recently hired, quit, leaving the team with Turner, Weatherly and Roberts. Another pilot was needed and Vogt suggested Ralph Moody, a former midget driver from Dighton, Mass., who had made some sort of a reputation after coming south, but who was now running a gas station in Dania, north of Miami. Red called him.

When the phone rang Moody had just sold his station and was trying to buy into a machine shop, so for the moment he was at liberty—and he was a race driver. Moody didn't even want to know the terms, but Red told him anyway. "You get $500 a month, plus 40 percent of anything the car wins, plus expenses."

Moody let out a slight gasp, but Vogt continued, "And since you're a good mechanic, I can get you another $500 a month if you want to work on the cars."

"You mean I can make $1,000 a month?" Moody said. "Sign me on!"

Although Moody turned out to be one of the best things that happened to Ford, he was almost the only good thing that transpired during the 1956 Daytona Speed Weeks. Parts were late, there was trouble setting up the cars, there was friction between DePaolo and Ford engineering.

Even in a large corporation like the Ford Motor Company, things like this have a way of getting home, and it wasn't long before McNamara heard about it. He called Chase Morsey, then in charge of passenger car marketing, and told Morsey to get with Joe MacKay, who was working on special projects for McNamara but was in Morsey's department.

MacKay came to work the next morning and soon found himself in Morsey's office.

"What do you know about stock car racing?"

"I think it's what Chevrolet is advertising," MacKay said, "but aside from that I don't know anything about it."

"Well, something, is wrong. We've got a bunch of guys down at Daytona Beach.... I don't know what the hell is going on, but would you please go down and find out."

MacKay left that night and got to Florida in the morning. When he arrived he found a Ford public relations man and said, "What gives? I'm here to find out although I don't really know why I'm here."

"Well, this thing is all in a mess: it's all terribly fouled up."

"Why?"

"Well, there's a constant argument over at the Fish Carburetor Company, nobody knows whether they're up or down, Bill France is changing the rules every hour on the hour, and we're not getting anywhere."

So MacKay went to the garage, and he found Dave Evans of engineering and DePaolo sitting at desks that faced each other, and he also found a wall of tension between the two so strong it was almost visible. He was about as welcome as the plague at this point; they didn't know him, he didn't know what was going on, and to make it worse, he didn't know what to do. So MacKay stayed there over the weekend, watched what happened, and went back to Dearborn convinced things were not right.

The next weekend MacKay and Tony Menkel, the Ford Division manager of administration, went back to Daytona for the races and fully expected to see the worst. They were pleasantly surprised and considerably relieved by the results. In the convertible event Saturday Turner and Roberts ran first and second, with their virtuosity behind the wheel making up for any shortcomings in the car. The old beach-road course, located south of town, has seen many great drivers, but few who employed the brilliant broadsliding tactics of the mountain man. Down at the south turn, where the course left the road and turned onto the beach again, the biggest treat of the day was watching Curtis throw the car sideways on the asphalt long before he ever got to the corner, then bring it on around in a great shower of sand and commotion, straightening everything out and heading north again while most of the spectators were still flinching, waiting for the disaster that never occurred.

On Sunday, as Tim Flock won easily in his Chrysler 300, Moody salvaged third place for Ford despite flipping during the event. He had been running second and pressing Flock going into the north turn when suddenly from the ocean on his right came Lee Petty, seeking to rejoin the race. Petty, his windshield blasted by the flying sand thrown up by other cars, had simply lost his way and wandered out into the water. Moody, attempting to avoid Petty, rolled it, fortunately with no vital damage to the car or himself. He finished behind Billy Myers, who took the runner-up spot in one of Stroppe's Mercurys.

MacKay went back to Dearborn happy over the results of the weekend but disturbed by the over-all picture. He knew Ford had not deserved to do that well; Turner's talent and a little racing luck had done the job, not the Ford Motor Company. MacKay then recommended that since the Ford Division was spending the money, control should be taken out of the hands of engineering and given to the division, preferably to Morsey's department. At this time the various divisions had no engineering function (as did GM's), and Morsey's office seemed the logical place.

The answer came back: "You've got it. You made the recommendation to bring it here, so you take it."

So Joe MacKay, ex-Marine, Yale man, electrical engineer by diploma, who had seen only two competitive automotive events in his lifetime, became a racer by decree. In his new role as the man from Dearborn he was to be instrumental in straightening out the program. But first he had to get his feet wet. He wound up getting them soaked before he had a chance to don his rubbers.

On March 4 at West Palm Beach, Fla., Myers won in his Mercury to give that division something to crow about, but that was all anyone won in the Grand National Division for a long time. On March 18 Herb Thomas, driving a Chevrolet, won at Wilson, N.C., and then the Chrysler era began. For the next 16 Grand National races everything in sight was won by either a Chrysler or a Dodge; Buck Baker, Speedy Thompson and Thomas (now switched from Chevy) won everything. The Fords were having trouble even finishing, and relations between Charlotte and Long Beach grew more and more strained. In the convertible division Turner followed his Daytona victory with back-to-back wins at Charlotte and Hillsboro, N.C., and then Ford was shut out for the next nine races.

Money was being spent, and nothing was happening. To make things worse, there was always the danger of the drivers—Ford's only strong point—getting disgusted and leaving. A retainer and expense money are nice, but they do not make up for inferior equipment and the lack of even a fighting chance.

MacKay was in Long Beach late in the spring, talking over the situation with DePaolo, when Daigh stuck his head into the office.

"Listen," he said, "John Holman is outside, and he'd like to be able to talk to you while Joe is here."

"Who's John Holman?" MacKay asked.

"Aw, he's a truck driver for Bill Stroppe," DePaolo said.

"What does he want?"

"Chuck says he wants to go to work here, and he's pretty good."

"Well, have him come in."

Holman did in fact no longer work for Stroppe. He had resigned almost a month earlier and taken a 30-day terminal leave while he decided what to do next. Now he knew what he wanted, and that was to run Ford's eastern stock car operation.

In the past Holman had done many things. Forced to go to work at 15 when his father died, one of Holman's first jobs included working on Gold Cup speedboats and race cars for Lou Fageol. He had been a tool and die maker and he'd had his own trucking business, an adventurous occupation that involved hustling loads of scrap from Texas to California and selling it fast to make good on the checks he had used to pay for it in the first place.

In a little more than two decades the burly Holman had learned several things that were now to prove helpful: He knew about cars, he knew about machinery, he knew about transportation, and he knew how to get things done. As an additional factor in his favor, the two men being considered for the Charlotte job, Daigh and Danny Eames, weren't anxious to leave California. So Holman made his pitch.

When he walked in, MacKay got his first shock. Holman had on white mechanic's pants rolled halfway up his leg, with brilliant purple socks showing underneath, and the sight of this getup on the husky Holman was something MacKay remembered vividly more than a decade later. But as soon as Holman started to speak, MacKay listened. Not only is Holman one of the great doers in the racing business, he is also one of the great talkers; when he went to work on MacKay this became evident, but the big thing was that Holman made sense. Among other items, he demanded there be no shortage of money to run the operation, and that he would have control. He did not mention any money for himself, however, and MacKay asked him about this.

"You guys don't know me from a can of worms, Holman said. "If I'm successful, then I'll stick my hand in your pocket." Two weeks later he flew into Charlotte with DePaolo, and Pete went to talk to Vogt. Unfortunately, he did not tell Vogt exactly what Holman's function would be.

"Do you know John Holman?"

"Yes," Vogt said.

"How would it be if I got John over here to get parts for you?"

"Well, I don't know of anybody who can get them any better."

Holman had stayed in the motel during all this, which took place late on May 24 while Vogt was putting the finishing touches on Curtis Turner's new 312-inch engine for a convertible race the next night at Roanoke, Va. Vogt wound up the job at 5 a.m. and went home for breakfast. When he got back to the shop, he found Holman adjusting a front wheel bearing.

Red didn't like the way Holman was doing it and said so, and Holman told him from now on that was how they were going to be done. Vogt demanded an explanation, and the two of them marched into DePaolo's office where the embarrassed Pete said, "Well, the factory sent him down here...." Vogt quit on the spot. Interestingly enough, within a few minutes of his return to his Charlotte home, Vogt was called by Kiekhaefer.

"I understand you quit."

"How did you know?"

"I have my ways and means," Kiekhaefer said.

So Vogt went to work for the other side, and Holman set about bringing order to Ford's house in Charlotte. They flew to Roanoke that night and Turner won. The

All alone at the head of the pack—Tim Flock and his Mercury on their way to winning the 1957 convertible race at Daytona Beach.

next evening saw a race in Columbia, S.C. and the Fords dropped out with engine trouble. After that Holman called a halt, deciding the cars would not be raced again until they were really ready to go—and to finish. So Sunday afternoon, with a race scheduled for the old Charlotte Motor Speedway, Holman went over to see what the others were doing. There he met France, and John laid it on the line. They needed new and heavier spindles, Holman said, and it was obvious they were not coming from the factory. It was not only a question of getting a race-winning car together, it was also a matter of safety, and Ford spindles had been snapping with a frequency that made flying wheels a not uncommon sight in NASCAR races.

France gave Holman the OK and they went to work, not only giving Ford a chance to do some winning, but affording France an opportunity to restore some sort of balance of power among his contestants; the Chryslers and Dodges had been taking everything, and a change of pace was needed. On June 10 everything was ready, and the team went to West Memphis. Moody won it, doing so after being knocked groggy on the last lap when the windshield blew in, and coming to just in time to guide the car across the finish line. Even then, the officials said Mercury pilot Jim Paschal was first and Holman had to file a protest, matching his lap count against that of the officials. A recheck showed Holman was right, so they gave Moody the race and infuriated the Lincoln-Mercury Division. Holman wasn't concerned with Lincoln-Mercury's discomfiture; he was getting paid to win races for Ford. This was the first Grand National sedan win for the Ford Division in the Southeast and the first since Stevenson had won at Willow Springs, Calif., on November 20, 1955.

From then on things got better, and the choleric Kiekhaefer did everything he could to stop the Fords. On July 4 at Raleigh, N.C., Roberts racked up the second win of the Holman regime, defeating Speedy Thompson in one of Kiekhaefer's Dodges, and the latter immediately asked Holman if he could buy the car as it stood. Holman told him the car wasn't his to sell, so they sent the Fords and the Chryslers to the inspection and Kiekhaefer invited Holman downtown for dinner. During the meal Kiekhaefer kept questioning Holman about specific parts of the car, and every time Kiekhaefer would ask a question John would turn to Vogt, who was also present, and ask, "Did you put those things in the cars?" or, "Is that what you did before I came here?" Kiekhaefer never did get an answer.

Finally, with dinner over, Holman asked Kiekhaefer, "Is there anything special you want to see in the cars?"

"No, nothing special," Kiekhaefer said, and then they went back to the garages.

When they arrived Holman found Kiekhaefer had filed a protest and his Fords were in the process of being taken apart, piece by piece.

The first thing he found was that NASCAR wanted the camshaft, and that Gus Davis, who along with Joe Blais was one of the engine men he had imported from California, was busy removing the cam.

Then Kiekhaefer strolled over and watched Davis at work.

Gus didn't like this, so he went and covered the engine up with newspaper—mostly to annoy Kiekhaefer—and worked by feel only, with his hands under the paper.

Kiekhaefer immediately shouted for a NASCAR official to make sure Davis wasn't going to slip another camshaft out from the folds of the paper.

Then chief inspector Norris Friel wanted a piston to go with the cam, and Davis got under the car to take care of that job.

While Davis was dropping the oil pan, Kiekhaefer decided he wanted to check the wheelbase, so he got the measuring equipment and some chalk and sidled up to the vehicle.

But whenever he made a chalk mark at one wheel, Davis and others would nudge the car backward or forward so when he got to the other wheel the car was no longer in its original position. Soon Kiekhaefer gave up on this ploy and tried to stick his head back in the engine compartment. Holman told Kiekhaefer if he didn't move away, he would call a cop. It was late, and things were getting tense.

Eventually both piston and camshaft were handed over to Friel, and they decided to continue with the inspection in the morning. But they weren't through yet. Kiekhaefer demanded the two mechanical parts be deposited in the safe of the local police department.

The crusty Friel turned him down and took them to his hotel room instead.

The first order of the continuing inspection was to check the wheelbase, both right side and left side. When it was found to be standard, Kiekhaefer exploded.

"When did you change the chassis on the car?" he demanded. "You must have sneaked a guy past the guard and worked on them last night!"

And then they checked the rest of it, piece by piece, through the long hot day.

Finally, around 3 p.m., chief steward Johnny Bruner came to Holman.

"The old man is willing to recognize you won the race, but he'd like to have the cam."

"OK, he can have it," Holman said, "but not before I get the money."

So the purse was handed over and then Bruner presented the camshaft to Kiekhaefer, who walked out of the garage. In a moment, he was back.

"What about the piston?"

So he got that too, and on taking a look, saw what appeared to be some extra grooves in it, and promptly blew up again. But the grooves were meaningless, and anyway, it was too late now.

Kiekhaefer didn't give up easily; that could be said for him—that and the fact he was understandably perturbed over being blown out of the saddle in NASCAR. He wasn't used to second place, and the Ford and Lincoln-Mercury divisions, counting both East and West Coast races, had taken eight Grand National events in a row, from Marvin Panch's win at Birmingham, Ala., July 29, through Roberts' victory at Myrtle Beach, S.C., Aug. 25. During the same period, Fords won seven of 10 convertible races.

By now Holman's operation was well organized. Turner and Weatherly were the stars of the convertible circuit; Roberts, West Coast flyer Panch and Moody were the Grand National drivers, and Bill Amick, like Panch imported from the West, was the short-track man. Davis and Blais, the engine experts, helped in that department, and Moody was invaluable working with the chassis modifications in addition to driving. Not only were Fords finishing, they were also winning, and the entire team had a distinct air of professionalism about it.

The California division of DePaolo was also getting straightened away, with one of the most valuable men there being Eames, who left the Chrysler Corporation to join Ford in April of the year. Eames was the administrative manager for DePaolo, and technically had Daigh—responsible for the cars on the USAC circuit—and Holman under him. Eames, a veteran racing man, not only kept the papers shuffling and the money flowing, but was also responsible for the organization of several other promotions undertaken by Ford that year. In June Ford broke the 500-mile stock car mark at the Indianapolis Motor Speedway, in September Fords set hundreds of world and international class records in a 50,000-mile run at Bonneville, and in November Eames and Daigh set a coast-to-coast driving mark of 47 hours and 37 minutes. Ironically, they made the Los Angeles to New York trip in a little over 40 hours, but picked up a speeding ticket that nullified the attempt. When they turned around to do it the other way, heavy weekend traffic in several places slowed them down. Their car was the same one that averaged 108.16 mph for 50,000 miles at Bonneville.

With things going well, at times the Fords found their strongest competition came from their sisters under the skin, the Mercurys. Holman's crew usually managed to get the better of the outfit run by his old boss, Stroppe, but there were times when the tables were turned—like in the Grand National race held in August on the four-mile Road America circuit at Elkhart Lake, Wis.

Part of that one was run in the rain and somehow Stroppe had managed to come up with tires more suited for the wet weather than were those on the Fords. In addition, NASCAR then allowed the use of funnels for refueling, so Stroppe's boys found a 20-gallon garbage can and connected a large hose to its bottom. When the cars came in they simply ran up with the can, jammed the hose in the gas tank, and the can enabled three men to pour in gas at the same time, thus saving valuable seconds. Tim Flock and Billy Myers finished 1-2 for Stroppe, with Roberts placing third for Holman.

But the day wasn't finished yet. There was a convertible division race scheduled that night at Flat Rock, Mich., just south of Detroit. As soon as the Elkhart event was done, Turner, Weatherly and Holman jumped into Turner's plane and took off—downhill—from the main straightaway of the circuit and flew east across Lake Michigan. They arrived in Flat Rock near dark, and by the time they landed and hurried to the track, the race had already started, with Holman's mechanics driving the two convertibles. Turner and Weatherly jumped the fence, dashed between the speeding cars and into the pits, from where they signaled the mechanics.

By the time Curtis and Joe got into the cars they were too far behind to win, but they gave the fans a great show, lapping everyone in the place in a vain attempt to catch up.

Next came Darlington. The Southern "500," the only race of that distance on the Grand National circuit in those days, was the big one, the race Ford had to win. It was also the race Turner and Weatherly had made up their minds to win, not for themselves, but for Shuman. The year before, after Buddy's death, they had promised themselves they'd go back in 1956, complete with the wild hogs on the sides of the cars, and take the one Shuman wanted so badly. This sort of thing, when it happens in a grade-B movie, is so trite it is nauseating. But when it happens in real life, it can be touching. And when it happens to a pair of rough, ready and unromantic characters like Turner and Weatherly, it is even more than that.

Darlington was the big push. Every car and every driver that could be gotten ready was on hand, as a win here would make the season a success. A loss would make it a failure. Ford had Turner, Weatherly, Roberts, Moody, Panch, Amick, Tim Flock and Joe Eubanks, who was getting partial support. Mercury had Fonty Flock, Jim Paschal, Bill Blair and Billy Myers. As their primary opposition they had Paul Goldsmith, Jim Reed and Herb Thomas in Chevrolets, plus Kiekhaefer's team of Buck Baker and Speedy Thompson in Chrysler 300s and Frank Mundy in a Dodge. The Chevrolets were advertised at 225 horsepower, the Fords at 260 and the big Chryslers at 340, but the public figures didn't bother anyone. They knew Ford and Chevy were considerably over those numbers, and still short of the hemi-head Chryslers. What the Fords and Chevrolets had going for them, however, was the extremely high weight of the Chryslers.

Baker set a Darlington record qualifying, with a 119.659 mph average for his four-lap trip, and Speedy Thompson, who qualified on the first day, sat his Chrysler on the pole with an average of 118.683. Turner's average was 118 plus, but in this one qualifying speed didn't mean much. All you had to do was be near the front of the pack. In that respect Ford was in good shape. There were eight Fords and two Mercurys among the first 15 cars.

On race day there were 75,000 fans packing the place when Panch dove into the first turn ahead of Thompson, with 364 laps to go. Thompson took the lead back the next time around and held it through the 16th lap, when Tim Flock, coming up from the fifth row, charged into the lead with Turner riding his tail.

Turner finally got by after 33 laps. Then it was Flock for two. Then Turner for two. Then Panch, always running near the front, slipped into first for four laps. It was an all-Ford show once the flag dropped and the giant crowd loved it. In the pits, DePaolo, MacKay, Holman and the rest sweated out the possibility of one Ford running another off the road.

At 105 laps Fonty Flock, with his Mercury, challenged teammate Paschal for the lead but blew a tire just as he was about to get it and crashed into the wall. Paschal held first until lap 131, heading for the pits at that juncture and letting Roberts into first. Roberts was well in front when suddenly, on lap 161, Dink Widenhouse and Roy Bentley collided right in front of him. Fireball had two choices: hit the two cars or hit the wall. He chose the wall, and it put him out of the race. When he walked back to the pits some over-eager tire company man ran up to him.

"Didja blow a tire, Fireball?"

Roberts glared. "Hell, no. I wrecked. It's possible to wreck out there, you know!" Then he stalked off in the noonday heat.

When Roberts departed Turner took over, and when he pitted Panch moved into the lead until lap 202, when Turner regained first. From there until the finish, for the last 162 laps, Curtis stayed in front, roaring down the hazy, smoke-filled straights, charging into Darlington's one high-banked turn, just missing the retaining wall as he accelerated out of the infamous flat curve at the other end of the speedway, passing the wrecked and broken-down cars that littered the sides of the track. With 50 miles to go Curtis let up; he was so far in front he could afford to take it easy. He stroked it home, the winner by more than a minute over Speedy Thompson. Panch was third, Goldsmith fourth, Paschal fifth.

Ford was overjoyed, the fans streamed up the two-lane highway that would be jammed with traffic until the late hours, and as the dusk fell over the track, a plane buzzed the nearly deserted pits, wiggling its wings in salute.

It was Turner, flying away. "Let's have a party," DePaolo said.

Darlington had been the big one, but there were still two months of the season to go and the rivalry was just as strong.

In late September, at Columbia, S.C., Holman suspected Baker's winning Dodge of oversize fuel tanks, and he protested immediately after the race. There were no United States Government measuring vessels on hand—Kiekhaefer insisted on them—so they sealed the cars into the Kiekhaefer trucks. There was no time to inspect them the next day as there was a race at Occoneechee, N.C., that night—which Roberts won in a Ford. This time it was Kiekhaefer who filed a protest, and the caravan headed for Charlotte. By now, what with the protests and counter-protests, there were eight cars to inspect.

The next morning Holman got the word from Norris Friel.

"The old man had to leave early on business," he was told, "but before he left he said he'd withdraw his protest if you'll withdraw yours."

Holman shrugged and said yes. They never did get a look at Baker's fuel tank.

Kiekhaefer went out the hard way. He protested the Fords the next week at Newport, Tenn., and the week after that at Charlotte—the latter coming even after a Kiekhaefer car won. At least Kiekhaefer had the satisfaction of seeing his automobiles take the last five races of the season. By this time Chevrolet was practically forgotten by those responsible for winning races on the Grand National circuit. They had made the Fords go faster against a far tougher opponent. They had also spent a lot of money, and made numerous mistakes. But now, at the end of the year, things were rolling. Ford had a strong team ready for the 1957 season, and they would have even stronger engines.

Flying mile trials at Daytona Beach, vintage 1957. A Corvette starts its way down the hard-packed sands while the famous Henry (Smokey) Yunick, complete with the sign on his back, watches the takeoff.

NASCAR—1949–1955 RESULTS

Hudson—79	Dodge—8	Studebaker—3
Oldsmobile—69	Lincoln—4	Buick—2
Chrysler—36	Mercury—4	Chevrolet—2
Plymouth—10	Ford—3	Nash—1

a. Ford Motor Company individual winners:

Lincoln

Jim Roper (Charlotte Fairgrounds, 6/19/49).
Jack White (Hamburg, N.Y., 9/18/49).
Harold Kite (Daytona, 2/5/50).
Tim Flock (Charlotte, 4/7/50).

Mercury

Bill Blair (Vernon, N.Y., 6/18/55).
Lloyd Moore (Winchester, Ind., 10/15/55).
M. Burke (Oakland, Calif., 10/14/55).
B. Norton (Gardena, Calif., 1/11/55).

Ford

Jimmy Floria (Dayton, Ohio, 6/25/50).
Speedy Thompson (W. Memphis, Ark., 10/9/55).
Buck Baker (N. Wilkesboro, N.C., 10/23/55).

NASCAR—1956 RESULTS
Grand National Division

Chrysler—22	Dodge—11	Chevrolet—3
Ford—14	Mercury—5	Oldsmobile—1

a. Ford-Mercury individual winners:

Ford

Fireball Roberts—5 (Raleigh, N.C., 7/4; Chicago, 7/22; Myrtle Beach, S.C., 8/25; Hillsboro, N.C., 9/30; Newport, Tenn., 10/7).
Ralph Moody—4 (W. Memphis, Ark., 6/10; Old Bridge, N.J., 8/17; Spartanburg, S.C., 8/23; Charlotte Fairgrounds, 9/12).
Curtis Turner—1 (Darlington, 9/3).
Eddie Pagan—1 (Bay Meadows, Calif., 8/19).
Chuck Stevenson—1 (Willow Springs, Calif., 11/20/55).
Marvin Panch—1 (Montgomery, Ala., 7/29).
Lloyd Dane—1 (Portland, Ore., 9/23).

Mercury

Billy Myers—2 (W. Palm Beach, Fla., 3/4; Norfolk, Va., 8/22).
Jim Paschal—1 (Oklahoma City, 8/3).
Tim Flock—1 (Elkhart Lake, Wis., 8/12).
Lloyd Dane—1 (Sacramento, Calif., 7/8).

b. Beginning with Moody's victory at West Memphis June 10, there were 25 Grand National races in the east. Fords won 11 of these, Mercurys won three—or 14 of the 25. On the West Coast there were five races after this date. Fords won two, Mercurys one.

c. Grand National champion—Buck Baker (point total included 14 victories, nine with Chrysler, five with Dodge).

Convertible Division

Ford—27 Chevrolet—10 Dodge—10 Buick—1

a. Ford individual winners:

Curtis Turner—22 (Daytona, 2/25; Charlotte, 3/18; Hillsboro, N.C., 3/25, 10/14; Roanoke, Va., 5/25; Norfolk, Va., 6/22; Wilson, N.C., 6/24; Flat Rock, Mich., 7/1; Syracuse, N.Y., 7/4; Belmar, N.J., 7/14; Abbotstown, Pa., 7/21; Fort Wayne, Ind., 7/28; Winston-Salem, N.C., 8/3; Columbia, S.C., 8/4; Raleigh, N.C., 8/25; Greenville, S.C., 8/30; Asheville, N.C., 9/5; Chicago, 9/9; W. Memphis, 9/16; Shelby, N.C., 9/18; Spartanburg, S.C., 9/29; Weaverville, N.C., 9/30).

Joe Weatherly—5 (Hamburg, N.Y., 7/7; Heidelberg, Pa., 8/17; Rochester, N.Y., 8/19; Atlanta, 9/2; Martinsville, Va. 10/28).

b. Beginning with Turner's victory at Norfolk, Va., June 22, Fords won 23 of the last 29 convertible division races, including 18 by Turner, who together with Weatherly finished 1-2 14 times during the season.

c. Convertible champion—Bob Welborn (point total included three victories, all with Chevrolet; won title primarily due to great number of finishes in top 10—40 against Turner's 29. Turner placed second).

Short Track Division

Chevrolet—25	Mercury—2	Oldsmobile—1
Ford—11	Dodge—1	Corvette—1

a. Ford-Mercury individual winners not available.

b. Short track champion—Jim Reed (point total included 14 victories, all with Chevrolet).

U.S. AUTO CLUB—1956 RESULTS

Stock Car Division

Chevrolet—11 Ford—4 Mercury—4

a. Ford-Mercury individual winners:

Ford

Johnny Mantz—2 (Milwaukee, 8/19; Birmingham, Ala., 10/21).

George Seeger—1 (Clovis, Calif., 7/7).

Troy Ruttman—1 (Schererville, Ind., 8/29).

Mercury

Sam Hanks—2 (Milwaukee, 8/23; Paramount Ranch, Calif., 11/4).

Jimmy Bryan—1 (Milwaukee, 9/16).

Troy Ruttman—1 (Milwaukee, 7/15).

b. Chevrolets won first six races, Fords and Mercurys eight of last 13.

c. Champion—Johnny Mantz (entered nine races, won two, placed second three times, third once. Clinched championship in last race at Paramount when he drove relief for Jerry Unser and finished second).

d. Pike's Peak Hillclimb—winner Jerry Unser, Chevrolet, 16:07. Runner-up: Chuck Stevenson (Ford), 16:27.

e. Walt Faulkner became first factory-sponsored driver fatality, being killed at Vallejo, Calif., 4/22/56.

f. Troy Ruttman, driving Chevrolet and Ford, was winner of six-race USAC short-track title. Five of the events were in California, the sixth was held on the quarter-mile track on 16th St. in Indianapolis the week before the "500."

g. Sam Hanks, driving a Mercury, won the Pacific Coast Division championship. This was a title awarded to the most successful driver in the four stock car championship races held on the West Coast, plus the five short-track division races there.

19

SHUTDOWN

Preparation for the 1957 season started in the summer of 1956, and that was a good sign. This time Ford planned everything in advance—everything except the one item that was to blow the company out of the game just as it got going. The first full year of factory-sponsored stock car competition had been one of trial, error and frantic attempts to catch up. The second was to be an all-out attempt to flatten Chevrolet and thus restore to Ford its quarter-century dominance in the V8 field. One of the basic elements, the production car itself, was still weaker than the Chevrolet, but Ford was now able—through organization—to more than offset this shortcoming. The various field groups had shaken themselves down to the point where every man was in his proper job.

The drivers signed up for 1957 were probably, within their own frame of reference, the greatest collection of talent ever assembled to pilot one make.

And on top of it all the Grand National entries were now supercharged; the blower, used with the 312-cubic-inch engine, produced 325 horsepower, although it was advertised at only 300 to keep the demand from private customers at a minimum. The supercharger, as long as it was used, was to give Ford superiority in the horsepower department for the first time (and for the only time in the next 10 years). The Mercurys, though not blessed with this device, were now equipped with an engine of 368 cubic inches and 335 horsepower; it had previously been used in Lincolns only.

The supercharger was indicative of the lengths to which Ford was willing to go to re-establish an image. NASCAR rules at that time called for a minimum number of units to be scheduled during the year before it could be considered "stock"; this made it a considerable investment for the company. McCulloch, one of the better-known manufacturers, was to produce the items—with the first examples to be handmade, as there was not enough time to get some sort of production line going before the early-season races. Blowers, throughout racing history, have had a checkered reputation: Although they produce more power, fuel consumption goes up, and engine reliability almost always goes down. On top of this there are maintenance and preparation problems which are considerable, due to the many parts in the supercharger assembly. Although it was listed in the parts catalog, the blower was obviously intended for factory use only, and even then the company hedged its bet by running normally aspirated (with one four-barrel carburetor) 312's as back-up cars for Grand National races and on the convertible and short-track circuits as the number one engine (blowers were banned in these divisions).

As opposition, Chevrolet's V8 was now enlarged to 283 cubic inches and was equipped with a fuel injection system that gave it perhaps the best power curve of any of the engines competing in NASCAR during the 1957 season. Horsepower for the injected Chevy was approximately 310. Although these two were the main contestants, there were also others in the picture. From General Motors, Pontiacs started to make their appearance, this year with a V8 of 347 cubic inches and 325 horsepower in racing trim, and Oldsmobile showed with 371-inch engines and 325 horses. Kiekhaefer had pulled out just before Christmas, leaving the Chryslers without a protagonist and practically out of the running: The cars were too big and too heavy to compete with the lighter Fords and Chevys, now that the latter two had reached a higher stage of chassis development. Because of a lack of factory support, neither Dodge (with a smaller version of the Chrysler Hemi which had 354 inches and 330 horses) nor Plymouth (with a 318-incher which produced at best 300 horses) made more than token appearances. Along with Dodge's withdrawal came the switch of Lee Petty, that firm's best driver outside the Kiekhaefer organization, to Oldsmobile.

For Ford the lineup was as follows: In NASCAR the primary assignments were Roberts and Panch in the Grand National cars, Turner and Weatherly in the convertibles, and Amick and Reed were to take care of the short-track circuit. Moody, whose considerable talents for car preparation were invaluable, had been elevated to a sort of field engineer status, and was also available to drive whenever and wherever needed. This end of the operation, in Charlotte, was under the command of Holman, whose team still included Davis and Blais on the engines and Wayne Mills and Herb Nab as two of the chief mechanics. Each driver had two cars, and a 10-man team of mechanics was assigned to each of the divisions— meaning 10 men had four cars to worry about during the season, but no more than two at any single race.

On the West Coast, where the USAC program had its home and sedans were the only models used, Ruttman, Chuck Stevenson and Jerry Unser—also hired away from Chevrolet—were to be the top drivers. A limited amount of support was to be given drivers on the IMCA and MARC circuits, both of which were strong in the Midwest, and this was also to come from Long Beach. Daigh was in charge of all this, with Eames above him as operations manager, and DePaolo was the nominal head of the whole works. A new addition in Long Beach was Fran Hernandez, one of the best engine men in California—or anywhere else in the hot-rodding world, for that matter. Hernandez, who had been shop foreman for Vic Edelbrock and a partner of Fred Offenhauser, was to be in charge of engine development, and had joined DePaolo in the summer of 1956.

MacKay, by now well versed in the racing business, was still Ford's man in charge, and now he not only had the stock car program under his wing, but was also responsible for a small advanced development group at the shop of Jim Travers and Frank Coon, another California operation. These two, who in later years were to develop a reputation as the finest engine builders in the business (preparing Chevrolets, to the dismay of Ford), were now working on a secret project that was the pet idea of Harley Copp, the most sophisticated of the racing fans in the Ford hierarchy. Copp's dream was to run a Ford at Indianapolis, and he had initiated plans for a 32-valve, overhead cam V8 which would carry the company's colors in America's premier race. At one time during the year, arrangements were made with Mercedes-Benz (which retired from racing after having won everything in Europe in 1955) to let Travers and Coon examine one of their famous straight eights to see how the desmodromic valve gear functioned.

Stroppe's Mercury operation had also grown in size, and the lineup for 1957 looked like this: for NASCAR, Tim Flock, Billy Myers and Jim Paschal; for USAC, Jimmy Bryan, Sam Hanks and Marshall Teague.

As is normal with a factory racing operation, there were a certain number of private pilots who received a degree of help, usually in the form of free parts, from either DePaolo, Holman or Stroppe. But the attempt was made to keep this to a minimum for a good reason: Experience had shown that privately entered cars stood little or no chance of winning, regardless of how much assistance they were given.

By the time of Speed Weeks at Daytona in February, the company had a veritable Armada assembled in Florida. Holman was in charge of the Ford Division race cars, of which there were 11, and had 28 men under him. Eames and Daigh had a collection of 15 cars which were to be used for the straightaway runs on the beach, and they had 29 men to work on those. Add to this Stroppe's crew, which had both race and straightaway vehicles, plus the various Ford engineers and public relations men, and the number came to more than 100.

The Ford forces were confident. Not only was everything ready to go, but in a tuneup Grand National race on the airfield road circuit at Titusville, Fla., December 30, they had run 1-2-3-4 with Roberts, Turner, Panch and Moody finishing in that order. Then disaster hit. In the 160-mile convertible race on Saturday, a steering linkage fault showed up and slowed all four Ford entries. An improper heat treat of certain parts had caused the wheels to assume an exaggerated toe-in during the race, and driving was just like pushing a snowplow down the beach. Tim Flock won the event for Mercury and Billy Myers finished third for that make, with Weatherly sandwiched in between. Panch finished seventh, Roberts eighth, independent Glen Wood was ninth in a year-old car, and Turner was thirteenth.

On Sunday the steering problem was worse. The little-known Cotton Owens, driving a Pontiac, won the 160-miler, with Chevrolet pilot Johnny Beauchamp next. Fonty Flock, making one of his now-infrequent appearances, took third for Mercury—and the snowplowing Fords were nowhere. The various titles accumulated during the straightaway runs on the beach did little to ease the shock of defeat, which was rubbed in again when Pontiac tied the Owens victory together with a "drive the champ" sales promotion campaign that included the giveaway of 100 cars in various parts of the country. Although they were new to the racing business, Pontiac showed right from the start they understood the need for merchandising high performance in order to gain marketing value.

The Daytona setback for the Ford Division proved itself to be only a minor stumbling block on the road to almost total domination of NASCAR. The early part of the year was a near sweep. In the Grand Nationals, from the beginning of the point season in November through May 5, Fords won 12 of the 16 races. Roberts took five of them, Panch three, Paul Goldsmith two, and Moody and West Coast independent Art Watts one apiece. In the convertibles, it was all Ford. Tim Flock's Daytona win for Mercury was the only thing that stood between the Ford Division and an unprecedented sweep of the first 17 events of the season. Turner won nine of them, Weatherly four, Wood (later to be acknowledged as one of the finest mechanics in the business and head of the fastest pit crew) took two and Roberts won the biggest one, the first Rebel "300" at Darlington.

In short-track competition the company won eight of the first 11 events, Reed taking five, Roberts one, West Coast driver Eddie Pagan also winning one, and California independent Bob Ross taking one in a Mercury. The over-all plan of attack was working, and Chevrolet was being wiped out, at least on the stock car tracks, if not the sales window. Ford led every race, with the ones they lost being due only to supercharger problems.

On the list of early-season 1957 winners there is one well-known name seemingly out of place in a Ford product—Goldsmith. He got there by virtue of one of the bigger racing coups pulled during this period. After the Daytona Beach races in March, negotiations were begun with Goldsmith and his chief mechanic, Henry (Smokey) Yunick, in an effort to switch them from Chevrolet to Ford. Although Goldsmith's talents as a driver were considerable, the services of this tall, taciturn pilot from the Detroit suburb of St. Clair Shores were not the main item at stake. Yunick was the plum. Starting with his preparation of Hudson Hornets in the early 1950s, with which Marshall Teague and Frank Mundy won three straight AAA stock car crowns from 1952 to 1954, and with which Herb Thomas and Tim Flock won three straight NASCAR championships during the same years, Yunick had earned a reputation for being the best in the business. His Daytona establishment proudly proclaimed itself as "The Best Damn Garage in Town," and it was—in a town where having the best garage is somewhat akin to being the best skier in Kitzbühl, Austria, or being the top mountain climber in Chamonix, France: If you are the best there, you could very well be the best anywhere.

Smokey, a secretive type who preferred to work alone, had been one of the stronger men in Chevrolet's camp. Goldsmith had been one of their better drivers. In April a two-year contract was signed which sent both of them to Ford, and sent considerable cash and equipment (including a full dynamometer rig) to Daytona. At times the feature of having Holman's team and Yunick's team running in the same race had its disadvantages. At North Wilkesboro, N.C., on April 7, Roberts won, Goldsmith was second, Moody was third and Panch fourth, and there was little competition during the latter stages of the event. The Fords were well out front, and in order to avoid their pushing each other and possibly breaking up a car or two in the process, the Ford men present had the pit crews tell the drivers they would each collect a sum equivalent to first-place money if they held their positions until the checkered flag.

This little bit of on-the-spot maneuvering was the beginning of an education for a new member of the Ford organization, watching his first race that spring day in the northern reaches of the Carolinas. His name was Jacque Passino, and after several years with Willys in his home town of Toledo, the prematurely gray, bespectacled engineer had applied for a job with Ford and gone to work there in January. Assigned to the sales promotion office under Morsey, he was there six weeks before he ever laid eyes on MacKay, who then appeared sporting a Florida tan. Had Passino looked a little closer he might have detected the marks of fatigue under the outward signs of good health, for racing, to the factory liaison man, was much the same then as it is now—a round-the-clock job. Soon afterward Passino heard MacKay was resigning; figuring the job was more interesting than being chained to a desk in Dearborn, he applied for the position and got it. In the next decade he was to become the one man in the corporation who was always in constant touch with the racing fraternity, but that day at North Wilkesboro he was just another sales promotion man getting his initiation. One thing he saw that afternoon was never forgotten: The excitement and partisan feelings the cars caused among the fans. Passino learned that racing could sell cars; had more members of the corporation seen this first-hand, the events of the next few months or the next few years, for that matter, might never have taken place.

The week after Wilkesboro came Langhorne, the one-mile circle north of Philadelphia which was the fastest dirt track in the country. Again, Roberts and Goldsmith were on hand. Fireball led the first 27 miles, then Goldsmith took over for the next 48 of the 150-miler, bringing them to half-distance. The rest of the field wasn't even close. When Goldsmith went into the pits, his car wouldn't restart after taking on fuel, and he lost 52 seconds. Fireball then proceeded to lose his gas cap, so his stop took 49 seconds. In the latter half of the race, after Goldsmith had recaptured the lead, he slowed slightly and Roberts charged past. Goldsmith was never able to catch him, finishing second. After the race Yunick said his driver had slowed because he thought Roberts was on the Ford team too. Obviously Fireball didn't think so, and there were some temporary hard feelings. Ford, privately, was happy with the 1-2 finish, and Roberts was on a hot streak. He won a few days later on the half-mile dirt oval at Charlotte for his third straight, then finished second to Panch at Spartanburg, S.C., fifth (Goldsmith won) at Richmond, and then came the inaugural running of the Rebel "300," which was to give Darlington two major events each year in stead of only one.

Ford assembled six drivers: Turner, Weatherly, Roberts, Panch, Amick and Goldsmith, who sat his car on the pole; Mercury had Tim Flock, Paschal, Billy Myers and his brother Bobby. Weatherly, Turner and Roberts were right behind Goldsmith in the starting lineup, and it looked as if the Fords would romp home—until the 29th lap. Then Paschal blew a tire and Buck Baker hit a spinning car. Baker managed to get out of his vehicle and clamber over the wall, but Paschal, stuck in the middle of the track, watched the field thunder down on him. His car was clipped by several others, each one knocking a piece off, until Paschal was left sitting in little more than a seat with the remnants of a race vehicle lying around him. Through some miracle he wasn't hurt, but nine cars were involved in the accident, the track was blocked and the race had to be stopped for 50 minutes.

When it started again there were three Fords (Turner, Amick and Panch) missing, as well as Paschal's wreck. Roberts, who had just avoided the smashup, went on to win easily, with Flock and Bobby Myers running second and third, respectively. Fireball's car was notable for two things at Darlington: It was the only factory-sponsored entry still running at the end, and it went the distance on one set of tires. Holman had come up with the idea of using hard-compound tires on the outside and soft ones on the inside. Daigh, who had left the DePaolo team and joined the Chevrolet operation in Atlanta, spotted the difference by checking tire serial numbers before the event and screamed long and loud, but it was legal. Holman had found a loophole in the rule book, and made it pay off.

After Darlington the Fords rolled on. In USAC, for example, a Ford or a Mercury had won every race—but this was not to last for long. Before another month passed they were to be shut down, due to the decision that many Detroit observers still consider an adroit piece of General Motors maneuvering. It started at the February meeting of the Automobile Manufacturers Association, that group which includes GM, Ford and Chrysler. It was almost over, with nothing of consequence having come across the table, when GM President Harlow (Red) Curtice pulled something out of his pocket.

"Say, there's one other thing ..." he said, and before Curtice was finished that day, he had proposed what a few months later wound up as the AMA ban on factory-sponsored racing teams, on advertising horsepower—or on anything to do with speed. It proved to be about as successful as the Volstead Act, but was not nearly as noble an experiment. Although few persons knew it at the time, it was not the first attempt in this direction. On June 27, 1956, when the Ford racing program was beginning to pose a threat to Chevrolet, the executive group of the engineering advisory committee of the AMA met with the engineering committee

The opposition: (Top) Cotton Owens, third from right, after winning the 1957 Daytona feature in a Pontiac. Others are, from left, chief mechanic Ray Nichels, then Pontiac boss and now Ford president Semon E. Knudsen, General Motors styling vice-president Harley Earl, Time *executive Maynard Womer and Bill France. (Bottom) Ed Cole, then head of Chevrolet and now president of GM, with his drivers at Hillsboro, N.C., in 1957. From left: Cole, Jim Rathmann, Buck Baker, Speedy Thompson and Jack Smith.*

of the American Association of Motor Vehicle Administrators (AAMVA), the group which represents the vehicle commissioners of the various states—and therefore the desires of those who license what Detroit builds.

Earlier that day there had been an administration committee meeting at Ford, and E.S. MacPherson, the company's vice president for engineering, had expressed his opinion that the best thing to do was to get the entire industry to not advertise horsepower or high performance or the winning of contests "having to do with speed and acceleration."

"The horsepower figure," MacPherson said, "should be found, as it used to be, in the fine print among other specifications of the car and nowhere else." In the afternoon MacPherson, GM Engineering Vice President Charles Chayne, Chrysler Director of Engineering Paul Ackerman and others met with the AAMVA, and the first major item for discussion was the recent criticism the heads of the various states had leveled at the auto industry and its performance campaigns. The engineers were quick to agree ("Heartily," MacPherson's later memo said) to a proposal to the AMA directors to de-emphasize racing.

Although at first glance it seems incongruous that mechanically minded men would want to discontinue what was basically a technical exercise, the reasons for it are clear. Now, for the first time after years of building automobiles in the privacy of their factories, and after years of having these cars subjected to no more abuse than Aunt Mimi turning 2,300 rpm on her way to market, the monkey was on their backs. Production automobiles—*their* production automobiles—were now publicly subjected to stresses and strains they could not stand. The responsibility, basically, was that of the engineers; more specifically, that of the chief engineers, and they didn't like it.

The men in command of Detroit's engineering departments at this time had spent most of their professional careers working in those two decades (1935 to 1955) which saw American automotive progress in one of its more stagnant periods. The last piece of original engine thinking to come from Ford was the flathead V8, which Henry himself personally supervised in 1932; it took GM 17 years (1949—Cadillac and Olds) to come up with a better one. Now the public, which previously had looked only at an automobile's styling and price before making up its mind, was getting a peek at other qualities of the car. It had to be reprehensible to the management engineers, and when they found a willing ally in such organizations as the AAMVA and the National Safety Council, they were quick to take advantage of it.

It was remarkable. On the lower levels there were young men straining every nerve to improve their products to the point where they would be better than those of the competition, men who had suddenly discovered a whole new avenue of engineering endeavor, and who realized how important it was—not only to a racing program, but to making the series production vehicle that much better for the consumer. On the upper levels there were some persons who just didn't want to be bothered—or be shown up in a contest they had always been able to lay off on the sales department. That was what happened toward the end of June, while the companies were spending millions in both money and manpower to accomplish their aims in this very direction.

When Curtice offered the proposal in February, the groundwork had been laid, and his idea fell on receptive ears. The racing programs were costing a lot of money, and sales figures (on a national basis) did not seem to be affected by the results. The Ford Motor Company had only recently joined the AMA and did not want to go against the majority feeling of a club in which it was a new member. At the beginning of April James O. Wright, then assistant general manager of the Ford Division, was called upon to explain—and justify—the performance program to A.A. Kucher, who had succeeded MacPherson as vice president of engineering staff. Wright described how Chevrolet had taken advantage of it to grab a healthy chunk of the youth market away from Ford, the advertising and sales promotion techniques used by Ford to complement its racing counter-attack, remarked on the benefits to the dealer organization, explained the finances of the program, and included a key paragraph which in later years proved to be one of the best predictions ever made in Detroit:

"It is probably true that other manufacturers will decrease their performance advertising emphasis for the balance of the year primarily because they will not have anything to advertise. We feel that competitive statements to the effect that performance advertising may be abandoned for 1958 and subsequent years probably springs from a feeling that Ford's 1958 engine program will continue to keep it in a position of supremacy in stock car racing [note: Ford had scheduled its 390-inch engine for 1958. The racing ban made it 1961 before the engine was introduced]. Our program must be continued to ensure that this situation will continue to exist in the years to come since we have every reason to believe that if we should lessen our efforts, other manufacturers will quickly increase their already sizeable interest in this field to the detriment of our sales and dealer morale."

Then he added a remark that engineering should have already realized was true: "Finally, over and above any merchandising consideration, the program possesses great potential for real benefit to accrue to our product engineering activities, and it is entirely possible that this benefit could ultimately become even greater than that applying to sales." It is encouraging to realize that despite the many criticisms leveled at Detroit for being solely profit-motivated, there is proof such as this of individuals in the industry who are interested in putting out the best possible product, even though the subject has nothing directly to do with this history.

Opposition to the AMA ban, at least from a few executives, continued. On May 8, C.R. Beacham, the Ford Division general sales manager, wrote to McNamara, at that point in his whirlwind career still the general manager of the division:

"We would like to recommend the Ford Division continue to participate.... Racing will not stop as a result of any AMA resolution; and because of the peculiarities of the Ford and Chevrolet products, the Ford car—unless in the hands of capable mechanics with adequate equipment and parts, and driven by the best drivers—cannot outperform the Chevrolet ... because of this, an individual or a dealer cannot devote the money necessary to assure a winning Ford ... we believe General Motors recognizes these facts and is using the AMA as a guise for drawing us away from our objective, knowing full well that they will achieve superiority in all the race sanctioning organizations purely on the basis of having a car more easily adaptable to racing than the Ford."

It accomplished nothing. By mid-May the various divisions had received copies of the AMA resolution that would be adopted at the next meeting, June 6. In the same communication the divisions were ordered to comply with the ban in letter and in spirit, and to do it in a hurry. It said, in effect, get out of racing. It was signed by Henry Ford II, the man whose name was on the building.

The job of cleaning house at the Ford Division now fell to Morsey and Passino. "The one thing I was convinced of," Morsey says, "was that Ford, [Lewis D.] Crusoe and McNamara did not want to do anything in any way that violated the spirit of the agreement; so this was one thing in which we could not get caught, but we nevertheless ought to be good businessmen and work to our advantage—do something that will benefit us beyond this time."

The first recommendation, written May 17 by Passino, was that Travers, Coon, Eames, Hernandez and Holman be retained by the company on a permanent basis. Although the political climate of the time obviously prevented anyone from coming right out and saying it, Passino was convinced some day his company would be back in auto racing. And when they returned, he knew talented personnel of this type would be invaluable. The recommendation included the following:

"There will still be the necessity for intelligent appraisal of the capabilities of our products ... were we to dissolve our entire performance program, we would be faced with the necessity of handling each project involving car performance on an individual basis with a ... hastily gathered together group of individuals ... talent we have is, as the performance shows, the best available in the country ... in this group we have the nucleus for almost any kind of endeavor involving an automotive product ... as we know, the racing program will probably in some respects expand after the manufacturers withdraw and we will be besieged with questions that, to preserve the reputation of our product, must be answered. I believe this could be done without violation of the conditions of the resolution."

Morsey and Passino were not the only ones concerned about the withdrawal. The resolution was anything but good for France, whose stock car circuit had profited greatly by Detroit participation. "Why come out with a public statement and such a stiff rule and then have to break it?" France asked. Whether or not France realized it at the time, Morsey was in agreement with him, but as an employee he went along with the corporate decision. The conversation got France nowhere, as Mersey wasn't in a position to do anything about it, but one item France mentioned was the key that was eventually to draw the manufacturers back: There will be races conducted anyway, Bill said, and as long as they are going to be conducted, it would seem that the manufacturers would be interested in the showing of their products. But in May of 1957 he got nowhere.

Passino got little further with his. Eames and Hernandez were retained to work on Ford's round-the-world sales promotion expedition which was to serve as an introduction for the 1958 models, but they were the only ones. Travers and Coon dropped the Indianapolis engine project and went back to work on other things. Holman, who was now involved in winding things up, would also be cut loose.

Ford had to dispose of the physical assets of the racing team; not only the cars and tow trucks, but also the machinery used to equip the shops in both Long Beach and Charlotte, and a large inventory of racing parts which were now of no use to the Ford Motor Company. In a memo of May 21, Holman was one of several men mentioned as possibilities to take over the stable as a private operation. Interestingly, Kiekhaefer's name led this list.

On May 23 a meeting was held at which steps of the phase-out were discussed, and on the same day information was received that indicated Chevrolet was merely going underground once the ban was imposed: They were not pulling out. Morsey sent a memo with the particulars of the intelligence he had received to McNamara, but nothing was done about it. On May 29 a meeting was held between Ford and Chevrolet. The result of this disarmament discussion was an agreement that:

(1) The resolution would cover all vehicles produced by both divisions, with no exceptions for Corvettes or Thunderbirds.

(2) No parts peculiar to racing would be supplied or engineered by either manufacturer.

(3) Inquiries from racing enthusiasts would be answered with a form letter that said, in effect, "We build passenger cars, not race cars, and besides, we don't know what you are talking about."

The same day Wright sent a memo to Henry Ford II stating the division was ready to comply, and outlining the steps that had been taken. He included the three points from the Ford-Chevy talks earlier in the day, then added a fourth one: a suggestion for some sort of policing organization to make sure everyone stayed honest.

On June 6 the AMA had its meeting, and the resolution was passed unanimously. For the record, it read as follows:

"Whereas, the Automobile Manufacturers Association believes that the automobile manufacturers should encourage owners and drivers to evaluate passenger cars in terms of useful power and ability to provide safe, reliable and comfortable transportation, rather than in terms of capacity for speed,

Now therefore, this board unanimously recommends to the member companies engaged in the manufacture and sale of passenger cars and station wagons that they:

(1) Not participate or engage in any public contest, competitive event or test of passenger cars involving or suggesting racing or speed, including acceleration tests, or encourage or furnish financial, engineering, manufacturing, advertising or public relations assistance, or supply "pace cars" or "official cars," in connection with any such contest, event, or test, directly or indirectly;

(2) Not participate or engage in, or encourage or assist employees, dealers or others to engage in, the advertising or publicizing of: (a) any race or speed contest, test or competitive event involving or suggesting speed, whether public or private, involving passenger cars, or the results thereof; or (b) the actual or comparative capabilities of passenger cars for speed, or the specific engine size, torque, horsepower or ability to accelerate or perform, in any context that suggests speed.

The whirring sound heard that night in Dearborn was that of old Henry spinning in his grave, at a considerably higher rate of revolutions than the agreement intended for his engines.

The 1956 Ford team for NASCAR, with John Holman sitting in the car. The others, from left: Curtis Turner (hat), Joe Weatherly, Ralph Moody, and former West Coast stars Marvin Panch and Bill Amick.

NASCAR—1957 RESULTS
Grand National Division

Ford—27   Chevrolet—19   Oldsmobile—5   Pontiac—2

a. Ford individual winners:

Fireball Roberts—8 (Titusville, Fla., 12/30/56; N. Wilkesboro, N.C., 4/7; Langhorne, Pa., 4/14; Charlotte, 4/19; Shelby, N.C., 5/4; Newport, Tenn., 7/15; Newberry, S.C., 10/12; Concord, N.C., 10/13).

Marvin Panch—5 (Willow Springs, Calif., 11/11/56; Concord, 12/2/56; Spartanburg, S.C., 4/27: Charlotte, 7/12; New Oxford, Pa., 8/10).

Paul Goldsmith—4 (Greensboro, N.C., 4/28; Richmond, Va., 5/5; Lancaster, S.C., 6/1; Raleigh, N.C., 7/4).

Eddie Pagan—3 (Portland, Ore., 5/26, 7/14; Los Angeles, 6/8).

Ralph Moody—1 (Wilson, N.C., 3/17).

Art Watts—1 (Portland, Ore., 4/28).

Lloyd Dane—1 (Eureka, Calif., 5/30).

Bill Amick—1 (Sacramento, Calif., 6/22).

Marvin Porter—1 (San Jose, Calif., 9/15).

Parnelli Jones—1 (Bremerton, Wash., 8/4).

Whitey Norman—1 (Langhorne, Pa., 9/15).

b. There were 21 Grand National races before the AMA ban, of which Fords won 15. There were 32 after the agreement took effect, of which Fords won 12. Chevrolets won five before the ban and 14 afterward.

c. Grand National champion—Buck Baker (point total included 10 victories, all with Chevrolet).

Convertible Division

Ford—26   Chevrolet—12   Mercury—1   Oldsmobile—1

a. Ford-Mercury individual winners:

Ford

Curtis Turner—11 (Greensboro, N.C., 3/17; Greenville, S.C., 4/13; Hickory, N.C., 4/20; Winston-Salem, N.C., 4/22; Norfolk, Va., 4/28; Langhorne, Pa., 5/5; Charlotte, 5/17; Asheville, N.C., 5/18; Spartanburg, S.C., 5/25; Concord, N.C., 6/23; Columbia, S.C., 7/19).

Joe Weatherly—6 (Jacksonville, N.C., 11/11/56; Manassas, Va., 3/24; Hillsboro, N.C., 3/31; Wilson, N.C., 4/14; Raleigh, N.C.; 7/4: Columbia, S.C., 10/30).

Glen Wood—4 (Fayetteville, N.C., 3/10; Richmond, Va., 4/7; Chicago, 6/29; Charlotte, 8/23).

Bill Amick—3 (Raleigh, N.C., 8/2; Norfolk, Va., 8/6; Martinsville, Va., 8/11

Paul Goldsmith—1 (N. Wilkesboro, N.C., 9/22).

Fireball Roberts—1 (Darlington, 5/12).

Mercury

Tim Flock—1 (Daytona, 2/16).

b. There were 20 races before the ban, of which Fords and Mercurys won 17, the first 17 of the season. In the 20 post-AMA events, Fords won 10. Chevrolets won three before the ban and nine afterward.

c. Convertible champion—Bob Welborn (point total included eight wins, all with Chevrolet).

Short-Track Division

Ford—14   Chevrolet—13   Mercury—1

a. Ford-Mercury individual winners:

Ford

Jim Reed—7 (Gardena, Calif., 1/1, 3/3, 5/4; Bakersfield, Calif., 4/27; Jeffersonville, Ind., 5/21; San Diego, Calif., 7/4; Winston-Salem, N.C., 7/27).

Eddie Pagan—3 (Gardena, 5/29; Santa Rosa, Calif., 6/1; Atlanta, 8/23).

Lloyd Dane—2 (Pacheco, Calif., 6/15; Los Angeles, 8/31).

Fireball Roberts—1 (Fayetteville, N.C., 11/4/56).

Clyde Palmer—1 (Merced, Calif., 6/29).

Mercury

Bob Ross—1 (Gardena, 11/25/56).

b. Fords won eight of the 13 events before the AMA ban and six of 15 afterward; Chevrolets won four of the first 13 and nine of the last 15.

c. Short track champion—Jim Reed.

U.S. AUTO CLUB—1957 RESULTS
Stock Car Division

Ford—12   Mercury—4

a. Ford-Mercury individual winners:

Ford

Jerry Unser—4 (Schererville, Ind., 7/24; Williams Grove, Pa., 8/10; DuQuoin, Ill., 8/31; Riverside, 12/1).

Ralph Moody—4 (Milwaukee, 7/14, 8/22, 9/15; Birmingham, Ala., 10/20). Troy Ruttman—2 (Clovis, Calif., 3/10; Paramount Ranch, Calif., 4/28).

Mike Klapak—1 (Trenton, N.J., 9/2).

Sherman Utsman—1 (Knoxville, Tenn., 8/3).

Mercury

Sam Hanks—3 (Pomona, Calif., 2/24; Vallejo, Calif., 3/31; Trenton, N.J., 6/23).

Jimmy Bryan—1 (Phoenix, 1/20).

b. Champion—Jerry Unser (entered 15 races, won four, placed second in three. Runner—up Ralph Moody entered eight races, won four, was third in one).

c. Pike's Peak Hillclimb—winner: Jerry Unser (Ford), 15:39.2. Runner-up: Nick Sanborn (Ford), 15:48.8.

20

LIONS' DENS AND COTTON PICKERS

BY THE TIME the resolution was official, Ford's racing effort, including that of the Lincoln-Mercury Division, was out of business. Although it was hoped they would be able to run through June 30, this was scotched by top management and the last Ford-sponsored entries ran June 1 at Lancaster, S.C., where Paul Goldsmith won in Yunick's car, and on the same day at Santa Rosa, Calif., where Eddie Pagan won in a Long Beach vehicle. But these were merely the death agonies.

The more farsighted executives of both Ford and Chevrolet, now able to look at the AMA ban from an objective viewpoint, were able to see three main weaknesses:

(1) General Motors, even if the agreement was carried through in both the letter and spirit of the law, had much less to lose in the deal. Chevrolet had stolen a march on everyone by using racing as a new and exciting medium through which to introduce its V8. This had been accomplished in a relatively short span of time—and could not now be undone. Tactically speaking, GM called a cease-fire after it had won the war. From an engineering standpoint, since GM knew it had a better engine in the Chevy than anything Ford or Chrysler could offer, the racing support to introduce the engine bad been sufficient; from now on, private persons who went racing would purchase Chevy products before all else and thus further enhance the performance reputation of the make.

(2) The agreement was open to interpretation, and depending on how you read it, short of racing you could do damn near anything you wanted. Ford chose to interpret it literally, Chevrolet went ahead and did more or less as it pleased—and built up an even healthier position in the marketplace. Chevy even had an additional good business reason for doing this. The Corvette, the closest thing Detroit ever produced to a European grand touring car, came equipped with various high-performance parts. To amortize tooling costs, it was logical to make the parts available in all other Chevy products. And then there were other items: The AMA agreement never specified, for example, that fuel injection, or a set of three two-barrel carburetors, or mechanical valve lifters were classified as racing equipment. And who said

you couldn't put miniature checkered flags on the sides of your car? There was no law against that, and Chevrolet did it.

(3) The most important weakness was that the resolution went against the law of inevitability. Anyone who glanced at the population and birth-rate tables could see that by the 1960s the country was to have more young people than ever before. It is axiomatic that young people are impressed by performance. It was obvious the day would come when the resolution would have to be repudiated.

That was the academic state of the art in June, 1957. On a pragmatic level Ford was closing everything down. Each of the drivers was given his two race cars, a tow truck and a supply of parts as a bonus. The rest of the material, of which there was considerable, needed a home, By now Morsey and Passino had decided on Holman as the man who could best make use of the equipment, and who would best be able to carry Ford's colors without any factory backing. By June 19 Holman had made his plans. He wanted to set up an independent operation, using the best personnel from the Ford-sponsored days, and made the company an offer for all the machinery located in Charlotte, plus the Long Beach dynamometer and some other equipment, and for all of the racing parts. In addition, Holman had contacted numerous suppliers and assured himself of distributorships. While he was still involved in dismantling the Ford operation Holman went into business for himself, and he did it by the simple expedient of picking up the phone (he was in California at the time) and calling Moody in Charlotte.

"We have a chance to buy all this stuff," Holman said. "Do you want to buy it?"

Moody said yes and Holman-Moody was born—without even so much as a piece of paper for the first five years of its operation. It was not until Ford came back officially in 1962—and came back to Holman-Moody—that incorporation was necessary. But that was in the future. Now the pressing problem, in addition to raising money to buy the equipment from Ford, was to build a reputation as an independent operator. The best and quickest way to do this was to go and win a race—not a NASCAR race, where Holman and Moody were well known, but a USAC race. It was an anomaly, but even though the USAC stock car circuit was not as well organized or as highly developed as that of NASCAR, in certain ways it was a better proposition. USAC had the benefit of the Indianapolis drivers, and they always drew a little more ink in the nation's papers than did the men who limited themselves to the South. Also, from Holman and Moody's standpoint, a good showing in USAC would open up a whole new market for them, and it was a market for which they had some goods: The superchargers, outlawed in NASCAR at the end of April, but still legal in USAC. Most of the blowers and their spare parts were in the Charlotte warehouse. A good deal of the ability to make them work was housed in Holman-Moody's staff, and that was no small advantage. So they headed for Trenton, N.J., and the 300-miler on the one-mile oval which had recently been converted from dirt to asphalt. The event was scheduled for June 23 and the big name on the

Speed merchants since 1957: John Holman (left) and Ralph Moody. (Bottom) Troy Ruttman leads Moody for a moment during the 150-miler at Milwaukee in 1957, soon after Holman and Moody started their business. Moody won the race, Ruttman finished second, and the infant company picked up enough prize money so it could continue operations.

card was Sam Hanks, who had just won the Indianapolis "500" and who was set to retire at the end of the season. Hanks was running one of Stroppe's Mercurys, now also entered as independents. Holman and Moody brought two cars, one for Ralph and one for Ruttman. They had chosen the USAC star as the other team driver with malice aforethought: Everybody knew Ruttman was good—and Moody knew *he* was faster in a stock car. The sight of one of USAC's own hot dogs being beaten by an unknown would further enhance the infant company's reputation.

The two Holman-Moody cars were such late entries that in the program Moody was listed merely as "driver and car number to be announced at post time." When they arrived they found not only Hanks, but Jimmy Bryan, Jim Rathmann, Johnny Parsons, Marshall Teague and Johnny Mantz—all also driving Mercurys. Moody started in the middle of the pack, but after a minute or two of the 300-mile grind it was apparent the race would be no contest. By the 50-mile mark Moody and Ruttman were running 1-2 and had lapped the field. Then, at 60 laps, Moody was forced into the pits by a broken bolt on his supercharger. By the time the trouble was corrected, he had lost five laps and was seemingly out of it. But Moody charged back anyway, taking up a hopeless chase. In the ensuing 240 miles he lapped Hanks four times to finish third (Ruttman retired) and was the hero of the boiling hot day. After the event was over Hanks was so exhausted he needed medical aid, and all the other Mercury drivers had requested relief during the event. Moody looked fine.

From there, as Holman puts it, "We went into the lion's den." The next stop was Milwaukee July 14, for a USAC 150-miler. Again it was no contest, with Moody and Ruttman running first and second all the way. When it was over Bryan, one of the great drivers this country has produced, was perplexed. "Nobody," he said, "is supposed to come flying out of the blue and beat everything in sight." Moody's car won $14,000 that day, money that was badly needed in Charlotte: Holman and Moody had put themselves on the payroll at only $75 a week until things got going, and every penny helped. Milwaukee, in August, was the scene of a USAC 200-miler, and again it was the supercharged Ford with Moody behind the wheel that showed the way home. In September at Milwaukee the distance went to 250 miles. Again, Moody was the winner. In October, there was a 100-miler at Birmingham, Ala. The winner—Moody.

"And out of that," Holman says, "customers came our way and bought our equipment, and we took the money and bought more machinery and made more equipment." The new firm was on its way, on the strength of Holman's initiative and Moody's heavy foot. Even though the two men were not personally close, they complemented each other: Holman the promoter, the idea man, the student of Clay Smith; Moody the lean New Englander who in his brief bigtime career proved himself to be one of the best—and least publicized—stock car drivers the sport has known. His contributions were to be primarily in running the racing team itself—the cars that were to maintain Holman-Moody's reputation.

Moody saw his first race in Boston Garden, where a mid-1930s form of micro-midget was being used, and built his own racing car when he was 15. His parents screamed but Ralph kept at it, running on the minor-league tracks that filled New England in those times—West Springfield, Fall River, and New Bedford, in Massachusetts; Thompson, Conn., and even down to Castle Hill and Freeport in New York—dozens of places. Sometimes a guy would take a blade and scrape it around a cornfield and they would run on the makeshift track—if the remaining boulders weren't big enough to rip out the undercarriage. At the end of the war Moody was so deep in Austria with the 13th Armored Recon that the fighting had been over several days before the news caught up with them. Then he came home, and while in California waiting for his discharge, Moody would sneak out of Camp Cook at night to race at nearby Bakersfield. Back in New England, he ran a repair shop and raced at the same time. Although he had as many as 20 people working for him, the race cars were the big thing, and there never was a better time for the midgets. "You could run seven nights a week and Sunday afternoon, too, just in New England," he says.

Like most of the drivers in his area, Moody was running a V8-60 in his midget; they were goers, and the times were good. At Lonsdale, R.I., a high-banked third of a mile with 30,000 seats, you could make real money with them. One night Moody came home with $8,888 as the result of his efforts. On another night at Lonsdale, driving a modified, the three-time New England stock car champ picked up $5,500. Lonsdale was pretty much the center of it, and the Ford-equipped midgets were the hot ones. You could average better than 90 with one of them, and the local drivers were tough to beat on their own track. Occasionally some stranger would show up with an Offy, and he would go home a bad loser. Even one-legged Bill Schindler, the great midget driver of the New York-New Jersey-Pennsylvania area, needed several races at Lonsdale before he was competitive. After the first one, in which he wasn't even a factor, he turned to Moody and expressed his amazement at the speeds they generated. "I didn't know you guys ran Indianapolis every night," he said.

Then racing went to hell with itself in that part of the country, Moody sold his body shop and started going south each winter. The girl he was going to marry was now in Fort Lauderdale, so that was as good a reason as any and besides, there was racing there. After three years of winters in the South and summers in Taunton, Mass., Moody settled in Dania in 1951 and stayed until Speedy Thompson quit and Red Vogt remembered Ralph was looking for a ride. Moody not only got a ride, he got a new career as well.

Holman and Moody, as events transpired, were the only successful part of Passino's plan to retain the racing talent in some form or other. Travers and Coon, as mentioned, went their way after engineering could find no place for them in the budget. Eames, after running the round-the-world expedition in 1957, also left, and it was only through a stroke of good fortune that he came back to the Autolite Division of Ford several years later (and eventually became head of Autolite's racing operation).

Coincidentally, when he joined Autolite Eames went to work for Hernandez, who after the ban was imposed went with Stroppe, then joined the Electric Autolite Company (its pre-Ford name) as racing manager in 1959. Hernandez left the Autolite Division to become Lincoln-Mercury's performance man in the fall of 1962, when Eames succeeded to his position.

But this was all coincidence; the Holman-Moody move was planned. Morsey and Passino did everything in their power to ensure they put in the highest bid for the shop equipment, and it was on their recommendation that H-M got the racing parts inventory. The price they paid for this enormous stock of pieces was a tightly kept secret, with guesses on it ranging from as little as $1 to as much as $10,000. It was actually $12,000, but that is of little importance. In Ford's bookkeeping setup, the pieces were written off as expendable the day they were produced, so it cost the company nothing. As later events showed, Holman-Moody's use of the parts, in keeping the Ford name alive in a sport which the corporation had temporarily forsaken, was worth many times the original cost of the pieces—whatever that figure might have been.

The other outside factor in Ford's racing effort, Yunick, was just starting a two-year contract. He was paid off for the remainder of the pact, and also kept the equipment he had in his shop. Yunick, as the operator of a GMC truck dealership, could not have been expected to enter into any non-racing alliances with Ford. But since he had taken the company's money, he wanted to live up to his part of the bargain for at least the remainder of 1957. Smokey, with Goldsmith and Turner as his drivers, was shooting for the Southern "500." Then as now, there is no race that gives a car owner, mechanic or driver more satisfaction in winning, and it would have been a coup for a Ford to have come through in the South Carolina classic after the company withdrew.

The pole at Darlington, giving another indication of things to come, was won by Cotton Owens in a Pontiac, but both Turner and Goldsmith were in good positions in Yunick's black and gold Fords when the long grind got under way. Then, suddenly, on the 28th lap, Fonty Flock, making his only start of the season, spun out in another Pontiac. He was hit by Bobby Myers, whose Oldsmobile flipped end for end. Goldsmith, running right behind Myers, was clipped by the flying car and also crashed. Myers died within minutes and Goldsmith spent several days in the hospital, though not seriously injured. When the race was restarted after an hour's delay, Roberts, driving the lone Holman-Moody entry, took the lead. On the 101st lap he spun into the wall and out of the race; the event roared on, shaking itself down to where Turner and Petty, in an Olds, were battling for the lead.

On the 281st lap Petty put Turner into the wall and the Ford's chances were done. Speedy Thompson, driving a Chevrolet, won by three laps from Owens and became the first man to top the 100-mile-an-hour mark at Darlington, averaging 100.1 for the distance. In third, a lap behind Owens, was Panch, with Reed four laps astern in fourth. That was as close as the Fords could get.

Tony Bettenhausen (top) didn't drive Fords very often, but this time he not only drove one, he finished first as well: Milwaukee, the 150-miler in July 1959. (Bottom) Fred Lorenzen (28) fights off Nelson Stacy (2) and Don Oldenberg (1) during the same USAC event.

Yunick was burning. Although used to the rough-and-tumble driving of the NASCAR circuit, this time, he felt, Petty had gone too far. He registered his complaints in a letter to France, a letter of which even Ring Lardner's famous rookie would have been proud. It was dated September 7, and Smokey sent a copy to Morsey:

"Dear Bill,

"This is a request that you look into—investigate—the Curtis Turner crash at the 'Cotton Pickers 500.'

"I did not see the accident, but Curtis Turner and about 200 other people have told me that during and after the combination Hell Drivers thrill show and part-time race, that it appeared as though Lee Petty, America's favorite driver, had a hell of a dislike for black and gold Fords with 31s on them and kind of crashed it into the fence. Now this may not seem serious, but let me explain just how Lee's attitude has affected my whole life.

"To start with, everyone said that if I took my cars to Darlington Sept. 2 there would be a race there, and that I would win from $12,000 to $20,000. So after months of work and quite a bit of money spent we arrive at the Racer's Paradise. There we had to sweat out the gnats, inspectors, a dirty hole called the inspection station, and the local female cotton pickers.

"After many anxious moments in the inspection station I finally won the title of the biggest cheater, not to say anything of the mental hell we were going through as we staggered into our beds at the motel. As you know it was very crowded there and finding a place for everyone to rest was not easy.

"By this time, after reading the paper and listening to the radio and TV, I am so sure we will win that I start spending the money.

"Finally the great day arrives. Just before the race starts we change our clothes so we will look nice in the pictures, and we are off. About the 28th lap I hear a hell of a crash and notice that one of my little Fords is missing. Of course you know why, so I won't go into that. About this time I am getting a little suspicious, maybe the newspapers had the wrong dope. But anyway, we still have another Ford left, and I didn't spend the whole $20,000 yet, so I figured Curtis would just win the $12,000. So I stand on the wall and push the watches and give signals so Economaki [Chris Economaki, the announcer] can tell everyone what a good kid I am.

"We had the lead at this point, so I figured I would just stay around till the last gas stop and then go and lay down so I'll look fresh for the movies, have enough strength to carry the money and the trophies, and to kiss Miss Cotton Picker of 1957. All of a sudden my car is missing and finally I see it staggering around the bend like a bowlegged Memphis beauty queen just hit by a train on the way to the Town Park Motel. I rush to the window and Mr. Turner is purple and hollers 'Lee put me in the fence.'

"I notice you don't stop the race and wait for me to fix the car. And now I realize that I am in one hell of a mess—boy, I really got troubles now.

"So we fix the car up and get it back out again, but in the meantime they are long gone. As I stand on the wall now I'm sorry to even be living; the papers and the radio were just a bunch of liars. I won't get back the money I spent, I don't have any more race cars, and Paul is in the hospital.

"After the thing is finally ended, as I sit down people slap me on the back and tell me what a good job we did. Some say Lee should get a trophy for the beautiful style he has of putting a car in the wall; others compliment me on having the best-looking wrecks at the track. Myers' car looked a little better, but Turner's looked worse than Petty's, so I still won that event. But not only did I win this year, I won last year also, so I got that sewed up. I only wish Petty could have done it sooner so we wouldn't have had to use so many tires and do the pit stops. Last year we had much better luck. Paul and Herb [Thomas] were well wrecked long before the halfway mark. So Bill, you can see why I seemed a little upset. Of course I realize I don't have any right to, but I guess I am not quite broadminded enough.

"A lot of people go to the races to see the wrecks, and after all we have to keep them happy. You sure have a swell guy in Lee. He has done a beautiful job for almost two years now, but I'm afraid you will lose him one of these days. I guess someone will come along to replace him, though. I hope when it happens it will really look good, so everybody can always remember him as the best. Maybe he can get up into the grandstand and really put on a show.

"Besides all the things that happened up there, I can't work since I got home. Everybody keeps calling up and coming here to see and talk about the wrecks. Also, I am having to walk around. I was driving a black and gold Ford, and ever since Monday any time I drive near an Oldsmobile the damn Ford runs into a ditch and stops.

"So you see, Lee really messed up my whole life. Also, like a damn fool, I got mad about it, and won't race any more for a long time. Look at all the fun I'm going to miss.

"If you would care to discuss this with me any evening you can find me around Second Avenue getting a reversing treatment—as this is the fourth time this has happened.

"Do you think you could advertise in your newsletter for me? A two inch square of Curtis's or Paul's car for $1 as a souvenir of the 1957 eighth annual You Name It."

That was the way it really ended—not with a whimper but a bang.

There were two other items of incidental information, buried deep in the records of NASCAR and USAC, that were of interest to practically no one.

In NASCAR's West Coast activity it was noted a certain young Californian won the August 4 event at Bremerton, Wash. Known only on the Coast, it is not surprising that his name was misspelled. They had it "Parnellie" Jones. In years to come, NASCAR, Ford and many others were to find out exactly how it was spelled.

In the USAC stock car standings, the man in 21st position was a Ford driver who entered six races, finished second in one, and earned $2,497 for the season. His name was Fred Lorenzen, and he was getting up in the world. The previous year, when he entered only one USAC race and was 46th in the standings, they spelled his name "Lorenze."

21

DARK DAYS

WHILE FORD WAS BUSY eliminating its racing program other manufacturers were intensifying or revising their own efforts in this area. Those with limited vocabularies used a simple definition for it: cheating. A broader view would be that all's fair in love and war, and the battle among the various automakers had very few rules—and besides, the terms of the AMA agreement were unworkable. A great and growing segment of the buying public was in interested in performance and couldn't have cared less (in fact had no knowledge) about any agreement among manufacturers.

There was one bit of irony involved in those muddled days of the late 1950s, and that lay in the Pontiac Division of GM. The driving force behind Pontiac's change of image and rise on the sales ladder was Semon E. (Bunkie) Knudsen, who made the car into a hot item through (among other things) the establishment of a performance image through racing. More than 35 years earlier his father, William S., left the Ford Motor Company because it was not progressive enough and built Chevrolet into a bigger seller than Ford. Now the son was following in his father's footsteps (and in early 1968, in a surprise move, he was to assume the presidency of Ford).

At first there were only rumors—talk that involved Pontiac and Chevrolet and even Ford. Most of this occurred during the fall of 1957, when Ford dealers were loud in their complaints about the lack of a racing program, and when men in Detroit were eyeing each other warily, seeking even the slightest sign of deviation from the agreement. Eventually McNamara had enough of the rumors and ordered an investigation. The confidential report, which covers inquiries and interviews made during January, 1958, is a thick and detailed affair, which better than any other collection of documents illustrates the situation at the time.

At Jim Rathmann's shop in Miami, where the great Indianapolis driver had set himself up in business, they found a Chevrolet being prepared for stock car racing, and they found numerous engines and the other paraphernalia that go with a race car. This in itself was no evidence of anything, as Rathmann was certainly entitled to purchase a vehicle and prepare it as he saw fit. But what *did* raise some eyebrows was the fact that the car arrived in stripped (no interior upholstery, etc.) condition, and there were crayon marks on a fender indicating the car was intended for Rathmann. These marks were made in the manner in which they are made at GM assembly plants; in other words, GM had gone out of its way to provide a racing-type car for someone. Suspicions were heightened a few days later when Holman stopped by the shop and saw a crate of intake and exhaust valves arrive from "someplace in Michigan." It was observed the box had an addressograph label, indicating an open account, and it was also learned that Chevy engineers were now designing camshafts for private companies, from which they could be purchased by racing-minded persons.

The activity in Rathmann's shop could have indicated almost anything. No correspondence was seen, and therefore nothing could be proved. It was an assumption based on the old premise where there is smoke, there is fire. If you were a racing man and had seen the operation, you would know if it was factory supported or not just by the smell of it. If you were an investigator and were reporting your observations to a group of non-racing corporate executives, it was impossible to draw any conclusions.

Rathmann, they also found, was convinced Ford had not withdrawn. Yunick's Darlington operation, plus the mass of equipment Holman and Moody now had under their command in Charlotte, led Rathmann to believe they were still involved, but attempting to cover it. It was a logical assumption. No one had ever attempted to set up a private, profit-making racing operation on the scale of Holman and Moody's venture—nor had anyone ever been the recipient of so much racing equipment. It was simply hard to believe the two former Ford men were that ambitious.

More disturbing to Ford was the intelligence that Pontiac had been staging a series of high-speed tests ever since June, 1957. These started at the old Packard proving grounds at Utica, Mich., where they ran most of the summer, then switched to Dallas municipal airport and in December were conducted on the GM proving ground at Mesa, Ariz. Pat O'Connor, another star Indianapolis pilot, did most of the driving. By the time they got to Mesa, speeds were in the 150-mile-an-hour range. They were obviously not testing for fuel economy. Further investigation revealed well-known California camshaft grinder Ed Iskenderian had been producing special cams for Pontiac (more than 100, in fact), and that piston manufacturer Art Sparks, also of Los Angeles, had made a few hundred sets of special pistons for Pontiac. To make the picture even blacker, Sparks had also provided Oldsmobile with racing pistons.

More news from Pontiac involved Jack Zink, the Tulsa millionaire and successful car owner at Indianapolis who had an idea in which he hoped to interest the nation's Pontiac dealers. Since they could not now receive performance help from the factory, if they would chip in 25¢ for every car they sold, the money would be used by Zink to achieve performance results (mostly in speed trials) with their car. They would be provided with publicity and advertising help to let the public know about these hot items. Zink's idea was a good one, and it was accompanied by a letter from the Pontiac national dealer council endorsing it. There was, of course, no letter from the Pontiac Division, but it was obvious they knew about it and did not disapprove. That the entire project never amounted to much is irrelevant; the important thing was that this type of activity was going on, and Ford was standing still.

On the Chevrolet side an expedition to the sports-car Grand Prix of Venezuela, held at Caracas in the fall of 1957, came in for scrutiny. Three Corvettes ran there, and they were the property of Dundee, Ill., dealer Dick Doane. Two were 1958 models—and had been shipped by Doane to South America before any had been seen by other United States dealers. In addition, one of the vehicles was referred to as "the factory car," and the investigators wondered where an individual dealer got the money to mount a 14-man attack in Caracas. No fire, but more and more smoke.

They even investigated Yunick's latest project, a Pontiac which he was building for Goldsmith to drive at Daytona Speed Weeks. Yunick and Goldsmith had been to the Pontiac Division in mid-January, it was found, but they said later no contract was signed. Instead Daytona Pontiac dealer Jim Stephens, a racing and promotion-minded businessman and friend of France's, was sponsoring the car. Stephens, when contacted, stated he was providing the car, various parts and several thousand dollars.

That was a private deal, as near as could be found, but it was also discovered Knudsen was on the march. In January he held at least three dealer meetings in the Southeast—at Jacksonville, Fla., Columbia, S.C., and Charlotte, and although he stated the ban would be observed, he also said that at the first sign of any cheating on the part of the other automakers, Pontiac would jump in with both feet. It was clear to Knudsen that stock car racing was the way to go, and corporate decisions were not going to prevent him from making a success of Pontiac.

McNamara, who interpreted the AMA agreement literally, was not pleased—either with Chevrolet and Pontiac, or with the alleged Ford activities. He passed the material along to the Ford Division with a note that included: "The report implies that, directly or indirectly, Ford Motor Company has supported racing programs in violation ... please take whatever action is necessary to insure that we adhere strictly ..." The ex-racers in the company who read this were shocked. They knew they were staying away; they were surprised at McNamara's directive. Years later, one of them reflected on this and said "Perhaps he was just making sure we stayed away." About the only concrete evidence Ford found as a result of its gumshoe activities was that Chevrolet had not removed certain racing parts from its catalog. On page 492, for instance, could be found such items at 5.83 to 1 heavy-duty ring and pinion sets—scarcely the thing for cruising down the Pennsylvania Turnpike. The young Turks in the corporation wanted Ford to include similar stuff in its catalog offerings, and among those who made the recommendation was Lee Iacocca, a tough, hustling engineer-turned-salesman who was the car marketing manager of the Ford Division. On Jan. 22, 1958, he wrote one of his first memos on this subject. It said, in effect, if they are doing it, we should do the same.

But instead, on Feb. 18, the Ford Division sent a letter to Chevrolet pointing this out. The letter was mailed just before Daytona. On March 5, after Daytona, there came a reply apologizing for the violation and informing Ford the parts would be removed from the catalog. When, a year later, Ford observers at the first Daytona "500" reported Cole, members of his staff and Chevy engineers all over the place, they did not bother to send another letter.

But that was later, when the giant high-banked track emerged from a swamp adjacent to the Daytona airport. This was still the winter of 1958, and it was time for the gathering of the faithful down on the beach.

Yunick had spent the weeks before the race in preparation. They would work all day on the car, then late at night Goldsmith would practice. It was against the law, this high-speed running on public roads and beaches, but Yunick and Goldsmith got in enough of it to convince them their car was a contender—if their engine, at that time still not as reliable as those in later Pontiacs, would stand the test. They knew the opposition, consisting mainly of Fords and Chevys, could be expected to last the race.

And the opposition, among other things, included a pair of Holman-Moody Fords for Turner and Weatherly. Holman had rounded up some money by soliciting the Ford dealers in the Carolinas, had also gotten sponsorship from the as-yet unbuilt Atlanta International Raceway, and had two vehicles ready. They were zipper-top, which meant he could run them in a convertible event one day, then fasten a roof to the body and enter them as sedans. It wasn't strictly according to the rules, but when the factories withdrew good cars became hard to find, and France wasn't going to reject someone of this stature. In the 160-mile convertible race Saturday, it was all Turner. He led most of the way in the 39-lap event, won by 14 seconds, and at the finish had lapped all but five of the 29 starters.

The next day, complete with bolted-on tops, Turner and Weatherly went out to race Goldsmith, the fastest qualifier at 140.57 mph. At the beginning it looked as if they didn't have a chance. Goldsmith jumped into the lead and at half-distance was ahead by a minute. Then slowly, at first almost imperceptibly, Turner started to shave the margin. Waiting even later to back off for the turns, roaring through the soft sand there at even higher rates of speed every time around, Curtis closed the gap. He was passing slower cars on the inside, on the outside—everything but driving over the top of them. Then, going into the north turn on the 30th lap, Turner was attempting to pass Johnny Allen in a Plymouth. Allen shut him off and Turner, to avoid an accident, was forced to continue up the beach. He lost 10 seconds on that maneuver, but whipped his Ford around and continued the chase. With one lap to go, Curtis was only 10 seconds behind Goldsmith and the 30-odd thousand fans lining the course were going wild. Goldsmith, aware of what was behind him, stuck his foot into it as he headed up the beach. Then, in his anxiety, Goldsmith spun in the last turn. Fortunately for him it was not a serious one, and he was able to accelerate again almost immediately. He crossed the finish line a length in front of the flying Turner. Jack Smith was third in another Pontiac, Weatherly was fourth.

Turner, in pushing Goldsmith to the line and then losing, was a symbol of the private-entry Fords that season. When Holman-Moody cars ran, they stood a good chance—but they only ran when they could get some sponsorship. Then, while Holman and Moody were getting the cars ready for the Rebel "300" May 10, Weatherly and Turner talked them into another venture. Joe was promoting a NASCAR convertible race on the dirt half-mile at Wilson, N.C., May 4, and well, it would really help the gate if ...

Holman took his team there, Turner and Weatherly ran first and third, and the cars were a mess. When Ford was the sponsor this would have been no problem; you simply dropped the cars off in Charlotte, picked up a fresh pair and headed for Darlington. Now there were no other cars, and the mechanics slaved to get these ready. As it was, they didn't arrive at Darlington until the day before the event. In qualifying, the cars ran poorly; things looked even worse. But the mechanics worked all night again, and this time they passed some sort of miracle. When the flag dropped, the Ford pair soon charged to the front and started to leave the pack behind them, making it strictly a race between friends.

The casual onlooker would never have known they were buddies. Turner and Weatherly pulled every trick in the book, ramming each other from behind, side-swiping, closing the gate going into corners—the works. It would have been rough driving on a quarter-mile dirt oval, where speeds never get too high. But here, where they were turning laps at better than 115 mph, it was frightening to watch, and for Holman and Moody even more so. The cars being subjected to this high-speed demolition derby were theirs. Somehow, both machines stayed in one piece, Turner winning, Weatherly finishing second, with Panch third in another Ford and Pagan fourth in still another. From a long-range standpoint, the important item in the final results was the fifth-place finisher. It was Roberts, and he was driving a Chevrolet, not a Ford. Before the season was out Fireball was to prove himself in this make as well. Despite his late start in a competitive car, Roberts was to win eight races (both Grand National and convertible) for Chevrolet before the season ended, including the Southern "500." It was a long year for Ford: In Grand National races held in the South, the only Ford driver to win after May 15 was a heavyset youngster from Ingle Hollow, just up the road from Ronda, N.C., on the outskirts of North Wilkesboro. His name was Bob Johnson, but everyone called him Junior and remembered he had been a promising driver a few years earlier, then disappeared from the scene. Wilkes County, which is where Ingle Hollow is located, is the heart of the Carolinas boot-legging industry, and well, Junior had gone and got himself caught. It was ironic, too; he'd forsaken the business a few years earlier. When the revenuers picked him up at his father's still, he'd just gone there for a day to help. But that was a few years ago. Now Junior was back, and was making his presence felt. In June he won two races in a row, and at the end of the season he won his second straight event on the five-eighths mile paved track at North Wilkesboro. Ford fans needed a new hero, too—not only were their cars getting beaten, but after Darlington Turner had gone into the hospital with back trouble.

It was a disappointing season; some of the spark had gone out of it when the Detroit high rollers left the scene. It wasn't only the money they spent, it was the sudden sense of urgency that accompanied southern stock car racing in those days. When they were present, the events were no longer dusty happenings in out-of-the-way places; there was symbolism attached, and every Ford and every Chevy out there was representing a multibillion-dollar corporation, and the crowd sensed this.

Now they were back to the good old boys running their own cars. Taken by itself it was great, and it was faster than anyone had ever run before. But compared to the previous season it was just a little bit tattered around the edges. Stock car racing, without open factory participation, would never again be quite that exciting.

What little hope there was for Ford in 1958 was found in the North, where the USAC stock car circuit was still making an effort to establish itself. The excitement came in the form of a good-looking blond youngster who was so nervous he seemed to be walking two feet off the ground. His name was Fred Lorenzen, and he could win races.

A decade later, when he had become the biggest stock-car money winner in history, and when he had won more races on super speedways than anyone else, Lorenzen would often belittle his emotional involvement with the sport. It was only a business, he said, and he didn't know where else he could work so little for so much money. To anyone who had known him since his early days, this was laughable. Lorenzen may have taken a businesslike attitude toward racing, but racing was also his life, and had been since he was 11 years old.

First he had a miniature single-seater powered by a lawnmower engine mounted in the back. Some of the older kids in the neighborhood helped him build it, but it was Freddy's idea, and when it was finished it was a great thing for buzzing around the streets of the Chicago suburb of Elmhurst, where he was born and raised. Eventually the police made him put it away, as it was so low motorists couldn't see him streaking along behind the high weeds. But Freddie was already hooked. During high school he worked in gas stations afternoons and evenings, and every chance he had, he would take something apart and put it back together again, discovering which parts went round and round and which went up and down. When he was 14 he got his hands on a Plymouth of mid-1930s vintage, and he and his friends took it to a makeshift racetrack they had set up in a cornfield, and Lorenzen got his first chance to play full-size driver. Within a matter of minutes he rolled the ancient buggy. A year later there was the summer afternoon when he listened to a broadcast of 'the inaugural Southern "500" at Darlington. Red Byron, Fireball Roberts, Curtis Turner, Johnny Mantz ... they were all big names to Freddie, and the money at Darlington loomed even bigger to the 15-year-old. That's where he wanted to be.

In high school it was a succession of gas station jobs and two-wheeled vehicles—motorbikes, motorcycles, anything that would run, and then he switched to a used Ford convertible, which was followed by other, better examples of the genus hot rod. To earn money for the cars Freddie started working as a carpenter for his brother-in-law, who was a contractor, and it wasn't long before he got his union card. It was to be more than a decade, after he had become a big money winner, before he gave it up again. But back then thoughts of big money from racing were in an altogether different frame of reference.

It was 1955, and big to Freddie meant the $100 his buddy earned while winning a demolition derby at Soldier Field in Chicago ("I worked all week for $100, and here he was making it in 10 minutes"). Lorenzen's father didn't like the idea but his mother was amenable, so Freddie entered the next one of the series, which was run by Andy Granatelli, expanding from his speed shop operation. Fred didn't win that night, but he finished close to the top—if that phrase can be used for such a dubious form of the sport—and he came back again practically every time Granatelli staged another. For 1956 Lorenzen organized a Chevrolet, and with the help of his friends, including a local mechanic named Jack Sullivan, they got the car ready and took it to Langhorne in April for his first race, a NASCAR event. Had Lorenzen known anything of Langhorne, he would have found a more forgiving arena for his debut. The Pennsylvania dirt track, built in the form of a one-mile circle with semi-high banks and its infamous "Puke Hollow" a quarter mile past the starting line, was a most difficult place to drive. A slightly frightened Lorenzen brought up the rear of the pack as Buck Baker, Speedy Thompson, Fireball Roberts and the rest zipped past him on almost every lap.

But at least he finished, and with his hopes buoyed, Freddie headed South with his buddies as the crew. He ran at Columbia, Concord, Hickory, Martinsville and Greenville—and then ran out of money. About the only thing spectacular was Lorenzen's getting upside down at Hickory and Greenville. Then it was back to work, pounding nails and raising enough money to get the car into shape. When it was ready, he returned to racing on a lower level—the short tracks at Soldier Field and O'Hare Stadium, the latter only a few miles from home. On these, and with a taste of the big time behind him, Freddie was a terror. He won, and won, and then he won some more. Soon his name began to appear in those two and three-paragraph stories which the publicity men for the minor-league ovals sometimes manage to plant in area newspapers, such as this literary item from the Chicago *American* of July 8, 1956: "Fred Lorenzen, Elmhurst daredevil, and Stewart Joyce, intrepid Indianapolis petrol pusher, tonight resume a feud that started Independence Day at O'Hare Stadium...." History does not record what became of Mr. Joyce. Lorenzen kept on winning.

For the 1957 season Lorenzen walked into an Oldsmobile dealer and organized a car ("I told him I was the greatest thing since popcorn") for the longer races, and a buddy, Jake Talarico, got hold of a Chevy for the short-track events. Jake did it the

The beginning: (Top) Lorenzen's first powered vehicle, which he built when he was 11. (Bottom) Lorenzen, his sponsor and the track clown at O'Hare Stadium, Chicago, in 1957. At right: (Bottom) Lorenzen after winning his first race in his own car at O'Hare, May 1956. (Top) When the factories pulled out of NASCAR, the machinery took on a somewhat shabby patina—Hillsboro, N.C., in 1959, with Buck Baker's Chevrolet and Joe Weatherly's Thunderbird occupying the positions of honor in the front row.

easy way: He put $100 down for a new car, then they took it home, stripped it and got it ready for the races which were going to pay off the balance. Later in the season, when the dealer saw what they had done to his vehicle, he was staggered. For the Olds, Freddie sold a gravestone manufacturer the advertising space on the flanks. It was the fastest ad Peter Troost Monuments ever had—until Lorenzen wrecked the car at Trenton and almost got sued. The dealer thought it was to be raced in the Chicago area only.

By midsummer 1958, after cleaning up at Soldier Field and O'Hare, Lorenzen switched from gravestones to pizza pies. He found another angel, and this time it resulted in a new Ford with "Lou and Ev's County Line Pizza" emblazoned on its side. Freddie, Jake and their friends worked night after night to get the car ready, they practically hocked their souls to get a Holman-Moody engine for $980, and took the results of their handiwork to Milwaukee for the USAC 150-miler, where Horatio Alger was forced to move aside.

Lorenzen sat it on the pole, then won the race going away ("It meant the world to me; here I was, racing against Jimmy Bryan, Marshall Teague … Johnny Parsons—all the big wheels!"). A month later he won another 150-miler at Milwaukee, then over Labor Day weekend he took two races within three days. On August 30 he won the DuQuoin "100" in the southern part of Illinois: That night they loaded the car on the trailer and headed for Trenton, almost 1,000 miles away. On Labor Day, at the Jersey circuit, Lorenzen chased Teague for most of the 300 miles, and when the Chevy's engine blew with 24 miles to go, the 23-year-old won again. He clinched the title in a 226-mile road race on the Meadowdale circuit outside of Chicago on October 19—his fifth win in seven starts. The next year he won the USAC title again, with six wins in 13 starts (five of them after September 1), and then he went south again to try his luck in NASCAR. He had already accomplished something important for Ford: In the depths of their withdrawal, Lorenzen had provided some excitement when it was most needed.

While Lorenzen and a few others were chasing across the country on their own, a private drama was unfolding inside the corporation, and it centered around McNamara. One of the famed "Whiz Kids" management group who came from the Army Air Corps to Ford as a team led by Tex Thornton (later the head of Litton Industries), McNamara made invaluable contributions in the areas of organization and management, and his speedy rise up the ladder reflected his talents. Now, as he neared the top, McNamara was caught in a minor dilemma. He had little personal use for auto racing and the multitude of unforeseen contingencies that went with such a harum-scarum activity, but as a realist had seen that the company got involved when it became necessary to offset the Chevrolet effort in 1955.

But when the AMA ban took effect in 1957, and with his company's signature on the industry agreement, he did his best to uphold it. But despite the willingness to go along with the ban, things started to change in late 1958. It was nothing you could put your finger on, and there is little in the company files to indicate this, but the top management attitude was becoming more amenable; it was still not positive toward racing, but it was not quite so negative. One reason was that business was bad; after outselling Chevrolet in 1957, Ford fell behind again in 1958, and its troubles were compounded by the economic recession of that year. The company was barely able to pay a dividend to its stockholders, and no bonuses were handed out to executives.

Now, even if the company had wanted to go racing, there was no money. They could only think about it, and one of the foremost thinkers (and doers) was Iacocca. He learned his lesson in the Philadelphia district in 1956, when Ford decided (a decade before Ralph Nader) that a safety theme would be the thing to push the sale of new cars. "I as a guy in the field," Iacocca says, "gave the safety thing hell; I promoted it for all it was worth, but the Chevy V8 was beginning to take off—and they were promoting that. What I learned was simple; a puppy's got to like what he's being fed." And Chevy's diet was more appealing than was Ford's.

In 1959 the attitude became faintly aggressive. The major reason was a sudden jump in Ford sales, thanks in part to a rare styling slip on the part of Chevrolet; 1959 was the year of the bat-winged monstrosity. The next reason was the inaugural 500-mile race at the Daytona International Speedway in February. Now there was more money to spend, and there was a report which showed spending was necessary.

Through 1958 the only Ford Motor Company employee allowed to attend races was George Merwin, then in the sales department. Merwin watched what the other manufacturers were doing, and also kept Dearborn informed of the progress of Bill France's new plant in Florida. Now, with a new level of publicity to be opened for stock car racing, Ford sent Merwin and Bob Graham to Daytona for the inaugural race in February of 1959. Graham, one of the brighter young lights in product planning at the time, did not know anything about racing, but he had the sense to keep his eyes open and add two and two. Graham did not have to look far. During the 500-mile race he was sitting next to Chevy boss Cole—and was given one of the box lunches prepared by a catering firm for the large group of Chevy and Pontiac executives and engineers who attended. At one stage of the race, when a Thunderbird was momentarily leading the field, Cole kiddingly told Merwin that if the T-Bird won, Cole would make him pay for the meal!

Graham left Florida with two conclusions: The factory racing ban was as good as dead, and that Ford's performance reputation was about to suffer the same fate. In the flying-mile runs on the beach for standard cars, the Fords were more than 10 miles an hour slower than the Chevrolets and Plymouths. In the runs for highly modified stock cars the Fords weren't even entered; no one could buy any parts with which to modify them. At the track Pontiac pace cars, plus Duntov's engineering team and Super Sport Corvette show car, were everywhere a potential buyer could turn. The Olds and Cadillac experimental sports cars were also on display and were also used for demonstration runs. In the race itself there was only one rather weak-kneed 1959 Ford, and it did not last as long as a Studebaker Lark which had somehow found its way into the starting lineup.

Then there were the Holman-Moody Thunderbirds. Six of them started, four of them finished, and one—driven by the practically unknown Johnny Beauchamp of Harlan, Iowa—lost in a photo finish to Lee Petty's Oldsmobile. Even these, however, did not give the situation an aura of anything except despair. The T-Birds, running with 430-cubic-inch engines, did not meet NASCAR standards, and had been admitted only to lend some extra interest to the race. In addition, the big, heavy and low-revving engines, despite extensive modifications, did not turn out nearly the 340 horsepower produced by Chevy's 348-inch V8; it was tapped out at a little more than 5,000 rpm while the Chevys could run at 6,500. Ford didn't have the basic hardware, regardless of what miracle men like Holman and Moody could perform. Chevy, on the other hand, not only had a good high-performance package, but it was available through dealers, and Chevrolet engineers were constantly developing new and better equipment.

Graham's recommendation was to develop a high-performance package for the Ford, and when he delivered the proposal to McNamara three days after the race, the erstwhile Whiz Kid looked over the mass of information and made up his mind in a hurry.

McNamara's actions that day were the first steps toward the restoration of a factory-sponsored program. Hans Matthias and an aide were in McNamara's office during the Graham presentation, and when they left, Matthias was succinct. He merely turned to the other man and said, "You're it."

By that afternoon Donald N. Frey was working on the infant plan, the guts of what was eventually to bring the company back to racing in a manner undreamed of at the time.

The Thunderbirds were another story. The appearance of so many of them at Daytona, their high standard of preparation and their operation under the aegis of the erstwhile Ford racing team led many to believe the company was back in, and McNamara wanted to discover how this came about. An investigation found Holman had purchased most of the parts he needed from Ford, and had bought much of it as scrap. At any large auto manufacturing facility there are always a number of parts which are damaged in some way or another, yet would be perfectly serviceable if repaired. They are of no use to the company involved, as they will not put repaired items on new cars. Holman knew this, and knew his mechanics would have to dismantle and completely rebuild a car anyway to make it fit for racing, so he hit upon this way of getting what he needed for a reasonable price. Armed with a letter of credit and pointed in the right direction by some of his former associates at the Ford Division, he purchased literally hundreds of items (including complete bodies, engines, etc.) from the Thunderbird assembly plant at Wixom, Mich.

When the non-racing-oriented scrap and financial administrators at Wixom were told what had happened to the pieces they sold that nice gentleman from North Carolina, they were staggered. All they knew was he had money, knew exactly what he wanted, and was willing to pay several times as much as they could have gotten from their usual sources. And besides, they added, was he not sent to them by someone else in the company (they were not sure who, and that was a good thing for the parties involved)? Before the investigation was done the entire scrap disposal policy of the corporation was rewritten. But Holman and Moody had their cars, and Beauchamp's battle with Petty bad given the image another much-needed shot in the arm. The average speed of 135.521 mph, for what was ostensibly a stock car, gripped the imagination of many persons who previously thought little of stock car racing, and the delay in determining the winner added even more to the event from a publicity standpoint. Due to the lack of a photo-finish camera at Daytona, it took officials 61 hours to study films and still photos (and reap the publicity benefits) before they finally gave it to Petty. Beauchamp hadn't been in doubt. After they crossed the line and were on their cooloff lap, he eased alongside Petty on the backstretch and with a wave of his hand congratulated Lee on winning. At the finish line, where Holman had been watching, he had known immediately his driver had lost. But the ink helped everyone, including NASCAR, which ran only 39 Grand National races that year.

The proof that General Motors had been hard at work violating at least the spirit of the AMA agreement was a hard nut for Henry Ford II to swallow. He had entered into the agreement in good faith, and had kept watch over his company to make sure its actions would be as good as his word. Now, with all the facts of the matter laid out before him, Ford decided on a direct course of action. He went to Frederic G. Donner, the new chairman of General Motors, and started talks on the subject of upholding the ban in a sensible—and workable—manner. When Donner went to Europe in late April, Ford pursued the matter with John F. Gordon, then the GM president, and on April 27 wrote Gordon a lengthy letter, outlining what had happened, offering suggestions as to what could be done about it, and offering to have his men meet with a GM group.

To reaffirm his intentions of acting in good faith, Ford concluded: "On a short-range basis, we intend to develop those high-performance components for the Ford car that are presently offered by Chevrolet and Pontiac. We believe this action is mandatory to assure the competitive position of our products.

"On a long-range basis, we are most anxious to work out a more satisfactory agreement with other members of the industry." The message was clear: Through your actions you are forcing us to act in violation of the agreement we both signed; we've got to do this simply to stay alive in the marketplace. But we would prefer to stand by our word—if you would do the same.

Henry Ford II never received the courtesy of a reply.

When it became apparent he would not get one, the company was as good as back in racing. The biggest mistake it made from then on was (at first) to attempt to do so on a restricted scale. This was akin to the biological impossibility of being a little bit pregnant. When the corporation finally got this message, it proved itself better at waging an all-out racing campaign than anyone else.

In the meantime what was to grow into that effort was confined to three men in the basement of the engineering building, with a former University of Michigan professor as their boss. Frey had earned his bachelor's, master's and doctorates in engineering at Michigan State and Michigan, and in the fall of 1951 went to work for Ford in the just-born scientific research laboratory. By the time he and Matthias left McNamara's office in the winter of 1959, Frey was the executive engineer of Ford Division product planning. A fan since the Lincoln successes of the mid-1950s, Frey's first step was to place Dave Evans, who had been involved in the former stock-car effort, in charge of a three-man group, and to assign the engine responsibility to one of the major contributors to the racing history of the company, Don Sullivan. One of the small team which designed the first flathead Ford V8 and the V8-60, Sullivan had also been in on the 1935 Indianapolis project, and on practically everything where more horsepower was needed in a hurry.

Frey was short a man, so he asked for a suspension engineer. A few hours later a tall, thin youngster by the name of John Cowley showed up. He had been asked if he would like to work on a new project for developing heavy-duty police car suspensions. That was the cover story for the project, and it took Cowley a month or so before he realized what was really happening. It was a ridiculous group, when viewed in relation to the over-all manpower and finances of the company. Only three men— Frey primarily occupied with the normal engineering program—and with no money. Sullivan, Frey says laughingly, laid out the new intake manifold on the kitchen table, and since they were not able to command the use of dynamometer facilities, they relied strictly on Sullivan's know-how and the way the engine sounded. Bill Innes, then on his way up through the ranks of the Engine and Foundry Division, took an interest and managed to make what parts they needed. When it came to getting a car in which to install the engine, the trio had to scrounge some more. There are 20 hand-built prototypes of each model made several months in advance of regular production for testing purposes. It was vital that the embryo racing group get their hands on one of these. They found enough extra sheet metal for the body, made sure there were enough spare suspension parts, installed their own hand-built engine, and although the Ford Motor Company never recorded it officially, there were 21 prototypes built that year.

Before they got the new car built, some of the components were dropped into a 1959 model, and Cowley and Sullivan would sneak the car to Detroit Dragway and check it out against the Chevrolets and Pontiacs that populated the place. They would always go home before the official runs started, so as not to draw attention to themselves, but eventually they were caught. Inadvertently, they had left the manufacturer's license plate on the vehicle—and got hell for it. When the prototype was finally ready, another problem arose: With Curtis Turner in the hospital, they were short a test driver. They were so unsophisticated about it, Cowley recalls, that "we simply looked in the NASCAR newsletter and we saw that a guy named Cotton Owens was near the top of the standings, so we called him." Any association with

Holman-Moody, the known purveyors of Ford speed equipment, was out of the question. So the Wood brothers, who were able to move in a more inconspicuous manner, were brought in to crew the car when it went to Daytona at the end of August, and the announced purpose of the affair was tire testing for Firestone. Within a few days, and despite the "normal" heavy duty suspension which was designed for street use, Owens was able to crack 145 mph. This was faster than any lap during the first Daytona "500," and the Ford crew was ecstatic. Had the suspension been a full-race affair, Owens told them, he could have gone faster—and then he inquired about a ride for the 1960 season.

Now that they knew the engine would run, the next problem was to get a suspension package in shape, and the already weary prototype was shipped to the rough dirt track at Concord, N.C., where Turner and the Wood brothers spent most of the fall thrashing around the half-mile oval. At the beginning, Curtis would tear a wheel off the car within 10 laps, and the engines would blow after about 20. "It got to be laughable," Cowley says. "You could predict it almost down to the lap." It was a time of rebuilding engines in the sand and the dirt, of replacing broken spindles, of chasing after flying wheels which had disappeared into the piney woods around the circuit. By late October the high-performance package was ready for release in its single four-barrel (oval-track) configuration. A three two-barrel carburetor version was developed for drag racing and street use, and at least it was a start. In the meantime Lorenzen, complete with pizza pies on the sides of his car, was all Ford had going for it.

The first steps of the comeback had been made just in time; in 1960 stock car racing took on an entirely new look as two more super-speedways went into business. These were the 1½-mile, high-banked ovals at Atlanta and Charlotte, and they changed the complexion of the sport. Now, with these two plus Daytona and Darlington, a super circuit appeared within the larger framework of the NASCAR organization. With two races per season at each, there were eight events at which the speeds went far over 100 mph, drawing large crowds and national publicity. Boiled down, it meant the proposition was that much more attractive to the manufacturers. Unfortunately, there were few persons at Ford who realized this. At Pontiac, where Knudsen The Younger was holding sway, he used the major speedways as a vital link in reshaping his car's image.

In January of 1960 Ford personnel were not looking that far ahead. They were still concerned with the development work done on the 352-inch engine and with the optional pieces now in the catalog. People were buying the car and then ordering the special pieces, and Holman and Moody were even advertising a prepared version of the vehicle. "T-Bird Power Products suggest a way of going 150 miles per hour," was the headline in the H-M ad, and the body copy indicated that for $4,995 the Charlotte outfit would deliver one of the hot Fords in full-race condition. The more naive members of Ford's management assumed this type of thing would be enough; their "limited re-entry," as it was called in internal company memos, had been accomplished. All you had to do was build a few pieces, sell them over the counter, and the racers would take them and stop bothering everyone. Besides, wasn't the 360-horsepower rating of the 352-inch engine the highest in the industry? And didn't it outsell Chevy last year?

Then came Daytona Speed Weeks. By the time they were over, Ford realized how far it still had to go. In the beach trials Fords were not the fastest, and in the 500-mile race there was disaster: No less than 32 Fords were entered, 28 made the race, and none of them came even close to winning, with all but a few dropping out.

That was the substance of the winter on the east coast of Florida. The details will illustrate why things went the way they did. First, there were the beach runs. Evans, Cowley and Sullivan had prepared a 360-horse Starliner for this event, and it was being run in the guise of a private entry to be driven by a magazine editor. In December trials, thanks to Cowley's use of a fast stop watch, the car was clocked at 142.5 mph—and the Ford men knew it would go faster if the driver would only stick his foot into it. Then, in late January, when it appeared the editor wasn't going to drive it any harder, Evans got behind the wheel. On his first run he spun out, winding up with the hindquarters of the car in the Atlantic Ocean and a beautiful target for the numerous photographers in the neighborhood. When the picture appeared in the Detroit papers, McNamara gave Evans and Cowley six hours to get out of Florida. Sullivan was allowed to stay, but was told exactly where he could and could not go. His instructions read: "Your only activities will be to assist and train the personnel of the Ford dealership ... you will exercise extreme care to avoid any association with the speed week events, including attending any of the races either at the beach or the speedway." Giving advice to race car mechanics over the telephone was an obvious impossibility. Without any on-the-spot technical help, Ford's new engine modifications, never before subjected to 500 miles of full-speed running, proved something less than durable.

Junior Johnson won the wreck-strewn event in a year-old Chevrolet after the Pontiacs had proved themselves fastest in practice, and the compact car races added insult to injury. France staged these as a television package, with the cars using most of the high banks plus the infield course for 10-lap events.

Starting in the fall, some outside work had been done on the Falcons, primarily in the form of a three-carburetor manifold developed by Holman-Moody and also by Bill Stroppe working in conjunction with Edelbrock. This boost in horsepower for the 144-inch straight six, from its stock figure of 85 to 130, was figured to be enough. But the Chrysler Corporation's Valiants also had a kit of sorts. The difference was that these cost somewhere over $500, had to be installed by an excellent mechanic—and produced more than 200 horsepower from 170 cubic inches as opposed to the standard 101 horses. The TV races were a Valiant picnic, and another example of how escalation was setting in.

Although the 1960 season statistics show Fords took more NASCAR races than any other make, it was a poor affair from a Dearborn standpoint. The Chevy

When the Daytona International Speedway opened its gates, a new era began for stock-car racing. (Top) Cars at speed on the track during the 1960 event. (Bottom) An aerial view of the place in 1964. The smaller oval at lower left is a dog track; the open space in the infield is a lake.

victories were backed up by a thorough dominance of the top 10 positions through the season, and neither make was the one to provide the real excitement. This plum fell to the oncoming Pontiacs, which were getting more and more numerous and were the undisputed kings (when their engines didn't blow) of the super-speedways. Ford was scratching, as was Lorenzen, spending his first full season in the South. He had worked on his car himself, setting it up at Holman-Moody, and then gone racing with little success and a lot of peanut butter sandwiches and nights spent in the back of his car. By the tail end of the season he was ready to quit, and after breaking an axle at Martinsville, Va., headed for home. When he got there, a telegram from Atlanta was waiting. It included the promise of a motel room and some much-needed parts, if he would race. Lorenzen hooked up the trailer again and headed south. He finished 10th and earned $1,000 then went home and sold his rig. He would go back to hammering nails, he thought.

Slowly, the more innocent members of the corporation were learning. In August, when a good look at a Pontiac engine was available, it was discovered the motor not only was totally non-stock from the cylinder block on, but it violated at least 14 NASCAR rules. At first there was righteous indignation. Soon this changed to an awareness of the real name of the game: win.

Then in the fall of the year John Fitzgerald Kennedy was elected President of the United States and he wanted the newly chosen president of the Ford Motor Company, Robert S. McNamara, to be his Secretary of Defense. He left the company in January, approximately two months after another man had been named general manager of the Ford Division. This was Iacocca, who just a few weeks after his 36th birthday had been jumped over the heads of many senior men to the biggest general managership in the corporation.

Iacocca moved fast. He was acutely aware that the person soon to be in the rnajority was the young one, and he knew younger people didn't think much of Ford. ("When they heard the name Ford they just associated it with their parents and things that were fuddy-duddy; they hadn't lived through the prewar era.") Iacocca started a series of meetings aimed at finding a theme. First there was the selection of an image; Chrysler products had an image, GM products had an image. Ford products (with the possible exception of the low-volume Lincoln) had none.

They decided on the "total performance" image, and although the slogan was soon done to death in Ford ads and press releases, this was (and is) something more than a mere phrase. It was what they knew they had to do. General Motors had a virtual lock on the auto industry. Its cars appealed to a broad spectrum of the population—and the only way to get back in a contending (much less superior) position was to build better ones and let the people *know* they were better. Iacocca decided to do it by creating excitement. ("When you don't have anything the quickest way to generate something is excitement. Earlier it had really built up inside of me that we were going to go racing on all fronts.... I wasn't as interested in stock cars per se as I was on all fronts—a more sophisticated approach.")

Those early meetings revolved to a great extent around the problem of how to get back with the kids, and racing was the most obvious way.

The activities of the previous year were now stepped up slightly, and at the same time Iacocca started discussions of the racing program at the highest level. ("I had to do it of necessity, but Henry Ford was the man who had to do it, and if I couldn't sell it to him, we just couldn't do it.") Iacocca's ideas fell upon receptive ears, and everything a restricted budget would allow was done.

Why wasn't more accomplished at this time? Primarily because the company was preparing to bring out a new type of vehicle: the Cardinal, scheduled to be the American Volkswagen. It was a small, plain-Jane type auto with no frills, designed as basic transportation, and much effort was being expended on it. Iacocca devoted all his energies to stopping the project. ("The greatest thing I ever did for this company was killing the Cardinal at the beginning of the youth boom; we would have gone back to basic transportation and bombed!") As an alternative he offered an item first introduced by Frey, now the Ford Division product planning manager, in early 1961. This was the Mustang, which originally showed up as a sophisticated, midships-engined sports car, and which Iacocca and Frey tailored into a marketable item. (Iacocca: "It was the first of the long-term plans to put something together for the kids. The components were in the system; all we had to do was put a youth wrapper around it, and this was done for less than $50 million.") Although the potential success or failure of the Cardinal in the United States market can only be guessed at, the sales triumph of the Mustang is a matter of record. One of the things that helped "preframe" the Mustang image, it should be noted, was the intensive competition program undertaken by the company in the two years prior to the Mustang's introduction April 17, 1964. But that was later; at the beginning of 1961, things such as the end-product Mustang and the domination of any type of racing were merely dreams. Some of them, such as Holman-Moody, came close to slipping away. After an unsuccessful 1960 season, in which they had been reduced at times to running a team of Studebaker Larks in compact car races, and with little promise of help from Ford in the future, the situation was bleak. Autolite was the principal Holman-Moody sponsor at the time, and Autolite (not yet a part of the Ford Motor Company) wanted to run a Dodge in 1961, so Moody had mentioned this to Lorenzen when he called him just before Christmas 1960 and surprised Freddie by asking him to be their driver. Passino, knowing help would be coming in the near future, talked Holman into staying with Ford, even though at the moment things looked bad.

Then came the season itself. Ford went in hoping its V8, by now out to 390 inches and advertised at 375 horsepower (410 in stock car racing trim) would be the answer to the 389-inch, 440-horse Pontiacs. They rarely stood a chance. The Pontiacs, after several seasons of working out the bugs, and with the "experimental" engine of 1961 now available to all who wanted to race it, were the biggest power producers on the circuit. They established a NASCAR record by winning 30 races, and there were times during the year when Pontiacs would occupy the first four, five and even six rows of the starting grids.

Typical of much of the season was the Daytona "500." For the first time there were numerous cars over 150 mph in qualifying and Roberts' Pontiac, prepared by Yunick, was the quickest at 155.7. In the race itself Roberts was making a runaway of it, leading from lap 43 through lap 187, when his engine blew and let Panch, in a year-old Yunick Pontiac, through to win at 149.6 mph as Daytona passed Indianapolis in the average speed department for the first time. Goldsmith was third in still another Pontiac, and back in fourth was Lorenzen in a borrowed car. Holman was unable to finance the construction of a vehicle for Freddie but Lorenzen came to the beach anyway, as did Passino, now making his public return. Passino and Holman scouted among the private entries and finally found what they wanted—a good-running Ford with a slow chauffeur. His name was Tubby Gonzales, and he was a contractor and part-time race driver from Houston. The rotund, loquacious Holman and the lean, reserved Passino set to work on Gonzales with the aid of Bob Tasca, the competition-oriented dealer from East Providence, R.I., who runs one of the country's most successful retail sales operations. Finally Tasca offered to give Gonzales a new station wagon if he would let Lorenzen drive his entry. When Tasca called the Houston Ford dealer and arranged to have the car waiting on Tubby's doorstep when he got home, Freddie had a ride, even if only a fourth-place one. At that he did considerably better than two other Fords which showed flashes that day. One of them was the property of Nelson Stacy, a rugged World War II tank driver who had been spending his summers on the dirt tracks of the MARC circuit in the Midwest and now wanted to try his luck at the big time. Stacy had received a few free parts from Ford in the past and was also getting them now, but aside from that he was strictly on his own. His vehicle blew on the 80th of 200 laps. The other car belonged to a bespectacled youngster from Asheville, N.C., who had made some sort of a reputation driving in NASCAR's minor league of sportsman and modified races. His name was Edwin (Banjo) Matthews, and after the race sorted itself out, he found himself in second place behind the flying Fireball—until his engine blew, five laps before Roberts' did.

On April 9 Lorenzen won his first NASCAR race, an event on the half-mile paved oval at Martinsville, Va., in which he dueled most of the way with Rex White in a Chevy, and which he won when it was halted by rain. Lorenzen was starting to move, and almost exactly a month after his first trip to the winner's circle he finished first again in his most satisfying victory. It was in the Rebel "300" convertible race at Darlington, the place a teen-age Lorenzen heard about on the radio. Now he was there, running alongside Roberts in his hot Pontiac and the legendary Turner in another Ford. Freddie was thrilled, and when the flag dropped he charged off from his pole position as if the 300-mile grind were a 10-lap sprint.

Each time he tore past the pits, Lorenzen noticed Moody standing near the track pointing to his head, and Lorenzen couldn't figure why. Then, practically before be knew it, he was forced in for an unscheduled tire change; the hot pace he was setting had blown one, costing an extra pit stop. In the meantime Roberts charged to the front of the pack. With 40 laps to go, coming out after another tire change, Lorenzen started running at record speeds in an attempt to take second place, figuring Roberts was long gone in the lead. With 25 laps left Lorenzen was on Turner's bumper, fighting for what be thought was the runner-up spot, not knowing Roberts had dropped back due to mechanical difficulties. Freddie was faster than his idol, but the peculiar configuration of the Darlington track makes it virtually impossible for one car to pass another of roughly the same speed range unless the slower man moves over.

Turner wasn't about to do that. Every time they came off the second turn Lorenzen would try to pass him on the outside and Curtis would close the gate, moving up to the retaining wall and sometimes shouldering Lorenzen's car aside in the process. Again and again, at speeds in excess of 130 mph, Lorenzen's white Ford tried to pass Turner's black one to the outside and failed. Then, on the next to last lap, Lorenzen faked to the outside.

Turner moved out.

Lorenzen cocked his wheel to the left and went low, going past on the inside.

Turner came down too, trying to hold Lorenzen back.

Lorenzen's right front fender shoved Turner back up, both cars shuddered for a moment, then the drivers regained control.

Fred was past, He'd given as good as he'd gotten from the master of race-track roughhousing, and he won by a few seconds, although he didn't know it until he got to the pits.

Turner was so infuriated that on the cool-off lap he pulled alongside Lorenzen and gave him one more shot.

When the two cars got to the pits Turner clambered out and beaded for Lorenzen. Holman, quick to act, stepped up to the giant lumberman, said a few quiet words, and it was over—not the newspaper part of it, in which the Southern press had Turner swearing eternal vengeance and making dire predictions about the next time this high-speed morality play was presented, but the serious part. The most laughable thing about it was that on Monday morning, one segment of the racing faction at the Ford Division was barely speaking to the other. Lorenzen's car had been backed by marketing and sales promotion money. The Wood brothers' car, which Turner drove, had been an engineering department vehicle.

Lorenzen also never forgot Moody's finger pointing at his head. From then on, any Holman-Moody race car Freddie ever had included the lettering *Think! W.H.M?* on the dashboard. The initials stood for "What the Hell's the Matter?" and their presence contributed to Lorenzen's seldom running anything other than a carefully planned race.

At Daytona's Firecracker "250" July 4, Lorenzen again showed he had a nose for the big money. He was leading this one with two laps to go when Joe Weatherly, in one Pontiac, pulled in front of David Pearson in another and gave the rookie an aerodynamic tow past Lorenzen. Pearson won by less than a car length, as the art of high-speed slipstreaming and team tactics worked for the opposition. Although Weatherly had one of the fastest cars on the track, he had been delayed by pit stops and had no chance to win. Pearson was running second, however, and when Weatherly hove into view just in front of him, their combined efforts put a precious few extra miles an hour on Pearson's vehicle.

Five days after Daytona, the re-run of the rained-out Atlanta "250" was staged, and Lorenzen finished first in the only race of this distance at the Georgia bowl. He almost didn't make it, cruising around with a near-empty (gas tank the last few laps and coming across the line with nothing left. A lot of the Pontiacs had engine trouble at Atlanta and it was just as well, because when the activity returned to the world of the smaller ovals they won seven of the next eight races leading up to Darlington and the Southern "500."

In one sense Ford now had even less going for it. Turner, the idol of the Southland, had been removed from the scene. In financial difficulties with his newly created Charlotte track, Turner had gone to the Teamsters Union seeking a loan. He was promised the money, but one of the conditions was that he organize the drivers. In mid-July the movement gained momentum. When France got wind of the project in early August he put a stop to it in a hurry. The creator of this budding empire was not about to see control turned over to another party, and he brought the Turner-NASCAR-Teamsters maneuvering to an abrupt halt on the night of August 9, when he talked to all the drivers, car owners and mechanics who were on hand for a race in Winston-Salem, N.C. France talked for more than an hour in his classic, persuasive style; he appointed a committee to investigate a pension plan for the drivers, and he gave everyone on hand an opportunity to resign from any union commitments. After that came the blast. He threatened to plow up the Daytona Speedway before he would let any union men get their hands on it, and as his ultimatum he said:

"After the race tonight, no known union members can compete in a NASCAR race, and if this isn't tough enough, I'll use a pistol to enforce it. I have a pistol and I know how to use it. I've used it before."

There wasn't a man in the crowd who doubted his words. The union threat stopped, and both Turner and Tim Flock were banned for life, leaving Ford without one of its better symbols.

At Darlington on Labor Day the heat was more oppressive than ever, with the thermometer hovering near 100° as the 60-car field accelerated toward the first turn, filling the flat expanse of the infield with an almost terrifying combination of noise, dust and exhaust fumes. Lorenzen, up front along with Roberts, grabbed an early lead as he used the better handling of the Ford to outrun the more powerful Pontiac.

Lorenzen managed to hold on for a while, but he ran himself out of brakes while doing so and fell farther and farther back, finally dropping out after 158 of the 364 laps and leaving Roberts in command. Then, amidst the pack of Pontiacs at the head of the field, another Ford made its appearance. It bore none of the glossy sheen that accompanies factory-backed equipment, but it was moving as fast as anything on the track. It was Stacy, in his own car.

Stacy and Roberts now made the running, with Stacy leading from laps 113 to 123, then Roberts taking over again, then Stacy for a dozen laps starting with the 170th, then again for 14, starting with 226. Finally Roberts, weak with the flu, gave his car to Panch with 87 laps to 20 as Stacy took the lead again. Stacy worked his way back up front from laps 277 through 302, then it was Panch once more as Stacy came in for a pit stop, the last one before the run for the checkered flag. Down in Lorenzen's pit, where they were equipped with a team of lap scorers, Holman had watched the goings-on and had seen the minimal number of helpers that comprised Stacy's crew. He knew what the race situation was, but he wasn't sure Stacy realized he could win. Holman walked down the line to Stacy's pit, where the driver's young son was in charge.

"Does Nelson know how to read?" Holman asked.

The boy nodded, looking somewhat startled.

"Do you know how to write?"

The boy said yes.

"Then take that blackboard and write 'Stand on it' and show it to him."

Nelson stood on it. With six laps to go Stacy passed Panch in a daring maneuver and he was in front to stay. It was the closest finish in the history of the Southern "500," with only 2.6 seconds separating Panch from the record-setting Stacy. His beat-up, much-traveled car had averaged 117.8 mph for the distance, more than six miles better than the old mark, and that gave Ford some small consolation for the season. It was just as well. At the ensuing major races in Atlanta and Charlotte, the Pontiacs filled not only the forward sections of the starting grids, but also most of the higher places in the final results. They were first through fourth in the Atlanta race, and the only non-Pontiac pilot in the top four at Charlotte was young Richard Petty, who was capably filling his father's shoes since Lee was seriously injured at Daytona in February.

It hadn't been a good season, but it hadn't been that bad. With the budget limiting participation to a relatively few races, Lorenzen had driven in 15 events and won three of them. Ford was now filling the role Pontiac had played a few years earlier: Only enter the big ones, and you'll get more ink out of those than you will from all the smaller races put together. But it was obvious work had to be done on the numerous disinterested parties in the corporation. Throughout the year Passino had been the author of what were called "technical evaluation" reports. These reports were basically an information service he set up to let everyone know what was going on in the racing world: results, interesting newspaper clippings, figures on sales of high-performance parts, incidental intelligence, etc. The reports were disseminated to widely varying types—some were in the sales department, some were in engineering, others were in marketing or product planning. It was Passino's own private campaign to make the various factions at the company performance-oriented, and it was a great help in laying the groundwork for the seasons to come.

NASCAR—1958 RESULTS
Grand National Division

Chevrolet—22   Ford—16   Oldsmobile—9   Pontiac—3

a. Ford individual winners:

Junior Johnson—6 (N. Wilkesboro, N.C., 5/18, 10/19; Columbia, S.C., 6/5; Bradford, Pa., 6/12; Reading, Pa., 6/15; Atlanta, 10/26).

Jim Reed—4 (Old Bridge, N.J., 4/27; Roanoke, Va., 5/15; Hamburg, N.Y., 7/19; Belmar, N.J., 7/26).

Curtis Turner—3 (Fayetteville, N.C., 3/15; Atlanta, 4/13; Charlotte, 4/18).

Parnelli Jones—1 (Sacramento, Calif., 9/7).

Shorty Rollins—1 (Busti, N.Y., 7/16).

Eddie Gray—1 (Riverside, 6/1).

b. Grand National champion—Lee Petty (point total included nine victories, all with Oldsmobile).

Convertible Division

Chevrolet—13   Ford—6   Oldsmobile—2

a. Ford individual winners:

Curtis Turner—4 (Daytona, 2/22; Wilson, N.C., 5/4; Darlington, 5/10; Birmingham, Ala., 6/22).

Joe Weatherly—2 (Richmond, Va., 3/23; Nashville, 8/10).

b. Convertible champion—Bob Welborn (point total included 10 victories, all with Chevrolet).

Short Track Division

Ford—12   Chevrolet—7   Oldsmobile—3

a. Ford individual winners:

Parnelli Jones—5 (Gardena, Calif., 1/1; 4/20, 7/3; San Diego, Calif,, 6/4, 7/4).

Jim Reed—3 (Roanoke, Va., 5/15; Buffalo, N.Y., 7/19; Belmar, N.J., 7/26).

Eddie Gray—1 (Gardena, 3/9).

Curtis Turner—1 (Fayetteville, N.C., 3/15).

Junior Johnson—1 (Bradford, Pa., 6/12).

Shorty Rollins—1 (Busti, N.Y., 7/16).

b. All the eastern short track races (14) were run in conjunction with the Grand National events in order to fill out the fields, hence the duplication in victories in the two divisions.

c. Short track champion—Lee Petty (point total included three victories, all with Oldsmobile).

NASCAR—1959 RESULTS
Grand National Division

Ford—15 (Ford 9, Thunderbird 6)   Chevrolet—13   Plymouth—9
Oldsmobile—5   Pontiac—1

a. Ford-Thunderbird individual winners:

Ford

Junior Johnson—5 (Wilson, N.C., 3/29, 6/20; Reading, Pa., 4/26; Hickory, N.C., 5/2; Greenville, S.C., 6/13).

Ned Jarrett—2 (Myrtle Beach, S.C., 8/1; Charlotte, 8/2).
Jim Reed—1 (Winston-Salem, N.C., 3/30).
Eddie Gray—1 (Sacramento, Calif., 9/13).
Harlan Richardson—1 (Los Angeles, 5/30).

Thunderbird

Curtis Turner—2 (Hillsboro, N.C., 3/1; Concord, N.C., 3/8).
Tom Pistone—2 (Trenton, N.J., 5/17; Richmond, Va., 6/21).
Johnny Beauchamp—1 (Atlanta, 3/22).
Cotton Owens—1 (Richmond, 9/13).

b. Grand National champion—Lee Petty (point total included 14 victories, four with Oldsmobile and 10 with Plymouth).

c. Raw numbers were deceiving in 1959; five of Ford wins were recorded by 3/30; Thunderbird victories did little to establish performance image for a car that had just been taken out of the two-seater class.

Convertible Division

Ford—10 (Ford 5, Thunderbird 5)   Chevrolet—9   Plymouth—2   Oldsmobile—2
a. Ford-Thunderbird individual winners:

Ford

Glen Wood—3 (Winston-Salem, N.C., 5/23, 8/21; Martinsville, Va., 9/27).
Shorty Rollins—1 (Daytona, 2/20).
Ned Jarrett—1 (Charlotte, 8/23).

Thunderbird

Joe Weatherly—3 (Charlotte, 4/24; Hillsboro, N.C., 4/26; Daytona, 7/4).
Curtis Turner—1 (Hickory, N.C., 3/22).
Tom Pistone—1 (Martinsville, 6/7).

b. Convertible champion—Joe Lee Johnson (point total included four victories, all with Chevrolet).

Short Track Division

Ford—9 (Ford 7, Thunderbird 2)   Chevrolet—1
a. Ford-Thunderbird individual winners:

Ford

Parnelli Jones—4 (Los Angeles, 11/16/58, 5/30); Gardena, Calif., 7/3; San Diego, Calif., 7/4).
Jim Reed—3 (New York, 4/25, 7/11; Hamburg, N.Y., 7/18).

Thunderbird

Scott Cain—2 (Belmont, Calif., 6/13; Fresno, Calif., 10/4).
b. Short track champion—Marvin Porter.

NASCAR—1960 RESULTS
Grand National Division

Ford—15   Chevrolet—13   Plymouth—8   Pontiac—7   Dodge—1
a. Ford individual winners:

Ned Jarrett—5 (Columbia, S.C., 11/26/59; Greenville, S.C., 4/23; Spartanburg, S.C., 5/28; Birmingham, Ala., 8/3; Sumter, S.C., 9/15).
Joe Weatherly—3 (Hickory, N.C., 4/15; Wilson, N.C., 4/17; Darlington, 5/14).
Glen Wood—3 (Winston-Salem, N.C., 4/18, 6/25, 8/23).

Speedy Thompson—2 (Charlotte, 10/16; Richmond, Va., 10/23).

John Rostek—1 (Phoenix, 4/3).

Marvin Porter—1 (Hanford, Calif., 6/11).

b. Grand National champion—Rex White, Chevrolet (point total included six victories, 25 finishes in top five).

c. Convertible and short track divisions discontinued after 1959 season.

d. Four of Pontiac's seven victories were on "super speedways," one at Darlington, two at Atlanta and one at Daytona.

e. Of Ford's 15 eight were on dirt tracks, three (all by Glen Wood) were on the quarter-mile oval at Winston-Salem, and one was on the West Coast, away from the mainstream of NASCAR publicity.

NASCAR—1961 RESULTS
Grand National Division

Pontiac—30   Chevrolet—11   Ford—7   Plymouth—3   Chrysler—1

a. Ford individual winners:

Fred Lorenzen—3 (Martinsville, Va., 4/9; Darlington, 5/6; Atlanta, 7/9).

Eddie Gray—2 (Los Angeles, 5/27: Sacramento, 9/10).

Joe Weatherly—1 (Charlotte, 11/6/60).

Nelson Stacy—1 (Darlington, 9/4).

b. Grand National champion—Ned Jarrett, Chevrolet (46 starts, one win, finished in top five 22 times, in top 10 32 times).

U.S. AUTO CLUB—1958 RESULTS
Stock Car Division

Ford—6   Mercury—3   Chevrolet—3

a. Ford-Mercury individual winners:

Ford

Fred Lorenzen—5 (Milwaukee, 7/3, 8/17; DuQuoin, Ill., 8/30; Trenton, N.J., 9/1; Meadowdale, Ill., 10/19).

Mike Klapak—1 (Langhorne, Pa., 5/18).

Mercury

Jimmy Bryan—1 (Phoenix, 2/9).

Johnny Mantz—1 (Pomona, Calif., 2/23).

Norm Nelson—1 (Milwaukee, 9/14).

b. Champion—Fred Lorenzen (entered seven races, won five, placed third in one. Runner-up: Mike Klapak entered eight races, won one, had one second, two thirds, two fourths).

c. Pike's Peak Hillclimb—Nick Sanborn (Pontiac), 15:49.7. Runner-up: Bob Korf (Pontiac), 16:09.0.

U.S. AUTO CLUB—1959 RESULTS
Stock Car Division

Ford—10   Chevrolet—5   Pontiac—2

a. Ford individual winners:

Fred Lorenzen—6 (Langhorne, Pa., 4/19; DuQuoin, Ill., 9/5; Milwaukee, 9/20; Atlanta, 10/25; Clovis, Calif., 11/22; Las Vegas, 11/29).

Don White—1 (Salem, Ind., 6/14).
Tony Bettenhausen—1 (Milwaukee, 7/19).
Rodger Ward—1 (Milwaukee, 8/23).
Mike Klapak—1 (Langhorne, 9/13).
b. Champion—Fred Lorenzen (entered 13 races, won six, placed second, third and fourth once each).
c. Pike's Peak Hillclimb—Nick Sanborn (Chevrolet), 15:45.2. Runner-up: Louis Unser (Pontiac), 15:53.6.

U.S. AUTO CLUB—1960 RESULTS
Stock Car Division

Ford—8   Pontiac—1
a. Ford individual winners:
Norm Nelson—3 (Milwaukee, 8/21, 9/25; DuQuoin, Ill., 9/3).
Tony Bettenhausen—2 (Milwaukee, 7/24, 8/25).
Don White—2 (Nashville, Tenn., 6/12; Terre Haute, Ind., 8/14).
Rodger Ward—1 (Salem, Ind., 10/9).
b. Champion—Norm Nelson (entered 8 races, placed first three times, second twice, fourth twice).
c. Pike's Peak Hillclimb—Louis Unser (Pontiac), 15:36.6.

U.S. AUTO CLUB—1961 RESULTS
Stock Car Division

Pontiac—14   Ford—7   Chevrolet—1
a. Ford individual winners:
Don White—3 (Concord, N.C., 4/2; Indianapolis, 5/29; Schererville, Ind., 6/28).
Norm Nelson—2 (Indianapolis, 7/4; Milwaukee, 8/13).
Eddie Sachs—2 (Milwaukee, 7/16, 8/17).
b. Champion—Paul Goldsmith, Pontiac (entered 19 races, won 10, finished second three times).
c. Pike's Peak Hillclimb—Louis Unser (Chevrolet), 15:06.0 Runner-up: Curtis Turner (Ford), 15:08.4.

Part 4

(The 1960s)

ADVANCE TO THE REAR

FORD BROADENS OUTLOOK:
LOTUS AND THE 500, COBRAS,
RALLIES AND DRAGSTERS

22

How It Happened

THE POPULAR ASSUMPTION HAS been that at some point during the early 1960s someone at the Ford Motor Company sat down with a clean sheet of paper in front of him, and after contemplating his navel for a while, proceeded to outline just how the corporation would go about expanding its racing activities. With an organization of this size, with such great amounts of money available and with advance planning the *modus operandi* for most of the company's other endeavors, it would have been the logical way.

This was not the case. Somewhat like Topsy, it more or less just growed.

There *was* a guiding (or perhaps overseeing) hand through the expansion process, and that was Iacocca's. He was the one who first broached the idea of an all-out performance campaign, and he was the one who sold it to top management. But at the beginning the idea was only sketched out in broad, general strokes; things were taken more or less as they came up, rather than to fill an assigned spot in a prearranged plan.

By 1963 Ford was involved in the most ambitious competition program in the history of the industry, either domestic or foreign. By 1966 this program had become the most successful in the annals of any American manufacturer, and a good argument can be made that it was the most successful for any automaker anywhere, the possible exception being the Mercedes-Benz effort of 1955, when that firm's cars won both the Formula I and world manufacturers title. In 1966 Fords or Ford-powered equipment:

Won the world manufacturers championship with triumphs at Daytona, Sebring and Le Mans, with the latter being the first 24-hour victory here for an American vehicle.

Won the Indianapolis "500," dominated the remainder of the oval-track, single-seater racing in this country, and was the engine used by the USAC champion.

Were the main source of engines for international Formula II and Formula III racing, and dominated the latter.

Were a major factor in international rallying.

Made their presence felt in big-time drag racing.

Won the SCCA's Trans-American sedan racing championship.

Were as usual one of the major factors in NASCAR and USAC stock car racing, although one of the almost-annual disputes over the rules caused the company to withdraw its sponsorship in this area for a good part of the season.

Although often accused of accomplishing this with what has been referred to as rectangular dollars instead of cubic inches, on a proportionate basis Ford actually spent less than did Daimler-Benz during its glory years of 1954 and 1955. Whatever the exact sum is, before it was spent, the Ford car had lost its image. After it was spent (and this process is still going on, as the performance campaign is one to which the company has a long-term commitment), Ford's products *had* an image. Without it, they could not have been sold as successfully as they have been.

The development from a program directed solely at stock car racing (and that in a *sub rosa* fashion, thanks to the AMA ban) to an all-fronts attack took place in a period starting with the early spring of 1961 and running through the early summer of 1963.

Interestingly, the primary obstacles to the development and eventual success of the program were not the speed of the opposition's vehicles. The obstacles were internal, and were the following:

The bastard-child status of the thing.

A certain lack of advance planning and organization, part of which stemmed from the first point.

The "System."

The last point was (and is) the most important. In any large corporation, regardless of whether its products are automobiles, cigarettes, soap or suppositories, there is a System. There are committees and subcommittees, numerous copies of memorandums, operative procedures, intricate budgets, the big-brotherism of personnel departments, executive isolation fostered by private bathrooms and dining rooms and also a great number of lower-level persons who seek havens in this inherently conservative atmosphere because here they can find security—here they can bury their mediocrity behind a welter of forms and procedures and operate on the principle of not doing anything wrong by the simple process of not doing anything.

Practically everything in these large corporations is weighed carefully. It is passed through several committees, it is examined by all departments, numerous multiple memos are written, and after a suitable gestation period the project is finally undertaken. This is especially true of the auto industry, where vehicles containing more than 15,000 individual parts must be designed four and even five years before they are driven off the end of the production line and sold to the general public. The System, despite its many weaknesses, is the strength of the company. Its shortcomings, the insular thinking it creates and the time spent by individuals attempting to circumvent it are all part of the bargain.

Now, suddenly, along came racing, and it was diametrically opposed to The System.

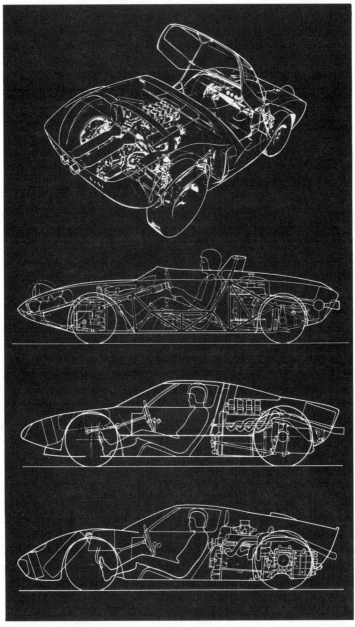

A part of the evolution of the Ford GT prototype. (Top) The original concept sketch of the GT40, made in early 1963. Below are three drawings showing the path through the Mustang I to the GT40 to the Mark II.

The original GT40, below that a cutaway drawing of the Mark II and photographs of the Le Mans-winning Mark II, front, rear and side views.

Although racing takes as much advance planning as does anything else (if not more), once the planning is over and activities begin it turns into a shoot-from-the-hip operation, fast-moving and full of unexpected contingencies. That is the nature of the beast, and making it compatible with the other activities of the Ford Motor Company was a difficult process—in fact it is doubtful it will ever be fully accomplished. Racing is an activity in which the abilities of the persons involved are completely exposed to the public every time the starter's flag drops, and there is no substitute for first place. It is axiomatic, from a psychological standpoint, that the average person in a large corporation would be at the very least resentful of that small, ambitious group confident enough to lay its accomplishments out in the open and have them compared with the performance of others.

Sometimes, getting The System to accept the racers was almost laughable. Once, when Frey's small group was attempting to assemble its low-budget stock car package of 1960, they went to the Ford forging plant at Canton, Ohio, and sweet-talked some of the plant personnel into making heavy-duty spindles. This was done by the simple expedient of using worn-out (and therefore oversize) dies, which had been scrapped. After weeks of maneuvering through Canton and through various departments in Dearborn, they had their stock of heavy-duty spindles, the spindles had a part number, they were listed in the catalog and were on a shelf waiting for the orders to come. At the same time the company was adopting a computerized perpetual inventory system. When the computer discovered this minuscule supply of spare spindles, it scrapped them.

The strength of the performance program came from several factors:

The first was the increased interest on the part of top management;

Another was the corporation's engineering divisions, the ones that supplied new hardware and developed the old far beyond original expectations

Third was the ability to align the corporation with the most talented outside personnel, such as Holman and Moody and the Wood brothers in stock car racing, Colin Chapman and Lotus for Indianapolis, and with drivers such as Jimmy Clark, Dan Gurney, A.J. Foyt, Mario Andretti, Fred Lorenzen and Ken Miles.

And finally, a lot of hard work. For certain persons in the company, it was more than just a job.

It was most difficult to equate The System and the special vehicles activity in the early stages, when the racing efforts were run by an amorphous group which had little substance, even less form, and did not have the attention of top management. Passino, for example, was dividing his time between the advertising department and the racing; Merwin was doing the same thing from his position in sales; Evans and his group had to operate on their own with little budget money. Had the corporation been farsighted enough to organize the operation properly in 1961, or even as late as the spring of 1962, it would have been much ahead of the game when things went into high gear in 1963. The biggest reason for delaying any organizational move of this type was the AMA agreement, which Ford did not publicly repudiate until mid-June of 1962. Although the agreement had long since outlived its usefulness (if it ever had any), Henry Ford II was reluctant to break it and in doing so possibly stamp his company with a "bad guy" label in the eyes of the public, Congress and the National Safety Council. In mid-1961 he once again tried to get a more workable agreement—and without success. But by spring of 1962 it was more obvious than ever that not only GM, with its all-winning Pontiacs, but also Chrysler (and of course Ford) were making a mockery of the thing.

There was one last conference on the subject, this meeting being held in mid-May. When members of other corporations questioned GM's senior executives about the Pontiac and Chevrolet activity, the answer was they were having "difficulty" controlling the general managers of these divisions.

Henry Ford put an end to it. "We're going in with both feet," he said. After that, there was really nothing left to talk about.

Although the other automakers knew of the Ford decision, for some unexplained reason there was no announcement of it for almost a month, and the public disavowal was made only because of the detective work of one of the better automotive journalists in the country, then-UPI auto editor Bob Irvin. As a careful observer of the Detroit scene, Irvin was aware something was going on, and had contributed fuel to the fire earlier that spring in South Bend, Ind., when he quoted Studebaker President Sherwood Egbert as saying Detroit was "two-faced" about racing. On June 10, when Irvin was covering the Atlanta "500," he got word that Henry Ford had been there a few days earlier and had told a group of southeastern dealers the company was in again. On Monday, in Detroit, Irvin set about cornering the chairman. In the afternoon, while Ford was at a dealer meeting in downtown Cobo Hall, Irvin waited in the kitchen until the proceedings were concluded. Then he approached Ford and Charley Moore, at the time the corporation's vice president for public relations. Moore saw him coming and tried to steer his boss away, but it was too late. "Has there been any change in your position on racing?" Irvin asked. Ford started to give him a roundabout, diplomatic answer, so Irvin told him of Egbert's opinion.

Ford took a look at Moore, then turned back to Irvin and said, "All right, let's be honest about this."

He proceeded to give Irvin the biggest automotive scoop in years. Irvin never did get it as an exclusive, as Moore prevailed upon him to let the company announce it generally, but it was now out in the open. The announcement, made later that day, read as follows:

> "The so-called 'safety resolution' adopted by the Automobile Manufac-turers Association in 1957 has come in for considerable discussion in the last couple of years. I have a statement to make on this subject.
>
> "I want to make it plain that I am speaking in this instance only for Ford Motor Company. I am not speaking for the AMA, of which I am currently president, or for the other manufacturers.

"Following the adoption of the AMA resolution, we at Ford inaugurated a policy of adhering to the spirit and letter of the recommendations contained in the resolution. We tried very hard to live with this policy. We discontinued activities that we felt might be considered contrary to the principles embodied in the resolution, and also modified our advertising and promotion programs appropriately.

"For a while, other member companies did the same. As time passed, however, some car divisions, including our own, interpreted the resolution more and more freely, with the result that increasing emphasis was placed on speed, horsepower and racing.

"As a result, Ford Motor Company feels that the resolution has come to have neither purpose nor effect. Accordingly, we have notified the board of directors of the Automobile Manufacturers Association that we feel we can better establish our own standards of conduct with respect to the manner in which the performance of our vehicles is to be promoted and advertised.

"This action in no way represents a change in our attitude toward highway safety. Indeed, I think everyone is aware that Ford has been a pioneer in the promotion of automobile safety. We will continue with unabated vigor our efforts to design, engineer and build safety into our products and to promote their safe use. We will also support every legitimate program—both inside and outside the automobile industry—which we believe contributes materially to safer vehicles and safer driving."

By now the activities of the racing department had grown and they were soon to grow some more. Basically, this is how the various projects got started (aside from the stock car program, which was there from the beginning, and which for an American automobile manufacturer must of necessity remain the cornerstone of any effort):

Drag racing—It began in the early part of 1961, when it became apparent to Ford that a great segment of the youth market was more interested in this form of competition than it was in oval-track activity.

Indianapolis—Thoughts of this activity started stirring in Frey's head when he was at the 1962 running of the "500," and within a few weeks there was the fortunate coincidence of Dan Gurney and Colin Chapman walking in with a proposal. By the end of July, the first Indianapolis effort was under way.

Long-distance sports car racing—In 1961 Carroll Shelby, the ex-Le Mans winner now retired from active racing due to a heart condition, wanted to install American production V8s in light European chassis and sell them. After being turned down by GM, in the late summer of 1961 he went to Ford. They said yes, and from this was to stem the Cobra, the Shelby Mustang, and the idea to enter a car at Le Mans.

Rallies—The suggestion to get involved in this area came from J. Walter Thompson, Ford's advertising agency, as part of the plan to change the image of the Falcon from an underpowered six-cylinder car to a hot item equipped with V8, four-speed transmission and the like. The proposal was made in the summer of 1962, and the 1963 Monte Carlo rally was the first undertaking.

Until the late winter of 1967, all competition programs within the company were carried on independent of each other; the Ford Division ran its own show. Lincoln-Mercury did likewise, etc. The long-overdue reorganization as a corporate effort was effected at that time—although competition activities of Ford of Britain and other international divisions were still left under the operational jurisdiction of these groups.

Before the reorganization, the various divisions conducted the following activities:

Lincoln-Mercury—They came back to stock car racing in 1963, participating on both the NASCAR and USAC circuits, and after two years of full-bore activity (in which they bumped heads with the Ford Division), stock car activity was cut back. In 1965 and 1966 the degree of participation varied from partial support to none at all; then it was back to two factory-sponsored cars at the beginning of 1967. This ceased when the program went corporate, and Lincoln-Mercury then made an all-out drive for the Trans-American sedan championship.

Lincoln-Mercury also carried on a continuing program in drag racing, which in its own small way was perhaps the most successful of the company's domestic performance activities, and made one abortive attempt at international rallies. Other Lincoln-Mercury efforts, not strictly speaking racing but run by the performance department, included the well-received 100,000-mile endurance run at Daytona in the fall of 1963 (in which 458 international records were set by Comets), and another long-distance jaunt that involved driving from Cape Horn to Fairbanks, Alaska.

Autolite—Already the possessor of a racing program when this firm was absorbed by the Ford Motor Company in the spring of 1961, its activities continued without interruption, except Autolite now had the advantage of seeing its sparkplugs in all Ford-sponsored equipment.

Economy tests—For want of a better place to put them, the participation in the Mobil Economy Run and the Pure Oil (later Union Pure) Performance Trials have always been handled by the various racing departments—which could easily have spent the time and money involved on more conclusive demonstrations of one make's superiority. They had little choice, however. The oil companies had long since established their events, and the automakers were practically blackmailed into competing. With the reorganization in the winter of 1967 both Ford and Lincoln-Mercury activities in this area came under the new corporate structure.

There was one avenue of endeavor, possibly the most successful one, that was divorced from Dearborn at its beginnings and remained that way. This was (and is) the British Ford program, and action here stemmed not from any great plans, but from being in the enviable position of having the best product. Although this part of the company had for years been producing small displacement four-cylinder engines, in the fall of 1959 a brand new one was introduced, and it proved to be a winner in both the literal and figurative senses of the word. Not only did sales of the cars it powered show a steady rise, but the engine soon became the darling of British tuners and race car designers. Within a year it became all conquering in its class, and thus sparked the British Ford involvement with racing that led to the introduction of the world's most successful Formula I engine in 1967.

The other major overseas car producer, Ford of Germany, has never had a program of any magnitude, primarily because its products are not suited to all-out competition. What activity there has been (and again, operated independently of Dearborn) has been primarily in rallies.

On the next level, such organizations as Ford-France, Ford of Canada, Ford of Switzerland and Ford of Australia have conducted their own programs during the past five years, but these were campaigns undertaken with equipment built and developed by other divisions, and the impetus for them came from the general competitive feeling of the company rather than from any self-starting nature.

That, in the broadest of terms, is what happened. The facts of the matter, which provided some of the genuinely great moments in the 70-year history of the sport, are related in the ensuing chapters. For the sake of clarity the involvement in the various types of racing are treated separately. Actually they all were happening at one time—in the biggest and fastest three, four and even five-ring circus auto racing has ever seen.

23

GREEN PAINT AND REVOLUTIONS

JUST LIKE THOSE MULTIMILLION-DOLLAR Hollywood spectaculars, *The Indianapolis Story* was a wide-screen technicolor affair, larger than life, with a cast of thousands and with numerous principal actors.

There was Daniel Sexton Gurney—handsome Dan, the personification of the all-American boy. He started a love affair with the automobile almost as soon as he was old enough to know what one was, and when he grew up he became one of the fastest drivers in the world. But his foremost contribution to American automotive competition was more important than any races he won or lost. Before this opera singer's son came on the scene, the three varieties of United States autosport were almost totally divorced from each other. But he wanted to drive, and he didn't care what kind of a car it was as long as there was a race to be run and money. Gurney was the first man to be successful in single seaters on oval tracks, in stock cars on both oval tracks and road courses and in European-type grand prix and sports cars. The example he set encouraged others to try the same thing, bringing the sport closer to the long-awaited "one world" concept.

Dan had ideas, lots of them. One was that a rear-engined car could win at Indianapolis. He knew the man who built a rear-engined racing chassis better than anyone, and he thought he knew a factory that could stuff a V8 into it.

There was A.C.B. Chapman, Esq., B.Sc. (Eng.), the head man of a company with the unlikely name of Lotus. A trim-mustached Englishman in his mid-thirties who bore a faint resemblance to David Niven, his primary outward feature was his arrogance. He had, however, a right to that attitude; from the time he left the Royal Air Force in the late 1940s and started welding up ridiculously light vehicles of his own design, they usually held the road better than anyone else's. They didn't always win, because sometimes the execution of the design was rather sloppy, and most of the time he didn't have a competitive power plant, but persons who understood these things knew Chapman was *the* forward thinker in the business. By 1962 Chapman had introduced a new concept in grand prix design with his monocoque body-cum-chassis, and by 1962 he had a driver with the talent to push the car to the world championship. He wasn't interested in Indianapolis, until Gurney talked him into it.

There was Jimmy Clark, a slim young Scotsman from the Berwickshire hills. By 1962 it was obvious he was a great driver and might eventually be the best of them all. At first he knew little and cared less about Indianapolis, but as he got more and more involved with the event it became of prime importance to him. Within a few years he was not only to become the dominant driver at the Speedway, but he would also revise many American opinions about the abilities of European pilots.

There was Bill Gay, a cigar-chewing engineer on his way up at Ford, who perhaps best exemplified the New Breed in the corporation. He didn't know much about racing, but he knew how to build engines. He was confident of his ability to build a good one, and he didn't mind someone taking his engine and running it as fast as they could. After Gay moved on (and up) there was another man who took over, A.J. (Gus) Scussel. First he had to take what Gay had started and convert it into a more sophisticated power plant. Then he had to take this engine and teach a lot of mechanics how to maintain it. The engine demanded more and better care than they had ever given anything before, and the behind-the-scenes work was as great an accomplishment as winning the race itself. The only trouble was neither Scussel nor his men ever got credit for it.

Then there were Parnelli Jones, A.J. Foyt, Rodger Ward and Bobby Marshman. They were all Indianapolis heroes of the old school.

Cast in the bad-guy role, despite his habitual white Stetson, was J.C. Agajanian. The archetype of the Establishment that ran USAC, the sanctioning club, and one of the leading car owners, the likeable millionaire from California was castigated for standing in the way of progress when all he was trying to do was protect his own interests.

One of the most important was a tall, dark-haired, hard-faced veteran of the company named Leo Beebe. Raised practically in the shadow of the Rouge plant, Beebe wasn't interested in college until a few months of manhandling bodies on a Ford assembly line convinced him the University of Michigan was better. By the time he was graduated in 1939, he'd won six letters and the Big Ten award for athletes who excelled in scholarship.

After college Beebe wanted to be a coach and wound up in Leslie, Mich., where they let him coach to his heart's content. He coached football, baseball, basketball and track, taught English, math, science and gym, and took care of a homeroom—all for $1,500 a year. Soon after the United States entered the war, he joined the Navy as a chief petty officer in the Gene Tunney physical fitness program. The next thing he knew he was back in Dearborn as part of the cadre for a machinists mates, pipefitters and technicians' school at the south end of the Rouge. When he arrived, along with several other CPOs, they were assigned as seconds in command to the various ensigns who were barracks officers. Beebe was sent to Barracks G, where he was told he would find Ensign Ford. When he got there, he discovered the ensign's first name was Henry.

Four years later Beebe went to work for Ford, this time as the man who set up the company's employee recreation program. In the next 20 years he did various things, and many of them were jobs in which he had to clean up. He was the last man on the Edsel payroll when he played a role in shutting down the ill-fated venture. Twice the company turned him loose, at Washington's request, to help the government. The first time he resettled 33,000 Hungarian refugees after the mid-1950s revolution in that country, and when Florida threatened to become jammed with Cubans fleeing the Castro regime in 1961, he was called on to bring order there. By the spring of 1962 he was car and truck marketing manager for Ford International, working out of Brussels. Two years later, on an afternoon in early April, he was visiting a dealership in Switzerland when he got a telephone call from Harold Jones, the European group director.

"It was suggested that you be special vehicles manager at Ford Division," Jones said. "Are you interested?"

Beebe thought he might be, so Jones told him to hold the phone. In a moment Leo found himself talking to Iacocca on the transatlantic wire.

Iacocca described the position for him, saying it was primarily racing, with some promotion and public relations also involved.

"Are you offering me the job?" Beebe asked.

"Yes."

"I accept."

Within 10 days he was back in Dearborn and Iacocca told him the rest. It was simple: All he had to do was win at Indianapolis, Daytona and Le Mans, and also win the races leading up to these major efforts. Beebe had never seen a racing car, and did not know any of his assistants.

And when he got his first look at the races themselves, his thoughts were mainly how to get out.

To lend a Greek touch to the drama, the outcome of the first two acts was decided by an automotive form of *Deus ex Machina*. First it was a leaking oil tank, and the next year it was a defective set of tires.

When it came time for the third act, things had reverted to a more melodramatic interpretation. Justice—and the revolution—triumphed, and the hero went roaring off into the evening sun accompanied by the cheers of the crowd.

The scene, naturally, was the Indianapolis Motor Speedway, that giant, almost monolithic structure rising out of the plains of the Midwest. What tradition there is to American racing is almost all bound up with this 2½-mile rounded rectangle. More than just a race, the May 30 proceedings have become a sociological phenomena, and the crowd that assembles to watch is the world's largest one-day live audience for a sporting event.

DAN GURNEY AT POMONA

Almost as soon as Dan Gurney got into a really fast car, he became the darling of the fans and the magazine editors. (Top) He and his Ferrari grace the cover of the California Sports Car Club journal in early 1958. (Bottom) As an established international star, Gurney drove for the Porsche team in Formula I races in 1961 and 1962. At right: As long as it had wheels, Dan would drive it—here after the Big Bear cross-country race of 1958. (Inset) Working on the engine of his Cobra at Sebring, 1963.

When Gurney was a high school boy, growing up on Long Island in the years right after World War II, the midgets were a big thing, and the biggest of the midget stars was Phil Walters, later to become known as a sports car driver for the Briggs Cunningham team but then famous on the oval tracks under the steering-wheel pseudonym of Ted Tappet. There is a photograph extant of a bunch of kids standing behind the first turn at Freeport Municipal Stadium holding up two sheets joined together, and painted on them is "Ted Tappet Fan Club." Dan is at one end of the sign, which came out of Mrs. Gurney's linen closet.

When the family moved to California, life became a succession of such hot-rod staples as a 1927 Model T, a 1932 rail, a five-window chop top.... the dry lakes, unofficial, informal drag racing: They were the normal steps of an auto-oriented youth, with nothing to distinguish him from thousands of other kids in Southern California. A few years after he got back from Korea Dan had a Triumph TR2 and he drove his first race with it at Torrey Pines, north of San Diego. ("I finished, but at the end the wheels were so loose you could turn the lugs with your fingers.... I didn't know how to heel and toe, so I had a hell of a time getting slowed down and into the right gear for the corners....") From the TR2 he graduated to a Porsche 1600 Speedster, and soon the Mercedes 300 SLs in the area were having a hard time getting away from Dan at Pomona, Palm Springs and the other local courses. Then, in 1956, he had to quit; not enough money to raise a family and race at the same time. Instead he would go out on the dirt roads around Riverside at night, practicing for when he would get another chance. He picked up a ride here and there, and in one of them, a Corvette, he broke several local records. Then he got his break—a chance in a 4.9-liter Ferrari, a brute of a car which even experienced drivers found difficult to handle. His first race with it was in the fall of 1957 at the Riverside Grand Prix. He finished second to Carroll Shelby only when slowed by mechanical trouble at the end. The next race, at Palm Springs, was all Gurney's.

In the summer of 1958, with less than a dozen starts behind him, Dan was driving a Ferrari at Le Mans. He had it up to fourth after five hours when his co-driver was involved in an accident with a car that spun in front of him. From there Dan went to Monza, to watch the second invasion of the Italian autodrome by the Indianapolis cars and drivers. Oddly, it was his first look at America's premier machinery, and although he was impressed by the sight of his heroes, the obsolete design of the equipment was a surprise. In the next few years, as he drove grand prix races for Ferrari, for BRM and for Porsche, Gurney was in on the evolution of the Formula I car from a front-engined to a rear-engined vehicle. It was obviously the better way, and was proved to be time after time as lap speeds went up and up.

Then, in 1961, Jack Brabham took a 2.7-liter Cooper-Climax to Indianapolis and finished ninth despite a lengthy pit stop and a notable lack of power. Although some sports car fans got excited, Brabham's performance caused scarcely more than a ripple among the members of the tradition-bound Establishment. One of their solid-axle, Offenhauser-powered roadsters had won, and that was the way it was supposed to be. To Gurney, the outcome of the race showed that a rear-engined vehicle, built according to European ideas and propelled by a decent engine, must of necessity win the race. The next year was to be the key one, in which Gurney got his first ride in a rear-engined Indy car, and in which Dan got Chapman and Ford together.

The introduction to Ford (which many claim was an inevitability, considering Gurney's talents and their expanding program), came through coincidence: In the winter of 1962 the Daytona "500" followed on the heels of the Continental, Bill France's then-struggling sports car event. In order to bring about a closer association between the two, at the conclusion of the first race France asked Ford if they would make a car available to David Hobbs, a British driver who had competed in the Continental. No one seems to know the reason for picking him, but when Hobbs tried a Holman-Moody Ford on the high banks, it soon became evident he wasn't going to cut it. Then Holman suggested they get Gurney. Why not? He won the Continental, didn't he? The fact that Gurney, after doing well in practice, had his engine blow during the race, was of no importance. The big thing was that a contact had been made, and Gurney had met Passino. Now, if he were to call Dearborn, he knew someone there.

The next step in the course of events took place during the third week of May in Holland, where the Grand Prix of The Netherlands was being run at Zandvoort. Gurney was there as the number one driver on the Porsche team, and Chapman was there with Clark and the brand new Model 25, the first of the monocoques. The possibility of running something like this at the Speedway excited Dan so much he volunteered to pay Chapman's way to the race so the British designer could see it for himself. Chapman took him up on it, and on Memorial Day watched Gurney, in an underpowered, rear-engined car, built by Mickey Thompson and equipped with a modified Buick V8, run 92 laps before the transmission failed. On the way from Indianapolis to Monaco that night Gurney and Chapman were already working on basic dimensions, as was Don Frey on *his* way home from the same event.

Frey, his brother and Dave Evans had driven down the night before, spent the morning looking at the machinery, the afternoon watching the race, and were headed north again that evening when Frey finally gave voice to thoughts that had been going round in his head.

"Wouldn't it be great to build a Ford engine for Indianapolis!"

They talked about it the rest of the way home, then Frey got it moving. "You go to Misch (Herb Misch, the vice president of engineering) and get $50,000," he told Evans. "I'll find $50,000 and we'll see if we can't get something going."

Frey went to Bill Innes, then chief engineer of the Engine and Foundry Division, which had been doing some experimental work with Fairlane-sized aluminum blocks. "Why don't we take an aluminum engine, stick some Webers on it and see if we can't get an engine to go to Indy?"

"You're on," Innes replied, and the first steps were taken in that department. Within a few days, while he was outlining the proposition to Iacocca, Frey sent a memo to Evans requesting him to find a man to build the chassis, and the project was taken one step further. The initial approach of those in the Ford Division was conservative; the only constructors to enter the discussion were Americans, men with Indianapolis experience. Lujie Lesovsky, Quinn Epperly, Eddie Kuzma, Clint Brawner and A.J. Watson, with the latter's name predominating, were the men they discussed. Also among those discussed, and in this case brought in for a brain-picking session, were longtime Indianapolis car owner Lindsey Hopkins and Jack Beckley, his chief mechanic. Hopkins was already convinced, they found, that a rear-engined machine would win. After watching the Cooper in 1961, in fact, he had tried unsuccessfully to buy one. A few weeks later Gurney and Chapman came walking through the door, strictly on their own, on July 23. Since his visit to the Speedway Chapman had done his homework, and now he had a proposition that included necessary engine weight and minimum horsepower—the outlines of a Lotus he could build that would win the 500-mile race. Chapman met Frey and Passino first, then sat down to discuss his project with Innes and Gay. Gay knew only the barest details of Chapman's background and was somewhat nonplused by the simplicity of his demands and his assurance that he could win at Indianapolis. (Gay: "I was skeptical. Here was some Englishman who'd never raced there, and he said all he wanted was 350 horsepower and gasoline when all the others were getting 400 on methanol and nitromethane.")

Chapman, as a sophisticated European designer, had seen what stagnation of development had done to the Speedway vehicle. He could beat them, he reasoned, by making fewer pit stops for tires and fuel, and would accomplish this by making a smaller, lighter car that would also hold the road better in the sweeping turns. The conclusions he drew were so obvious they were almost painful. But the mystique that had been built up around the track was of such proportions it made persons automatically suspicious of anything not cast in the age-old, four-cylinder roadster mold. Gay was so dubious (after Chapman went back to England with a rough agreement to let him proceed) he brought in Watson. His views, naturally, were almost diametrically opposed to Chapman's—and his cars had won the 500 several times. Gay started to attend USAC races to check the level of competence for himself, and to see what Watson could do. One Monday, after a weekend of playing spectator, he told Passino, "If Watson hangs a wienie on the side of his car, within two days every car in USAC will have a wienie hanging from its side." It was plainly a game of follow the leader.

While Chapman, Clark and Gurney (still with Porsche) were back in Europe chasing the world championship (which Clark was to lose in the closing laps of the last race of the season), Gay and his small design team worked on the engine. They had the Indianapolis Motor Speedway surveyed, the first time this had been done in decades, to find out exactly what the course was like. They purchased an Offenhauser engine and ran it on a dynamometer to see what the opposition had. The Offy, they found, produced 407 horsepower at 6,000 rpm, and also turned out a healthy 383 pound-feet of torque at 4,800 rpm. They brought in Rodger Ward, a two-time winner, to have discussions on driving technique; where did one accelerate, and where did one brake? As insurance against what they felt was Chapman's impractical scheme of outrunning the Offys on less horsepower (Gay smiles about it now), a concurrent program was conducted to develop the engine for methanol. They got 400 horses at 6,800 rpm in this manner against 351 hp on gas. (Gay: "We felt that regardless of who was right, Watson or Chapman, we now had the horsepower.")

At this stage, despite a rumor or two that had circulated through the racing world, the project was still a small affair: The company had invested little money, contracts had not been signed, and Gay, Tom Landis, Ed Pinkerton, Gordon Ellis, Joe Macura and the rest of the engineers were working more or less in seclusion. Then, on the first Sunday in October, Clark won the United States Grand Prix at Watkins Glen and made quite an impression on the engineering department. From Watkins Glen, the Lotus was shipped to Indianapolis for testing. It was to be Clark's first meeting with the storied Speedway, and he did not care much for the manner in which he was received. As he wrote later in his autobiography, "Jim Clark at the Wheel":

"Everyone was very interested in our ploy. After all it was not every day that someone arrived with a puny little 1.5-liter racing car that produced only 175 b.h.p. on their sacred track and just to see that I was a good little boy the officials had invited a number of drivers along just to watch me go round and see that I did the correct thing at the correct time. This is one thing which really annoyed me. They treated me like a kid who had never raced before. On this first occasion I took things easily and tried to get the hang of driving around left hand corners all the time. Remember, the car had come straight from Watkins Glen so it was running on normal racing tires and was not set up for left-hand turns only and the banking. I did about 100 laps on that occasion and I remember thinking that it was all a bit dull. My fastest lap of 143 m.p.h. average made most people sit up and take notice but what made them even more interested was the speed at which I was taking the turns. The Indy cars rely on their acceleration between the bends to give them their high lap times and the fastest time an Indy car had recorded in the turn was something like 138 m.p.h. Our Lotus was doing over 140 on the corners...."

From there the car was shipped to Dearborn, where Lotus mechanics took it apart for Gay and his staff to examine before it went to Mexico City for the next grand prix. Ford wanted to buy it to use as a mobile test bed and Chapman agreed to sell one, but the idea was discarded when they realized there was no driver around who was familiar enough with the rear-engine configuration—and who would be available for extended tests. As an alternative, one of the early prototypes was installed in a Galaxie and taken to Daytona, where Nelson Stacy got it around in the high 140s on gas and in the mid-150s on methanol.

In late October Gay flew to England to finalize the engine design with Chapman so the power plant and the car would fit together properly. Then he went on to Bologna, the home of Weber carburetor. At Weber he had trouble getting in the

(Top) Don Branson, Leader Card Special, 1963.
(Middle) Jimmy Clark, Lotus-Ford, 1963.
(Bottom) Jim McElreath, Forbes Special, 1963.

(Top) A.J. Foyt, Sheraton-Thompson Special, 1963.
(Middle) Rodger Ward, Kaiser Aluminum Special, 1963.
(Bottom) Parnelli Jones, Agajanian's Willard Battery Special, 1963.

The big one: The Borg-Warner
Trophy, emblematic of
victory at Indianapolis.
(Below) How Ford engineers
viewed Gurney's fast lap at
Indianapolis—the lap that
saved the project from being
thrown into the wastebasket.
At right: (Bottom) The
development of the intake
and exhaust systems for Ford's
double overhead cam Indy engine.
(Top) A cutaway diagram of
the power plant, showing
how the valves are actuated
by the camshafts.

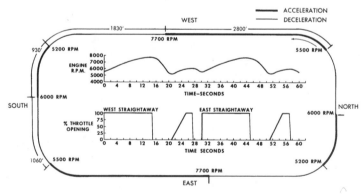

FORD LOTUS VEHICLE—INDIANAPOLIS TRACK

MARCH 27, 1963
AVERAGE SPEED 150.501 M.P.H.

door. When Gay called from London, chief engineer Francesco Bellicardi told him he was wasting his time; Weber didn't see any opportunity to transform this project into something they could sell at a profit, so what was the use?

But Gay talked Bellicardi into at least seeing him. When they met in the reception room, the first thing Bellicardi said was "I remember you." He and Gay had lunched together several years earlier, when Bellicardi was on a tour of Detroit manufacturing facilities, and the Italian hadn't forgotten. "I was in a strange country and I didn't know much of the language," he said, "and you helped me. So now I will help you. What do you want?"

The pair stayed up most of the night designing a set of 58-millimeter carburetors for the engine. Ford got what it needed thanks to a chance meeting.

But when Gay returned to Dearborn he found the program had budget trouble. Added to this was the constant argument over gas versus methanol, magnetos versus battery ignition, carburetors as opposed to fuel injection—with management and Chapman wanting to go the route most similar to that used on a production car, and the engineers in favor of maximum horsepower. So the program was canceled. No work was done after November.

Then, one day in January, Innes walked into Gay's office. "We're going to Indianapolis," he said, "and we're going second class." That meant gasoline and the rest of the low-power (and better fuel consumption) equipment. They resurrected an engine and quietly installed it in a Cobra Gurney was to drive in the Daytona Continental. The engine gave nothing but trouble, the engineers worked right up to the start of the race—in fact until after the race was started, as Dan got away late—and the car was not competitive. Gay went back to Dearborn more depressed than ever.

"What's the problem?" Innes asked.

"Lots," Gay answered, and proceeded to list them.

"Fine," Innes told him. "I'll give you what you need to fix them."

At this stage, in February, there were still only two prototype engines in existence, and the design was a long way from finalization. By mid March Chapman had completed a car and it was flown to Kingman, Ariz., for tests on the Ford proving grounds. Although they got the vehicle up to a speed of 165 mph, the tests were a flop; the engine was not reliable. From Kingman, Chapman and Gurney went back to Dearborn and confronted Gay.

"We don't want to go with you," they said. "You've got major problems." Gurney wanted to turn the prototypes over to a California group he felt could get them ready. Chapman was generally unhappy; after all, it wasn't the chassis that was causing the trouble. Gay is at his best in a crisis, and here was the entire Indianapolis program going down the drain right in front of him. So he did the only thing he could.

"You're right," he said, "but I have the corrections to the problems, and I'd like to go to Indianapolis next week and establish that we've got a competitive vehicle."

He talked Chapman and Gurney into it, and that afternoon they presented a united front when they met with Frey and Innes. It was agreed—one last shot.

A few days before the lone revised engine was to be shipped it was being run in on the dynamometer. Suddenly the camshaft broke, and there was the harsh sound of twisted metal. Gay went home, crushed.

Late that night, while sitting around the house, he was still thinking about the engine. There hadn't been too much damage, but how was he to correct the trouble? In his hand he had one of his son's toys, a working plastic model of an engine, and as he looked at it, he worked out in his mind the changes that would have to be made. Early the next morning they were back at it again, and when the rest of the engineering department went home that night, they stayed. With 48 hours of nonstop effort this small group of men, some engineers and some mechanics from the engine-build shop, had effected a complete design change and build on the valve train, and the engine went up to 365 horsepower in the bargain.

Hurriedly, the last-chance engine was loaded on a chartered aircraft and flown to Indianapolis, where Chapman, Clark and Gurney were waiting. The rush was so great that when they arrived it was found several vital parts were missing—so they rented two Fairlanes, which had a more mundane version of the engine under their hoods. Wiring harnesses, ignition brackets and the like were cannibalized and sneaked into the garage while local newspapermen waited for the debut. When the car was wheeled out on the afternoon of March 24, the long-awaited end product of a supposed mass dollar expenditure and all-out engineering effort by one of the world's largest corporations, there wasn't an outsider in the place with even the slightest suspicion this was strictly a shoestring, last-gasp effort.

One of the newspapermen looked at the Lotus, looked around the garage, and then turned to Gay. "Where are your spare engines?" he asked.

Gay shrugged. "I can only see room for one engine and one driver in that thing. If you can show me a place for another engine..." The reporter backed off, sheepish after Gay's matter-of-fact answer and totally unaware of the true state of affairs. On March 25 Clark got up to 146 and a fraction, then they were shut down by wind and rain for 1½ days, and Chapman and Clark flew back to England for a race at Snetterton. On the 27th, Gurney slowly worked his way up to 149-plus, and that night they changed the final drive ratio from 3.295 to 3.477. The next day, after trying Firestones (which were slower), he switched back to Dunlop and shortly after 5:30 that afternoon he cracked the magic 150 mark. The official watch read 59.78 seconds. The average, second fastest in the half-century history of the Brickyard, was 150.501.

By the time the engine got back to Dearborn it had covered 457 miles, including 390 at racing speeds, with little or no difficulty.

Within a few days contracts were signed with Chapman, three entries (one a spare) were made for the race, and the project got moving in earnest. Two new cars were built for the race and the "mule," or development vehicle, was entered in case anything happened to the first two. The design of the modified pushrod engine, dubbed AX230-2, was frozen two weeks after Gurney's run, and work was in progress on the engines to be used in practice and the race. From here there was no turning back, and the company's engineering reputation now rested on a small batch of pushrod-operated V8s, down on power to an established, well-developed double-overhead cam racing design, running in proven vehicles.

And the Ford Motor Company wasn't a particularly welcome guest.

There were few places in the racing world more provincial than the Indianapolis Motor Speedway and environs in the spring of 1963. They were used to doing things their own way—widely advertised, naturally, as the best way—and the Establishment didn't take to this sudden invasion of the premises by a large corporation, a revolutionary design and a bunch of foreigners with strange accents. Even the color of Clark's car was abhorrent. It was painted the Lotus shade of British Racing Green—and green had for years been a strictly bad-luck color in American oval-track competition.

Although varying reasons were given for the dislike, the basic one was simple: Ford had a better idea, to paraphrase one of the corporation's advertising slogans of a few years later, and almost everyone at the Speedway knew it. The tiny green car, looking ludicrous when compared to the big, flashily chromed roadsters, had gone 150 mph practically right out of the box, and it had them confused. It had, in those 59.78 seconds Gurney took for his quick lap in March, told the Establishment they had been worshipping false idols. Nobody likes to be told they have been stupid, hence the reactions that followed. About the only Indianapolis veteran smart enough to realize the jig was up (or would be in short order) was Ward. A month before the race, and even before official practice began, he said, "The cars to watch are the Lotuses. The only way we can hope to catch them is on the pit stops. We'll be able to keep them in sight, but if they run the race with only one pit stop, and it's a quick one, they can beat us." The rest of them should also have realized the situation—especially since in April Lloyd Ruby, driving an older-model Lotus with a relatively weak 2.5-liter Climax engine, had set a record qualifying at Trenton.

When the new Lotuses arrived at the track, they showed several improvements that were not on the practice car that went so quickly in March. For one thing the suspensions were offset, allowing the vehicles to make the steady diet of left turns at a somewhat higher rate of speed. For another, the cars were sporting brand-new 15-inch Firestone tires instead of the Dunlops used through most of the early testing. Firestone had been in possession of a virtual lock on the tire business at Indianapolis for four decades, and although its domination at the Speedway had been primarily by default of the other manufacturers, the company nevertheless used its annual victory as the subject of a big-budget advertising campaign. As is normal when any company has a monopoly in any field, development had slowed to a crawl. The only models available were 18-inchers for the rear wheels and 16s for the front. Now, suddenly, here came Lotus, looking like a threat, and with a car designed for 15-inch wheels. Firestone quickly made suitable tires available, and the rest of the Establishment screamed. The last straw, the one that set the drivers off, was Gurney's 149-mile lap on May 6. In short order there was a petition from the car owners asking Firestone to withdraw the 15-inchers or make them available to everyone. (The company had also produced a batch of extra-wide 12-inch doughnuts for Mickey Thompson's new rear-engined vehicles, but since Thompson's entries were not going quickly, no one said a word about them.) Firestone at first demurred, which caused no end of commotion among the drivers in general and A.J. Foyt in particular. This led to meetings at which nothing was accomplished and to Foyt's contacting Goodyear for a supply of their 15-inch stock car rubber. Between Goodyear's appearance and the general bad press the situation was receiving, Firestone finally consented to make the new tires available to everyone and the focus shifted to wheels. Ted Halibrand, the regular supplier to the Speedway crowd, had only a limited number of 15-inch models available. Although he promised to work overtime for the next two weeks it was unlikely he could make enough to outfit all the cars.

It was better than a three-ring circus: tire problems here, funny-looking Lotuses there—and in the middle of it Chapman and Clark flew back to England for the *Daily Express* Formula I race at Silverstone on May 11. Clark won, as he did in 20 of the 32 races he entered that season, but the sight of their prize package (and prize designer) shuttling back and forth across the ocean to do non-Indianapolis things was quite unsettling to Ford.

By the week before qualifying it was apparent the main opposition to the Fords would come from one man—Rufus Parnell (Parnelli) Jones, who a half-dozen years earlier had been a young Ford stock car driver in California. Every so often there appears at Indianapolis a man who almost immediately dominates the place, and Parnelli was one of these. In his debut year of 1961 he qualified fifth fastest and was leading the race when slowed by ignition troubles. In 1962 he became the first man to crack the 150-mile barrier and was comfortably in the lead when he was hampered by brake line failure and finished seventh. This time, once again at the wheel of Agajanian's car, he made it clear he was number one. On May 12, aided by the 15-inch tires (about which he had said little), he topped 152, and on May 15 and 16 he was over 153. It was ironic that the Ford computers, which reckoned 150.5 mph as the top speed for an Offenhauser-powered roadster, had not been able to take into account any tire improvement for the Offys; the tires that had been built for the Lotuses were also adding speed to the opposition.

Wheels, not tires, were the Lotus problem. The Dunlop rims with which the cars were originally equipped were inferior to the wider Halibrands. They managed to get a pair of the Halibrand rears from Yunick, after Curtis Turner wrecked Smokey's car in practice, and they had them remachined to fit the Lotus hubs. The improvement in roadholding was noticeable. The problem rested in the fact that there was

At left: (Bottom) Jimmy Clark giving the Lotus-Ford one of its first test runs at Silverstone, England, in the late winter of 1963. (Top) A few weeks later he and the car were at Kingman, Ariz., for further trials. (Above) Gurney and his car at speed during the 1963 running of the "500." (Bottom) Clark and Ford's first USAC single-seater victory— on the way to the checkered flag at Milwaukee in August 1963.

(Top) Johnny Boyd, Vita-Fresh Orange Juice Special, 1964.
(Middle) Jimmy Clark, Lotus-Ford, 1964.
(Bottom) Dan Gurney, Lotus-Ford, 1964.

(Top) Eddie Sachs, American Red Ball Special, 1964.
(Middle) Bobby Marshman, Pure Firebird Special, 1964.
(Bottom) Rodger Ward, Kaiser Aluminum Special, 1964.

(Top) A.J. Foyt, Sheraton-Thompson Special, 1964.
(Middle) Dave MacDonald, Sears Allstate Special, 1964.
(Bottom) Lloyd Ruby, Forbes Special, 1964.

(Top) Clark brings his crippled Lotus to a halt in the first turn after dragging his broken rear suspension the length of the straight and somehow managing to keep control. (Bottom) Ward at Trenton in 1964, driving A.J. Watson-built car that was one of the first American designs to employ the Ford engine. The vehicle was only partially successful.

only one set of wheels for two cars and no way to get more before qualifying, 48 hours away. It was decided to let Clark and Gurney share the set. Gay also wanted the cars to run their 10-mile efforts with injection systems and methanol (this would give them an additional 2.5 mph) and then switch back to carburetors and gasoline for the race. Then the weather took over. The day before qualifying brought rain, closing the track and making it impossible to undertake shakedown runs with the injection system. In addition it was found the British fuel bags in the Lotuses would not handle methanol. "We'll run the race setup," Gay said, and that was that—except the problems had just begun.

The biggest sporting event in the United States is the Indianapolis "500." The second biggest also takes place at the Speedway, and is the first of the four days of qualifying trials, the one on which the fastest man gets the coveted pole position. Almost 200,000 persons were sitting in the giant grandstands or lay sprawled around the infield on a chill, windy May 18 as warm-up runs began shortly after 9 a.m. Soon most of them were watching Gurney, whose white Lotus, complete with its blue stripe and a big number 93, was starting to move quickly. He hit 151, then 152—and then he hit the wall in the first turn. Gurney was unhurt but the car was a mess, and so were the only pair of wide-rim 15 inch wheels owned by the Ford Motor Company. Clark had to qualify on the narrower Dunlop wheels, and the mechanics, engineers and everyone else who could lend a hand set to work taking usable pieces off the wrecked car to get the "mule" in shape.

While this frantic activity was going on in Gasoline Alley, Clark went out and qualified at 149.750 mph for fifth best time, and was greeted with the gratuitous comment, "that's pretty good for a rookie," as the public address announcer informed the crowd of his achievement. Jones was the fastest, setting a record of 151.153 despite the winds, and joining him in the front row were Jim Hurtubise in the supercharged Novi (150.357) and Don Branson (150.188). Ward had the inside spot in the second row with 149.800, then came Clark, and Jim McElreath (149.744) was the outside man in the second row. At least Jimmy was in, and as soon as he finished the car was wheeled back to the garage to be stripped of various pieces needed for Gurney. Late in the afternoon they somehow had the car ready and Dan went out. He turned in three laps at close to 150, and then, on his fourth, with everyone waiting anxiously for his time, he headed for the pit lane. Gurney's foot had caught on the throttle strap and in disentangling it he had lost valuable time. Then the six o'clock gun sounded. It was over for the day, and if Gurney did not qualify on Sunday he would have to miss the Grand Prix of Monaco, scheduled for the following weekend. He made it, coming in Sunday with an average of 149.019 to squeeze into the fourth row. Then Chapman, Clark and Gurney dashed for a helicopter, while Gay and the mechanics were left with the cars. The trio could have stayed at the Speedway. For Clark, Monte Carlo proved to be the only world championship race he failed to finish in 1963 (he won seven of the 10), retiring while in the lead after 79 laps. Gurney lasted only 26 of the 100 laps before the gearbox in his Brabham failed.

Meanwhile, members of the Establishment and its hangers-on were busy trying to find reasons why the Ford could not finish, and the cars were being readied for the race. The local Ford plant had machined enough 15-inch wheels to fit the Lotus hubs, so at least that worry was out of the way. But on the day before the race Gay found another one. Being unfamiliar with the starting procedure, he asked someone how it was done. They explained you had just so long to get your car going, and if it was not accomplished in that time, the car was pushed aside and the vehicle always held in reserve got its chance instead. Gay turned around and saw only one battery cart for two cars. So he went out and borrowed one from Mickey Thompson, who had an extra. When they brought it back to the garage, the mechanics went through a dry run to make sure everything worked. The starter shaft snapped off inside the transmission, and they spent some time fishing it out and getting another. At the same time, because the British mechanics had no comprehension of Indianapolis' high-speed pit stops, and because they hadn't time to practice, the task of getting a pit crew together was begun at almost the very last minute. Pete Wiseman, a transmission designer from Chicago, was given the assignment of handling the hose; a hurried call was put into the Atlanta base of Bill Stroppe's Mercury stock car operation, and the rest of the crew was assembled and put on a plane for Indiana. When they arrived, the evening before the race, they found they had to work the night through to get things in some sort of readiness—and they had never seen a Lotus before, much less worked on one.

On the morning of the big event the Speedway was the focal point of the annual frenzy that grips Indianapolis. The entire event is larger than life, with the hundreds of thousands of holiday-mood spectators, the dozens of bands, the convertibles filled with minor—and some major—celebrities, the singing of "Back Home Again in Indiana," the playing of "Taps" and the traditional call of "Gentlemen, start your engines!"

There are numerous great moments in sports: the sight of a Kentucky Derby field breaking from the gate, a Willie Mays making a great World Series catch in the outer reaches of the Polo Grounds with his back to the plate, a Herb Elliott making the world's best look like amateurs as he sprints home to win an Olympic 1,500 meters or a pack of unlimited hydros kicking up rooster tails as they streak across the waters off Seattle. All of these pale in comparison with the start of an Indianapolis "500," with the sight of that 33-car field coming roaring and streaming down the front straight, exploding in a cacophony of high-speed color and even higher drama as they set out on that 500-mile chase. It is an emotional, even visceral experience, with the sound level assuming such proportions it is almost a physical weight.

And this time, toward the front of the howling maelstrom, there were two spiderlike contraptions, almost lost in the shuffle, bearing the hopes, the fears and the reputations of both Lotus and Ford.

Hurtubise, thanks to the extraordinary power of his Novi and his own personal courage, led the first lap, and then Jones took over and started to pull away. By

50 miles Parnelli, running at 150, was leading the field by 22 seconds and was being chased by a six-car pack which included Hurtubise, Roger McCluskey, Jim McElreath, Marshman, Foyt and Ward. Gurney and Clark, right behind, were running 10th and 11th and were seemingly making no attempt to catch up. Yellow caution flags for various minor accidents kept Jones from stretching his advantage, and when he went in for his first pit stop after 63 laps, McCluskey, driving the race of his life, moved into the lead. Four laps later McCluskey went in to refuel, and the pair of tiny Fords, which had worked their way toward the front, were running first and second.

(Clark: "I never really stuck my neck out the whole race. During the first 30 laps, in fact, I ran very easily because I was in the big draft of about 11 cars and I could see everything that was going on in front of me.... I could count every car ... that was going to have to stop before I was. Parnelli was a little farther ahead, but as long as he wasn't too far out in front I didn't worry about it.")

Running at a steady 148, Clark and Gurney maintained their lead until lap 92, when the word came in from the track observers that Gurney had tire trouble; they could see the white of the carcass. On lap 93 Gurney came in, changed tires and took on fuel. Chapman had calculated the tire wear at something over 100 laps, but as was found later, Gurney's poor chassis setup, caused by the lack of time with a rebuilt car and Dan's Monaco trip, had caused a much higher rate of wear. His relatively long stop of 42 seconds, plus the knowledge that he would have to stop at least once more, put him practically out of contention. Fearing Clark's car might be in the same trouble, Chapman called him in after lap 95. When Jimmy charged into the pits, he stopped with his front wheels on the marks painted for the rear ones, and it took 10 seconds of yelling to get him to move. Clark had a peculiar expression on his face, looking almost as if dazed, and it was not until Wiseman inadvertently spilled some of the fuel on him that he seemed to come to life. In another 33 seconds the job was done and Jimmy was gone again, making up with his four-speed transmission what the pit crew had lost through its inexperience. When he rejoined the race, now behind Parnelli, a look at the tires showed Chapman they were not nearly as bad as Gurney's and there would be no trouble running the rest of the way nonstop. The refueling, unknown to anyone at the time, had led to a humorous mixup which could have been disastrous. Gay, in charge of calculating this, was so excited he used the car numbers for his figuring instead of the number of laps left. "It was a good thing they were 92 and 93," he said later. "When I checked the tanks after the race Clark had four-tenths of a gallon and Dan a little less than a gallon!"

At the halfway point Jones was first and running strong, Clark was second, and the rest of the field was nowhere—including Gurney, who had dropped to ninth. Then two laps later the black flag went out for Hurtubise, running third. At the driver's meeting the day before, chief steward Harlan Fengler had cautioned the assemblage about leaking oil, be it from tanks or engines, and warned that any car found dripping *anything* liquid on the race track would be summarily banned. "And if you don't believe me," Fengler wound up, "just try me." Now he was sticking to his word. Hurtubise's car had a leak, and it was pushed back to the garage area.

Jones came in for his second stop on lap 126, and got lucky; just as he pulled in Lloyd Ruby smacked the wall and the yellow caution flag went out, causing the field to run at reduced speed until the track was clear again. Parnelli was able to get back out before Clark came around, and he returned to building his lead, knowing he would have to make still a third pit stop while Clark could run the rest of the way. By the 400-mile mark it was obvious only Clark stood even the remotest chance of catching the flying Jones. Foyt, in third place, and Gurney, who had worked his way back up to fourth, were too far out of it—and besides, Gurney had that other pit stop scheduled. At 163 laps Jones pitted again (and again under the yellow flag) and was back in action in only 21 seconds. Now Clark was a mere 12 seconds astern.

Then the picture changed. In the previous instances as soon as Parnelli came out of the pits, he had gone faster and moved ahead. Now Clark started to shave the margin, at first imperceptibly, then in big chunks. By lap 172, the difference was 10 seconds. By lap 176 it was only six seconds. The next time around it was only 4.5, a matter of several hundred yards, and the crowd was going wild. And then the yellow light went on again. Eddie Sachs had hit the wall in the first turn, and as the field slowed and Jones went past the start-finish line, McCluskey pulled alongside the leader and pointed to the side of Parnelli's car, trying to direct the starter's attention to something. That something was the oil tank on the big number 98, which had cracked and which was laying a stream of the stuff on the side of the car, on a rear tire and on the ground. All of this was not obvious to the main grandstand or the press box (the oil tank was on the left side), but those in the pits could see it, and in a flash Chapman was standing next to Fengler. "You know what you've said about oil leaking," Chapman yelled. "Now what are you going to do about it?" Someone handed the black flag to starter Pat Vidan, but before Jones could come around again Agajanian had run up to join the discussion and was defending his driver, saying the leak had stopped now that the oil had run down to the bottom of the crack, saying anything he could think of to keep his car in the lead. Regardless of what the situation was, with his car out front just minutes from the end of the world's richest auto race, Agajanian could not—in retrospect—be blamed for doing everything to keep it there. The fault was with the officials, who were vacillating. With Aggie being a member of the Establishment, and with Chapman an outsider, Parnelli stayed where he was.

(Clark: "I could see Parnelli up front and I could see that he was losing oil. I really can't say if it was all from Parnelli or not, but even on the straights at 180 I could see lines of oil. I figured well, if I can actually see the oil on the track he must be losing it something shocking. I suddenly went completely sideways, and I was lucky to collect it again. Then, in the next turn, I saw Sachs do the same thing, only he wasn't so lucky. I said to myself, 'We've come this far, its bloody silly to pile into the wall in the last 20 laps.'")

Eddie Sachs: Always a comedian, and everybody thought all his exits were laughing ones, but at Indianapolis in 1964 he went out in a ball of flame and a giant smoke cloud. When his partially incinerated car was towed away, there were many in the pits who couldn't look at it.

Pit stops were one of the Lotus team's main weaknesses in both 1963 and 1964. (Top) Clark gets ready to take the track again after his lone pause for gas and a change of tires, 1963. Chief mechanic Jim Endruweit has his back to the camera, while Bill Stroppe is on the left rear wheel and Pete Wiseman (at right) has finished the refueling. (Bottom) Gurney during one of his 1964 pit stops, in which everyone seems to be confused. As it turned out, tire trouble made Gurney's lengthy stays in the pits academic.

(Top) Clark taking the flag that signifies the winner after leading from wire to wire at Milwaukee in 1963. (Bottom) An exhausted Scotsman and Colin Chapman (left) after finishing second at Indianapolis the same year.

Leo Beebe, the man who never saw a race—until he became directly responsible for winning a lot of them for the Ford Motor Company.

Parnelli Jones pulls away from his pit during the 1964 "500," not knowing his fuel tank is on fire. The shimmering waves above his head are the burning of the alcohol-based substance. He was lucky to get out of it.

Jones, once he got used to the Lotus in 1964, was practically unbeatable in the car. Here he is on his way to winning the September race at Trenton that year. Clark, driving the other team entry, did not finish.

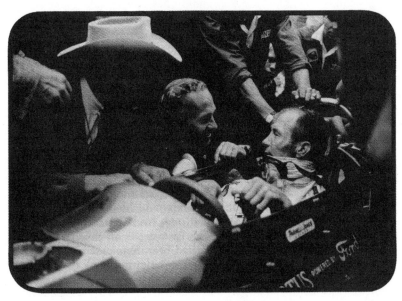

Chapman (center) and J.C. Agajanian, complete with his usual Stetson, congratulate Jones after his late-summer victory at Milwaukee, 1964.

Not only oil, but the constant use of the yellow flag was going to cause more comment after it was all over. On Europe's road courses, when the yellow flag is shown this is done only in the immediate vicinity of the accident, and drivers slow down only in this area of the circuit. Clark, who had spent his entire career under these rules, was now faced with something new; at Indianapolis, when the yellow goes out, it is displayed all around the track, and the law says there shall be no passing. What Clark was not aware of is that you can pass a car that is markedly slower than yours, or one that is not in contention—and also that practically everyone cheats on the backstretch at Indianapolis (providing the accident is not there), running at near-racing speeds for as long as the officials in the pits can't see it.

(Clark, after the race: "I wouldn't have known about it yet, but I was running on the yellow with A.J. Foyt toward the end and he *passed* this bloke. I said to myself 'Hey, he hadn't ought to do that,' but within one or two laps he had the length of the bloody straight on me, and I figured I'd better get going before he came all the way around and caught me. So I passed this bloke myself, and nobody said anything about it.")

By the time the green replaced the yellow again, Jones had wisely stretched his lead a bit by running hard down the back chute, and that was it—except that three laps from the finish the yellow light went on for the ninth time when McCluskey spun out trying to pass Jones going into the third turn—a foolish maneuver considering he was running third, a few laps behind, and the track was slippery. The actual margin at the finish was 33.83 seconds, and Gurney was seventh despite two late pit stops (including one caused by the crew failing to tighten a wheel properly and forcing him to come back).

When it was over, the reactions were varied. Gay, for one, was just exhausted ("I didn't think we had done anything miraculous; I was just plain tired"), and most of the other Ford officials were disconsolate. (Passino: "It had been a lifetime chance, and I was crushed. First it had been 'If we can just get them qualified,' and then when we qualified it was 'Oh boy,' then it was 'If we can only win' and then, toward the end of the race, it was 'We must win' ... and then it ended the way it did.")

Considering the situation, the company had come out of it with the best possible image. Had Fengler black-flagged the Agajanian car, accusations of Ford money buying the victory would have been inevitable and the victory would have been a tainted one. And the fact remained, Parnelli had been the fastest driver in the fastest car on that particular day, even though the rest of the roadsters had been outclassed by the Lotuses. It was unfortunate his performance had to be dimmed by the accusations and counter-accusations which went on for months. Jones himself added fuel to the fire the day after the race, when the voluble Sachs goaded him at an Autolite luncheon. Sachs eventually called Parnelli a liar, and when Jones asked him to repeat this, he did. Parnelli then finished (or started, depending on your outlook) the proceedings by hitting Sachs in the mouth, decking him. What Jones had not realized was the free meal had attracted almost as many newspapermen as did the race, and they had a ringside seat for the bout. The resultant publicity did not help the affair.

Chapman and Clark were understandably miffed. They felt the muddled yellow flag rule had cost them valuable time (someone estimated it to be 59 seconds), and they were bitter over the oil incident, even though they managed to be diplomatic about it. Clark, tired of the condescending treatment he had received as a rookie and a foreigner, let loose with a few opinions on the race, now that he had shown what he could do. "What beat us?" he asked. "Well, I think it was the yellow flag, and the black flag, and the rules and things. Given an equal chance and a break or two, we should have lapped Parnelli. I'm not really keen to come back, except that it is quite a lot of money. Don't get me wrong, I enjoyed doing it. But for me, personally, as a driver, all the ballyhoo and hoo-ha doesn't have much to do with motor racing. I think I'd really rather run in Europe ... I think the grand prix circuit is tougher; I have blisters from last week's race at Monaco but none from this one." He did, however, have his share of the $55,000 earned by his car. It was not nearly as much as the $149,000 collected by Jones, but it was considerably more than he'd ever earned for winning anything in Europe, and Ford threw in another $20,000 for qualifying two cars and another $25,000 for finishing second. In addition Ford had paid all expenses, and when the company added the bill the feeling in Dearborn was that while Chapman might be a great designer, he was an even better businessman.

The primary result of Ford's participation in the "500" was to provide Iacocca's favorite word—excitement. After almost two decades in which the race had degenerated into a landmark of engineering rigor mortis (and turned into more of a holiday affair than anything else), Ford had now lent a new dimension to it. The Indianapolis "500," as it richly deserved to be, once more became an international proving ground for new ideas. It didn't make any difference that the ideas being tested had been tried successfully in Europe several seasons earlier. The big thing was that Ford had brought them over here. With this effort the Ford party line, which emphasized "open competition," was given real meaning. It had been years since a major American manufacturer (coincidentally Ford, in 1935) had been courageous enough to lay itself open for criticism at America's biggest race. It was more than coincidental that Gay later that year received an award from the Racing Fraternity of Greater New York. It wasn't that this organization was capable of awarding anything comparable to a Pulitzer Prize—it was the fact that American fandom had been made engineering conscious. That was almost as satisfying to Gay as was the condition of Clark's engine after the race. When run on a dynamometer, it was found to have actually picked up horsepower during the race: The 500 miles of extra "running in" had boosted it from 365 horsepower to 376.

If there was any doubt in anyone's mind as to the potential of the Lotus-Ford combination, it was dispelled 10 weeks later at Milwaukee, where the two cars were entered for the second time. Both Clark and Gurney had been to a mid-July practice session at the one-mile paved oval, and the results were encouraging as both circulated at speeds better than the track record. Now, in mid-August, they figured to be even faster, as Clark's car was equipped with new 48-millimeter Webers (the only set available; Gurney had to make do with the old 58 mm version) and Dunlop tires, which stuck better than the Firestones and wouldn't take an Indianapolis-type beating in this slower race. They were ready. In practice Clark shattered all marks by clicking off a best lap of 32.93 seconds, an average of 109.3 mph. Gurney was next at 33.09, and Foyt had the fastest of the front-engined dinosaurs with 33.74. In the 200-mile race Clark was just as dominant. He led right from the flag and was never in danger, lapping everyone in the field save for one car. Gurney, who ran second to his teammate for the first 80 laps, was troubled by poor carburetion in the turns and was passed by Foyt at that point on the course. For Clark, the remainder of the event was a brilliant *tour de force* as he swept cleanly, almost majestically, through Milwaukee's two wide bends, while all the others were working twice as hard to make it through only half as quickly. As a final bit of adding insult to injury, when Clark came up behind Foyt, rather than pass him, he contented himself with staying right there, taking it easy while Foyt drove harder than ever to save himself from being lapped. There were a few of the opinion that Clark hadn't gone around A.J. for another reason: At Indianapolis Foyt had taken the Scotsman right to the wall when Jimmy passed him, and perhaps Clark wanted to ensure that this wouldn't happen again. But it made little difference, and his staying behind the Texan made the situation all the more humorous. Gurney was third and grudgingly, even the most reactionary of the old-line USAC supporters had to admit Clark and the Lotus were really something (the fact that Jimmy, in a similar Lotus but with Climax engine, had just clinched the world championship meant little to them; that was part of the "sporty car" business).

The Trenton "200," in late September, was scheduled to be a repeat of the triumphal procession at Milwaukee, and it started out that way. Qualifying saw Clark and Gurney both go under the record for the one-mile track and the start of the race saw them pull steadily away, until the 49th lap. Then Clark was through for the day. The car had burst an oil line that led from the dry sump system back to the engine, primarily because the hose should have been replaced after Milwaukee but was not. Then Gurney took over and with two-thirds of the event done, it was all his, he thought. Then Dan's car went out through a freak mishap: A tang on one of the pistons broke off, fell down into the lubrication system and blocked the pump that drove the oil from the pan back to the tank. The result was that the engine literally drowned in its own oil. Foyt wound up winning the race, which was of minor importance, and which was to be the last appearance for a pushrod Ford V8 in USAC oval-track racing. It was close to the end of the season, and back in Dearborn there was the start of a new phase of the engine program, both in organization and development.

Gay, who had been making his mark in the company, was promoted to be in charge of a new tractor engine design program, and responsibility for future work on the new double overhead camshaft Indianapolis engine was transferred to Scussel, who had been in charge of development work on stock car engines and who was now being put in command of a separate advanced group which would operate under Engine and Foundry Division and take care of all competition matters.

For 1964 Chapman was once again head of the main team for Indianapolis, with Clark and Gurney driving, and engines were loaned to others Ford figured capable of winning. The first to be taken into consideration was Hopkins, as a form of repayment for his assistance at the beginning of the program. Ford also sold him one of the 1963 cars (actually the one Gurney crashed just before qualifying, now rebuilt). This was not only to be used for racing in 1964, but was also to serve as a mobile test bed for engine development through the fall and winter months. It was a good choice: Hopkins had one of the better mechanics in Beckley, and he also had one of the bright young stars of American racing in Marshman. In his Speedway debut in 1961 Marshman had started 33rd and worked his way up to seventh at the finish. The next year he was fifth, and by the late summer of 1963 he was ready to make his bid for bigger things. The Lotus was the car that could do it for him, Bobby felt.

Watson and Ward, partially because of the help they gave at the beginning of the program, partially because of Watson's reputation and partially because of Ward's, were to get engines for one car. This was a new rear-engined machine which was Watson's first attempt in this direction. Sachs, one of the better drivers and great talkers of the Speedway, managed to convince Special Vehicles to give him one for a new monocoque being built by Halibrand, and then there was Mickey Thompson. Although the famous California hot-rodder had always gushed with good ideas, and although he had some experience building this type of machinery, Ford had not taken him into consideration. Mickey usually tried to bite off more than he could chew, and Ford was interested in working with persons who would follow through and pay attention to details. But Mickey had other ideas. Strictly on his own he was able to convince Executive Vice President Charles H. Patterson, then in charge of North American automotive operations, that he had a better way of doing it. The next thing anyone in the Special Vehicles Department knew, Mickey was to get five engines. Those who didn't get engines were an even better story. The leaders in this department were Jones, Foyt and Brabham. Although Parnelli and Agajanian made overtures, it was decided to go with out them; first let's beat them, was the attitude. Later on we'll sell them engines. Brabham, who was to build and drive a car for Jack Zink, didn't get one because Ford officials felt Zink was asking too much. The three time world champion from Australia was at this period practically in eclipse as a driver (from an American standpoint), and his efforts in Formula I car construction, although promising, had not yet been successful. So that was one less team. Foyt was another story. Negotiations were on—and off—at various periods through the end of 1963 and the early parts of 1964, with the upshot being there *was* no upshot. Foyt was busy trying out rear-engined cars (notably the MG

Liquid Suspension specials built by Joe Huffaker in San Francisco), but they never could get together. Soon Foyt was to have a big edge when it came to further negotiations, but that was to be a few months later; and at that time, as things were to turn out, he would need every edge he could find.

While everyone else had been negotiating, or in Chapman's case working with the designs of several cars at once, Marshman had been driving. Test work is lonely, boring and dangerous. Wherever it is done, the scene is usually the same: an empty grandstand, an empty track, a small group of mechanics and engineers standing in the pits and no other cars against which to measure yourself—only the ticking of a stopwatch. To make it worse, new things are always being tried, and it is up to the driver to go as quickly as he can to see if the new things are better than the old. Sometimes the new things just don't work; at other times they break, and then it can get deadly. Marshman knew little about driving rear-engined machinery, and Beckley was unfamiliar with their maintenance and adjustment procedures. On top of this the engineers were trying to develop a new power plant, and the combination of the three was often a frustrating one. But Marshman drove, Beckley turned his wrenches, and the engineers kept coming up with something better. That fall they ran at Indianapolis ... then it was Kingman ... then Phoenix ... then back to Indianapolis in the spring, when the snows left the ground. Slowly, over the winter, everyone got the hang of it; Marshman learned how to make the car go quickly, Beckley found what to do with the camber, the caster and the complicated plumbing, and the engineers kept producing more horsepower. By the time they arrived at the Speedway in early May, they were ready. Although Foyt had gone fractionally faster during tire tests in March, the rubber on his Offy-engined Huffaker car had been of the "gumball" variety, designed more for two or three quick laps for publicity purposes than for long-distance running, so his 154.1 wasn't taken too seriously. Marshman, on the other hand, had been over 153 for days at a time.

The Ford-sponsored cars weren't the only rear-engined ones that year. Watson had built a vehicle similar to Ward's (but equipped with an Offenhauser engine) for Don Branson. Len Sutton had another rear-engined Offy, constructed by Rolla Vollstedt, and there were the three Huffaker cars, including the one Foyt finally turned down in favor of his roadster and two that were eventually qualified by sports car star Walt Hansgen and Bob Veith, an Indianapolis veteran. Brabham had the only other rear-engined car to start which he managed to do after some frantic commuting between Europe and the United States for the two weekends of qualifying. The new cars that didn't make it were also interesting. The Lotus-Ford effort had shaken the American constructors, and in addition to those that lined up for the race there were 17 other rear-engined machines that didn't. Some, such as the back-up car for Clark and Gurney, didn't for obvious reasons. Others hit walls, and still others were simply too slow. But it was a start, and regardless of what the local press said, it was obvious the roadster was dead.

The paradoxical feature of the changeover process was that two of the quickest drivers in the place, Jones and Foyt, were still in roadsters. Parnelli, who had a rear-engined machine of dubious quality in his garage, preferred to stay with his 1963 winner because he was familiar with the car. Foyt, who switched from the Huffaker machine back to his roadster, had been approached by Ford early in the month about taking the Lotus back-up car, but negotiations kept stalling. Foyt wanted the car for the entire month. Chapman, wanting to protect himself in case Clark or Gurney crashed, didn't want to give it to him. Early in practice, the two supposedly out-moded roadsters were the ones that got the headlines. On May 5 Foyt hit 154.1, and three days later Parnelli turned a lap at 156.223, the fastest ever recorded at the Speedway. It wasn't until May 11 that Marshman got to 156, but the day after that, with everything working well, the crew-cut blond from the Pennsylvania dirt-track country pushed the record to 157.178. Ward was now over 155, Clark and Gurney were starting to move, and the situation looked much brighter. On the following day Marshman jacked it past 158 and Clark was right behind; hopes went still higher.

The commotion and press coverage generated by the Ford accomplishments at Indianapolis, plus the renaissance of stock car racing and the myriad other Ford competition activities in other parts of the country and the world, finally drew an official rise out of General Motors. A press conference was scheduled for GM's Milford, Mich., proving grounds two days before qualifying started at Indianapolis, and to guarantee a full house the corporation even used its own planes to fly in newspapermen from all parts of the nation. In the morning the assemblage was treated to a tour of the proving grounds and some exhibitions of the "performance" capabilities of GM cars. These were rather simple-minded exercises, such as brak-ing to a stop from 100 mph (the audience had no idea as to the true speed of the car or the actual stopping distance, nor did they know what had been done to the brakes), and one special goodie that was intended to show GM rims were capable of main-taining their grip on tires under extreme conditions. To illustrate this, the various models were driven at approximately 25 mph, then the cars made an abrupt turn with the driver's foot still on the gas. It did manage to show that with the tire tending to roll under the rim it still would not come off, but it also showed (to those who under-stood the basics of vehicle behavior) that the cars suffered from an acute case of understeer.

Lunch was better yet, with the seating arrangements being such that a GM vice president was acting as host at each of the more than 25 tables set up in a hall at Milford, while Board Chairman Frederic G. Donner and President John F. Gordon sat with a few of their aides at the head table. In his speech Donner left little doubt that racing had got under the corporate skin. "There is no question that racing as a sport may prove out racing cars," he said, "but certainly this does not prove out the qualities in our passenger cars that best meet the everyday needs of our millions of customers." No one, of course, had tried to intimate that it did. Donner went on to make a thinly veiled remark about the key item not necessarily being the quality of the car that is being raced, but the efficiency of the team that handles it. This was a tacit admission that Ford's (and Chrysler's) performance campaigns had caused annoyance. At the same time, GM corporate advertising took a new tack: Proving grounds, not race tracks, were the places on which to test cars—conveniently failing to mention that the other two major manufacturers also had extensive test facilities. Then, with this reaffirmation of the AMA agreement, General Motors lapsed back into silence.

On the morning of May 16, the first of the qualifying days and the one on which the forward rows are filled, both the Speedway and Ford were in a turmoil. The excitement at the race track was of the normal variety. More than 200,000 persons were expecting to see records broken once qualifying started, and to bring them to an even higher pitch, Marshman hit 160.1 in warm-ups that morning. In the Ford hospitality room there were two other subjects being discussed—tires and Foyt. Chapman had been using Dunlops in practice, but Passino was afraid the Dunlops wouldn't last the race and wanted the Lotuses to run on Firestones instead. The American tires might be slightly slower, his reasoning went, but their endurance qualities were superior to those of the softer British rubber. But Chapman, using his best diplomatic tactics, soon talked Ford out of the idea. He talked Iacocca out of it (Iacocca was sitting in as an observer, having come down to watch the trials), he talked the then Special Vehicles manager, Frank Zimmerman, out of it (Zimmerman was ready to leave the post). Beebe, still a neophyte, sat by and listened. So Chapman kept his tires, and he wound up keeping his reserve car in just that capacity when he talked the Ford assemblage out of loaning the vehicle to Foyt.

A.J., considerably upset by all the back-and-forth discussions, reached an even higher peak of frustration a short time later, when he took his roadster out for warm-up runs. The large percentage of nitromethane he had added to the fuel caused him to burn a piston. As his mechanics wheeled the car back to Gasoline Alley for a hurried engine change, one look at the volatile A.J.'s expression caused bystanders to back out of the way. Parnelli ran into the same trouble during warm-ups and he also went back to the garage, but both of them were quickly forgotten. When qualifying started Clark went out and shattered the record by more than seven miles per hour, recording an average of 158.828 to grab the pole position. Next came Marshman, whose 157.867 might have been faster had he not been so tense, and Ward filled out the front row with a 156.406. Ford seemed to be in solidly, and even though Jones (155.099) and Foyt (154.672) came back with new engines and made the second row, there didn't seem to be much cause for concern. Joining the two roadsters in the second rank was a minor Ford disappointment—Gurney. Dan, who could do no better than 154.487, had seemingly been at odds with Chapman and his mechanics all month, and little work had been done on his car. But even that was lost in the shuffle now. Clark alone was more than a second per lap faster than Jones in the fastest roadster, and this multiplied by 200 laps meant an advantage of three minutes at the finish. Added to this, of course, was the fact that the Fords would have to make fewer pit stops than the Offys.

The confidence lasted until Monday, when Gurney went out for practice with a full load of fuel (to check both the handling of the vehicle and the gasoline consumption). Soon the tires on Dan's car were scattering tiny bits and pieces of rubber around the Speedway, and when Gurney pulled into the pits, the word got around. The Dunlops were chunking, which in Speedway parlance means throwing pieces of rubber. Chapman, when descended upon by the press, shrugged it off. "We have no tire problems," he said, adding, "We plan to run the race on one set of tires." Chapman said it, and his words had to be taken at face value. But there was also the undeniable fact that Gurney had run into trouble. Chapman's public face was considerably different than his private one when Ford asked what the trouble was: This time Chapman said the air pressure hadn't been high enough.

The next intramural controversy involved Ward and Watson. Although Ford engineering had specified methanol for qualifying and gasoline for the race, the veteran pair had been demanding methanol for the race as well. They had an extra-large fuel tank in their car which would offset the mileage inferiority of methanol, and they were hot to use it for the extra power it would provide (approximately 475 horsepower as opposed to 440). Ford kept turning them down, but the night before the race Watson locked the doors of his garage and converted the fuel system to run on methanol. It was a decidedly uncharacteristic move for Watson, whose strongest point in the past had been to check everything a dozen times and be extremely careful in everything he did. Now he would have no chance to assess the quality of his adjustments until the race itself. When he wheeled the car out on the line, he would have no way of knowing whether he had been right or wrong.

Alongside Ward's vehicle that day were Clark and Marshman, with Gurney right behind them, and Dave MacDonald back in the fifth row in one of Thompson's cars. A fast-rising youngster from El Monte, Calif., who had done well in sports cars, MacDonald was making his debut at the Speedway, and although he was inexperienced at this sort of thing, during the month he had voiced his dissatisfaction with the manner in which his car was handling. In the sixth row was Sachs and back in the eighth was Eddie Johnson, a veteran of more than a decade at the Speedway, a slow but reliable driver who had been called on at the last minute to qualify one of Thompson's cars. The 11th-hour agreement with Johnson was typical of the Thompson operation. Although Mickey had slaved over the cars and gone night after night without sleep, everything was usually in a shambles, and the project never did get caught up. The only two cars he was able to qualify were not nearly as fast as the other Fords.

When the flag dropped it appeared as if Clark were running one race and the rest of the field was in another. Making full use of his four-speed gearbox he streaked away from the pack, and by the time he came around at the conclusion of the first lap, he was more than 100 yards in front of Marshman with the rest of the leaders strung out behind and the main group just starting to come through the fourth turn.

MacDonald, charging through the corner, attempting to get up with the front runners, hung the tail of his car out just a bit too much in the turn and spun to the inside, hitting the wall at better than 100 mph. The instant he made contact his vehicle exploded into a flaming ball of gasoline and ricocheted back across the track, flying squarely into the path of Sachs. The veteran Eddie had no place to go except into MacDonald's car. Although medical examiners later determined Sachs was probably killed by the impact, his vehicle was sprayed with gasoline from MacDonald's, and the rookie's mistake became the veteran's funeral pyre.

It all happened in less than two seconds and it was a horror: giant flames, black, billowing clouds, a few cars darting through the smoke, burning tires flying over the fence into a packed crowd, and the rest of the field braking to a halt as the red flag appeared. Through some miracle no other drivers had been seriously hurt, although Ronnie Duman sustained burns on his neck. Bobby Unser, Johnny Rutherford, Chuck Stevenson and Troy Ruttman had driven practically through the conflagration and couldn't figure out how they made it. Some of the drivers were almost in a state of shock as they sat there, waiting for the track to be cleared. Sachs had gone instantly. MacDonald, although technically alive, didn't have a chance and died within an hour. When the race was restarted an hour and 45 minutes it was done in single file, with Clark leading the way. Some drivers almost had to be talked back into their cars, but once they were running again they managed to push thoughts of the ghastly wreck to the back of their minds.

Clark led the first few laps after the restart, but on the seventh lap Marshman's white Lotus went streaking past the favorite, and surprisingly Clark could do nothing about it. Lap after lap Marshman extended his lead, running at 157 and better with a full load of fuel, leaving the field far behind him as all those lonely months of testing paid dividends. Then, on lap 37, while coming into the second turn, he suddenly found rookie Johnny White in front of him. Marshman dove down, intending to pass White in the middle of the corner; White did the same thing and Bobby had two choices: either put White into the wall or go even lower, down on the grass. He chose the latter alternative, and in the brief moment he spent off the track, the car bottomed and tore out the oil drain plug and ripped a water hose. Marshman was 28 seconds in front, and the lifeblood of his vehicle was running out through two jagged holes. The next time past the starting line, the officials saw what was happening and got the black flag out, but they never had to use it. Marshman pulled his car off the course and onto the grass inside the fourth turn, and the lead was taken by Clark.

Hopkins and part of the crew gathered up their equipment and trudged slowly back to the garage. Beckley and the others got a truck and went to retrieve the car. Marshman was nowhere to be seen, even after they towed the low-slung racer back to Gasoline Alley. Finally, more than an hour later, Bobby showed up, still wearing his uniform, with the marks of the goggles showing around his eyes—and with a program in his hand.

"What are you doing with that?" Hopkins asked.

Marshman looked sheepish. He had been wandering around in the crowd, he said, and "I thought if I bought it nobody would know I was a driver and they wouldn't ask me silly questions."

He was a picture of dejection: an entire year's work, the chance of a lifetime, all gone in one brief instant. For a while they just sat there.

In the meantime the number of Fords still running had dwindled to two. Nine laps after Clark took the lead, and while he was going into the fourth turn, he suddenly lost a great section of tread from his left rear tire. The enormous out-of-balance condition broke a radius rod, and in a matter of seconds the entire left rear suspension collapsed and the wheel, barely hanging on the car, was splayed at crazy angle. Somehow Clark managed to keep his car under control and bring it down the main straightaway, looking almost ludicrous with that rear wheel hanging on as some sort of useless appendage, and with an enormous shower of sparks being thrown out behind by the transmission dragging on the pavement. He managed to bring the car to a halt on the infield grass and walked back to the pits, his race over. On his way, one of the racetrack hangers-on ran up to him: "My heart was in my mouth when I saw you like that!" he blurted.

Jimmy looked at him. "You should have been where I was, mate," he said. Then he kept on walking.

That moved Jones and Foyt into a battle for the lead, and for a few laps they put on one of the greatest wheel-to-wheel duels ever seen at the Speedway before Jones went in to refuel on lap 55. He never got back out, his fuel tank catching fire and the resultant mess almost consuming the car. Now it was Foyt in the lead with Ward, in one of the remaining Fords, in second place. What had started out as a day full of hope had now turned into a nightmare, and one that had a tragedy tacked on for good measure. That was the way the race ran itself out, for the last 145 laps, with Foyt cruising along in the lead and Ward unable to make a run at him. His fuel system was running much too rich for maximum power, and he kept having to make additional pit stops. At the finish he had made a total of five (one of them to check the chassis); one time he was even forced to return because there hadn't been enough methanol in the refueling tank. Watson's rebellion of the night before had proved to be a costly one.

Gurney, in the meantime, had dropped back due to an early pit stop, and never was able to get near the front. Forced to run at lower speeds after getting a warning about his tires, Chapman finally withdrew the car at the 110-lap mark when the Dunlop man refused to guarantee that what had happened to Clark's car would not happen to Dan's. Johnson's vehicle—Thompson's second car—had lasted through a mere six laps.

When the procession ground its way to the finish, Foyt was a minute in front of Ward—and he was crowing. On his way to the victory lane ceremonies he happened to roll past Patterson, and when he saw Ford's executive vice president he gleefully made a well-known gesture that involves the use of the middle finger. Almost as soon as he climbed out of his car the vociferous Texan was mocking the Fords (which he had wanted to drive, and which he never stood a chance of beating had luck not entered into it in large proportions), and praising what he called his "Li'l ole antique car."

On Monday morning in Dearborn, Iacocca was enraged. His division had been made to look foolish in front of several hundred thousand spectators and the nation's press, and bad luck or not he was going to get to the bottom of it. "I want to find out chapter and verse what happened," he said. "What control do we have over tires ... Chapman made himself and us look ridiculous ... how much did he get paid for using Dunlop tires? ... get the answers ... Why *did* Rodger Ward come in five times? Get Thompson out of your league—it was wrong going in.

"I want a detailed autopsy," Iacocca said, and then got into what the attitude of others in management was. It was one of indecision about what to do next. The hawk-nosed general manager snorted. "If you can't stomach it," he said, "then pull out!" He reserved some of his choicest comments for Foyt and Foyt's remarks after the race. A.J. would be out of Ford equipment from then on, Iacocca said (he had a stock car agreement at the time), but later in the day he relented somewhat and agreed to take him back at a later date. Frey, Zimmerman, Beebe and public relations man Bob Hefty filed out of Iacocca's office and headed for another meeting, this one with Chapman.

For once the dapper Englishman was neither condescending nor arrogant. He opened by saying "I'm desperately sorry things went the way they did ... it was my decision to use Dunlop tires ... the fault with these tires, in my opinion, was not a design fault, it was a manufacturing fault." Chapman explained this occurred after the initial tire troubles, and when Dunlop arranged to produce new tires with shallower tread patterns. The fact that mold revisions and production had to be squeezed into a high-pressure span of three or four days was what probably caused the error, he said. Clark, Chapman continued, had started to feel "something going bad" after about five laps, "but he felt that he could comfortably hold the lead after Marshman dropped out."

Frey asked Chapman what he proposed to do next.

"We would like to continue our program with these cars," he replied. "I am confident that these are the best cars and we can win with them."

Frey asked him about racing that weekend at Milwaukee, and Chapman said the provisional plan had been to go to Milwaukee if they had lost at Indianapolis, but not if they won. "Actually," he continued, we have no plans to run this weekend, but we would like to run the big ones [i.e., the 200-milers] at Milwaukee and Trenton."

Then Frey dropped his bombshell. "We would like to have you sell us all three cars immediately," he said. "Would you do that?"

"Yes," Chapman replied. "But we would like a chance to vindicate ourselves. We feel we've let you down."

"We agree with that—in spades," Frey said.

Chapman attempted to get the discussion back to tires. "I still think Dunlops are OK," he said. "They're still good tires." They talked about tire agreements (there were none prohibiting use of another brand), about the damage to Clark's car, about the fires and the gas-alcohol argument that was raging and about the Lotus team's shoddy pit work (Gurney had a two-minute stop), and then Frey started to wind it up. Turning to Beebe, he said, "Leo, you arrange the funds to buy these cars right away."

Chapman asked "Are you adamant that you will not let us race at Milwaukee or Trenton?"

"No," Frey replied, "our mind is not made tip, but Ford is determined to redeem itself."

When the meeting ended, the company personnel present understood that Ford would buy the cars immediately, and that Chapman would present, on paper, his proposal for the 200-mile races later at Trenton and Milwaukee. Then, on the basis of the written proposal, Ford would make up its mind whether Chapman's services were wanted.

They went from Frey's office to Beebe's for the purpose of finalizing the arrangements for the sale. But when they sat down again, a few yards and a few moments down the hall, Chapman maintained he had not understood Team Lotus was to sell the three cars to Ford immediately.

Beebe and the others were so shocked that for a moment they didn't know what to say.

Chapman had invoked the terms of the original contract, in which Ford was prohibited from exercising its option to buy the cars until after the September 20 race at Trenton.

"But you just agreed to sell them to us!" Beebe exploded, and proceeded to read back the stenographic notes taken of the meeting in Frey's office. It made no difference. Chapman refused to sell them. "I'll put them on the shelf before I'll lose the opportunity to redeem myself," he replied. For reinforcement Beebe called Zimmerman back into the meeting, but it made no difference.

Chapman got Ford to agree to run the cars at Milwaukee and Trenton, and they drew up a set of terms for those two events. Somehow, despite the catastrophe, Chapman had maintained his hold.

At the same time, however, he was aware that from now on it was a new ballgame, and not only because he had his own reputation to rebuild. The other reason was Beebe.

Leo made his debut, so to speak, at the World "600" stock car race at Charlotte May 23, and saw Fireball Roberts horribly burned. A week later at Indianapolis he watched MacDonald and Sachs die in another fire, and a week after that he saw Jim Hurtubise burned at Milwaukee. ("A whole world I knew nothing about was opening up, and then there was that smoke and fire ... I got that feeling in the pit of my stomach and thought there must be a better way to make a living.") At the beginning he was diffident, sitting around on the fringes, trying to learn. After the Indianapolis debacle, he began to take command.

The first thing necessary was a reorganization, and he took the racing part of his job (in the middle of 1965 Beebe was also made the public relations manager of the Ford Division) and stripped it of non-essential parts. The first move was to transfer such items as the air hostess panel, the custom car caravan, the college shows and driver education to the marketing and sales promotion departments. Then he took what was left on his desk, divided it into piles and called in Evans, Cowley and Ray Geddes. Each got a pile: Evans had Indianapolis, Cowley stock cars and Geddes the sports car activities, with Passino acting as second to Beebe.

The primary thing was Indianapolis, and there were several major problems here. The first was Chapman, and the second was Foyt. Although A.J. had been considered the king of the oval tracks for a few seasons, in 1964 he was having one of the greatest years any driver has ever experienced. Usually he was the fastest and won going away. But when he wasn't the quickest he turned out to be lucky as well, and he was winning everything. By mid-August Foyt had finished first in all seven USAC national championship events, had won a flock of sprint car races and had the satisfaction of winning the Firecracker "400" stock car race at Daytona in a Dodge after Ford got rid of him.

It was obvious: If Ford wanted domination of single-seater oval-track racing it would have to make some sort of agreement with Foyt, even though it did not think much of his speech-making abilities.

Through a series of coincidences, he rejoined Ford sooner than expected—only 11 weeks, in fact, after Indianapolis. The two Lotuses were scheduled to run at Milwaukee August 23, the same day as the Grand Prix of Austria. The previous winter, when Chapman had been apprised of the fact Clark might have to miss a world championship race to make Milwaukee, he had been the picture of confidence: Jimmy would be so far ahead in the point standings by that time, Chapman said, he could afford to miss one. Now, after six Formula I events, Clark was second in points to Graham Hill and wanted to go to the Austrian race. Gurney also wanted to pick up world championship points, and when he asked for a release from his contract, Ford said OK. (Passino: "We had the contract, but you can't put a piece of paper in the car.") So now there were two spaces to be filled. Negotiations with Jones and Agajanian took care of one of them, and Chapman preferred Walt Hansgen for the other. In his debut at Indianapolis the sports car star had for a brief moment risen as high as second when Ward pitted after Foyt took the lead, and had in general driven well until sidelined by mechanical troubles. In addition, he had rear-engine experience. Both men practiced with the cars at Trenton in mid-July and Hansgen crashed one of them, damaging it slightly. Then a few days before the race, during a practice session at Milwaukee, Hansgen crashed again. This time he was too badly shaken up to take part in the race, and the car was a mess.

And who was standing there, watching the proceedings and looking instantly available? Old A.J. He looked at Ford, they looked at him, and in short order it was arranged. Foyt would drive the spare car: It was a case of love at 741st sight, and the breach had been healed. Actually, Ford-Foyt discussions had gone on for a few weeks, but Hansgen's crash brought them to a head.

On race day, and with Chapman in attendance in the United States rather than in Austria with his Formula I team, it was all Ford. Parnelli topped Clark's qualifying mark of the year before, as did Ward in the Watson car and Foyt in the other Lotus. When the flag dropped it was Parnelli from wire to wire in record time, with Ward second. When it was done, and Parnelli took his triumphal lap sitting on the back of a convertible, he was flanked by Chapman and Agajanian. They even posed for gag photos, with Chapman wearing Aggie's Stetson and the latter with Chapman's conservative English cap. It was a long way from the screaming scene at Indianapolis on Memorial Day of 1963.

Foyt was not as lucky: his winning streak was broken the first time he stepped into a Ford. The shifting mechanism jammed between two gears at the start, and when A.J. pulled behind the pit wall to fix it, he was out of the race.

The next problem was not that simple. It was the matter of signing Chapman and Clark for the 1965 race, signing them to a contract which would give Ford more control over Chapman, and signing them cheaper. In 1963 and 1964 Team Lotus had cost Ford a young fortune, and Iacocca didn't intend to have it happen again. "Fix it—and cut the budget—and don't come back without Clark," were Iacocca's instructions to Beebe, and in mid-September Beebe flew to England to negotiate.

Although Chapman is undoubtedly one of the great talkers of modern times, as a negotiator he met his match in Beebe (although the Ford man admittedly had an edge; Chapman was anxious to finally win the race he could have won the first two times). Beebe didn't waste any words:

"Colin, I'll tell you what I'm going to do; I'm not going to make a contract with you like we had last year. I'm going to take my wallet out and lay it on the table and you can have all that to race for us and no more—and I'm not going to tell you how to spend it."

Beebe named a figure and Chapman said it was too low, and besides, he had other offers.

"I'm either going to work out a contract right here this afternoon," Beebe replied, "or I'm going to leave and get someone else and that will be the end of it. If you've got a better offer then by all means take it and let's both save time."

Chapman agreed—at Beebe's figure.

Basically, the deal was that Ford would put Chapman on the track. The sum they paid him included no bonuses for success, for qualifying or anything else. What he did with the money was his business, and all expenses were also his worry. The only items Ford would provide would be the engines.

Then Clark came in. "Would you drive?" Beebe asked him.

Jimmy wasn't eager. He didn't want to miss the Monaco Grand Prix, which conflicted with the 1965 race, his mother had raised objections after the double fatality in 1964, and he wasn't particularly happy over the way he had been treated in several matters relating to the cars. Slowly, Beebe persuaded him. Then Chapman turned to Leo and asked who would pay for Clark's services.

"I just gave you your contract, Colin. Who you pay is up to you."

Then Beebe called for a typewriter, pecked out a one-page letter of agreement and had Chapman sign it on the spot. A few weeks later a formal contract was signed, and between the two documents there was the Trenton "200," which was run under the terms of the 1964 pact. For Parnelli it was a repeat of Milwaukee. He established a record in practice, and won the race going away. For Clark, who was in America for the United States Grand Prix, it was perhaps the worst day he ever experienced in a racing car. In private practice a day before the event, he could never go as fast as Jones, and during the night they even switched some pieces from Parnelli's car to his in an effort to speed it up: It didn't work. Even the best of racing drivers has his off moments, and Jimmy's frame of mind was such that he could not run at competitive speeds. He qualified only seventh fastest, then dropped out after 96 miles.

When the year was over there was little doubt in anyone's mind that the Lotus-Fords were the fastest racing cars extant, but the record still showed Foyt winning 10 of the 13 events with an Offenhauser-powered roadster. Even Ward's car, which ran the full season on the paved tracks, was not fast enough, and Marshman had been plagued by a series of mishaps, starting with his bad luck at Indianapolis. The year that began so brightly for Bobby had turned into a dismal one. Soon it turned into tragedy.

On November 27, while testing at Phoenix, Marshman's Lotus suddenly dashed into the wall. By the time they were able to get the driver out of the flaming wreckage, he had been burned over most of his body. Flown to specialists at Brooke Army Medical Center in San Antonio, Tex., he lived for a week before he finally succumbed.

When they brought him home for burial, a procession of more than 160 cars followed the hearse from the church to the cemetery. Marshman was leading his last pack, a slow, silent caravan which wound its way through the John O'Hara country of eastern Pennsylvania, where he was born and where he learned to drive a racing car. Only a few weeks before his death he was sitting in his pretty new home one night, watching Olympic star Gerry Lindgren leading a 10,000-meter race on television. "I'd lead that one too," Bobby said, "and then I'd probably have a magneto fall off or something." There was no smile on his face when he said it.

Marshman was the third major driver to be killed at the wheel of Ford-powered equipment that year, and his death was the cause of considerable soul searching. Was the company morally responsible for the fatalities? Would the accidents reflect on the corporate image? It is easy to rationalize in either direction, but several somewhat brutal facts remained: regardless of who provides the machinery, men will always find another car to drive, and finally, no man was ever put behind the wheel of a racing car except of his own free will. The program continued, and grew in scope.

24

R<small>UNAWAY</small>

WITHIN A MATTER OF DAYS after the 1964 race Ford had another form of proof that the engine was a good one: There were telephone calls from various car owners, drivers and mechanics, asking to purchase engines for the 1965 season. They knew it was better than what they had, and now they wanted one. It was a practical impossibility for Ford to supply them and provide spare parts and service, so plans were made to set up an outside agency, one that would act as intermediary between the factory and the racing teams. The decision was easy: Louis Meyer, the three-time Indianapolis winner and partner in Offenhauser builders Meyer and Drake, was given the job. Meyer had been in contact with Ford for some time; only a few weeks after Henry Ford II publicly disavowed the AMA agreement in 1962, Meyer had written a letter congratulating him on Ford's stand—and offering to sell Meyer and Drake to Ford. Discussions between Meyer and the company had been carried on for more than a year, and now he sold his interest in the Los Angeles plant to partner Dale Drake and set up his own facility in Indianapolis, just a few blocks from the Speedway.

Getting someone to sell and service the engines was only part of the problem. The cost was an even bigger obstacle, and caused the comptrollers many headaches. In order to make the engine available at a reasonable price, at the outset the company took a tremendous loss on each one; the cost to Ford, for the 1965 engine series, rose rapidly during the winter months of 1965. Eventually it hit $31,400 per unit, with these being sold for $15,000 and the Special Vehicles Department absorbing the difference (Offenhausers were going for $12,000). When the engines reached the point of a production line item (in a racing sense), Ford was able to drive the cost down to $22,800, including a reasonable profit for Meyer. And when it got there, the company decided this would be the price charged to the racing teams. The system now was that Ford ordered the parts from specialty suppliers, exercised quality control over them, then had everything shipped to Meyer for assembly. The price was admittedly steep, but so were the charges of custom machine shops for doing low-volume work.

While engines were being built in America, and while Ford was holding seminars to acquaint Indianapolis mechanics with the details of timing and maintaining the power plant, Chapman was finishing his new chassis in England. In late April they were flown to the United States, and a few days before the early season race at Trenton, Clark and Roger McCluskey went there to practice with the cars. It wasn't long before the throttle linkage on McCluskey's car jammed and he leaned it rather violently against the wall, bringing an end to the testing. Rather than risk the remaining car in the Trenton event, Lotus packed everything and headed for Indianapolis. Now the number two car had to be rebuilt and held in readiness as the number three, and the hull that was intended to be the spare had to be prepared for use as the number two machine.

When practice opened at the Speedway the new Lotuses were almost lost in the welter of rear-engined machinery. It seemed as if everyone with a welding torch and a few photographs of an independent rear suspension had been busy over the winter, and now the many variations on Chapman's theme were in the majority. Of the total of 68 entries 45 were rear-engined, and 24 of these had Ford power. The outstanding examples of the art were the new Lotuses. Basically the same as those of the year before, their detail refinements included longer noses to prevent lifting at high speeds, a little wider track and more offset to the suspension. Team Lotus had them, with Clark in one and the other car still without a driver, and Gurney also had one. Relations between Dan and Chapman had been strained the previous year, and this time Gurney felt he would be better off going it alone. Ford never knew what the terms of his agreement with Chapman were, but when they parted Dan took a brand new car with him. Now it was the lead machine for the new All-American Racers organization formed by Gurney and Carroll Shelby. Two Ford-powered Shrikes, built by Ted Halibrand, were the other team cars, with McCluskey in one and former motorcycle ace Joe Leonard in the other. Foyt, who by now was getting an impressive amount of help from Ford, had one of the 1964 Lotuses (which the company arranged), plus a back-up Lola built by British constructor Eric Broadley, and a wide assortment of engines and transmissions. Jones, also the recipient of Ford support, had another of the 1964 Lotuses. There were various other Huffaker, Halibrand and Gerhardt chassis present, as well as two new Watson creations for Ward and Branson.

The car that created the biggest surprise was the one used by a rookie, Mario Andretti. In 1964 this 5-foot, 6-inch, 138-pound Italian immigrant who lived in Nazareth, Pa., had been a spectator at the race, a kid from the dirt tracks making his pilgrimage to Mecca and wandering around in Gasoline Alley, hoping for a ride. One of those he sought out was Clint Brawner, the veteran crew chief for Dean Van Lines and a man who had just lost his driver when Chuck Hulse was injured in a sprint car accident early in the month. Brawner had put together machinery for such greats as Jimmy Bryan, Sachs and Foyt, and the sight of this scrawny youngster was nothing much. (Andretti: "He was so dejected because of Hulse's crash ... we got into the garage area and I was introduced by Rufus Gray, who owned the car I was driving at the time. He hardly knew Clint but he was trying his darndest to get me a ride, so he says to Clint that I drive sprint cars, and Clint came on and said, 'Goddammit, sprint's a dirty word in this garage!'") Andretti left in a hurry, but a month later, while Brawner was beating the bushes for a new pilot, he saw Mario drive a sprinter at Terre Haute, Ind., and asked him if he wanted a big-car chance. (Andretti: "I was excited, very excited, because in major league racing there are only a few outfits worthwhile driving for ... they are going to produce a winner. I considered Dean one of these, so I thought maybe I'm finally getting into something good.") In the latter half of the 1964 championship season he was good, and sometimes even spectacular, in Dean's lightweight roadster. Then, over the winter, Brawner set about building a new car. Being a practical man he wanted a proven design, so he made a deal with Zink: In exchange for a chance to copy Zink's Brabham chassis, he would make an extra one for Zink. Brawner and his aides did their work well. Although the car almost literally never turned a wheel before it arrived at Indianapolis, from the time Andretti first went out on the track it was apparent that here was a combination with great potential.

Shortly after practice started, Chapman signed a driver for his second car. It was Bobby Johns, the stock car veteran who had not won a race of *his* type in some time, and whose only previous Indianapolis experience had been the year before, when he put Smokey Yunick's ill-conceived side-saddle car into the wall during practice. Ford wasn't happy with the choice, but it was too late to do anything else. The company's primary pick had been Jones, but negotiations fell through when it became apparent Agajanian would be part of the deal. The feeling in Dearborn was that with Lotus and Ford there were already more than enough sponsors. To the public, the Johns matter was of minor importance. From the day practice started Foyt and Clark were the ones who made the running, and were the ones who almost invariably had quickest time at the close of each session. Gurney was doing well after losing time early in the month rebuilding his car to his own stringent standards, Andretti was impressive, Jones was sidelined for a few days by a broken hub carrier, but it was all incidental. From May 1, it was a two-car battle.

Ford's biggest problems during May were on the engineering side. Scussel and his team, confident they had a reliable power plant after a winter of testing and development, were suddenly faced with something new: Many of the Indianapolis mechanics, they discovered, were not capable of handling an engine with this one's degree of sophistication—and some of them weren't capable of handling anything more complicated than a lawn mower engine.

The Lotus mechanics were among the major offenders, and since this was the factory team they naturally caused the most grief. Scussel's men found, incredibly, that in order to provide clearance for the power plant's installation into the chassis, one of them had literally taken a hammer and chisel to the engine and knocked pieces of metal off the cam towers, the front cover, and the oil filter mounting.

There was also a dangerous modification of the throttle control lever which they felt was responsible for McCluskey's accident at Trenton, fuel system maintenance was poorly handled, the plastic insulator on the distributor cap had been cut back a half inch, and minimum maintenance standards were not being followed. When Chapman arrived in town, a few days after his cars, Scussel arranged a meeting with the Englishman. From then on Ford men were the only ones who touched the Lotus engines.

Then, once practice got going in earnest, they were faced with a rash of blown engines. The trouble, they found, was basically that Indianapolis standards of engine and engine-accessory cleanliness were not those of the engine buildup and test departments at Dearborn. Tiny chips of paint, metal and the like had been left in the cooling and lubrication systems of the cars themselves and were now being sucked into the engines and causing the damage. The engineers soon built five system flushers to clean out the plumbing, and at the same time veteran Indy mechanic George Salih changed from the small Ford-designed oil filter to a much larger one. Salih's system was soon picked up by all, with an aircraft fuel filter (with a different element) being used for the job. It was another of the almost-traditional examples of factory engineers and their racing counterparts learning to communicate with each other, and after the improvements were made there was little trouble in this area.

On the first day of qualifying Foyt was so charged up he could have run around the track at better than 150, but he had to sit back and wait his turn; he was 13th in line. When it began at 11 a.m. the huge crowd was surprisingly quiet and anticipatory, and they gave the earlier drivers an almost perfunctory round of applause when their average speeds were announced. First came Len Sutton, in the Vollstedt-designed rear-engine Ford, and he was good for 156.121 ... Then came McElreath driving Zink's Brabham, still with an Offy engine. He did 155.878 ... and then Bob Christie, and Mickey Rupp, and George Snider ... and then Parnelli. The best he could do was 158.625, and when he came back to the pits, the expression on his face made it apparent he knew that wouldn't be nearly quick enough for the pole.

One after another, those who were ready went out, took their four laps and then came back with a spot in the race; there was Al Miller in a rebuilt 1963 Lotus with 157.8 ... there was Lloyd Ruby in a Ford-powered Shrike with 157.2, and rookie Gordon Johncock with a fast 155 in an old roadster, and then there were three more who couldn't go quick enough and had their crews wave them off, and all this time the little Italian with the big white car was coming to the front of the line. At 12:45 it was Andretti's turn, and as he headed onto the empty track there was a certain electricity in the air. In 3:46.63 it was done, with the hoarse scream of the Ford engine dominant over the yells of the crowd as he finished. His average of 158.849 was a record, and so was his fastest single lap of 159.405.

Andretti hadn't even started talking to reporters when his mark was shattered. Clark was next, and he turned four consecutive laps above 160 mph. For the first time in the history of the Speedway someone had officially gone over the 160-mile barrier, and the crowd was in a state of pandemonium. Chapman almost kissed his driver when he came back in; the over-all average was 160.729—and even Jimmy's mark didn't last for more than a few minutes.

Clark had started his bid at 12:51 p.m. At 1:04 Foyt roared out, full of adrenaline and his car's fuel tank carrying a seemingly proportionate amount of nitromethane. It didn't take long—screaming through the corners, getting up within a foot of the retaining walls as he drifted onto the head of the long straights, Foyt started off with a resounding 161.958, and although the car slowed fractionally on each of the next laps, he drove it for all it was worth. His average was 161.233, and from the crowd reaction a disinterested observer would have thought he just saved the American flag. Speeds at Indianapolis have gone up considerably since then, but when considered in its time and place, Foyt's performance that day must always rank as one of the great qualifying efforts. By the time he rolled into the pits, however, he had reverted to his sometimes cool and collected self. A habitual practitioner of the psyching art, Foyt's main comment was a matter-of-fact "We'd hoped to run a little faster; we were a few rpms off, but everything should be OK by race day." Then he smiled, shrugged and let the army of photographers fire away.

When Gurney went out a few minutes later to turn in a 158.898 and move Andretti back to the second row, he did so practically unnoticed. When Canadian rookie Billy Foster, driving a year-old chassis with an Offy engine did 158.416 in mid-afternoon, hardly anyone turned around. That's the kind of a day it was; the word fast had been given a new perspective at a track which had been intended, at its birth, for velocities that might eventually increase to the neighborhood of 100 mph. It was a day on which failure was to create more excitement than middling success. Ward, the two-time winner and participant in 14 straight events, pulled off the track after not being able to get up to speed. Eventually, as the following weekend would prove, the combination of Ward and Watson's new chassis were not fast enough to make the event. It was a remarkable comedown for both of them.

It had been a good day, Scussel thought, as he walked down the pit row late in the afternoon. His engines had the top five spots in the race, and the speeds of Foyt and Clark made him even more content after the hectic activity of the past few months. Then Chief Engineer Emmett Horton walked up to him.

"I just found out you're going to rebuild all the engines," Horton said.

Scussel was shocked. "But I don't have part one!"

Between qualifying and the race itself the engines have to be taken apart, examined and put back together again, with new pieces installed where necessary (and after the use of nitro, new pieces are usually the order of the day). If Scussel, his engineers and the engine buildup men in Dearborn thought they had worked hard before, it was nothing compared to the activity of the next 10 days. The word had been given: Bring them home. A total of 18 engines (17 that qualified, plus one for the 34th, or alternate car) were flown back to Detroit, stripped, checked, new parts were found, old ones were renovated, it was all carefully reassembled, they were run in on dynamometers, and then flown back to Indianapolis on planes standing by solely for this purpose. It was part of the Indianapolis effort which for some reason—possibly embarrassment to Meyer—was never publicized. But it was one of the most self-satisfying, from a company standpoint, in the annals of Ford and racing. The men who did the work were assigned to a six-cylinder truck engine one day and were on the racing program the next, and when it was all over they went back to their humdrum existence of piecing together stuff that had come off a production line. The curse of an auto manufacturer in this day and age is the lack of pride of workmanship. Finding that the men in this section of the company were proud of their talents and treated the hectic rebuild as more than just a job was one of the most encouraging things to come out of the racing program.

Later Scussel was able to laugh about the night-and-day rush to get the engines ready. "All spring," he said, "people would approach us looking for special goodies for their engine, and I don't think we ever convinced some of them that even if we wanted to give them something special, there were no such items. Goodies? Heck, if they had seen how we took them apart and put them back together they'd have *known* there weren't any!" As a point of interest, when Clark's rebuilt engine was run in on the dynamometer (on straight methanol) it produced 505 horsepower; Foyt's had 495, with the negligible difference coming because fewer pistons had been changed in Clark's. Both had run 20 percent nitro for qualifying, both ran methanol for the race.

But engines, in the two weeks between pole-position qualifying and the race, were a relatively minor worry. The big one was tires, for the second year in a row. Goodyear, America's largest manufacturer, had for decades made no attempt to break the Firestone grip on the Speedway. Then, when Foyt brought Goodyear stock car rubber in as ammunition during the 1963 tire rebellion, the company decided to add oval-track activity to its recently established stock and sports car programs. By 1965 the struggle between Goodyear and Firestone had grown into a full-scale war, with both paying high prices to get name drivers under contract, and with both thinking nothing of flying planeloads of their latest developments to races in any part of the nation. Although the Goodyear participation gave greater impetus to tire development than any other factor in the history of racing, in 1964 the newcomer was all but shut out in Indianapolis. In 1965 Goodyear came back strong, and this time they had Foyt and Gurney (among others) qualify on their rubber.

On the Monday after he took the pole, Foyt went out to practice with a full load of fuel, intending to check fuel consumption and tire wear. After approximately 15 laps at speeds in the 154–155 range, Foyt came back in and observers sitting on the pit wall noticed small pieces of rubber missing from his rear tires. It was the chunking business all over again, and when the Goodyear men hustled the car back to Foyt's garage the word flashed around Gasoline Alley in a matter of minutes. Branson and Foster were also reported to have experienced the difficulty, and the panic started. Goodyear men were busy saying there was nothing wrong, and Firestone men were busy whispering in everyone's ear. When Passino got word of it, he grabbed the phone and called Akron. There was nothing to worry about, he was told; the tread depth of 7/32 of an inch was just a little too much. When they buffed it down to 5/32, it would be fine.

And all this did absolutely nothing to pacify him or anyone else involved with the operation. Ford had blown the race the year before after being told there was nothing wrong with tires. Passino and the others in Dearborn sweated out the days until the race, while back at the Speedway the controversy resembled something out of a comic opera. Foyt refused to surrender the questionable tires until he was finished with them, and he allowed as how he might run them around on a pickup truck for two or three years before he would consider them finished. Goodyear announced it could cure the problem by taking the tread depth down to 5/32, and USAC said you couldn't do this by buffing, but only by running them around on a track, and so on, *ad nauseum*. It was beautiful. As things turned out in the race, those who rode on Goodyear tires had no trouble whatsoever, but the exercise did manage to liven up a dull spot in the month of May and add a little more gray to Passino's head.

There was also more gray to come. Parnelli, out practicing with his Lotus a few days after he qualified, again broke a rear upright and spun into the wall. Fortunately he was not injured and the car looked to be repairable, but this was the second material failure of this type and the USAC safety committee quietly grounded all the Lotuses until the problem could be resolved. Although Chapman complained (with some justification) that the failure had occurred only on older models that were now out of his jurisdiction, the safety committee insisted on stronger uprights for all the Lotuses. A telephone call to England produced a hurried revision in the pattern and heavier cast uprights for Gurney and Johns, while a special set was welded together for Clark's car. In Detroit a new design for a fabricated set was made up at Ford and flown to Indianapolis, where new uprights were welded together for Foyt and Jones. It was getting to be one nightmare after another, but this seemed to be the last of it, if for no other reason than the month was drawing to a close.

And as it did, the Wood brothers flew into town—Glen, Leonard, Clay and Delano and their cousins Ralph Edwards and Ken Martin. After the pit-stop histrionics of the past two years Ford wasn't taking any chances, and early in the spring Beebe's office started casting about for a good pit crew. At first they talked about getting a team from Holman-Moody, then Cowley suggested the Wood brothers. Why not? They were the best in the business, and besides, they were connected with Ford. When the lean, almost angular men arrived from the Virginia hill country, it was feared they would need an interpreter to communicate with Chapman. But their southern drawls and Chapman's clipped English accent caused little difficulty once each had seen what the other could do. Although the Woods had never worked on an

(Top) Mario Andretti, Dean Van Lines Special, 1965.
(Middle) Parnelli Jones, Agajanian's Hurst Special, 1965.
(Bottom) Jimmy Clark, Lotus-Ford, 1965.

(Top) Dan Gurney, Yamaha Special, 1965.
(Middle) A.J. Foyt, Sheraton-Thompson Special, 1965.
(Bottom) Al Miller, Jerry Alderman Ford Special, 1965.

Indianapolis Lotus, they were professionals, and after a few days' practice (using an orange crate with a fuel valve bolted to it), Chapman was duly impressed.

Refueling and general pit procedure were to be even more important this year. After the fires of 1964 the rules had been amended to limit the fuel capacity of the cars to 75 gallons, to insist on a minimum of two pit stops for each car, and to eliminate the high-pressure refueling equipment. From now on, refueling would be done by gravity only, and the speed of the pit crew was to be vital to the entire operation. Things were looking better, and one of the items that made them look that way was the number of Fords in the starting lineup. Of the 33 cars ready to go on Memorial Day, 17 had Dearborn-built engines in the back. (And there were 10 more Offys mounted aft of the driver, making 27 cars of this type.) The two years of frustration and the months of work for this one were all put aside now. There was nothing left to do for anyone except the drivers. Now, when the pace car got out of the way, they were the ones who counted.

When the flag dropped and the pack darted for the first turn, Clark outran Foyt for the corner and led him around the opening lap, with the rest of the field strung out behind. The next time Foyt was in the lead with Clark on his tail, and the crowd roared with anticipation of a battle between these two giants. On lap three it was Clark again ... then Clark by a little more ... and a little more ... and slowly it began to dawn on everyone there would be no struggle, that Clark was in command and would do as he pleased. It is not very often that a driver can lead at his own pace in something like the Indianapolis "500," but that was just what was happening. The low green car, with the dark blue helmet barely peeping out of the lay-down cockpit, had no opposition. Lap after lap Clark increased his margin, then he headed for the pits on lap 67, ready to refuel and giving the number one spot to Foyt.

The Chinese-firedrill stops of the past two years were little more than a memory as the Wood brothers swarmed over the car: In ... stop ... hoses hooked up—and out again. It took only 19.8 seconds to stop, pick up 50 gallons through a gravity refueling system and get out, and crews in nearby pits were goggle-eyed. It should not have been possible but it had happened, and Clark was roaring away, going through the gears as he ran for the first turn. The usually reserved Chapman was so ecstatic he hugged Glen Wood. What the startled onlookers didn't know was that Ford had been working on aid for the laws of gravity ever since the new type of refueling had been announced. Danny Jones, whose primary job was liaison between the factory and the racing teams, contacted Ford's hydronics laboratory and outlined the problem to them. In short order they came up with a special tank. When it was discovered standard tanks would be employed, they went to work on the nozzles and developed one through which the fuel flow actually increased in velocity.

Foyt held the lead until the 75th lap, when in an ill-judged attempt to make his fuel last as long as possible, he ran out on the back side of the course and was forced to coast to the pits with a dead engine. It took them 44 seconds to refuel A.J. and restart him, and by that time Clark was long gone. Foyt could do nothing about it, and when he came into the pits at the end of his 115th lap with his transmission shot, the event lost even the slightest resemblance to a contest for first. From here on it was merely a high-speed cruise with the scream of the green Lotus, its big number 82 flashing in the sunlight, echoing around the giant arena. The next time Clark came in for fuel it was 58 gallons in 24.7 seconds; there was no hurry now.

Behind Clark there had been some interesting battles. Some of the better cars and drivers had fallen by the wayside, and there were sonic surprises among the front-runners. Gurney had held third place for most of the first 100 miles, but an engine failure sidelined him, and Jones, who had been running fourth, moved up a notch. It had been a bad month for the 1963 winner, but when the race started Parnelli figuratively said the hell with it and decided to go as fast as he could for as long as he could, and was driving his older-model Lotus at speeds it had never before registered.

Andretti, who had been with the leaders from the start, was driving like a veteran. Although troubled by a faulty fuel valve which took the methanol out of one tank but then refused to switch to the other, the little rookie hounded Jones throughout. But it was all more or less of a sideshow. The man everyone was watching was Clark, flying along two laps in front of the rest. Slowly, the remaining miles were ticked off; Clark was so far ahead he was down to running at 148 after opening with laps of 157 and more. Could it happen now, after all these miles? Some of the Ford officials in the grandstand grew nervous, and those in the pits started pacing back and forth. Their fears were unwarranted. A few minutes later Clark's car streaked across the line, with the little Scotsman's fist raised in triumph as he saw the checkered flag. Even taking it easy for almost half the race, he had averaged 150.686 mph. The new era, delayed a few years by such things as oil leaks and tires, had officially begun, and Chapman did a little dance of joy down the pit row as he ran toward victory lane to greet his driver.

For the record, Clark's margin over Jones was 1:58, and Parnelli managed to give the crowd something of a thrill at the finish. His car had been running low on fuel for the last few laps, but he didn't dare stop. Andretti was only 20 seconds astern, and to pit would have been to lose second place. Carefully, running at part throttle, he nursed the car around, hoping it would last to the finish. Then Mario's crew saw what was happening and gave him a signal; Andretti set out in pursuit. He missed by six seconds as Parnelli zig-zagged down the finishing straight the last time around, attempting to slosh what little fuel was left into the pickup. Those six seconds were the difference between $64,700 for Jones' car and $42,500 for Andretti's, but neither came out of it exactly destitute. The lion's chunk of the $628,000 purse went to Chapman and Clark. Jimmy led 190 of the 200 laps (at $150 a throw), and the car's total earnings were $166,000. Al Miller managed to finish fourth in one of the 1963 cars, giving Lotus three of the top four and British designs *all* four, and Johncock placed fifth in his Offy-powered roadster. Of the 11 cars running at the finish, eight were powered by Ford, including Johns, who had a trouble-free drive to seventh place.

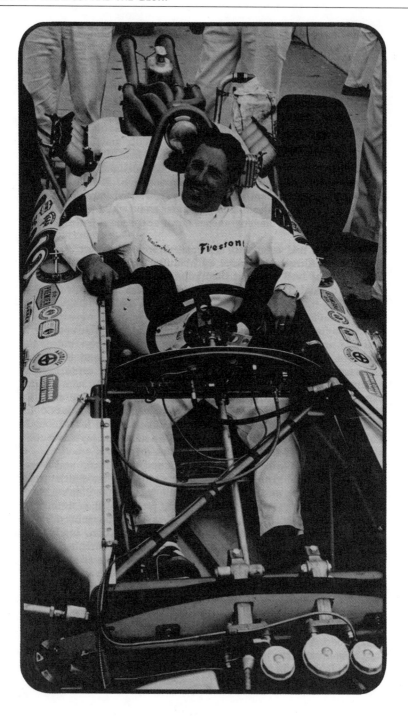

At left: With the cover off, Andretti stretches out in his Brabham-chassised Dean Van Lines Special, 1965. Most drivers have trouble fitting in the tiny cars. For the 5-foot, 6-inch Andretti there was no problem. (Top) Clark at speed during the 1965 race, in which he led 190 laps and was never threatened. (Bottom) The end of the first lap in 1965, with Clark outrunning Foyt and Gurney close behind in third place.

Quick work: The Wood brothers' pit crew, well known as the best in the South or anywhere else, for that matter, refuels Bobby Johns' Lotus, 1965.

Finally: Chapman, with both hands raised in the air, greets Clark after the 1965 race as the Scotsman drives past the pits to the winner's circle.

Almost literally jumping for joy, Chapman starts to run alongside Clark as the car heads for Victory Lane. Clint Brawner, crew chief of the Andretti car that placed third, is at left in cowboy hat.

Now it becomes a race between the man carrying the Borg-Warner Trophy and the "500" Festival Queen to see who reaches the hero first.

Half submerged: Clark in Victory Lane at Indianapolis, 1965, with the radio announcer's microphone in his face practically before he stopped.

As Clark crossed the line both Beebe and Passino experienced the same feeling, and it was one of relief. The exhilaration, the excitement, all of that was to come later. At that moment it was merely thankfulness that the job had been done. The engineers got their real satisfaction a few days later, when a post-mortem was done on the 17 engines. Only three of them, it turned out, had left the race because of failures in the engine itself, and one of those was running a high percentage of nitromethane. Eight finished, three (Foyt, Johnny Boyd and Johnny Rutherford) went out with transaxle failures, two (Leonard and McCluskey) were victims of clutch failure, and Bud Tingelstad lost a wheel. Ironically, one of the three sidelined by an engine fault was Gurney. A part of the cam gear drive had somehow missed the heat-treat (hardening) operation. Gurney, the man who was the catalyst in the program, was also the man who through coincidence got the short end.

The morning after the race, when Beebe was back at his desk in Dearborn, the telephone rang. It was Clark, calling from his Indianapolis motel. "Leo," he said, "I just want to thank you for flying over to London last year and talking me into the race." Clark hadn't forgotten their September discussion in Chapman's office.

Understandably, after the victory the Indianapolis program became anticlimactic. There were even persons in the corporation who were in favor of a complete withdrawal, but this was impossible from a public relations standpoint; now that Ford had made obsolete the normally aspirated Offenhauser engine, the least the company could do was to continue to make available its new V8. Meyer gradually began to take over all of the business, with Jones acting as liaison and responsible for the sourcing of parts. From the experimental stage in a back room of the engineering building to being an over-the-counter item, the double-overhead cam V8 had taken a little more than two years.

As the 1965 championship season went on, the USAC mechanics grew more familiar with the engine and it also became dominant on the mile tracks where the bulk of the events are run. Of the 13 races held on paved courses, Ford-powered equipment won eight, and three of the other five were taken by McElreath and his excellent Brabham chassis. With regard to flat-out speed, Fords were the fastest qualifiers 11 of the 13 times. The championship also—for that matter inevitably—went to a Ford-powered driver. The winner was Andretti, who was spending his first full season on the Championship Trail. At this stage of his career Andretti had not yet attained the almost frightening skill with which he and Foyt were to dominate USAC; he won the title on reliability instead. Mario participated in 16 races and won only one, when Foyt ran out of gas on the last lap of the Hoosier Grand Prix on the road circuit at Indianapolis Raceway Park. But he finished second six times, third three times and fourth twice. Foyt won five races and was second three times and third and fourth once each, but the rest of the time he dropped out. Andretti drove his lightweight roadster in the two races preceding Indianapolis, and in two more events after he lost a wheel and crashed his Brabham in July, giving him a total

(Top) Mario Andretti, Dean Van Lines Special, 1966.
(Middle) Graham Hill, American Red Ball Special, 1966.
(Bottom) Jimmy Clark, STP Gas Treatment Special, 1966.

(Top) Jackie Stewart, Bowes Seal Fast Special, 1966.
(Middle) Lloyd Ruby, Bardahl Eagle, 1966.
(Bottom) Gordon Johncock, Weinberger Homes Special, 1966.

of nine starts in the rear-engined machine. Of these he finished lower than fourth only twice—once after dueling for the lead with Gurney in the Milwaukee "200," and then a week later at Trenton when he was slowed by mechanical troubles.

By the next season Andretti was ready to take over the world, and as the month of May got going, hardly a day went by in which he didn't record the fastest practice speed at Indianapolis. When it came time to qualify, he sat his car on the pole with a record four-lap average of 165.899 mph, well ahead of second-place man Clark's 164.144 in the newest Lotus. Had Andretti been able to run his own race, it is doubtful anyone would have caught him. As it turned out, he was hit by valve trouble right at the start. After a wild accident that wiped out 11 cars before they reached the first turn of the first lap, and after they got the pack going once more with Mario at the head of the single file, an ominous stream of smoke started issuing from his left-hand exhaust pipe, and soon it was all over. The race itself was one of attrition, with Clark unable to hold the lead due to his car's poor handling on an extremely slippery track. Then Lloyd Ruby lost what was almost total command of the race when a bolt attaching the front cover to the cylinder head broke and was thrown out through the cover by the cam gears. Jackie Stewart, the young Scots grand prix star making his Indianapolis debut, took the lead from Ruby at the 150-lap mark, and as the long day ground its way to a conclusion, he appeared an easy winner. But even this was not to be. With 10 laps remaining Stewart was forced to shut off his engine as he lost all his oil pressure and the lead went over to Englishman Graham Hill, another of the European contingent attracted to the race through Clark's success. Hill, like Stewart driving one of Broadley's Lolas, thus wound up the winner in a confused finish—some persons thought Clark, who placed second, had actually won—and by now the fact that the victor was powered by Ford became almost academic. The chassis selection and tire competition were the main themes, and interestingly enough in this race Chapman-built cars rarely led. The vehicle Ruby was driving was one of Gurney's Eagles, and the man responsible for it was Len Terry, the former Lotus chief designer who had gone to California to work for Gurney's All American Racers. On the engine side, there were 24 Fords on hand at the start, and they were in the first four cars to come across the line (and in five of the seven still running at the end). Hill's average speed was only 144.317 mph, well down on Clark's 1965 performance due to the many yellow flags and the oily condition of the track. As a further indication of the kind of day it was, the car that finished fourth, driven by Gordon Johncock, actually spent less time on the track than did any of the others. Johncock's vehicle was damaged slightly in the first-lap melee, and according to USAC rules he was not able to effect repairs until the race was restarted. He lost several laps in this manner, and although he was the fastest man on the course once he finally got there, the deficit was too great to make up.

Indianapolis was one of the few places Andretti was not successful in 1966, as he almost literally ran off and hid in the chase for the championship. Of the 15 races

*Mario Andretti, who became a star almost from the day he first put a wheel
on the surface of the Indianapolis Motor Speedway.*

held during the season he won eight, and of the 11 on paved tracks he took seven. At
one time or another he led 12 of the 15 and was the fastest qualifier 10 times. As a
further indication of his superiority, he lost the first race at Trenton by running out of
gas and having to make an unscheduled pit stop, and he lost the first race at Phoenix
when he made an error in judgment and chopped Foyt while both were lapping a
slower car. It was a remarkable year, and it was much the same for Ford as it was for
the man who made the engine move the fastest. All but one of the paved-track
events were won by the engine, which was also in the top qualifier's car on each
occasion.

Dominance is fine, but there is one thing wrong with being on top in a technically oriented activity: There is no place to go but down. When the corporation first
decided to make an Indianapolis effort, the V8 engine configuration was dictated by
the fact that Ford also happened to have V8s for sale to the general public. To take
an objective (and somewhat cynical) viewpoint, all the Ford did was to reaffirm the
timeworn engineering truism that eight cylinders are more efficient than four. A V12
or a V16 might have been even better, but this was out of the question.

Then, in the year of Ford's first triumph at the Speedway, another factor was thrown into the pot. In 1965, for the first time, the rules called for two mandatory pit stops. This in effect canceled any mileage advantage a non-supercharged engine would have over one that was supercharged, and the USAC ratio of 4.2 liters unblown to 2.8 liters blown had long since shown itself to be heavily weighted in favor of the blower. It was a relic left over from the 1938-1939-1940 Formula I proportion of 4.5 to 3.0 liters, which blown Mercedes and Auto Unions had made ridiculous.) By 1966 both supercharged and turbocharged versions of the Offenhauser began to appear, and it became obvious, in theory at least, that they could be competitive with Ford. Rodger Ward actually won an early season 1966 race at Trenton with the supercharged engine when most of the Fords were sidelined by various troubles, and Parnelli Jones was among the front-runners at Indianapolis the same season before wheel bearing failure put out his supercharged car. In 1967 the turbocharged (exhaust-driven) version of the supercharger had taken over, and Ruby was able to qualify one for the "500" at 165.229 mph, leaving little doubt that if a Ford-type development program was put behind the engine, it would become even more powerful.

But by this time the Fords and the reworked Offenhausers had been eclipsed by something else, a jet engine running in a chassis equipped with four-wheel drive. It was typical automotive irony: The development impetus provided by Ford (and Chapman) made other persons think in terms of vehicles not limited by traditional ideas, and now someone had come up with an even more advanced design. It was Andy Granatelli, who over the course of two decades had graduated from the role of sometime race driver and Chicago speed shop operator to the presidency of the Studebaker Corporation's STP additive division. Granatelli had been coming to the Speedway as a car owner for almost 20 years, at first with a clapped-out and partly refurbished survivor of Ford's 1935 Indy effort (this was in the late 1940s), then later with a conventional Offy roadster. After that he bought the Novis and milked them for all possible publicity, but he had never been near the ownership or sponsorship of a winner until 1966, when STP was the entrant for Clark's runner-up Lotus-Ford. The year before that, however, marked the start of an even better idea. It was the season in which Granatelli combined one of the Novi engines with the British Ferguson four-wheel drive system. Although the vehicle did not last for any length of time, the four-wheel drive had propelled the car around the Speedway faster than any Novi had gone before.

Now this time he had the new machine, dubbed the STP Oil Treatment Special, painted a brilliant day-glo orange, and equipped with a 260-pound Pratt and Whitney aircraft turbine (the Ford engines weighed slightly over 400) that put out 550 shaft horsepower and enormous amounts of torque.

The car was constructed around a sort of I-beam center section split at both ends and looking suspiciously like Chapman's designs for the Lotus Elan and Europa models, and had the engine mounted to the left of the beam and the driver sitting on the right, and the thing created more commotion than did the Lotus-Fords when they first arrived. With Parnelli driving in early spring tests, the car hit 164 on its 10th lap at the Speedway, a fantastic accomplishment, and it also caused numerous drivers to hit the roof. The turbine was illegal, they said. It was an airplane, or something like that, and they did not want it racing with automobiles. The sounds were vaguely similar to those of 1963.

In point of fact there was very little wrong with the car. It was the rules that were wrong. Some years earlier, in an effort to make the rules correspond with the idea that the Indianapolis "500" was the world's greatest auto race, someone sat down and included, in the fine print of the entry blank, conditions under which such exotic power plants as turbines, rotary piston engines and even fuel cells could be entered. This was all well and good, but the trouble was no one ever accurately figured the proper proportions that would limit turbines, etc., to the same horsepower as a four-stroke, non-supercharged piston engine.

That was where the fault lay, and Granatelli had merely been smart enough to see the obvious discrepancy. When Jack Zink had shown up with a turbine in 1962, or when Norm Demler brought one in 1966, no one had complained because neither car had run well. Now a turbine-powered machine was really flying, and the grumbling of the opposition was considerably louder than the turbine's exhaust.

Andretti, picking up where he left off the previous year, was once again the fastest during the month of May as the turbine car, plagued by gearbox difficulties, did little running. On the first day of qualifying trials Andretti turned in a four-lap average of 168.982 mph to grab the pole. In 1962, the last non-Ford year at Indianapolis, Jones had sat on the pole with a mark of 150.370. In five years the average speed for the fastest qualifier in the race had thus gone up more than 18.5 mph, the greatest increase over any such period in the history of the track. Gurney, who for one of the few times in his career pronounced himself satisfied with his car, was second with an average of 167.224, and Gordon Johncock filled up the front row with still another Ford-powered machine which averaged 166.559. Foyt and Joe Leonard, the number two driver on Foyt's Coyote team (they looked remarkably Lotus-like), picked up two of the positions in the second row, Foyt with 166.289 and Leonard with 166.098. Then came Parnelli. No one was sure if he was driving his machine to the hilt or not, but when the red car was finished, he had turned in four laps at an average of 166.075, and the rest of the field was still wondering. As an indication of the progress made, when the 33-car lineup was set, the average for the group was 164.173 mph, and the slowest vehicle had turned in a performance that would have been good for a spot on the front row in 1966.

Interestingly, among those who had the greatest difficulties during the month of May were Clark and Hill. Chapman, expecting an Indianapolis version of the BRM H-16 grand prix engine, had designed his cars with this powerplant in mind. When he discovered the BRM would not be available he had to switch back to Ford, and the resultant chopping and changing on the chassis left both cars in less than optimum condition.

The first-lap accident of 1966. Somebody made a mistake, and as a result a good portion of the field never got as far as the first turn.

Lloyd Ruby and his Ford-powered Bardahl Eagle: He led more of the 1966 race than anyone else, but a mechanical failure sent him to the pits.

A.J. Foyt, the winner of more big races than any other American, at Indianapolis after winning the "500" for the third time in 1967.

The pole-sitter: Andretti was the fastest qualifier for the "500" in both 1966 and 1967. Here he is during the 1966 edition of the race.

(Top) Graham Hill, STP Oil Treatment Special, 1967.
(Middle) Denny Hulme, City of Daytona Beach Special, 1967.
(Bottom) Al Unser, Retzloff Chemical Special, 1967.

(Top) Jimmy Clark, STP Oil Treatment Special, 1967.
(Middle) Mario Andretti, Dean Van Lines Special, 1967.
(Bottom) Jim McElreath, John Zink Special, 1967.

(Top) Parnelli Jones, STP Oil Treatment Special, 1967.
(Middle) A.J. Foyt, Sheraton-Thompson Special, 1967.
(Bottom) Joe Leonard, Sheraton-Thompson Special, 1967.

Added to this was the fact that for once Chapman did not have Ford engineers maintaining his engines, and the Lotus (also sponsored by STP) operation was suddenly one of the weaker ones. Clark made the field at 163.213, and Hill managed to make it on the last day with 163.317. In the race both dropped out early with engine difficulties, Hill being placed 32nd and Clark 31st.

Their departures were scarcely noticed. When the flag dropped Jones shot out of the second row, passed a few cars in the first corner, passed a few more in the second, shot past Andretti on the back straight and was in command. When the race was called after 18 laps due to rain, Parnelli was still in the same place, running comfortably ahead of the field. When everyone pulled in and the cars were wrapped in plastic covers, Jones exchanged his helmet for a straw cowboy hat, lit a cigarette and comfortably observed the world around him. "Ain't no use for everybody to risk their necks in the rain," he said. "If the car lasts through the race she'll beat everybody easy, and if she don't you ain't got a thing to worry about."

Foyt, a calmer, more mature person after his consistent streak of bad luck for the past 18 months, had been running in third place at the time of the red flag, with Gurney having proved himself the best of the piston-engine field ("first in class," he said with a grin). But Foyt was confident. That night, while eating dinner with Speedway owner Tony Hulman, he was so loose he kidded Hulman about the first postponement in the history of the track. "I'm so sure I'm going to win this race," he told Hulman, "that I ought to charge you for keeping my money overnight."

When the race restarted the next day it was more of the same. Parnelli took off in front, with Gurney vainly attempting to keep up and slowly pulling away from Foyt in third place. Andretti, who had clutch trouble the first day, was no longer a factor, and the rest of the field was strung out behind. About the only thing that kept Parnelli from lapping everyone else was the yellow caution flag, which came out frequently for minor accidents. Once it was for Parnelli himself, who was forced to spin to avoid a gyrating Lee Roy Yarbrough on the 52nd lap. Gurney got by into the lead for two laps at this point, but Jones soon took over again, and by lap 58 Gurney was in the pits for an extended stay. The selector valve designed to switch from one fuel tank to another had frozen. Running with the stuck valve, and with little fuel coming through when the tank was nearly empty, had resulted in a very lean mixture, which caused Gurney to burn a piston. Foyt moved into second, and Gurney, although he ran 250 more miles, did so on seven cylinders. Foyt took the lead when Jones went in for fuel on the 80th lap, but three laps later Parnelli was out front again. Now it was a high-speed, noisy waiting game, with Jones and the turbine slipping silently along in front of the field, going only as fast he had to, with no one able to match the turbine car. Early in the race Parnelli had turned a lap as high as 164 mph, and it seemed as if he could do it for all 200 if that became necessary. So it went, the race wearily running itself out, with the turbine in an unassailable position. By the time Jones completed his 192nd lap, even though the race had been run under the caution flag for a total of almost an hour (allowing Foyt to close on the leader each time it waved), Parnelli was 52 seconds in front, the "easy" sign had long since been hung out, and the winner seemed to be a forgone conclusion.

Almost.

On the 197th lap a bearing in the car's gearbox failed and Parnelli came slowly into the pits, rolling to a stop and climbing dejectedly out of the car. It was over. The gearbox trouble, seemingly cured, bad cropped up again. The only other driver to lead so many laps and lose (191 in Parnelli's case) was Ralph DePalma, who led 195 in 1912 and lost when his car broke down two laps from the finish. (The all-time one race lap leader is Billy Arnold, who led 198 when he won in 1930.)

When Foyt sailed past he realized what had happened and he gave his pit a sign he knew he was in front, then settled down to cruise for the final three laps, taking it easy, waiting for the checkered flag. Then, somehow, A.J. was reminded of a few crazy thoughts he'd had the night before, when he started wondering what would happen if the race ever ended with a multiple crash on the last lap. ("Man, I don't know what it was, but I just had this instinct, and I put the binders on her and slowed down. I must have been going only 100 miles an hour; hell, I could have *walked* faster than I was going. But I knew there was going to be this crash.")

Foyt was right. While he was coming out of the third turn on his final lap, a group of also-rans was already in the fourth one. Then Bobby Grim hit the fourth turn wall. In an instant Chuck Hulse and Carl Williams were also involved in the mishap and there were spinning cars all over the track. Foyt threaded his way through the wreckage and across the line, his fist raised high as he became the fourth man to win the Indianapolis 500 three times.

Foyt won (at a record average of 151.207 that was almost incidental), and so had Ford. But the turbine and the four-wheel drive had made their point. The screaming after the race was even louder than before, and it reached a crescendo when USAC belatedly revised the rules on June 26. The change came through a limitation on the size of the annulus, or air intake: This was now limited to 15.999 square inches, as opposed to the 23-inch maximum under which the 1967 race was run (curiously, the exact dimension of the annulus on the turbine Granatelli used). Granatelli thereupon threatened the club with everything from lawsuits to a bolt of lightning from on high, but his complaints had little effect.

Whether or not Granatelli's turbine car ever ran in another race, it had done its job. It had proven itself to be the fastest vehicle ever seen at the Indianapolis Motor Speedway, and it had provided further impetus to the advancement of design. Despite the new intake limit, other persons started working on turbine-powered cars, and at Ford, engineers started casting about for ways of preserving the company's leadership in the field. They had to come up with something better—which is what racing is all about.

25

SOLEMN SWEDES AND AD CAMPAIGNS

OF ALL THE FORD MOTOR COMPANY Cars in the early 1960s, the plainest was the Falcon. It had a six-cylinder engine and Grant Wood styling, and although it was a great success during the economy-minded year of 1960, the ensuing trend toward performance and better body design left the company with a major overhaul job. The first part of this was mechanical, including installation of the new 260-inch V8, making four-speed boxes available, etc., for the 1962 edition. The Mustang was still a few years away, and until that was introduced, a hot Falcon would have to carry the load. The second part of the task was to change the public's opinion of the car, to let potential buyers know (through advertising and the like) this was really something good. One of the ideas for this latter part of the project was what got Ford into the rally business (there is no "e" on the end of it unless you are French).

The original proposal for participation in rallies was made in June of 1962 and was designed as a tie-in with the introduction of the 1963½ models the following February. The idea was to present the new cars (which featured a fastback roof) in an exotic, sporting setting, and the man who came up with the pitch was the same one who had been instrumental in getting Chevrolet to go stock car racing more than a decade earlier. At that time Barney Clark worked for Campbell-Ewald, the Chevy advertising agency. By 1962 his travels had taken him to J. Walter Thompson, which had the Ford Division account, and Ford's new-found interest in performance activities was made for Clark. His proposal outlined the benefits of having spectacular, international-type scenery as background for the new advertising, and added that if several of the cars were entered in the Monte Carlo Rally (coincidentally scheduled for late January) any sort of decent performance by the vehicles would "Give us the validity we need to support our shots of high-speed motion on challenging, unusual and exciting roads."

Had anyone at Ford Division an idea of just how tough a European rally was, it is doubtful they would have undertaken the project. In the United States rallies are

The various routes of the 1964 edition of the Monte Carlo Rally.

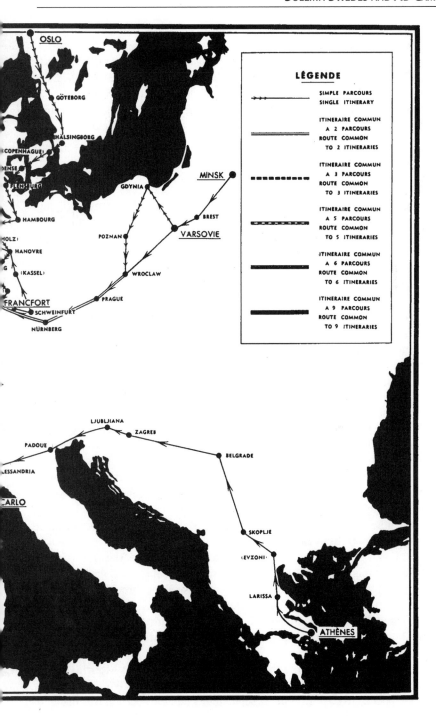

mostly Sunday afternoon romps through the country in standard cars, with involved mathematical calculation necessary to maintain such averages as "17.4 mph for 5.6 miles, then turn right and begin 18.2 mph average for the following 10.3 miles." If you have a doctorate in mathematics and several hundred dollars worth of calculating equipment in the car, you might have a chance to win. Driving ability is normally so minor in importance that your grandmother could take care of the duties. In Europe the only thing that remains is the basic principle of completing a multistage event held on public roads, and arriving at the end of each stage at a predetermined time which is established by the required average speed. But although the principle is the same, the rest is another story: The major European rallies are held over distances of 1,500 to 3,000 miles, are nonstop affairs and are held on roads that would make goat paths seem like autobahns by comparison. The favorite rallying areas of Europe are the twisting mountain passes of the French Alps and the unbelievably bad byways of Yugoslavia. To maintain the normal rally average of 60 kilometers per hour (37.5 mph) over these requires driving at almost racing speeds. Then, in order to make the events even tougher, the organizing committee usually throws in what are known as special stages. These are normally the most difficult sections of road, are closed to regular traffic and are where the competing cars have flat-out races, with the fastest receiving no penalty points and the rest getting points corresponding with the number of seconds they were slower than the leader. Many outstanding European racing drivers refuse to go on rallies; they say it is too dangerous.

There are numerous classic events in Europe, such as Liege-Rome-Liege, the Coupe des Alpes and the Rally of the Midnight Sun, but the big one is the Monte. It is the second oldest, having started in 1911, and it has the advantage of being the only major automotive event held on the Continent in midwinter. As a result it gets far more publicity than the rest, and it also offers a good excuse to spend a week on the Riviera when the remainder of Europe is eyeball-deep in snow. European auto manufacturers also go for it in a big way, because an over-all victory here is worthy of considerable sales promotion (and again, there is no event two weeks later which another make can win and publicize). The normal format for the modern-day Monte is to give the entrants a choice of eight or nine starting points, including such places as Minsk, Stockholm, Frankfurt, Paris, Glasgow, Lisbon, Athens and Monte Carlo itself, then trace a path from each that runs approximately 1,900 miles to a point from which all cars follow a common 500-mile route through the Maritime Alps to Monte Carlo. On this section the roads are much more difficult, and there are also five or six special stages. Then, those that manage to struggle through will participate in a three-lap race around the Monaco grand prix circuit. Any number of things can happen along the way, including dropping several hundred feet down the side of a cliff or picking the wrong starting point and getting trapped in a blizzard halfway across Yugoslavia.

The man tagged with running the rally for Ford was George Merwin, partly because he was a member of the three-man special vehicles activity, and partly because he happened to be in Europe in September when the decision was made to add rallies to the program. Earlier in the month Passino told Merwin if the program was approved he would probably be asked to form a rally team, and that he should start thinking about it. Then, on the Sunday evening after the Italian Grand Prix at Monza, while he was packing to leave, Merwin received a telegram from Dearborn: "Proceed to Monte Carlo. See Tom Tierney." The latter, one of the brighter young men in the public relations department, was already on hand making arrangements for the new-model press conference to be held three months later. He filled Merwin in on a few details, then George called Dearborn. Passino told him to assemble a team of three cars and to figure out what money and materials would be needed and what modifications would have to be made to the cars. "And remember," he added, "you'll have to get them homologated."

"Homolo-who?" Merwin asked. That was his introduction to the intricacies of the International Automobile Federation, which has an involved set of rules and regulations regarding what can and cannot be done to a standard production car and still keep it eligible for events such as the Monte. Any non-standard parts put on the Falcons would have to be made in a minimum of 1,000 examples and placed in catalogs as optional extras if Ford expected the FIA to approve them (homologate is the "official" word).

Merwin met with the rally organizers in Monte Carlo the next morning, flew to Paris to have lunch with the competitions manager of Ford-France, then went on to London to have dinner with the competitions manager of Ford of Britain. The first thing he discovered was that most of the good rally people were already under contract for the season, and the second was that one team boss was still available. His name was Jeff Uren, he was the former competition manager of British Ford, and he was a good one. Uren eventually proved to be one of the best things that happened to Ford in this venture. A martinet and somewhat officious, he drove his team hard from the beginning of practice to the end of the rally. But he always knew what he was doing, and his organizational plan was almost faultless. Then there was the problem of the drivers, and again, most of the top ones had been hired for the season and Uren and Merwin had to scrounge from what was left. Anne Hall, a veteran British pilot with a good record, was hired, and Margaret McKenzie was signed up as her co-driver; Peter Jopp, another British veteran, was put in the second car with Trant Jarman, the Midwest advertising manager for *Car and Driver* magazine, as his copilot. Jarman had considerable rallying experience in Canada, where winter conditions approximated those in France, and had helped Ford with a preliminary report on what rallying was all about. So that left one car to be filled. Uren, who had done some events in Sweden, remembered watching an ice race there in which one particular driver had been quicker than all the rest. Uren thought he might be the man, so he was hired.

His name was Bo Ljungfeldt. He was a tall, partially bald, enormously powerful man in his early 40s, he was silent and moody—and he proved to be the sensation of the Monte both that year and the next. Gunnar Haggbom, another Swede who was the navigator on the 1962 winning team, rode with him.

(Above) One of the 1964 Falcons during practice in the Maritime Alps. At right: (Top) The winner of the 1962 and 1963 Montes—Erik Carlsson and his front-wheel-drive Saab. (Middle) Bo Ljungfeldt at speed on the Monte Carlo grand prix circuit during the speed test that wound up the 1963 event, and (bottom) after taking his own pictures of graffiti.

Ljungfeldt's talents first became apparent during the practice runs made in December, which concentrated on the roads between Chambery, the start of the common route, and Monte Carlo. During the pre-Christmas weeks, running on metal-studded Dunlop tires through the icy sections, he was unbelievably quicker than everyone else—and still complained he wasn't going fast because the tires weren't good enough. Ljungfeldt and his co-driver knew a Swedish firm that made even better spikes, they said, and when he went home for Christmas Ljungfeldt arranged for a set to be shipped to Ford, a set with well over 600 spikes installed in each tire. As soon as these were put on the cars times on the special stages dropped sharply. Ljungfeldt could almost fly on them, and for the first time the team thought in terms other than merely hoping to finish. Ljungfeldt was so happy with the spikes (the development of which were a fortunate coincidence for Ford, whose relatively big cars would have been lost in the snow without them) that he even thought he could win. From what the rest of the team had seen of Ljungfeldt, they were beginning to believe it. On the snow and glare ice he could drive faster than they could on the dry pavement, hurling his car around the narrow mountain roads at frightening speeds. As is usual during these month-long practice sessions, natives in the area came in for at least one close call each day. Once Ljungfeldt had Jarman in the car with him and was demonstrating his ice-driving technique, doing nearly 100 mph down a narrow mountain pass, when suddenly a tiny Citroen appeared around a corner. There was no way to miss the French car, and as he prepared to duck Jarman saw Ljungfeldt cross himself. Fortunately the Citroen driver had presence enough to head right into the snowbank on the mountain side of the road and somehow Ljungfeldt scraped by on the open side, where a slip would have sent them down a cliff. When they got stopped, Bo turned the Falcon around and headed back to the little car. He got out, grabbed it by the front bumper and pulled the forward half out of the snow. Then he went round to the back, yanked on the rear bumper and dragged the car back on the road. The girl in the passenger's seat had fainted and the driver was white-faced, but they recovered quickly when they discovered it was a rally team practicing, and spent the rest of the afternoon at the top of the pass watching the three cars speed back and forth.

By the time the rally was ready to start the team was in good shape. Their new cars, built at Holman-Moody, were equipped with 260-inch V8s that produced 240 horsepower and far more torque than any of the other entrants. With disc brakes in the front, heavy-duty suspensions, four-speed gearboxes and the spikes, the Falcons appeared to be as tough as anyone. To back them up Uren had established an intricate service organization which would keep track of the cars and be available to help at almost any point of the rally. Sam Croft-Pearson, a veteran driver, was in charge of the service crews, and Uren had hired racing and rally drivers to ensure the service vehicles would move as quickly as the rally cars themselves should the need arise. Australian Paul Hawkins and a pair of East African Safari winners, Bill Fritschy and Johnny Manussis, were the ones who got these jobs; Holman came over for the rally itself.

Due to the tie-in with the new-car presentation in Monaco (Ford flew more than 100 press, radio and TV people over for the thing), the Falcons started from Monte Carlo even though some of the drivers—notably Ljungfeldt—would have preferred Stockholm. Eventually, the choice of starting point was to cost the team the over-all victory. Although the event began on a clear but cold afternoon, by the time the sun went down and the cars were in the mountains it started to snow heavily, and the white stuff was settling on top of a glare-ice coating. Ljungfeldt soon went off the road, but fortunately Croft-Pearson was nearby and somehow managed to haul him out as the snow got thicker. By midnight there was more than a foot of it packing the narrow trails, and up ahead a car bogged down while climbing through one of the more difficult sections near Montauban. The road was too narrow to pass, so all the cars behind him also got stuck, including Ljungfeldt and Jarman. While they were waiting for the road to clear they changed to spiked tires, and at the same time Anne Hall came up behind them and also stopped. Maurice Gatsonides, a former Monte winner, was behind her, and he suggested they attempt to find an alternate road which would lead around the blockage. The two of them took off—just before the road finally opened a bit and the other two Falcons were able to squeeze past the remaining cars. Anne never did find a good alternate route and arrived at the next control outside the maximum time allowance. One car down, two to go, with both of them now penalized for time lost while being blocked. Although Ljungfeldt had driven like a madman, he was still six minutes late at the control, and Jarman dropped 13 minutes. They kept going through one of the more wintry Montes of recent years, and then, the next day, Ljungfeldt lost another 25 minutes when he had to get his gearbox rebuilt. The situation looked bad, but the other teams were also having difficulties. Of the Monaco starting contingent of 32, for example, only eight managed to finish the rally and only one of those went unpenalized on the road section. The entire Athens group of 13 starters was holed up in a little Yugoslavian town where snowdrifts halted them, and the teams that had to run through Holland told stories of frost so bad that even the special fluid in the windshield washers had frozen; some cured it by substituting gin, which doesn't solidify as easily.

At Chambery, where the special tests were to begin and where the various factory teams were able to get their last good crack at servicing the cars, the two Fords heard the word; if you can finish, you can win the large touring car class, as all the big-bore opposition has dropped out. When they roared off into the night, heading for the 30-mile race across the Granier pass, Ljungfeldt acted as if he didn't care if he ever finished. Throwing the big Falcon into the corners, seldom backing off the throttle, Ljungfeldt turned in a 40-minute, 42-second clocking, 12 seconds quicker than Finland's Pauli Toivonen in a hotted-up, front-wheel drive Citroen which was better suited for the job. The more powerful GT class could do nothing about coming even close. On the next section, this one of 22 miles including the Uriage hillclimb, Ljungfeldt again was fastest. Then they drove on through the night, headed south for the famous Mt. Ventoux hillclimb, which was to be run before dawn.

In Provence, where the brooding mountain sits above the tiny town of Bedoin, and with perhaps 120 cars still left in the rally, the drivers found two things: The first was that the road was shrouded in fog, and the second was that Ljungfeldt didn't mind if he could see or not. His time on the 10-mile climb was 12:59. The second fastest vehicle (again Toivonen) was 13:46—an almost ridiculous margin.

Then, as the sun came up, the remaining cars turned toward the mountains behind Monte Carlo and the last three races—and again, it was Ljungfeldt each time. About the only two things he didn't take were the rally itself and the three-lap timed run around the town's grand prix circuit (in which he was second to a factory Austin-Healey). But even though he didn't win, due to the 31 minutes lost on the road sections, Ljungfeldt had established a mark that could never be beaten; for the first time in history, one driver had posted fastest time on every open-road special stage. Ford, which went into the rally as neophytes, hoping merely to finish, came out smelling like a rose. Jopp and Jarman, who finished 35th over-all, were the winners of their class, and Ljungfeldt (who was 43rd in the general classification) had grabbed most of the headlines. In addition two of the three had finished—a batting average far better than the norm for the event, which was completed by 100 of 292 starters. The Ford publicity drums beat so loudly and so often that Saab, the sponsors of Erik Carlsson's winning car (the second straight year for the pair), had to produce ads saying, "Only one car *won* the Monte Carlo rally."

From a technical standpoint the performance of the relatively big-engined, relatively bulky Falcon on low-adhesion road surfaces was a surprise to many pseudo-theoreticians. In recent years front-wheel drive cars, and especially small ones, have had a decided edge in bad weather events such as the Monte. The top seven spots in the final standings in 1963 were occupied by front-wheel drive cars. Yet the conventionally packaged Falcon, making use of its horsepower and torque advantages was actually faster.

But to the Great Unwashed, the finer points of who beat whom or which beat what were of no importance. The Falcon had been faster than anything else, and J. Walter Thompson was able to generate enough mumbo-jumbo copy to hide the fact that Ljungfeldt hadn't won. Since he was the moral victor, it wasn't too much of a smokescreen. From an over-all viewpoint, and despite the rally being almost unknown in the United States, Ford got nearly as much publicity mileage out of this venture as it did from any other. The ads ran for months, and the newsmen who had been flown over earlier helped to generate interest when they got home.

With the conclusion of the rally the team was disbanded; to continue the program and try to sell successes in lesser-known events would have been stretching it. Then, surprisingly, the successes came without any help at all. One of the Falcons had been left with Ford of France for use by Henri Greder and Martial Delalande in their domestic rallies, and they had driven it in four between the end of the Monte and mid-April. Now they took the car into the European championship Tulip Rally, and when it was all done, the somewhat road-weary car (it was originally Anne Hall's) wound up as the winner.

The Tulip, which is Holland's biggest event, covered 2,000 miles through France, Belgium, Holland and Germany, and although the road sections were fairly easy, there were 14 special tests, including laps of the grand prix circuits at the Nürburgring in Germany and Zandvoort in Holland. Greder won his class in every one of the speed tests, and won by such large margins that he was given the over-all title. It was the first major European rally win for an American car in the post-World War II era, and was made even more interesting by Mercedes-Benz' actions. When the Stuttgart firm heard Greder had entered the event, that company withdrew its big sedans, not wishing to bump heads.

That news worked Dearborn up again to the extent that the Swedish Rally of the Midnight Sun got an entry of two cars, and neither of them did well. After that came the French Coupe des Alpes, or Alpine Rally, and Ljungfeldt and Greder were entered in that. Only 24 of the 78 starters managed to finish, and Ljungfeldt was not among them. Greder made it to the end, but was far behind in the touring car section, in 14th place.

Spa-Sofia-Liege, the revised version of the classic Liege-Rome-Liege, was next. Ljungfeldt and Greder made up the two-car team for this one, and Fords began finding trouble almost a month before the event began. Greder and Maurice Foulgoc, his mechanic, were in Yugoslavia in July, checking out some of the more critical sections when on the 26th of the month they stopped in the town of Skopje. More through coincidence than anything else their room in the Hotel Macedonia was near the top floor, and that saved their lives; while they and the hundreds of other guests were sleeping an earthquake hit that part of Yugoslavia and destroyed a good part of the town, including the hotel. The two Frenchmen suddenly found themselves catapulted into the bowels of the building, where they were trapped in the rubble for 24 hours. They were lucky to come out of it unscathed (1,011 persons died in Skopje, 3,350 were injured), but neither was in any shape to return for the rally and veteran French driver Jean Vinatier took over. Neither Vinatier nor Ljungfeldt made it to the finish of this 3,000-mile car breaker, but that was nothing unusual. Of the 119 starters only 20 completed the grind. The rally included no special stages—just the worst roads in Europe and high average speeds for three days, three nights, and all those miles. They don't call it the "Marathon de la Route" for nothing.

At the same time the rally Falcons were making their presence felt, another interesting phenomenon was taking place in Britain. This was the rise of the big-engined American car as the favorite in British sedan racing, and the new winners were all Ford Galaxies. The idea had started the year before, and typically, had begun with Dan Gurney, who brought a 409-inch Chevrolet to a race at Silverstone where he left all the Jaguar sedans far behind before losing a wheel on the last lap.

This time the invasion was brought about by John Willment, one of England's largest dealers, and Uren, now his competition manager. Working together with Holman, they imported one car in the spring of the year and at Silverstone in May veteran touring car driver Jack Sears whipped the Jaguars. He repeated the trick in June and in July led a 1-2 Ford finish in a preliminary race to the British Grand Prix, with Sir Gawaine Baillie placing second. Even Jimmy Clark got a crack at the Galaxie, driving it to a midsummer victory at Brands Hatch, and that fall Gurney and Graham Hill ran first and second at Oulton Park. Prior to this, Jaguar had been dominant in the touring car division of the week-long Tour de France, and the success of the Galaxies in Britain almost inevitably led to a two-car entry for the 1963 Tour, which takes place in September.

The Tour, which is the automotive equivalent of France's famous bicycle race, is a 3,600-mile event stretched over 10 days which in 1963 included nine races and seven hillclimbs. There are four overnight stops involved, and the event is split into touring and grand touring classes. Ljungfeldt, Greder and Jopp were entered in three Galaxies, and Holman was brought over to help with the servicing problems that would be encountered; the rally-cum-race made an almost literal circle of the country, and the service trucks would have to run hard to keep ahead of the competitors.

The 1963 Tour started in the evening at Strasbourg, headed south for a few miles to take in a night hillclimb near Colmar, then went north and crossed the German border on its way to the Nürburgring, the fabulous 14-mile German circuit where a one-hour race was scheduled in the morning. Greder and Jopp finished first and second and Ljungfeldt was finished for good, blowing his engine part way through the event and disappearing into the bushes, car and all. From there they went to Belgium and Spa-Francorchamps, scene of the Belgian Grand Prix, where the Galaxies again placed first and second in another hour event that afternoon, and then it was on to Dinant, where the drivers had a night's sleep. On the following day the rally moved back into France and Greder won at both Rheims and Rouen before another rest stop, and when the two-hour race at Le Mans on the next day was almost over, Greder had a commanding lead with one lap to go. Then he made a silly mistake, put his car into a sandbank on the outside of a corner, and lost so much time digging out that he incurred the maximum number of points. Greder kept going for the sake of individual wins at the various races and hillclimbs, but as far as a chance for the class victory was concerned, he was out of it. That left Jopp, together with co-driver Baillie, at the head of the class and with a comfortable lead over French Jaguar driver Bernard Consten, a three-time winner. A few days later, while heading out of the Pyrenees and toward the closing stages of the Tour, the two Britons went roaring over a railroad crossing at high speed. Their route notes had indicated caution, as there was the possibility of bottoming on the not-too-level crossing. They ignored the notes, ripped the oilpan out—and Ford was finished with the Tour de France. The 1963 Tour was one of the toughest ever run, with only 31 of the 122 starters managing to complete it; but to lose two cars through mental error was inexcusable.

Greder and Delalande, on their own and back in one of the refurbished Monte Carlo Falcons, brought Ford back out front in the next major European test, the Geneva Rally, which is Switzerland's contribution to the championship circuit. This one, run mostly through the French Alps, saw the two Frenchmen edge 1961 European titleholder Hans Joachim Walter of Germany (Porsche) and star driver Gunnar

Andersson of Sweden (Volvo), and that was enough to pump up enthusiasm for another Dearborn-sponsored crack at the Rally of Great Britain in November. They should have stayed away. The tiny forest roads on which the RAC ran its special stages were too narrow for the Falcons, and Anne Hall, Jopp and eventually Ljungfeldt went off the road and never got back on it. But by late November the RAC was of minor importance. The big push was to be the Monte Carlo Rally of 1964.

After the near miss of the year before, and with the experience picked up through the 1963 season, it was decided to make an all-out effort. By walking the thin edge of the homologation rules Ford was able to get its new 289-inch engine and numerous fiberglass body parts admitted; the cars dropped several hundred pounds in weight and picked up 40 horsepower. The team manager this time was to be Alan Mann, a young Englishman who had been successful running cars in British events the previous year, and there were to be eight entries. The top driver, logically, was Ljungfeldt, and one other Swede, Bjarne Lundberg, was also signed. From Britain came Anne Hall (paired with Denise McCluggage, America's fastest woman driver), Jopp, veteran rally star Peter Harper and even Graham Hill, the 1962 world champion. Greder and Jo Schlesser, the latter one of the top drivers in his country, would handle the two French entries.

Ford had some of the fastest cars and some of the best drivers, yet the chances for an over-all victory, they realized, were slim. Ljungfeldt's performance of 1963 had shown the rally organizers the true capabilities of a big-engined car. So this time they reintroduced an item used a few years earlier—the coefficient. This meant everyone's times on the special stages would be multiplied by a previously determined factor designed to equalize the performance of the little cars with the big ones. The only trouble in this mathematical paradise was that the factor was more advantageous to the small cars—with Ford being a synonym for the word big. There were numerous reasons for loading the factor, and the main one was that the French auto industry's rally-suitable cars were small. The French-oriented Monegasques, therefore, had a rooting interest. What they were forced to swallow, however, was that when they loaded the system in favor of small vehicles, they also favored the British Mini-Coopers and Swedish Saabs.

According to the handicap system, on a special stage that would take a Ford 20 minutes to cover, one of the Minis could make it in 20 minutes and 47 seconds—and still be one second ahead. It was an almost impossible task, but it was worth a try, and on the evening of January 17 four Fords rolled out of the Oslo starting point, heading south toward France, where they would meet up with four more Falcons which started from Paris a few hours later. By the time they all joined up at Rheims everyone would have covered about 2,000 miles, with another 500 to go before they reached Monte Carlo. There were 299 starters, and for the first time in several years the weather came up warm and dry. As the Fords roared across Denmark, Germany, Holland and Belgium, there was little to do but drive, sleep, and wait outside the various controls. Starters from the other points found the same conditions, and

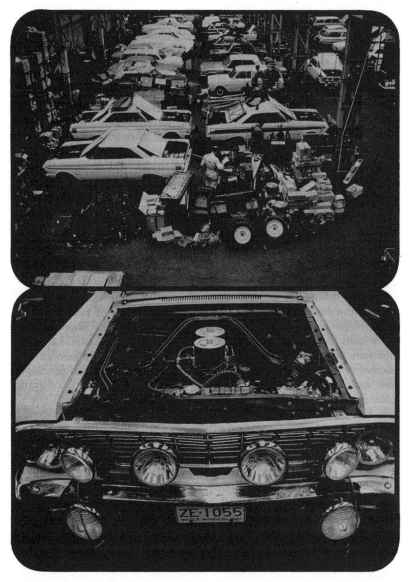

At left: By the time of the 1965 Monte, some of the cars were using tires with as many as 1,200 spikes in them. They wouldn't last more than a few miles on dry pavement, but in the snow and ice they permitted the teams to run at racing speeds. Here is a Goodyear model used by the Cortinas.

Above: (Top) Ford entries for the 1964 Monte undergoing preparation in London. (Bottom) One of Europe's first looks at two four-barrel carburetors sitting atop a husky American V8. The lights include two standard, two spot, two for cornering and two for fog.

when the cars arrived at Rheims on the morning and early afternoon of Monday, there were still 274 running, many of them unpenalized and eager to head south (with nearly 100 of them being factory entries from most of Europe's manufacturers). As the year before, Ljungfeldt showed the way, making fast time on the first special stage. But right behind was Irishman Paddy Hopkirk in a hotted-up, stripped-down Mini-Cooper, and the coefficient put Hopkirk ahead of Ljungfeldt on points. On the second stage, the Swede was again quickest. Somehow, Hopkirk managed to tie Ljungfeldt in scratch (non-handicap) time on the third stage, then the Swede took all the rest of them. When they rolled into Monte Carlo Tuesday morning, the coefficient had relegated Ljungfeldt to fifth place. Hopkirk was leading and had it locked up, unless he crashed in the final three-lap event. Erik Carlsson, the two-time winner, was second in a Saab. His wife Pat (Stirling Moss' sister and the finest woman rally pilot in history) was third in another Saab, and Finnish star Timo Makinen was fourth in another Mini.

A check showed if Ljungfeldt could drive markedly quicker than either of the Carlssons or Makinen, he could make it into second place, as times recorded on the grand prix circuit were not multiplied by the factor, but merely added to the total as one penalty point per second.

Hammering the car around the tight corners in big slides, with the bellow of the V8 echoing off the walls of nearby buildings, Ljungfeldt posted fastest time of the day—and got his hoped-for second place behind Hopkirk. For the second year in a row he was not the winner, but he was unquestionably the hero. All eight of the Ford entries made it to the finish (as did 163 of the 299 starters), with Schlesser placing 11th, Greder 19th, Anne Hall 39th, Jopp 50th, Hill 107th and Harper 115th. Hill lost his chances through crashing and suffering body damage in one of the stages. Harper, in 20th place on arriving in Monte Carlo, was involved in an accident during his three-lap race when a Citroen spun in front of him, and lost thousands of points as a result. They still remember the mishap on the Riviera: the flying fiberglass was something to see. In addition to the good over-all placings, Ljungfeldt (who for the second straight year drove the entire way, his copilot attending strictly to navigation) won the large touring car class, and Anne Hall took the large grand touring category, helped by Denise McCluggage. The latter victory was the result of a move made in the fall, when Ford got the news Chrysler was entering three Valiants in the GT class. Chrysler's reason for entering touring cars in the supposedly faster (but with weaker competition) class was to have a better chance of winning something—and thus have something to advertise. Ford switched its girls and also the Jopp car into GT to halt the Valiants and they did this easily, with the women proving themselves faster drivers than the men on their own team.

Success in Europe, on the part of the Ford Division, was soon to be offset slightly by the biggest failure Lincoln-Mercury ever had in a performance event. As the next step after the successful 100,000-mile record run of late 1963, some promotional genius at Lincoln-Mercury decided there was United States sales value in winning the East African Safari, a 3,180-mile car destroyer that ran through jungles, over mountains and past such movable obstacles as lions, giraffes, elephants and rock-throwing natives. Not only were the Comets short on experience and long on weight, but they were also, months before the start, to find themselves in an intra-corporate dispute. Ford of Britain, which had embarked on an extensive rally program for 1964 (and which *could* make good promotional use of a Safari victory), was involved in an all-out attempt to win in East Africa. When Fran Hernandez flew to Britain in the fall of 1963 to ask for advice, the first thing he was told was "Don't."

The suggestion turned out to be a wise one. There were 10 Comets entered, then four had to be withdrawn to act as service cars. Of the other six only two managed to finish, one 18th and one 21st. There were 94 starters.

The lighter Cortinas wound up first and third over-all, first through fourth in their class, and also took the team prize. Lincoln-Mercury shot enough movie footage and came out with enough ballyhoo to obscure the basic facts of the matter from the general public, but it had been a bad proposition from the beginning. High horsepower, heavy cars stood little chance where only 300 miles of the route was paved, and the rest included waist-deep river crossings, miles of sticky African mud and rocky paths which eventually pounded suspensions to pieces. About the most welcome sight in Africa, for the Lincoln-Mercury crew, was the Nairobi airport when they were headed home.

Back in Europe Ford made no major move until midsummer. Greder, driving for Ford-France, attempted repeating his Tulip Rally win of 1963, and this time he finished fourth. In the middle of June Ljungfeldt tried his own country's rally with a Falcon, despite knowing the event would favor small cars. He wound up seventh over-all, but won his class. Later that month Ford made a big push in the French Alpine rally, but when the cars showed up at the starting line they were disqualified—the cry over the homologation of the lightweight Falcons had caused the International Automobile Federation to take another look at the proceedings, and through an *ex post facto* decision, they were now ruled out. It made little difference, except for the inconvenience of the moment. Mustang production was in full swing, and the Mustang was eminently better suited for competition work than was the Falcon.

The first trial for the Mustangs was Spa-Sofia-Liege, with Ljungfeldt and Fergus Sager driving one car, and top British pilots Peter Proctor and Peter Harper in the second. As the previous year, the effort came to naught; Ljungfeldt went off the road somewhere in Yugoslavia, and the two Englishmen also retired before they ever got out of that part of the world. It was an inauspicious debut, but one for which they were to get even in the Tour de France.

This time not only were Ford-powered touring cars involved, but so were a trio of Cobra coupes, driven by Bob Bondurant and Frenchmen Maurice Trintignant and Andre Simon. If the Cobras could sweep the top spots in the grand touring category, the world manufacturer's title would go to Shelby American. After leading through the first few stages they all retired with mechanical difficulties, the Ferrari GTOs going on to win that portion of the event and retain the title for their Italian factory. The 1964 Tour was, as usual, about 3,600 miles in length and included eight races

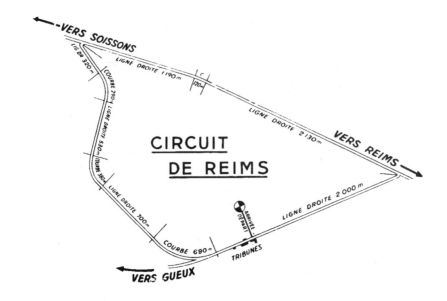

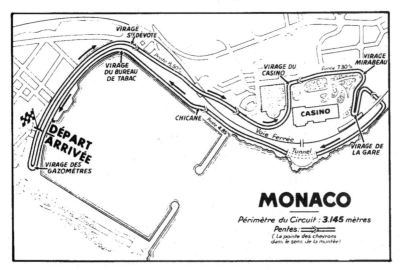

Above: (Top) The road course at Rheims, sometimes used for the French Grand Prix and also employed for speed tests in the Tour de France. (Bottom) The grand prix circuit at Monaco, used for speed tests in the Monte Carlo Rally and the Tour de France. At right: (Top) Ljungfeldt on his way out of Rheims, 1964. (Middle) 1964 Tour de France index of performance winners Vic Elford (left), David Seigle-Morris and their Cortina. (Bottom) 1964 Touring category winners Peter Proctor (right) and Andrew Cowan with their Mustang. Another Mustang was second.

and eight hill climbs, with the Nürburgring and Spa of the year before being dropped, and Monza and Cognac (an airfield circuit in the area where they squeeze the grapes) being included. Going in, the Mann-led team figured it had a good chance to win, especially if it ran as a team and the drivers didn't try to "race" each other. Mann had three cars, driven by Ljungfeldt, Proctor and Harper, while a fourth Mustang, entered by Ford of France and sporting two four-barrel carburetors instead of one, was handled by Greder.

Through the opening stages, including an hour and a half race at Rheims, a hillclimb at Bramont, an hour's race at Rouen and a two-hour event at Le Mans, the Mustangs occupied the first four spots in the touring class, with Mann's three vehicles running—as planned—neck and neck, and Greder some distance behind. In fifth was Consten, looking for his fifth consecutive win in the Tour and knowing his Jaguar could do this only if the Mustangs blew up or crashed. It was not going to happen, at least not to all of them. Ljungfeldt was disqualified after he pushed his car—as per a gendarme's directions—through a shortcut after he stalled during the race at Pau, and Greder blew his engine after the race at Clermont-Ferrand. But Proctor and Harper, with a commanding lead in the class, took it easy on the closing stages and finished well ahead of Consten and right next to each other, with Proctor in front due to Harper's being penalized once for an illegal start. But that made little difference. The main thing was the Mustangs had been impressive, and in Europe, at least, they got considerable publicity mileage from their accomplishment. At home the event received little notice. Rally participation for 1965 was already out of the question, as the budget made no provision for it: the only 1965 activity to be conducted in Europe in the coming year was to be racing—synonymous with Le Mans.

There were aftermaths to the rally program, in fact several: Greder, using one of the 1963 Falcons, managed to win the Geneva Rally for the second straight time in October, and there was the Monte Carlo rally of the following January. It had two Mustangs entered on a more or less private basis, one by Mann for Ljungfeldt and one by Ford-France for Greder, and neither of them did anything worth writing home about. But they did do something worth filming and using for background sequences for a movie.

The name of it was *A Man and a Woman,* and it was a French production, starring Jean-Louis Trintignant and Anouk Aimee, which was one of the more sensitive love stories of 1966 and an Academy Award winner. The hero of the film happens to be a Ford factory rally driver, and although this is never blatantly pushed forward in the story, it is inescapable, just as is the fact he drives a Mustang in the Monte Carlo Rally, various other Fords in other things and still other Fords for his personal transport. To get your product in a movie is no bad thing for an auto manufacturer. To get your product as one of the major actors in a movie that managed to play one New York theater for more than two years, and to receive wide critical acclaim in the bargain; if all the 1963 and 1964 rally programs did was set the stage for the film, they were worth it.

26

BIB OVERALLS, MAGAZINE COVERS AND BILLIE SOL

IN THE SUMMER of 1956 and the winter of 1957 there were two unrelated occurrences. The first was a memo written by Joe MacKay, then getting his indoctrination as a stock car racing man. MacKay still didn't know much about racing, but he was a thinker and he was looking to explore all the possibilities. The memo read in part, "On several occasions comments have been made ... concerning the merits of internationally flavored performance events for the Ford car." MacKay went on to suggest running 1957 Fords at such well-known European circuits as Monza, Spa and the Nürburgring (not in races, just for the cameras), and then using the resultant footage for a promotional campaign. "I fully realize this may be just a wild idea," MacKay concluded, "but I would appreciate any comments you might have." In the conservative world of Detroit, vintage 1956, MacKay's suggestion stopped right there.

That was also the year a skinny, smiling ex-chicken farmer from east Texas was making the Sports Car Club of America racing circuit his own personal property. Carroll Shelby had a wealthy sponsor, a hot Ferrari, and something even more important: style. He'd show up with that big smile, his curly hair and his cowboy boots, climb into a pair of bib overalls and proceed to blow everybody off. Then he'd vanish into the sunset again, like as not with a good-looking girl on each arm. Nobody was quite sure where he'd gone; either on to another party or back to Texas to count his patron's oil wells, or buildings, or some other property. The SCCA allowed only amateurs to race in those days, and the standard story was that Shelby's angel kept him within the letter of the law by paying Carroll to make sure none of the wells picked itself up and walked away.

By the end of the year Shelby had made it apparent that the smile, the overalls and the girls weren't the only things he had going for him; he could also drive fast, and had won just about everything he'd entered. Among those who watched Shelby that season was Luigi Chinetti, the Ferrari distributor in the United States; Chinetti soon arranged an audience with Enzo himself. It was held in the commendatore's almost theatrically barren office in his Maranello plant, and when Shelby mentioned he had won 20-odd races the year before, Ferrari sarcastically asked him who had come in second. When Shelby wanted to know how much money he would earn, Ferrari told him $40 a month and 30 percent of the purses, if he happened to win anything.

Shelby wanted 50 percent.

No, 30 percent, Ferrari said.

"Do I get to drive all the races?"

"You drive when I say so," Ferrari replied.

Shelby stood up. "I'll blow your ass off some day," he said. Then he walked out and went across town to Maserati, where he picked up several cars for his sponsor of the year before.

Four years later, in the summer of 1961, Shelby's racing career was finished. Although he had never made it into the exclusive group of regular grand prix pilots, Shelby had been a good, heady driver who had never lacked for a factory-sponsored ride at any of the major races such as Sebring or the Nürburgring 1,000 Kilometers, and who had driven an Aston Martin to victory in the 24 hours of Le Mans in 1959. He was good enough to get his picture on the cover of *Sports Illustrated* when they named him sports car driver of the year in 1957, but now he was 38 and sidelined by a minor heart ailment. His assets included the Goodyear race tire franchise for the far western states, a high-performance driving school and an idea. The tire distributorship was located in a corner of Dean Moon's speed equipment business in the Los Angeles suburb of Santa Fe Springs, the driver's school was held at Riverside, some 50 miles to the southeast, and the idea was in Shelby's head.

Basically, it was to combine a mass-produced American engine with a lightweight European chassis to make a sports car—one that was good enough to be raced successfully, yet flexible enough to be sold as a street machine. Shelby's idea was little more than a pleasant pipe dream, one which many other mechanics, drivers and other would-be car constructors had thought of in the past. Such wealthy ones as Briggs Cunningham and Lance Reventlow had been able to transform their dreams into reality as far as the racing part of it was concerned, but even they had to give it up over the long haul as it invariably turned into a losing proposition. But Shelby was not burdened by Cunningham or Reventlow-type financial problems. He didn't have any money to begin with, so he didn't worry about that. What he *did* have was his own personality, and that was worth considerable.

You-all know Ole Shel?

Why man, he could sweet-talk the leaves right off the trees, if'n he was of a mind to, and remember the first time you met him?

Why he had you laughing inside of two minutes and after five you were his buddy, right? And what about all them good-lookin' ladies he had around him and all them rich millionaires who used to give him fancy cars to drive.... man, he could sure promote up a storm, couldn't he?

Timing, it is said, is everything in life, and Shelby, when he made his first few contacts with Ford, couldn't have picked a more opportune moment. The reason he went to Dearborn was that he found General Motors unwilling to make a deal for the aluminum V8 then used to power the smaller Oldsmobiles and Buicks. Ford, Shelby had heard, was getting ready to introduce a somewhat similar engine with its 1962 model line. Although it would be a cast-iron proposition, new techniques had enabled them to keep the walls thin and the weight down.

What Shelby didn't know was that Ford was ripe for performance ideas and the company was looking for something that would give it an exciting image. In a large corporation, or in any large undertaking, it is always difficult to place responsibility for success or failure on the shoulders of one man, but in the case of Ford's efforts in the sophisticated world of long-distance international racing, there is little question that the spark was in many ways provided by this Texas promoter. Nobody has ever been able to put his finger on just what it is that Carroll Shelby has, but whatever it is, he has lots of it. Perhaps it is an ability to get others to do things for him, or the ability to seize an opportunity and make use of it for his own advantage (there were several persons who always refer to him as Billie Sol, a kidding reference to Billie Sol Estes, another Texas wheeler and dealer who had the misfortune to get caught).

So Shelby went and made deals and did things, and whenever he got in too deep Ford would have to come around and straighten him out again, but the main thing was that in 1963, 1964 and 1965 he got results, and he gave them an image. At first it was a loud, raucous, blaring image of an Anglo-American hot rod called the Cobra. By 1965, the Cobra had won the world manufacturer's championship. By the next year Ford's ultra-sophisticated, ultra-expensive GT had won at Le Mans, and although by now there were hundreds of people in the act and control was far from Shelby's hands, the car had been entered in his name, and when it was all over, there were still a lot of photographers and reporters who ran to Billie Sol.

Personality ... and image, and all those good things.

At the beginning it was innocent enough. Shelby had met Dave Evans at the Pike's Peak hillclimb July 4, 1961, and that brief introduction gave him his first contact with a member of Ford's performance department. A little over a month later Shelby called Evans, told about his plan and hit him up for a few of the new engines. Evans, who knew little of sports car racing and even less of Shelby, said he'd think about it. (Evans: "Those first few phone calls, why, I thought I was talking to a corporation president instead of a guy who was working out of a garage!") Shortly after Labor Day, and for reasons he still can't explain, Evans decided to ship two of the new 221-inch V8s to this unknown on the West Coast. The project was of such minor importance that Evans didn't bother to tell Frey, and things dragged so that it was nearly November before Shelby got not only the engines, but also such accessory pieces as starters, fans, fan belts and fuel pumps. As soon as he shipped a complete one, including the four-speed transmission, Shelby shipped it to AC Cars in England for installation in the prototype and continued his

The many faces of Billie Sol. At left: (Top) Shelby on his way to winning at Le Mans, 1959, and (bottom) practicing for the Targa Florio in 1955. Above: (Top) The overall-clad Shelby, plus (from left) Roy Salvadori, Jack Fairman and Stirling Moss after the Aston Martin team swept the Tourist Trophy in 1959. (Bottom) Curly hair and that big smile—Shelby at Le Mans in 1954, where he shared an Aston Martin with Belgian Paul Frere.

wheeling and dealing, keeping Ford interested on one hand and keeping AC anxious on the other side of the ocean. Evans then told Frey about it; the latter, a sports car fan, *knew* who Shelby was and from then on watched the project personally.

Frey, however, was laboring under the impression Shelby was another of those Texas oil millionaires, and was curious to know more about him. A few days later Ray Brock, the editor of *Hot Rod,* was in Detroit and both Frey and Evans started quizzing him about their new-found friend.

"We understand he's one of those rich Texans," Frey said.

"Well, he's a Texan," Brock told him, "but he sure as hell doesn't have a dime—all he has is a good idea."

A few weeks later Shelby heard about the conversation, and at the bottom of one of his letters to Evans made sure there was no longer any doubt. Referring to what Brock had told him, Shelby wrote, "I am a poor man who has spent everything in trying to put my automobile together. I have driven race cars and worked hard to see this through to the end, it is all my money so far, but I must either ask you for help or I will have to take in some investors, which I would rather not do."

Evans showed the letter to Frey, and within a few weeks Ford was taking care of Shelby's expenses. The shipping of the engines was the first concrete step in the relationship, this was the second—and still, no one had any idea where it would lead.

By the beginning of January, unknown to Shelby, his little project had created enough interest that Ford was merely waiting for the tests of the prototype before negotiating an agreement with the would-be constructor. But the car wasn't ready and tests, originally scheduled for Riverside in mid-January, had to be rescheduled for the end of the month in England. Shelby flew over to track down missing axles and to keep AC's interest alive with one hand, and with the other he would write to Evans ("I'll get the job done") and maintain the relationship in Dearborn.

On January 30, a chill day in the middle of a typically damp English winter, the erstwhile race driver climbed into the cockpit of his new baby, and in a few moments, the peculiar minor-key roar of an American V8 echoed across the green expanse of Silverstone. It ran, and once it was pointed in the right direction, it ran fast.

Within a few days the Cobra was on a boat headed for the States and Shelby was in Dearborn, equipped with movies of the test. On the strength of these, accompanied by Shelby's oral report of the car's behavior and potential, on February 5 Ford and Shelby signed their first papers, a letter of agreement in which Shelby agreed to use "Powered by Ford" labels on all his cars in exchange for the engines and other parts he would receive.

Things were rolling, and in a few weeks they were to pick up all the speed the project would need to become a full-blown reality. When the prototype (dubbed the CSX1001) arrived in Los Angeles, Shelby got on the telephone to his large collection of friends who worked for automotive enthusiast publications. They flocked to see—and write, and photograph—the new Cobra. By the beginning of

March Shelby was able to call Ford and report his creation would be the subject of a number of articles and would even grace the covers of several magazines. When the news got to Iacocca, that was all Shelby needed. For the past year one of Iacocca's sore points had been the lack of this type of exposure for Ford products. He would constantly leaf through the various "buff books" and see that Chevy and Pontiac had a virtual monopoly, not only on the covers, but on the stories contained therein. No one at Ford had been able to get Iacocca any of the covers, and now here came this curly-haired farmer out of the Texas weeds and with one stroke he managed to get the Ford Division more editorial exposure than it had received in years. Shelby and the Cobra were home free (at least in principle), and when Ford included the car as part of its exhibit at the New York auto show, the reaction it caused served to solidify the deal.

The main contracts were signed at the beginning of August, and basically the agreements said Ford just about owned Shelby American, Inc., and what Ford wasn't financing in one way, Ford was financing in another (such as the racing program Shelby was to conduct). In addition, Ford undertook an exhaustive study of the new car to determine what could be done to make it better. Danny Jones was in charge of this segment of the operation and soon came up with a bookful of recommendations for changes in the basic model, most of them worthwhile, and many of them soon to be incorporated into the design. The original plan of simply dropping in a 260-inch high performance Ford V8 and a four-speed transmission proved to be overly optimistic; there was a great deal of work to be accomplished before the car could be sold as a reasonably roadworthy package, and production slowed while this was achieved. The original financial forecast that Shelby American could become self-sustaining as early as December of 1962 also proved optimistic; throughout the time Shelby's manufacturing operation was located on the West Coast (until the summer of 1967, when the 1968-model Shelby Mustangs were assembled in Ionia, Mich.), this part of the business was never in the black.

Although they are nebulous and subject to opinion, there are other ways of measuring profits besides in dollars and cents, and what the manufacturing side of Shelby's dream lacked in this respect was more than made up by the racing activities of the Cobras. Here the profit was to be counted up in quantities of ink, that good black kind used in newspapers and magazines; Shelby's racing Cobras got exposure like no other American competition car in the decades before them, and every time the word Cobra was mentioned, there was bound to be the word Ford somewhere nearby. The idea to race the car, naturally, was Shelby's, and he was the man who made sure the basic power-to-weight ratio of the vehicle was a favorable one. But the person who more than any other was responsible for the Cobras running as well as they did—and for all other Shelby racing equipment being successful—was Phil Remington, who came along with the store.

When Shelby moved out of his Santa Fe Springs location in the summer of 1962, he took over Lance Reventlow's facility in Venice, where Reventlow had built his Scarabs (including the unsuccessful Formula I car and the practically all-conquering Chevy-powered sports car). The heir to the Woolworth fortune was engaged in closing down the operation at this time; he hadn't been able to turn a profit, and the government was ready to start nailing him for income tax. Among those working for Reventlow was Remington. When Shelby moved in, Remington stayed where he was. The arrangements were simple: Remington asked Shelby what he was going to be doing, and Shelby told him they were going to go racing. That was enough.

If Remington is a mechanic, then at least 99 percent of the others who carry that title are imposters. Remington is called a mechanic (his official title at Shelby American eventually became chief engineer) mainly by default, as he does not have an engineering degree. His formal education, which included two years at Santa Monica City College and six months at UCLA, was interrupted by World War II, and when that was over a diploma didn't mean much. Phil just wanted to race and he did, going back to what he had done as a kid on the dry lakes of the Mojave. He worked on this race car and that one, spending some time with Jim Travers and Frank Coon when they maintained midgets and Indianapolis cars for oil millionaire Howard Keck, and in 1949 wound up in San Francisco as shop foreman on Sterling Edwards' sports car project. Edwards had one of the first postwar notions that you could build a limited production car at a profit. Edwards soon found he couldn't, and Remington moved back to Los Angeles where he worked on injection systems for Stu Hilborn, on chassis for Lujie Lesovsky, and for Ford on its round-the-world promotional project of 1957. Then he went with Reventlow, where he spent five years and where he was when the shop changed hands.

At the beginning Remington was occupied with getting cars ready to race on one hand and improving the production models on the other. When the first Cobra (still with the 260-inch engine and a single four-barrel carb) made its competition debut at Riverside in October, the only improvements were wide-rim wheels and racing tires, a larger fuel tank and a roll bar in case driver Billy Krause should get upside down. Krause, faced with a bunch of California's better Corvette pilots and the newest, independent rear suspension version of Chevrolet's sports car, had little trouble. He pulled away from the pack, and after an hour was rolling along with a comfortable lead when a rear hub carrier broke. The car hadn't finished, but the potential had been shown. The next appearance, at Nassau Speed Weeks in December and again with Krause driving, was also unsuccessful—but again the word spread. If they ever got it to finish, the Cobra would be a winner. (This race also marked the debut of a privately entered Cobra; Ed Hugus, a Pittsburgh driver and foreign car dealer, had picked up the franchise for his area the previous summer, and took one of his own cars to Nassau. He didn't do any better than Krause.)

The next man to join the team was Ken Miles, and what Remington did for Shelby American with his mechanical talents, Miles did with his abilities as a development and racing driver, not only with the Cobras, but later with the Ford GTs.

Miles was already something of a legend among the Southern California sports car crowd by the time he joined Shelby. An almost cadaverously lean Englishman in his mid-40s, with jug-handled ears, a large hooked nose, a long, pointed chin and graying hair, Miles always kept his strong British accent even though he had emigrated in 1952. He started driving races almost as soon as he arrived in the United States, and was a consistent winner from the start. Miles specialized in small-displacement cars, starting with MGs and MG-powered specials he designed and built himself, then switching over to Porsches in the late 1950s. By the time he arrived at Shelby's, Miles' reputation as the fastest Porsche driver in the country was well established; he had won just about everything, had gone through as many as 60 straight races without dropping out and had been beaten only by the very best of the big-car drivers. Why hadn't Miles made the logical step to a bigger, faster car? There were some who said he didn't want to take a chance on losing (he was soon to disprove this nonsense), but the main reason was there weren't too many sponsors who wanted Miles. This ascetic Englishman was a difficult man with whom to get along. He was brutally frank, could be terribly sarcastic and also had a considerable ego. He once refused to take an SCCA driver's test (he had already amassed a considerable reputation in outside races) because he claimed there was no one in the club capable of driving as well as he, and therefore no one capable of passing judgment on his talents. But with it all, and despite the number of sponsors and jobs, Miles was a topnotch driver and also a warmhearted human being to the few who ever managed to pierce the barriers he set in front of himself. Shelby was one of those, Remington was another.

In January at Riverside the Cobra collected its first victory. It was only a small, SCCA divisional affair, but it was nevertheless a first. Dave MacDonald, the Corvette hotshot of the year before, but now driving for Shelby, was the winner with Miles in close attendance in second. From there the team went to Daytona and the Continental, at that stage of its growth still a three-hour race. It was to be the first meeting between the Ferrari GTO, at that time the fastest grand touring car extant, and the Cobras (now with four double-choke Weber carburetors), and the Ferraris had an easy time of it. Shelby had three cars—one for Gurney, one for Skip Hudson and one for MacDonald. Gurney's vehicle was being used as a secret trial horse for Ford's Indianapolis engine project and ran into a myriad of problems during practice. The final one came when a Welch plug blew out of the engine 80 minutes before the start and the entire unit had to be changed. He started two laps after the rest of the field, never ran well and eventually retired with ignition problems. Hudson was running second when his flywheel burst, shattering the steering and Hudson's ankle and causing the car to crash. MacDonald lost time when his starter had to be replaced and finished fourth. It was an inauspicious debut in bigtime racing, and the next appearance in a major event was no better.

MacDonald and Miles again finished 1-2 in a small SCCA race held on the Dodger Stadium parking lot in March; then a major effort was mounted for Sebring—

five cars, including one entered by Holman-Moody. Sebring was a failure, despite the advantage of having Ford's new 289-inch engines for the first time. Not only the cars, but the team was also in need of a shakedown. Mechanics worked night after night getting ready for practice and then had to work more long hours making adjustments for the race. Phil Hill, in one of his first drives for Shelby, actually led the race for a while, but soon was forced in with a brake caliper welded to a disc when the air scoop was ripped away as he ran over a rubber course marker someone else had knocked onto the track. Gurney was as high as fifth after six hours, but then his steering had to be replaced, and the rest of the cars dropped out or suffered long delays for various reasons. Ferrari won the race for the fifth time in six years, and the Cobras finally decided to do away with the worm and sector steering, switching over to rack and pinion. A car driven by Miles, Hill and Lew Spencer managed to limp in 11th, another was 29th, and another 41st—and the bright spot was still there: While the cars were running, and despite the obvious weaknesses, the Cobras had been quicker than anything in their class. The problem was to keep them running.

The major objective for the Cobras in 1963 was to win as many titles as possible in Sports Car Club of America competition, and there were several available. This was the first year of the United States Road Racing Championship (USRRC) series, which had divisions open to both manufacturers and drivers. Since the Cobra had been classified as an A production category car by the SCCA, there was also that championship to be considered. For his team Shelby collected Miles, MacDonald and Bob Holbert, the veteran Pennsylvania Porsche driver who had the same sort of record on the East Coast that Miles had compiled in California. Their first USRRC race was in late May on a bumpy airfield course at Pensacola, Fla., and the results were even more disheartening than anything that had happened so far. All three cars were clearly faster than anything else, and all three dropped out when their differentials overheated. On the SCCA national championship level, the Cobras were also having trouble: Holbert lost one race at Danville, Va., when he had a flat tire, and Bob Johnson, of Columbus, Ohio, lost another at Marlboro, Md., when he crashed. It was not until May that anyone picked up national championship points and then it was Johnson who did it, winning consecutive races at Cumberland, Md., and Bridgehampton, N.Y.

The factory Cobras got healthy in a hurry in early June at Laguna Seca, Calif., where the second USRRC event of the season was to be run. During a preliminary event on Saturday, which MacDonald won easily, there were indications of the differential trouble that bit the team at Pensacola. Overnight, oil coolers were installed in all three cars and the next day they won with ease, running 1-2-3 for most of the 150 miles with Holbert winning, MacDonald second and Miles fourth due to an unforeseen pit stop.

It was as if someone had thrown a switch. From then on the Cobras rarely came close to losing; with their big exhausts blaring forth all sorts of loud noises as they charged down the straights, and with their primitive suspensions making the cars skip and slide as the drivers took them through tight corners in dirt-track style, the Cobras were the heroes of the sports car circuit. The manufacturers' races of the USRRC series soon became little more than exhibition tours for the Cobras, but it was something to see; the three factory cars, usually accompanied by Johnson and another private entry or two, would charge off at the drop of the flag, with the only race of any sort being among the team cars themselves. It wasn't even a race—the drivers always split the pot equally, regardless of who won, and the decision as to which man would win was normally made before the start. Any passing or repassing was done mostly to give the fans a thrill; watching the trio roll around, nose to tail for the 150 miles of each race, would have become boring. After Laguna Seca came Watkins Glen, and here Johnson actually beat the factory team in the manufacturer's race (primarily due to a better choice of tires) as Cobras finished 1-2-3-5, and then Miles decided to run in the 200-mile driver's championship event for modified sports cars. They refilled his car with gas, changed tires, quickly put out a small fire in the engine compartment, and he finished third behind two sports-racing cars. At Lake Garnett, Kan., where the factory cars went to help Johnson in his bid for the class A production title, MacDonald and Miles finished behind Johnson, and then Miles again decided to enter the modified event. Before the production race someone complained about the Cobra's differential coolers, maintaining they were not a production item and forcing the team to discontinue them. When that event was over Miles went to the officials and told them he proposed to run the car in the modified race—with the differential cooler once again connected. Miles proceeded to run away from various older-model Chaparrals, Ferraris and Cooper Menaces to win the Lake Garnett Grand Prix (perhaps the only time anything in Kansas has ever been given such an illustrious name).

At Kent, Wash., MacDonald, Miles and Holbert ran 1-2-3 in the manufacturers race. They came back in the modified event and were running 2-3-5 before rain (and the lack of rain tires) dropped them to 4-5-6 (Holbert, Miles, MacDonald) at the end. Both races were 150 miles, which meant by the close of the day Cobras had run 900 miles under racing conditions without so much as a pit stop. Pomona, Thompson, Meadowdale, Harewood Acres in Canada, Watkins Glen again, Santa Barbara, Candlestick Park, Mid-Ohio, Bridgehampton again and Riverside too—almost everywhere they went they were winners. The factory cars alone—and this includes the early season failures—won 11 of the 16 grand touring class races they entered.

Gurney, who drove for the team when his European schedule permitted, also had the satisfaction of recording the first Cobra success in an international championship event when he won the 500-kilometer race at Bridgehampton in September. Miles and Holbert, sharing the wheel of one car, just missed winning the Road America "500" on Labor Day weekend, this being one of the country's premier road-racing events. The team won the USRRC manufacturer's championship easily and Holbert and Miles were 1-2 in the USRRC driver's standings, thanks to their activities in the modified races they ran as extracurricular activity. By the end of the season this phase of Shelby's operation was so successful the team even took on two Ford-powered Cooper Monacos (soon dubbed King Cobras) for the big fall races at Riverside and Laguna Seca. MacDonald won both of them, beating some of the world's best in both places and enhancing his own reputation as the hottest young driver in the country.

Then there was Le Mans.

It was an innocent enough proposition the first year. The chassis builders, AC Cars, entered one in the race, and Ed Hugus, a regular competitor at Le Mans, entered another. Remington was there, as he had been pried loose from Shelby (for the second time that season—he had already helped Ford with the Indianapolis testing) to install a V8 in Eric Broadley's new Lola coupe. Remington acted as chief mechanic, gave advice and did what he could with his own hands, and the two cars took off with the rest of the pack. The Hugus entry expired after 10 hours with engine trouble, but the other one, driven by Scotsman Ninian Sanderson and Englishman Peter Bolton, kept right on rolling. At the end it was seventh, behind six Ferraris. It was not only a finish for the car, it was the start of considerable hope for Le Mans success on the part of Ford.

Despite the victories there were two serious setbacks during the year, items much more important than any race losses during the surprisingly short growing-pains phase. One of these was visible to the public, and took place in the Bahamas in early December, when the annual Speed Weeks were held. The Shelby team showed up with its usual collection of Cobras and Cooper-Fords and soon found itself running a poor second to a collection of Chevy-powered equipment, ostensibly owned by private individuals, but accompanied by a group of Chevrolet engineers who coincidentally chose Nassau for a December vacation. As opposition for the Cobras there were several "Grand Sport" Corvettes—ultralight, space-frame cars equipped with giant disc brakes and with their normal 327-inch engines bored and stroked to 377 inches. They were examples of what GM had intended to build in small series before the no-racing edict was reinforced in the early part of 1963, and they were fast. On an average, they were nine to 10 seconds per lap quicker than the Cobras. On the racing sports side there was the sole Lola GT coupe ever to get out of Ford's hands, this one equipped with a Chevrolet engine, and there were two Chaparrals and A.J. Foyt with one of the old Scarabs, also complete with Chevy power. Not only were all of these faster than the Cooper-Fords, but neither the Cobras nor the Coopers even managed to make it close.

The Chevrolet equipment won so easily there was even some embarrassment on the part of their factory personnel, who had hoped the journey south would escape unnoticed. But at the same time, they were smirking. One of the engineers, when approached by a reporter with a technical question, laughed and said, "You realize, of course, you're talking to a man who isn't here." All of them received lectures when they returned to Detroit, but the mission had been accomplished: Ford was shown it had a way to go.

The other setback was of a more permanent nature: In June of that initial Cobra racing campaign, at approximately the time the cars started to show their potential, the Cobras (at least in their present form) were written off as interim vehicles. There were various reasons for this, all of them justified in the light of developments at that time (and all of them dealt with in later chapters). The negotiations to purchase Ferrari had fallen through in the middle of May, and as a result the decision was made in Dearborn to build a long-distance sports-racing car capable of beating the Ferrari at its own game. The logical extension of this program would be the build of a limited-production passenger car which would employ the same basic design (mid-engine, as per the best and latest racing principles) as the competition cars. This would be the vehicle to replace the Cobra as the image-builder for Ford products, much, and even more so, it was hoped, as the Corvette did for Chevrolet. So the Cobras became much like the bumblebee, which no one ever bothered to tell its wings are too small to allow it to fly. Not knowing this, it simply goes ahead and flies anyway.

For 1964 it was obvious the Cobra would have to fly faster than the previous year, and in the fall of 1963 work was started on a coupe body. The original open roadsters might have been fine for the tight circuits of the SCCA, where speeds of perhaps 140 mph were hit for a second or two each lap, but for sustained high-speed running in Europe a more aerodynamic enclosed form was a must (and it was legal: the FIA grand touring rules of the time specified a minimum of 100 cars built in 12 consecutive months, but left the form of the body free). Pete Brock, the young stylist, race driver and jack of all trades who was Shelby's first employee, made the drawings. Remington was in charge of most of the construction, when he could find time to get away from Ford's GT40 program (he spent most of the fall of 1963 and the winter of 1964 in Europe, working on the prototypes of this new series). They didn't use computers and they didn't use wind tunnels; they relied instead on Brock's talent and on the craftsmanship of their own mechanics. When it was finished, the aggressive-looking machine gave Shelby a genuine 180 mph from 370 horsepower, despite an extra 150 pounds due to the body. The car not only went 20 miles an hour faster than the roadsters, but was considerably more economical in fuel consumption (again, thanks to the slippery shape).

The first appearance of the coupe was in the Daytona Continental at the beginning of February (it got its name from this race), and as opposition there were numerous Ferrari GTOs, including a factory-sponsored entry to be driven by Pedro Rodriguez and Phil Hill. The race had grown in length to 2,000 kilometers (about 1,240 miles), and for most of it there was little question who had the fastest car: It was the Cobra coupe, with Holbert and MacDonald cooking inside the poorly ventilated cockpit, but pulling away from the Ferrari. After a third of the race was done the Cobra took a commanding lead when the Hill-Rodriguez car lost three laps with a blowout and resultant repairs. When two-thirds of the event was over the Cobra was four laps in front and it came in for a pit stop. The differential cooler had ceased to function, and when mechanic John Olsen crawled under the car to check the rear

Above: (Inset) Ken Miles, who made the Cobras go. (Bottom) Phil Hill at Sebring in 1963, in the Cobras' first big-league race. (Top) Bob Holbert, driving the prototype Cobra coupe, leads eventual winner Hill during the Daytona Continental of 1964. At right: (Top) The first coupe again, as it was shared by Holbert and Dave MacDonald at Daytona. (Bottom) The first Cobra to take part in the 24 Hours of Le Mans, driven by Ninian Sanderson and Peter Bolton in 1963. It finished in seventh place.

end, other members of the Shelby crew held their breath. Suddenly, gas spilling out of the refueling hose dripped on the overheated differential, and the rear of the car burst into flames. The firemen put it out in time to prevent serious damage to either the vehicle or Olsen, who went to the hospital with first and second-degree burns, but the car was done for the day. Ferraris took the top three spots in the 13-hour race. Gurney and Johnson, in a roadster-type Cobra, finished fourth.

Sebring, that flat, featureless airfield circuit that is a collection of drag strips connected by Mickey-Mouse corners, was next. This time it was 12 hours, and this time the Ferrari first team was on hand: rear-engined racing sports cars for John Surtees and Lorenzo Bandini, for Mike Parkes and Umberto Maglioli, and for Lodovico Scarfiotti and Nino Vaccarella, and a similar distributor-sponsored entry for Graham Hill and Joakim Bonnier. The Cobras didn't stand a chance for an over-all victory, and went in knowing this. They came out of it, after 12 hours in the burning Florida sunlight and the somewhat cooler night, in fourth, fifth, sixth, eighth and 10th positions, and with an even more enhanced reputation for speed and dura-bility. The Ferraris, as expected, finished 1-2-3. Right behind them came Holbert and MacDonald in the coupe, then Spencer and Bondurant, and Phil Hill with French-man Jo Schlesser—and then the first Ferrari GTO. But for a late accident, in which Bob Johnson tangled with a slow-moving Alfa right in front of the pits, the Holbert-MacDonald car would have been relegated to fifth place; the vehicle Johnson shared with Gurney was running a strong fourth at the time, with little more than an hour left in the race. Buried in the results, but very obvious to those who were there, was the Cobra that carried number 1 on its side and was driven by Miles. As noisy as the other Cobras were, their sound was nothing compared to the bellow emanating from this one: It was the 427-inch prototype. Miles managed to bump into what was probably the only tree in all of Sebring during the first practice session, they never did repair it properly, and the car eventually retired with engine problems. But again, it was a start in a new direction.

When it was all over, Shelby said "Next year, Ferrari's ass is mine." He hadn't beaten the Italians yet, but Shelby had some consolation from the 1964 race. It was the second event of the season (Daytona was the first) counting toward the world championship for manufacturers of grand touring cars, and according to the involved mathematics used to determine the standings, the Cobras were now ahead of the Ferrari GTOs. Ford and Shelby weren't worried about the 275P and 330P models which had finished in the top spots at Sebring. The GTOs, the coupes Ferrari had used to dominate this sphere of activity for the past few seasons, were now slower than the Cobras; the next step would be to try and lift this crown from Ferrari's head. From here on the history of the cars would be split: There would still be an American effort to win in the USRRC series and in the SCCA's A pro-duction category, but the emphasis would be in Europe, where most of the FIA championship events would be run.

In the United States the Cobras had little trouble. There were nine races counting for the 1964 USRRC manufacturers title and the Cobras won all of them, with Miles taking seven and sharing the seat in another victory, and West Coast veteran Ed Leslie (a midseason addition to the team) winning the other. The SCCA A production championship went to Johnson for the second straight year, and the Cobras were dominant wherever they ran and almost regardless of who drove them: All you had to do was get it around the corner one way or another, point it down the next straight and go. The car would take care of the rest. Shelby's other American project, the Cooper-Fords, were no longer successful. The cars were now usually outclassed by the Chaparrals, and once Jim Hall's automatic transmission came into public view (or at least the tarpaulin covering it every time the rear bodywork was raised; Hall was remarkably tight-lipped about what went on inside the gearbox housing), the Cooper-Fords were practically a thing of the past. Technological progress wasn't the only thing that helped shuttle the cars into the background—accidents to two of Shelby's top drivers also helped. Holbert was the first, when he lost control in practice at Kent, Wash., in early May, skidding on a puddle at the entrance to the main straight and careening into the pits, destroying his own car and two others and injuring himself seriously. Although Holbert recovered, he chose not to drive again. The other accident had nothing to do with Cobra equipment, but only with the driver. It was MacDonald, who on the strength of his 1963 and early 1964 performances with Shelby, had got a ride at Indianapolis in one of Mickey Thompson's cars. MacDonald never lived to complete the first lap of that event as one of the brightest—and briefest—careers in American racing came to a fiery end.

The European invasion, while it served to establish a beachhead, also resulted in the by-now usual opening-day catastrophe. For their first 1964 race in Europe the cars were shipped to Sicily, where the main competition was to come not from the Ferraris but from the twisting, turning, almost never-ending Madonie circuit, a 45-mile nightmare of bumpy Sicilian roads that wind from the seacoast into the hills and back down again. The stiff suspension of the Cobras, everyone knew, were not suited for this type of thing. But points were points, so the attempt was made with four cars, plus Tommy Hitchcock's private entry.

Somehow, with their giant vehicles spending more time in the air than they did on the ground, the drivers managed to stay up with the head of the pack and after six of the 10 laps (450 miles), the Cobras had attained the impossible: The Gurney-Jerry Grant car was actually running second, another car driven by Hill and Bondurant was fourth and the car shared by Sicilians Vito Coco and Enzo Arena was fifth. It was too good to last: Hill's car broke its suspension, an oil pipe fractured on the Sicilian vehicle, and then Gurney, still third with two laps to go, also broke his suspension. Somehow he managed to limp around and finish eighth. Hitchcock's car, plus the factory entry shared by Innes Ireland and Masten Gregory, were never close, the latter eventually crashing and Hitchcock being delayed by a variety of ailments.

Cobras—and more Cobras. Above: (Top) Dan Gurney at the Targa Florio, 1964. (Middle) Ken Miles in the 427 prototype at Nassau, 1964. (Bottom) The Gurney-Bob Bondurant car after Le Mans, 1964.

(Top) Bondurant in the Nürburgring 1,000 Kilometers, 1964. (Middle) Bondurant again, in the coupe he shared with Jo Schlesser during the 12 Hours of Rheims, 1965. (Bottom) Bondurant once more, at Spa, Belgium, in 1964.

Above: (Top) Chevrolet was out in force at Nassau in 1963, with several Gran Sport Corvettes (background), the Chaparral (right), and with the Lola prototype owned by Texas oilman John Mecom, Jr. (00), and powered by a Chevy engine. (Bottom) The almost biblical downpour that nearly drowned everyone at Sebring in 1965. At right: Two of the Cobra coupes on their way to first and second in class in the Monza 1,000 Kilometers, 1965.

From Sicily the cars went north to Belgium for the Grand Prix of Spa, a 500-kilometer (310-mile) event, and from there it was a two-hour drive through the Ardennes and the Eifel to the Nürburgring in Germany, where the 1,000-kilometer race at the end of May was the last major event before Le Mans. The Cobras did nothing to distinguish themselves in either race, as the suspensions were not right for the courses and no one had the hang of setting them up properly. Ferrari moved farther ahead in the chase for points.

Le Mans was something else. You can prepare cars for the Nürburgring and you can prepare cars for Spa and all those other places, but when you're part of an American team, and you've heard all those stories about Jimmy Murphy and his Duesenberg, and about how Briggs Cunningham tried for years, and you know how much it means to your boss, who drove the winner here in 1959, and how much it means—well, it gets to mean a lot to you, too. You may not like the town, or the idea of staying up all night just to watch a bunch of cars roar by every four minutes or so, but that's the way it goes on the Circuit de la Sarthe, and you kind of get worked up over it....

The Ford Division had three of the new GT40s entered, and Shelby, operating in the shade of the excitement caused by the new cars, had two of his Cobras, and AC also built up a car for the event. One of Shelby's was the original Daytona coupe, now equipped with a spoiler at the rear, and it was to be driven by Chris Amon, the young New Zealander, and Jochen Neerpasch, an excellent German driver. The second car was a new one, another coupe, and it was to be driven by Gurney and Bondurant. Remington had been in Modena, where he had some Italians making a coupe body for the chassis he had built in England, and between the inevitable delays in getting the body built, the chassis hung underneath and the engine and running gear installed, the car was actually finished in a night-and-day session in the Le Mans garage. It never turned a wheel until it set out for the technical inspection station in the middle of the week. The British car, which had its body made at home, was similar to the two Shelby entries, and had Englishmen Jack Sears and Peter Bolton as drivers. It was an odd thing: All three coupes had chassis that were considerably reinforced compared to the older roadster types, and this was obvious to anyone who cared to take a look underneath. Yet all three went right through the pompous, exhaustive Le Mans technical inspection and the Shelby cars did likewise through every other technical inspection for the rest of their careers (including a few in Italy, where the pro-Ferrari organizing clubs would have been only too glad to throw them out). As opposition for the Ford GTs and the Cobras there were 12 Ferraris, including four GTOs which were the Cobras' main concern.

Right from the start the Cobras left the Ferrari grand tourers behind and were up running with the racing sports cars. The British entry was having difficulties, but at the end of six hours Amon and Neerpasch were running fourth and the Gurney-Bondurant car was fifth, both of them blasting down the Mulsanne Straight at speeds of 180 mph and better, and both of them outrunning a lot of more sophisticated equipment. Just before midnight, almost eight hours after the start, trouble in the form of a dead battery hit the lead Cobra. When they replaced it with a new one, in violation of the rules, they were disqualified. The British Cobra had crashed after six hours, so that left only one still running—Gurney and Bondurant, who moved up to fourth and stayed there through the night, rolling along with the flat blast of the exhaust pipes waking up even the soundest sleepers among the thousands who lined the eight-mile circuit. At a little past 7 a.m., with all three Ford GTs long gone by this time, the car rolled into the pits. An oil cooler line had broken. Remington hurriedly rigged a bypass, the driver was sent out again with instructions to take it easy, and the car rolled away, still in fourth place, with a pair of Ferrari GTOs some distance astern. Then trouble hit again. With less than an hour to go Bondurant came in with the engine misfiring at high revs. This time it was the dual-point distributor (a stock item on the high-performance 289) that had gone bad. The mechanics blanked off one of the contacts and sent Bondurant out again, crossing their fingers. The team's charting crew was not sure if the closest Ferrari was on the same lap or a lap behind, and as Bondurant kept pushing, going as quickly as the malfunctioning ignition system would allow, every time he saw a red car come up in his rear-view mirror he got nervous until the car went past and he saw it wasn't the one he was worried about (what the Cobra team didn't know was that the pursuing Ferrari was in trouble with fading brakes, and was making no attempt to catch them). Finally, as it always does despite seeming to take forever, the checkered flag dropped. They were home free in fourth place, with only three Ferrari prototypes in front of them. They recorded an average speed of 116.3 mph for the distance, which is not bad for a car that was put together five days before the race, had a cumbersome, outmoded chassis which called for the engine to be installed up front, and had what was basically a production, pushrod-operated V8 for power.

It was unquestionably the high point of the year for the Cobras, and to make the triumph even more complete, there was a car in 18th place that was a great testimonial for the make. This was a privately entered, French-owned Cobra which was strictly a street machine (with the exception of the large gas tank), and didn't even have the four double-choke Weber carburetors. The car, which stayed out of the way of the faster vehicles throughout and ran at a steady pace, wound up averaging 100.7 mph, with its race preparation consisting primarily of the gas tank installation and a general tuneup. The Gurney-Bondurant coupe was the one that got most of the headlines (and it was fortunate Ford had something to talk about after the GTs all retired), but the French car should have been placed right up there on a pedestal with the other.

The Cobras did not win the manufacturer's championship that year, although they managed to keep it close until the finish. At the Rheims 12-hour race both coupes retired when the tailshafts on the transmissions broke (the only time this ever happened), then Bondurant won his class in both the Freiburg hillclimb in Germany and the Sierre-Montana climb in Switzerland. They also finished 1-2-3 in the grand touring section of the Tourist Trophy, run at Goodwood, England, at the end of August (and 3-4-5 over-all, with Gurney leading Britain's Jack Sears and Bob Olthoff). By mid-September the Cobras still had a mathematical chance to win the title if they won the 500-kilometer GT race at Bridgehampton and the Tour de France. This was a highly unlikely proposition, as no Cobra had ever run something as varied as the 3,600 miles, the eight races and eight hillclimbs that compose the Tour. Bridgehampton was no problem, with Miles leading a group of Cobras into the first four positions, but by that time it was all over. The Tour, which had started 10 days earlier, saw three Cobras lead through the opening events, then retire with mechanical troubles. There was always next year.

Next year already looked good; the 1965 Cobras were bound to be improved, both in the horsepower (to 380–385) and roadholding departments, and the build of the Daytona coupes had continued until there were now six of them. In addition Shelby had something else up his sleeve—the 427-inch engine for the car. The experiment (and it was purely that) of Sebring 1964 had progressed so well that Miles had run a "proper" 427 Cobra at Nassau in the fall of the year, and it had looked promising. On certain circuits the 427, from which at this point 460 horsepower could be achieved (as well as more torque than most cars could handle), would be vastly superior to the 289. Part of this came from the new rear suspension, which was designed by Ford's Klaus Arning and which gave the vehicle considerably improved manners at high speed. From a commercial standpoint a bigger engine for the street machines was a must: Corvette was soon to offer a 427-inch V8, and the Cobra had to stay in the same displacement range.

Shelby started pulling strings to get his new car homologated as soon as possible. On the other side of the ocean Ferrari started to do the same thing with his newest GT project, a mid-engined 3.0-liter coupe dubbed the 250LM. The homologation committee of the FIA was already wary of Ferrari, as the Italian had pulled a fast one with the GTO: After they had accepted the car as having been built in a minimum series of 100, the committee discovered that approximately 20 of them had actually been built, and they were forced to save face by acknowledging the changes over the standard 250 GT model as "minor" ones—minor in this case including such items as completely different gearboxes and no less than six double-choke Weber carburetors sitting atop the V12 engine. So when Ferrari tried to get his latest car recognized as a standard production model, he was watched closely. The committee turned down his first request in the spring of the year, and continued to turn him down through the summer while the ravings in Maranello got louder. In the end they could find evidence of no more than 55 or 60 of the cars being built, and Ferrari was given a final no. The reaction was a violent one, and it even included the old man's temporarily "resigning" from the Italian Automobile Club (at the 1965 Italian Grand Prix, all the Ferraris that ran were painted in the white-with-blue-stripe American colors and were entered by Ferrari's United States distributor). Shelby, who had a little more than 50 of the race-chassis 427s built by May, didn't stand a chance to get these homologated either, as the Ferrari troubles were making committee members wary of all applications. By the time he built 100, and got them recognized, it was too late (the SCCA, which does not run its classes according to international rules, had approved the car for the A production category at the beginning of the season).

Ironically, despite the maneuvers on both sides to get something better with which to win the manufacturer's championship, both Ferrari and Shelby wound up with their older-model cars. And in 1965 not only were the Cobra coupes vastly superior to the Ferrari GTOs, but Ferrari did not lend official factory support to the grand tourers carrying his name. The Cobras roared through the season with scarcely a setback.

The first race was the Daytona 2,000 Kilometers, and the coupes finished second, fourth and sixth (the factory cars) with 10th going to a private entry. Schlesser and Hal Keck shared the leading coupe, which finished ahead of one of the Ford GT40s after that vehicle was slowed by starter troubles. It was a good beginning, and at Sebring a month later the coupes took fourth, seventh, 13th and 21st, with a privately entered roadster 19th. That was the race of the almost-biblical downpour, and at one time it got so bad Phil Hill was actually driving waist-deep in water that had come in through the ventilation holes. When he opened the door, it was like pulling the plug in the bathtub as all the water ran out of the car. Schlesser was again one of the drivers of the lead car, sharing it this time with Bondurant, and after that the scene of the action moved to Europe, where Alan Mann was given the responsibility for running two of the coupes.

Bondurant and Allan Grant, who had a few factory rides in the United States, were to drive one car, with Englishmen Sir John Whitmore and Jack Sears in the other. In late April at the Monza 1,000 Kilometers they were 1-2 in their class, with Bondurant and Grant in front, and finished eighth and ninth over-all despite a cautious drive to make sure they picked up all the points. At Oulton Park a week later Whitmore won his class in the Tourist Trophy and placed fourth over-all, with a Ferrari fifth and Grant sixth. Two weeks after that, at Spa, the Cobras were finally beaten: Whitmore crashed one of them and Bondurant, in the other, finished just behind a GTO Ferrari after being delayed by a broken pushrod. That gave Ferrari 49 points to Cobra's 60—the closest the Italians were to get.

At the 1,000 Kilometers of the Nürburgring, with Bondurant and Neerpasch driving the lead car, the Cobras were a vast improvement over those of the previous year. The aforementioned two, with Bondurant turning in a shattering 9:18.5 in practice, finished seventh over-all in the race, with Sears and Australian Frank Gardner placing 10th and Schlesser and Andre Simon 12th. Three weeks later, in the Rossfeld Hillclimb near Hitler's former Alpine retreat at Berchtesgaden, Bondurant edged Bo Ljungfeldt, back for his only ride in a Cobra, as they placed first and second in the large GT category.

Even the disaster at Le Mans, where 11 Fords of all descriptions started and only one finished, did little to delay the Cobras. The lone Ford running at the end was a Cobra coupe shared by Sears and Dr. Dick Thompson, the former SCCA Corvette star, and despite their eighth place they were no worse than second among the big grand tourers (behind one of Ferrari's new 275GTB models). The championship was a certainty now, and a few weeks later it was clinched at the close of the 12-hour race at Rheims, when Schlesser and Bondurant won the large GT class easily and finished behind four Ferrari sports models. It was a good day for an American team to win the first international automotive title ever brought to this country: The date was July 4.

That was about the end of it for the Cobra, at least from an international standpoint. Bondurant won his class (and finished third over-all) in a 500-kilometer race at Enna, Sicily, in August, and the odd privately entered Cobra showed up now and then at various European affairs, but once the championship was won, the situation in mid-1965 demanded that all efforts to put into other programs. The failure of the Ford GT40 and the 7.0-liter Mark I at Le Mans had caused a reorganization of the Dearborn performance aims, and from now on Shelby's crews would concentrate solely on the rear-engined coupes.

At home the Cobras won the USRRC manufacturer's championship for the third straight year (and the last it was offered, as the Trans-American sedan racing series replaced this), partially through the efforts of factory cars and partially through private drivers who received some factory support. In the SCCA's A production class, split up into six championships by geographical region, four of the titles were won by Cobra drivers, two with 289-inch engines and two with the new 427s. But now even these were being overshadowed to a degree by Shelby's newest creation—the Mustang GT350. This was the first year of the Shelbyized Mustang and the SCCA put it into B production, where it promptly proceeded to dominate its class and to win five of the six regional-cum-national titles. The outstanding driver of the GT350 that season was Johnson, who split his time between running Cobras for the factory and driving the Mustang for himself, both with considerable success.

You can still find a Cobra or two at almost any of the smaller SCCA races and sometimes you'll find them at the bigger ones as well, but they aren't quite as popular as they were a few years ago: Advancing technology has made it practically impossible for anything but a rear-engined car to win these days, and in the bigger events that's all there is on the starting grids.

But if you were at Le Mans back then, when Gurney was roaring through the night, rolling along Mulsanne with his exhaust pipes belching flame when he shifted down for the tight corner at the end, or if you were at Schauinsland when Bondurant went charging up the hill, playing the gas pedal like a concert violin as he kept the big brute on the road ... that's what the Cobras were really like.

They built 900 of them—75 with the 260-inch engine, 515 with the 289 and 310 with the 427 and 428—and the last of them was sold just a few days before January 1, 1968, when the Federal emission and safety laws went into effect. Cobras weren't the kind of cars that were built for being purposely detuned through anti-smog devices, and they had rollbars and the like long before the government ever thought of it.

Granted, they never made money out of it, but taking Carroll Shelby's Cobras under its wing was one of Ford's better ideas.

27

WIN ON SUNDAY, SELL ON MONDAY

IT WAS SUMMER, and the asphalt on the Baltimore-Washington road was sending up shimmering heat waves on a stifling, sweltering afternoon, and although it was only 4:30 there was a stream of cars turning off at a ramshackle sign saying "Capitol Raceway," with an arrow pointing up an oiled dirt road leading through the trees.

The road, with the dust rising where the builder hadn't laid enough top dressing, leads for a half mile through a wilderness that resembles the Argonne of 1919 and then suddenly, surprisingly, it turns into a neat, well-ordered area surrounded by chain-link fences, with paved parking lots. High above everything stands a two-story cinder-block structure that is the headquarters of the place and behind this, stretching off into the distance and with a slight uphill slope after it goes past the timing lights, is the strip, maybe 60 feet wide and bordered by grandstands, then by a forest at the end. This is drag racing, mid-1960's style.

Many of the 300-odd cars that would make up the night's field, most of them strictly stock with the hubcaps removed in an expression of youthful independence, were already in the huge staging area below the tower, their owners tinkering with the engines. Some are just lounging around, sitting in the front seat, trying hard to appear nonchalant with one arm draped in a stylishly negligent fashion around a teen-age girlfriend who is complete with bare midriff, practically adhesive hip-huggers and a beehive hairdo. Up the hill, in a fenced area between the tower and the starting line, where the grandstands can see them and where they won't have to associate with the more commonplace entries, are the reasons for the large group of early arrivals. There are two of them, a pair of double-A fuelers, the *ne plus ultras* of the sport. One is painted black, has a giant supercharger rising out of its midsection and has "Don Garlits—Wynn's Jammer" lettered on the sides. The other, a gleaming bronze, is equipped with a 1,600-horsepower supercharged version of Ford's single overhead camshaft V8. Its identifying marks say "Connie Kalitta—Bounty Hunter."

The slim nose glistens faintly in the lowering sun while the kids crowd against the fence to stare at it. This is it, the living end, the alpha and the omega, Nirvana for every teen-ager who ever tried to get the drop on somebody else at a traffic light. Freud would have a picnic.

Garlits is the big daddy of drag racing, the kid who came out of Florida in the late 1950s to stand the West Coast hotshots on their collective ear and give a new dimension to the sport. He was the first man past the 170 and 180-mile "barriers," he was the first to use extra-wide tires, and wherever Garlits goes he and his blown Chrysler Hemi are the team to beat. He is the first of the touring pros, the star of the small group that rolls across the country week after week, running best-of-three match races with anyone if the price (at least $1,000 to appear) is right. Kalitta is another top-rank veteran, a laughing, wisecracking funny man from a Detroit suburb, who since the beginning of 1965 has been Ford's high-speed guinea pig. He is the only man on the circuit running the overhead cammer, the only one trying to dent the Chrysler phalanx, and for Connie it has been a cut and try operation, a frustrating process of running hard to find out which part will break next. His engine puts out more horsepower than anyone else's, but getting that horsepower to the ground— and getting it there at the right time—has been a major problem.

The two are old friends, and they lean against one of the two trucks, passing the time until the first run while the kids look on hungrily, eyeing the dragsters, watching every move. Suddenly a girl clambers over the chain-link fence, accompanied by a roar from the kids, and just as quickly she is with the drivers and their crews. She is about 17, black-haired, complete with the painted-on hip huggers and big breasts, and she is panting, half from the exertion of getting over the fence and half from excitement. Just what she was after—Connie, Don, the cars or maybe all four— wasn't clear, but she wanted to be a part of the scene so they stuck her in one of the rails. She almost disappears into the cockpit that hides behind the looming supercharger and there was an involuntary shudder when she sees her groin resting practically on the differential and she realizes what would happen if it exploded. Then she was hauled out again and joined the party, and the two crews started jockeying for position. One of them, they figured, was going to get a little of that, and everyone was trying to be first on line.

It is time for the first run, and the drivers climb into their aluminized fireproof suits, suddenly becoming faceless behind masks of the same material and warlike under their crash helmets. The trucks push the dragsters to get them fired up and then they scurry for cover as the two monsters, flames shooting out of their stubby, upswept exhausts, roll to the line. The "Christmas Tree" device that gets them going blinks yellow, yellow, yellow … and then green and they go.

What does a dragster in action look like? What does it sound like? There is almost no separating the sight and sound of a fueler in full cry. It explodes in a peculiar kind of automotive violence which approaches the threshold of pain in its intensity and in sudden, unbelievable motion with fountains and mountains of smoke streaming out behind. It is an eight-second mechanical orgasm—multiplied by two.

Then suddenly it is over, the engines shut off, the fighter-plane-type drag chutes blossoming, and the vehicles braking to a stop down near the forest with the push trucks scurrying to catch up with their homemade rockets and the crowd cheering the one that got there first. Then some of the onlookers go back to the staging area, returning to their own Fords and Chevys and Pontiacs, to wait for their turn. There is a class for every type of car and a trophy for each of the classes, and as the kids return to their equipment, the smoke from the tires and the fumes from the nitromethane are still in their eyes.

It is night now, and the area where the two headliners park is bathed by flood-lights and they sit there, Kalitta good for perhaps $50,000 a year, Garlits making nearly twice that. They sit in silence for a few minutes, then Kalitta speaks.

"Hey. There ain't no way to get out of it, is there?"

"Huh?"

"No way to get out of it."

"Nope. You can't quit. You got to cut the cars in two with a torch, that's how you quit."

"Yeah. You get a job running a punch press or something, you come in and you ..."

"You'd last six days and then you'd punch somebody in the mouth and slide down the elevator cables."

And in the background, out on the starting line just behind the wall of bright lights, brace after brace of sedans goes charging down the strip, and the constant chatter of the announcer makes sure the brief gaps between the sound of the engines is not to be left in peace.

Garlits goes to check something on his car and Kalitta eyes the ground. "I'll tell you, it's pretty good money," he says. "It's hard to turn it down ... it's all that him and I are gaining right now ... You see, he's got 10 years behind him and I've got five ... When he first made a big one he went to California and I went out with him ... I went along with another buddy from Detroit, and I was a stooge, and I got out there, and you know, I said some day I'm gonna be king of this game ... and I'm a-swingin'!"

Connie laughs, the lights glare, the engines roar, and the hungry-eyed kids lean over the fence.

"You can't stand still in life ... That's the way I feel about it ... If you don't gain nothin', if you don't learn anything, and if you don't meet people, what's the use of bein' around? I could never punch a time clock ... I'd commit suicide before I'd do that ... " There is silence, broken by the roar of an engine warming up. "It's a hard way to go ..." The engines howl again and drown him out. Connie gets up and goes to his car.

In another half hour it is over and both vehicles are loaded onto their trailers and soon they roll into the night, Garlits headed for a race the next evening at Lebanon Valley, outside of Albany, N.Y., and Kalitta pointed toward Winston-Salem, N.C. The girl went along with one of the crews.

On that night Capitol was where the action was—at Capitol and hundreds of other places just like it: at Lions, Carlsbad, Irwindale or Fontana in California; at Great Meadows, Atco or Westhampton on the East Coast, at Amarillo, Tex., or Great Bend, Kan., at Thunder Valley in South Dakota, or at Fairmont, W. Va., or you name it. This is what drag racing has evolved into since the days of street racing and weekend trips to the dry lakes of Southern California, and since the days when they used up the lakes and started running at airports in Santa Barbara and Santa Ana. Today there are more than 40 drag strips throughout the nation and more than 10 million persons a year pay to watch. The biggest of all the enthusiast magazines, *Hot Rod,* is read by more than a million persons a month, and total dollar volume done by speed equipment manufacturers is near $500 million annually. Drag racing, that short and sometimes not very simple process of getting to the other end of a quarter mile before the opposition, is the grass-roots level, the starting point for any American manufacturer trying for the youth market.

It is also the activity in which basic product superiority is most evidenced by the results, and the one in which the Ford Motor Company was far behind from the time General Motors introduced its overhead valve V8s in the early 1950s.

Organized drag racing got going with the founding of the National Hot Rod Association in 1949, and during the 1950s it grew, spreading across the country and slowly but surely getting the kids and their cars off the streets and onto the strips. It wasn't always easy to get the necessary cooperation of the civic authorities, as the very name "hot-rodder" carried, and still does, the aura of a black leather jacket. Perhaps the biggest step toward getting national recognition for the sport was the "Safety Safari," a Mobil-sponsored caravan originated by NHRA President Wally Parks which crossed the country in 1954 and again in 1955 to meet with the kids and the police and explain this was really a good thing. Right after the 1955 Safari the NHRA held its first national meet at Great Bend, Kan., and the top eliminator title was won by Calvin Rice, driving one of the first true "rails" with a modified Mercury engine supplying the power. But by then the flathead was already on its way out. The Olds, Cadillac and Chevrolet V8s were better for high-rpm work, and so was the hemispherical combustion chamber Chrysler, which would eventually hold a monopoly in the top-line fueler class. By the latter half of the 1950s Ford's share of drag racing, which by now had expanded to include a circuit run by the American Hot Rod Association (AHRA), was almost nil. Until the close of the 1950s, the Chryslers, Chevys and the rest slowly built up their dominance over the quarter-mile. Then, when Parks brought his national meet to Detroit in 1959 and 1960 and gave the auto industry a look, GM was quick to see an opportunity and took an even greater interest. High-performance parts for General Motors engines had always been easy to buy. Now, despite operating under the AMA ban, the various divisions (especially Chevrolet and Pontiac) started making even more parts available. Ford, on the other hand, had little to offer the private customer, and the West Coast speed equipment manufacturers were naturally concentrating on making goodies for the GM and Chrysler cars. It was turning into a vicious cycle, and by the time Ford got back into the performance field in 1960 and 1961, the picture was a dark one, punctuated by only a few spots of light.

One of these was veteran West Coast rodder Les Ritchey, a man so devoted to Ford he even had a cat named Fairlane. Like so many others a product of the lakes, Ritchey was in charge of all high-performance tuning work at the racing-minded Ford dealership in Torrance, Calif., and for a while was chief mechanic on Parnelli Jones' stock car. By 1961 Ritchey had gone on his own, establishing Performance Associates in the Los Angeles suburb of Covina, and soon he became the oracle for many of the Ford-equipped drag racers in the area. Ritchey and a few others like him were the only ones keeping the company anywhere near the business in those times, and when the program became a regular one in 1962 his relationship with Dearborn turned into something more formal; he spent a month helping prepare cars for the NHRA Nationals on Labor Day at Indianapolis Raceway Park, and things began to roll.

From a manufacturer's angle, and especially from the viewpoint of a corporation trying to re-establish a reputation in drag racing, the program must be twofold: On one hand the brand name must be carried by exotic equipment (such as supercharged rails) to build the image, to be the headliners at the various strips and to be interesting enough for the enthusiast magazines to publish stories on the car. The second part of the activity is to make sure the basic product, the one the kids will buy and drive from the showroom to the drag strip, can be purchased in a competitive configuration. In other words. in Ford's case, the big-engined Fairlanes and Comets had to be able to run as well as the Pontiac GTOs, the Chevelle 396s and 427s, the Olds 442s and the various Dodges and Plymouths.

Success in such other forms of competition as Indianapolis or long-distance sports car racing is difficult to measure. The cars and engines used for these are expensive, sophisticated creations which bear little or no resemblance to the production item, and the best that can be, said for winning at either the Speedway or Le Mans is that success there contributes to the general over-all engineering and romantic images of the corporation. There is no clear-cut way in which victories in those events can be checked against sales gains (or conversely, against losses after a defeat). But in drag racing, it is different: The car strongest at the strip on Sunday will show a measurable sales increase in the surrounding dealerships on Monday. Many of the kids who come in to buy have no intention of dragging the one they have purchased; but it is their badge, their announcement that they own the *hot* car—even if they purchase a cheaper, somewhat lower-horsepower model of the same family. Added to this are the principles of retention: If you can sell them when they're young, you have a good chance of keeping them as customers for a long time to come. By way of a convincing argument in support of these principles, the

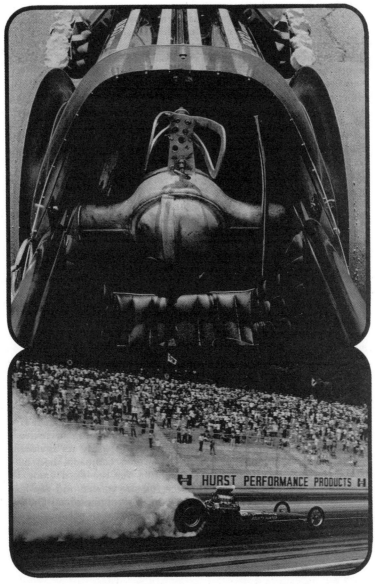

At left: (Top) In the old days at Bonneville, they used to tow the timing stand all the way from Los Angeles. (Middle) Roadsters digging out of the hole at Santa Ana, 1950. (Bottom) By 1955, some of the equipment was a little more sophisticated—early "altereds" and "rails." Above: (Top) The view from the bridge—the seat of a modern-day dragster, complete with miniscule steering wheel. (Bottom) Connie Kalitta blasts off during the 1965 NHRA Spring nationals at Bristol, Tenn.

company has its own best example in Tasca Ford Sales of East Providence, R.I., a somewhat illogical location for a dealer who sells more than 2,500 cars annually. Bob Tasca, the owner and driving force behind the operation, has for years been convinced that a performance image is a great aid in capturing the youth market, and he has always sponsored his own drag racing cars and made an effort to provide good service for the owners of the hotter machinery he sells. As a result in 1966 Tasca did 127 percent of the business written by the closest Chevy dealer (as opposed to a 1966 nationwide Ford average of 93 percent).

When the first Ford Division attempt was made at the NHRA Nationals in 1962 it was a hurried affair, with Ritchey and personnel from the experimental garage managing to prepare 10 lightweight Galaxies equipped with the 406-cubic-inch engine. Most of them were put into the hands of performance-minded dealers, and the venture was unsuccessful. Perhaps the most depressing thing about it was that the cars *did* run well. They were quicker than the opposition off the line, but ran out of revs at the far end of the strip, where the stronger GM and Chrysler vehicles would go right past them. But at least it was a start, and it was also the time when the division began a working relationship with many of the drivers who would become the *de facto* factory team for the next few years. Ritchey and Gaspar (Gas) Ronda were two of them, and among the others who took part in the 1962 Nationals under Ford aegis were Dick Brannan and Phil Bonner.

With more money available for the 1963 season, the division scheduled a production run of 50 lightweight Galaxies at the Atlanta assembly plant, these being the first equipped with the high-performance 427-inch engine and sold to private individuals. In that season sales of the Galaxie 427 package went well, not only in the lightweight version, but also in the steel-bodied configuration. Part of this was due to the good styling of the 1963½ fastback models, and part of it was due to the fact it was truly one of the hotter street cars. Chrysler wasn't going to revive the Hemi until the following year, Chevrolet was still using its nondescript 409-inch engine, and none of the high-powered compacts had yet made their appearance. The only competition for the Ford came from the Pontiacs, which were 421 inches in the full-size version and 389 inches when packaged in the GTO, which was the forerunner of all the other compact "muscle" cars, and which was in its first year of production.

For the moment, Ford had as good a basic product out there as did the next manufacturer, and when Frank Zimmerman came in to reorganize the special vehicles activity in the summer of that year, things looked even better. Zimmerman recognized the value of the drag-racing program, and his first step was to initiate the construction of the Thunderbolt, an ultra-lightweight, ultra-fast exhibition car which still looked something like a stock vehicle, and to relate this to the dealers. This latter project involved the formation of the Ford Drag Council, an eight-man group composed of some of the better drivers in the country and Ritchey, who although he drove was best known for his mechanical talents. Most of the members represented a dealer and drove and worked out of that location. They were missionaries in several senses. For one thing they would each have one of the new cars and would drive it as often as possible; for another, some of them would be salesmen for high-performance cars. During 1963 these men, both before and after the formation of the council, drove the lightweight fastback Galaxies, and sold a lot of cars as well.

But the 1963 season, plus the introduction of the Thunderbolt, was to prove the last high-water mark of this end of the program. There were several reasons: Drag racing was moved down the list from being number two in priority (behind stock car racing) to below the Indianapolis effort, below the Le Mans effort, below the continuing stock car campaign and perhaps even behind the international rally activity. Therefore not only was there less money available, but top management interest was always focused on other items. Such events as the Indianapolis "500" or Le Mans were glamorous and received widespread press coverage and were also pleasant places at which to personally represent the corporation. The drag strips were mainly in out-of-the-way locations, and the venture rapidly fell into the death-and-taxes category (this, too, would always be with them). The relegation to a minor role, plus the emergence of truly hot street machines from competitors, were what slowed the program after it had made a good start. The various Chrysler Hemis, the Chevelle 396 and the others were much too strong for the 390-inch Fairlanes and Comets, and it would have taken a top management decision to either install the 427 (a financially bad proposition, as the engine was produced in limited quantities) or accelerate development of the new series V8 which was introduced to the public in the fall of 1967 in the Thunderbird.

But the Thunderbolts, when considered within the framework of their time, were really something to see. Equipped with wide racing slicks on the rear wheels and slim tires up front, the much-modified Fairlane had a purposeful look about it which was added to by the installation of a 427-inch engine complete with multiple carburetion and ram-air induction. The cars were designed at Ford, built by Dearborn Steel Tubing, then brought back to Ford and finalized during the late summer and early fall. Danny Jones, who was soon to spend most of his time on the Indianapolis project, had a hand in the final modifications and took advantage of his own driving talents as a former CRA sprint car champion to test them all on the Dearborn proving ground. The cars were due for delivery at 9 a.m. on October 22, and Jones didn't get them for a final checkout until late in the afternoon of October 21. Starting at 4 p.m., he drove, adjusted, then drove some more, until he was satisfied the vehicles were as close as possible to each other in performance. Jones would drive, the mechanics would replace a transmission or adjust a carburetor, and then he would drive some more. By the time they got through with all seven vehicles (the eighth was retained as a factory test car) it was 6 a.m. The elapsed times of the cars varied between 12.05 and 12.19, the top speed clocked through the trap that straddles the end of the quarter-mile varied from 120.48 to 121.29. Then the cars went off to compete in the factory experimental class at the major meets—later in the super stock class, when enough were built to satisfy the minimum requirement of 50—and to barnstorm the rest of the time.

During the same period Lincoln-Mercury was also getting into drag racing as the next step in its low-budget performance program (starting with the 1963 season, Mercury had returned to stock car racing). Later in the year Mercury staged a 100,000-mile record run at Daytona, there were plans for the 1964 East African Safari, and for a run from the tip of South America to Alaska, and all of it had been administered by one man: Fran Hernandez, the veteran hot-rodder. Now he had drags tacked on, and it became mandatory to hire someone else. As is normal in large corporations, Hernandez went through channels. Personnel records failed to show anyone with a drag racing background, and Hernandez was still without an assistant. So eventually, almost as a last resort, he reminded himself of a tall blond kid who worked in the Lincoln-Mercury service department, who owned a Chevy-powered rail, and who had been bugging him about drag racing. Hernandez called him in, talked about the project for a little while, and then made it brief. Al Turner still recalls his words: "Fran said 'You're here. Here it is.' It was just dropped on me and it was either sink or swim."

The veteran Hernandez is one of the great pragmatists of auto racing. He had established in his own mind that Turner knew what he was doing. Now all he wanted was to get the job done, and he did not want to be bothered by details. In Turner he found a kindred soul, and between the two of them they were to eventually make the Comet team the best factory-sponsored outfit in the country, and the most successful regardless of how much budget money was available.

The first step, late in 1963, was to start the build of 50 Comets of the same configuration as the Fairlane Thunderbolts, and four of them were kept as factory cars and taken to Lions drag strip in Long Beach, Calif., for final shakedown in preparation for the NHRA Winternationals in February at Pomona. Hernandez had rounded up a good collection of drivers—Don Nicholson, Tom Sturm, Ronnie Sox and Bill Shrewsberry, and now they had to get things sorted out. At first they were running in the 12.40–12.50 bracket and the outlook was dim. But slowly, through various suspension adjustments, they got the cars working, and finally, two days before the big meet, the word got around to the racers coming into town: Sox had turned an elapsed time of 11.08. It was so far superior to anything the opposition had that when the Pomona proceedings opened, various factory-sponsored Plymouths and Dodges were left in motel parking lots. Just as predictably, the factory stock eliminator final was contested between Sox and Nicholson, with Sox the winner in 11.49.

It was an auspicious start for the pair, as they were to go through the season unbeaten in exhibition match races, except when they lost to each other. In those days the Plymouth opposition included such drivers as Hayden Proffitt and Dick Landy, Tom Grove in the "Melrose Missile" and Roger Lindamood in "Color Me

Gone." The Dodge forces were led by Al Eckstrand in "Lawman" and Jim Thornton in the Ramchargers' car. Although the Plymouths and Dodges—MoPars for short—were by and large capable of taking the measure of the Thunderbolts, they were no match for the Comets, one of the reasons being the location of the airscoops on the leading edge of the Comet hoods. Working on the proving grounds with bits of yarn glued to the hood to show airflow direction, they worked out the proper location for the intakes—and cut two-tenths, of a second off the elapsed time in the quarter mile, a remarkable amount to be gained merely by chopping a hole in the right place. The styling of the scoops on the drag car, incidentally, was picked up and made standard (although non-functional) on the 1966 Comet Cyclones.

Then Dodge, which could always be counted on to do something in the space-grabbing department, came up with the predecessor of the "funny" cars and started getting all the magazine ink. It was done by the simple expedient of building two nonstock, but extremely loud and colorful cars, naming them "Chargers," and sending them on an exhibition tour in the spring of 1964. The two vehicles, complete with bold red, white and blue stripes and a supercharged engine running on nitro (with the blower sticking through the hood) weren't that fast—but they were different, and the kids flocked to see them.

It was imperative something be done quickly, and it was Jack Chrisman, the owner of Shrewsberry's car, who came up with the solution. A veteran California hot-rodder and the 1962 NHRA Nationals top eliminator, Chrisman had been out of action due to an accident in 1963, and now he was ready to come back. His Charger-stopping creation consisted of a lightweight Comet with a fuel-burning, supercharged 427-inch engine mounted in the standard location, and with liberal use of fiberglass for body panels. Once it was ready, Chrisman set out after the Chargers and chased them across the country, week after week. When Dodge saw what it had to contend with, the Chargers were pulled off the circuit. Chrisman's car was such a success that strip operators soon had him booked for the season at $1,000 per show, a new high in appearance money for a stock-bodied vehicle.

The Fairlane Thunderbolts were doing well while running in class—and enough of them had been built (127 were eventually produced) to permit competition in the super stock category. Ronda, with 7-inch rims instead of the 10-inchers the Comets used to compete in the factory experimental class, won the top stock title at Pomona and then piled up enough points through the season to be declared the national title-holder (T-Bolts also won six of the seven NHRA divisional championships). But on the grass-roots level Fords and Comets were falling farther behind. The Hemi-powered Dodges and Plymouths and the Chevrolets and other GM cars were clearly quicker. There *was* something, however, that could be done to improve the exotic end of the image. This was the 427-inch engine with the new single overhead cam-shaft conversion which had been developed during the winter and spring of 1964. Although originally intended for stock car racing it had been turned down for that purpose by the sanctioning bodies. Now here was a chance to make some use of it in a rail and go for the position of having the fastest all-out competition vehicle in the country.

The man who got the first engine was Kalitta, and he got it not because he was the best driver (at that time either Garlits or Don Prudhomme), but because of a combination of circumstances: Connie was *one* of the leading pilots, he was good mechanically, and his base of operations was nearby Mt. Clemens, Mich., conveniently close to the factory.

Along with the engine came many problems. Although factory engineers were available for advice, the only practical way to develop a supercharged, exotic-fuel drag engine is to run it in the car. To test the engine on a dynamometer would be impossible, so the cut-and-try process is used. When Kalitta first pulled the front cover off the engine and saw the forest of gears and chains, it was a depressing sight. He was used to the relatively simple innards of the pushroad-actuated Chrysler, and now he was a one-man campaign to beat that same Chrysler—an engine that had the benefit of years of drag racing development.

In the late winter of 1965 he became the first man to pass the 200-mile mark at an AHRA national meet, doing this in his first run at Phoenix. The connecting rod troubles experienced during the shakedowns earlier in the year were seemingly cured—until the next day, when he blew the engine. Within the next few weeks they managed to get the rod and bearing problems solved, but in the summer the trouble cropped up again. This time they stopped it for good: A new crankshaft was machined to accept Chrysler rods, and that was the end of problems in that area. The engine was now considered reliable, and by the late summer of 1965 Pete Robinson, the 1961 NHRA top eliminator and another star touring pro, became the second man to get one of the engines, plus the advantage of the knowledge Kalitta had accumulated. (By late September the engineers found a way to get an accurate estimate of the horsepower the engine was producing. Working with data accumulated from a Kalitta run which produced a 7.85-second elapsed time and a 200-mph trap speed, they arrived at a figure of 1,607 horsepower at 8,500 rpm.)

Kalitta wasn't the only one having difficulties: Both the Fords and the Comets were in trouble, not only on the lower level but also with the factory-sponsored cars. On the production side, the newly introduced 390-inch engine package for the Fairlane GT and Comet Cyclone (with both four-speed and automatic transmissions) proved itself to be non-competitive. Not only did sales suffer once the word got around, but so did the image the company had worked hard to build through activity in other types of racing. On the exhibition circuit the factory-sponsored entries were faced with the sudden evolution of the stock-bodied car into a genuine match-racing attraction. Drag strip operators throughout the country were willing to pay good money for hot machinery that still bore a reasonable resemblance to the production-line versions, and the situation became obvious. At the match races, it was a case of "run what you brung," and if one of the cars was a little lighter than the regulations allowed, or a little more modified in the wheelbase or the engine compartment, it didn't make any difference. All the spectators wanted was a good show. Since a car could run upwards of 100 match races a year, but only compete in a half-dozen major meets, the practical thing to do was to build a "cheater" for the match races and not worry about the national meets. The publicity and good will created by the match races, plus the graphic demonstration that your car was faster than the opposition, far outweighed the exposure that could be gained at the big events (where the AA fuelers got most of the publicity anyway).

So the rule-bending started, and Dodge and Plymouth showed up with cars that had been lightened by dipping the body panels in acid baths, with altered wheelbases to give better weight transfer under hard acceleration, and with a dozen other items calculated to increase speed and lower elapsed time. In the same period both Ford and Mercury were switching to the single overhead cam engine for their exhibition cars. They were faced with new problems caused by added weight, there were new chassis problems and there was a power deficiency caused by the Chrysler products switching from gas to alcohol-based fuels. In addition, there were the normal growing pains associated with a new engine.

Bending, stretching and even breaking the rules is an old story in automotive competition, and when you get a bunch of competitors as mechanically minded and as innovative as drag racers, those who enforce the regulations have a difficult job. Stories in this area are legion, and guys who think they are being original by filling their spare tires with cement (for added weight on the rear wheels and therefore better traction) have a lot to learn; it was being done, and being detected, years ago.

There are thousands of tricks and every weekend, somewhere around the nation, one more technical inspector is uncovering one more example of American ingenuity. There was, for example, the driver of a stock-class car who had a tiny tank of alcohol fuel hidden in the chassis rails and used his windshield wiper motor to act as a secret fuel pump, and there was even the guy who brought a pair of identical cars to the strip; he'd run the illegal one in competition, and when it came time for technical inspection, he would somehow get back to where he had the other car hidden and make a quick switch. At times the "bump car" technique would crop up, this being a ploy in which one illegally modified car would eliminate the opposition in its class—until it got to run against its teammate. Then it would slow just enough to get whipped—and as a loser, not be inspected. Even some of the factory teams appeared to be guilty of this, although proving it would be difficult.

Despite the problems the Ford Division managed to come away with something from the 1965 Winter Nationals at Pomona when Bill Lawton beat Len Richter in an all-Mustang showdown for the factory experimental crown. Both cars were of the single overhead cam variety, normally aspirated, running on gas, with fiberglass forward of the firewall, with fiberglass doors, with a two-inch alteration in the wheelbase and with an altered front suspension due to clearance problems with the new engine.

But out on the road the MoPars had the jump with their "funny" cars, the name first being given them by Hernandez. The stopper, for the second year in a row, was

At left: (Top) Drag-racing veteran Jack Chrisman and his topless Mercury Comet "funny car," 1966. (Middle) Chrisman and his more standard (?) Mercury with the innards exposed, 1966. (Bottom) One of Hubert Platt's modified Falcons at Irwindale, Calif., 1966. Above: Les Ritchey, one of the early mainstays of the Ford drag-racing effort. (Inset) "Sneaky Pete" Robinson at Irwindale, complete with an airfoil mounted up front, 1966.

to be Chrisman. His 1964 Comet was stripped, the sheet metal was changed to update the appearance, and extensive mechanical changes were made underneath. The engine was moved backward in the chassis for better weight distribution, the superchargers disappeared under the hood to preserve the stock look, a lightweight dragster-type front axle was installed, the driver's seat was moved to the back of the car, and the magazine photographers and booking agents got in line. The rest of the overhead cam engines available were being used by Nicholson, George DeLorean, Proffitt and Arnie Beswick, while factory-sponsored Comets with unblown pushrod engines were being run by Eddie Schartman and Ed Rachanski. The pushrod versions, of which 20 with 427s and 20 with 289s were built, were less than successful. Turner and Hernandez had trouble finding dealers to buy them at wholesale.

It was that kind of a year, with the rules changing from meet to meet, new classes springing up and no team really able to establish a clear-cut superiority. About the only thing that season did accomplish was to get in idea going round in the heads of Hernandez and Turner. By the fall Hernandez had it figured, and sat down with his drag racing man.

"I want you to go out and think how you would build the most way-out car ever built—we would be the ultimate cheaters. The weight objective would be 1,700 pounds."

"You can't build a car that light!" Turner exclaimed.

"I didn't ask you that," Hernandez said. "Just do it."

"We're not going to pick up anything we've done in the past," Hernandez added. "We're going to take the attitude that we're the dumbest guys in the world ... We're not going to use anything because 'so-and-so's using it, so it must work ...' and everything we do we're going to have to justify to ourselves on paper before we do it."

Within a few weeks Turner had a plan and they sat down again and dissected it, knocking weight off every place they could. Then they went looking for someone to build it. Most of the constructors turned them down, claiming the thing would never work. Then finally they got Logghe Stamping, in nearby Fraser, Mich., to do the job. ("They were hungry," says Hernandez. "That's the only reason they took it on.") When the car was finished it was perhaps the most deceptive-looking vehicle ever built. At a casual glance the car appeared to be a standard Comet with skinny wheels in the front and the extra-wide drag slicks on the rear. But upon closer investigation it could be found that the entire fiberglass body was a mere shell that lifted easily at the front, and when it was, revealed what was essentially a tube-framed rail.

The prototype was taken to Florida for shakedown tests, and in short order the skies fell. The car wouldn't run nearly as well as they had expected. Getting it right was a slow, sometimes agonizing process. Nicholson, the test pilot, had never handled anything that quick before and had to revise his whole approach to driving. The car made revs so quickly, for example, they destroyed several engines merely because no driver could ever have reflexes quick enough to shift it. That called for a switch to an automatic box, and the transmission and chassis division started developing an automatic strong enough. Eventually they came up with boxes that would last, and at the same time Turner was getting the spring rates and weight distribution to where the car would work, and slowly the project began to look good and other cars were built.

Then, at the *Hot Rod* magazine meet at Riverside, Calif., in June, the whole thing caught fire. Chrisman, driving the "topless" car that was the lead exhibition vehicle, ran 8.32 and 184 mph and astounded the rest of the drag racing world. From then on, with Nicholson, Schartman and the Denver team of Kenz and Leslie handling the standard-body cars, there was no other vehicle of the same type that could even touch them. Through the year the Comet drag racing team, including the five stock cars that were also sponsored, won 86 percent of the races in which they participated. Nicholson, the most successful of the group, wound up with a 130-10 record, which at one time included a match-race streak of more than 30 straight. The cars, which started the season at 1,950 pounds in the case of the sedans, at the end of the year were closer to Hernandez' original goal, now weighing in at 1,875 ("We found that anything lighter than that is dangerous," Hernandez says). The elapsed times, by the fall, were consistently in the 8.10–8.20 bracket, and the speed through the time trap was in the neighborhood of 175 mph. By the spring of 1967, running basically the same cars as the year before, they broke the eight-second barrier consistently.

The Ford Division team, after enjoying a successful 1966 AHRA Winternationals with their own "funny" Mustangs, suffered a serious loss a few weeks later. The date was May 1 and the scene was the strip at Fontana, where Ritchey was running a match race against Proffitt, who had switched to Chevelle. Ritchey's car got off the side of the strip, hit the guard rail and flipped. Ritchey, who for years had been skeptical of seat belts and had always worn his loosely, was thrown out and was decapitated. All the harness buckles were still fastened when the wreck was examined. Somehow, a week after his 43rd birthday, Ritchey, had been yanked right through the loose straps. The craftsman had been killed by something he built with his own hands.

The rest of the season, from the standpoint of the Ford Division, was galling due to the superior; performance of sister (and much smaller) division Lincoln-Mercury's funny cars. To Ford they were not at all humorous. And in a long-range sense, the performance of both the Ford and Lincoln-Mercury exhibition vehicles, whether outstanding or mediocre, had little effect on improving the over-all image. The reason was simple: Down in the stock, private-owner classes, the Chevrolets were still quicker, and the kids knew it. Ford got back into the performance picture in 1960 with the first 360 horsepower kit for its 352-inch engine. Yet since that time, and regardless of what was done, the company failed to make a dent in Chevy's domination of this segment of the market. Although there are hundreds of ways to prove or disprove this, the following series of figures are as good as any. They are taken from the National Hot Rod Association's Summer Nationals meet, which is generally considered the biggest, most prestigious and most popular of the various events held around the country, and are therefore fairly indicative of the total situation:

NHRA SUMMER NATIONALS

		Entries		Total	Wins	
Year	Total	Chevy	Ford	Classes	Chevy	Ford
1960	530	262	32	46	14	4
1961	610	442	65	58	31	4
1962	746	422	60	60	34	2
1963	901	535	79	61	36	4
1964	970	553	115	64	42	5
1965	988	575	111	69	39	2
1966	1,113	649	119	92	50	10
1967	1,547	865	161	92	50	6

At the top of the drag racing heap, from a publicity and individual prestige standpoint and despite the over-all situation, are still the fuelers. From this class comes the top eliminator, the man who gets to the other end of the quarter quicker than anyone else. He is the man who gets the newspaper and magazine ink, and Ford managed to get some major-meet exposure in this department for the first time in more than a decade.

The groundwork was laid by Kalitta, who suffered through the early stages of the overhead cam engine's development for drag racing. Then, when Robinson obtained his, the odds on a Ford winning one of the bigger titles got better. Later in 1966 still a third top-line car and driver combination was obtained when Lou Baney, an oldtime hot-rodder who became a California Ford dealer, signed Tom McEwen to drive his dragster and made a deal with the factory. McEwen, long one of the West Coast kingpins, soon came close, losing in the finals of the AHRA Nationals in August (Kalitta had done the same at the NHRA Spring Nationals in 1965). Then, in October, at the NHRA world championships in Tulsa, Robinson was a winner. The elapsed time was 7.27 and the top speed at the end of the quarter was 203.16, neither figure being outstanding, but good for the strip conditions that existed.

It was the first major top eliminator title for Ford-powered equipment since Rod Singer had won the 1959 NHRA Summer Nationals crown, driving a gas rail powered by a supercharged Lincoln engine. That car, which recorded an elapsed time of 9.76 seconds in the championship final, was tuned by Karol Miller, the almost legendary (in a hot-rod sense) Texan who got such surprising speeds out of his Fords at Bonneville in the mid-50s. The only other Ford winner was Rice in the 1955 inaugural, with an E.T. of 10.30 and a top speed of 143.95 mph. There are literally dozens of classes that produce better performances today.

Kalitta, who had never lived up to his exhibition tour promise in the major meets, made up for two years of frustration a few months later, at the start of the 1967 campaign. In the brief span of a few weeks in February, he won the top elimi-nator title at three major meets in a row, becoming the first man ever to achieve this feat. Kalitta finished in front at the NHRA Winternationals in Pomona, then went east to the AHRA winter meet at Phoenix, where he won again. He capped his hot streak with a win at the end of the month in Deland, Fla., scene of the NASCAR winter championships.

The McEwen-Baney combination did not work out as well as had been hoped, and by the time 1967 came around, Baney had a new driver, It was Prudhomme, who after establishing himself as the nation's best in the Chrysler-powered "Hawaiian," had left that team and was looking for another ride. It was a natural combination. On May 5 in an NHRA regional meet at Carlsbad, Calif., Prudhomme broke the seven-second barrier with a 6.92 performance. A short time later, Robinson turned in a 6.92 at Pelion, S.C., and then in early June the lean and lanky Prudhomme put on a precedent-shattering performance at the NHRA Spring Nationals at Bristol, Tenn. En route to the meet's top eliminator title he turned in three successive runs under seven seconds—6.99, 6.97 and 6.92 in the finals, where he was timed at 222.76 mph through the lights as he defeated Robinson in an all-Ford showdown.

Unprecedented to run under seven seconds three times in a row? Then, yes. By the end of the season Garlits had made a spectacular comeback to win the NHRA Summer Nationals with a 6.77 clocking, and on a good day, at a good strip, a sub-seven-second performance would draw nothing more than a healthy round of applause. Tomorrow, there is no telling where the so-called barrier will be, if there ever was such an obstacle, except in men's minds.

Bob Tasca's factory experimental Mustang, driven by Bill Lawton, at Tulsa, Okla., during the 1965 NHRA world championship finals. Note the low air pressure in the rear tires, which makes for better traction.

28

The Best Engine They Ever Built

FORD HAS A FACTORY in Britain and for years they built plain old everyday cars, most of them equipped with an asthmatic flathead four designed in Dearborn during the early 1930s; even Don Sullivan had a hand in its birth, back when he also contributed to Ford's first V8.

The engine would get you here and take you there, as long as you weren't in too much of a hurry, but when the postwar auto racing boom took place in Britain, any successes registered with this engine were more or less by default. People seeking a proprietary power plant for their home-built racing cars would look at almost anything before they would consider a Ford. As a result British racing came to include a set of regulations for cars powered by Ford engines only. This was the "1172 Formula," and all the cars racing under these rules had only similarly handicapped vehicles to beat. They were all right for buzzing about the various deserted airfields which now littered the island, but no one would ever think seriously of taking one and trying his hand at serious international competition. Motorcycle power plants such as Nortons or JAPs were the thing to have in the tiny Formula III machines popular in the late 1940s and early 1950s, and after that someone discovered an overhead cam fire-pump engine made by Coventry-Climax, and soon it became The Thing To Have.

One thing you could say for the 1172cc (about 73 cubic inches) Ford; it was light, and because of this it became popular with that peculiar minority of Britishers who participated in what are known as trials—a somewhat masochistic sport in which spidery looking, featherweight homebuilt specials attempt to climb muddy hillsides on cold, rainy days. Among those who went in for this sort of thing in 1950 was a young engineer who had just built his own special, rescuing the engine from a Ford that had been destroyed by fire. He also ran the car in a race in June of that year, beating a Type 37 Bugatti to win. His name was A.C.B. Chapman, and he was busily thinking about building a newer, better car.

Chapman soon became known as Colin and his cars as Lotuses and they won a lot of smaller races, but even he switched over to the Climax when it came time to get involved in international events. In such things as rallies Fords were also a minor factor. Somehow or other Ken Wharton won the 1949 Tulip Rally with one of the old side-valve Anglias, and the next year he did it again with a flathead V8 Pilot (the engines were shipped from the United States). One of the new six-cylinder Ford Zephyrs even won the Monte Carlo Rally in 1953, the year it was more of a clock-reading and mathematical exercise than anything else. If your sister said she was going out with a bloke who was driving a Ford ... well, at least you wouldn't think he was much of a sport.

Then came the fall of 1959, and almost hidden in the waves of acclaim that greeted the radically new, front-wheel-drive Mini-Minor of the British Motor Corporation, there also appeared a revised Ford Anglia. It had a new engine of wildly oversquare dimensions, with so little bottom-end torque that for the first time in the history of British Ford the engineers thought it necessary to equip a car with a four-speed transmission. It was an odd little engine of 997cc (about 60.5 cubic inches) which produced 39 horsepower at 5,000 rpm, with each of its four cylinders having a bore of 80.9 millimeters and the pistons having a stroke of only 48.4. There were some jokers who said the crankshaft didn't even revolve; all it had to do was lie there and vibrate. The unit weighed only 217 pounds complete with accessories, and the extremely short stroke made it possible for the cylinder block to be only 7¼ inches deep. It had nice big valves, an excellent intake and exhaust port arrangement, and despite only three main bearings, had a rigid bottom end.

Many production engines have been designed and built in the period since World War II, some of them good, a few unsuccessful and most of them nondescript, capable of doing their jobs only because the general level of technology makes it almost impossible for a really bad design to see the light of day in a production automobile. But none of them, the good, the bad or the mediocre, ever approached the development potential of this one. The Ford engine, refined and hopped up all out of proportion to anything that had ever been done to a production engine, gave British racing car constructors a great power plant to install in their new models. With it they were to dominate Formula Junior, Formula III and Formula II racing, and lessons learned from it were eventually to be carried over to success in Formula I, or grand prix events. The fall of 1959 was a most auspicious time for it to come along, as the popularity of automobile racing was at a new high in Britain.

Stirling Moss, the uncrowned king of the drivers, was a national hero and was known all over the globe. Mike Hawthorn had won the world championship in 1958, and Australian Jack Brabham was about to do the same in 1959.

British-built Vanwalls had won the Formula I constructors' cup the previous year and this time the honor would fall to Cooper, which had built Brabham's 1959 car. An Aston Martin had just won at Le Mans and had also taken the world manufacturers championship for sports cars. British constructors such as Lotus, Cooper, Lola and others were looking for new and better engines and Ford, coupled with the talents of some outside tuners and designers (especially the brilliant young Keith Duckworth), was about to give it to them.

By 1967, still with 997cc and restricted to one carburetor with a venturi of only 36 millimeters, the engine was producing 110 horsepower. By the same year, in 1.6-liter form and equipped with double overhead camshafts, the engine was capable of more than 220 horsepower—more than five times the original output.

The engine wasn't the only thing necessary. A class in which it could be exploited to its fullest potential was also needed, and that had been invented a few years earlier in Italy. The father of it was Count Giovanni Lurani, a wealthy former gentleman driver, magazine editor and Italian representative to the International Sporting Commission of the FIA. As early as 1956, when he was troubled over the lack of a cheap single-seater racing car in which young drivers could gain experience, he evolved a set of regulations for a new class. By 1958 they were in force as an Italian national class, and the experiment was a success.

It was called Formula Junior, and the basic regulations were simple: The cars would be single-seaters, with minimum dimensions for wheelbase, track and width of body, and their choice of power plants would be limited to pushrod-operated engines taken from production touring cars. The maximum allowable displacement was 1100cc (67 cubic inches) and carburetion was more or less free, meaning you could go all the way to one per cylinder. No limited-slip differentials were allowed, pump gas had to be used, and the minimum weight for the cars, with oil and water but without fuel, was 400 kilos (882 pounds) or 360 kilos (791 pounds) if an engine with a displacement of 1000cc was used.

In 1959 Formula Junior became an international class and this not only made Lurani happy, but also created considerable joy in the Italian speed-equipment business. The Fiat 1100 was obviously the best engine for the job, and there were dozens of shops in Italy with experience in tuning it for competition They envisioned orders from all over the world, and for a while, as the class gained in popularity through 1959, the orders came. Stanguellini built the best cars and one of his won the Formula Junior grand prix at Monaco, and there were also Conrero, Taraschi, Volpini, Dagrada, Branca, De Sanctis and many more, and they dominated the racing. About the only thing Britain had to offer that season was a front-engined Elva, with some of them powered by a two-stroke German DKW engine and others by BMC's veteran four-cylinder. Then along came the Ford, and Chapman was interested. By Boxing Day of 1959 (the day after Christmas, when traditionally a race meeting is held at Brands Hatch, near London) the first rear-engined Lotus appeared in public. It was the Lotus 18, it was driven by Alan Stacey, and it did nothing to speak of. The chassis had been put together practically on the starting line, and the engine which Duckworth had prepared for the car (with perhaps 75 horsepower) had broken down and a last-minute substitution had to be made.

But by spring the Lotus-Fords were ready and so were their drivers, two youngsters by the names of Jimmy Clark and Trevor Taylor. Their first serious opposition was at Goodwood, where they ran up against many-time world motorcycle champion John Surtees, making his automotive debut in a Cooper with BMC engine. It was wheel to wheel all the way, with Clark edging Surtees for the win, and Taylor close behind in third with the satisfaction of having driven the fastest lap. At Monte Carlo a short while later the Lotuses were again impressive, with Clark's pole-grabbing practice time of 1:45.5 actually being faster than the fastest lap of the grand prix race on the same circuit in 1957. Henry Taylor, who was later to become Ford of Britain's competitions manager, won the race in a Cooper-BMC after Clark retired while in the lead.

That was one of the few times the engine lost anything: Of the 19 major Formula Junior races held in 1960, Lotus-Fords won 13 (six by Clark, four by Trevor Taylor), and the Cooper-BMCs won four (three by Henry Taylor). The only two events won by Italian cars were held in that country and did not receive any top entries from Britain. By the end of the year the engine, in its best Formula Junior tune, was producing 90 horsepower at 7,500 rpm.

In 1961, with Clark having graduated to the Formula I ranks, Trevor Taylor and Peter Arundell were the team pilots and their record was even more convincing than that of the previous year: There were nine major Formula Junior races and Lotus-Fords won seven of them, two going to Taylor and three to Arundell. Halfway through the season, when it seemed the others might make it close, Cosworth came out with an 1100cc version of the engine, which produced 95 horsepower and a comparable increase in torque. They were really something to see, those Formula Junior Lotuses—ridiculously slim and low-slung when compared to other vehicles of that era, they were also probably the cleanest looking race cars ever built, as the engines were so slim the body would even cover the mouths of the two double-choke Weber carburetors. When they were being warmed up the Fords gave forth that hoarse bark characteristic of four cylinders, but when they were in full song there was no longer a resemblance to any other engine with the same number of pistons; the shrill scream of the Lotus-Ford was a cry unto itself as the rev counter worked its way up to 9,000. No other four-cylinder engines, with pushrods, had ever successfully been wound as tight as the Fords used for Formula Junior at that time. The engine had developed such a monopoly in the class that even Italian constructors ordered them.

Formula Junior wasn't the only type of competition in which the Ford engine created a sensation; the next was to be small-capacity sports car racing, where Chapman would drop his newest bomb. The first Clark knew about it was in the winter of 1962, when he had just returned from winning three races in South Africa and stopped by the factory to pick up his Lotus Elite coupe before heading north to Scotland. The car wasn't ready and Jimmy wanted to get home, so Chapman said, "Tell you what; I'll lend you an Anglia."

Clark didn't think much of driving several hundred miles in what for him was an underpowered car, but Chapman said it was the only thing available, so he took it.

(Top) A typical early-day Continental Formula junior, this one a 1960 Stanguellini powered by a Fiat engine. (Middle) Jimmy Clark's first single-seater ride, in the Formula Junior event at Brands Hatch, England, the day after Christmas, 1959. Clark (30) is driving a Gemini. (Bottom) The first rear-engined Lotus, driven by Alan Stacey, was in the same event—and also had a Ford engine.

(Top) The start of the Formula Junior race at Monaco, 1961.
(Bottom) Formula IIIs at Monza, Italy, 1965.

No sooner did he turn the key than he was aware this was no ordinary Anglia. Instead of the slim-line four-cylinder pushrod engine under the hood, Clark saw a hefty-looking double overhead cam conversion sitting atop the original block. On the way north the combination of Clark and the Q-ship on wheels made life miserable for numerous Jaguar owners, who were cruising along at 100 mph—and were passed by this innocuous little beast. Clark's newfound toy was equipped with the first example of the double overhead cam Lotus engine, with cylinder head designed by Harry Mundy and the block underneath it being the new five main-bearing unit intended for the 1,500cc version of the standard engine. It was scheduled for use in the new Cortina, to be introduced in the fall of the year, and Chapman, Cosworth and Mundy had been able to get one of the five preproduction examples cast at the factory. The overhead cam design was originally intended for use in Chapman's new Elan models, but at some point between Clark's trip to Scotland and the spring, Chapman had thoughts about installing it in still another new machine—the Lotus 23.

In today's frame of reference the Lotus 23 is still one of the smallest racing sports cars ever built; when it showed up at the Nürburgring in late May of 1962, it looked so small it was almost laughable. Porsches were considered the proper size for a medium-capacity sports racer—yet the Porsches looked like trucks compared to this green thing that was barely taller than your kneecaps. About all anyone knew of the car was that it arrived at the course in pieces and most of the first two practice days were spent assembling the flimsy bits of fiberglass while Phil Hill was busy making fastest time of 9:25.5 with a 2.4-liter Ferrari. Willy Mairesse was next with a 4.0-liter Ferrari at 9:34.8, and then there was Dan Gurney with one eight-cylinder Porsche at 9:36 and Graham Hill with another at 9:42. When Clark finally took the 1.5-liter, 925-pound car out on Saturday afternoon he raised a few eyebrows with 9:48.9, but there was still precious little attention paid to the vehicle. It was another of those Chapman creations that would fall into pieces on the first lap, someone said, and besides, how did a pushrod Ford engine ever get that thing around so quickly? The timekeepers must have made a mistake (and the critics never bothered to see if the engine had pushrods or overhead cams).

It rained the night before the race, and when the field lined up for the Le Mans start at 9 a.m., the 14-mile circuit was still wet in many places. A good number of the 350,000 spectators were standing under trees still dripping with moisture when Clark beat the rest of the field at the start and shot through the south curve, up the back straight, and then disappeared over the hill and into the woods.

Watching a race at the Nürburgring is different from other circuits because of its length. Once the cars go out of sight, grandstand spectators are dependent on the scoreboard and the announcer, who gives the positions of the leaders at various points. At the top of the scoreboard is a diagram of the track, and as the lead car proceeds around the course bulbs on this replica light up so those in the main grandstand will have some idea when he will arrive. As Clark had a good lead at the start, the fans were not surprised when the announcer said he was in front at Adenauer

Forst, or even when he got to the Karussell. But by the time he passed Galgenkopf, at the head of the 1½-mile, up and downhill straight, it was something of a surprise to hear the Scotsman was still ahead. From that point to the finish line there are no trackside reporting posts, and you wait until the pack bursts into view.

This time there was no pack, merely that little green car buzzing past the pits and down into the south turn. People looked at each other. This wasn't real, was it? The other cars, the Ferraris and the Porsches, one of them must have crashed and blocked the track or something.... Then, just as Clark was coming out of the south curve and heading down the back straight, Gurney's snarling Porsche, with Hill's Ferrari hot on its heels, came speeding into view; Gurney was 28 seconds behind Clark. The next time around the margin was 47 seconds, after three laps it was more than a minute, and even the pro-Porsche crowd was going wild over Clark and his tiny bomb. It was too good to last; on his 10th lap, driving easily to save wear and tear on the ultralight car, Clark had the shift lever jump out of gear. What he didn't realize was that a lap or two earlier the exhaust manifold had cracked slightly, and gasses were being sucked forward into the cockpit, deadening his reactions. When the lever jumped out, the groggy Clark wasn't quick enough to catch the sliding car and he went off into the bushes, unhurt, but out of the race. But both the engine (putting out barely over 100 horsepower at the time) and the car had already made their point, to Ford as well as to the racing fans. The performance of the Lotus 23 with the overhead cam engine led to the first official cooperation between Ford of Britain and Lotus, as plans were made for a Lotus-modified and overhead-cam-powered version of the Cortina. (Note that Chapman and the Ford Division in Dearborn were getting together on the Indianapolis project at almost exactly the same time. The Lotus balance sheet for 1962 must have been a great improvement over that of 1961.)

The first big step toward giving Ford of Britain a performance image had been the 997cc engine. It was an outstanding example of the better mousetrap principle: If you manage to come up with something markedly superior to anyone else, then you hardly have to promote it. People will come to you and pay you money for your superior product, and in using it successfully will promote it for you. Ford of Britain was in this position with the Anglia in particular and with its entire line in general, as newspapers and magazines all through Britain and the continent would week in and week out list Ford engines as winners. It was free advertising in its finest form, and it didn't cost the factory a figurative dime.

The second big step, the one that refined and improved the image, was the Cortina. Introduced in the fall of 1962, it was not exactly a triumph for the styling department, but it was a pleasant-looking car, and it went like hell, especially when a little bit of the know-how gained with the smaller, earlier engine was applied under the hood. The original car had 59.5 horsepower in untuned form, then a GT version with a double-choke Weber carburetor appeared in the spring of 1963 and was good for 84 horses. The Lotus version was introduced in the fall of the same year, and the stock horsepower figure was 105, with a special-equipment version giving 115. Those last two numbers were probably the most conservative ever announced for an engine, as most of those that were raced had at least 140 horses, and in some of the no-modifications-barred classes more than 180 horsepower was extracted, using everything up to and including fuel injection. (Today Ford sells fuel injection as an optional extra.)

Within a few days after the car was introduced it won its first race, with Jack Sears nipping the reigning British saloon car champion (saloons are what the British call sedans, not where they go to drink), and eventually winning that title himself. Although the overhead-cam version was not yet homologated, the Cortina GT, pushrods and all, managed some remarkable victories: Sears and Bob Olthoff, driving one car, and Henry Taylor and Jimmy Blumer, sharing another, beat some Holman-Moody Falcons and the rest of the field to take the annual 12-hour race at Marlboro, Md. In Europe, the Cortinas became the car to beat in the medium-sized sedan events. In Britain they even bored out the 1,500cc engines to 1,650cc, installed them in Anglias and then raced the result. In international rallies the Cortina soon became a car to reckon with, and an intensive factory effort that first year gave Ford of Britain the RAC world manufacturers rally cup.

The bigger engine also had a beneficial effect on Ford power used for Formula Junior racing: The five-main-bearing block was now employed for 1100cc Juniors, and the increased rigidity of the bottom end made it possible to turn it even tighter. By the end of the season the better Formula Junior Ford engines were producing as much as 115 horsepower at 9,000 rpm. As in previous years, at any of the bigger races for this type of car, the dominant make was Ford: They won 17 of 17 events, and ran 1-2-3 in 16 of them.

As far as speed was concerned, what was originally intended as a cheap stepping stone class had now become nearly as fast as the Formula I cars. When Clark won the 1963 British Grand Prix at Silverstone, driving a Lotus equipped with Coventry Climax double overhead cam V8 engine of 1.5 liters displacement and about 210 horsepower, his average speed for the race on this medium-speed circuit, replete with fast bends, was 107.75 mph. The best lap, achieved by John Surtees in a Ferrari was 1:36.0, or 109.76 mph. In the Formula Junior curtain-raiser (admittedly a shorter race, requiring the cars to carry less fuel), Arundell won at an average of 104.1 mph and established fastest lap at 1:39.4—106.01 mph. The only thing wrong with Formula Junior was its name.

There was a more serious weak point in its structure, however, and that was the cost. To go racing with a fully prepared, top-line car, and to compete against factory entries, was becoming prohibitively expensive. So the classes were changed. For 1964 the Juniors were abolished and split into two divisions: Formula III allowed a minimum weight of 881 pounds, a maximum displacement of 1,000cc, and only one 36-millimeter carburetor. Formula II was basically the same except the minimum weight was 420 kilos (924 pounds), the 1,000cc engine was limited to four cylinders and the method of valve actuation was free. As a consequence Cosworth designed and produced a single overhead cam version. At the beginning it produced 115 horses at 8,750 rpm, and was far and away the best thing going. In 1964 Ford-Cosworth engines not only won all of the 17 races held for this formula, but also placed 1-2-3 in 16 of them (Brabham chassis took eight, Lotuses seven, Lola and Cooper one each). At Enna, in Sicily, the winner averaged 126 mph; at Rheims, in France, the winning average was 119—considerably faster than the legendary combination of Juan Manuel Fangio and the 2.5-liter streamlined Mercedes when he won the Grand Prix of France in 1954.

One of the two setbacks to the tidal-wave approach of Ford occurred in 1964 in Formula III, partly because of a single driver and partly because of Cosworth's paying most of its attention to the Formula II engines. The Formula III driver of the year in 1964 was unquestionably Jackie Stewart, the young Scotsman who was following in the footsteps (or was it tire tracks?) of Clark. Although there was an unofficial agreement among major manufacturers not to take part in the Formula III events, leaving this open to the private teams, Stewart was driving a Cooper powered by a BMC-blessed engine. Cosworth did not market a new model for the year, and Holbay had only a mildly tuned version. So the BMC four-cylinder, which had been pushed into the background during Formula Junior's peak period, came to the fore again. The combination of the factory-tuned engine, Stewart's talents and the lack of attention on the part of Ford resulted in BMC-Coopers winning 12 of the 23 major Formula III races held in 1964, with 11 of these going to Stewart. Only eight were won by Fords, with three staged in France that drew more or less local fields being won by cars with Renault-based power plants.

The temporary shortage of victories here did little or nothing to hurt the image; an even better source of ink had been found in the Lotus Cortina, which was homologated after 1,000 were built at the end of 1963 and which was now race ready. Clark won the British saloon car championship with one, spending much of the summer cornering on three wheels, and Sir John Whitmore took another and dominated the European touring car championship with it. Things got to the point where the Lotus Cortinas were not only the fastest cars in their class, but also the fastest cars in the race. About the only exception to this rule in Britain came when a well-driven Galaxie appeared. Ford even had the satisfaction of running Mercedes out of sedan racing, as the German factory's 300SE models, despite excellent preparation and good drivers, were not as quick as the light little Fords. One of the 300SEs won the six-hour touring car race at the Nürburgring, with Lotus-Cortinas second and third behind it and forced to slow down because of the pounding the course was giving the suspension. But when they got to England for the six-hour race at Brands Hatch the standings were reversed, with two Cortinas finishing in front of the first Mercedes. Badgered on one side by the Cortinas and on the other by the big-engined Ford Falcons which ran the Monte Carlo and other European rallies, Mercedes got out. The Jaguars, which had dominated British sedan racing until the Galaxies

(Top) The start of a Formula III race at Brands Hatch, 1966. By this time almost every good car of this type had a Ford engine in the rear. (Bottom) One of the few to crack Ford's grip on Formula III—Jackie Stewart and his BMC-Cooper at Rheims, 1964.

(Top) The prototype Lotus 23, fifth from left, at the start of the Nürburgring 1,000 Kilometers of 1962. (Inset) Clark in the lead during the same race. (Bottom) Ford-powered Formula II cars at Brands Hatch, 1966.

(Top) A Ford Zodiac plowing through on its way to a class win in the 1964 East African Safari. (Bottom) Clark shortly before he crashed the Lotus 23 at the Nürburgring 1,000 Kilometers, 1962.

(Top) Roger Clark testing his Cortina in preparation for the 1967 Shell 4000 Rally in Canada. (Bottom) The start of the six-hour race at Brands Hatch, 1964. The Cortina in the middle outran the Mercedes to win.

shocked them the previous year, were now having to face the additional embarrassment of watching the tail-lights of the Cortinas, and they also faded away.

Not only were the Cortinas now the fastest, but the British saloon car championship was rapidly becoming an all-Ford affair; Sears started it in 1963, Clark took it the next year, and in 1965 Roy Pierpoint won it in an Alan Mann-entered Mustang, Mann also being responsible for running the Continental effort that won the 1965 European touring car championship, running the Falcons so successfully in the Monte Carlo Rally of 1964, the winning Mustangs in the Tour de France the same year, the Cobras in all European events counting for the international manufacturers championship in 1965 and various other projects for Ford on both sides of the ocean. In 1964 two of his Lotus-Cortinas repeated the 1963 success of the Cortina GT at Marlboro, placing first and second, and in 1967 one of his Falcons (actually one of the 1964 rally cars), with Frank Gardner driving, took the British saloon car title. In 1966, just to keep the string intact and to give one of the other British Ford models a chance, John Fitzpatrick won the same championship in a 997cc Anglia.

On the international rally scene, British Ford scored its greatest success in 1964 and it was with the Cortina GT, not with the higher-powered version. The cars finished first and third in the 1964 East African Safari and also won the team prize (this was the same event in which the Comets had so much trouble). Although the Safari attracts little attention in the United States, a victory in East Africa is one of the biggest profit-makers of them all for a British manufacturer. Not only domestic sales benefit, but the considerable investments these companies have in African outlets get impetus from a win in what is the biggest and toughest event of the year on that continent. If that wasn't enough, in 1964 the Cortina GT won the touring car category of the Alpine Rally and the Lotus Cortina won sedan car handicap honors in the Tour de France.

By the end of 1964 important decisions had been made in Paris and Coventry that were to govern the future of British Ford in racing: Starting with 1966, it was announced, Formula I would no longer be for 1.5-liter engines, but for 3.0 liters (or 1.5 supercharged, with which no designer was to bother). Starting with 1967, another decision said, Formula II would increase from 1,000cc maximum displacement to 1,600cc. Series production engine blocks (from either touring or grand touring cars), which had been made in a minimum quantity of 500, and which had at most six cylinders, would be allowed. At the same time it was known that Coventry-Climax, the primary supplier of Formula I engines to the various British teams, would not build any engines for the 1966 season. Would it be worthwhile for Ford to back any efforts in this direction?

By the fall of 1965 the company was working in both areas, and a great deal of the favorable influence at Dagenham had been exerted by Walter Hayes, Ford of Britain's promotion-minded director of public affairs, and by Harley Copp, one of Dearborn's biggest racing protagonists during the mid-50s and now the man in charge of engineering and product development in Britain. The decision was to compete, to use Cosworth Engineering for both Formula I and Formula II projects, and to tie in the Formula I effort with Lotus.

Formula II came first, despite its going into effect a year after the new Formula I rules; it was felt lessons learned in the construction of the four-cylinder engine could then be readily transferred to the V8. Also, they could see what the others were doing in Formula I before getting their feet wet. Preliminary discussions on the design were undertaken by June of 1965 (during which year the old 1,000cc Formula II units won 13 of 14 races, with only one going to BRM's newest double-overhead cam effort). By February of 1966 the first engine was installed on a dynamometer and fired up. It was run in at low speeds for 2½ hours, then Duckworth boosted it to three-quarters throttle. It produced 170 horsepower, then was taken down for an inspection of the moving parts, which looked fine. It was assembled again, put back on the dynamometer and revved to 8,500. The engine produced 202 horses, just about what Duckworth had estimated for the beginning,

The two new engines, while promising great things for the future, at the same time made it impossible for any manpower to be available for further development on the current Formula II entry, which went into 1966 with 130 horses at 10,000 rpm—and ran smack into something Honda had rigged for the Brabham team. This Japanese four-cylinder, complete with double overhead cams, produced upwards of 150 horsepower; in the hands of Jack Brabham and Denis Hulme it was practically unbeatable that season. That 150 horsepower, representing the highest specific output ever obtained from a normally aspirated automobile engine running on pump gas, was enough to let Brabham and Hulme win the first 12 Formula II races in which they competed in 1966, and it was not until the end of the season at Brands Hatch that Austrian Jochen Rindt was able to beat them—in a Brabham equipped with a Ford. It was with a figurative sigh of relief that Ford saw the Formula II season and the 1,000cc maximum expire. For the three years of the formula, however, Ford power won 35 of the 48 major races. As further consolation in 1966, Ford-engined Formula III machinery won 37 of the 39 important races for cars of this class—and finished 1-2-3 in 34 of them. By this time Cosworth had lost some of its stranglehold; Holbay, Britain's second most important tuner of Ford engines, also built many of the winners. Some drivers even combined Holbay cylinder heads with Cosworth blocks, thus gaining more horsepower with the combination than either of the individual companies ever achieved.

In the meantime the new Formula II engine was going through that tedious process of picking up two horsepower today, losing one tomorrow, then finding four the next day. They call it development work, and the time from the day the engine first runs and the day it is considered race ready can often be the most agonizing period in its life. This one was ready for vehicle installation by midsummer, and it was put in an older-model Brabham chassis and run in several minor formula libre events with Mike Costin driving. By September it was judged ready and Ford made the announcement that 40 engines would be sold. The buyers (Lotus, Brabham, Cooper, Matra and others) had been standing in line for some time.

*The Ford Formula I engine, which made its debut at the Dutch Grand Prix of 1967,
shown in both cutaway drawing and in the metal.*

Clark—before, during and after: (Top) The victory procession after the 1967 British Grand Prix. (Inset) Before the start of the 1967 Belgian Grand Prix. (Bottom) Clark ahead of Denis Hulme in Holland, 1967.

Before the 1967 season started the Ford engine was considered no better than an even-money bet (if that). BMW of Germany had a fine four-cylinder engine to which they had fitted a four-valve head with the two intakes diagonally opposite each other and the two exhausts the same, and even as early as January reports of 225 horsepower were common. The Germans thought so much of their chances, and so did Lola, the two made an agreement whereby Lola was to get engines for two cars and also provide two chassis for BMW to run out of Munich. In addition, Surtees was scheduled to drive one of the two Lola-BMWs, giving them an extra edge. The other strong competitor in the field was to be Ferrari, which had developed one of its small-capacity V6s (they ran this configuration in 1.5-liter form as far back as 1957, when Peter Collins won a race at Rheims with it) for incorporation into a Fiat production car. In this manner the four-cam engine would be built in a minimum series of 500, some people who just wanted a car to drive on the street would be happy with their hot new toy, and Ferrari's engine would be "legal" for the new class.

But once spring came and the cars started running, it was all Ford. The BMW engines developed so many problems they were withdrawn from competition. The Ferraris, for one reason or another, appeared only at a few races. By that time the Fords were untouchable. Not only were they race-proven power plants putting out more than 220 horsepower, but every good British driver, plus some of the better Continentals, were using them. Ford's bet was hedged in both directions, and to make domination in this field even more complete, many of those who weren't able to purchase the engine (it wasn't the $7,000 price tag, it was the fact that only 40 were sold) resorted to modified versions of the Lotus-Cortina engine.

How good was the engine? In a field where every serious contestant is powered by the same brand it is hard to draw comparisons, but the capabilities of what is technically known as Ford's FVA model was shown in an interesting manner during practice for the 1967 German Grand Prix at the Nürburgring. In order to provide a suitable field for the large circuit, the organizing club invited a group of the better Formula II cars to run along with the Formula I machinery; included in this bunch was Jacky Ickx, the brilliant young Belgian. Clark, driving the new Lotus-Ford Formula I car, was clearly the fastest in practice, shattering the record for the winding, twisting course with a time of 8:04.1. Second fastest was Hulme, the leader for the world championship, at 8:13.5 in his Repco-Brabham. After him came such stars as Stewart (BRM, 8:15.2), Gurney (Eagle, 8:16.9), Bruce McLaren (Eagle, 8:17.7), Surtees (Honda, 8:18.2) and Brabham (Brabham, 8:18.9).

The fastest of the Formula II cars was Ickx in a Matra-Ford with a time of 8:14.0, an unbelievable performance.

By way of comparison, Clark's vehicle weighed 1,170 pounds and had about 415 horsepower at its command. Ickx's weighed 900 pounds and had the aforementioned 220 horses. (Neither Clark nor Ickx finished the race, due to suspension problems, but both were leading their respective classes when they went out.)

The engine with which Clark shattered the absolute record at the Ring got started in the fall of 1965, when the basic design of the car was agreed upon. Since British Ford was now selling passenger models (such as the Corsair and the Zodiac) with engines of V configuration, there was a degree of rationale for their sponsoring a V-type racing engine. At the same time it was known that the BRM H16, the Honda V12 and the Gurney-Weslake V12 would in all likelihood put out more horsepower than anything a Ford-Cosworth collaboration could bring forth from a V8. The

Clark and his mechanics talk things over before the 1967 British Grand Prix at Silverstone, which Clark won in his Lotus-Ford.

solution to the problem was to build a better V8 than anyone had in the past, and also to make sure it was installed in a car that was at the minimum weight limit of 500 kilos. They banked on the fact that the constructors with the heavier 12 and 16-cylinder engines would not be able to build vehicles that light, and that the lack of weight would more than make up for any possible shortage in the power department.

The chassis was left to Chapman, a past master at weight-saving, and he and Duckworth (who got his first job with Lotus after graduation in 1958) worked out where the rear suspension would mount on the engine block, for that was to be the secret of the car: The body, as such, would end right behind the driver. From there back the engine would be a load-bearing member of the structure, and everything usually fastened to the rear of the vehicle would simply be bolted to the engine.

Duckworth and Costin didn't get started on the Formula I engine until November 1966, when the Formula II project was signed off, and by which time they had already seen their theories were correct: Brabham won the 1966 world championship not on horsepower, as he had less than almost anyone else, but through having the lightest and most reliable vehicle. Thanks to experience gained in the four-cylinder project, such items as combustion chamber shapes and the like were no problem and the new engine moved along amazingly quickly, so quickly in fact that the first one was handed over to Chapman April 25. There was no time to get a car ready for the Grand Prix of Monaco May 7 but by the end of the month, while Chapman and drivers Clark and Graham Hill were at Indianapolis, two cars were made ready and Hill flew back to give one of them a shakedown run at Snetterton.

Clark never saw his until four days before the Dutch Grand Prix on June 4, where they made their debut. They were beautiful little things, so slim the bodies were only 27.5 inches wide, so sleek the other makes looked almost trucklike by comparison. In practice the Lotuses spent most of the time making adjustments, and it wasn't until late in the final session that Graham Hill went out and grabbed the pole position with a record lap at 1:24.6, more than five seconds quicker than the old mark and a half second faster than Gurney in his new lightweight Eagle. Clark, whose car had wheel-bearing problems, barely had time to get familiar with it and was on the third row of the grid with a 1:26.8. The bearing troubles came in part from the use of what must be the first "square" wheels in auto racing; they were of 15-inch diameter, and the rim width was also 15 inches. For the race itself, to insure no recurrence of the problem, the Lotuses ran on 13-inch rims.

When the race started Hill jumped off in front of the pack—and after 11 laps was out of it, a broken timing gear having finished his mount. But Clark, who had been with the leaders since the beginning, was now getting the feel of his car. By lap 16 he was in front and he stayed there the rest of the way, winning comfortably while Copp, Hayes, Duckworth and Chapman chewed their fingernails in the pits. To find the last time a brand new design won a world championship event in its first appearance you had to go back 13 years to 1954, when Mercedes took the Grand Prix of France with its straight-eight streamliner.

First start—first victory: Jimmy Clark after the Grand Prix of the Netherlands, 1967.

(Inset) Clark during the 1967 German Grand Prix.

*Graham Hill's Lotus-Ford dices with the Brabhams of Denis Hulme and
Jack Brabham during the Italian Grand Prix at Monza, 1967. (Inset) Hill with
engine designer Keith Duckworth, who was responsible not only for Ford's
Formula I and II engines but for many others as well.*

To make it even more depressing for the opposition, all of them could see that the development work necessary to catch up with the Lotus-Ford could not possibly be done during the season. They were right: From that day, the only thing that beat the Lotus-Fords in a world championship race was mechanical failure. Following is a brief breakdown of the season, starting with the Grand Prix of the Netherlands (they missed the Grand Prix of South Africa January 2 and Monaco May 7):

EVENT	FASTEST QUALIFIER	WINNER	REMARKS
G.P. Holland	Hill	Clark	
G.P. Belgium	Clark	Gurney (Eagle)	Clark leading, slowed by faulty spark plug.
G.P. France	Hill	Brabham (Brabham)	Both Clark and Hill led, retired with faulty differentials.
G.P. Britain	Clark	Clark	
G.P. Germany	Clark	Hulme (Brabham)	Clark led, retired with broken suspension.
G.P. Canada	Clark	Brabham (Brabham)	Clark leading, retired with water soaked electrical system.
G.P. Italy	Clark	Surtees (Honda)	Hill leading, retired with mechanical failure near end; Clark lost lap due to pit stop to change tire, repassed entire field, ran out of gas on last lap while in lead.
G.P. U.S.	Hill	Clark	
G.P. Mexico	Clark	Clark	

As a final plus the V8, which should have been down on power (theoretically) to the 12 and 16-cylinder opposition, was producing between 415 and 420 horses by the end of the year. Gurney's V12 Eagle, probably the fastest of the non-Ford-powered cars, was also getting about 415. The Ferraris spent the entire season trying to get over 400, and Brabham and Hulme, who won on reliability, made do with much less.

Less than a decade earlier British Ford engines had been renowned for practically nothing.

By the close of 1967 British Ford engines dominated—indeed, practically owned—Formula I, II and III racing.

And it all started from an innocuous-looking little four-cylinder with big valves, nice ports and a rugged bottom end.

Of course there were those who put the knock on it at the beginning all that business about no low-end torque; that's why they put a four-speed transmission behind it.

29

PORCUPINES, HEMIS
AND ESCALATION

IN THE FALL OF 1961, with Pontiac the king of big time stock car racing and Ford trying to find its way back to the top, six men from the Engine and Foundry Division sat down to help with the job. They were A.J. (Gus) Scussel, the section head; Norm Faustyn, Joe Macura, Al Rominsky, Bob Schwender and Don Sullivan. On paper the six were just another of the numerous special engine groups of the division, and with the notable exception of the veteran Sullivan most of the rest had never seen a race, much less built a power plant for one. Lack of experience wasn't their biggest handicap: they were engineers, and for this project only the parameters of what was expected of the engines had changed. The main hang-up came from the raw material. Stock car racing engines, regardless of how much modification they undergo, are limited in their potential by the basic design of the production version from which they stem. In Ford's case this special group was working with something not as good as the engines used by their competitors. Accused by some of being little more than two old-time Chevrolet four-cylinders hung on the same crank and starting life in 332-inch form in 1958, as it progressed through 352-inch and 390-inch versions it was always a step or two behind the others.

In the next five years, with basically the same personnel doing the work, the special engines men managed to somehow add 200 horsepower to the output and (for certain applications) almost 48 hours to its race durability. As an important adjunct, in the course of development of the engine as a racing unit many items were found which could also be used to improve the more pedestrian versions. It was a peculiar cycle: The assembly line engine was taken, and in the process of refinement and modification for racing, pieces were replaced or redesigned in favor of other parts more favorable to high-speed running. Then, with the new racing part providing the impetus, a better version of the production item was developed. Rudolf Uhlenhaut, who was responsible for much of Mercedes-Benz' competition success in the 1930s and 1950s, summed it up best when he likened automobile racing to war. You don't develop anything through racing that you wouldn't have developed anyway, Uhlenhaut said, but through the accelerated pace demanded by the sport you develop it a lot faster. At Ford not only the pieces, but also the manner in which they were tested underwent great improvements as a result of the racing program.

And development was necessary. For 1962 Ford's largest V8 had grown to 406 cubic inches as the industry continued to make the big ones even bigger. Pontiac, the defending champion in both NASCAR and USAC, was up to 421, and even previously non-racing Chrysler now offered optional 413-inch engines for both Dodge and Plymouth. Chevy had its 348-inch model up to 409, but this one was never particularly successful for high performance activity, its ancestry as a truck power plant managing to show at critical times. From a muscle standpoint the unquestioned leader was Pontiac, which was now estimated to produce in the neighborhood of 465 horses. The best Ford could do, at the beginning of the season, was 430. With the engine in that configuration it would only last for 39 minutes when being run on the dynamometer at its full-throttle rate of 6,200 rpm.

The difference in horsepower and durability was most apparent at Daytona, at the start of the season. The high banks and the 2½-mile length of the course enabled the cars to be driven flat out, and practice had barely begun when Roberts hit 159 miles an hour in Yunick's Pontiac. At that moment school was out; if Roberts' engine stayed in one piece there was no one who could catch him. The other Pontiac drivers spent the next few weeks of practice figuring ways to do this, while the Ford team was trying to find ways of lasting. Scussel and his crew had built 11 new engines, and soon after they arrived the blocks started cracking. Fortunately, from a tactical standpoint, they found the first crack before the engine spread its guts all over the race track; from then on, this weakness was kept a secret from the other teams. Every time a car would come in, they would drop the oil pan and Scussel would send one of his engineers underneath for a look. If it showed signs of a crack the engine was yanked before it got any worse and the news never got out—until the race. Then the cars had to run for 3½ hours, and there was no way of keeping it quiet. Roberts led almost from start to finish and behind him, one by one, the Fords were dropping out with blown engines. The only one to last was Lorenzen; he finished due to a cracked fuel line that made it impossible for the engine to run at high revs during the later stages of the race. Freddie placed fifth, and the engineers went back to work. By the time of the Atlanta race in early April, the engines had cross-bolted main bearings and no more blocks were split.

The year, for Ford, was somewhat similar to the ones Pontiac had when it was developing its racing engine a few seasons earlier. Although the budget had been stepped up from the previous season it was still not enough to permit entries in the majority of the 53 Grand National events (although cars did make most of USAC's 22 races). Lorenzen and Stacy, who had been hired on the strength of his performance as an independent in 1961, composed the Holman-Moody team. Marvin Panch, one of the Ford mainstays in the mid-1950s, came back again in the spring when he joined up with the Wood brothers, led by ex-driver Glen. In the USAC circuit Ford still had Norm Nelson and also picked up the veteran Don White, who was driving for the Zecol-Lubaid team out of Milwaukee. Turner, now banned from NASCAR, made arrangements to drive in USAC, and he was also to receive support. Others in both USAC and NASCAR were to receive spare parts and technical advice, including Larry Frank, a veteran of the Southeastern scene; Bill Cheesebourg, one of the better USAC drivers, and Mike Klapak, who was driving in the minor-league MARC (later renamed ARCA) circuit.

The lack of money, plus the lack of horsepower, had an inevitable effect: With some notable exceptions, the General Motors cars took home everything except Ford's hubcaps, as Fords managed to win only six of 53 races. That half-dozen, however, included four of the eight super-speedway events, and those provided enough excitement, and enough ink, to make up for the lack of victories on the smaller tracks. It was a propitious time: Pontiac had been the boss for more than a full season, and the fans loved to watch the favorites get knocked off. In 1962 the Fords were the underdogs, and by the time a third of the season had gone by they were really dark horses; it took 20 races before a Ford won anything, and then came Darlington, in early May.

The Rebel "300," run for the last time with convertibles, was the event. The cross-bolted main bearings had given the engines durability and the Darlington track, thanks to Moody's talents for adjusting the chassis, was the only "big" speedway where handling would be more important than power. In addition, Ford had a pair of drivers who had won the last two races at the saucer in the middle of the tobacco fields. After practice the outlook was even brighter as Lorenzen took the pole with a qualifying average of 129.8 mph, with Roberts second and Stacy third. Macura was so confident that before the race, when he spied a broom in Roberts' pit Joe told him "We'll be by to pick that up after the race."

Macura was only kidding, but he was prophetic. Not only did Roberts crash on the second lap and rid the Fords of their main adversary, but the cars for which Macura had helped refine the engines dominated the event. At the finish it was Stacy, Panch and Lorenzen, in that order, with the latter having lost a lap through penalty by passing the pace car during one of the yellow-flag periods. Stacy, in winning, was involved in the same type of duel he and Panch staged at the finish of the Southern "500" the previous fall, with Stacy passing Panch two laps from the end and winning by a length and a half. When it was over Macura gleefully ran to Roberts' pit, grabbed the submariners' emblem of a clean sweep and carried it all the way back to Dearborn, where it was suitably decorated.

Darlington was not the first time the convertibles appeared. Early in April they made their appearance at the Atlanta "500"—complete with fastback-style hardtops bolted to the body. This ploy began in Dearborn, when the 1962 body styles were finalized. The members of the embryo Special Vehicles Department saw there was no fastback model in the line, and realizing this would present a serious aerodynamic handicap at the faster tracks, they asked that one be added. Since they had about as much influence as a gnat on an elephant, the line went without the fastback. At Daytona they had too many engine problems to worry about the body shape, but once the engines were straightened out the fastback moved to top priority. By the Atlanta race, after some unofficial huddling with NASCAR, Ford showed up with its latest creation. There was even sales literature on the new car, and there was actually one of them sitting in the showroom of a local Ford dealer, but aside from that model and the ones at the track, you couldn't have found another for love or money. The other competitors screamed, and finally NASCAR made the Ford crew weld convertible X-members into the chassis; if it was a convertible, they reasoned, it should have the standard convertible frame. Holman found some Fords in a junkyard, the Wood brothers cut the X-members out with torches and welded them into the race cars—and then it rained, postponing the Atlanta proceedings until June.

When the cars showed at Charlotte toward the end of May, the protest raised by the competition forced NASCAR to ban them. Starting Wednesday afternoon, both Holman and Moody and the Wood brothers had to work day and night, reconditioning some older cars for use in the Sunday race.

Roberts, as usual, was the fastest qualifier, a fraction over 140 mph for the 1½-mile track. But Howard DeHart, then Stacy's chief mechanic and now the general manager of Holman-Moody, felt the pace of the 600-mile event would be much slower. He and Stacy decided something between 132 and 133 would be about right. Soon after it got going, from his position in the pits DeHart saw that wouldn't be nearly fast enough, so he hung out the "plus" sign ("plus" and "minus" were two of the few signs this crew ever used, preferring to keep it simple and avoid any possible confusion). When Stacy came around and saw it, he raised his speed.

On the next lap the sign was still there, so Stacy went faster.

On the next lap it remained there, and Stacy went even faster.

DeHart didn't pull in the sign until Stacy was running as fast as he could.

By the last half of the race it had settled down to a duel between David Pearson in a Pontiac and Stacy in his Ford. Stacy was pitting every 100 miles and through the speed of the crew, would get back on the track quicker than Pearson. Once they were running it would take Pearson about 50 miles to recapture the lead, and then he would hold it until the next pit stop, when Stacy would move in front again. On his last stop Stacy got an additional worry. When Paul Norris, who was changing the right front tire, yanked his wrench away from the last lug nut, the socket somehow got hung up on the nut and stayed there as Nelson charged back into the race. Within a lap, as the imbalance in the wheel became evident, Stacy slowed and made signs to his pit he was in trouble. Stacy had no idea what was wrong and wanted to come back in for a check, but DeHart was just as determined to keep him running.

First he held up a blackboard with the word "socket" on it, but this was unintelligible to the driver. Then he tried other words, but none of them worked. Finally

DeHart wrote "We Know" on the board, added a big plus sign and held up that. Stacy shrugged and went back to driving, with Pearson on his tail and getting ready to pass. Soon after he did, with less than 40 miles to go, his engine blew and Stacy was home an easy winner with Lorenzen third.

When Stacy rolled into the victory circle, exhausted by the effort, the first thing he said to DeHart was "What the hell was making that thing vibrate?" The socket had been jammed on so firmly it stayed there to the end.

Within two weeks Ford had won another big one, and this time it was at Atlanta with Lorenzen in front at the finish. Originally scheduled for 500 miles when it was rained out in April, this latest attempt ended after 327 miles with more rain. At the climax it was Lorenzen and Banjo Matthews in a Pontiac fighting for the lead, with Lorenzen keeping his eye on the clouds as they moved in over the race track. When he and Banjo made their next pit stops, Freddie was convinced it would rain any minute, and was sure whoever got out of the pits first would be able to hold the lead until it rained hard and the race was stopped. Lorenzen's crew was the quicker one; he was the winner.

By the time they got to Daytona for the Firecracker "250" July 4, the zipper-tops were a long-dead issue and the combination of bad aerodynamics and not enough horses made it an all-Pontiac show. The top 10 qualifiers were Pontiacs, led by Matthews' 160.499, and when the checkered flag dropped the car it waved over was also a Pontiac, this one driven by Roberts (the same one he had driven for Yunick in winning the Daytona "500," but now owned by Matthews and painted red and white). The best any Ford driver could do was Panch's third, two laps astern, while Lorenzen and Stacy were both eliminated through Stacy's crash on the 34th lap.

Lorenzen's Atlanta victory in June was the start of a dry spell. Through the rest of that month, July and August, over a span of 20 races, not one Ford finished in front. Darlington, the sauna bath and kingpin of the southern tracks, was to be a different story, and another one that would have been bad theater had it happened anywhere but in real life.

By the time the 364-lap, 500-mile grind got to its critical stages there were only three cars left in contention: Johnson's Pontiac, Richard Petty's Plymouth and a privately owned Ford driven by Larry Frank, a muscular veteran from Greenville, S.C., who had never won anything of note. Had Johnson not lost three laps after a tire blew on the 200th lap, there is no question the race would have been his. Now, with 30 laps left he was third, 1½ laps behind the leading Petty and a lap behind Frank, and each of the top two still had a pit stop to make. On lap 341 Frank pitted. On lap 346 Petty pitted, and when he came out again, he was only nine seconds ahead of Johnson. Steadily, Johnson shaved the margin, until with four laps remaining he was only a car length behind. Just as Johnson was about to pass, Petty's car blew a tire and he was forced to the pits, leaving the husky Junior an easy winner with Frank limping home behind him, crossing the line on a flat tire and with a broken tie rod.

Frank's fans almost tore down the scoring stand. Their man had won, they yelled, and the scorekeepers started a recheck. It took eight hours, and at 11 p.m. the announcement came: The scorers had missed a lap. Frank was the winner. It was to be the only Grand National race he won.

The season was almost over. Johnson had little trouble winning the National "400" at Charlotte, then Rex White took the Atlanta "400" in a Chevy when Panch ran out of gas in the final stages. Ford's only successes in the latter part of the year were far removed from the super-speedways; Lorenzen won his first (and only) dirt-track event on the half-mile oval at Augusta, Ga., and Stacy took the 250-mile race at Martinsville, Va., after Lorenzen and Roberts eliminated themselves. Lorenzen had pulled up behind the leading Roberts and started tapping Fireball's bumper. Roberts wiggled a finger at him, warning Freddie to lay off.

Lorenzen wagged a finger back.

Then Roberts waved him away again.

Freddie kept right on tapping.

"I didn't tell him again," Roberts said later, "because I knew how to get him off me."

Fireball simply hit the brakes. The resulting damage to the Ford's radiator put it out within a few laps, and Roberts also retired soon after, giving Stacy an easy win.

By the end of the season most of the action on Ford's part was not on the tracks, but was involved with getting ready for 1963, which the company intended to make a banner year. Part of the work was done by the engineering department, part of it was political, and this latter segment consisted of helping NASCAR to fix a displacement limit. Ford knew that GM would soon have several engines capable of displacements close to 500 cubic inches, and they did not want to get involved in racing with engines which would be much larger than those used in passenger cars. One of the by-products of the possible "big-big" engines was a 483-inch model the company had produced by boring and stroking a 406. When it became known that nothing of this size would be needed, in the fall of the year Lorenzen drove a car equipped with it, first at the Ford proving grounds in Romeo, Mich., and then on the Bonneville Salt Flats. The car, which was one of the outlawed zipper-top convertibles, averaged 172 mph for 25 miles at Romeo, with a trap speed of 182, and at Bonneville, with Moody and Don White sharing the driving, it averaged 164 mph for 500 miles.

At the same time that the 483 actually ran, preparations for 1963 were being rushed in the special engines section. By now the reports said NASCAR's limit would be set at 6.5 liters (396 inches) and as a consequence the engineers went to work on an engine of this capacity. Then, when the 7.0-liter limit (428 inches) was announced, there was a rush to complete development work. By November they had six engines ready and they were taken to Daytona for a test. Five failed almost immediately, a few within 10 laps. It was time to head home, and this included picking up all the various pieces that bad been scattered over the garage floor in an effort to determine what broke first. In order to pack the engines for shipping, a banding machine was needed—and banding machines are not something a racing engineer carries as normal equipment. A quick search of the Daytona area showed that Smokey Yunick, of all people, had one in his garage, so the problem was even more complicated. The engineers did not want to let Yunick know of their troubles, so before taking the engines and crates in for banding, they were hurriedly reassembled and labeled with tags reading "removed at 350 miles, removed at 600 miles," and the like.

By January everything was ready, the 427's problems had been cured, and the engine was ready to go, not only as a racing power plant, but also as a production item. The company had decided to merchandise what it raced, and during the 1963 model year was to sell 4,978 examples of this latest evolutionary step, complete with mechanical lifters, crossbolted main bearings and the like. At the beginning of the year, in racing trim, it was producing close to 450 horsepower, and the factory would now install it not only in the racing Fords, but in Mercurys as well. The smaller division of the company, the one that had begun the modern-era participation with its Mexican road race victories, was coming back with a team headed by Stroppe, and that, at the start at least, bore a resemblance to a family reunion. Hernandez, the former engine development expert for the DePaolo team, was now the performance man for Lincoln-Mercury. Stroppe, who still had Vern Houle and Chuck Daigh with him, had rounded up a team that included such old-time Ford luminaries as Troy Ruttman and Parnelli Jones, who had now advanced to genuine star status at the Indianapolis Motor Speedway. The Ford Division, in addition to Lorenzen and Stacy running under the Holman-Moody banner, and Panch driving for the Wood brothers, had added Ned Jarrett, a former NASCAR Grand National champion—and for the season opener, at Riverside, Calif., had also given Gurney a ride.

The Riverside race was something new for NASCAR. Although the stock car drivers had been on road circuits before, they had never been on one for a race of this magnitude: It was for 500 miles, or 185 laps on Riverside's 2.7-mile course. There were many who felt the heavy sedans would not be able to take 500 miles of heavy braking, constant gear changes and both left- and right-hand turns. The drivers were also a problem, some of the skeptics said. They might be great at turning left, but they didn't have the finesse required for road racing. Curiously, the one who had the most trouble adapting (on a relative basis) was Gurney. By now an established international star in sports and grand prix cars, Gurney had only limited experience with the stockers and had never driven one on a road circuit. Even though he had practically learned to drive on the Riverside course, at the start he couldn't get the hang of the different style that was needed.

Moody tried to explain to Dan that he had to set the car up for the corners considerably earlier than he was doing, and Gurney would say yes, then go out and continue trying his own way.

Above: (Top) Fred Lorenzen's crew changing tires during the 1963 Firecracker "400" at Daytona. (Bottom) Lorenzen's crew again, this time at the World "600" in Charlotte, 1964. At right: (Top) The opposition stops at the pits during the 1964 Daytona "400," Bobby Isaac's Dodge is overheating. (Middle) Nelson Stacy, complete with cigarette, during the 1963 Firecracker. (Bottom) Veteran Marvin Panch in the 1964 Daytona "500."

Once Gurney, exasperated, offered to let Moody drive the car if he knew so much about it, and when Ralph replied "Well, I can do that, too." Both of them calmed down, and then took advantage of a break in practice to drive around the circuit in a passenger car, with Moody explaining just what he meant.

When practice resumed Gurney went out and tried it Moody's way. When he came into the pits after a few laps, and they told him the times he'd been turning, Gurney didn't believe it. For a few moments he sat there alone, thinking about what he had been doing, and rationalizing what the difference in driving styles had done to the stopwatch.

Then he went out and set fastest qualifying time.

In the race itself the only man who could come close to Gurney was Jones, but when his Mercury had transmission trouble at the 87-lap mark, Gurney coasted the rest of the way. Dan led 120 of the 185 laps and averaged 85 mph despite five caution flags. The stock cars had not only managed to complete 500 miles, but they had looked impressive doing so and thus lent a new dimension to the sport. So, for that matter, had Gurney. Until Riverside, 1963, no road racer had ever won a major NASCAR event.

As the teams headed east for the month of activities preceding the Daytona "500," the Ford crew was confident. Riverside had shown the Dearborn cars to be as quick as the Pontiacs had been the year before, and none of the others were expected to be in the picture when it came to the major races. When they arrived on the coast of Florida, they found nothing could have been further from the truth. Chevrolet was at Daytona, and was ready with an engine that made the others look anemic by comparison.

It was a peculiar engine in several ways, most of them from an engineering standpoint: It had staggered valves, which gave it the nickname "Porcupine Head," and as an extra added attraction it took in fresh air for the giant four-barrel carburetor from a low-pressure area just beneath the windshield. The elongated air intake, plus the radically new area from which the air was obtained, served to give the engine a mild supercharger effect, as if it wasn't strong enough in the first place.

The other peculiarity was in its pedigree, and the peculiar thing was that it had none.

Engines used in NASCAR stock car racing were supposed to be at least limited-production engines, yet here was a power plant no one had ever seen before, and which was not, to anyone's knowledge, available in any Chevy the public could buy. Somehow, the division had obtained an OK to return to racing and NASCAR, in its anxiety to get factory-sponsored teams from GM for the first time since 1957, had winked at the rules.

There were four of the cars, two from Ray Fox's Daytona garage with Junior Johnson and G.C. Spencer driving, one from Yunick (who didn't have a pilot when the month started), and one driven by Rex White, the 1960 Grand National champ. While the best Fords were working up to 161 mph the Chevys were running at 164, and it was plain that if the Chevrolets could keep running, it would be no contest. The screams over the engine could be heard all the way to Orlando on a windy day.

When Holman went to the local Chevrolet dealership to purchase one, he was told none were available; they scarcely knew what he was talking about. Finally, through the intervention of France, Holman got his hands on one. When they brought it in, the paint on some parts of the outside was still tacky. When they dismantled the engine, it was obvious it had been hastily put together the night before, and had been assembled out of every rejected part they could find. As far as its production ancestry was concerned, they could still see the scribe marks on the intake manifolds. (Late that summer, when Johnson was running out of spare parts, he stopped by Holman-Moody headquarters in Charlotte in an effort to buy the engine. When Holman showed it to him Junior took one quick look and said "Nope, that's not the one." Holman laughed. "I knew that when I bought it," he replied.)

The Chevys were so quick that when Yunick picked young USAC star Johnny Rutherford to drive his, the latter hit 166 mph almost as soon as he sat in the car, despite being totally unfamiliar with the Daytona track. Spencer, never considered a threat in earlier seasons, was now showing his exhaust pipes to everyone except the other Chevy pilots, and Johnson was even clocked at an unofficial 168. In the two 100-mile events that preceded the "500" the Chevys won almost as they pleased, Johnson taking one at an average of 164 mph, and Rutherford winning the other with 163. The Fords, led by Lorenzen at 161 and a fraction, were still around the 160-mile mark, and the Mercurys weren't even that fast. Stroppe had brought a large contingent, including USAC drivers Ruttman, Jones and Rodger Ward, and neither they nor the cars were getting the hang of the banks; the Mercurys were only in the 158 bracket.

Engines weren't the only thing bothering Ford. Halfway through the month the team had lost one of its better drivers when Panch was injured while testing a Maserati sports car equipped with a 427-inch Ford, and he escaped with his life only because of the heroism of five men. Panch's car got out of control in the third turn and wound up on its back in the east bank of the Speedway, burning with the driver trapped inside. Somehow, braving the flames, drivers Tiny Lund, Ernie Gahan and Bill Wimble, plus tire engineer Steve Petrasek and mechanic Jerry Raborn, managed to get Panch out of the holocaust. Although his back was badly burned, the veteran driver would recover. But in the meantime the car he had qualified for the "500" was without a pilot. From his hospital bed Panch suggested to the Wood brothers that they employ Lund, a huge hulk of a man (6 feet, 5 inches, 265 pounds) who had spent the last several years on the periphery of bigtime racing. All five were awarded Carnegie Medals for their bravery, and Lund got Panch's ride as well. Still, scarcely anyone looked at Tiny, in a figurative sense. He was at best the fourth or fifth car in the Ford lineup, and even though the Fords were now sporting a new fastback body which would add a few miles an hour, they were hardly quicker than the flock of Pontiacs on hand.

On race day, after an almost two-hour delay because of a rainstorm, the first 10 laps were run under the caution flag to help dry the track. Then, when the green flag fell, Johnson charged to the front, seeking to get there in a hurry and thus shake off anyone who had dreams of hanging on in his slipstream. Junior got away from all but one car, Goldsmith's Pontiac remaining glued to his bumper as they opened up a lead on the pack. Neither lasted, Johnson going out with mechanical trouble on the 26th lap, Goldsmith departing on the 39th while the Fords that were chasing them started to move up. By the 175-mile mark Lorenzen and Pontiac driver Bobby Johns were battling for the lead, and when Johns ran out of fuel at 300 miles there was nothing left up front but Fords.

The fight for the lead now became an argument between Lorenzen and Jarrett, with Lund, surprisingly enough, right behind. Although he had a reputation for driving only with his foot, in this race Tiny had been paying strict attention to orders. The Woods were having Tiny slipstream other cars, conserving his fuel, and they were bringing him in every 40 laps (100 miles) just like clockwork, for more gas. Lund had never been involved in the fight but now, because of attrition and a smart plan, he was right there, and when he roared out of the pits on the 160th lap, with a full tank of gas and obviously finished with his stops for the day, the crowd of 75,000 paid attention. Jarrett and Lorenzen, still up front, had not been getting the mileage that Tiny had been coaxing out of his mount and they had made their previous stops with 44 and 43 laps to go. They would have to come in one more time and when they did, Tiny would be a winner. On the 193rd lap Lorenzen dove into the pits and Jarrett and Lund roared past, Jarrett dropping behind Lund to run in his slipstream and to save enough gas on which to finish. Three laps later he knew he couldn't make it and Jarrett also headed for the pits, leaving Lund all alone.

When Jarrett stopped Lund slowed his pace slightly and crossed his fingers. On the same lap in which he took the lead, his engine started missing in the corners, as the little fuel he had left sloshed away from the pickup in the tank. Tiny started sweating.

On the straights the engine would catch again, and now there were only two laps to go ... then one lap ... then the engine quit again in the fourth turn as Lund rolled toward the finish. It caught once more just before he crossed the line on his last teacup of fuel. Lorenzen was 24 seconds behind, Jarrett had missed by 30 seconds, Stacy was fourth and Gurney, imported for the occasion, finished fifth. Lund, who averaged 151.566 mph, was so happy he cried. Auto racing had a new hero, and Ford had scored the greatest victory in the history of its stock car efforts.

For the moment Lund's win and the 1-2-3-4-5 sweep made everyone forget the Chevrolets. But the morning after the race, and for most of the season, the Chevys were uppermost in Ford's mind. They were faster, there was little doubt of it, and if they overcame their growing pains reasonably quickly, there was little Ford could do. Then, shortly after Daytona, Ford got what turned out to be a double-edged sword: Chevrolet, on orders from the executive floor of the General Motors building, was told to get out of stock car racing, and to get out in a hurry. The factory support disappeared. Johnson and the rest were left with what equipment they had on hand, plus what little they could sneak out the back door of the GM Technical

Center in Warren, Mich.—a back door that now had a corporate watchdog sitting in front of it. Since the Pontiacs were shut down at the same time as the Chevys, and since the Plymouths were not competitive with the Fords on the longer tracks, it looked to be the greatest Ford year since the early part of 1957.

The catch in the setup was the sudden change of image brought about by Chevy's withdrawal. Ford, which had worked long and hard to get itself into a position of strength, suddenly found itself cast as the wealthy bad guys, with Johnson and his lone Chevy in the role of the white knight and the embodiment of all that was good and noble. Johnson had become an automotive version of the Lone Ranger and Chevy, from the standpoint of public image (and therefore spectator identification with brands) could not lose. If Junior won, he was great for having beaten the Fords single-handedly. If he lost, well, at least he'd led the race and besides, everyone knew he wasn't getting any more factory help.

The problems of image and the like were of no concern to Lorenzen. His job was to win races; the more he won the more money he made, and his next big chance to earn some was at the Atlanta "500," in mid-March.

He won it, too, taking the race for the second straight year by some sharp calculations on his fuel consumption and by some quick thinking in his choice of tires. Lorenzen had started the event on Firestones, but in the early going he soon found the Goodyear-equipped cars were exhibiting much better roadholding characteristics and he decided to switch brands in the middle of the event. Although there was nothing in the rules against this, switching makes in the middle of the race was something that had not been done. In the past, whenever a driver found he'd made a bad choice, he simply suffered with it. Now Freddie wanted the others, and he wanted to let his pit know. He found a crayon in his shirt pocket, and as he tore around the 1½-mile oval, his bouncing, vibrating car running at lap speeds of close to 140, Lorenzen started to write Goodyear, backwards, on his window, while driving with one hand.

Freddie's reverse penmanship, coupled with the handicap under which he was writing, left something to be desired. Although his crew was aware something was happening they couldn't read the message and it wasn't until his next pit stop, when Lorenzen came in screaming for the Goodyears, that they knew what he wanted. Due to a lack of time they sent him back without them, but on the next caution flag Freddie came zooming into the pits again and his tires were changed without the loss of a lap. In the latter stages of the race, with the car handling beautifully, and with Lorenzen having conserved fuel by riding in the slipstream of everyone and anyone, he was left with no competition. He won by a lap, with Roberts edging Bobby Johns by a bumper-width for second place as Pontiacs ran second and third.

It was Fireball's last race in a Pontiac. Passino had been dickering with the star driver for some time, and now that General Motors had pulled back its *sub rosa* support, he was looking for another ride. Coincidentally, Stacy had broken his pelvis in a practice accident at Atlanta, so there was a seat open on the Holman-Moody team. By the 250-miler at Bristol, Tenn., two weeks later, the famous number 22 was emblazoned on the side of a lavender Ford, and Roberts was back where he started his big-time career a decade earlier. His return was something of a sensation, not only because everything Roberts did merited headlines in the Southeast, but also because he won the Bristol race, doing so after a long duel with Lorenzen when the latter was forced to make an extra fuel stop with seven laps to go. Lorenzen, who was just coming into his own as a star and who never got along with Roberts anyway, was resentful of the move and managed to tap Roberts' bumper once or twice during the affair. The next week Holman told both drivers what he expected of them in the future; although the two were never exactly friendly, the mutual respect they had for each other, plus the watchful eye of their bosses, prevented any recurrences of the Martinsville incident of 1962.

With a twosome such as Roberts and Lorenzen added to their vastly improved cars, Ford was going to be even tougher to beat, and with few exceptions that was the way it went for the remainder of the season. At Darlington's Rebel "300," run for the first time with sedans rather than convertibles, and run for the only time in two 150-mile heats, Weatherly gave Pontiac its last major win when Johnson blew, Lorenzen crashed and Roberts finished second. Lorenzen made up for this in early June, when he and Johnson hooked up in a thrilling duel at Charlotte's World "600." The two of them led for 365 of the 400 laps, Freddie winning on an empty gas tank, coasting across the line at 30 mph after Johnson blew a tire while a car length ahead of Lorenzen with less than four laps to go.

At the Atlanta "400" in June it was Johnson's turn, his car staying in one piece this time as he beat Lorenzen back to second, and at Daytona a week later, in the Firecracker "400," Johnson burned a piston after two-thirds of the event and from then on it was all Ford. Roberts won it in a three-car blanket finish, edging Lorenzen by half a length, and Panch, healthy again, by a length and a half. By this time Stacy was also back, and as chief mechanic for him Ford had obtained the services of Matthews, who had given up his dual role of both driving and servicing Pontiacs. A few weeks after Matthews joined the operation, another important addition was made. This time it was Weatherly, the 1962 Grand National champion, who was well on his way toward retaining his title. Weatherly was signed by the Lincoln-Mercury Division, and with him came his car owner, Walter (Bud) Moore of Spartanburg, S.C., who in the long run was to prove even more important to the operation than was his star chauffeur.

On Labor Day at Darlington it was Roberts' turn. For the first time in the history of the Southern "500" the entire affair was run without so much as one caution flag and when Fireball flashed under the checker, his average of 129.8 mph was 12 miles quicker than the old record as he led a parade of eight Fords and Mercurys. Panch was second, running the last half of the race without brakes, and Lorenzen was third, 37 seconds behind Roberts as an extra pit stop cost him the victory. Stacy, in one of his last major appearances on the NASCAR circuit, finished fourth, and Darel Dieringer was fifth in a Mercury prepared by Stroppe. Roberts finished with a gallon of gas in his tank and the cord on his right front tire showing, and was bothered throughout by the pain of a chipped spine he suffered in an accident at Bristol in July. It was a near thing that he won, but near things were, and are, the order of the day in NASCAR.

Johnson, still bucking the odds, gave the Chevy its swan song at Charlotte in mid-October, in the National "400." This time the car stayed in one piece, and although Lorenzen chased him throughout, there was no catching the chicken farmer from Ronda, even though Fords and Mercurys occupied the other spots in the top five. After Charlotte Junior switched to Mercury, which was looking to bolster its sagging NASCAR forces. The smaller division of Ford had not been able to register a victory, and when it did so a few weeks after Charlotte, Johnson had nothing to do with it. Dieringer, a capable driver who usually operated out of the limelight despite his considerable talents, was the man who came home with the decision. He won the only running of the Golden State "400" at Riverside.

After the opening events of the 1964 season, one of the publications that follows stock car racing felt constrained to run a story that started "Is this the year Ford takes it all?" From the way the campaign began, and from a look at the Ford and Mercury lineups, it seemed a reasonable proposition.

When it started November 10 on the half-mile dirt oval at Concord, N.C., Jarrett finished in front. A week later, in the five-hour race on a road circuit at Augusta, Ga., Roberts outlasted the field to lead a 1-2 Ford finish, Dave MacDonald coming in from the Coast to fill the runner-up spot in one of his first stock car events. When they got back to Riverside in January, Gurney won the 500-miler for the second straight year. This time, instead of piloting a Holman-Moody entry, he was behind the wheel of one built by the Wood brothers, but it made little difference to Dan. As in the 1963 race, the only man to give Gurney a run for his money was Jones in one of the Mercurys, and once Jones went out shortly before half distance it was easy. Behind Gurney came Panch (giving the Wood brothers first and second), Roberts, old-timer Bill Amick (who now confined his activities to West Coast races and driving a year-old Mercury) and Jarrett.

One of the drivers who did not finish was Weatherly. Delayed by various troubles early in the event, he was on his 87th lap (Gurney was already on his 110th) when he struck the steel retaining wall in the number six turn. The car hit the wall broadside, and did it so perfectly that the big number 8 on the side of the vehicle left its imprint on the barrier. At the moment of impact Weatherly, who wore a safety belt but refused to don the almost standard shoulder harness, had his head snapped out the window and against the wall. The first man to drive a Ford Division-sponsored car in a racing event, the man who brought Curtis Turner to the Ford team and who apologized to Buddy Shuman when his suspension fell out from under him at Darlington, was killed instantly.

Lorenzen, who finished well down after losing much time with clutch trouble, summed it up best at the close of the glum day. "There's no sense in chasing Gurney unless there's something wrong with his car; there's no catching him when everything's right." Weatherly never stood a chance of catching the leader or surviving the crash.

Even without him, the Ford-Mercury lineup was one of the strongest imaginable. For Ford the team was led by the Holman-Moody pair of Roberts and Lorenzen, and there was also an extra car available if someone happened to come along at the right time. Panch was still driving for the Wood brothers, Jarrett was still affiliated with Bondy Long, and such drivers as Gurney and MacDonald could be called upon when needed. In addition Foyt was now a Ford regular with Matthews as his crew chief, and although A.J. would be spending most of the season on the USAC circuit, he could be counted on to enter the major NASCAR events (those in which driver interchange was allowed). In USAC Foyt would be the big gun, backed up by White, while Whitey Gerken would also receive support as Ford intensified its efforts in this direction. (Norm Nelson, the long-time Ford stalwart, had joined Plymouth at the beginning of the 1963 season.)

For Mercury, Stroppe was still trying to run both a NASCAR and a USAC operation, with Jones and Ward his primary drivers in USAC, running out of Stroppe's home base of Long Beach, Calif. For NASCAR, Stroppe had set up an Atlanta garage, and had Dieringer as his top man. Moore had hired rookie Billy Wade as a backup driver for Weatherly, and when the latter was killed Wade moved into the top spot. Rex White, still operating as an independent, got his parts through Moore. The Johnson-Fox combination, which had come to Mercury in the fall of the previous year, lasted for just one race, the Riverside "400." Then they were gone again, and at the beginning of February, when everyone got to Daytona, the reason for the switch became apparent.

Johnson and Fox were there with a brand new Dodge equipped with a 426-inch version of the Chrysler Corporation's famous old "Hemi," or hemispherical combustion chamber V8. The engine, which had originally been produced from 1951 through 1957 and used primarily in Chrysler 300s (Kiekhaefer's cars had it), was dropped at the end of 1957 as an economy move, although there was little question its horsepower potential was far above any other American production V8. Dodge and Plymouth hadn't scared anyone on a race track in years but now Chrysler, watching the way Ford was rebuilding its image through racing, was ready to grab a piece of the market for itself. All through 1963 development work had been done on the old Hemi, increasing its displacement and modernizing it generally. Once it was ready, they took it west to the giant tire testing oval at San Angelo, Tex., to measure it against the fastest car of the 1963 season—Johnson's Junior's well-worn Chevy, unbeknownst to most of the racing fraternity, ran its last race on the Goodyear proving grounds five-mile track, acting as a baseline for the Plymouths and Dodges. When the session was over there was little doubt the Hemi-equipped cars were the fastest stockers ever seen. To give their introduction even more of an impact, Chrysler brought its 1963 models to Riverside and held the new ones for Florida, where they knew the publicity benefits would be manifold.

At Daytona they were out in force. Plymouth's effort was led by Petty, Goldsmith, Jimmy Pardue, the veteran Buck Baker and his son Buddy. For Dodge there were Johnson, Pearson, Bobby Isaac and Jim Paschal. It was an impressive crew, and almost as soon as practice started speeds went over 170 mph.

Artistically, it was beautiful. Legally, it was questionable. No one had yet seen a "new era" Hemi for sale in a Plymouth or Dodge dealership, and no one was likely to for some time to come. The Ford personnel on hand were enraged. For the second year in a row someone had skirted the rules in the most obvious manner and NASCAR, in an attempt to get as many manufacturers as possible into the act, had let it go. NASCAR rules at the time said at least 1,500 of the engines had to be scheduled for production in that year, and it was clear from the beginning that Chrysler had no such numbers in mind. (For the record, Chrysler sold a total of 493 Hemis in 1964 models, all of them equipped with the twin four-barrel carburetors favored by drag racing enthusiasts, Plymouth accounted for 246 of the total, Dodge sold 247.)

In qualifying runs during the early part of the month Goldsmith led the way with an average of 174.910 mph, Petty was next with 174.418, and the rest were nowhere. The fastest Ford qualifier was Jones in his Mercury at 169. Ron Householder, the mid-30s king of the midget drivers who was now Chrysler's stock car chief, simply tilted his cigar at an even jauntier angle and smiled. Holman went downtown to a Chrysler-Plymouth agency and asked to buy one of the so-called production engines. They didn't have any. Then Holman went to the local Dodge dealer. They didn't have one either, so a day or two later Holman managed to get his hands on one through France. It was the same story as in 1963, the paint on the engine was barely dry, and when it was dismantled they found almost every part was hardly good enough to survive at low revs.

This marked the real start of the escalation of hostilities in big league stock car racing. Prior to February of 1964 engines used for competition bore at least some resemblance to those sold in the showroom (or at least they did before the mechanics got hold of them). The cars themselves, although strengthened considerably to take the enormous stresses and strains, were also at least vaguely similar to those you could buy. Within a few months that sort of conduct was considered naive. Cars were being chopped down, noses were being dropped, weight was taken out: In short, anything and everything that would add another mile an hour was considered justifiable.

Ford's first move, a week before the big race, was to apply for NASCAR's approval of a new engine—the 427-incher complete with single overhead camshafts. The request came as a surprise to almost everyone in racing, because no one outside the company had any idea Ford was in possession of such a power plant. Even after the request was made, thus bringing the engine into the public eye, there was still one major point: The engine had barely been completed, and had not, at this date, been run in an automobile. It didn't make any difference, as France turned down the overhead cam request.

The race at Daytona, or what there was of it from a Ford standpoint, was all Plymouth and Dodge. Petty won easily, leading Pardue and Goldsmith across the line in a 1-2-3 Plymouth finish and averaging 154.344 mph, despite three caution flags and despite stroking it during the late stages. The only Ford driver to poke his nose in front was Foyt, who led for two laps while the other cars were refueling at the 100-mile mark. Petty led from the 52nd lap through the 200th and final one, and as his electric-blue Plymouth dashed around the high-banked oval, among the 80,000-odd spectators were Henry Ford II and Lynn Townsend, the president of the Chrysler Corporation. Ford stayed until the end and when it was all over he shook Townsend's hand, but then he told Patterson what he thought of the defeat, and the troops soon got the message. The next day, almost as soon as the crowds cleared out of the Speedway, the Holman-Moody crew was testing a model they hoped would be the successor to the Galaxie.

The idea was to install the 427-inch engine in a smaller, more aerodynamic Fairlane and race that, as the combination would at least be equal in size and body shape to the Plymouths (which were smaller and thus aerodynamically cleaner than the big Fords). The Fairlane wheelbase, which at 115 inches was an inch below the minimum allowed by NASCAR, would even be stretched an inch on all models to make the Fairlane legal. It didn't work, as the heavy 427-incher in the nose of the light Fairlane made the car handle poorly at high speeds, and the idea was shelved for the time being. Instead, a two-pronged program was initiated, with half being done at the Charlotte shops of Holman-Moody, and the other half in the special engines office in Dearborn. The southern end of the operation involved taking out as much weight as possible, and within a few weeks the cars were close to 3,600 pounds. The engineers developed a new lightweight valve train that would enable the drivers to run at 7,000 rpm, and by Atlanta, the next big race, the cars were ready to go faster.

Even prior to the installation of the valves and cams, however, they whipped the Plymouths and Dodges in the next big one, which took place at Bristol March 22, and consisted of 500 laps around the half-mile oval. Lorenzen, whose car was handling better than anyone else's, led the last 493 laps and coasted home at slow speeds when his engine developed trouble at the end. Roberts was second, and heading for Atlanta and the new engines, things looked better.

In Georgia it was all Lorenzen. He won it by two laps over Isaac's Dodge at an average speed of 134 mph, and it was the third straight time Freddie took the Atlanta "500." Only 10 of the 42 starters managed to finish, and among those who retired were most of the other Fords and Mercurys, some with blown engines, some—including Gurney, Jones, Dieringer, White and Roberts—through accidents caused either by themselves or someone else.

The Ford engines now had 500 horsepower in race configuration for the first time in history, but even with the extra muscle under the hood, the difference at Atlanta had been proper chassis setup and superior race preparation. Throughout

It was all Hemi: The start of the 1964 Daytona "500," with Plymouths and Dodges occupying the first seven spots at the beginning and the top three at the end. (Inset) Junior Johnson's hot Chevrolet of 1963.

Pike's Peak, the classic American hillclimb. Parnelli Jones, whose Mercury dominated the USAC stock-car scene in 1963 and 1964, setting a record on the hill in the former year. (Inset) Ak Miller, the veteran hot-rodder and a veteran of the hill, winning the same year in a Ford-powered special.

Winners: Curtis Turner at Meadowdale Raceway, outside Chicago, in 1962.
(Inset) Fireball Roberts after he took the Firecracker "400," 1963.

Tiny Lund after the Daytona "500" of 1963.

the remainder of the season, and despite the lightweight valve train, durability and preparation were what won for Ford; 1963 had been only a brief interlude in the history of Ford's power shortcomings. This season, regardless of the record, was to be well by the mechanics and the drivers.

North Wilkesboro, N.C., in the heart of white lightning country, was the next place Lorenzen proved himself, Fred winning his third straight race as he led 368 of the 400 laps and limped home with no water left in his radiator, a few hundred yards ahead of Jarrett with Panch third. Again it wasn't the horsepower, it was the handling qualities of the car; Lorenzen went deeper into the corners of the five-eighths mile track than any other driver.

A week later Freddie tried for number four, this time on the half-mile oval at Martinsville, Va., and the shape of the opposition had changed somewhat. Johnson, after his brief relationship with Dodge, had switched back to a Ford. Considering he had just gotten into the car, Junior did well, finishing third in the vehicle Matthews had originally prepared for Foyt. At the finish Johnson was the middle man in a five-car Ford sandwich which swept the top spots in the race, and which ran so well that a non-Ford product never made it into the top five during the entire 250 miles. The winner, and by now news of his streak had made him the biggest drawing card in NASCAR, was Lorenzen, who again did pretty much as he pleased. Panch was next, Jarrett was fourth and Roberts fifth. Lorenzen led 485 of the 500 laps—in a car that was weighed by the NASCAR technical inspectors before the race and found to be 3,630 pounds. Jimmy Pardue's Plymouth, which also went on the scales, tipped them at 3,750, and was 125 pounds lighter than any of the Dodges weighed at the same time.

The next time Freddie tried his luck it was in a USAC race a week later, the Yankee "300" on the three-mile road circuit at Clermont, outside Indianapolis. This was the only USAC stock car race of the season open to NASCAR drivers, but when a man is on a hot streak such as Lorenzen was, it doesn't make any difference who sanctions the event. At Indianapolis Raceway Park, where Parnelli Jones was well ahead of the field in his Mercury, Jones ran into mechanical trouble and Lorenzen won on the last lap. That made it number five, and next was Darlington and the Rebel "300."

In practice, at least, the Chrysler products were again competitive with the Fords. Lorenzen took the pole position, but Richard Petty was right alongside. Pardue made the second row together with Johnson, and Pearson was in the third row next to Roberts. In the race, the only two cars to lead were Lorenzen's and Petty's, and the two of them exchanged the lead nine times before Petty pitted on the 139th of 219 laps with overheating problems. From there Lorenzen cruised home, and all the excitement took place in the pits. With the race in its closing stages and with Fords 1-2-3-4, Holman ordered both Lorenzen and runner-up Roberts into the pits for a look at their left-side tires. Jack Sullivan waved Roberts in, his car was checked and sent on its way. Herb Nab, Lorenzen's chief mechanic, refused to do so, fearful his driver might lose the race. A brief arm-waving scene ensued, and in short order Nab joined the ranks of the unemployed.

Lorenzen stayed out on the track and at the finish had an almost bone-dry gas tank and only a few laps worth of rubber on the left side of the car. In was his sixth in a row, and two days later Holman rehired Nab.

That was the end of it. The streak of six straight in major events was unprecedented in NASCAR history, and if nothing else, Lorenzen was finally due to lose. In addition, the Dodges and Plymouths were due to find solutions to their problems. As a third factor, the next big race was scheduled for the 1½-mile banked track at Charlotte, where horsepower is more important than at any other place save Daytona. Lorenzen's hot streak, plus the Ford-Chrysler duel, had worked the race fans of the Southeast into a frenzy of interest, and even several hours before the start of the "600" it was almost impossible to get near the Speedway.

The crowd of 68,000 was the largest ever to see a sports event in North Carolina, and many of them were barely over the thrill of the thunderous, 44-car flying start when they got excitement of another kind. On the seventh lap Johnson, trying to fight his way up through the pack, started to spin coming out of the second corner and finally did so halfway down the back straight, blocking the paths of both Jarrett and Roberts. Johnson's car wound up in the middle of the track, and he clambered out. Jarrett's car slammed into the inside retaining wall and started to burn, but Jarrett also climbed out in time.

The rear of Roberts' car, as it spun into the inner wall, hit a sharp abutment. The force of the blow, delivered at more than 100 miles an hour, drove the fuel tank halfway into the driver's compartment and in a second the car was a holocaust with Roberts unable to free himself. Jarrett, as soon as he got out of his own vehicle, ran to Roberts' aid and helped drag the still-conscious driver away from the flames. Roberts, who had never flame-proofed his uniform, saying he was allergic to the solution then used for the purpose, was burned over 75 percent of his body, and much of the damage was of third-degree intensity. While the ambulance took him to a hospital the race roared on, with the proceedings resembling a Roman holiday. The huge crowd, full of cold beer and hot sun, included a few hoodlums who thought it would be funny to throw a can on the track and see what happened when a car ran over it. Petty and Panch, running nose to tail in the early stages of the race, ran over the same can; the report of their tires exploding sounded like two cannon shots in rapid succession. Both hit the wall, but Petty was able to rejoin the race after a lengthy pit stop. Panch wasn't that lucky. The right side of his car was wiped out and he suffered minor injuries.

The winner, after a race of attrition, was Paschal, the veteran driver who was running the number two car on the Petty team. Of the 17 factory-backed entries in the race, his was the only one that did not encounter some kind of difficulty. Petty was second, White was third in a Mercury and Lorenzen was fourth, seven laps back. Freddie had been either in the lead or near it for most of the race, and just as he was about to make his bid in the closing stages he ran over a piece of an axle that had been dropped by one of the slower cars. His pit stop cost him nine laps, in which his crew repaired damaged steering and the front suspension.

Roberts managed to live six weeks before he succumbed to his injuries. When he finally went NASCAR lost its biggest name, the idol of the fans—and surprisingly, many of the other drivers found, their own personal hero as well. Although he was only 35 when he died, he was one of stock car racing's links with the past; when he was a teen-ager at the University of Florida he would cut classes to drive in the races on the beach, and eventually the driving became more important to him than anything else. A tall, athletic-looking man, one of Roberts' greatest ambitions, from the time he was a youngster, was to play a competitive sport. But Roberts was an asthmatic, and this was the reason he turned to auto racing. That, with its high cockpit temperatures and long hours behind a heavy steering wheel, was just as demanding (if not more so) than any of the physical contact games, but Roberts never quit trying. Sometimes sick in the car, sometimes barely able to breathe, he kept quiet about his affliction and kept his foot down on the throttle. When he died, a few days before the Firecracker "400" at Daytona, everyone had the usual nice things to say, which was expected. But three years later Lorenzen, who never particularly got along with him, was asked to name his top competitor. He was unhesitating in his answer: "Fireball. He was the best. He did everything the way it should be done."

Between the time Roberts was injured and the time he died the only Ford pilot to win anything was Jarrett, who took two more of the short-track races in which he specialized, and added the Dixie "400" at Atlanta. This was his first major victory and he got it when Lorenzen and Johnson both retired early with valve troubles, and then Ned had to outrun Petty and Goldsmith. At Daytona, during a preliminary race the day before Roberts' funeral, Ford lost its second star driver in seven weeks. This time it was Lorenzen, who was involved in an accident caused when Goldsmith spun coming out of the fourth turn, but he was considerably luckier than Roberts. Lorenzen's injuries included a cut tendon in his left wrist and compressed vertebrae. They operated on the wrist almost immediately, and the damage was only of a temporary nature, but the near miss caused the money king of the southern tracks to do considerable soul searching; there was talk of his retiring, and much conversation about the rising speeds making it almost suicidal. But it was like veteran Buck Baker said after the Roberts accident: "You still have brakes, you know, and nobody ties a race driver's foot to the accelerator. It's a matter of judgment. A man can make his own decisions."

At Daytona one of those who decided to stick his foot in it was Foyt, who had made a midseason switch to Dodge after the Indianapolis disagreement with Ford, A.J. becoming one of the few non-NASCAR drivers to win a major race on the high-speed ovals. Foyt nipped fellow Dodge pilot Bobby Isaac by a car length at the finish, Dodges or Plymouth occupied most of the top spots in the results, and most of the Fords retired with blown engines incurred while trying to keep up with the Chrysler products. The Dodges and Plymouths did not possess the standard of roadholding or preparation shown by the Fords, but at Daytona, where it was all flat out and belly to the ground, the latter two qualities were not as important.

Another man who made a decision was Lorenzen. On July 10 he was quoted as saying "When I return and just how long I continue in racing will be affected a great deal by what they decide to do about speeds. That incident down there has taken a lot out of me." Within 10, days, with the stitches in his wrist just recently removed and the injured member still swollen, Lorenzen arrived at Bristol, ready to drive. Halfway through the 500-lap race the effort became too much for him, and he let Jarrett, who had been sidelined earlier by mechanical failure, take over with the car running fifth. Lorenzen's doctor had told him not to drive, and the doctor's orders seemed to be right. Moody took Lorenzen and hosed him down with water, then brought him back to an air-conditioned trailer for a change of clothes. When Jarrett made a pit stop with 57 laps to go, Lorenzen climbed back in, now running second and three laps behind Petty. The latter had the race all but won as he was less than 30 miles from the checkered flag, but when Lorenzen tried to pass him, for some reason Petty started to race with Fred, seemingly forgetting Lorenzen's passing would merely make the margin two laps instead of three. The pair tore around for lap after lap in the best nose-to-tail tradition until finally, with three laps remaining, Petty's engine failed. The Plymouth driver threw it into neutral and coasted along. Lorenzen flew past and started eating up the difference between the two cars. Petty's momentum was only good for two laps and he came to a stop just past the finish line, having completed 499 laps. The only lap Lorenzen led was the 500th.

Lorenzen's car had been the only Holman-Moody Ford to take part in the race at Bristol, as the attrition rate in vehicles and drivers had been unusually high in the past few months. Roberts had wrecked cars at North Wilkesboro, Atlanta and finally Charlotte; Jarrett had lost a car at Charlotte, Lorenzen's Daytona car was almost totaled, and there had been others that suffered minor damage. On the driver side, Holman and Moody had hired Rutherford to take Roberts' seat at Daytona, as USAC pilots were eligible for this race, and afterward picked up the veteran Bobby Johns and rookie Cale Yarborough for the remainder of the NASCAR season.

Driver problems, and also organizational problems, were much more serious in the Mercury camp during 1964. Weatherly was lost almost before the year started and Moore was left with Wade. Stroppe was still trying to stretch himself between Long Beach and Atlanta, with Dieringer as his number one driver for NASCAR races and with USAC talent coming down for the big ones. For one reason or another neither Stroppe nor Moore was able to win a major event, though Dieringer had impressive leads in several races before succumbing to mechanical difficulty or an accident. At Atlanta in June both Dieringer and Johns, who joined the team for that race, crashed while in good position, and after the event Mercury told Stroppe to close down in the Southeast and concentrate on USAC for the rest of the year. Dieringer moved over to Moore's stable, and soon afterward Moore's other driver, Wade, hit a hot streak that saw him win four races in as many starts in a 10-day period. The only other Mercury driver to win a NASCAR race that season was Dieringer, and he waited until November before coming home first in a 150-miler at Augusta, Ga.

On the USAC circuit Mercury enjoyed the best season it ever had, with the combination of Stroppe and Jones. Not only was Parnelli an outstanding talent and Stroppe one of the best car builders, but the two also understood each other perhaps better than any other mechanic-driver twosome in racing. Jones finished fourth in the season opener, a 150-miler on the one-mile dirt circle at Langhorne, Pa., and then was nipped by Lorenzen on the last lap of the 300-miler on the road circuit at Indianapolis Raceway Park. Then, once the Indianapolis "500" was over and the USAC stock cars began running on a regular schedule, there was no touching him.

Parnelli won on the road circuit at Castle Rock, Colo., in June, and the next week shattered the stock car record at Pike's Peak with an unbelievable 13:52.2, taking 25 seconds off the mark he set the year before. From there the Stroppe-Jones-Mercury combination moved on to Milwaukee, where the Wisconsin State Fairgrounds are the hub of Midwestern stock car racing during the summer and where Parnelli won the last three races of the 1963 season. Stroppe had two cars for Jones to drive in 1964, identical as to paint job and the big number 15 on the side, but underneath the sheet metal they were considerably different. One of them was the "Milwaukee" car, the other was the vehicle used in the remaining races. The Milwaukee vehicle was the car that won at Pike's Peak, and after that adventure it was shipped straight to Wisconsin, where Stroppe and Jones spent long hours getting the suspension, brakes and the like tailored to the peculiarities of the track. Once it was ready to go they never touched the suspension again, the only work done on the car being in the engine department. Between races the vehicle was stored on the grounds.

When the first race was run at Milwaukee in July, Jones was the fastest qualifier and went the 200 miles almost unopposed. When it was over, Stroppe got the news from Lincoln-Mercury: The budget was being cut back even further, and they were withdrawing their support for the USAC circuit as well. Stroppe and Jones were stunned to hear the division would contemplate such a move when they were leading the championship, but financial considerations outweighed any other in Dearborn. Stroppe, a professional to the core but paradoxically an amateur at heart, asked for a chance to run the remainder of the season on his own, and the request was approved. Although there were no longer any financial ties between Long Beach and Dearborn all the Mercury-owned equipment, all the cars, tow trucks, spare parts and the like were turned over to Stroppe, and he continued to run Rodger Ward and Jones as a two-car team. In mid-August, when they ran the 150-miler at Milwaukee, Jones won again, and a few days later when the second 200-miler was held at the height of the state fair, Jones dropped out with mechanical trouble, but relieved Ward in the second Mercury and brought that car up to win again. That made it six straight over

(Top) Joe Weatherly's fatal crash at Riverside, 1964. (Middle) Fred Lorenzen at speed, Charlotte, 1964. (Bottom) The man to beat: Richard Petty and his Plymouth, 1964.

(Top) Two-time Grand National Champ Ned Jarrett, Charlotte, 1964.
(Middle) Marvin Panch in the Wood brothers' Ford, Charlotte, 1964.
(Bottom) Junior Johnson, back in a Ford again: Charlotte, 1964.

a two-year period, and the sight of Parnelli and his flying orange, white and blue Mercury was creating considerable intramural jealousy on the part of the Ford Division. It would have been bad form to register a protest, and since both the Mercurys and the Fords, along with every other make competing in major-league racing, were now far removed from stock configuration, Ford decided to run in a ringer. They showed up at Milwaukee with one of the old 483-inch engines installed under the hood of Whitey Gerken's Ford. It didn't make any difference. Parnelli was still the fastest, his big brakes enabling the Mercury to be driven deeper into the corners than any of the other competitors, and his big foot enabling him to get around those same corners quicker than anyone else. When Parnelli won the 250-miler at Milwaukee in September, that made it seven straight. From there he went on to win a 200-mile event on the road circuit at Wentzville, Mo., just outside St. Louis, to win the 50-miler at Ascot, in Los Angeles, and to finish second to Foyt's Dodge in the 200-mile race that closed out the season at Hanford, Calif. Jones had driven in 15 of the 16 races, won eight, finished second twice and fourth once.

Lorenzen, after his short slump in the middle of the season, was back at it again in the late summer, and as Labor Day and the Southern "500" grew near, his wrist was completely healed when Ford gathered every car and driver it could for the oldest, most prestigious race on the NASCAR calendar. It was not to be a Ford race. By the time it was halfway over most of the top-line Fords had departed either with engine trouble or due to accidents. When it was all done the winner was a surprised Buck Baker in his Dodge, Baker having finished first because of the remarkably high attrition rate among the others. Jarrett, in fourth, was the first Ford. After going into the event with high hopes, the defeat was a blow, but it also had its compensations as Darlington proved to be almost the last hurrah of the season for the Chrysler forces. Pearson and Cotton Owens, his boss, won the next two minor races, then the Fords came back to win eight of the last nine. Jarrett won the first two, at Manassas, Va., and Hillsboro, N.C., then at Martinsville Lorenzen took his third consecutive win on the Virginia track, leading 492 of the 500 laps and outrunning Petty, who finished second. At Savannah it was Jarrett again, at North Wilkesboro Panch scored one of his few wins that season as he edged Lorenzen, and then at Charlotte the Fords and the Chrysler products met for the last of the big ones.

Based on qualifying times it should have been all Plymouth, or at the worst all Dodge. Lorenzen was the only Ford pilot among the top seven, and when the race got going the situation stayed that way, with Goldsmith and Petty battling for the lead. Then Goldsmith dropped out, and slowly Lorenzen worked his way up, taking advantage of every pit stop and every caution flag. With 80 miles to go Lorenzen was on Petty's tail, and the two of them staged the most furious race of the season, dogging each other into the corners, riding bumper to bumper at record speeds. Lorenzen wasn't able to get by, but as the race drew to a close, from his cockpit he could see the right front tire of the Plymouth, and it was smoking. Fred knew it couldn't last, but he also knew it didn't *have* to last much longer.

Then with a little more than a lap left and the two cars charging into the third turn at 150, the tire went and Petty slammed into the wall, with Lorenzen ducking underneath to go past. The show was over. Lorenzen, the man who could win races, had done so again.

It had been a good year, and it was to be the last good year that stock car racing enjoyed for the next several seasons, as the rules were to become more important than the action on the track.

(Top) The man who could win the big ones—Fred Lorenzen after the National "400" at Charlotte, 1964, flanked by Linda Vaughn (right) and another, less well-endowed beauty queen. (Bottom) Charlotte, aerial view.

Part 5

(The 1960s)

GRAPES
INSTEAD OF
WRATH

VICTORIES
AND RECORDS
AT LE MANS

30

MARIA McNALLY, MUDDY AND MUSS

HAD ENZO FERRARI placed an ad in a newspaper, it could have read like this: "For sale—modern auto manufacturing and sales facility in northern Italy. Production approximately 500 units per year; ready market with high prices and good profits. Subsidiary to manufacturing is small group of company-owned vehicles of sophisticated design, most in good shape, driven only on weekends."

But when you want to sell the world's most famous high-performance auto factory, that is not how you go about it. The brief interlude in which the Ford Motor Company almost bought SEFAC Ferrari began like an international spy thriller and a few months later ended abruptly with a unilateral decision that encouraged Ford to build the fastest long-distance car in history.

It started in early February of 1963, when officials of the Ford-Werke AG in Cologne received a letter from the German consul in Milan, mentioning no names but referring to the consulate's recent discussions with a man representing a "small, but nevertheless internationally known Italian auto factory," which was looking to make some sort of cooperative agreement. The consul assumed the party was one of many troubled by the then current economic depression in Italy, and concluded the subject for the cooperative agreement would probably be the Taunus 12M, the smallest of the passenger cars produced by Ford's German subsidiary.

On February 20 Robert G. Layton, then the director of finance in Cologne, advised Ford's business planning office in Dearborn of the situation. Layton had done some checking and discovered the factory in question was Ferrari, but being far removed from the performance-minded group at the Ford Division, Layton had no idea how appealing the offer would be. His communication of the 20th read, in part, "For what it is worth, I am attaching a letter ... while I doubt whether this is of special interest, there may be angles that I do not know of ... before re-contacting, I want to bring it to your attention."

Within a few days the business planning office sent the matter over to Ford International with a note: "With reference to the attached, does Ford International have any interest?"

On the next day Ford International sent its reply to Layton: "We agree with you that it is not of particular interest to pursue the matter...." When the message got to Layton he simply passed it along to the consul in Milan and forgot about the matter, and Ferrari was informed Ford was not interested.

But in a corporation the size of the Ford Motor Company the left hand does not always tell the right what it is doing. At the time Ford International was busy saying no, at the Ford Division Iacocca was planning a Ferrari move of his own. Iacocca understood fully the importance of labels, and he had in the past sought to provide a class label for the Ford. At one time, struck by the scuff plate on General Motors products that was embossed with "Body by Fisher," he even toyed with the idea of purchasing Rolls Royce so that Ford scuff plates in particular and the image in general would go one-up on GM. Now he was looking for a label that would not only add some class, but would also have practical advantages. He fixed on Ferrari as his target. Iacocca and Frey had played with the thought in previous years, but it had never gone past the level of idle talk between the two. Now, a few weeks after Ford International had declined the offer, Iacocca, still unaware of Ferrari's availability, sent out feelers through Filmer M. Paradise, then head man of Ford of Italy. Ferrari was receptive. For all he knew, the overtures represented Ford's second thoughts on his February proposition.

From there things moved fast. By mid-April a Ford fact-finding team complete with engineers, product development personnel and finance men, descended on Maranello, the little town just south of Modena where the factory is located. They went through both the factory and the books, and in the process made what is probably the only complete inventory of Ferrari's assets. It is a detailed document, listing such items as vertical milling machines, horizontal milling machines, scribing plates, boring machines—right down to and including the number of iron pipe chairs and wooden desks. Today a copy of it rests in the Ford files.

When the team returned to Dearborn they had seen enough to know that Ferrari was the sole owner, that the factory was a money-maker (despite many rumors that he was subsidized by the Italian auto club, by the government and by Fiat) and that the deal Ferrari proposed was as follows:

Ford would get exclusive rights and control over the Ferrari name and trademarks.

Ford would get the rights to all patents, technical developments, etc., owned by Mr. Ferrari or by his companies.

Ford would get 90 percent of the stock of SEFAC, the parent manufacturing and development company. The name would be changed to Ford-Ferrari. Mr. Ferrari's stock participation would be in the form of nonvoting preferred stock with a fixed dividend. Ford would have an option to buy this stock at its adjusted nominal value

*Commendatore Enzo Ferrari, seen with friends in top and bottom photos,
and one of his thoroughbred cars, on its way
to victory at Sebring in 1963.*

*The men interested in buying Ferrari's holdings were Henry Ford II
(top), Donald N. Frey (left) and Lee Iacocca.*

at Mr. Ferrari's death. There would be no restrictions on Ford in the operation and management of the company, which would have Mr. Ferrari as a vice president.

The racing and related development work would be transferred to a new company, to be known as Ferrari-Ford, Mr. Ferrari would own 90 percent of this undertaking, with the other 10 belonging to Ford. This company would obtain restricted rights to the Ferrari and Ford names through a limited licensing agreement—or in plainer language, Ford would tell this company the type of racing in which it was to participate, and the extent, and it would be Mr. Ferrari's responsibility to achieve the results.

The basic reasons for the original proposal, the report continued, were Ferrari's advancing age (he was 65 at the time) and his lack of an heir, his son having died almost a decade earlier. He had never been as interested in building his high-speed luxury cars as he had been in racing, and now he wanted to spend the rest of his years strictly on the competition side of the business—with Ford paying the bill.

From Ford's view, the Ferrari factory looked like a reasonable investment, and not only from a racing standpoint.

On the street-vehicle side, the Ferrari grand tourers that would continue to be produced would give Ford a brand vastly superior in prestige to anything General Motors or Chrysler had.

On May 2 Iacocca made his recommendation to top management: The Ford Division wanted to buy it. The image that Ford would buy (along with the physical facility) would be invaluable, and the division could merchandise it in many ways, The ownership of Ferrari would give Iacocca the excitement he sought.

The asking price was $18 million, and a few days after Iacocca's recommendation, teams of lawyers were on their way back to Maranello for the negotiations. There were Ferrari's own lawyers, there were Ford lawyers from Dearborn, Ford lawyers from the company's Italian affiliate and even Ford lawyers from Switzerland, as some of Ferrari's corporations were registered in that country. As the first week went by the price dropped from $18 million to $10 million, and coded cablegrams flew back and forth across the Atlantic: "To Maria McNally,* Fordmotor Dbn: The corporate argots of breed and flaky should include both muddy and muss ... provisions requested by muss may also conflict with existing qualms and dunces of relic in deceit field," and so on, day after day (with Henry Ford kept personally informed of every step in the negotiations).

By the time Frey (then assistant general manager of the Ford Division) arrived May 13 to close the deal, Ferrari's back was up. He had spent the last week in the hands of the lawyers and he didn't like it. Frey's presence helped for a while, as Ferrari felt here was a man who would understand him on an engineering level, and the commendatore took great pride in showing Frey around the plant and taking him for hair-raising rides on the winding mountain roads south of Maranello. (Frey: "I never let on that I was in the least impressed or frightened, but there were times,

---

*A secretary in the company's legal department.

when he had my side of the car practically hanging over the edge of a cliff, when I thought we'd had it!")

Negotiations were slowly collapsing. The more Ferrari saw of the battalions of Ford men on the premises, and the more he saw of the accumulation of legal documents, the less he liked it. A man accustomed to operating as his own boss and making his own decisions, Ferrari now found himself about to be absorbed into the corporate system of the Ford Motor Company, and he was unable to accept it. The beginning of the end came a few days after Frey arrived, when Ferrari started to impose new conditions in the long, drawn-out negotiating sessions that usually took place at night. One of them was that Ford would not be able to compete through anyone but Ferrari, which would have in effect done away with the Cobra operation (it seemed Ferrari had as much of a dislike for Shelby as Shelby had for him), and every day there would be another condition. To make it worse, every time Ford acceded to a request, Ferrari would then come up with still another demand. Finally, on May 21, Ferrari broke it off with an impassioned speech at the last of the night-time marathons. Frey recalls his saying "My rights, my integrity, my very being as a manufacturer, as an entrepreneur, as the leader of the Ferrari works, cannot work under the enormous machine, the suffocating bureaucracy of the Ford Motor Company."

The next morning the negotiating party left for home, Frey with an autographed copy of Ferrari's autobiography as a gift. The next time representatives of the two companies would meet, negotiations, such as they were, would be conducted at 200 mph, with the scene of the discussions being the long straights and various corners of the circuit at Le Mans.

Despite Enzo Ferrari's high-handed slamming of the door on a deal which he had originally suggested, there were two brief epilogues. The first came at the beginning of July, less than six weeks after the proposed merger had fallen through, and came in the form of an intermediary who was a personal friend of Ferrari's. He contacted Ford's Italian lawyer, attempting to see if Ford was willing to re-open negotiations. The reply came back—We are not interested.

In the spring of 1966, when the Ford-Ferrari negotiations were little more than memory and a veritable Armada was preparing to depart the United States for Le Mans and Ford's first victory there, another contact was made. Again, the letter came from a friend of Ferrari's, and this time it was addressed to Henry Ford II: "Mr. Ferrari assured me he is ready at any time to reconsider and close the deal with you at conditions already discussed...."

Again, the same answer: Not interested.

By then it was too late to think about buying Ferrari. Ford was ready to beat him instead.

31

GROWING PAINS, PUBLIC AND PRIVATE

WITHIN 48 HOURS of the time Iacocca heard his proposed purchase had fallen through he had a memo out to his staff: "Prepare a presentation of plans we propose to implement in view of the suspension of Ferrari negotiations."

A week later Iacocca had it in writing—a proposal to establish a high-performance special models operation, one that would come up with the concepts, then work with outside sources to bring them into being; in other words, a group that would be responsible for building a car to dominate the world of long-distance racing. Going a step further, the group to build the racing car and eventually the street machine were only part of it. From a corporate standpoint the most important part of the recommendation was that for the first time performance activities were to be carried on by a unit designed for that purpose. This was the beginning of the special vehicles department, with Frank Zimmerman as its first manager. Passino, Evans and the others who had conducted programs in the past were now transferred to the group, and the "new" man, who had no previous connection with Ford performance activities, was Roy Lunn.

An Englishman who came to Dearborn in 1958, Lunn had been an engineer with Aston Martin, Jowett and Ford of Britain, and was one of the few persons in the company with a working knowledge of what was necessary to build the type of car Ford wanted. Lunn, who was in the advanced concepts department of engineering research, had been in charge of the build of the Mustang I (complete with Lotus suspension parts) when that vehicle was constructed in 1962, and when Iacocca and Frey were looking for recommendations on how to set up their own group, Lunn was the man to whom they turned (they had already considered him when the Ferrari purchase was being negotiated; Lunn was one of the first to make the trip to Modena to survey the facilities, and probably would have been chief engineer of the Ford-Ferrari factory had that deal been consummated). Within a few days after Lunn gave the Ford Division his ideas on the nature and organization of the car-building group, Iacocca had him transferred.

By early June the plan had been OK'd, and Lunn, Ray Geddes (now in charge of the care and feeding of Cobras), Shelby and Hal Sperlich, from Ford Division product planning, left for Europe. Their first stop was Le Mans, where they watched what they would have to beat (Ferraris finished first through sixth that year); then they headed for England, to find someone to build the car. At this time in the United States there was no free-lance engineering outfit with this capability: For that matter there was no one anywhere, outside of a few persons employed at Mercedes-Benz, Ferrari, Porsche and a few other places. The choice was a simple one—either Colin Chapman, Eric Broadley or John Cooper, three of the men who had given Britain its dominant position in racing car design.

Although Shelby already had an arrangement with Cooper to purchase several of his Monaco sports-racing chassis for use with a 289-inch Ford engine, Cooper soon faded out of the picture. His Formula I cars had been in eclipse for the past few years (and were to remain there, as events of the next four seasons proved), and he had relatively little experience with projects of this type. At the start the most obvious choice was Chapman. Not only did the Ford Division and Ford of Britain both have contracts with him, but he was generally considered the finest chassis designer in the world. It should have been no contest, but there were things militating against Chapman. There was the question of how well he would take direction, whether or not he and Shelby would rub egos, whether the capacity of his plant was such that it could absorb the Ford GT along with the other things under development, and just how much publicity Chapman would seek. At one stage during the trip, which was more of a scouting venture than anything else, Chapman surprised his visitors by offering to sell them the place. Ford would then run the production side of the business, Chapman said, and he would stick to the racing. They never got around to discussing price.

Then there was Broadley, a quiet, somewhat retiring ex-architect in his early 30s. Broadley came upon the scene in 1959, when his 1,100cc Lola sports car dominated this popular British racing class which had been the personal property of Lotus. Although his ensuing designs for Formula I cars were not as successful they were nevertheless good, and a few months earlier, at the London racing car show in January, Broadley had displayed something sensational. It was the Lola GT, the lowest (42 inches high), sleekest, most compact long-distance competition car ever seen. For power, mounted in the rear was a 260-inch version of the new Ford V8. (Note: the 289 had not yet been announced. Broadley's engine was one he had got merely by contacting Passino, who thought it sounded like a good idea and sent him one. That decision to turn loose one Ford V8, at a figurative cost of pennies, was to prove the start of the long trail leading to victory at Le Mans.) Not only was it the first European competition car to be designed with an American engine in mind—or at least the first that anyone could remember, not counting such minor items as Dutchman Maurice Gatsonides' flathead "Gatso" of the late 1940s—but in general concept it was far ahead of anything else. The body appeared truly aerodynamic. It was of monocoque (aircraft type) construction, and it was the lightest car ever built for an engine of this displacement. For the first time, people started talking in terms of a vehicle strong enough to last 24 hours (all cars of this type are built with Le Mans in mind), and also capable of topping 200 miles an hour in a straight line.

Broadley's car had run twice during the 1963 season, at the 1,000 Kilometers of the Nürburgring and at Le Mans, and although it had suffered from a lack of development time and money, it obviously had possibilities. The Lola GT was almost exactly the type of car Lunn's group had envisioned—the question of which came first, the chicken or the egg, was often brought up at the beginning—and it was available for use as a departure point. To make Broadley even more attractive he was a good engineer, he was eager to join forces with the corporation (as he had little money), he would give 100 percent of his time to the project, and he did not care about publicity. It would be a Ford-Ford, not a Lola-Ford.

The visitation team went back to Dearborn, and in a few weeks it was settled. Frey, accompanied by Geddes and Lunn, returned to make final arrangements with Broadley, who was signed to a one-year contract beginning August 1, and to add one other man to the organization, John Wyer. The general manager of Aston Martin-Lagonda Ltd., Wyer had also been that firm's racing manager for several years, and had been in charge of the Aston team when it won at Le Mans in 1959 and when it won the sports car manufacturers' championship the same year. Shelby had been one of Wyer's drivers, and it was through Shelby that Ford got together with the haggard-looking, autocratic Englishman. While in Los Angeles on a business trip that April, Wyer had visited Shelby. Geddes, who was there at the time, asked Wyer to stop in Dearborn on his way home and see Frey, which he did, filling him in on general racing conditions in Europe. Ford knew that Wyer was leaving Aston Martin, and they needed a man to head the overseas racing effort. Wyer was signed to a three-year contract during Frey's trip to Britain. His job would be not only European operations manager for all competition there, but he would also, when the street-version successor of the GT car was designed, deal with suppliers who would provide the parts for this new vehicle.

Now the GT effort was a three-pronged one—Broadley, Wyer and Shelby. Broadley would design and build the car, with help from Lunn and other Ford engineers. Wyer would race it, and Shelby would act as front man in Europe, race the cars in the United States, and distribute the street machine in the United States when it became available.

Thus began the great adventure, for that it was for Ford, the same as it would be for any Detroit manufacturer entering a new world. The last effort of this type by an American automaker had been Chevrolet's abortive try with specially designed Corvettes at Sebring in 1957; that venture, which lasted for just part of one race, had not been nearly as impressive as was Ford's the first time its car appeared in the company of other makes. Now, between the signing of the contract and the initial race there were to be 10 months of intensive work—months in which Ford tried to accumulate the knowledge that Ferrari and others had spent decades gathering.

Debut: Phil Hill (inset) and Bruce McLaren drove the first GT40 (top) in its initial race at the Nürburgring 1,000 Kilometers in 1964, where it is seen (bottom) completing the first lap. It didn't finish.

At the beginning of August Lunn, plus engineers Len Bailey, Ron Martin and Chuck Mountain moved to England and went to work in Broadley's tiny garage at Bromley, south of London. Broadley and Bailey did the chassis design and redesign, Martin took care of the body engineering, and soon Remington came over to help with the engine installation. (At this time they were using the pushrod version of Ford's Indianapolis engine; five of these were scheduled to be increased in displacement to 280 cubic inches and then shipped to Shelby for evaluation and final preparation, and a minimum of five of the new double overhead camshaft Indy power plants were to be made available for use at Le Mans in 1964. The 280-inch project never got off the ground, and delays in development of the DOHC engine resulted in no Ford GT ever running with one.) The first tests of the car were at Brands Hatch in late August, when the vehicle was merely run around to check on cooling systems and to see if the new suspension components would not fall off (this car was one of Broadley's original Lolas equipped with the new pieces, as were all the fall 1963 test cars). By the time they got to Goodwood a week later Bruce McLaren was established as the test driver for the operation and here, for the first time, an attempt was made to go quickly. But they couldn't; the fuel system was not functioning properly. Remington effected an on-the-spot redesign and in order not to lose the day, they wound up with Remington sitting in the passenger seat, holding a can of gasoline with a line running back to the engine, and hanging on for dear life while McLaren opened it up.

From Brands Hatch and Goodwood they moved to Snetterton, and then when the weather turned bad in Britain, they went to Monza. Despite the high-speed nature of the circuit the project was still moving slowly. Both understeer and oversteer became apparent on the Italian course, once the back part of the body flew off on the straight (with Broadley driving), and Remington spent a few long evenings in an Italian machine shop making new pieces. Typical of the Italian testing was the Hilborn fuel injection system Remington had installed; it finally worked well, but then they had to discard it as too difficult to start. But at least, they figured, they had Ferrari worried; strangers with stopwatches could be seen checking the Ford's performance. By the late fall, construction was started on the first of the new cars, which got the name GT40 merely by being 40 inches high. By April 1 the first was ready, and it was hurriedly grabbed out of the hands of its builders and flown to New York for a press conference, as the image-building part of the program took precedence for a few days. With some round-the-clock work the second one was completed within 10 days and both were taken to Le Mans for the annual trials on the weekend of April 16. Both Jo Schlesser, Ford-France's top pilot, and veteran British driver Roy Salvadori found the new car to be a handful on the long Mulsanne Straight. As soon as the cars would near their top speed they became "light" in the back end and almost unmanageable, as the aerodynamics proved to be a weak point of the car. Although the vehicle was still almost completely untried, it was nevertheless the fastest racing coupe ever built, and as such ran into aerodynamic problems which had never been encountered before. The high-speed flow of air washing over the rear created a situation in which there was very little downward thrust on the rear wheels; in fact there was considerable aerodynamic lift. The answer to this was to affix a device to disturb the airflow at the back—a spoiler. This consists merely of a strip of metal a few inches high and as long as the body is wide, which is riveted or bolted to the hindquarters and sticks up into the airflow. But there was no spoiler available, and Schlesser proceeded around the circuit at a sedate 4:21 while the Ferraris ran hard right from the beginning. For a few hours on that first morning the track was dry and John Surtees, in an open-top 4.0-liter 330P, established a lap record of 3:45.9. Then Lodovico Scarfiotti, with the slightly smaller 275P that had won at Sebring two weeks earlier, got around in 3:43.8. Just before lunch, with Schlesser driving in wet weather, the car failed to come past the pits at the appointed time, and then suddenly the telephone started to ring; he had lost it on the Mulsanne Straight, spinning several times and bouncing off various immovable objects. Schlesser was only shaken up, but the car was a wreck. Scratch one Ford. The next morning, with the rain still conning down, Salvadori lost the other, failing to get slowed enough at the end of Mulsanne and going, albeit slowly, nose first into a sandbank. Scratch the other.

By the end of May, now complete with spoiler, the GT40 was ready to make its competition debut. It did so at the Nürburgring, the toughest closed circuit in the world when it comes to pounding a chassis and suspension to death. The course, built in the 1920s as a sort of German WPA or anti-poverty project in a depressed area of the country, winds through the Eifel mountain region, a sleepy area between the Rhine and the Belgium-Luxembourg border. The circuit is 14.2 miles in length (17.5 miles counting the seldom-used south portion), and twists its way through pine forests and up and down hillsides, with 75 left-hand turns, 73 right-hand turns and an altitude difference, between its lowest and highest spots, of about 1,000 feet. Less than 10 percent of the course is level, and about half of those 148 turns, which vary from perhaps 45 to 150 miles an hour, are blind. On the Ring a great driver can make up for a lot of deficiencies in a race car—it is where Tazio Nuvolari beat the might of Mercedes and Auto-Union in 1935, where Fangio came out of nowhere to overhaul Mike Hawthorn and Peter Collins in 1957, and where Stirling Moss, with 20 percent less horsepower, beat Phil Hill and Wolfgang von Trips to win the Grand Prix of Europe in 1961. Roadholding is the key to success on the Nürburgring, and for this reason Wyer and his team figured they had a chance, even if the car was on more or less of a shakedown cruise for Le Mans. The Ford's handling had finally been sorted out to where it was better than that of the Ferrari, and to take advantage of it they had McLaren and Phil Hill as pilots. McLaren had done the bulk of the development driving, and Hill was perhaps the world's finest long-distance chauffeur with three Le Mans wins, three Sebring wins and almost literally dozens of victories in other endurance races, from Sicily to South America and back again.

At first there was trouble with the gear ratios, the car being equipped with the wrong ones despite many in the Ford party having considerable Nürburgring experience. They went around the first day in 9:50.5, almost a minute slower than Surtees, who took the top factory 275P around in 8:57.9 to better the Ring's sports car record by almost 18 seconds. The next day, with the proper ratios in the box, Hill managed to do 9:04.7 for second quickest time, and things looked better. When the race started on Sunday morning, with 44 laps and 623 miles to go, Surtees jumped off quickly after the Le Mans-type start while Hill was slowed by having to get into a closed car and then slowed again by having to buckle the safety harness. At the end of the first lap Surtees was in the lead by 21 seconds, with Hill next despite having to carve his way through good chunk of the 66-car field. Right behind were Graham Hill and Scarfiotti in cars similar to the Surtees machine, and by the next lap they had managed to get ahead of the Ford—one of the advantages of having multiple entries when you are going long-distance racing is to keep a few back to watch the opposition.

It was soon clear that regardless of whether his teammates were bothering Phil Hill, Surtees was too much for the rest, and the next two Ferraris were also too quick for the Ford if Phil were to drive in a manner that would ensure it finishing the race. At the end of 11 laps, when he came in for his pit stop and to hand over to McLaren, Hill was riding in a frustrating fourth place, unable to do anything about the three red cars. When McLaren went out it soon became worse. Four laps later he was back in the pits, as the right rear suspension was tearing loose from the chassis. Ford's race was over, Ferrari went on to win, and the 300,000 or so who jammed the forests around the Nürburgring saw the much-heralded duel between Europe and America turn into a runaway.

Three weeks later came Le Mans.

The main highway from Alencon to Tours carries the designation N158, and like any one of a thousand other leftovers from Napoleon's administration, the sleepy, tree-lined road is as straight as the landscape allows. Fortunately for its builders, western France has no real hills and N158 has many sections that will allow speeds of 100 mph and more if you are of a mind to go that fast. Just south of Le Mans, a drowsy city with a population of 130,000, the road passes through the outer edges of town, and then it suddenly widens and becomes almost dead straight for 3½ miles. On any given afternoon the population of this stretch will include farmers' wagons, with a few of them being pulled by horses; a few salesmen hurrying along, the inevitable Citroen 2CV crammed full of children and perhaps a tourist or two stopped by the roadside, looking at the monument to the Wright brothers (this is where they made the first airplane flight in Europe, and the feat is duly noted). That is the scene for 51 weeks of the year. During the other week Le Mans, a nondescript municipality complete with a cathedral and a railroad yard that was a target during World War II, becomes the racing capitol of the world. This particular piece of N158 becomes the Mulsanne Straight, the fastest stretch of road ever incorporated into a closed circuit.

Le Mans became involved with automobiles in 1906, when the first Grand Prix of the Automobile Club of France was held on a 65-mile circuit east of the city. When this race returned to the Sarthe River basin in 1921, it was held on a new 11-mile course south of town which was an elongated version of the present track. In 1923 the Sarthe circuit was used for the first of the 24-hour races, and from then on it became a regular part of the European automotive scene; not a large part at the beginning, as in the 1920s and 1930s big time racing in Europe was for single-seater cars, but it was there, and slowly it grew into something traditional. When the race resumed in 1949 one amendment to the rules made Le Mans important: From now on not only catalog models were eligible, but so were prototypes. Within a few years Jaguar and Aston Martin were leading an annual British invasion, Mercedes and Porsche were visitors from Germany, Ferrari (which built its first car in 1948) and Maserati came from Italy, and there was even the romantic attempt of the early 1950s by American millionaire Briggs Cunningham. All of this, plus higher than ever average speeds (and an intensive British press and propaganda campaign to make a race their cars could win the most important race of all) contributed to its stature. By the time Ford showed up in 1964 it was more than a race; it had become an institution.

It was not a race liked by the better drivers. Among the 55 cars turned loose every year there was a speed differential, between the fastest and the slowest, of nearly 80 mph, and the slowest were also sure to be driven by amateurs who didn't know enough to get out of the way of the grand Prix pilots in the big ones. That, plus the night driving, and the fact that it was more of a "car" race than it was a test of driving skill, was what turned them against it. But it didn't make any difference, as Le Mans kept growing in stature until it was to Europe what Indianapolis is to the United States. It was The Thing To Do, and if you got bored with watching the cars, you could always go to the carnival set up along the perimeter, complete with Ferris wheels, lady wrestlers and all the rest. The track itself, 8.36 miles in length, is one of Europe's faster ones despite a 35-mph corner at the end of the Mulsanne Straight, and another of 40 mph at Arnage.

From the pits, located just past the finish line, the road is uphill and curves gently to the right, with the cars hitting about 180 through here, then increasing in speed slightly as they crest the hill and start diving down toward the Esses, a left-right turn between earth banks that can be taken at about 80. After they get through there is a short straight on which they hit 120 or so before having to brake down for Tertre Rouge, the 65-mph right-hander at the head of the Mulsanne. From there, for the next 3½ miles, it is a matter of standing on it, with the fast cars in 1964 just touching 200—except, for some, at one point about a mile from the end. Here, in the middle of a pine forest, there is a gentle right-hand bend, one that even rank amateurs can go through at 125 and think nothing of it. But at 200 this is something to be treated with respect.

Only the very best drivers do it flat out. Almost as soon as the driver gets through, and he's used all the road in the process, he has to set up for the corner at the end, and about 600 meters from there starts a series of signboards indicating the distance to the apex.

Back off the throttle, hit the brakes, start down through the gears, breathe the brakes a little, down to first gear and go through, being careful not to get sideways, as that only costs time and rubber.... On the next straight the cars get up to 175, then it is down to third gear for a right-hander, and then down once more to second for the slow left turn known as Indianapolis (years ago it was paved with bricks) ... Accelerate up to 100 and then shut down once more, brake and go into first for the right-hander at Arnage.... Accelerate again, heading back toward the pits, whipping through some curving bits at 165, braking to 120 for White House corner, then speeding away again, hitting 180 as you flash through what seems to be a tunnel of pits and grandstands. This exercise would have to be completed at least 350 times in 24 hours, in daylight and in the darkness, in sunshine and quite probably in rain, if a Ford were to win the race. The record average was 118 mph, and that included pit stops.

For its first attempt Ford brought three cars. Hill and McLaren were to drive one, Richie Ginther and American veteran Masten Gregory the second, with Schlesser and Englishman Richard Attwood in the third.

As opposition there were four factory-entered Ferraris (Surtees-Lorenzo Bandini, Jean Guichet-Nino Vaccarella, Scarfiotti-Mike Parkes, Umberto Maglioli-Giancarlo Baghetti) and two more distributor-entered cars (Graham Hill-Joakim Bonnier, Pedro Rodriguez-Skip Hudson) which were just as fast. There were also eight other privately entered Ferraris of varying types and displacements to act as backup for the front line, and to compete with the Cobras for grand touring honors. Although the chances for a Ford victory were less than slim, at the outset they looked surprisingly good. Surtees, as expected, was the fastest in practice with 3:42.0, a record average of 135.6 mph, but next, and freely admitting be could have gone five seconds quicker, was Ginther with 3:45.3. Rodriguez followed with 3:45.5, then came Phil Hill at 3:45.8, while the Schlesser-Attwood car was ninth fastest with 3:55.4. The top 13 cars were either Fords or Ferraris, so it was clear no other make would have a chance.

When the flag dropped and the drivers ran for their cars the Ferraris got away first, followed by Ginther, then Attwood farther back. Hill's car remained parked as its driver tried frantically to start it. More than a minute passed before he was able to get going, with the entire field having disappeared under the Dunlop Bridge and the leaders by now roaring along Mulsanne, four miles ahead. Within a few minutes the front-runners appeared in the distance, and the first cars that came out from behind the farmhouse at Maison Blanche were all red—Rodriguez, then Bonnier and Surtees—and then Ginther, right on their heels. As they shot up the hill and under the bridge he came closer, and by the time the quartet was on Mulsanne again they were nose to tail, slipstreaming each other in a high-speed caravan with Ginther bringing up the rear. As they got halfway along the straight Ginther, using the momentum built up by being sucked along in the other cars' vacuum, ducked out from behind Surtees and drove past all three, to the accompaniment of startled glances from Bonnier and Rodriguez. As he went into the lead, Ginther felt his steering get a little light and he looked at his rev counter … It said 7,200 rpm, which he knew was somewhere close to 210 mph.

The next time past the pits the white car with the blue stripes was still in front, and for the first time a European crowd got a look at a Ford leading the world's best cars. It was only the second lap of a 24-hour race, and from a tactical standpoint leadership at this stage meant nothing, but to a small group of Le Mans veterans, who had been crossing the ocean for almost a decade to watch European machinery competing against itself, it was an emotional experience. At this point it was no longer a sales-promotion affair, or an attempt to build an image for a mass-production business, or anything else of a commercial nature. It was a sport, pure and simple, and their baby, carrying their colors, was out front. Americans, because of their isolation between two oceans, are not possessed of the same type of nationalism that affects Europeans, who live within elbow-rubbing distance of foreigners from the time they are born. This isolation was even more pronounced in auto racing at the time, as the United States type was primarily for American-built equipment, and the Americans who drove European-style events did so in European vehicles. Now here, suddenly, was a Yankee car, and it was out front, and to those Americans who were watching it, for the short while it stayed in that position it was more than just machinery. It was graphic evidence the day would come when Americans would build a car that would win this race.

Ginther stayed ahead, pursued closely by Surtees, until his first pit stop, after 1½ hours. The Ford took 2:07 to refuel, the Ferrari spent only 1:28, and as a result took the lead when its tanks were filled. Ginther was now second, then came three more Ferraris and then Attwood, rolling along in sixth. Hill, after finally getting his car started, had been troubled by a persistent misfire and made five pit stops in the first hour. It wasn't until the last one that the mechanics found the cause of the trouble, a blocked main jet in one of the carburetors. When that was fixed he roared off with his engine finally sounding healthy, but the car was in 44th place, and its situation looked hopeless as Hill started lapping faster than anyone in a vain attempt to make up for lost time.

At the end of four hours, with the pace still far above anything seen at Le Mans before, Surtees was still in front, now a lap ahead of Ginther, with the three Ferraris behind him and then the Schlesser-Attwood car. Hill and McLaren, driving as hard as they dared, had moved up to 23rd, and in a few minutes were going to have the only Ford left in the race. The first one to depart was Attwood, who saw flickering lights in his rear-view mirror. When he looked again he saw the lights were a fire that had broken out in the engine compartment. As soon as he got around the next corner Attwood parked it and bailed out just in time. A cracked fuel line had been

The start at Le Mans, 1964. (Bottom) The drivers sprint across the track to their cars, and then there is a moment of silence as they clamber into the cockpits.

*(Top) Pedro Rodriguez' Ferrari is the first
away, and within seconds is followed by the howling pack.*

dripping gas onto hot metal. The next to leave was Gregory, who had just taken over from Ginther. Within a few laps he was back in the pits. The Colotti gearbox had gone bad, and he could only find first and second speeds. Ferrari had also lost two cars by this time, but Ferrari had another 11 left. Ford had only Hill and McLaren (plus the Cobras, which weren't figured to win).

It got dark, the headlights came on, the night grew suddenly cold, and there was nothing to do but sit there shivering and watch the lone Ford, with Hill and McLaren pushing it along ... 11 o'clock and they were eighth ... Midnight, and they were sixth ... They moved up to fifth by 1 a.m., still roaring through the blackness, trying to catch the leaders ... Sometime after four in the morning, with the sun starting to rise, Hill tore through a light ground fog that enveloped parts of the course and set the lap record at 3:49.2 (131.375 mph) ... And an hour later, while in fourth place, succumbed to the same gearbox troubles that had sidelined Ginther and Gregory. The numbed mechanics pushed the car away, Hill took off his helmet and just stood there for a moment, and the sleepy crowds in the stand opposite the pits gave him a little cheer. It didn't help. The Ferraris, with which Hill had scored three victories on this course, were snarling along, their peculiar high-pitched whine echoing across the countryside, on their way to a fifth consecutive victory at Le Mans.

Among those who stayed up that night (and through the afternoon to watch Gurney and Bondurant bring their Cobra home fourth behind three Ferraris) was Leo Beebe. He had never seen a race of any sort before May, and he hadn't even laid eyes on his Le Mans cars until a few days before the event. Beebe didn't say much, partly because long-distance racing was totally new to him, and partly because he had no engineering background. But he watched, he saw what was going on, and he left France with the feeling that Ford was much farther from victory in this type of racing than was the consensus, which tended to be overly optimistic because of the speed of the car. ("You could lay it to a gearbox—but if the gearbox didn't work how could we know anything else would work?")

In Detroit the results of the race caused little or no reaction; it was, after all, a first try for the jackpot and the car had produced a record lap, hadn't it? The gearbox was the only part that had shown any public signs of being weak, and the small crew that was running the GT program was left to its own devices.

Two weeks later they tried again, this time in the 12-hour race at Rheims, a flat, roughly triangular course of five miles per lap laid out on highways through the wheatfields of the Champagne district, some 60 miles northeast of Paris. What could be fixed after Le Mans had been, and as an experiment this time the Schlesser-Attwood car was fitted with a bigger engine, the Cobra version of the 289. It weighed 100 pounds more than did the aluminum-block Indy model, but as compensation it produced 30 more horsepower. Everyone crossed his fingers that this time the gearboxes would hold.

Surtees was again the fastest in practice, driving a 3.3-liter 275LM complete with roof (the factory-entered Le Mans Ferraris had been open-topped). His best lap was 2:19.2 (about 133 mph), and right behind came Ginther in the first Ford with 2:20.0, and Hill in the next one with 2:20.3. Graham Hill, in the other 275LM, was at 2:22.0, and the Attwood-Schlesser Ford was a few seconds slower than Gurney's top GT time in a Cobra (2:24.2 to 2:23.9). At least now there were three front-line Fords to only two Ferraris, and both of the latter had been entered by distributors rather than by the factory.

The start, odd in the normal frame of reference but *de rigueur* for Rheims, was at midnight. When the Automobile Club de Champagne (there was more of that at the race than water) stages its annual midsummer event, it throws a big one; the long-distance section of it in 1964 was only a curtain-raiser for Formula III and Formula II races the next afternoon. Surtees was the first to shoot into the darkness, with Ginther right behind him and Graham Hill another few feet astern, and for the first hour the trio staged a bumper-to-bumper sprint that resembled a trophy dash at a quarter-mile oval. McLaren and Attwood were a bit farther back and then, after 32 laps, Ginther's gearbox went again and the two Ferraris moved farther in front.

When the cars came in for their first pit stops McLaren reported clutch trouble, and lost 20 minutes. Attwood and Schlesser were now third, and the distance between their car and the two Ferraris that were struggling for the lead grew steadily greater. As the night wore on, and the Ferraris kept swapping positions every few laps or so, the Attwood-Schlesser car was resigned to its position. Then even that was not to be. At 4:10, with streaks of dawn showing, a drain plug in the transmission worked its way loose. As the oil surged out the final drive expired and the car was parked. Ten minutes later the McLaren-Hill car blew its engine as it went past the pits, and the race was over for Ford. The Ferraris went on to a 1-2-3-4 finish. (The two Cobras entered, which were decidedly faster than the Ferrari GTOs, both retired with transmission difficulties of another nature; it was a bad night all around.)

Not only was the race over, so was the season. Regardless of what the other weak points of the GT were, it was useless to go racing with a transmission that would not stand up, and there were no other proprietary units. The Colotti was the only one available. When Ford went to Germany's famous ZF transmission builders, the best they were able to do was order units for the 1965 season; ZF had nothing on the shelf that would fulfill Ford's immediate needs. The cars were taken back to what was now called Ford Advanced Vehicles, Ltd., at Slough, just west of London airport. (The operation had moved there in the fall of 1963, and the new corporation, needed for housekeeping purposes, had been formed in the winter of 1963–1964.) The record now was seven cars started and none finished, much less finished first, and as the mechanics did what they could in England, the outlook of the operation began to change. First Broadley left. The brilliant designer, Lunn and Wyer had not been able to get along, and with his contract running out and various new, non-Ford ideas in his head, Broadley again set up his own shop. Martin and Mountain had already gone back to the United States, and in November Lunn followed, leaving Wyer alone with the cars.

The problems were thus taken back to Dearborn, as Beebe felt design decisions and control should be in the home office, especially since the primary need at the moment was for more power. In the fall Beebe, Frey, Innes, Scussel, Passino and Lunn sat down to review Ford's range of engines to see what was available or to perhaps build a new one. Innes, proud of the success his engineers had achieved with the Indianapolis engine, was anxious to build something new and exotic— a V12 which he was certain could be made to produce a higher specific output than the Ferraris. But because of the time factor involved, it was decided to go with a modification of a production power plant, and to go with a big one—the 427.

It was a bold step, and one that was received with scorn by the purists. No one had ever successfully put a 7.0-liter engine in the rear end of a competition car. The weight alone (approximately 600 pounds) was enough to dissuade even an amateur constructor, they said, and even if it could be installed the 450, horsepower couldn't be put on the ground ... Or you couldn't get the brakes to make it stop ... Or the fuel consumption would be too high ... And besides, whoever beard of a pushrod engine lasting 24 hours? Innes was determined to make it run that long, or twice as long if need be, and from then on he kept a close check on the project. (He was not one to stand on ceremony. Once, when some poorly cast blocks showed signs of porosity, Innes grabbed a saw and started cutting one apart to find where the weak spots were.)

From an over-all design standpoint Lunn also thought he could make it work, and his engineers (notably Ed Hull) sat down to modify the GT40 center section and to create a transaxle capable of taking the torque and horsepower of the big engine. (They even used the gear clusters from the four-speed transmission that was standard equipment on the big Ford sedans.) To make the prospect even more depressing, everyone concerned was fully aware the 427 would be strictly a back-up measure for Le Mans in 1965. There were only eight months left until the race, and that was clearly not enough time in which to design, build and develop an almost totally new car. The 1965 season would have to be carried by the GT40s and their 289-inch engines, if they could get a transmission that would live. Development work on the GT40 continued in England, and then it was decided to bring two of the cars to Nassau at the beginning of December for Bahamas Speed Weeks. More than four months had passed since the cars had last been raced, and this non-championship event would be a good place to see what progress had been made.

When the two cars arrived at Nassau they were in a begrimed state and more than 100 pounds heavier than at Le Mans, and the men who were working on them looked little better than the machinery. Once they got running (both now with 289-inch engines), it was evident their appearance wasn't the only thing wrong. In the matter of horsepower they were far behind the formula libre potpourri of machinery that had showed up for the annual drinking and driving sessions sponsored by the Bahamas Ministry of Tourism. McLaren had brought his new Olds-McLaren racing sports car to drive in a few of the events, and it was faster; Gurney brought his Lotus 19B equipped with 325-inch Ford, and it was faster (the 325 was a stroked version of the 289, and Gurney was using it as an unofficial trial horse for Shelby). The two Chaparrals were quicker, and for that matter so was the 427-inch monster Cobra that Miles was driving as an experiment. The use of Nassau as a shakedown race was looking more and more like a bad idea, and even before the first big event got going it looked terrible. In one of the warm-up events the front suspension on McLaren's Ford came apart and he went zooming off into the bushes. Then Hill, who was struggling along in third and fourth behind Miles and Roger Penske's light-weight Corvette (a holdover from 1963), had the same thing happen, and he involuntarily parked the second Ford a few yards from McLaren's. In both cases, it was found, someone had forgotten to install big enough retaining washers when the front suspension was bolted together.

From the time Beebe took over the Special Vehicles Department in May, he had a habit of prefacing many of his remarks by saying "I don't know anything about racing, but ..." and then giving his opinion. Now he had seen enough, and late that afternoon, after the race had run itself out, he called a meeting in one of the local hotels.

"I don't know anything about racing," he started out, "but there is one thing that has become increasingly apparent to me in the past few months—you don't either!" A good deal of what he said after that was unprintable, but the gist of it was clear. Things were going to change.

Shelby was given operational control of the race cars, and Wyer set to work building the 100 cars that were intended for sale to private customers. A few months earlier the design center had shifted from Europe to the United States; now the vehicles did the same, with the 1965 season only two months away.

When the cars arrived in California they received a Shelby paint job (dark blue, with two white stripes) and were trucked to Riverside to find what was wrong. Miles was getting his first chance at being the development driver for the GT, and he soon found there was much that needed development. (Miles: "The handling was atrocious. They had been taken apart and put back together again so many times the design settings had gotten lost. When we reset the suspension to the original specifications, the cars improved enormously. It may sound odd, but our first job was actually to get the cars back to where they had started.") So now they behaved when going around corners. In the 10 weeks between getting the cars and Daytona, other weaknesses were attacked: aerodynamics, weight and brakes. The aerodynamics, Shelby's crew found, with help from California-based Aeroneutronics, a part of the Philco Division, and from the Dearborn wind tunnel, were a lot worse than they appeared. Many of the ducts bringing air into the body, leading to such things as radiators, had no exit for the air. It was found that at least 76 horsepower was being eaten up in this manner. (It made observers wonder just how bad Ferrari's aerodynamics were; he had more horsepower and less weight, yet the Fords were still faster in a straight line.) Remington rearranged the ducting so that it worked better, and he was also the one who took the gamble of using a wet-sump lubrication system for the car, saving about 60 pounds. No one remembers who ripped out the "air-conditioned" seats, but they went in a hurry; the fancy ducting to pump air under the driver's behind had never worked anyway. Magnesium wheels were ordered, lighter-weight fiberglass was ordered, wider tires were employed, brake problems were taken to Kelsey-Hayes, and a hundred other minor items were fixed. In the space of a few weeks the GT40 began not only to look like a racing car, but to perform like one.

Shelby's first try was at Daytona February 28, where the Continental was to be run over the 2,000-kilometer distance for the last time. Ford had two cars (plus the Cobras), with Miles to share one with USAC veteran Lloyd Ruby, and Ginther in the other along with Bondurant. As opposition Ferrari had one really hot car, plus one more that could be dangerous. The leader was the newest Ferrari 330P2 model, sleeker than those of the year before, and with its V12 engine sporting four overhead camshafts instead of the traditional Ferrari two. For drivers it had Surtees and Pedro Rodriguez, and going into the race it had to be considered the favorite. The backup car, like the first entered by the North American Racing Team rather than by the factory, was one of the 1964 4.0-liter cars with veteran Walt Hansgen and Englishman David Piper doing the driving. Then there was one more car that would figure in the running—Ford's mechanical rabbit. Shelby, knowing his 380-horsepower machines still weren't fast enough to force the pace, had an idea: They would use Gurney's much-modified, somewhat ancient, but still very fast Lotus (they still called it a Lotus for want of a better name; it had undergone so many Gurney-inspired modifications there was little of the original left). Gurney's car, as at Nassau equipped with one of the experimental 325-inch, 420-horse versions of the 289 and now co-driven by Jerry Grant, would take off in front and attempt to make the Ferraris keep up. If things worked as intended the Ferraris would break down, Gurney would slow down, and one of the GT40s would come on to win.

Practice on Daytona's 3.81-mile course, which includes almost 2¼ miles of the high-speed banking used by the stock cars and an infield section of 1½ miles that features slow turns, showed the Ferrari to be faster and the Fords to be cautious. Rodriguez, using all the engine revs allowed, came up with a best lap of 2:00.6, an average of 113.7 mph, while the Fords were timed in 2:01.8 (Bondurant) and 2:03.0 (miles). Hansgen recorded 2:03.8 while Gurney's car, which was still undergoing various adjustments, could do no better than 2:11.0 (in 1964 he had set the lap record with the same car and a weaker engine—1:59.1). In order to save the engines Shelby limited his drivers to 6,000 rpm in practice, with the exception of two qualifying laps during which they could use 6,500 rpm; the race would be run using 6,000 as a maximum, which meant laps at 2:06 or 2:07. If the cars were to last the 327 laps that went into this 13-hour grind, that was as hard as they could safely go.

This time there was hope they would last, as many improvements had been made: Dana joints had been substituted for the Metalastik "rubber doughnut" couplings at the inboard end of the halfshafts, and the Colotti transmissions (ZFs were still not available) had undergone a thorough overhaul through a combined Ford-Shelby operation. Modifications included the installation of a new Ford-built ring and pinion, and the respacing of the gears in the box. What had not shown any improvement were the brakes, which at the start of practice were a new ventilated rotor design being developed by Kelsey-Hayes. They were much better, but they showed so many cracks in practice that they were taken off and Girlings were used for the event (eventually, the Fords were to have the finest set of brakes ever installed on a long-distance racing machine, but that was still two seasons away).

When the race started Gurney performed as expected. By the second lap the ultra-light Lotus was in front, and slowly but surely he was pulling the Surtees-Rodriguez Ferrari into lapping a second or two faster than it had intended. Within a half hour this was the only Ferrari to worry about, as Hansgen ran over some debris left on the track and blew a tire at 170 mph. The force of the blast ripped apart the left rear section of the body and sent Hansgen spinning wildly down the track, fortunately missing the wall as he went; for the first time the Ferraris, regardless of for what reason, were dropping out before the Fords, which were still rolling along behind Gurney and Surtees. By the 2½-hour mark, well after the first pit stops had been made, Gurney had a lead of 50 seconds over Rodriguez when the Ferrari burst its left rear tire while speeding along the backstretch. The car spent more than an hour undergoing repairs, then fell out with a broken rear suspension soon after rejoining the event. There was a slight bit of irony connected with the incident: In 1964 at Indianapolis the Fords were forced out of the race by the inadequacies of their Dunlop tires. Now, less than a year later at Daytona, with the factory Fords on Goodyears, they got their biggest break when their opposition used Dunlop. The latter company had again failed to run a comprehensive test program.

From the time Rodriguez pulled into the pits the race, as such, was over. The Fords immediately slowed their pace and from then on all they had to worry about was finishing. For a while it seemed as if they would both wind up behind Gurney's Lotus, but after eight hours of running, and with a lead of several laps, his experimental engine finally broke a piston and the Fords were all alone at the head of a pack of Shelby's Cobras. They got their first scare a few minutes later, when the Ginther-Bondurant car was hit with starter trouble. Seven laps were lost getting it going again, and more time was lost each time it made a pit stop after that. This dropped the car to third behind a Cobra, but the two kept right on rolling, their exhaust pipes spitting out long flames as the drivers shifted down for the slow corner just past the pits, and some 12½ hours after the start, the Fords came home first and third (with a Cobra in between and more Cobras behind them). The 1965 season had started auspiciously. At least now they were capable of finishing.

*(Top) The director—Carroll Shelby and some of his crewmen give
instructions to the drivers during the 1965 Daytona Continental.
The signboard is self-explanatory.*

*(Top) The start of the 1965 Continental, with Ferrari star
John Surtees on the pole and Bob Bondurant alongside. (Inset) The Ken
Miles-Lloyd Ruby GT40 at speed, Daytona, 1965. (Bottom) Gurney and his
mechanical rabbit. It forced the pace, then broke down.*

A month after Daytona there was Sebring, which left a bad taste in everyone's mouth. The race was ostensibly one of the series counting for the manufacturer's championship for GT prototypes (of which the Ford was one), and these are vehicles that had to be built to minimum weight limits, with space for luggage, etc. When the championship series was set up, the International Automobile Federation agreed that basically faster cars—such as racing sports cars—would not be allowed in these events so as not to take anything away from vehicles competing for the championship. But Alec Ulmann, Sebring's head man, thought otherwise: The hottest car in the United States during 1964 had been the plastic-chassis, automatic-transmission Chaparrals of Jim Hall and Hap Sharp, and now the Texas team wanted to take a crack at long-distance racing. It would mean a bonanza at the gate if Ulmann could get this Chevrolet-powered (and General Motors sponsored, in a *sub rosa* fashion) entry to compete against the Fords. So he simply opened the race to them. The Chaparral was little more than a two-seater grand prix car, weighing about 700 pounds less than the Fords (1,450–2,150) and having about the same horsepower (380). If the Chaparral could last the distance the Fords could do nothing about it, and the special vehicles department knew this at the start. But, as Beebe said later, "We had nine good reasons *not* to come and one good reason to come, so we went." Ferrari thought otherwise and stayed home, limiting his participation to some distributor support for several of the 1964 racing sports cars.

Right from the start of practice the fastest things on the somewhat motheaten airfield were the Chaparrals. Hall's car, which would be shared by Sharp, was clocked in 2:57.6 for the 5.2 miles, and Ronnie Hissom, teamed with Bruce Jennings in the second machine, did 3:00.0. The Ford GT shared by Miles and McLaren did 3:07, the Ginther-Phil Hill car was at 3:08.3, while Gurney's Lotus, now even painted in the Shelby team colors, was at 3:08.4 and expected to go much quicker when the flag dropped. Practice times for a long-distance race can only be used as relative figures, as no one would attempt to run the entire 12 hours as hard as both car and driver could go. But the speed differential in practice, assuming no one held anything back, is important: If during the race the Chaparrals could circulate at seven seconds per lap faster than the Fords, and if time spent in the pits for refueling and driver change was equal, at the end of the 12 hours the Chaparrals would be more than seven laps in front, if they did not slow the pace at the end after having built up a good lead. By race morning the standard joke was that at the Le Mans start the faster sprinters among the drivers would jump into the Chaparrals, while the slower ones would be left with Fords.

It turned out that way. Ginther managed to lead the first lap, but came in at the end of it to report a strange noise. The mechanics discovered the brand new magnesium wheels flown in that morning were contacting the brake calipers, so they had to change back to the older aluminum models. It was an indication of things to come: The handling of the car deteriorated, the shock absorbers collapsed, and before two hours were gone the car was out, the final blow having been a radius rod mounting bracket tearing loose. (This was the Attwood-Schlesser Le Mans car that had been rebuilt, and it was felt the fire probably caused heat embrittlement of the chassis. It had been used because of an acute shortage of cars.) While Ginther and Hill were spending most of their time in the pits Hall was charging along at record speeds, with Gurney making him hurry from his runner-up position, and Hissom was third in the other Chaparral. Miles was running fifth behind the 3.3-liter Ferrari shared by Rodriguez and Graham Hill and he was stuck there, lapping to orders at 3:11 to 3:12 with his only hope being that the others would fall out. Some of them did; one of them didn't. Hall and Sharp didn't, and Miles and McLaren finished second after what developed into one of the oddest races of the year.

Gurney, who managed to lead Hall twice during the opening stages, finally went out after 2½ hours with a broken oil pump drive. This time, the mechanical rabbit ploy didn't work as the Chaparral was still steaming along in great style, its light weight giving it excellent acceleration out of the corners, and its brakes seemingly up to the many applications per lap and the 95-degree day. Then, after three hours, the Hissom-Jennings car dropped back with various problems and Miles moved up to third, still on the same lap as the Ferrari, but falling steadily farther behind the Chaparral. By the end of seven hours Hall and Sharp were seven laps ahead of both cars; from there on they could cruise. And then the skies to the north got gray ... then almost black, and the 40,000-odd persons scattered around the course, plus the apprehensive drivers speeding up and down the runways, could see the rainstorm marching in on them. It hit at 5:25, and within a minute visibility was reduced to zero, and cars that had been streaking around in three minutes were taking more than nine. As the airfield was not adequately equipped for drainage the torrent of rain simply lay on the runways and soon was more than six inches deep. It was so bad it was impossible to make out cars as they crawled past the pits, obscured by the rain and the spray they were throwing tip. The Chaparral pulled into its pits for more than 10 minutes at the height of the storm and simply sat there, waiting. They were so far in front they could afford that luxury. After a half hour the rain abated, speeds started to pick up again and the Chaparral, extra cautious now, picked its way through the puddles to victory. Miles and McLaren, four laps behind at the end, were second because the rain had drowned the ignition of the Graham Hill-Rodriguez Ferrari.

From Sebring the two race-weary cars, with the broken suspension on Hill's vehicle now fixed, were air-freighted to France for the practice session at Le Mans. Shelby had one more car flown over, and Ford of France was present with the first of the cars equipped with the ZF five-speed gearbox. Wyer came with a brand new open-top version, on which he had been working the past few months. Ford spent the weekend trying 289 engines and 325-inch engines, trying various-shaped noses, various tires and almost anything else they could squeeze into the time allowed.

Ferrari spent the weekend going fast and Surtees led the pack with a resounding 3:35.1, the first-ever lap at better than 140 mph. The other Ferrari drivers, including one in a privately entered car, all managed to get under 3:40; the fastest Ford pilot was Attwood, who managed a 3:40.9.

Between the practice session and the race at Le Mans that year there were 10 weeks, a time span in which it was obviously impossible to do anything to the basic configuration of the car. Beebe, Shelby and the others knew it, and they were stuck with it. The only thing to do was to keep going. After Daytona and Sebring Ford was, after all, in the lead for the manufacturer's championship.

The 1,000 Kilometers of Monza April 25 reaffirmed the practice weekend at Le Mans. Ferrari had three of the P2s with all the front-line drivers, while Ford had cars for Miles-McLaren and Umberto Maglioli-Chris Amon. They used the 10-kilometer (6.2 mile) circuit, complete with the high-speed banking, the road course, and even threw in a chicane for good measure, placing it at the entrance to one of the banks so the cars wouldn't pound their suspensions to pieces. In practice McLaren's best was four seconds slower than Surtees, three seconds slower than Parkes, and he was also slower than Bandini and Switzerland's Herbert Mueller in a private Ferrari. To make it worse the suspension was bottoming on the rough banks, and it was felt the cars would be fortunate to finish, much less win. Strategy was simple: McLaren and Miles were to lap at 2:55, Maglioli and Amon were to run at 2:57-59. Everyone was to keep his fingers crossed that the cars would stay together, and hope the Ferraris blew up.

Neither happened, at least not completely. The Ferraris ran first and second, as expected; McLaren and Miles placed third, two laps back, and Maglioli crashed when a ball stud failed. The Ferraris won as they pleased.

It was a bad situation, and it was now to get worse for several reasons: for one, the California-based Shelby operation had to rely on help (for its supplies and its European campaign) from Ford Advanced Vehicles in England. It was one of the world's longer umbilical cords for a racing team and besides, relations between the Shelby forces on one hand and the Wyer group on the other—remember, they had recently lost the job to Shelby—were not of the best. When Carroll Smith came over to manage a team for Monza, the Targa Florio and the 1,000 Kilometers of the Nürburgring, cooperation between the two fell to a new low. The clincher to the situation was that Ford officials, because of other programs, were not giving the GTs their primary attention: May of 1965 was the month of the all-out push at Indianapolis, and America's largest race, practically on Ford's doorstep, was the only topic of conversation in Dearborn.

The Targa was undertaken as an experiment to test the new ZF gearbox and to check out the open-top car. It was strictly a one-vehicle effort, with Sir John Whitmore and Bondurant being the drivers and Smith taking care of the team. It turned out to be a total loss, not only of the race, but of the car as well.

It was a peculiar event. They had the wrong gear ratios, they were missing a quantity of spares which should have been on the truck. They were up all night fixing things that had broken and making modifications to the car, and nevertheless, when the flag dropped the Ford, despite running on seven cylinders most of the time, was actually among the leaders. Bondurant drove the first three laps and kept the car in third. Whitmore, still running well on the fifth lap, had a wheel come off at speed, and although he brought the car to a stop without any damage, neither the wheel nor the three-eared wing nut could be found. Somehow, Whitmore got to a telephone and called the press box at the start and told a reporter to inform the pits. Smith then set out over back roads to find Whitmore and give him a new wing nut. In the meantime a Sicilian gendarme had forced one of the local souvenir hunters to cough up the original spinner so Whitmore mounted his spare wheel and took off again, in 13th place. When he came by for another check after the sixth lap (Smith had returned to the pits by this time—Targa Florio laps take about 40 minutes apiece) the car was looked over, pronounced OK, and while a group of Goodyear personnel created what Smith later termed "a monumental diversion" at the rear of the car, he managed to sneak a new spare tire into place (when Whitmore lost the wheel the tire had disappeared; the rules insist spares be carried at all times). It came to naught. On the ninth and next-to-last lap, while running ninth and still on seven cylinders, Bondurant slid on some gravel another car had scattered across the road and went into a ditch. It was over, a Ferrari had won, Porsches took the next four places, and the wrecked Ford was carted back to England.

The week after the Targa, in mid-May, the 427-inch prototype was finished, and Tom Payne drove it first. A veteran SCCA pilot from nearby Ann Arbor, Mich., Payne had practically no experience with this type of high-powered machinery (nor, for that matter, had anyone else). But he could drive well, and because of his proximity he did the first two days of testing on the Ford track in Dearborn. Payne drove the car on the low-speed ride and handling circuit and also on the "dogbone" loop, which allowed top speeds of 150 or so. The big test was to come that weekend at Romeo, Mich., where the company had a five-mile high-speed oval (they had to wait for the weekend; from Monday through Friday the facility was used to test passenger cars and trucks). At Romeo they would find out if the car was fast.

Miles and Remington flew in from California for the test but at the beginning were just onlookers, standing to one side and watching as Lunn's crew made the final adjustments and Payne did the driving, which was tricky; it was a good day, but there was a 20-mile crosswind, and if the car lacked anything in lateral stability it would be dangerous. Through the morning Payne drove and the mechanics adjusted, and shortly after 11 a.m. the car started to go quickly. When it hit a lap speed of 180, everyone got excited. The GT40 would not have gone that fast on this track, and they knew it. Just before lunch Miles took over the driving, and after a short break for a sandwich, they got going again.

Spoilers were put on, others were taken off, and slowly the speeds rose. Finally, just before 4 p.m., Miles turned in a lap at 201.5 mph, with his speed on the straight being 210. That was it. The car *would* go fast. Strangely subdued, perhaps by the almost-frightening speeds they had seen, everyone was getting ready to pack up when Payne asked for another ride. He wanted to try it in its final form. On his second lap, while streaking past the pits at over 200 for the first time in his life, Payne was caught by a crosswind, and the car suddenly moved over one full lane. Lunn, who was standing at trackside, jumped out of the way. When Payne came in, his face was almost the same color as his white helmet.

I suppose you'd like to know what the dials were reading?" He said to Lunn.

Lunn said yes.

Payne gave him a weak grin. "Well, I didn't have the nerve to look down at them!"

When they got back to the hotel, with everyone gathered in one room, Lunn opened up the post-mortem. "Well, what does everybody think?"

Miles ended the discussion almost immediately with one sentence: "That's the car I want to drive at Le Mans this year."

At that point there were four weeks left before Le Mans, and on Monday morning the race to get there began in earnest. The decision was made to get two cars ready, in France arrangements were made to switch entries, in Dearborn another car was being built in day-and-night sessions, and the original car, meanwhile, was flown to Riverside, Calif., for more testing on a road circuit. As soon as that was over it was flown back to Dearborn, taken apart, checked, rebuilt and prepared for shipment to France. ("Here's where I made the decision I think cost us the race that year," Lunn says. "The transmission, when we checked it, looked good, and I was faced with the choice of simply putting everything back, or of replacing the gears with new ones. We replaced them, and in the general rush to get everything done a scrap gear somehow got into the box.")

While the engineers in Dearborn were rushing to get the big car ready, the European campaign of the 289s, such as it was, kept grinding its weary way from circuit to circuit.

At the Nürburgring the panic continued. Smith had two cars (the rebuilt Monza entries) with a 325-inch engine for Hill and McLaren and a more normal 289 for Amon and Ronnie Bucknum, making his first start for the team. Wyer showed up with another of the open-top cars (Whitmore and Attwood) while the Ford-France entry, like Wyer operating on its own, had veteran Maurice Trintignant and Guy Ligier. The story was the same: Nights without sleep for the mechanics, and fastest practice lap for Surtees in the Ferrari at 8:53.1, a record. Next came Graham Hill in another Ferrari at 8:58.8 and Parkes in the third factory car at 9:00.0. Only then came the Fords—Hill with 9:00.2, Amon at 9:06.3, Attwood with 9:07.3, and Trintignant behind a group of Porsches with 9:17. The race went much as the others: Surtees and co-driver Scarfiotti led it just about from start to finish, and Parkes and Guichet were second. The Fords started dropping out on the sixth lap and the first to go was Hill (broken halfshaft), who had been running second to Surtees. Trintignant, who once was as high as seventh but was never a challenger, dropped out at the halfway mark and the Whitmore-Attwood car, which was running third at the midpoint, dropped to ninth before departing with the same trouble that hit the French entry—broken motor mounts. The only car to last was Amon's, and that one had an adventurous time. The little New Zealander failed to see the signal that told him to come in for gas, and the next time around he ran out of fuel about a mile from the pits. Somehow Amon managed to push the car uphill to the pits and collapsed, exhausted, while McLaren and Hill took over the vehicle; before Amon had run out, he was in third. When McLaren took off again, the car was 21st. The best Ford's top two drivers could do with it was an eighth-place finish, hampered by having to run on seven cylinders a good deal of the time, and winding up behind a Cobra.

When Beebe flew back from Indianapolis to Dearborn a few weeks before Le Mans, he got his first concrete evidence the French campaign was headed for trouble. On the plane one of the engineers told him the Indianapolis effort had made it impossible for them to devote any time to the Le Mans engines, and that the power plants being used for the 24 Hours were strictly unknown quantities. It was too late to do anything now but go ahead, however, and the attack on Le Mans was to be a massive one. There were the two 427-inch cars, with Hill and Amon in one and Miles and McLaren in the other. Behind them it had been decided to run two cars with the unpredictable 325-inch engines, and one was given to Bondurant and Maglioli, the other to Switzerland's Herbert Mueller and Bucknum. The open-top car, with 289-inch engine, was to be handled by Trintignant and Ligier, while another 289 was installed in the coupe scheduled for Whitmore and Innes Ireland. That made six, and as backups there were five Cobras, driven by Gurney-Jerry Grant, Schlesser-Alan Grant, Peter Harper-Peter Sutcliffe, Bob Johnson-Tom Payne and Jack Sears-Dick Thompson. That was 11 in all and Ferrari had the same number, with five being factory entries and the rest sponsored by distributors.

The Ford entry was as confused as it was big. The last-minute rush to get everything ready, the indecision as to 289- or 325-inch engines in the smaller cars, the virginal condition of the 427s, these things were only a part of it. To add to the complexity of the problem, several of the Fords were, for the record, running under the aegis of private individuals. Due to a shortage of entries Ford had arranged to take over the places in the starting field already given to British whiskey magnate R.R.C. Walker and Swiss millionaire Georges Filipinetti. Ford-France was also in possession of an entry, another car was being run by Ford Advanced Vehicles, one of the Cobras was under the sponsorship of A.C. Cars, and finally there were the two biggest GTs and two of the Cobras listed by Shelby-American. It was a mess, and the administrative problems involved did little to help the effort.

But when practice was over the Fords had finally, for the first time during the 1965 season, been the quickest. Despite the all-night work sessions and the rest it was an encouraging sign. Hill, whose big 427 had not turned a wheel before it got to Le Mans, spent most of the first night having its suspension adjusted and having

(Top) The 1965 Sebring winner—Jim Hall's Chaparral. (Middle) Shelby and four of his drivers. From left, Jo Schlesser, Ken Miles, Bruce McLaren and Phil Hill, at Sebring the same year. (Below) McLaren in the 1965 Sebring runner-up, which he shared with Miles.

*Looking up from the Esses at Le Mans, with the leader
just coming over the hill.*

spoilers attached to practically every flat surface. Then, on Friday night (the usual Wednesday session was canceled by a violent windstorm, so the cars were given the full Thursday evening practice, plus three hours on Friday). Shelby told Hill to let it out. "All the way out?" Hill asked. Shelby said yes, and within a short time the veteran star had shaken the place with a staggering 3:33.0, more than five seconds faster than the lead Ferrari on Thursday, and a record for the circuit. Faces in the Ford pits, haggard and tense from the work of the past few weeks, grew brighter. By the time the session was over three of the four fastest times belonged to Ford: Hill, then Surtees (none of the Ferraris appeared Friday), then Bondurant at 3:38.7 and Mueller at 3:39.2. But the mechanics went back to the garage for another all-night session that included taking the 325s out of the Bondurant and Mueller cars—the engines had given trouble toward the end of practice, and it was decided to go with the more reliable 289s.

The morning of the race, with everyone hollow-eyed from the last-gasp effort, found the cars and the equipment gathered at the circuit; everything was put into place, the cars were lined up in front, and the time dragged through the early afternoon hours while the various ceremonies that led to the start took place. One of them consisted of the playing of the national anthems of every country involved in the event, and when they got to the "The Star-Spangled Banner," there was something wrong with the recording and it wouldn't play. They tried it several times, but the result was the same—silence. If there ever was a bad omen it was that faulty record. But just as it was too late to pack up and go home, it was too late to go out and find another one. Ready or not, the race was about to start.

When the 51-car field streamed away from the pits it was paced by the two biggest Fords, with McLaren in the lead car and Amon in the other, and they stayed that way through the first pit stop, McLaren finally leaving the lap record at 3:41.2 and the pair building up a lead of 50 seconds over the first Ferrari. But when they got to the pits, Amon's car stayed there for 38 minutes as the mechanics worked on the clutch. Dirt had strayed into the slave cylinder. By the time Hill took off he was 35th, 10 laps behind the leaders. Then in the fourth hour the McLaren-Miles car was retired with a fault in the transmission. It was the fourth Ford to go, Trintignant having lasted not quite an hour, and both Bucknum and Bondurant having gone out in the third hour with engine failures. By the end of four hours Ferraris were in their accustomed places at the head of the pack, running first through fourth with the Gurney-Grant Cobra fifth.

After five hours it was Whitmore's and Ireland's turn—again, engine failure. After six, and after having established a lap record of 3:37.0, the other 427 rolled to a stop. Curiously, the newest, most untried car had lasted the longest. But now all the front-line Fords were gone and all the Ferraris were still running, chased only by the Cobras. Slowly, the pits began to empty as the mechanics packed their tools and headed back to the hotels. Beebe stayed on and watched the Cobras, which had a chance only for the GT category.

The Ford team at Le Mans, 1965. Front row, from left: Allan Grant, Bob Johnson, Guy Ligier, Ken Miles. Back row: Dr. Dick Thompson, Bob Bondurant, Umberto

Maglioli, Jack Sears, Bruce McLaren, Jo Schlesser, Maurice Trintignant, Chris Amon, Innes Ireland, Tom Payne, Sir John Whitmore and Ronnie Bucknum.

It got dark, the race rolled on, and suddenly the Ferraris started making unexpected pit stops. The pace had told on them, too, and the factory cars were having trouble with cracked brake discs and broken gearboxes. By 2 a.m. every front-line Ferrari had stopped and a private Belgian-entered 275LM, a last year's model, was leading the race. Had they been running well, the Cobras would have had a shot at it—but the Cobras were also dropping out. Schlesser's car was gone by 2 a.m. and so was Harper's, both with engine trouble. Johnson and Payne lasted until 4 a.m., and Gurney and Grant, who had been traveling at a reduced pace for the last several hours, made it through until morning before finally retiring.

The lone ship left in the Ford navy was the Sears-Thompson Cobra, and it was going slowly; a minor collision with an Alfa Romeo sometime after midnight had damaged the cooling system, and unless it was driven at a sedate pace it would overheat. It limped through the remaining hours and finished eighth at an average of 105.5 mph, more than 11 mph slower than the Gurney-Bondurant car of the previous year and just ahead of an innocuous, Chevy-powered Iso Grifo. As a small consolation, and there was nothing that would console anyone that Sunday afternoon, all the factory Ferraris had also expired. The only trouble was that five private Ferraris *had* finished—in first, second, third, sixth and seventh. Ironically, one of the drivers of the winning car was Gregory, who had shared one of the Fords the year before.

That evening Beebe called everyone together in the breakfast room of the Hotel de Paris, which the team had been using to house most of its members.

"This," he said, "is a victory meeting! Next year we're going to come back here and win, and we might as well start right now."

The men who were there glanced at each other in amazement. It took them a few minutes to realize he wasn't kidding. In a few months they would think so too. For this small group the race at Le Mans was to become an intensely personal thing.

32

STAR-SPANGLED RAIN

NORMALLY, the loss of a single automobile race would not evoke any reaction from top management. For obvious reasons this one did, and when Beebe returned to Dearborn he was asked to explain. He made no excuses, but added that a concerted effort for 1966, he was convinced, would result in victory. The operating committee of the company listened to what he had to say and decided Le Mans was worth another try.

The reorganization that followed saw operational control for the Le Mans effort transferred from Geddes to Cowley, who had previously been occupied only with stock cars. Shelby American, up to now the only team responsible for racing the cars, was to be joined by Holman-Moody and by Alan Mann; experience had shown three cars were the maximum one team could be expected to run efficiently. Although Holman-Moody was inexperienced in long-distance sports car racing, the mechanical talent and the organization were there. Mann's reputation as a team manager had grown in the past year, and his connections with both Dearborn and Ford of Britain made him a logical man for the job. Kar Kraft, the small shop in Dearborn that had been taken over by the special vehicles department, would continue to design and build the basic car, under Lunn's supervision, and the semi-finished vehicles would then be shipped to Shelby's plant in Los Angeles for the final touches. Shelby's crews, led by Remington and Carroll Smith, would continue to conduct all development tests.

There was also a new organization established, the Le Mans Committee. Beebe had decided to turn around the very system which sometimes throttled racing efforts and make it work to his advantage. The Le Mans Committee was composed of, among other persons, the heads of the various divisions that were involved (e.g., Innes for Engine and Foundry, Hans Matthias for the General Parts Division, Ted Mecke for Public Relations). The committee was to meet every two weeks to assess the situation, and at these sessions anyone who had a complaint or a suggestion was free to air it. In this manner, they were able to slash through vast amounts of red tape. There was now support from all sides. (Patterson told Beebe, "Anything you want, let me know. We'll gold plate the gearboxes, if necessary.") The various departments started work on restoring Ford's tattered reputation, and by late August the first track test was held at Daytona Beach. Although no single part of the program could be considered more or less important than any other, these tests were the guts of the thing.

The man from Ford who was to live with the cars for the next 10 months was Homer Perry. A 26-year veteran of the company, Perry had spent the majority of his career at the proving grounds. He moved to the Special Vehicles Department a few years prior to the Le Mans effort, and had spent most of his time there preparing and testing cars for such events as the Mobil Economy Run and Pure Oil Performance Trials. Although he had little racing experience Perry knew automobiles, and he knew what it took to make them run. His job was to coordinate the activities of Remington, Smith and the rest of the Shelby crew with the designers, the engineers, with Holman-Moody, with Mann and with the dozens of other persons who played a vital part in the operation. Everything that had anything to do with the tactical part of the program was eventually funneled through Perry.

His counterpart at Shelby American was Al Dowd, who was one of those fortunate coincidences that happened to the performance program. A chief warrant engineer in the Coast Guard, Dowd had retired after 20 years of service at the end of 1962, and was still only in his late 30s. Dowd heard Shelby was looking for help, and in February of 1963 he went to work on the Cobras as a mechanic in the back of the shop, washing parts. It did not take Shelby and Remington long to recognize his talents and in a few weeks Dowd was in charge of a car that ran in smaller West Coast events. By Sebring of 1964 Dowd was in charge of the administration of the entire Cobra team and handled the business and administrative side of all Shelby racing, while Remington took care of the technical end. Had Dowd not been there the 1966 result at Le Mans would have been the same, but at least four men would have been required to do his job; his capacity for work was amazing.

After the Daytona test it was clear that not only Perry and Dowd had a lot of work to do, but so did everyone else. In four days Miles and Phil Hill managed to accumulate only 9½ hours running time, after which a rear hub retaining bolt failed. Before it did, they found significant problems in the areas of suspension, tires, vehicle cooling, transmission, electrical system, driver comfort, fuel system and brakes. There wasn't much that was right. By mid-September they had a revised model (called Mark II) in the Dearborn wind tunnel, and by mid-October they were back at Daytona. They found the improvements satisfactory, but they also discovered the basic chassis would have to be replaced by one employing heavier-gauge metals. In December they were back at Daytona again, in an attempt to make the new car last 24 hours. It didn't, as there were failures in both the engine compartment and the brakes. A week later Miles did some top-speed testing at Kingman to check out a new short-nose body configuration which added 8 mph to the top speed, and by mid-January the team conducted its last preseason test at Sebring. The car lasted 18 hours, and the part that failed was in the gearbox. The box and the brakes were the only major problems now. Thousands of miles and thousands of hours after the comeback decision had been made, the team was going racing.

The public beginning of Ford's new era was Daytona, and this time it was for 24 hours. If the cars were to win in June, and if the new organizational plan was to prove itself workable, early February was as good a time as any to find out. There were five of the Mark IIs (with 460 horsepower for this one), three being run by Shelby American and the other two by Holman. For opposition there was a brand new Chaparral coupe—and none of the front-line Ferraris. The Italian factory kept its first string home, with the best anyone could muster being a pair of rebodied 1965 P2s, equipped with 4.4-liter, single-cam engines. Pedro Rodriguez had one and his partner was Mario Andretti, as the young oval-track star was seeking experience in other fields. It was Andretti's second sports car event, Ferrari importer Luigi Chinetti having given him his first chance at Bridgehampton the previous fall. A similar car was entered by the Ecurie Nationale Belge, and was not considered as much of a threat as its sister vehicle or the Chaparral. The latter was equipped with new bodywork which gave it an enclosed cockpit and also room for what were sarcastically known as the FIA suitcases. Hall and Sharp were embarking on a European campaign for 1966, and because of this they had modified their vehicle to comply with all the international regulations. They had also changed drivers: With so much work to be done at home, and with veterans of the European circuit needed, Hall had hired Phil Hill away from Ford and had paired him with Joakim Bonnier, the veteran Swede.

But the main opposition for the Fords was not the Chaparral or the Ferraris. It was the circuit itself. If the cars could run well for 24 hours, they would win.

Shelby had Miles and Ruby, seeking to repeat their triumph of the previous year; Gurney and Jerry Grant in the second car and McLaren and Amon in the third. Holman had Walt Hansgen and young Mark Donohue, both making their first start for the company, with Richie Ginther and Ronnie Bucknum in his second car. The latter was the lone non-standard item on the team, as it was equipped with the experimental automatic transmission; Ford knew it was not quite right, but Daytona was a chance to test it under race conditions. (The others had the four-speed manual transmissions they were to use for the rest of their careers. The big engine put out so much torque that a five-speed box was unnecessary.)

Miles was the quickest. The days he spent with the cars, while many higher-priced drivers such as Gurney were flying from race to race, had given him an intimate knowledge of just how he wanted it set up, and he was also blessed with a fine co-driver in Ruby, who was never fussy about camber and caster settings, being content with whatever combination Miles chose. (The importance of this type of teamwork is often underestimated; too many times the drivers spend the practice period attempting a compromise between their different views on how the vehicle should be adjusted, the end result being that when the race starts neither is happy.) Miles had clocked 1:57.8, with something still in reserve, while Bonnier had a 1:58.0 and Hansgen 1:58.2. Rodriguez' 1:59.2 was the best any Ferrari could muster, with the Fords stringing out back to 2:04 (Gurney, who was still busy with his interminable chassis adjustments). With five cars to one for Hall, the strategy was simple: Miles and Ruby went out to run with them, and the other cars would run a second or two per lap slower. All were given their choice of what speeds they wanted to maintain. Miles chose 2:04, Hansgen and Gurney took 2:06 to 2:07, McLaren took 2:08 and the automatic was to lap at whatever speed it felt comfortable.

The end, as far as the race was concerned, came less than an hour after the beginning. Bonnier, taking advantage of his car's lighter weight (about 2,300 pounds with fuel and driver to 2,900 for the Fords), led the first lap, but Miles pulled in front as they hammered around the banking the next time and was never headed after that. The Chaparral made one quick pit stop, then came in with frozen steering a little while later. That cost an hour, and when it rejoined the race it was in 53rd place and out there merely for the exercise as the Fords roared ahead. Rodriguez knew he couldn't run with them and was content to stay back and hope the Fords blew. And so it went, through 24 hours which included the coldest nighttime temperatures seen in that part of Florida in decades; at 25 degrees the weather even knocked out the electronic lap scorer.

When it was over Miles and Ruby, their car never missing a beat, were eight laps ahead of Gurney and Grant. They covered 678 laps—2,750 miles—at an average of 108.02 mph. Their car had made 13 pit stops with an average time of 1:30, and aside from the expected brake disc change in the middle of the night, the rest had been only for oil, gas and tires. Gurney's car had run as well, being that far behind only because of its slower pace and an unexpected stop to check collision damage after Grant nicked a slower, smaller vehicle that got in his way on the banking. Hansgen, in third place, had encountered some brake trouble, dropping from second to third after 19 hours, and the McLaren-Amon car finished fifth behind Rodriguez and Andretti despite going the last nine hours with a broken limited slip in the differential. The only car that failed to finish was the one with the automatic, and it lasted 13 hours.

One of the few close calls took place in the pits during the night: Miles had gone back to the garage to get his overcoat, and when he tried to return the gate guard demanded to see his pit pass. Miles found he had lost it, and attempted to reason with the man.

He even opened his coat to display his electric-blue coveralls, complete with a large "Ken Miles" embroidered over the breast pocket, and said "Look here, you don't think I'm wearing this silly getup just to walk around this place, do you?"

At the same time the public address system was blaring forth the latest information on Miles' accomplishments. The guard was adamant, so Miles tried to push past him and two deputies came running. They were hauling him off to the local jail when someone from the Ford pits happened to spot the commotion and rescued Miles just in time

After the race, perched on top of the car in the winner's circle, Miles had as much of a smile as he ever permitted himself, and his eyes were sparkling despite not having slept at all. The outwardly phlegmatic Ruby, who had gone straight to sleep after his night-time driving stints, was as different from Miles as could be imagined. But together they were turning into a great team.

This race also marked the first en masse appearance of the GT40s, now being sold to private entrants. They were no more successful in those hands than they were under factory supervision: Four started, one was as high as sixth after 17 hours and none were running at the finish, departing with a variety of engine and transmission ailments.

Although the Daytona sweep did much to boost everyone's confidence, the result did not settle a difference of opinion which had existed since the previous summer. Despite the great strides made by the new car, there were still persons who felt it was impractical to attempt Le Mans with something that big and heavy. The 289-inch engine and the GT40 were still the answer, they maintained, and it was only necessary to do a little development work on the GT40 to make it a winner. Sebring, at first considered only for a token entry, now became the proving ground. Mann, who along with a few members of top management was an exponent of the lightweight car, prepared the two lightest GT40s ever built, using aluminum bodies instead of the standard fiberglass and bringing them in at approximately 2,025 pounds instead of the normal 2,200. He had the additional advantage of using the same brakes as the heavier Mark IIs, and he would also have an edge in fuel consumption. His cars, he thought, with 385 horsepower, would he better than the bigger Fords, now with 470 horses and weighing 2,450 pounds. For drivers Mann had some of the best in the business: Graham Hill and Jackie Stewart in one car and Sir John Whitmore and Frank Gardner in the other.

The problem of weight, coupled with the severe workout the brakes would get on a stop-and-go circuit like Sebring, had militated against sending any cars to the race. But since Mann's 289s were going, four other full-sized vehicles also went along. From a budget standpoint it cost proportionally more to race two cars than it did six, the company had to maintain the reputation it started to build at Daytona, and there also had to be cars with which to compare the 289s. Shelby American entered two, and so did Holman-Moody. Shelby had Gurney and Grant in one of the Daytona cars, plus Miles and Ruby in something new: this was the X1 roadster, which had been known as the GTX when Ford Advanced Vehicles, Kar Kraft and McLaren's own shop combined to build it the year before. It had been run unsuccessfully in the fall sports car series, and had been crashed and then rebuilt at Shelby's. The object of its appearance at Sebring was twofold: first, to see if the car's lighter weight (2,300 pounds) would offset its poorer aerodynamics on a course that featured acceleration and braking, and to serve as a trial horse for the latest of the automatic transmissions. It finished the latter half of the assignment in practice, as

Miles and Ruby went through three automatics before finally talking Ford into a four-speed for the race.

Holman's two cars were also varied, with Hansgen and Donohue in the normal one and A.J. Foyt (in his first GT ride) and Bucknum having an automatic transmission. For a change the opposition included one brand new Ferrari, a 330P3 to be driven by Parkes and Bondurant (switched over from Ford) and two Chaparrals. The team was finally going to get a look at its Le Mans opposition, and it got an impressive one as Parkes established a lap record of 2:56.6 on the second day of practice. The Fords, at that time, were still running around three minutes. They waited until the final day, when Gurney went out and carved another two seconds off Parkes' figure, and then Graham Hill turned in a 2:57.4 with the smaller-engined car. Hansgen was at 2:58.0, Miles at 2:58.6, and it was Daytona all over again: If the cars could finish, they could win. One Ferrari was not enough to hold off six Fords.

This time it was to be Gurney and Grant out front, running 2:59 laps, with Hansgen and Miles two to three seconds slower. The automatic and the 289-inch cars were to set their own pace.

The winner: The X1, which ran in only one race and won it. The car was driven to victory at Sebring in 1966 by Ken Miles and Lloyd Ruby.

The loser: The Mark II shared by Dan Gurney and Jerry Grant, which looked to be a certain winner at Sebring in 1966 and which suffered an engine failure on the last lap before the checkered flag, letting the X1 win.

But when everyone ran across the track, jumped in and drove away, there was one car left on the line. It was Gurney, who in the excitement couldn't locate the switch. After a full minute he found it and screamed off, leaving long black trails of rubber on the concrete. He passed 26 cars on the first lap, went by another 10 on the second, and by the ninth lap was running eighth and still moving up. Before 1½ hours had gone by Gurney was in front, lowering the record to 2:54.8 in the process. In the early stages the leaders were split into two groups: the two Shelby-managed Fords and the factory Ferrari up front, then Hansgen, Graham Hill, one of the Chaparrals and Rodriguez in the erstwhile Daytona Ferrari (again with Andretti). Soon both Chaparrals, which had spent the practice days looking for oil leaks and fixing transmissions, were out of the race. That left the Ferraris, and there were now a few less Fords to deal with them: Hansgen and Foyt had both run into brake troubles and although still racing, were far behind. The pair of 289-inch lightweights, although going well, were not quick enough to outrun the top Ferrari. They just kept rolling along in a high-speed three-car caravan—Gurney, Parkes and Miles—and when Bondurant, Ruby or Grant took over the situation remained the same, with the race unfolding at record speeds and the Ferrari sounding like it would run forever.

Forever, at Sebring 1966, was nine hours. It took that long for the car's transmission to start breaking up, and by seven in the evening the Ferrari was dropping back and getting ready to retire. Everyone in the Ford pits relaxed a little, and the slow sign went out to Gurney and Miles.

It was ignored. They had forgotten about team orders and were now staging their own private scrap with the only two Fords still in contention. The slow sign was given again, and the pair again paid no attention.

The next time they went by Shelby was on the pit wall waving a hammer at them.

A lap later Miles had dropped back, and as he went past the pits he smiled and made a rude gesture in Shelby's direction. The two of them settled down to run the race out, with the lightweight 289s now retired, with Hansgen moving up but miles astern, and with the Foyt-Bucknum car still having its journey interrupted by lengthy pit stops to cure brake troubles (one of them for 52 minutes). With a few minutes to go, and the crowd already gathering at the finish line, Gurney was a lap and perhaps 15 seconds ahead of Miles, the two cars were still droning along, and the newspapermen in the press box were already through the first several paragraphs of their stories, looking to get a head start and make an earlier edition. Those who had really tight deadlines had already sent information bulletins saying Gurney and Grant had won. The starter picked up the checkered flag, and everyone waited.

Suddenly, instead of Gurney, Miles came past, and at the same time, down at the corner before the finishing straight, there appeared the headlights of a car moving at perhaps two miles an hour. It was Gurney's big blue car, and Dan was out of the vehicle, pushing it.

On what would have been his last lap, or at worst his next to last, Gurney's engine had ceased to function and the car rolled to a halt only a few hundred yards from the line. He got out, wondering what to do, when a minor official told Dan to try and push it across.

While Gurney was pushing, Miles unlapped himself and went on to win the second consecutive event for himself and Ruby. Gurney's, who would have had second place if he had left the car sitting where it was, was disqualified for committing one of the bigger *faux pas* of the season: The international rule against pushing dead cars anywhere but off the track had been in force for more than five years. Gurney was almost speechless in his disappointment and frustration. It was a rod bolt that let go, after running 11 hours and 57 minutes. Ford finished 1-2-3, but that was little solace for Dan.

The Miles-Ruby car covered 228 laps at an average of 98.067 mph—a record, with Hansgen and Donohue having completed 216 laps for second place. Third, and the first of the private GT40s to do anything of note in an international championship event, was one of the Essex Wire team cars, driven by Robert (Skip) Scott and Peter Revson. They covered 213 laps and were the principal exception to the remarkable attrition rate among the GT40s—counting the pair from Mann, there were nine entered and only two finished. Despite a 1-2-3 conclusion it had been a bad race from many angles, the main one being the five deaths that accompanied it. The first involved Canadian champion Bob McLean, driving one of the two GT40s entered by his country's Comstock Racing Team. It was about the five-hour mark when McLean took over the car after a 13-minute pit stop, and for the next three laps he recorded times consistent with those the car had been doing from the start (3:15–3:16). Then, on his fourth lap, McLean somehow lost it going into a hairpin turn. The exact cause of the mishap was never determined, but the car flipped end for end and exploded as it hit a utility pole. McLean never got out. The other accident came with two hours to go when Andretti, steaming down on one of the corners in the back section of the course, had his gearbox selector mechanism malfunction and instead of putting the car into third gear got it into first instead, locking up the rear wheels and throwing the Ferrari into a spin. Porsche driver Don Wester, right behind, hit Andretti's car a glancing blow and went flying off into a non-spectator area. The only trouble was that spectators were there and Wester's car killed four of them. When Andretti came back to the pits, still not knowing of the tragedy, his car burned while the mechanics attempted to repair it. The morning after the race was a gray one.

The last-minute engine failure of Gurney's car, while a shock to the two drivers involved, turned out to be a fortunate occurrence. It drew the engineers' attention to a problem they had not known existed, and modifications were made for Le Mans. The race was 11 weeks off and there was time for this, but the traditional spring practice on the course was held the weekend after Sebring. Several of the cars and crews went practically from the finish line to the airport. Two of the Mark IIs went, the two GT40s went (although the 427-289 controversy had been settled, Ford did not know if the Le Mans organizers would allow a last-minute change of entries, so the smaller cars practiced as an insurance measure), and the fifth vehicle was the first of the J-Cars.

Introduced in clay-model form in December of 1965, the J-Car was the first Ford sports prototype to be designed and executed entirely in the United States. It had a peculiar shape, looking like a high-speed bread van due to the configuration of its hindquarters, and employed sheets of a lightweight honeycomb aluminum sandwich as the basic material for its monocoque chassis. Designed and built by Lunn's group at Kar Kraft, it was intended to be the successor to the Mark II. If it went well during the trials there was a slim possibility it would be entered in the race.

The first practice day brought rain, the thought of which had nagged at the team ever since the start of the Mark II program. The great power of the car, plus the extra-wide tires (which would tend to aquaplane, or ride, on top of the film of water on the road) would be a handicap in extremely wet conditions. Now they were going to get a chance to test in this type of weather, and the driver who pushed the hardest was Hansgen. As the rain abated he went faster and faster. When he came into the pits Cowley and Perry told him to take it easy, it was only a test, and they would prefer slower times to a bent automobile. Hansgen kept on pressing, and after five laps they called him in again. This time Carroll Smith repeated the advice. The 46-year-old veteran of 15 years of racing went back onto the track, with the rain practically stopped but the surface thoroughly soaked.

His first lap was 3:59, then the next time around he dropped sharply to 3:48.5. The next one was even quicker, 3:46.8. As Hansgen roared past again, most of the pit crew was occupied with the other cars and didn't look up until someone shouted. The car went out of control heading into the long, sweeping right-hander after the pits, and Hansgen tried to point it up the escape road instead. He almost made it, but the car, traveling at better than 150, clipped the wall on the right, bounced against the one on the left, and flipped over before finally coming to rest. The safety fuel tanks prevented a fire, but the vehicle was crushed. It took almost 20 minutes to cut Hansgen out, he was rushed to a local clinic and that afternoon was flown by helicopter to the U.S. Army hospital 80 miles away at Orleans, where the latest facilities were available. The doctors said afterward that only his strong constitution kept him alive for five days, in which he never regained consciousness. Hansgen had been involved in several spectacular (and car-destroying) accidents in the past. This was the first one in which he suffered anything more than a scratch.

Hansgen wasn't the only Ford driver to be involved in an accident the first day, although the other was strictly minor: Miles ran the second Mark II into a sandbank, filling a good portion of the undercarriage with grit and ruining a Gilmer belt (another was located in Switzerland and flown in that night, so the car practiced again on Sunday). It had been a bad day from many standpoints, starting with Hansgen's accident, followed by Miles', the wet weather which prevented flat-out running, and the absence of both the Ferraris and the Chaparrals. The latter team was home, still trying to straighten out its Sebring difficulties, and no one knew why Ferrari hadn't shown. But his cars weren't there, and it was going to be even more difficult to draw pre-race comparisons.

On Sunday the J-Car, loaded with instrumentation, made its first appearance. McLaren took it out first, and after various adjustments had been made and readings taken, Amon got his chance and in four laps achieved a 3:34. There were still many things wrong with the car, but it was a promising start. The best any of the Mark IIs could do was a 3:36.0 by Miles, and there was much work to be done on the suspensions before the middle of June. The year before Phil Hill had taken the untried predecessor of this same vehicle around the track in 3:33.0. This meant in its present form the car had taken a retrograde step.

The lack of faster times in practice, it was felt, was no reflection on the basic car. Except for brake problems there was nothing wrong that some careful adjustments wouldn't cure. Work in these areas increased in intensity, work on the J-Car continued as one faction wanted to run it in the race, and Beebe took stock of the championship situation. In 1966 there were seven events for the manufacturers' championship of unlimited displacement sports prototypes, with the best four performances by a manufacturer counting toward his total. The complicated scoring system, which acknowledged the top six finishers (but only the best car of each make) awarded points on the following basis:

Le Mans: 12-9-7-5-4-3.

Monza 1,000 Km., Nürburgring 1,000 Km., Targa Florio, Daytona and Sebring: 10-7-5-4-3-2.

Spa 1,000 Km.: 9-6-4-3-2-1.

Ford had established a clear lead with its wins at Daytona and Sebring, but in order to take it all, the company would have to participate in at least one more race besides Le Mans. Since Mann was now preparing two of the Mark IIs, and since his team still lacked race experience with the car, it was decided to send one of his vehicles to the 1,000 Kilometers of Spa May 22; if he finished first or second, that—plus Le Mans—would be enough for the title.

In the meantime final development tests were carried out at Kingman (where the Mark II was fractionally faster than the J-Car in a straight line), and at Riverside, where Miles, Donohue and NASCAR drivers Marvin Panch and Dick Hutcherson put both vehicles through a 24-hour durability test the first week in May. The test, run in three eight-hour segments in daylight only, saw the Mark II come through in fine shape. The J-Car lasted only through part of the first day, and proved that it was far from being race ready. The J-Car proponents quieted down, the build of the Mark IIs speeded up, and Mann took one of his vehicles to Belgium.

The 1,000-kilometer race at Spa was scheduled for the same day as the Grand Prix of Monaco, so instead of having Graham Hill and Stewart, Mann had to use Whitmore and Gardner. They were good, but they were not as fast as Ferrari's second string, composed in this instance of Parkes and Scarfiotti. To make the difference even bigger than usual the high-speed bends of the Ardennes circuit, located in erstwhile Battle of the Bulge country, give the better drivers more of an edge than does a course filled with slow corners. The 8.8-mile circuit has one hairpin, and the rest of it is filled with curves of anywhere from 100 to 175 mph. Even the Masta Straight, just over the hill from Malmedy, has a kink in the middle.

The big Mark II, outfitted with Le Mans gears and with the drivers holding to Le Mans revs (6,200), was never in front, the Ferrari leading from the start and helped to a degree by high winds that blew the Ford back and forth on certain sections of the course. It was close until the end, when the Ford threw a tire tread and had to come in for an unscheduled pit stop that gave Parkes and Scarfiotti a 132-mph, one-lap victory. The lone consolation for Ford was that the GT40s did well, with Scott and Revson placing third, Englishmen Peter Sutcliffe and Brian Redman fourth, and Innes Ireland and Amon fifth. In this category, for "Sports 50" cars, which had to be built in a minimum series of at least 50 examples, the Fords were already well on their way to the title, with most of the work being done by Scott's Essex Wire team.

By the end of May every department of the corporation that could possibly help the Le Mans effort was doing so. The word was out: This was no longer just another automobile race; it was something in which the prestige of the company was at stake, and there could be nothing short of victory. Although hindsight is the easiest kind, a backward look at the preparations shows it was more a triumph for organization than for any individual. For the months before the event there were numerous persons in Dearborn whose existence was interrupted by a project foreign to their normal preoccupation with passenger cars and trucks. Although most of them had never seen a Ford in a race, nor would ever travel to some of the glamorous places where the cars appeared, they were almost as important to the effort as the drivers themselves.

Some were dynamometer mechanics, some were electricians, some worked in the scientific research laboratory and there were some who only trucked parts to the airport. All of them knew what they were doing now was more than just another job.

The engine engineers had been working on a combination of durability and power ever since the first Mark II ran in May of the previous year. This time the engines were to be *known* factors: The target for Le Mans was an engine that had lived—under race conditions—for 48 hours. Although they had worked with the engine for almost five years, it had been used almost exclusively for stock car racing on oval tracks, and its conversion into a road-racing power plant presented numerous problems.

After durability the primary one was weight, as the location of the engine made this even more critical than it was in a sedan. There were new cooling requirements, ground clearance, oil capacity, new intake and exhaust systems, transistor ignitions and dozens of other things. They wound up with a weight saving, over the standard production 427-inch high performance engine, of 40 pounds, achieved mainly by using a magnesium oil pan, aluminum water pump, aluminum cylinder heads, a lighter flywheel and an aluminum front cover. (Had it not been for the penalty incurred through use of a dry-sump lubrication system, the weight saving would have been approximately 100 pounds.) Little by little, through the various track testing periods, through Daytona and Sebring and through the weeks that followed, the engine was brought to an optimum state. Night after night the dynamometer in cell 17D would tremble as another engine roared its way around a phantom circuit: The testing department of Engine and Foundry had simulated the Le Mans course on tape, and now the engines and transmissions were running laps at 4:02, shifting up and down, accelerating and decelerating as if they were in a car on the circuit. On some nights the engines would break down and on others they would blow up, but they kept getting closer to their target. Finally, the last week in May, it was achieved. The engine was producing 485 horsepower at 6,400 rpm, and it would live for 48 hours. Then they built 12 engines to the specifications of the test model, ran them in on the dynamometer for four hours, and shipped them to Shelby, Mann and Holman. The 12 showed a variance of 35 horsepower, with half being over the target of 485. In order to avoid bickering among the drivers, who would be seeking every extra horse, the engineers kept this data to themselves. They felt any one of the engines was capable of winning the race. As it turned out the best one, which produced 505 horses at the conclusion of its running-in process, never got out of a crate. The weakest engine, with 468.7 horsepower, was the one in the McLaren-Amon car. When it was returned to the factory and tested again after the race, it had loosened up to the extent that it produced 480 hp.

The people with the biggest problems were still those who dealt with the brakes. The Mark II was the heaviest and fastest car of its type ever built, and stopping it—and stopping it often—seemed to be an insurmountable problem. Both Ford and Kelsey-Hayes had worked overtime on it since the first car in 1964, and now the development pace was increased. Joe Ihnacik, at Ford, and Ken Caskey, at Kelsey-Hayes, complete with large testing staffs, had finally gotten the GT40 brakes to an acceptable standard. Then they were presented with the Mark II. This meant a weight increase of 400 pounds, plus an increase in velocity, to be hauled down to the proper cornering speeds every time the driver hit the brake pedal. The half-inch thick solid rotors on the GT40 were replaced by three-quarter inch models which were ventilated as well, but that wasn't enough. The brake fluid would boil, the rotors would warp or crack or both, and the brake pads would wear down in a hurry. Slowly, better materials were found for rotors, better pads were obtained, and as insurance Remington developed a quick-change system for the calipers and Holman built a quick-change setup for the rotor. Now, even if the entire assembly were unserviceable, it could be changed in two or three minutes. New ducts for cooling air were developed, other items were refined, and every time the engineers thought they had it licked, the cars would run harder and the brakes would show the effects. Even during the victories at Daytona and Sebring, several of the cars experienced brake problems. The copper matrix spray coating used on the Daytona discs was not good enough, and the nodular iron discs used at Sebring were better, but not by much. For Le Mans, and for the battle with the first-string Ferraris, they were improved some more.

From a technical standpoint the job of the brakes is to convert energy into heat. With the Mark II, using a gross vehicle weight of 2,860 pounds, the development engineers worked out the following:

Circuit	Distance	Lap Time	Number of Brake Points	Total Kinetic Energy to Be Dispelled on Each Lap
Daytona	3.81 miles	2:05	5	7,975,900 foot-pounds
Sebring	5.2 miles	2:58	9	14,502,200 foot-pounds
Le Mans	8.36 miles	3:35	6	12,597,900 foot-pounds

This would have to be done repeatedly for 24 hours at Daytona, for 12 hours at Sebring and for 24 more at Le Mans, with each course presenting its own peculiar problems. Although Le Mans did not require as much total braking effort per lap, and although it spaced fewer applications per lap over a longer time span, in one way Le Mans was more difficult. The corner at the end of the Mulsanne Straight is the grandfather of all. To slow the car from approximately 215 mph to 35 mph requires the conversion of 4,095,600 foot-pounds of kinetic energy to heat—and this would have to be done again and again, every 3:35, for 24 hours. The temperature of the brake disc would rise from 700 to 1,500 degrees Fahrenheit in seven seconds, then gradually drop to 700 degrees by the time the car got halfway down Mulsanne again. A heat fluctuation of this magnitude was simply too much for the discs to take. By way of comparison, to stop a 4,300-pound Ford sedan from 70 mph requires conversion of 700,000 foot-pounds of energy into heat—and no one expects it to perform this maneuver for 24 consecutive hours. The brakes, everyone knew, were the critical point.

The army—and by racing standards it was that—was ready to move overseas, and the logistics were staggering. Most of it had been handled by one man, Dowd. Starting the previous fall he had made several trips to Europe and had arranged for all the rooms, all the transport vehicles, the customs clearances, all the catering, garage space—everything that would be needed to take care of 100 persons and eight cars, plus the more than 20 tons of spares and equipment. Several weeks before the race a 40-foot tractor-trailer, outfitted as a machine shop on wheels and with "Holman-Moody-Stroppe" on its sides, was delivered to New York for shipment to France. In the weeks before the race the finishing touches were put on the cars in Los Angeles, in Charlotte and in England, they were taken to the nearest road circuit to be run for an hour and given a final check. Then the six cars from America were loaded on planes and flown to Paris (Shelby American alone shipped 167 pieces of freight). Before the cars arrived in France mechanics from both teams flew over, picked up trucks and trailers and drove them to the airport, where everything was loaded and taken to Le Mans (each of the race cars was transported individually, so as to minimize the loss if one should be involved in a traffic accident). The rolling machine shop came down from Le Havre, the mechanics came in with the cars, the engineers and designers flew in from Detroit, the timekeeping crew gathered, Frey, Beebe, Passino and the other administrators arrived, and the day before the race Henry Ford II appeared. He had been named honorary president of the event, and would drop the flag for the start.

The only persons not on hand were some of the drivers, as the first crisis developed. After starting to plan almost a year in advance, and after rounding up some of the finest long-distance pilots in the world, Ford now saw its staff whittled away on the shortest possible notice. The first to go had been Hansgen, but that was early April, and there had been time to get a replacement. Then, a few days after the Indianapolis "500" and two weeks before Le Mans, Ruby was flying a light plane from that city to Milwaukee. He crashed on takeoff, fortunately not killing himself, but sustaining injuries that would keep him out of a car for several months. Two days later at Milwaukee Foyt's car caught fire and he was forced to bail out, suffering hand burns in the process. That made three, and at the Grand Prix of Belgium the Sunday before Le Mans, Jackie Stewart was involved in a crash that put him in the hospital for some time. There was a quick scratching for drivers, some promotion of men who had been listed as reserves, and the lineup came out like this:

Shelby American: Gurney-Grant, McLaren-Amon and Miles-Denis Hulme of New Zealand, at the time the backup driver on the Brabham team for single-seater events.

Holman-Moody: Donohue-Paul Hawkins, Andretti-Lucien Bianchi of Belgium (the former Tour de France and Sebring winner) and Bucknum with Hutcherson, the NASCAR star who had never driven in a sports car race and whose only experience with the vehicle had been gained in the 24-hour run at Riverside.

Mann: Whitmore-Gardner and Graham Hill-Dr. Dick Thompson, the SCCA veteran and an experienced Le Mans driver. The sole spare now available for the eight cars was Bob Grossman, a slow but steady type who had been in SCCA competition for more than a decade, and who had finished at Le Mans six times in six tries.

The team cars were backed up by five privately entered GT40s, with Scott and Revson having the one most likely to succeed. But none of these, it was known going in, would be of any value if the front-line Ferraris ran well for the entire race: The factory cars would have to do it. They had 11 Ferraris to beat, and they lined up like this:

330P3 (4.0 liters, twin overhead cams, fuel injection): Surtees-Parkes, Bandini-Guichet and Rodriguez-Ginther.

365P2 (4.4 liters, single overhead cam): Willy Mairesse-Herbert Mueller, Attwood-David Piper, "Beurlys"-Pierre Dumay, and Gregory-Bondurant. "Beurlys" was the driving pseudonym of a millionaire Belgian contractor.

There was a variety of other Ferraris—275LMs, 250LMs, 275GTB grand tourers and even three of the 2.0-liter Dinos. But any fight would come from the top seven, or from the single Chaparral. That car had Phil Hill and Bonnier as its drivers, and was fresh from winning the 1,000 Kilometers of the Nürburgring, the first major win for an American car in Europe in more than four decades.

Three's a crowd: Walt Hansgen's Mark II leads the Chaparral of Joakim Bonnier and the Ferrari of Pedro Rodriguez during the early stages of the 1966 Daytona Continental. The winner was piloted by Ken Miles (inset) and Lloyd Ruby, while Hansgen and Mark Donohue placed third and Rodriguez and Mario Andretti were fourth. The Chaparral retired.

Ill-fated: (Top) The J-Car, shown here during its maiden voyage during the Le Mans practice session of April, 1966. (Bottom) The wreckage of Walt Hansgen's Mark II, taken after it crashed on a wet track.

On the morning of the second practice day, Ford got an additional edge when Surtees found Scarfiotti had been listed as a third driver of the car he and Parkes were to share. When he demanded to know why, the Ferrari team manager loftily told him if he didn't like it, he didn't have to drive. These two had been at odds for some time, so Surtees interpreted it as a move to squeeze him out and he called his manager's bluff, packing his helmet and going back to the hotel. Almost before he got there, Shelby sent a message inviting him to drive a Ford (there had been some negotiation between the two the previous winter). Surtees turned him down, hoping to save the situation when he got back to Maranello and could talk with his boss. In the meantime, the Ferrari team lost its best driver and the only man fast enough to stay up with the Fords.

On the first evening Gurney was the quickest with 3:33.3, Whitmore was next at 3:33.7 and Surtees had 3:36.3. Everything was going well and even Hutcherson, inexperienced in night driving or road racing, showed his stint at Riverside had been enough for him to handle a back-up car. The next night, while Gurney was lowering the practice mark to 3:30.6 and Miles was right behind with 3:31.7, another crisis occurred. It was right after 9 p.m. and dusk had fallen when Thompson came storming up to White House Corner behind the reserve-entry GT40 of Dick Holquist, a Pittsburgh driver whose previous experience included an undistinguished career in smaller SCCA events, and who had already been warned to keep out of the way of the faster cars. As Thompson arrived at the entrance to the corner, Holquist, who had been on the right, suddenly cut in front, blocking Thompson's path with a car moving perhaps 20 miles an hour slower. Thompson had no choice but to ram him, sending the GT40 flying, destroying the vehicle and injuring its driver. By the time Thompson got his car under control he was halfway to the pits, which are located about 800 yards up the road. He pulled in and reported the accident to the pit marshal while the mechanics and the curious checked the car, which miraculously had only shredded the fiberglass on the right front corner.

A few minutes later an emissary from headquarters appeared at the Ford pits and requested Thompson's presence before the stewards. When Thompson appeared he was informed he had acted in an unsportsmanlike manner in not stopping at the scene of the accident and again in not reporting it when he came into the pits. Both he and the car were disqualified. When Mann came rushing in to protest, the committee was adamant. Thompson and the car were out and that was final. Mann went back and explained the situation to Beebe.

Beebe grabbed Bill Reiber, then president of Ford-France, to act as his interpreter, and the two of them went to the committee. When they arrived they found the kangaroo court still assembled and obviously expecting them. One of the officials told Beebe that since he was not the official entrant, he had no business there.

"Let's not kid each other," Beebe started, and then he cooled down, realizing if he lost his temper now he would never get the car back in the race. Beebe explained (as if an explanation was necessary) that Mann was acting as Ford's agent, and therefore he deemed it proper that he appear. That seemed to satisfy the French sense of protocol, and the fencing began with a review of the rules. Thompson and the car had been disqualified because of unsportsmanlike conduct, Beebe was told.

"What, in your estimation, constitutes unsportsmanlike conduct?"

The officials said he should not have moved his car from the spot where it came to rest after the accident, and he should have reported it the moment he came in.

"I thought he did a wise thing, coming into the pits," Beebe replied, "and it is untenable to expect the driver involved to report the mishap. I would think the track officials should be in a position to see everything that went on at the circuit."

Then he paused for effect before delivering his ultimatum.

"If that were the case, if the officials could not see everything, then Le Mans is not a safe place to race. And if that is so, we would have to withdraw all the Ford entries."

Some of the group understood English and they didn't have to wait for Reiber's translation. As Beebe's words hit them, they started. They had never expected—or for that matter believed Beebe had the authority to order—a mass withdrawal. Leo kept right on talking.

"It was no secret this transpired. The car came in in front of thousands of people. It would be incredible to think they could see the damage and the officials could not." Beebe then asked them to reconsider their ruling.

The Frenchmen looked at each other. "Let us have a meeting," one of them said, and the group retired to the next room while Beebe and Reiber sat there, wondering what would happen. Beebe had placed his career on the block, betting the French wouldn't have guts enough to call his hand. In five minutes he got the news.

The committee had reconsidered, he was informed. They would leave the car in the race but would maintain their disqualification of the driver.

The car alone was no good, Beebe told them. He had no reserve drivers (Grossman had been offered a ride with another team, and had accepted, and if he were to keep the car in the race, he would have to get permission to bring in another pilot. The club agreed, and Beebe left. If there was one thing he regretted it was the sacrifice of the driver, but the club had to save some semblance of face and Beebe realized this. The first man he spoke to at the pits was Thompson, and when he did it was to apologize.

All eight cars were still in the race but it had been a near thing. Beebe hardly slept that night, agitated over the peremptory manner in which Thompson had been made the scapegoat for Le Mans inefficiency, and the next morning Mann contacted Brian Muir, an obscure Australian driver who was spending the summer in England and who was the only man available. He was flown in and on Saturday morning the club closed the circuit so Muir could familiarize himself with a car that had a speed potential far above anything he had ever driven. Muir was given two laps and the officials then declared him competent to drive a 200-mph vehicle on a course he had never seen before. These were the same officials who had declared Le Mans veteran Thompson incompetent less than 48 hours earlier.

But Graham Hill's late-arriving co-driver was of minor importance by then. It was race day, and the eight cars, which had undergone a painstaking final check the evening before, were lined up in front of the pits, tools and spares were laid in their proper places, the thousand last-minute things that always have to be done were accomplished, threatening clouds came moving in on the circuit, it started to rain, and the race began.

When the annual rush to the cars and the world's fastest traffic jam occurred after the flag signal, Ford almost lost two entries at the start. Whitmore's car jumped off the line and then stalled in front of Miles. The latter, starting alongside, nicked Whitmore's right front fender with his left, leaving a slight scar on each. Had the blow been even a little more severe, neither would have had the requisite two head-lights for the night driving.

It was a Ford race from the beginning. On the first lap it was Graham Hill, followed by Gurney, Whitmore and Bucknum, with Parkes fifth, and with both Miles and Hawkins heading for the pits. Miles' complaint was a minor one; the door wouldn't shut properly and this was fixed in seconds. Hawkins' problem was some-thing else. A halfshaft had fractured as he started and he was forced to make a slow, careful lap to get back to his pit. They lost an hour replacing it, dropping him to last place and writing the car off as a challenger. Whitmore had also come in early, making a 10-minute stop to repair a brake line. The Fords that hadn't stopped were running like trains, but two were already in trouble.

An hour went by, with Miles breaking the lap record again and again as he strove to make up for the short time he spent in the pits, an hour at the end of which the Fords were running 1-2-3-5-8, with Rodriguez pushing from fourth place, Parkes sixth and the Chaparral seventh ... The enormous crowd sat and watched, waiting for the Fords to break up and the Ferraris to come on, just as they had done for the last six years. There had been other cars in those years, cars faster than the Ferraris, but when 4 p.m. on Sunday came around, one of the red ones had always been in front.

The race kept rolling, unfolding at a record pace as the track dried, and after the first pit stops it was Gurney, Miles, Rodriguez, Bucknum, Graham Hill, Parkes and McLaren—Fords 1-2-4-5-7 and Ferraris 3-6 ... By the two-hour mark Whitmore's car was far behind after another long stop to fix clutch troubles ... The Hawkins car was in difficulty again, the tail section having blown off on Mulsanne, Donohue chasing after it and wiring it back on ... One P2 Ferrari was already out, but the P3s were running strong ... Soon Whitmore and Hawkins were gone, leaving six Fords, and as the race neared 7 p.m. Miles was first, with Ferraris now second and third ... The first three cars were on the same lap, with the next four one lap behind ... Everyone was still flying, and the Fords were not pulling away from the three top Ferraris. By 10 p.m. it looked worse, as Rodriguez and Scarfiotti were first and second, followed closely by four Fords, two Ferraris and two more Fords ... A few minutes later a third Ford was out, the Andretti-Bianchi car with engine trouble;

three down, five to go ... The Chaparral, delayed several times by long pit stops to change from rain tires to dry tires and back again, dropped out shortly after 11 with a dead battery ... Seven hours gone, 17 to go, and the field continued to roar past while the Ferris wheel and the rest of the carnival attractions gleamed brightly in the damp evening.

At 11 the Fords were out front again, with Miles leading Gurney, and within an hour the opposition began to disappear: A sudden shower put rivers of water on the track and two small cars spun and crashed at the Esses ... Scarfiotti came steaming along behind them and had no choice but to crash into the other two vehicles ... He wasn't hurt seriously, but that left only two first-team Ferraris.

The Hill-Muir car was also out by midnight—a front upright had disintegrated ... It was the right front; the blow it received in the Thompson accident was more serious than it had appeared ... That left four Fords, and all of them already on their second set of front discs. The unexpectedly hot pace of the first six hours caused an epidemic of cracking, and a shortage of spares forced the crews to cannibalize the cars that were already out.

The pace also did away with the opposition. Between the hours of midnight and 4 a.m. they fell out, one by one ... Gregory and Bondurant retired right after 12; Rodriguez and Ginther had their transmission go bad around 2 a.m. Mairesse and Mueller were next, packing it in after 3 a.m., and the others were too far behind to matter. When the Mairesse car was pushed off into the darkness one of the Ford mechanics looked at another and smiled. "Maybe we ought to go wake up Mr. Ford and tell him we've won the race." With half of it completed Fords were running first through sixth, with the four factory cars on top, followed by Revson and Scott, and then by Englishman Peter Sutcliffe and Dieter Spoerry, a Swiss.

The word was given to the signaling station at the exit from Mulsanne Corner: slow down. All we have to do is finish. The race was over; now it was a question of durability. The pace dropped from 3:38 (Gurney had set the lap record of 3:30.6 during the third hour) to a more sedate 3:50, and the weary faces in the Ford pits relaxed a trifle. Through the night, and through the gray dawn at 4:30, with a sprinkle of rain coming every so often, they kept right on rolling ... Gurney, Miles and McLaren's cars running practically neck and neck, the Bucknum-Hutcherson entry six laps behind and taking it easy; by 8 a.m. the closest Ferrari was in 11th place, 185 miles behind the leader, and Porsches were occupying eighth through 10th ... Scott's GT40 was out with transmission troubles, and Ford still had the first five spots.

The next to go was Gurney's car, and it went while in the lead. It was a few minutes after 9 a.m., and Gurney was sleeping in a trailer when Grant came into the pits, saying the water temperature needle had gone out of sight. The mechanics checked what they could see, poured an antileak compound in with fresh water and Grant took off again, with everyone's fingers crossed. In 45 minutes he was back, with all the water gone and the engine cooking under its fiberglass hood. Le Mans rules forbid replenishment of water at less than 25-lap intervals (about 200 miles). There was no choice but to push the car away.

The other three kept on rolling, their lap times around four minutes now, rolling past the damp grandstands which were beginning to fill again as the crowds returned for the finish, to sit there and watch the 20 cars still alive as they continued around the broad circuit, some of them as healthy as when they started, others streaked with oil on their flanks and with engines sounding rough ... The drivers and crews all hoping that after this much effort, the cars could keep going until 4 p.m. In the Ford pits the mechanics who had cars running moved slowly; the night had taken its toll and there was little left to do except fill them up with gas and oil, check the tires and wait ... The last six hours seemed like an eternity, and as the clock traveled past noon, the question of who was going to be the winner was discussed behind the pits. Miles was there, leaning up against the wall and waiting for his turn at the wheel. He smiled when someone asked him about it. It was a typical Miles answer.

"I work for the Ford Motor Company," he said, "and they pay me so much a month to do what they want. If they want me to win the race, why I'll do it ... and if they want me to jump in the lake, why I guess I'll have to do that too." Then he laughed again. Miles and Hulme were in the lead at this stage, a lap ahead of McLaren and Amon, and the lean Englishman assumed he would stay there. A short time later, he was told otherwise.

With approximately two hours left and the cars running 1-2-3, Beebe, Frey, Passino, Cowley and Shelby examined the possibilities for the finish. The Bucknum-Hutcherson car presented no problem, as it was a dozen laps behind. But the car driven by Miles and Hulme, and that shared by McLaren and Amon, were running almost in each other's tire tracks. The Ford officials were interested in their car winning, not in any special pair of drivers. The cars were the primary thing, and they came before any other considerations. There were three choices:

Let them race, with the winner determined in that manner.

Predetermine the winner and instruct the drivers accordingly.

Arrange a tie.

The first alternative was thrown out immediately. At this point, while the cars were still droning their way around the circuit, Reiber came up with a message: "Leo, the officials say if you want to do it, they can arrange a tie and they will cooperate with you."

This bit of largesse from a group of stewards who had been the losers in Thursday night's Thompson incident was surprising, but it was also welcome. There had never been a dead heat in the history of the race, and to someone interested in publicity it was the ideal solution. Miles and McLaren, both of whom were getting ready to drive the final trick, were called over and informed of the decision.

Neither liked it. Both wanted to race, but Beebe would have none of that. With a multimillion-dollar program on the brink of success, he would not take a chance on one of them going off the road in the rain, or on one of them blowing an already tired engine. They were given the procedure. they got in the cars and took off. Soon after they departed, Reiber came back.

"Leo, the officials *now* say a tie isn't possible." He went on to explain that because of the difference in starting positions, if both cars crossed the line together one would have actually covered a greater distance and would thus be the winner. Miles' car had been the second fastest in practice, McLaren's fourth. At the start they had been perhaps 20 feet apart, and now that would make the difference. The real winner, it seemed, would be Gallic logic. *Noblesse oblige,* although a French expression, seemed to be unknown in the western marches of the country.

Reiber's news came as a shock. "Oh my God, that's not what we wanted at all," Beebe said. "Is there any basis for appealing that?" There was none, and so there was more talk, and an incident that occurred several hours earlier played an important part. During the night Beebe had censured both Miles and Gurney for racing for the lead after all the Ferraris had dropped out, They also had trouble of this type with Miles at Sebring and now, at Le Mans, Beebe bad threatened to pull him out of the car if the intramural dicing continued. With one team or the other to be favored, these actions were to weigh against Miles and Hulme, as both McLaren and Amon had run strictly to team orders. Beebe's description of his thought process:

"We could let them go as instructed, or we could call them back and reinstruct them. If we did this, we could tell them to go ahead and race—obviously not a good choice—to let Miles win, or to let McLaren win. If you let Miles win, you were giving it to a guy who had given you a hard time. If you let McLaren win, you would take it away from a guy who had earned it over the years. From a public relations standpoint, if McLaren won it might look like we didn't know what we were doing. Someone might construe we had an anti-Miles attitude. On the other hand, if we let Miles win we might be thought of, by the foreign press, as being predisposed toward having an American driver up front. Anyone can question the judgment, but no one can say it was not a consciously arrived-at decision—and on grounds we considered valid and just. To have Ken win would have been more expedient and more popular. But the extent to which McLaren and Amon had played exactly according to our rules militated against Miles. The result was not necessarily even popular with me."

Two years later Passino was more philosophical about it. "If we had realized the whole world would take us on over it," he said, "we probably would have let Miles win."

But that was later. When the final decision was made Miles and McLaren were rolling along, each still thinking there would be a tie, both of them—but especially Miles, who had led for much of the race—in a bitter, frustrated state as the clock ticked slowly onward. Neither knew a dead heat was an impossibility, that McLaren and Amon would be the winners.

With two laps to go before 4 p.m. Miles slowed and McLaren and Hutcherson pulled up behind him, 100 or so yards away, and the rumbling caravan rolled past the pits and disappeared from view around the right-hand bend. The hands of the

Bruce McLaren waits for adjustments on the J-Car during the Le Mans practice session of 1966. The car was eventually succeeded by the Mark IV.

Ready to go: The Mark II Fords at Le Mans in 1966. The car in the foreground was shared by Miles and Denis Hulme, and the second one—the winner—was driven by Bruce McLaren and Chris Amon.

Watchful eye: Henry Ford II at Le Mans, 1966. (Inset) With Leo Beebe, who threatened to withdraw the cars over the Thompson incident.

*(Top) McLaren swirls through the wet on one of the closing laps. (Inset) The agony
of waiting for the checkered flag. From left, Roy Lunn (sunglasses), Ray Geddes,
Don Frey (raincoat), Beebe (hands in pockets), engineer Joe Macura (striped sweater),
John Cowley and Jacque Passino. (Below) McLaren finishes first as Miles backs off.
Dick Hutcherson is right behind on the track but is actually 12 laps in arrears.*

*(Bottom) McLaren (left) Henry Ford and Amon with champagne on the winner's
stand, while a disconsolate Miles offers a toast with a more mundane beverage (top).
Hulme, perhaps still not realizing what has happened (inset), waves to the
crowd after the finish of the record-breaking race.*

clock reached 4 p.m, and the race director raised his flag at the finish line as the first of the arrivals appeared from behind White House ... A few of the also-rans came across and then the three Fords showed up in the distance, with McLaren in the black car alongside Miles in the powder blue one, with Hutcherson a length or two behind.

As they came within a few yards of the finish line Miles suddenly backed off and McLaren went across a length ahead while Jacques Loste flashed the big checker in front of them and took his hat off in the traditional Le Mans gesture that greets the winner.

McLaren and Amon, or Miles and Hulme—or even Bucknum and Hutcherson; it didn't make any difference which car won the race. Three Fords had outclassed the finest field in the world in the most famous event of all, and had done it at record speeds. It was the greatest triumph in the 65-year racing history of the Ford Motor Company, and when they played the "Star-Spangled Banner" a few minutes later, with the rain falling gently on the hundreds of thousands of spectators, the small group of Americans at the Ford pits stood just a little straighter. Phil Remington was one of them, Bill Stroppe was another. It was a long way from the dry lakes of the Mojave, where they took their first Model Ts and flathead V8s. Muroc was three decades and 7,000 miles removed. It didn't seem that far.

The average speed of the first two cars was 125.4 mph, about four miles up on the previous record, and the two leaders covered 3,009 miles despite running conservative lap times for the last half of the race. The myth of Ferrari invincibility had been settled for good, and about the only one not happy with the result was Miles, who felt he should have won: His backing off just before the finish line was his form of protest against the management decision. If he couldn't be the first man to win at Daytona, Sebring and Le Mans in the same year, he didn't want what he thought would be a dead heat with someone else.

Almost lost in the shuffle that accompanied the Le Mans victory was the fact Ford had won the manufacturer's championship. With the best four results to be counted, Ford had three firsts and a second in the only races the company entered. Ferrari was close behind, thanks primarily to having picked up first-place points in races Ford had not attended (at the Targa Florio, for example, a Ferrari that finished 17th was credited with 10 points for being the first large-displacement prototype). Even the GT40s, all of which had again failed to finish at Le Mans, won the "Sports 50" over 2.0-liter title for Ford.

Three years earlier Ford had come to Le Mans beset by inexperience and confusion. This time the team went home with almost literally no more fields to conquer. It was a remarkable episode, not only in the history of auto racing and Ford, but for American industry as a whole. No other firm, not counting the isolated exception to the rule, had ever successfully challenged the Europeans at their own game; no other firm had ever, in so short a period, achieved dominance in an area almost totally foreign to it at the outset.

33

ON AGAIN, OFF AGAIN

THE MOST FRUSTRATING THING about Bill France, if you were a performance man from Detroit, was that he usually won the arguments. Even if you exercised the option of pulling your cars out and beat him for the moment, you knew, and so did the man in Daytona—you would be back.

From its humble beginnings, France had built NASCAR into an empire, and throughout the entire process he was the unquestioned leader. He built tracks of a size and scope unheard of previously, he provided healthy purses and a governing body, and he raised the stature and financial condition of the participants to respectable levels. There is a theory held by many students of political science which says the best form of government is a benevolent dictatorship, and they have numerous men scattered throughout history to prove their point. In automobile racing France was one of these. He was the boss, he was a brilliant negotiator, and in his wheelings and dealings with the manufacturers he was not hampered by having to check with anyone else before he made a decision (USAC, on the other hand, was run by a *junta* of promoters, car owners and drivers, each with different vested interests, and there was usually disagreement on everything except the time of day). Anything France did was unilateral; anything the manufacturers did had to be discussed, rediscussed and checked with at least two persons other than the negotiator. France was in a marvelous position: He knew his subject better than anyone else, and he was also in a seller's market, as the manufacturers wanted what he had to offer. The trouble was they all wanted to win.

This being an impossibility, Big Bill was left with the task of playing one off against the other, and every time a new rule was made it became the subject of hours of discussion and argument, for the basic specifications would usually be favorable to one automaker and would penalize another. The fact that one car, in showroom stock condition, was slightly heavier than another, or that a third car (like the rest with an engine designed to give good service at 60 mph) performed better at 150, while of no real importance to the average customer, became vital when the racers were involved. If your car wasn't as quick as the others, the next step was to build a few special parts to make it as quick—or quicker. If a private individual did this, the non-stock parts he installed would get him disqualified. When a factory did it, they simply stamped a number on each piece and gave the word "stock" a new connotation. The task of keeping a balance of power required the agility of a ballet dancer, and to compound the problem there was always the empty seat at the table—the one reserved for General Motors.

The spectators who made stock car racing prosperous wanted to see all brands of automobiles competing. France and NASCAR knew Ford and Chrysler were interested, but they also knew Chevy, Pontiac, Oldsmobile and the rest of GM's divisions were not, at least not officially, and therefore anyone who drove one of these was doing it on his own. Since stock car racing was long past the point where an independent could run with a reasonable hope of success, the privately entered Chevys and Pontiacs did not stand a chance. They were usually in the spear-carrier category, and this brought about a collection of symptoms known as the GM Syndrome.

More than anything else, after a 1964 season without Pontiac and Chevrolet, France wanted to get General Motors products back into NASCAR racing. To aid in achieving this, if it were at all possible, NASCAR's 1965 rules were bound to be such that GM would have an open invitation to return. It was only good business practice. Before the 1965 rules were announced, both Ford and Chrysler tried to have their say about them. The genealogy of the 1965 rules, or for that matter all NASCAR stock car regulations since 1964, starts with Ford's February, 1964, attempt to get its overhead camshaft engine accepted. This venture, though unsuccessful, was a warning to Chrysler that such an engine existed, and that Ford was fully prepared to go to war on an all-out scale should it be allowed. Accordingly, shortly after the Atlanta "500" in the spring of that year, NASCAR was in receipt of a letter from Chrysler requesting information on the 1965 specifications. It was evident to France that Chrysler was prepared to play the same all-out game, and with this much advance notice on the minimum number of engines and cars required, both Dodge and Plymouth would have enough time to build a special 1965 model that would be "stock"—and would be unbeatable.

France decided the best way to determine the rules for 1965 was to ask the manufacturers themselves. During the summer of 1964, while the Fords, Dodges and Plymouths were beating each others' brains out to the delight of the fans, both Ford and the Chrysler Corporation were asked to make suggestions. Beebe, by now the head of special vehicles, told France that Ford would not compete in 1965 if the rules stayed the same. Although his cars were winning the majority of the races, Beebe knew what would happen when the Chrysler entries got their problems solved, as they had an obvious horsepower superiority. The acceptable alternatives were either an OK for the overhead cam engine, or a return to a lower-cost engine which more nearly resembled what was sold to the public. Ford favored the latter route. Chrysler said it would like the 1965 rules to remain as they were in 1964, which meant France wasn't any better off than when he started. When officials of both companies arrived at Daytona for the Firecracker "400" July 4, France tried again, and he still couldn't get them together. Then came the race, and the power of the Hemi was evident as both Dodge and Plymouth ran away from Ford and Mercury. Worried that this high-speed display of muscle might sway NASCAR toward a "stock-stock" rule for 1965, before he flew home Chrysler Vice President Bob Anderson let word drop that if Ford's overhead cam engine was approved, that would be the end of it for his company: They would withdraw. Anderson's remarks guaranteed NASCAR would not announce anything for 1965 until after the last major race of 1964 (Charlotte, in mid-October). In this manner France would insure that neither manufacturer, in a fit of pique, would pull its cars out before the season ended.

In the meantime attempts continued to write the rules so they were acceptable to both parties. Late in July France met in Detroit with Frey and Anderson. They talked for three hours and neither side would give in, Frey insisting if the Chrysler Hemi was still allowed Ford would have to use the overhead cam, and Anderson saying if Ford did this Chrysler would do the same—except its version would have *double* overhead cams. Both admitted these engines would not be produced in great numbers, Anderson saying Chrysler would probably build no more than a dozen. In August France met with Iacocca, then still the Ford Division general manager, and the same old problems were discussed. Iacocca told him if NASCAR went the production-line route, Ford would race. Iacocca also revealed one more item not known by France: Plymouth would have a full-size car in its 1965 model line. NASCAR's previous basis for determining minimum vehicle size had been the wheel-base of the largest Plymouth, which in recent years had been 116 inches. With the advent of the racing Hemi, Plymouth's smaller size (the Ford Galaxies had a 119-inch wheelbase) gave it an aerodynamic advantage at high speeds, and gave Ford an excuse for wanting to run its smaller Fairlane even though it preferred, from a sales-appeal standpoint, to race the full-size Galaxie. Now, with the information on the longer wheelbase for the upcoming Plymouth Fury, the situation would change. France went back to Daytona and started to prepare the rules.

But the games were still being played. In September, Bob Rodger, the Chrysler Corporation executive in charge of the racing program, invited France to a missile launch at Cape Kennedy, and while he was there, asked if NASCAR would permit overhead cams in 1965. France said no, and then Rodger excused himself. In a few minutes he was back after having telephoned Detroit. "You just saved the Chrysler Corporation a million dollars," Rodger said. "I just canceled work on the double overhead cam engine."

The information on the overhead cam rejection wasn't the only item leaked to Detroit that fall. News of possible changes in wheelbase regulations for the faster tracks also traveled north, and in late September Anderson phoned France to tell him if NASCAR insisted the Herm be installed in the Furys and Dodge 880s and not in the smaller Belvederes and Dodge Coronets, Chrysler would not be at Daytona in 1965. Lynn Townsend, (then Chrysler's president) had asked him to convey the message, Anderson added. So France knew what the situation would be when the rules were made public.

France's one remaining problem was USAC. The ideal situation, from the viewpoint of the sanctioning organizations, was to have the same rules apply to cars that ran in both leagues. For one thing it would make car preparation easier for the factories (such groups as Holman-Moody and Chrysler's Ray Nichels built vehicles that raced in both). For another it would make driver interchange for major races easier, as the visiting firemen could then bring their own equipment. For a while it seemed as if USAC was prepared to go along with NASCAR, and so on October 19 France announced his rules.

They said, basically, that the limit of engine displacement remained at 428 cubic inches, that so-called "non-production" designs as the Chrysler Hemi and Ford's high-rise intake manifold were banned, and that the minimum allowable wheelbase on the four super-speedways would now be 119 inches instead of the previous 116. The 116-inch wheelbase cars would be legal on all other oval tracks and on road circuits, and there would also be a weight limit imposed, although just how much was not clear at the moment.

The protests from Chrysler, the praise from Ford, and the criticism from USAC were almost instantaneous. "Racing has always prided itself on being progressive," Anderson said, "and here we are now, backing up." At Ford, Beebe started his remarks with "NASCAR is to be congratulated for its efforts to speed progress...." It was remarkable how the connotation of the word progress changed as it moved from the east side of Detroit to the west. In Indianapolis, USAC competition director Henry Banks stated his 1965 rules would be the same as those of 1964, and that "We feel changing specifications without adequate prior notice works a hardship on our personnel and on the manufacturers." General Motors said nothing, and the lines were drawn: Ford with NASCAR, Chrysler with USAC. The Southern promoters could see the crowds dwindling and they screamed, but France held firm—even when on October 28 Chrysler's Ron Householder gave the official ultimatum: "Accordingly, unless the NASCAR rules for 1965 are modified or suspended for a minimum of 12 months to permit an orderly transition to new equipment, we have no alternative but to withdraw...."

France answered "If the Chrysler Corporation feels that its standard 426-cubic-inch automobiles are not competitive with comparable size cars of other American makes then I would be the last to criticize Chrysler on its withdrawal from NASCAR racing." As an alternative to the Plymouths and Dodges, he hoped to offer the fans something new from General Motors. It would not be equipment with direct factory sponsorship, France knew, but he also knew both Oldsmobile and Chevrolet had new engines, and he hoped they would at least be competitive on the smaller tracks. Oldsmobile's power plant was a 425-incher which turned out to be a bust where racing was concerned. Chevy's new one was something else. To be introduced as part of the 1965½-year package scheduled for a February debut, the engine was a 396-inch version of the 427 "Porcupine" which propelled Junior Johnson to the high speeds of 1963. Even without factory help it was bound to be a good thing, and as an aid to private entrants, the rules allowed engines of less than 428 cubic inches to be brought up to that figure by boring, stroking or both.

Then everyone proceeded to get ready. Ford had Lorenzen, Johns and former IMCA champ Dick Hutcherson running for Holman-Moody; Panch was again with the Wood brothers, Jarrett was still with Bondy Long, and Johnson was running his own car with Herb Nab as chief mechanic. Nab, who had taken care of Lorenzen's vehicle since the latter joined Holman-Moody, left Freddie in the late fall, as did Wayne Mills, the other mechanic who had been so vital to Lorenzen's success. Mills stayed with Holman-Moody in another position and Jack Sullivan, Lorenzen's schoolboy buddy from Chicago and Roberts' crew chief in 1964, took over the care and feeding of the famous number 28. The Lincoln-Mercury Division, no longer in stock car racing, was to be represented in a lefthanded manner by Moore, making the best of his 1964 equipment with Dieringer and Earl Balmer as drivers. In USAC Ford had nothing. If that circuit was to allow Hemis, it would get no cooperation from Dearborn.

The talking stopped just long enough for the season opener at Riverside, which Gurney won for the third straight time, again while driving for the Wood brothers. Then, at Daytona in February, the rules were again the prime topic of discussion. This time it was France who took the initiative, announcing the 1966 regulations almost a full year in advance so no one could say they didn't have enough notice. His newest rules were almost as complicated as the mumbo-jumbo that governs international sports car competition, and divided stock car racing into three categories:

Class I was for cars with a minimum wheelbase of 119 inches, with a maximum engine displacement of 430 cubic inches (increased from 428 to allow for "clean-up" reboring), and with a minimum weight of 4,000 pounds with gas, oil and water. These "full-size" cars would be the only ones permitted to run on the big speedways at Daytona, Atlanta, Charlotte and Darlington.

Class II was for cars with a wheelbase of from 115–119 inches, with a minimum weight of 3,500 pounds and a maximum displacement of 430 cubic inches. For every cubic inch over 405, however, the minimum weight would go up by 20 pounds. These cars could run anywhere but on the big tracks.

Class III was for compacts and sporty cars such as the Mustang, with a wheelbase of less than 115 inches, a minimum weight of 2,500 pounds and a maximum engine displacement of 335 cubic inches. For every cubic inch over 305, however, there would be a weight penalty of 20 pounds.

While the various companies were attempting to figure this out, the cars raced and the results were much as they were at Riverside, and as they were to be for the remainder of the season: Fords led the pack, with no one able to give them any real competition except the Mercurys when they happened to be running right. At Daytona, where the race was shortened to 332 miles by rain, Lorenzen came home the winner with Dieringer second after Panch had clipped Lorenzen while trying to pass and spun out on the last full-speed lap before the final caution flag. Lorenzen thus became the first driver in NASCAR history to win a major race on each of the four big tracks in the Southeast. It had been a great race, with Lorenzen, Panch, Dieringer, Johns, Balmer and Jarrett dueling right to the end—a better race, in fact, than the year before when Petty ran away from the pack. But the crowd wanted to see the different makes, and the all-Ford result did not satisfy them. Petty was there, but as a spectator; he had been spending the evenings prior to the "500" driving a Plymouth drag car at nearby Spruce Creek. The car was named "Outlawed."

With the new "medium-rise" intake manifold letting the engines produce as much power as the now-illegal high-risers they had copied from Chevrolet in 1963, it was merely a question of which Ford would win. As the season moved through April (when Panch, with relief from Foyt, won the Atlanta "500") and May (when Johnson took the Rebel "300"), the crowds began to shrink in size as the prospect of watching a Ford procession became less and less appealing. Not surprisingly, the prospect of winning every race became tasteless to Ford. In order to make victory meaningful, you have to beat somebody. But there was no one else around.

By the time of the Rebel "300" at Darlington, you could have fired a shotgun at the stands on the backstretch without fear of hitting anyone. A few weeks later at Charlotte (for the World "600," which went to Lorenzen) the same crowd conditions prevailed, and the promoters pleaded with France. In Dearborn and at the Charlotte offices of Holman-Moody, related problems were arising. All the Ford drivers, for one thing, wanted to race among themselves, and maintaining some semblance of discipline was difficult. The team would have been the laughing stock of the Southeast if it were beaten by a private entry, and for this reason, almost as much effort as if Chrysler were competing had to be put into every event. The number of races in which Ford was participating also increased. Although most of the cars still ran in only the top 17 events, Jarrett and Hutcherson entered all of them and Johnson ran in more than half as part of a tacit agreement to give smaller promoters help at the gate.

When the break finally came, it arrived in an unusual manner—with help from USAC. The Midwest-oriented club, which had vacillated over the rules before deciding to allow the Hemis, did not start its stock car season until the Yankee "300" the first week in May. When that race was staged USAC realized Beebe meant what he said when he refused to permit any of the Fords (or their star drivers) to participate. Soon after the race a delegation from USAC was in Dearborn to meet with Beebe; shortly after that, in June, USAC and NASCAR were huddling in an attempt to find rules acceptable to both. Considering the state of near-rebellion in which their promoters were at the time, it didn't take them long to reach an agreement. After the Dixie "400" at Atlanta (won by Panch, with relief from Foyt), the news was made public:

Effective immediately, the Hemi would be permitted on NASCAR tracks of over one mile in length—for the remainder of the 1965 season—in Plymouth Furys, Dodge 880s and Polaras. All 1964 Dodges (there were no full-size Plymouths that year) competing on the big tracks would be restricted to the wedge-shaped combustion chamber engine.

The Hemi would also be permitted in Plymouth Belvedere and Dodge Coronet bodies (the medium-size ones) on all USAC tracks, on all NASCAR tracks of one mile or less and on all road circuits.

A minimum weight rule of 9.36 pounds per cubic inch would be applied, meaning approximately 4,000 pounds (ready to run, with gas, oil and water) for a car with a 427-inch engine.

Since both France and Banks knew Chrysler had in recent years not built a full-size car with a hemispherical combustion chamber engine, both knew it was doubtful Chrysler would go to the trouble of building one now—thus leaving the big tracks and the big publicity to Ford, which had stuck by France through this last hassle. On the smaller tracks, France reasoned, he could give the Plymouths and the Dodges a chance without too much complaint from Ford. Since he knew the Chrysler Corporation's drivers were anxious to compete, he was reasonably sure he'd get them back. Up north, USAC was merely thankful it had Ford participation again.

Chrysler reacted in a predictable manner. The corporation rejected the idea of bastardizing a Fury with a racing engine for the few big-track events, but announced it would participate in the short-track proceedings. With the Firecracker "400" coming up at Daytona July 4, there were still no first-rate Dodges or Plymouths in the field, and Ford appeared to have a lock on it before the green flag ever dropped. But once the event got running, everything happened to the Fords. The first major setback was on the 100th of the 160 laps when Cale Yarborough, a recent replacement for Johns, blew his engine while leading. The oil he lost caused Dieringer, Hutcherson and Jarrett to crash, and there were three Fords and a Mercury on the sidelines. Lorenzen, who had gone out early, was now driving Panch's car in relief. On lap 136 a head gasket failed and he was forced out again, leaving only Foyt, several laps ahead of a field of independents. Foyt was cruising along while the Ford people were busy crossing their fingers when suddenly, with 15 laps to go, he came sailing into the pits. Chief mechanic Paul Norris rushed to the car and found the irrepressible Foyt laughing at him.

"Y'all want me for something?" Foyt asked.

Then he laughed again and drove away, leaving the crew with near heart failure and the field far behind.

As July wore on and the Pettys, Cotton Owens and the other Chrysler teams still hadn't made their appearance, the crowds stayed small and France needed another headliner to shore up his sagging circuit. At the end of the month he found one in Curtis Turner.

Whether or not France forgave Turner out of the goodness of his heart is a moot point. But one thing is clear: At the time he brought the Southland's stock car idol back to NASCAR, the circuit certainly needed him. At the time of his surprise reinstatement Turner was being billed as the star of an infant racing group trying to get going in the Southeast. It folded when Turner left. At the same time the Pettys came back and won their first race, a 200-miler before a record crowd at Nashville, Tenn. (breaking a streak of 34 Ford wins), and France's domain looked considerably healthier. By the time of the Southern "500" on Labor Day, the situation was again a rosy one for the promoters: Petty had won two races and been second in three, Pearson's Dodge had won once, and now their old hero, Turner, was racing again— even if he was in a Plymouth and not one of his customary Fords. Curtis, looking considerably older and heftier than in his salad days, started his comeback August 14 at Spartanburg, S.C., in a Petty-owned car and crashed. He did not figure to be much of a threat at Darlington and qualified well back in the field, but when the announcer was introducing the drivers before the race, the fans almost blew the roof off the grandstand with their enthusiastic welcome. Jarrett won the race, and Ford got the message. By the next big one, at Martinsville toward the end of the month, Turner was behind the wheel of a Wood Brothers Ford.

Curtis didn't do well at Martinsville, going out of the race on the 45th lap when his car tangled with one driven by Bobby Isaac, and he was made to realize it had been a long time since his salad days. When he climbed out of his car, Turner walked over to Isaac and asked the youngster if he had wrecked him on purpose.

Isaac was startled. "Why should I wreck you? This is the first time I've ever seen you!"

There wasn't much Turner could say.

At North Wilkesboro a week later he ran fifth behind three Fords and Pearson's Dodge, and in the National "400" at Charlotte in mid-October he placed third. This one went to Lorenzen after a heated duel with Foyt which saw the Indianapolis hero spin out five laps from the finish when an attempt to pass Lorenzen on the high side didn't work. The last big race of the season was on the new track at Rockingham, N.C., a one-mile banked oval that was the fastest course of its size in the nation and curiously enough, the only one-mile track in NASCAR. The race was for 500 miles and it promised to be tough, as it was the only major event of the year in which the full strength of Ford would be meeting Petty, Pearson and the rest of the Chrysler drivers (one-mile tracks were the largest for which the Hemis in the small chassis were eligible). Almost predictably Petty was the fastest qualifier, and as the race reached its middle stages he took the lead and looked as if he would stay there. He did until the 359th mile, when a tire blew and put the Plymouth into the wall. Petty was forced to pit, and ensuing distributor trouble finally forced the car out while Turner moved into the lead. Curtis was not in the best of shape; he had cracked a rib the day before and had gone back to Charlotte, gotten it taped, and returned to the scene. Now, with the race almost three-quarters over, he was beginning to tire and as he slowed slightly Cale Yarborough came from behind to challenge. For almost 50 miles Yarborough harried Turner, trying to pass him first on the high side, then on the low, knowing full well that if he ever got by the race was his. But Turner, relying on two decades of experience, wouldn't let the youngster pass. Every time Yarborough made a move, Pops was there to stop him. Finally Yarborough had to duck into the pits for fuel, and when it came Turner's time to pit, the Wood Brothers got him out faster. At the finish it was Turner by 11 seconds. Curtis was home again, the season was over.

The results of 1965, whether in NASCAR or USAC, were only incidental to the behind-the-scenes negotiations that continued even after the mid-season truce. Ford knew it was little more than a temporary cease-fire, and knew that when 1966 arrived it would be even worse off than it was at the start of 1964. Chrysler's Hemi, of which 493 were built in 1964 and a further 207 in 1965, would now be in production on a much greater scale, and would be available in both the Plymouth Belvedere and the Dodge Coronet. (Final 1966 totals were 1,826 for Plymouth and 1,800 for Dodge—and like all those built before, they were only delivered with two four-barrel carburetors, making Chrysler's single four-barrel for racing the most non-stock item on the circuit.) That meant both cars would be acceptable not only for races on NASCAR's shorter tracks, where they could run at 426 inches and 3,990 pounds, but on the four big speedways as well (where their engine size would be 404 inches and the minimum weight 3,780). In the past Ford had beaten the Hemi through superior preparation and durability, but development work, plus an expected improvement in the teams that used it, now gave Chrysler an edge.

By early July of 1965 Ford had told France it intended to use the single overhead cam engine in 1966. Realizing that this time his discussions had better be on a higher level, France sat down with Patterson, Iacocca, Frey and Innes. Iacocca told him Ford didn't think much of full-size cars competing against intermediates, and he was in favor of running the full-size models only; these were the sales leaders. This led to a further impasse, and when NASCAR announced its rules in the fall of 1965 the medium-size cars were listed as eligible for the big tracks, just as France had promised. Additionally, Section 20, Rule 1 D, relating to engine eligibility, stated "No overhead cam engines permitted unless approved by NASCAR. Volume production engines only (no limited production engines) and the volume production classification will be determined by spot checks of the various assembly lines when such checks are deemed necessary."

That should have been it as far as the overhead cam engine was concerned, but Ford was determined to run one and thought it saw a loophole in the rules, which did not specify, in numbers, just what volume production meant. At the company's motorsports banquet in Dearborn December 13, Frey stated Ford's stock car racing engine for 1966 would be the single overhead cam. He said it in a matter-of-fact manner, as if the wrangling of the past few months had never occurred and as if it were a *fait accompli*. From his delivery, a good many newspapermen in the audience thought it was—until they questioned France, who was also there. Although he was genuinely upset at someone's attempting to bluff him in this manner, France preserved his equanimity and would say only that "We have to be satisfied that the engine is in production, is generally available and meets our cost factors." At this stage Ford was planning to build 500 of the engines, which had recently shown 654 horsepower on the dynamometer, and to sell them for a price in the neighborhood of $3,000.

Four days later both NASCAR and USAC had something more definite to say about the engine, and the answer was no. It wasn't a production engine, they said, and was also outside the spirit of the rules. When this news reached Beebe, he announced the withdrawal of the Ford teams from the 500-mile race at Riverside in January and from the Daytona "500" in February, using the excuse that because of the refusal Ford wouldn't have time to adequately prepare cars for the early season races. Regardless of the ethics of the situation, it was a smart move: Ford stood a good chance of winning at Riverside, but practically none of finishing first at Daytona, where horsepower was the big thing. Since the cars couldn't very well run Riverside and not Daytona, they would pull out of both and wait until the lower-speed tracks used during the rest of the season came into play. On those, preparation and handling counted almost as much as power. Additionally, the temporary withdrawal would help put pressure on France through his promoters, who were fearful of having two poor seasons in a row.

Five days later signals were off. France needed Ford and Ford needed NASCAR, so France and Beebe sat down in Chicago. The result of their meeting was an agreement by which Ford consented to participate in the major races on the NASCAR circuit during the 1966 season, in exchange for consideration by both NASCAR and USAC when Ford felt it had fulfilled the requirements for production status of the new engine. France then checked with USAC to make sure it was in agreement, and on Christmas Day (perhaps as a present for all those drivers who were thinking they might be out of jobs) the announcement of the latest compromise was made from Daytona.

At Riverside the outlook for Ford was a rose-colored one: Gurney was back with the Wood Brothers again, and his prowess in a stock car on the California road course was such that he had most of the field psyched before the race started. During practice, as Dan was busy lowering the lap record, Junior Johnson watched glumly as Gurney sped past. Junior had retired at the close of the 1965 season and was now on hand as a car owner, running one vehicle for Foyt and another for Bobby Isaac. "We got about as much business bein' here as a one-legged man in an ass-kickin' contest," Junior said, and he was right. Five hours and five minutes after the green flag dropped, the first man home under the checkered one was Gurney, the only

(Top) Quick stop—Dick Hutcherson in the pits during the 1965 running of the Firecracker "400" at Daytona. (Middle) Dan Gurney on his way to victory at Riverside, 1965. (Bottom) Sometimes it can get rough—a crash at Daytona during preliminaries to the 500-miler of 1965.

*Lorenzen in action during 1965: (Top) In close quarters during the Southern "500"
at Darlington. (Middle) Running with a bit more room in the same race.
(Bottom) Ducking under Richard Petty at Bristol, Tenn.*

driver ever to win a major NASCAR event four consecutive times. It was according to the old formula: Pearson had just nipped Dan for the pole, and Pearson, Gurney and Turner took turns leading through the early stages of the race. But eventually the combination of Gurney's smooth, equipment-sparing style and the Wood brothers' pitwork made itself felt. Dan led the last 102 of the 185 laps, and at the finish Pearson was the only other man to complete the full distance.

At Daytona the first stock car to be towed through the gates of the giant speedway, and towed through the day after the Continental, was Petty's blue Plymouth. One of the track staff asked Lee what he was doing there so early in the month and Petty the Elder snorted. "We're a year behind already," he said. Almost from the moment Lee's son took the car out onto the broad expanse of the track, it was apparent the layoff had done little to impair his style. The following Sunday, when everyone tried for the two pole positions, Richard was the fastest with a record 175.165 mph, and the only car of any make that could even stay close was Hutcherson's Ford, which posted a 174.317 mph. Everyone else was either hoping to go faster once adjustments were made, or never had the speed in the first place. Oddly, the rest of the nine-car team from Chrysler (four Plymouths, five Dodges) was having trouble. Somehow the Pettys had found something in their engines the rest had not. Many of them called home—or Detroit—for new powerplants, Ford observers assumed it was something in Chrysler's new intake manifold, another one of a long series of so-called "production" goodies which somehow or other only showed up on race cars, and were impossible to find anywhere else except in the parts catalog. Chrysler's new one was just beautiful, being in effect a monster plenum chamber so rigged for high speed running that it was actually dangerous to start. After a few miniature explosions in the garage area, NASCAR supervisory personnel told Dodge and Plymouth mechanics not to start their engines unless the hoods were down. The Dodges had other troubles, too: The slippery new Charger fastback model, which should have been the quickest thing in the ballpark needed a sports car-type spoiler for the rear, and such an item was illegal. The Dodge speeds, therefore, were limited by the amount of good sense possessed by the drivers.

In the Ford camp, where Beebe and Passino were viewing the situation with an outlook that grew more glum by the hour (Beebe: "It'll take an act of God."), they tried to get even. The fact the various Ford mechanics knew they were coming in with a power shortage had led to considerable pre-practice innovation when it came to setting up the chassis, and many of the Fords were dropped so low in front that the bumpers were covering up half of the lower headlights. When the mechanics got a look at the Chrysler intake manifold and realized NASCAR was going to allow it, the contest to rig the cars for more speed became an affair in which few holds were barred; NASCAR chief inspector Norris Friel spent most of the practice period ordering crews to get rid of their latest modifications. When you are only number two you have to try harder, and in the desperate search for another mile an hour several crews went home to pick up a new car. Foyt, who by this time was barely speaking to Johnson, his car owner of record, went through three of them, finally winding up with the vehicle Jack Bowsher drove to victory in the 250-mile ARCA race that was one of the month's opening events. Bowsher had run his car in practice at 174 mph (and won at 164), but at one stage in his experimenting with various chassis setups Foyt had the car all the way down to 170.

By race time everyone had found a mile or two, Petty and Hutcherson had been timed unofficially at 177, and there were eight Fords ready for a shot at the blue Plymouth (Lorenzen, Turner, Yarborough, Jarrett, Isaac, Panch, Hutcherson and Foyt). When the flag dropped, and 90,000 fans saw the 44-car field thunder into the first turn, there were 43 of them that might just as well have stayed home. From the start it was all Petty, and the only reason anyone else could make it close was that the Pettys had chosen the wrong tire compound. At the 20-lap mark Richard stopped for a complete change and after 40 laps he stopped again for four more tires. This time his crew had been able to obtain the proper rubber and Petty started carving his way past the others, the only car able to stay with him being Goldsmith's similar Plymouth. Ironically, although the Fords had no tire trouble several of the faster ones were put out by a Plymouth that did. Jim Hurtubise, who was running on the same compound Petty had at the start, was throwing chunks of rubber from his rear wheels, pieces that had the velocity of a bullet. Through a coincidence, Hutcherson was behind him on the 38th lap, Panch was behind him on his 119th lap and Turner was directly astern on lap 122. All three had their windshields shattered. It probably wouldn't have made any difference. Petty worked his way back up to the head of the pack shortly after the halfway mark, and when Goldsmith was sidelined with driveshaft troubles the blue Plymouth had things its own way. Petty led from lap 113 through lap 198, when rain stopped it five miles short of the scheduled distance. He averaged 160.627 mph with a fastest lap at 176.8, and although Yarborough had driven a great race to finish second, he never stood a chance of catching the leader.

Petty missed the 500-mile race at Rockingham two weeks later. He was recuperating from minor surgery on a finger damaged, of all things, in a touch football game. But a Plymouth still won it, this time driven by Goldsmith, who edged Yarborough by less than four seconds in a race that could just as easily have been won by a Ford. But it wasn't, and that made it two in a row for the opposition. At Bristol the next weekend Hutcherson finished in front in the 250-miler to give Ford some satisfaction, but the goings-on at the tracks received scant attention. The fight to use the single overhead camshaft engine was the big thing, and within a week after the Daytona defeat Ford announced the SOHC was available to all. The cost of it, in a street machine ordered as an option, was to be $1,963 (the Hemi available to the public cost about $900), and the dealers were duly informed of this. "The price sort of exceeds the spirit of the deal," was all France would say, and he also didn't say much two weeks later in Dearborn, when he watched what passed for a production line for the new engine.

France was delaying the decision as long as he could to keep Ford's team running, and at the same time Ford was trying to get a decision as soon as possible. Even after an item was declared eligible, there was a 90-day waiting period before the new equipment could run in competition. If NASCAR and USAC approved the engine by April 4, it could run in Daytona's Firecracker "400" July 4, and the high-speed Florida track was the place it was needed most. If it wasn't OK'd by then there wouldn't be much point—from Ford's view—in admitting it. On the other tracks they still stood a decent chance.

When the Atlanta "500" was held March 27 there was still no decision, as France was waiting to take the matter up at the ACCUS meeting April 1 in New York. ACCUS (Automobile Competitions Committee of the United States) was ostensibly the governing group for motor sports in the United States, an organization to which NASCAR, USAC, the SCCA and the National Hot Rod Association belonged. A decision announced under the banner of ACCUS, the United States representative to the international ruling body of racing, would carry more weight than anything done by either NASCAR or USAC—and if it did not, at least it would sound better to the press. France had already stated NASCAR would accept the engine if it obtained ACCUS approval. What he failed to say was that he and USAC's Henry Banks would be on the committee to consider the proposal.

At Atlanta the largest sports crowd in the history of the state of Georgia, 71,000, had gathered to see the resumption of overt hostilities. It was a wild, charging affair, with the top five cars within a few lengths of each other for most of the race, and the Dodges and Plymouths were the fastest. Petty led for much of the first half, and when he went out it settled down to a race between the surprising Jim Hurtubise, the USAC driver making another of his few visits to the South, and Lorenzen. In even cars the three-time winner of the Atlanta "500" should have walked away from Hurtubise, who had not shown any great speed since his bad accident of mid-1964. But Lorenzen was driving a Ford and Hurtubise a Plymouth, and the closing laps saw the Chrysler car wrap it up with little trouble. Bob Anderson was among those in the stands, and the next morning he had breakfast with France. The NASCAR kingpin asked Anderson what would happen if ACCUS decided to approve the overhead cam engine.

Anderson smiled. "I've got mine already," he said. The, inference was clear. Even if Plymouth didn't win another race all season—and even if Plymouth didn't compete in another one—it had more than enough favorable racing publicity for 1966. The only possibility remaining was to turn down the Ford request. An approval of it, considering the price and general availability, would have cost France all of the considerable stature he had attained in the last three decades. A banning would result in Ford's withdrawal, but there was no other way.

Because of last-minute negotiations the only announcement to come from the ACCUS meeting was that the engine problem had been turned over to the car classification committee for "study." This took a few days, then the new rules were made public. As might have been expected, France still had an ace in the hole; they didn't ban the overhead cam engine, they merely handicapped it out of business.

The new rules, effective immediately, allowed the engine in the 119-inch wheelbase cars, but with a weight factor of 10.36 pounds per cubic inch, one pound more than the pushrod engines. This meant that an overhead cam engine of 427 cubic inches would have to propel a car weighing 4,427 pounds, while the more normal powerplants would have only 4,000 pounds to move. As a bonus to Chrysler, the category II cars (such as the Belvederes, Coronets and Chargers) would be allowed to run engines up to 430 cubic inches on the big speedways. Finally, and this eventually proved itself to be the most important addition to the rules, engines with wedge-type combustion chambers (such as the Ford) would be permitted to run two four-barrel carburetors instead of the previous one. The rules, which for years had been wonderfully simple, had now degenerated to where they were unintelligible to the average fan. Ford pulled out.

At first there was no announcement from the company, and although the cars were conspicuous by their absence from minor races April 7, 9 and 11, the press was looking for a statement. The lack of one was due to the fact that the Special Vehicles Department was still trying to save the situation, but on April 15 a statement came from an entirely unexpected source—Henry Ford II.

The groundwork for his action was laid when he personally got involved in the wrangling over the rules, France going over Beebe's head during the crucial stages and finding he would get no more satisfaction from the boss than he did from his delegate. That was the start of Henry Ford's disenchantment, and then on April 9 a story giving France's opinion of the Ford pullout appeared in the Detroit *News,* with France quoted as saying "They're acting like a kid who gets mad, doesn't want to play the game and takes his ball and bat and goes home."

The writer was Bob Irvin, the man who first got the news of the AMA ban repudiation five years earlier, and who had now switched from United Press International to the auto editorship of the *News.* Irwin was dissatisfied with what he considered the company's failure to take a formal position, and he decided to get some sort of a statement on his own. On April 15, at the dedication of a new plant at Woodhaven, Mich., Irvin bided his time until he could get Ford alone, and then popped the question.

"What are you doing about the rules? Are you out?"

"We're out of stock car racing," Ford answered. "We don't like Mr. France's new rules—we think the rules are unfair to us, so we're out for the year."

Irvin didn't spend 30 seconds with Ford before someone came up to join the conversation, but that was enough. The next day there was a banner headline in the *News* and the Special Vehicles Department discovered the boss had ended the negotiations. Anyone in Dearborn who called Daytona now did so strictly to pass the time of day. The Dodges and the Plymouths went on to win most everything, France had to put down an incipient rebellion by his promoters, and USAC never got a look at a factory-sponsored Ford, as that circuit's season hadn't opened by the time the company withdrew. Ford devoted its time to getting ready for Le Mans, and the drivers went their various ways. It was inevitable some of them would return to stock car racing before Ford did, and in May the first major break was made by Panch. He drove a Petty-owned Plymouth, with late-inning relief from Richard, as he won the Charlotte 600-miler. Turner was also one of the first to get another ride, showing up at several events in a Chevelle, and eventually Jarrett and Hutcherson were piloting privately owned Fords in minor races. But the ban, as far as the factory was concerned, was still in force. The hot cars stayed in the garages.

The change of attitude came in mid-July, during the Ford Operating Committee meeting at which the special vehicles budget for 1967 was approved. Beebe and Passino recommended a limited return to NASCAR for the rest of the season—along with a full return in 1967, when the rules, they already knew, would allow the single overhead cam engine without an additional weight penalty. Top management gave its OK and Ford was ready to go back, on France's terms.

Despite the 1967 approval of the SOHC engine, plans for using it were now shelved, and despite the company's desire to race only full-size cars, the vehicle of the future would be the medium-size Fairlane. The difficulties connected with using the powerful new engine stemmed not from racing but from the climate of the times. The company did not feel it was wise, considering the new wave of safety hysteria and the political opportunism it had generated, to lay the entire corporation open to possible federal criticism by building and selling (for street use as well) an engine capable of almost 700 horsepower. From the standpoint of a chassis, the new rules allowed a full-size "wedge" engine, complete with two four-barrel carburetors, to be installed in a smaller, aerodynamically cleaner car. This made the Fairlane the only way to go. Any roadholding problems created by the installation of the high-powered engine in the smaller car would be taken care of by the 1967 rules, which conveniently managed to forget 1966 rule number 28 ("Frames must be stock …"). If that weren't enough, the old NASCAR regulation banning locked differentials was also abolished for 1967, so the small cars were better roadholders than the big ones of earlier vintage. Iacocca may have been right in wanting to race his sales leader, but if he had, the Galaxie would have been strictly a tail-end Charlie.

By the beginning of August, coincidental with the public announcement of the 1967 rules, Ford came back. The first car to return was the one maintained by Junior Johnson, and at the Atlanta 400-miler August 7 it had Lorenzen as its driver. When the car made its appearance at the Georgia track it caused almost as much commotion as did Sherman when he marched through the area. The front-end sheet metal had been dropped so much the nose of the car looked like a snowplow, and the back end was swept up into what amounted to the world's largest spoiler. There were at least a dozen other modifications to the car, any one of which would normally have been enough to get it disqualified. It was the Special Vehicles Department's practical joke. NASCAR promoters were so anxious to get a factory-sponsored Ford with a big-name driver they would take anything—and Johnson's Yellow Banana, as it was soon dubbed, was what they got. There were some observers who speculated NASCAR would have OK'd a GT prototype if Lorenzen were sitting behind the wheel. Final approval for the car had to come from the upper levels of the NASCAR administration; technical inspector Norris Friel had refused to admit it. When he was overruled, he was never quite the same for the remaining few months of his life. Pragmatism had won out over the letter of the law. Friel was humiliated even more when he told Dodge entrant Cotton Owens to raise Pearson's car a quarter of an inch to make it legal. Owens took one look at Lorenzen's bomb and allowed as how if that was going to run, his quarter of an inch wouldn't make much difference. As a matter of principle, he loaded his car onto a trailer and went home. Had Lorenzen won the race the controversy might have gone on for months. As it was, he and Petty were fighting for the lead when Freddie went out shortly before the halfway mark, and the next time the Fords showed up at a race they more closely matched the accepted configuration.

At Darlington on Labor Day there was a Fairlane ready for Lorenzen. It was not the first factory-backed Fairlane, as Turner had run a prototype at Hickory, N.C., in early April after being turned down by the technical inspectors at Bristol. ("They didn't say anything until we started running faster than everybody else.") Lorenzen's car had the benefit of a solid month of testing and it was always up near the front, but Fred never led a lap of what turned out to be a typical wreck-filled Southern "500." The winner was Dieringer in his Comet, the first independent entry to win a major NASCAR event in several seasons. Dieringer, who lost the 1965 Darlington race through a bad break, received a good one this time as Petty blew a tire seven laps from the finish and limped home second. Lorenzen was fifth, and the car showed promise.

Three weeks later at Martinsville it was Lorenzen's turn. Starting in the front row alongside Johnson, who was making one of his infrequent returns, Lorenzen outlasted Junior and Petty and for the last 60 miles of the 250-miler had it his own way.

At Charlotte the National "500," upped from 400 miles for the first time, proved to be a Dodge benefit when Lee Roy Yarbrough outran the rest of the field with no Fords ever having a chance. Dieringer was second in a full-size Ford owned by the speedway itself, the USAC star Gordon Johncock was fourth in Johnson's new Fairlane. Lorenzen, Yarborough and the rest dropped out early, and Lorenzen had to wait until Rockingham, the last race on the schedule, for another win.

The sliding scale of weight to displacement and the success of many of the Chrysler cars running a 404-inch engine had led to considerable Ford speculation on the advantages of doing the same. For Martinsville, Wilkesboro and Rockingham Moody had installed a 396-inch version of the 427 in Lorenzen's car. With a powerplant this size the vehicle could come to the line at only 3,707 pounds, and the reduction in weight could make a critical difference in braking, fuel consumption and tire wear. Moody and Lorenzen discovered the latter factor during pre-race practice at Rockingham, when they ran almost 30 miles on "gumballs," high-adhesion, fast-wearing models normally used only for qualifying. At the end of the 30 laps a check showed wear to be surprisingly low, and Moody and Lorenzen decided to go with them for the race. The biggest problem now was to keep their secret from the other teams, so when the tire crews asked what they wanted for the race, Lorenzen kept putting them off till later. They didn't go to the tire fitters until late Sunday morning, and they didn't bring the car to the line until the last possible moment, fearful someone might check the rubber. By the time the other teams found out the race was half over, Lorenzen and Petty were dueling for the lead, and it was already clear Lorenzen would have to make one less stop than Petty.

The Plymouth driver dropped out after 320 miles, Lorenzen led the last 180 with ease as he averaged 104.3 mph, a remarkable figure for a stock car in a 500-mile event on a one-mile circuit. It was so remarkable, and his pit stops had been so few, the Chrysler people were having trouble believing it. Ray Nichels put up the $100 necessary for a protest and the inspectors started to check Lorenzen's car. Holman, knowing it was legal, immediately put up another $400, protesting not only the Dodge of Don White, who finished second, but the Fords of Jarrett, Yarborough and Johnson, who occupied the next three places. Holman was not interested in finding anything wrong with White's car, but in showing that not only Lorenzen's Fairlane, but also all the other leading Fords, were legal. By the time the inspection was over it was almost dark and practically everyone had left. Holman himself climbed into the cab of the truck carrying Lorenzen's car and drove it back to Charlotte.

The season was over, and so were the careers of several drivers. Johnson, who had made sporadic appearances since his announced retirement, now decided to hang it up for good, and he was joined on the sidelines by Jarrett and Panch. Still in his early 30s, the pleasant, personable Jarrett had been racing for a decade, had won the Grand National championship twice and now decided to start a business career. Panch, although only 40, also decided to quit while he was still a top contender. Turner, who was beginning to show his age despite a willingness to stick his foot in it, was to be dropped. The losses, especially of Johnson, Jarrett and Panch, were later to prove themselves of almost incalculable importance. A driver is at least one-third (the basic car is a third and the team that runs it is another) of the package, and now the company was losing three of its front-liners. Johnson, while perhaps not a consistent big winner like Lorenzen, was nevertheless as fast as any man. Panch was another first-class veteran and Jarrett, while possibly a shade slower on the big tracks, had for several years been the man who carried the Ford name to all the little circuits as well. On those Jarrett was as quick as anyone in the business, and the public relations image he and the other two provided for Ford was also a large part of their importance to the company.

For the start of the 1967 season Ford went in with its numerically smallest team in years. Lorenzen was the only Holman-Moody driver, with the other car left open for the moment. Hutcherson had taken Jarrett's place with Bondy Long, Yarborough was the Wood brothers' mainstay and Dieringer was driving for Johnson. In USAC Foyt, Andretti and Parnelli Jones would be the top three (with some or all of them scheduled to run in the bigger NASCAR races), while ARCA star Jack Bowsher had moved up to try his luck on this circuit.

In the horsepower department, Ford was working on one of its bigger break-throughs; a new intake manifold design dubbed the "tunnel port" which would add, it was hoped, as much as 30 horsepower. Although the engineers had been playing with the idea for more than six months, approval to proceed was not given until December 13, when Al Rominsky and Jon Bowers went to work. With the Riverside "500" scheduled for January 22, the best the designers could hope for was the Daytona "500" in February, if they worked nonstop. At Riverside, although the Fords would have to run with their older-model manifolds, the power problem was not as acute. What was considered a bigger worry, from the standpoint of the Ford Division, was that Gurney had signed a contract with Lincoln-Mercury that would involve the smaller division selling a Cougar with Gurney's name on it. As a consequence Gurney would be driving one of Moore's Comets at Riverside, where he had won the last four events. (Moore, who was to be in charge of the maintenance of the Cougars for the Trans-American sedan racing series, was also getting partial help for the two Comets he wanted to run in NASCAR. For Riverside, where he had the corporation's best driver for this particular event, he got full assistance in the form of cars, parts and expenses.)

To offset Gurney (and there were members of the Ford Division who would as soon see a Plymouth win as they would a Mercury), Ford had Jones, driving a car built by Stroppe (now working with Holman-Moody), Foyt, Andretti, Lorenzen, Hutcherson, and even added Lloyd Ruby for the race. The opposition consisted of everything Plymouth and Dodge could scrape together, but still, through the practice sessions most of the eyes were on Gurney. The race itself, which the previous year had been run in a little over five hours, this time took eight days. A heavy rain after the first 135 miles called a halt and they all waited until the next Sunday, Lorenzen flying home for a few days, then barely making it out of Chicago (via a helicopter and a chartered plane to Minneapolis, where a flight was being held for him) in the middle of the winter's worst snowstorm. In previous editions of the event, one man always near or in the lead, but never able to finish, was Jones. This time, as the race wore on, Jones found himself in front again and Gurney was busy trying to work his way back there after being penalized for passing under the yellow flag. Parnelli, by now a veteran road circuit driver as well as an oval track star, was uncatchable, and Gurney's engine succumbed to the strain on the 143rd of 185 laps. A Ford had won for the fifth straight year, and for the fourth consecutive time the car was crewed by the Wood Brothers, who had been switched from Yarborough's vehicle.

The start at Darlington, 1965, with Panch (left) and Lorenzen in the first row.
(Inset, top) Jimmy Clark in his only stock car race, at Rockingham in the fall of 1967.
(Inset, bottom) Mario Andretti and his wife after the USAC national champion
won the Daytona 500 in 1967.

No. 11—Mario Andretti at Daytona, 1967.
No. 26—Darel Dieringer at Daytona, 1967.
No. 27—A. J. Foyt at Daytona, 1967.
No. 15—Parnelli Jones at Riverside, 1967.

*(Top row, left to right) Cale Yarborough, Bill France, Mario Andretti.
Second row: A.J. Foyt, Richard Petty, Lee Petty. Third row: Dick Hutcherson,
Darel Dieringer, Parnelli Jones. Bottom row: Jacque Passino, Junior Johnson,
Ned Jarrett.*

The first team, lined up at Charlotte in the fall of 1965. From left, Dick Hutcherson, A.J. Foyt, Fred Lorenzen, Cale Yarborough, Ned Jarrett, Curtis Turner, Junior Johnson, Ralph Moody and John Holman. (Inset, left, above) Lorenzen getting new tires and

water at Charlotte, 1965. (Inset, right, above) Lorenzen in the pits at Rockingham, 1966. (Inset, right, below) Tire wear can be high: Charlotte World "600," 1967.

(Inset, top) Marvin Panch. (Inset, middle) Curtis Turner. (Inset, bottom) Fireball Roberts. And waving to the crowd, the man who won the big ones—Fred Lorenzen.

One of the also-rans at Riverside was Turner, who was driving Moore's other Comet and stuck it into the wall after only 15 laps. Old Curtis was about finished, everyone thought, and when he showed up at Daytona with Yunick's black and gold Chevelle, no one paid much attention. It had been several years since Smokey had produced a competitive car, and although everyone knew the Chevy engine had potential, to date it had not shown it. There were rumors the previous fall that Yunick, Turner and the car had done considerable testing at Daytona with some General Motors engineers in attendance, but that type of talk was common on the east coast of Florida. It rained at the beginning of practice, and as everyone talked about Ford's new intake manifolds, or eyed the almost *concours* condition of Petty's Plymouth, Yunick sat off to one side. On Thursday it was clear; after Petty worked up to 179 mph, and the Fords were running at 177, Yunick sent Turner out with the Chevelle.

In a few minutes Curtis had the other crews talking to themselves. The shining little Chevelle, its giant exhaust pipes screaming as it flashed around the oval, was turning laps at better than 181 mph.

Yunick, deadpan, waved the car into the pits, then parked it in a lonely corner of the garage area. He covered it with a tarpaulin, told his son not to let anyone near it and went home.

When Turner took the car out again Saturday, he was clocked at 181.5, and the factory teams were shaken even more. On Sunday, a damp, overcast day on which conditions were not the best, Turner recorded two consecutive laps at 180.831, and the pole was his. Petty was next at 179.068, while the best a Ford could do was Cale Yarborough's 178.660. Yunick, still expressionless, was busy psyching everyone with the news he had not been using one of his better engines, and all the Ford personnel were worried about the new manifolds. The rush job had resulted in two problems, the first being in the carburetion and the second concerning the manifold castings. In the hurry to get them done some of the cores had shifted during manufacture and now the engineers were busy trying to sort out the good ones.

It wasn't until a few days short of the race itself that the various problems were cured. When they were there was an immediate increase in speed, with the leader of the Ford crew being Andretti. The tiny USAC national champion was clocked unofficially at better than 182 mph, and he knew he was ready. Moody, the smartest of all the chassis men in the business, hovered over Mario's car like a mother hen, and between the two of them they arrived at a peculiar setup for a stock car. Andretti wanted to feel his back end drifting on the high banks, and when he was running alone he wanted to be able to drift from the second lane all the way up to the retaining wall. At first the mechanics thought it would not work, but when they saw Mario run they were convinced. This radical departure from the norm also had an effect on the other drivers, who were fearful Andretti wouldn't be able to control his car well enough when they were running side by side at 190. They weren't going to find out if he could or not until the race.

Friday was preview day, filled with the two 100-milers that are the traditional opener for the big weekend, and it was also a preview for the kind of speed that would be shown on Sunday. Lee Roy Yarbrough, in a Dodge Charger, won the first race at an average of 163.9 in a blanket finish with Foyt, but he had been running at better than 176 for the first 32 laps before a caution flag came out and slowed things. Every car in the race had to make a pit stop for fuel, the 22-gallon tanks not being enough to last 100 miles at those speeds, and as they called at the pits Lorenzen and Moody watched from the sidelines. In the second race, they decided, Fred would slipstream the leaders until the end in order to conserve fuel. Then he would try to make it on his own to the finish. He just did—coming across on an empty tank at an average of better than 174 mph. Andretti finished fifth, after wanting to try the same trick but listening to orders instead.

On Sunday, with more than 94,000 spectators jamming the place, Andretti charged off with the rest of the field in a frightening, awesome start which made the giant oval tremble with the vibration. At first it was Turner at the head of the pack, then Yarborough, then Foyt, then Yarborough again, then Buddy Baker in a Charger ... The top 10 cars were running bumper to bumper, passing and repassing at every point on the track in the fastest race ever seen. It was just as well, for the sake of the onlookers, that it was so liberally spiced with caution flags, as the yellow-light periods were the only ones in which the fans had a chance to catch their breath. The leaders were never more than a car-length apart ... And one by one, the favorites started dropping out. Yarborough damaged his suspension while avoiding a wreck on the 42nd lap, and Foyt's clutch went at the same time. Turner, still in contention, finally lost his engine after 143 laps, and the race settled down to a fight among Andretti, Pearson in a Dodge and Dieringer, with Lorenzen running right behind them and waiting to make his move at the finish. The next to go was Dieringer, who was slowed by shock absorber trouble ... Then Pearson fell out on the 159th lap while trying to keep in front of Andretti.

Now there were two Fairlanes alone at the head of the pack, the last pit stops had been made, and it was to be Andretti and Lorenzen in a duel to the wire. For the first 450 miles the various leaders and their closest pursuers had roared around as if there was a rope tied between them. Now Andretti was going to try to shake off Lorenzen. Within a few minutes he got his chance as the two cars came up on the Plymouth of Tiny Lund, who was running a lap behind, but whose speed was almost as fast as that of the top two. Rather than move aside Lund decided to race with the two Fords, and that gave Mario his break. While Andretti got past with comparative ease, Lorenzen had a little trouble doing the same. By the time he had Lund in his rear-view mirror Andretti was too far ahead to slipstream, and as the closing laps flew past, it was clear that the little kid with the big foot had the faster car. Lap after lap, he picked up a half second ... Sometimes a full second.... With two laps to go Andretti was 22 seconds in front, and when the blown engine in Petty's car brought out the caution flag, the final five miles were run in relative peace and quiet. The average for the race—146.9 mph—wasn't much due to the 54 laps under caution flags, but there was little doubt it was one of the closest, hardest-fought stock car events in history. Andretti had led 112 of the 200 laps; when it was all over the man who had driven the fastest was just as thankful as the rookies at the back of the field. "I had a few anxious moments out there," he said, "but if I were to tell you about all of them we'd be here all night." Andretti got his satisfaction on the track, and from the $43,500 his car earned. The engineers got theirs a few days later, when Mario's engine was placed on the dynamometer. Before the race it had produced 583 horsepower at 6,800 rpm. After the race, without so much as a valve adjustment, it turned out 575. A few years earlier a Ford racing engine wouldn't have withstood 6,800 rpm for five minutes, much less 500 miles.

It was a good start for the season, and when Pearson's Dodge won the 250-miler at Bristol a few weeks later, it made no difference. First Hutcherson and then Yarborough had that one locked up, but Hutch's engine went with 25 laps remaining and then Yarborough had a flat tire, and that sort of thing had to be counted as racing luck. Besides, Bristol had nowhere near the stature of Riverside or Daytona, or of Atlanta, which was next. Atlanta made it four major wins in a row for the Fairlanes, counting the Rockingham victory of 1966, and this time it was Yarborough out front after leading most of the way, losing the top spot to Andretti for a few laps, then taking it back again when Andretti hit the wall and damaged his steering. Andretti, who had shared the wheel of the winning Ford Mark IV at Sebring the night before, started in 22nd position and it took him 152 laps to get up to the front as he attempted the unheard-of feat of winning two major races in as many days. He didn't make it, and among the others who didn't was the Sebring runner-up, Foyt. His engine exploded on the 174th lap, and as it did, spraying oil in all directions, it dumped a liberal portion on the windshield of Lorenzen's car, directly astern. Instead of coming into pits to have it wiped off, Lorenzen drove to the impound area and parked. The public reason given for the retirement was "wrecked," but everyone in the pits knew otherwise. No one asked Fred about it, though; when you are the biggest money winner in the history of stock car racing and one day you decide you don't want to race any more, they figure that's your business.

Two weeks later at North Wilkesboro Lorenzen was missing. He had stayed in Chicago, bothered by his ulcers, and he was already hinting he might like to retire. Fred had mentioned retirement in the past, but each time he had done so it had been dismissed as just talk. While he stayed home, Fords ran 1-2-3, with Dieringer leading Yarborough and Hutcherson. Dieringer's engine was one of the so-called "374" versions of the 427. (Actually, it was 370.8 inches and the car weighed the minimum of 3,500 pounds, the lightest the rules allowed.) In the few days after Wilkesboro, Lorenzen's intentions became more clear. He really *did* want to retire, and as the big trucks were ready to roll out of Charlotte on Wednesday, heading north to Martinsville, Lorenzen made up his mind. This would be his last race, he said. Holman, Moody and the members of the Special Vehicles Department talked him out of that. If he was going to quit, they said, there would be no "just once more." Too many drivers had been hurt that way. Lorenzen saw the wisdom of the argument and agreed. The pearl-white car with the big 28 on its sides stayed home, and Lorenzen was done. At the age of 32 he had won more than $375,000 in the six years he had driven for Ford, and he had built a reputation as the best money pilot of them all. He had won more NASCAR races of 250 miles or more than anyone else, and he was the only driver in history to win an event at each of NASCAR's five big tracks.

It was a good way to go out, while on top. But Lorenzen's retirement also left a large hole in the ranks of the Ford drivers. Not only was he the fourth veteran to retire in the space of a few months, but he was the big one. Within a few weeks Holman-Moody hired David Pearson, who had recently split up with Cotton Owens, his long-time car owner under the Dodge banner. Pearson was unquestionably one of the fastest drivers on the circuit as well as the defending champion, but he hadn't won a major race since 1961.

It didn't seem to make any difference who drove or how quickly. Petty was winning the races. In every sport there comes a time when one man stands out above the rest and his natural superiority, during this period, is often enhanced by his getting every break in the book. The 1967 NASCAR season, despite its auspicious start for Ford, turned out to be the year of Richard Petty.

He started quietly enough, with a victory here and another one there, and even when he won three straight in the spring it created little commotion. After all, Richard was the fastest driver on the circuit and he had always been in one of the better cars, so why not? Then, when he took Darlington's Rebel "400" for the 55th win of his career, people began to take notice. Ford got some solace out of the Firecracker "400" (Yarborough) and the Dixie "500" (Hutcherson), but after that it was almost all Petty. In the late summer he won 10 races in a row, and by that time he had the opposition so confused for a while it seemed as if no one else would *ever* win again. When he took the Southern "500," he all but owned NASCAR. He finished with 27 victories in 48 starts, was in the top 10 40 times and finished 41 times as his car earned $130,275. In a sport where attrition rates are usually better than 50 percent and where a driver who can win 30 percent of his starts is looked upon with awe, Petty's record approached the unbelievable. And if you happened to be on the Ford side of the fence, it was worse than that.

The lone bright spot toward the end of the catastrophic season was Bobby Allison. For more than a year considered the outstanding independent driver on the circuit, for one reason or another Allison had never got a decent factory ride, In the fall, after registering one victory in a Dodge and three more in a Chevelle he owned and maintained personally, he was picked up by Ford—at Ralph Moody's insistence— and given a car that was managed by Lorenzen. With Allison doing the driving and Lorenzen dictating strategy from the pits the team won the final two races of the season, the 500-miler at Rockingham and a 250-miler at Asheville-Weaverville, in which Allison outran Petty to the flag.

What Moody had done for Lorenzen was now being done by Lorenzen for someone else. The wheel had come full circle.

34

ENCORE

A MONTH AFTER LE MANS top management decided the company would go back in 1967. Impressive though the initial victory might have been, they felt two in a row would drive the point home in an even more convincing fashion and slowly, the wheels began to turn again.

At first there was not much time devoted to the program, as the Special Vehicles Department was occupied with the problems of stock car racing, and there was the natural delay caused by a change of command: Beebe left late in the summer, when he was made general marketing manager of the Lincoln-Mercury Division (within a year he had been moved again, being named a vice president of Ford of Canada). Passino, after almost a decade, was now the manager, with Cowley being the *de facto* number two man and given the tactical responsibility for all racing programs. Perry, who had been involved with the Le Mans effort since the factory started taking a direct supervisory interest in the summer of 1965, was given charge of both the Holman-Moody and Shelby American efforts.

For the first few months the only work done with an eye toward Le Mans was the testing of the J-Car, which had run into many problems but was still considered the vehicle for 1967. It was lighter, it was more aerodynamic, it was everything it was supposed to be—if it would only behave properly. Perry, Remington and Carroll Smith were the ones running the midsummer development program, the object of which was to prepare a car for the Canadian-American Challenge Trophy, the new fall sports car series. Although the J-Car was not designed to compete against the lightweight Group 7 sports-racers, the feeling was that with such nonessential items as the FIA luggage holders and spare tire taken out, the car would give a good account of itself. The Can-Am series could then be used as a shakedown cruise for the new model. If all went well, by the time winter started the J-Car would be ready.

The work started at Kingman, Ariz., and then moved to Riverside. Located in the desert about 45 miles east of Los Angeles, Riverside gets hot in the summer and

August 17 was no exception. The thermometer had spent the afternoon at the 100-degree mark as the J-Car hurtled around the course, and everyone except Miles was wilting. Even though he was driving, and thus subjected to the heat of the cockpit, the slender old pro still looked fresh. Miles, at 47, was proud of his physical condition. He didn't drink, he didn't smoke, he ran several miles through the Hollywood hills every morning, and in the past three years he had shown many younger drivers what 24-hour endurance was all about.

They were winding up the second day of tests and Miles had just switched from the normal 15-inch wheels to a set of 16-inchers equipped with new, low-profile tires. He took off from the pits, heading for the Esses, while Remington and his small crew busied themselves with their watches. About a minute later they heard the growl of the engine as the car appeared on the back straight and then Colin Riley, who happened to be looking in that direction, yelled "Oh my God," and the rest of them whirled around.

They saw the car go sideways and then flip end over end with pieces flying in every direction. They started to run, knowing as they did that no one would be able to get there in time.

When Remington and the mechanics arrived the fire truck was already quenching the small blazes. Miles lay there, about 12 feet from the car. He had been torn out of the seat belt by the violence of the somersaults. The car came to rest about 300 yards from where it first went out of control. They spent weeks trying to find what caused the accident, but could never settle on a single item. The reason never brought up was pilot error: Miles was the original cool one, the development driver par excellence, the man who knew the car better than anyone else. It was impossible to believe he had made a mistake. When they buried him a few days later, there were hundreds at the funeral service. The sometimes cold, sometimes sarcastic, brutally frank Englishman would have been surprised to see how many persons there were who thought of him as a friend.

The accident caused the J-Car's stock to go down in a hurry, especially since the cause could not be found. The honeycomb structure, which had been considered stronger than the normal sheet steel or aluminum monocoque chassis, had torn in several places that no one had expected regardless of the force of impact, and the conservative element in the Special Vehicles Department fought for retention of the Mark IIs for 1967. By mid-September a compromise had been found: The new Le Mans effort would consist of six cars, three of them Mark IIs and three J-Cars, with the Mark IIs—due to their proven capability—considered the main part of the attack. "It is interesting to point out," the plan said, "that while impressive wins were posted at Daytona, Sebring and Le Mans, the Mark II was never pushed to its potential; while some engine and chassis failures were experienced, the Mark II can be very competitive again in 1967."

A six-phase program was initiated:

The engines would undergo further development work to improve both horsepower and fuel economy, with the investigation including the possible use of fuel injection or Weber carburetors, new camshafts, a new exhaust system and possibly an aluminum block.

Transmission work would consist of continuing development of an automatic, and of increasing reliability while reducing weight in the four-speed manual version.

The chassis of the Mark II would be the subject of a thorough study to find where weight could be removed.

The braking system was to be improved again. By this time the combination of Ford and Kelsey-Hayes engineers had produced a 12-inch ventilated disc 1¼ inches thick, and this promised to provide the answer to any stopping problems. In conjunction with brake development, 16-inch wheels would be tested in order to get more air circulation around the rotor.

Driver safety would also receive additional consideration. NASCAR-type roll cages were to be installed, as was an improved type of safety harness, and investigation was to be made into the feasibility of an automatic fire-extinguishing system. This was something never done before in a long-distance, sports-prototype vehicle. With designers fighting to take out every ounce of weight, here was Ford adding 120 pounds by the installation of roll cages and the like. No one would dare say anything in public, but there was *sotto voce* snickering in racing circles. (Eventually the roll cage was responsible for saving the life of at least one driver who crashed while testing. The car went end for end at better than 180 mph and was rolled up into a ball. Peter Revson stepped out with nothing more than a severe shaking.) As a final move in this direction, an "under 40" policy was instituted. The two drivers who died during the 1966 season had both been close to 50, and despite their reputations and talents, the company would take no further chances with anyone of that age. It was an arguable point; Juan Manuel Fangio, for example, did not win the first of his five world titles until he reached 40. But there were enough younger men to choose from and the move was considered further insurance.

The first full-scale test session took place during the second week of November at Riverside, with both a Mark II and a J-Car. Andretti, Ruby, Foyt and McLaren were the drivers, and when the nine-day expedition was over the Ford brake problems were a thing of the past. The new rotors were excellent, not only for providing stopping power but in the matter of durability. One item that did not make it through the test, and was temporarily shelved as a result, was the automatic transmission.

By December 1 Ford had its first indication of a Ferrari comeback. The Italian team showed up at Daytona with its newest 330 P4 model, a lighter and more streamlined version of the P3 complete with fuel injection and three valves per cylinder. Within a matter of hours after unloading, Ferrari drivers Bandini, Parkes, Scarfiotti and Amon, the latest addition to the team, took turns making hash of the lap record. Although the pits were closed to the public the grandstands were open, and the several hundred onlookers could see the car was experiencing a trouble-free run.

The Ferrari completed hundreds of laps at high speed, and among those who watched the red vehicle scream around the banks were several Ford men, who were getting ready to test as soon as the Italians departed. This was the first time the team had a good advance look at the opposition's capabilities, and it was a golden opportunity. A J-Car, supposedly improved over its Riverside configuration and with McLaren and Andretti as drivers, was ready to go.

It soon became apparent the car wasn't ready at all. It oversteered viciously in low-speed turns, the steering was too quick for the high banks, and finally the wheels started to crack. As a safety measure the test was reduced to using only the infield portion of the circuit, and to end the effort on an even more dismal note, there was a chassis failure that resulted in a suspension part tearing loose. At no time had the car come even close to the Ferrari performance. With less than two months to go before the Continental, the J-Car was given back to its designers, and the older Mark IIs were prepared for the race.

The Daytona venture ran into more trouble in early January, when the decision was made to try for more horsepower. The aluminum cylinder heads and the single four-barrel carburetor were shelved in favor of high-compression, bigger-valve cast-iron heads which were to be fed by two four-barrel carburetors. It was considered expedient, at this stage of the game, to add power rather than remove any of the recently added weight. In making these engine changes they incurred a further weight penalty of approximately 80 pounds. Now they had 530 horsepower instead of the 1966 Le Mans figure of 485. In addition, they placed a further load on the entire power train, including the transmission. Total vehicle weight, with fuel, oil, water and driver, was more than 3,100 pounds.

At Daytona, further difficulties arose. First a day of practice was lost while the high-rise intake manifolds were changed for a medium-rise version, then when the cars finally practiced they proved to be slower than the opposition despite all the changes. The quickest was the new Chaparral, complete with 427-inch Chevy engine and an odd-looking, wing-type spoiler that rode in the airstream several feet above the rear wheels, and which was connected to the rear suspension by a pair of struts. Phil Hill was still the number one driver, with Bonnier replaced by Mike Spence, a young British pilot. The lead Ferraris—and there were three P4s, plus a conglomeration of older stuff—were driven by Bandini-Amon, Parkes-Scarfiotti and Rodriguez with Frenchman Jean Guichet. They were going almost as quickly as the Chaparral, and it wasn't until the end of the last practice day that a Ford managed to grab the pole. Gurney was the one who did it, and he accomplished the feat by using "gumballs," and by using several hundred more revs than the engineers would have liked. Gurney, who was driving with Foyt, had a 1:55.1 to Hill's 1:55.3 and Rodriguez' 1:55.4. The rest of the Ford team, composed of Andretti Ginther, McLaren-Bianchi, Gardner-Bucknum, Donohue-Revson and Ruby-Hulme, was stretched out from fifth to 12th. It was a bit different from Le Mans the previous year, when the Fords had outqualified everything in sight, and done it with an engine they knew would last for 24 hours.

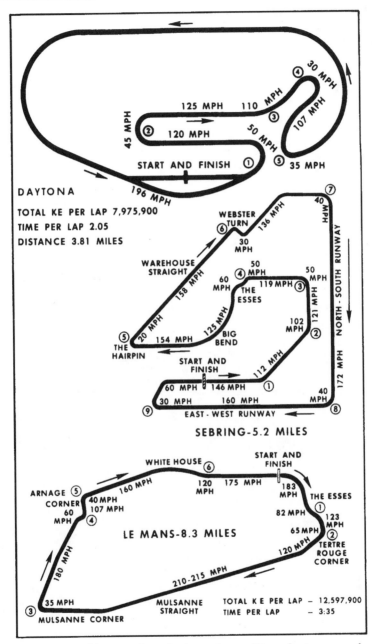

The braking problems, as shown by the engineers. These charts were made for the 1966 season. For 1967, with the increased speeds, the demands made of the anchors were even greater.

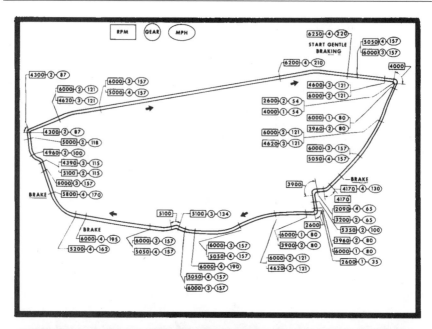

(Top) The course diagram used for setting up the dynamometer cell which tested the engines for durability. Note that speeds at various points of the circuit are slightly different from those used by the brake engineers. (Bottom) The Ferraris which knocked a hole in Ford's hopes at Daytona in 1967.

When the race started the Chaparral took off in front, with the Ferraris and Fords right behind. After 30 minutes, Bucknum came into the pits with transmission troubles. The only cure was to change the unit, which took 52 minutes and put the car hopelessly far back. And while Bucknum waited Andretti came in, complaining of instability at high speeds. They changed the front tires and sent him out again; two laps later he was back and they changed the rear tires. Mario, according to the prerace planning, was driving the car that was supposed to run hard and force the Chaparral and the Ferraris to increase their pace. Now he was well back, and the opposition was running away from the rest.

By the time two hours had gone the Chaparral was still leading, Ferraris were running 2-3-4, the Fords were next and still another Ford was in the pits, this one overheating. The head gaskets couldn't take it, and there was nothing that could be done about it. Soon the heads became a minor problem. One by one all the Fords were hit with the same type of transmission trouble that affected the Bucknum-Gardner car, and as the mechanics would change a box, they did so knowing it was only a question of time until the next car came in, or until they ran out of spare transmissions.

The Chaparral, meanwhile, had gone out at the four-hour mark when Hill slid into the wall while passing a car on a slow corner. Now the Ferraris were the leaders, and it looked bad. The little red wagon bringing transmissions from the garage was piling up more mileage than were some of the entries. The trouble was in the output shafts, which had not received a proper heat-treat after machining and which were being subjected to a heavier load than ever before. They were snapping off between third and fourth gears, and every transmission spread out on a table in the garage showed the same failure. Then someone remembered the two test cars sitting in a nearby van. They had older-model transmissions in them, didn't they? With output shafts from an earlier batch? Get them!

It was decided to save these for the two highest-placed cars. Gurney and Foyt got one, after having lost time earlier when a starter solenoid froze, and McLaren and Bianchi got the other despite their overheating troubles. When the two were finally changed the exhausted mechanics sat back and watched the cars circling through the night, roaring along like some sort of high-speed bugs on the high banks, with the red tail lights and the bluish glow from the exhausts making a color counterpoint to the brilliant white headlights up front. They sat there all night, as the car Gurney and Foyt were driving did not expire until morning and the McLaren-Bianchi car, despite frequent stops for water, managed to struggle home seventh, 278 miles behind the leading Ferrari and 30 miles behind a carefully driven GT40 which was sixth. It had been a ridiculous day: The cars that had so much care lavished on them were failures, but finishing in 12th place was another Ford which at the start had only the slimmest chance of ever seeing a checkered flag. This was a hotted-up Falcon that had blown its 289-inch engine in practice the day before the race. When its owners found no suitable replacement, they rented a Shelby Mustang from Hertz, took out the power plant, dropped it in their own chassis and went racing.

When it ended the Italian cars, the sound of their exhausts as healthy at the finish as it was at the start, rolled across the line in an impressive formation which their scorers never saw; the race had become so one-sided at the end that Ferrari's time-keeping crew had gone to lunch. For a team that was defending, among other things, its world manufacturers championship and its Le Mans laurels, Ford was in lousy shape.

By Tuesday morning everyone was back in Dearborn, a meeting was held, and Patterson made the decision: take the J-Car and *work* on it. Activity started at a pace that has seldom been duplicated in the history of any racing effort. Remington flew in from Los Angeles, and brought with him Bill Eaton and Dennis Gragg, his two sheet-metal experts. They moved into Kar Kraft, and the combined operation got going on a day-and-night basis. Perry, all the Kar Kraft personnel and various members of Ford's advanced styling department slaved over a new body design, with the drawings being transformed into metal almost the instant they were finished. At the end of 10 days the J-Car had a new body shape, and it was wheeled into the Dearborn wind tunnel. The improvement was surprising even to the bleary-eyed crew that stood in the control room and watched through the glass as a silent hurricane blew past their creation. Even at the relatively slow speed of 120 mph, the car had 100 pounds less drag. The project, which had reached its nadir less than two weeks earlier, was on its way back.

On March 4 the car, rechristened Mark IV due to the complete body overhaul (Mark III was the street version of the GT40), was run at Kingman to test its top speed against that of a Mark II. The Mark IV hit 215.8 mph, the best the Mark II could do was 211.8. From Kingman, after further modifications, the Mark IV and several Mark IIs were taken to Daytona for durability testing. Even though the new car had minor problems, it was the answer: Andretti got down to 1:52.4, almost three seconds quicker than Gurney's record effort in qualifying for the Continental. But there was no time to improve anything else. Sebring was next week. A Mark II was brought along as a base-line car, the trucks were loaded and the caravan set out across Florida. Sebring was to be a put up or shut up operation. If the Mark IV didn't make it, it would be shelved for good. For Le Mans, Ford would have to go with the refurbished Mark IIs.

At Sebring the only opposition was to come from the Chaparrals. Ferrari had decided to keep everyone guessing and stayed home, issuing such statements as "What good is Sebring? The Americans need me more than I need the Americans," and intimating if he could clinch the manufacturer's title before Le Mans, he might not show up there. So regardless of the outcome of the race, Ford would not have a chance to measure its new car against the Italians' best, and at Sebring would not even have a chance to test it against the older-model Ferraris: The North American Racing Team, always good for several entries, had decided not to come because of possible lawsuits over an accident at the track the year before.

It was even difficult to compare the performance of the car with that of the 1966 Mark IIs, the circuit had been changed slightly, making it several seconds faster. McLaren and Andretti, who were driving the Mark IV, got it around in 2:48.0.

(McLaren did it; Andretti spent several days commuting to Atlanta, where he was to drive in a 500-mile stock car race the day after Sebring. He was practicing for both, and by the end of the week was almost totally exhausted.) The winged Chaparral, with owner Jim Hall substituting for Phil Hill when the latter had an emergency appendectomy, was next at 2:50.6 and third was the Mark II of Foyt and Ruby with 2:53.6, just ahead of Bruce Jennings and Bob Johnson in the older-model Chaparral with 2:53.8. From the standpoint of possible winners, that was it; two from Ford, two from Chaparral. The only way anyone else could take it was if all four dropped out.

McLaren jumped off in front, the Mark II was running second, the older Chaparral third and the winged car was left standing at the start. Spence had trouble getting away and took almost 1½ minutes to get rolling and begin a chase that would last until evening. Hour after hour the yellow Mark IV roared across the runways, lapping between 2:52 and 2:53 while its pit crew watched the Chaparral draw steadily closer. They knew it was only a question of time before it got even, as the fuel supply system in the hurriedly rebuilt Mark IV was not functioning properly; the last 11 gallons in the tanks were not being picked up, and this meant the Ford would have to make two more pit stops than the Chaparral. The only obvious strategy was to maintain the 2:52 pace as long as possible, and if the Chaparral didn't break down, to race with it when it caught up, going as hard as possible and hoping the opposition broke first. Shortly after 5:30 p.m., with the race slightly more than half over, the Ford pulled into the pits for another stop and the Chaparral charged into the lead while its older sister stopped on the backstretch with ignition troubles. Minutes later the Chaparral went in to refuel and when it came out, the cars were running neck and neck. The race had begun, more than 700 miles after the starter dropped his flag. The two cars, McLaren driving one and Spence the other, went into the turns almost side by side, harrying each other as they went, slipstreaming down the straights and holding off until the last possible instant on braking. For five laps, or a little more than 14 minutes, the close-quarters duel continued.

Then smoke started pouring out of the Chaparral. Its automatic transmission had not been equal to the strain and it was through. The race was over, all that remained was to run through the darkness to the finish, with the Mark IV first and the Mark II second. The latter almost didn't make it. With 32 minutes to go Foyt brought it into the pits with engine trouble, and the mechanics soon found that a rod bolt had gone. While Holman's men worked to get the car moving again, the timekeepers checked the situation: The car had completed 226 laps, and was 10 laps (52 miles) ahead of the third-place Porsche. The Porsche, they figured, could never make up the 10 laps in the remaining time. It didn't. Andretti and McLaren finished first with a record-setting 238 laps, Foyt and Ruby were second with their 226 and the Porsche had the same number, but took almost three minutes longer to complete the final lap. As soon as it was over Andretti was bundled into a plane and flown north to Atlanta, where he would drive again the next day. The big yellow car was pushed back to a hangar alongside one of the runways. It had proven itself.

(Top) Birth of a new body—the prototype Mark IV in the wind tunnel at Dearborn in the winter of 1967. (Bottom) The end result—Bruce McLaren (left) and Mario Andretti with their Sebring-winning car.

The next step was the practice weekend at Le Mans in mid-April and at first it appeared to be a backward one. The fastest car, by far, was the hot P4 Ferrari driven by Lorenzo Bandini, who turned in a record 3:25.5. Parkes was next with 3:27.6, then came Eric Broadley's newest creation, a Lola coupe equipped with a new Aston Martin V8 that did 3:31.9 with Surtees driving, despite being a practically untried vehicle. The best the Fords could manage was 3:32.6 by Donohue in the older Mark II, and 3:36.1 by McLaren in the Mark IV. But it wasn't as bad as it looked. On Saturday the engineers had been getting information from the instruments with which each car was equipped for the occasion, and the mechanics had been getting the suspensions adjusted for the circuit. Sunday, when they were ready to go for the lap record, it rained. And by Sunday the Ferraris were already on top of the time sheets.

Without the Le Mans test session the cars would never have been successful in the race. The instrumentation showed the new "tunnel port" intake manifold, valuable in stock car competition where the engines operated in a limited rev range, was not as effective at Le Mans. Armed with this knowledge, the engineers installed an "over-under" intake manifold which solved the problem. The new manifold cut the horsepower slightly, but improved low and mid-range torque and gave the cars much better acceleration out of the corners. With the manifold and carburetion problems solved, the dynamometer durability tests approached their climax. The target was the same as the previous year—48 hours. But this time the engines had to last the distance at a lap speed of 3:30, a few tenths of a second quicker than the 1966 record (the shift points were now *7,000* rpm, and 6,600 rpm would be held on the long straight). By mid-May, the engines achieved 45 hours and 15 minutes, and that was deemed enough. A total of 10 were built, and when they were tested, all were within 10 horsepower of the desired 500. The system had started to move again, and the pieces were falling into place.

Then there was one last test—and again, there was a crisis. When the final-configuration car was taken to Daytona for a shakedown run at the beginning of May, the brakes, which had been so reliable, caused trouble. The company's metallurgists were the ones who solved the problem: There was nothing basically wrong with the design, they found. The trouble was in the material itself, as the batch of alloy mixed for the Le Mans discs had been faulty. A new batch was poured under the supervision of the metallurgists, and they had no more trouble in this area. During brake testing a disc had lasted for 48 hours on the dynamometer, and they had even run a cracked one for 12 hours to see how it would stand up *after* trouble developed. As a final fillip, all discs and brake pads to be used in the race or as spares were burnished on the dynamometer (each car went over with three sets of spares). The system was working, and the middle of June was drawing near.

Le Mans, to the aficionado, is the howl of the engines as they streak along the Mulsanne Straight, or the glare of the headlights, coming up from White House toward the pits.

Le Mans, to the drivers, is a long night and a long day of high speeds and hoping it doesn't rain. It is 24 hours of frustration; you can't run as fast as you'd like because the car won't take it—24 hours of seeking the proper combination of high speeds and keeping the car healthy, and sometimes less than 24 hours. Then there is only emptiness, and a broken car being pushed behind the pits.

To the engineers it is a massive problem, to the police it is a massive annoyance, and to the youth of Europe it is an opportunity for a holiday. To Al Dowd, whatever else it might have been, it was first and foremost an organizational task. Again he was the one who had to boil Le Mans down to pieces of paper, to sheets on which men and machinery were listed and moved according to timetables. He even issued condensed versions of the race regulations. The party included 14 drivers (two spares), 19 men from Shelby American, 27 more from Holman-Moody, 20 time-keepers and signalers, and another 34 from the Ford Motor Company, not to mention wives or Henry Ford II, who was traveling in Europe at the time. It was a massive undertaking, but by the Tuesday evening before the race Dowd's logistical exercise was almost complete. The cars were sitting in the Peugeot garage on the outskirts of town, piled high across the aisle were dozens of cases of equipment and spare parts, and parked outside was the latest Holman-Moody tractor-trailer with built-in machine shop.

Some of the men had been in Europe since the previous Friday, picking up the transport vehicles in England, driving to Paris, loading the race cars at the airport and bringing them to this humdrum provincial city. For several days the pace had been leisurely, but now it started to pick up. Wednesday was inspection day, and it was almost as if someone had pushed a button and brought the town to life: Rolls Royces and custom-bodied Maseratis and Ferraris appeared in the streets, with the latter two almost guaranteed to be driven by somebody wearing sunglasses and accompanied by a sleek-looking girl. Foreign license plates were as common as local ones, and in garages all over town cars were being given final touches in preparation for the first evening of practice. In one of them Franco Lini, the new Ferrari manager, watched his mechanics as they were replacing body, panels and thought about the race. He had been to Le Mans 17 times before as a reporter, Lini mused, and almost every time he had cursed the rain. Now it was different, he said. He was hoping for bad weather. If it got wet, he figured his cars would have a better chance. He thought about the Ford driver lineup and the possibility of rain and smiled. It was a tight, grim little smile. "They'll learn," he said. "You always put two rain drivers in a car. That way, if it rains, you know at least one car will do well."

Lini figured he had good rain drivers in *all* his cars. There were three of them directly under his control, all the latest P4 models and all occupied by pilots with Le Mans experience: Amon and Nino Vaccarella were in one, Parkes and Scarfiotti were in the second, and German Gunther Klass and Englishman Peter Sutcliffe had the third. Another P4, not under Lini but ready to do his bidding should the need for it arise, was driven by Belgian veterans Willy Mairesse and "Beurlys," the wealthy contractor. As back-up cars there were five other Ferraris of varying engine sizes and body shapes, but Lini wasn't concerned about them. They were private entries, and he knew if Ferrari was to have a winner it would come from the front four. His engines were now giving close to 450 horsepower, and at 2,160 pounds (with fuel, oil and water but no driver) they were considerably lighter than the Mark IVs or the Mark IIs.

In the Ford garage Passino watched his mechanics putting the last pieces back on their cars while reporters and photographers hung over their shoulders and made movement difficult. One of the writers asked him if he expected a recurrence of the brake problems of 1966, and Passino smiled. "We've got the greatest goddamn brake discs ever invented," he said. The giant rotors were at least as strong as any other part of the car. The driver pairings were giving Passino a much larger head-ache. Shelby had Gurney and Foyt in one Mark IV and McLaren and Donohue in the other. His Mark II was shared by Paul Hawkins and Bucknum. Holman's Mark IVs were set up with Andretti and Bianchi in one, Ruby and Hulme in the other. His Mark II would be driven by Gardner and by a newcomer to the team, Roger McCluskey, who had been picked up when Ginther announced his retirement just two days before Indianapolis. As reserves there were Scott and Revson, who had done so well with the GT40s the previous year, and there was another Mark II pre-pared for Ford-France which would be driven by Jo Schlesser and Guy Ligier and which would act as a back-up car. It was a strong team, but there were several weaknesses: Neither Foyt, Ruby nor McCluskey had ever seen the course before, much less driven on it. Neither Foyt, Ruby, McCluskey nor Andretti had much (if any) experience driving in rain. Finally, McCluskey, despite his abundant talent as an oval-track chauffeur, had never driven a Mark II, and had only minimal experi-ence in road-racing cars. If it rained for any length of time (and rain was two years overdue, despite a forecast that said the weekend would be dry), or if McCluskey's car was placed in a position where it would have to be driven hard, Ford was apt to find itself in trouble.

The cars, which had been as carefully engineered, assembled, checked and rechecked as anything Mercedes-Benz ever dreamed of in its racing heyday, were the strong point of the operation. They were built to last, and they were built accord-ing to the ancient theory that Le Mans is not a race, but an endurance contest. Any-thing on the vehicles that could be X-rayed, magnafluxed, safety-wired or cotter-pinned had undergone that particular process. Everything that could break had been made stronger, everything had been carefully pieced together, and they were ready to go. The Mark IVs were far from the lightest cars in the place, with the two Holman-built vehicles weighing 2,580 pounds (with fuel, oil and water) and Shelby's weighing 2,650. The Mark IIs were at 2,700—just what they were the previous year after a massive program of taking weight out, then adding it in other places. But the Fords were the best aerodynamically, and the combination of low-speed torque and high-rev horsepower built into their engines made them the cars to beat. They were, after all, the defending champions, and after the debacle at Daytona and the race-cum-test at Sebring they were beginning to look like it.

In the Chaparral garage Hall was looking forward to the event with a mixture of hope and fatalism. He had two cars entered, both now of the newest type complete with flipper, both weighing around 2,200 pounds and both equipped with 427-inch Chevy engines which produced at least as much horsepower as the Fords. He had a top flight two-man team in Hill and Spence, while Johnson and Jennings in the other car were, if not fast, at least steady. But he also had problems. The biggest one was still the transmission, the super-secret automatic with which he had stood the racing world on its ear two seasons earlier. Back then they had used 327-inch engines. With the 427 the resultant increase in torque had obviously been too much for the box—it had failed in race after race, and now they were going into a 24-hour event with no solution in sight.

Ford's turn to worry came a few hours later, soon after practice started at 7 p.m. About 45 minutes after the course was opened, Andretti drove into the pits with his windshield showing several lateral cracks. Everyone gathered for a look as the car was wheeled behind the pits. Either the glass had been improperly installed, or the chassis was flexing an extraordinary amount, or there was a flaw in the glass. For the moment it was nothing. Ford had brought three spare windshields despite four years of GT racing in which they had never once had to replace any, and it was a simple matter to switch one now.

Then it got serious. Within another hour Hulme's car was in with the same trouble and few observers started eyeing the Holman-Moody team, as both cars with cracked windshields had been built by the Charlotte crew. A few minutes later any suspicions in this direction were allayed as Foyt came in with a cracked windshield in one of Shelby's cars. A short time later the breakage was complete, as McLaren's cracked while the car was sitting in the pits. The problem was clear. The latest batch of windshields, which featured an extra-hard temper on the outside of the glass to minimize breakage by flying stones, was too brittle. A trans-Atlantic phone call was made to Dearborn, others were made from Dearborn to Corning, N.Y., and an emergency manufacturing operation was started. By Friday morning, Passino was told, you'll have your new windshields and they'll be good ones. In the meantime cross your fingers and use the spares for Thursday practice.

Wednesday had been almost a total loss. The only car which had done even a decent amount of running was the McLaren-Donohue machine, and it had reached 3:28.2. Hill had gone a full second faster in his Chaparral, and there were four Ferraris between 3:31 and 3:33, without broken windshields. Wednesday night had also seen the debuts of Ruby, Foyt and McCluskey and they were less than enthusiastic about the high-speed, tree-lined course. The trio had taken a ride around in a sedan during the afternoon and that evening, when McCluskey climbed into a Mark II for his first exploratory laps, Ruby gave him a friendly needle.

"Y'all remember which way to go?"

"I hope so," McCluskey said. He wasn't smiling. Foyt was a different story. His sports car experience had been on American road courses, which are relatively short and not noted for having trees along their sides. Although he didn't like Le Mans any better than the other oval-oriented drivers, Foyt's ego would not permit him to admit it. He got out and got running as soon as he could, if for no other reason, then simply because Andretti had driven here the year before and Foyt didn't want to be shown up by the little USAC champion. Whenever these two appeared in an oval track race in the United States, the winner was almost sure to be one or the other, and Andretti was the man who had taken away Foyt's national title. The rivalry between the two had developed into something big. Although they respected each other's talents, and although they were now on the same team, neither was about to let the other show him up.

McCluskey came rolling in after three laps and when he got out of the car Ruby laughed. "Tell us the truth!" he yelled.

McCluskey smiled. "No way!" he called back. Then McCluskey, Ruby and Foyt sat down with Andretti to figure out the circuit. They may not have liked it, but they were professionals and now the time for kidding around was over.

There was little horseplay of any sort among the drivers on Thursday afternoon. The windshield epidemic had affected them more than anyone else, and all were having thoughts of the glass collapsing at 200 or better. Most watched carefully as the mechanics replaced three of the cracked ones and backed them up with plexiglass to avoid such an occurrence. Then that night they all started running hard, even after all the windshields had cracked again within an hour. By 8 p.m. the Chaparral, with Hill driving, had cranked itself down to 3:24.7, but right behind it were three of the Fords: Hawkins had done 3:25.8, Andretti 3:26.1 and Gardner 3:26.4. Hulme was also getting faster, making one adjustment, then another. Finally, some time after 9 p.m, he turned a lap at 3:25.5, brought the car in and told Ruby it was fine now, and would he like to try it in the dark to get used to night conditions. The laconic Ruby sat there and smiled. "I'll be drivin' it Saturday night—you bring it in around seven, and that'll give me some time in the daylight. That'll be enough."

McLaren, somewhat slower than the others at the start of practice, was also moving quicker, giving Ford five well-adjusted vehicles and one that was still in trouble—the car shared by Gurney and Foyt. These two chassis engineers without portfolio, both of whom were famous for endless adjustments on the single-seater cars they drove at Indianapolis, had collaborated on making so many changes to their Mark IV it would hardly handle at all. Around 10 p.m., Gurney walked over to McLaren.

"Would you take ours out for a ride?"

McLaren couldn't believe it. "What?"

Gurney repeated his question, McLaren smiled inwardly and went out for a few laps in the number one car. When he got back and told the somewhat abashed stars what he thought, Bruce returned to his own vehicle and backed up his suggestions. He turned in a lap at 3:24.4, an average of 147.316 mph for the record and pole position, and everyone went back to the garages. Ford had five of the top six times, Scarfiotti had the fastest Ferrari at 3:26.9, and Gurney had struggled in with 3:29.8. The next morning the Gurney-Foyt vehicle was given the same camber, caster and ride-height settings as the McLaren-Donohue car, which meant Gurney and Foyt would race on a chassis setup they had never tried in practice.

The almost painfully slow process of inspecting every item on the car was carried out Friday. Shelby's men, armed with a 10-page, 124-item checkoff list, spent the day going through the cars for perhaps the hundredth time. After each section was complete, a factory engineer was called over for a final look and a sign-off on the check sheet. Working with precision, Remington and the others were fitting their high-speed jigsaw puzzles together again. With fuel and driver they would be 3,000-pound projectiles running at more than 200 mph. If one cotter pin were left off, or one nut were loose, it could mean disaster.

A few minutes after 1 p.m. a middle-aged man wandered in, looking like a tourist dressed in a business suit with a camera slung over his shoulder. He walked over to a group standing near the entrance. "I'm from Corning. I understand you've got a little problem with glass." He was welcomed as if he were the Pony Express that just outran the Indians to the fort. Parked outside was a truck with the new supply of windshields, and they were treated like gold. Taking no chances, two more specialists had been flown in by chartered plane from Brussels, the only European source of a special sealing compound. One problem had been solved. The one that remained would last 24 hours.

The morning of the race was a hot, clear one, but as the day wore on, and spectator areas began to fill with hundreds of thousands, it turned cool and low-hanging clouds appeared in the west. Passino paused in his pacing to eye them. "The weather bureau promised us it wouldn't," he said in a weak attempt at a joke. A hundred yards up the track Lini watched them too, and kept his fingers crossed and thought about strategy. Although neither Ford, Ferrari nor Chaparral knew for certain what the others would do, the situation was obvious: Ford, as the previous year, would go out and set the pace with one or two cars and let the remaining four or five hang back, each running a second or two per lap slower than the one in front. The lead Chaparral would run just off the pace of the leader, hoping something would happen to the Fords—and hoping its transmission would stay in one piece. The Ferraris would also run behind the front Fords, waiting for something to happen and for their chance to move. Lini was convinced the Fords would set a hot pace to try and draw his cars along and he was just as convinced the Fords would not— *could* not—last. He had to be convinced of this. If he wasn't, he might as well have stayed in Maranello.

While Passino paced, and while Lini looked at the sky and the mechanics laid their tools out on the pit counters, the thousands who had somehow or other wangled a pass strolled up and down, wandering from one car to another, doing nothing in particular until that time when the French police would clear them from the track. They watched the bands, the men looked at the models posing in front of the cars (only in front of those that didn't clash with their ensembles), and some of them turned to watch a small parade that was going past. It was a General Motors procession of eight cars, including a Corvette, a Firebird, a Camaro and various Opels, and as it went by the public address announcer was busy telling the crowd that GM was the world's largest manufacturer. For a corporation that publicly refused to have anything to do with racing, this automotive version of the guilt-by-association technique was humorous. Then everyone went back to looking at the race cars, or the girls, or to making sure all their tools were in place on the pit counters. It was getting close to 4 p.m.

The flag dropped, the drivers ran to their cars and the engines exploded into life, with Bucknum leading the pack as the cars screamed off, tearing up the hill and going out of sight around the bend. He hadn't bothered to buckle his safety harness, considering it more important to get ahead of the opening-lap traffic. Gurney was also one of the first away; he fastened his belt when he got to the Mulsanne Straight, holding the steering wheel between his knees at 195 to do so (Later he smiled: "Then I *really* stood on it"). The Chaparrals were among the last to get off, Hall insisting his drivers be completely buckled in before they hit the gas pedal.

On the first lap it was Bucknum, with Gardner a few hundred yards behind, then Rodriguez in an older-model Ferrari, then Schlesser, then Gurney, and then the pack. A Ford was out front, and by the third lap there were four of them—Bucknum, Gardner, Gurney and McLaren. The minor troubles started almost as quickly as the cars. First it was Hulme, making a 10-minute stop to repair a sticking throttle, and at the same time Gardner was in getting a new tire; the balance weights had flown off, and at 200 mph the vibrations were threatening to shake the car apart. After a half hour Bianchi brought a third in for a look at the windshield. A rock thrown up by a slower car had put a small hole in the middle, but it was good enough to continue. In the Chaparral pits Hall watched the flying pack, checked with his timekeepers and shook his head. The pace was too fast, he said. They would never last at this rate. Bucknum and Gurney were clicking off 3:29s, while McLaren was a second or two slower. The Shelby cars were running 1-2-3, the Holman cars had all run into those difficulties that make the difference between winning and finishing third or fourth. At 5 p.m., half an hour earlier than usual, the Fords started making refueling stops (the first one is always made early, to give a final check on fuel consumption under race conditions). When they took off again Bucknum was still in the lead with Gurney second. All the Fords were running between 3:29 and 3:33, with Hulme, Gardner and Bianchi trying to catch up after their extra stops. Within a half hour after he refueled Bucknum was back, his engine overheating badly. A cracked weld was discovered in one of the lines leading from the engine to the radiator. It was hurriedly pulled out, rewelded in Holman's trailer behind the pits, and as the mishap took place on the 23rd lap and regulations forbid replenishment before 25 laps, Bucknum had to make two more laps at low speed before they added more water. Then, finally, after losing many minutes, the car charged off again in 42nd place, with Hawkins driving and a hopeless task in front of him for the second year in a row.

At 6:30 the Ford team found DeGaulle wasn't the only Frenchman who didn't care for Americans. A small group of officials appeared, one of them carrying the 10-centimeter box (about four inches) over which all entries had passed during the ground-clearance phase of the technical inspection. Now they asked for Ford to bring all the cars into the pits. They wanted to check the ground clearance again.

For a moment everyone was stunned at the brazen attempt to stop them. Then Frey, who had been standing there watching the pit operations, stepped in. "Tell them," he said to an interpreter, "to go back and get the rule book so they can show us where it says they have the right to do this during the course of the race." He paused for a moment, then added, "And tell them that if they check *our* cars, we will insist on their checking every other car in the race."

The officials disappeared. They never came back, and the Fords roared on. As dusk neared, the lap record, which had been taking a constant pounding, was set at 3:23.6 by Hulme as he tried to get back up with the leaders; a little while later, once it got dark, Andretti equaled this as he tried to bring his car back into the lead. In addition to the windshield troubles Bianchi had been forced to have the shift linkage adjusted, and the combination of the two had slowed them just enough; after four hours they were second, running with the Chaparral and with McLaren. Up front, Gurney and Foyt were rolling along, still without missing a beat—until Foyt came slowly into the pits just after 8 p.m. Due to an error by the scorers he had been given the refueling signal two laps too late, and had run out of gas. Fortunately it happened on the approaches to the pits, and he had just enough steam to make it home. One of the mechanics looked at another and said "If Dan had been driving, with his luck it would have happened on the other side of the course." Gurney and Foyt were still in front, but behind them the others were dropping back. At 7:45 Ruby came in with a considerably altered nose and bellypan, the result of sticking them into the sandbank at Mulsanne. They lost 45 minutes fixing it, putting the car 17 laps (142 miles) behind. By 9:15, with the three Fords still running strong in front of the Chaparral and the Ferraris, McCluskey had been in the sandbanks twice, and had not been able to lap under 3:40. The three cars up front were the only ones that could win it. That much was clear after the race was only six hours old.

A little while later Ford lost its first car, and so did Ferrari. Ruby took care of the Ford, stuffing it deep into the Mulsanne sandbank. Amon was the driver of the Ferrari. The Italian cars, like the Chaparrals, were running without safety liners in their tires, preferring to save almost 10 pounds of unsprung weight per wheel and to take their chances on a blowout. Then Amon got a flat while shooting down Mulsanne, and was left with no alternative but to change it. As he swung an emergency hammer left in the car for loosening the wing nuts, the head flew off into the night, and he was stuck. The only thing to do was try and drive in on the flat, so he got behind the wheel. In a minute the sparks from the wheel started a fire, and the little New Zealander hopped out and stood there while the car burned. The year before he was a winner; this time his race ended with a burned-out car and a long walk home.

That left only the Parkes-Scarfiotti Ferrari as the challenger, and at midnight they were four laps back. The car driven by Klass and Sutcliffe was lapping at 3:40, and the Chaparral had been in trouble since 10 p.m., losing five to seven seconds per lap after its wing got stuck in the worst possible position for air resistance.

(Top) Ready to defend their title—the Fords at Le Mans, 1967.
(Bottom) Force of numbers—French police clearing the area in front of the pits.

*(Top) The start, 1967. Laying a trail of smoke as he charges away is Bruce McLaren.
(Bottom) The winged Chaparral of Mike Spence and Phil Hill.*

At Mulsanne Corner, where the signaling crews huddled on the earth bank, it was a different world from that of the pits. Here the only persons watching were those who were working, and the little island of light in which they gathered, a few for each car still in the race, was seemingly isolated from civilization, the only contact being the telephone lines running through the woods. At one station it rings, and the voice is in Italian ... "La ventiuno per favori ... tre giri ..." the signboard is hung out, and number 21 knows he has three laps left before he must refuel ... At the Ford station the phone rings, and the voice says "Number two in ..." The operator yells up to those sitting on the bank and the signboard is held out ... A pair of headlights comes streaking down Mulsanne and suddenly they begin to slow, the steady roar of the engine changing to a series of snarls as the driver shifts down from fourth, going through the gears to first just before he snaps around the corner and shoots away into the night, with those on the bank peering down to see if the man behind the wheel notices their sign. For a split second they think they see him nod, and then all that is visible of the yellow car are the tail lights rapidly growing smaller as they fade into the distance ... four red lights and the peculiar odor of hot oil.

A mile or so north lay the kink in the highway, a gentle bend in a pine forest during normal times, now the fastest corner on the longest racing straight in the world. The organizers had set up a timing trap on an earlier portion of the straight, and the Fords had been clocked at 213. Here, in the middle of the bend, they were going five to 10 miles an hour faster. It was pitch dark, with the only illumination coming from the countless stars and from the glowing end of a cigarette held by one of the three firemen sitting by their truck, until suddenly it began to get lighter up the track. The harsh glare came first, almost as brilliant as a pair of suns and throwing strange shadows through the trees. Then came the noise, starting as a low, pervading thing and then quickly, almost instantaneously, increasing in its intensity and turning into a roar as the car flashed past, its driver holding the gas pedal flat against the floor.

Just as suddenly there was darkness again, and the winking tail lights, with the blue flames of the exhaust pipe between them, disappearing, along with the sound and the light, down toward the corner. It was a cosmos unto itself and in the middle of it, at 2 a.m., was Frey. He stood there for a few minutes watching the cars stream past, punctuating the blackness with their headlights and making the earth quiver with their engines. Even at the rate they were going, and even without seeing the numbers on the sides, he had little difficulty picking out his own. When they came by even the pines trembled. Frey shook his head. He had known that these combinations of metal and rubber, these intricate pieces of machinery, could perform in this manner; but seeing them in full cry, at the height of their power, was an experience almost emotional in its intensity. Shelby stood next to him, also silent. The drawling, high-living Texan, the former playboy of the racing world who said he'd never drive unless he was well paid for it, who had laughingly said it was easier than working for a living, was watching too. He was reminding himself that this is what it was all about, this was what he had done almost a decade ago—and money had little to do with it. Then both of them turned and went back through the forest. The fireman put out his cigarette, leaned back against his truck and closed his eyes.

In the mess tent behind the pits Frank Gardner was sitting over a cup of coffee, rubbing the stubble on his chin, when someone asked him about his car. "This is wrong, that's wrong—it's like a bloody one-armed paperhanger in a thunderstorm! The Zed-F's not Zed-effing any more, and when you go around those slow corners ..." Gardner shrugged. McCluskey had been in the sand several times and once he had to bring it into the pits to have the exhaust pipes straightened. Gardner had already told Cowley the car couldn't race any more, but would have to cruise the rest of the way if it were to have any chance of finishing. Outside, in the pits, weary mechanics were drinking coffee out of plastic cups or were sitting slumped against the wall, hoping to sleep for a few moments before their car came in again. Ford was in a commanding position, with three good cars running on top, and with six in the first 11.

It was the dark of the night, that time between 3 and 4 a.m. when there was nothing to do but sit and watch, and hope nothing went wrong. Then McLaren brought his car in with a recurrence of earlier clutch troubles. While the mechanics replaced the slave cylinder Bianchi came in with the second-place car, ready to hand over to Andretti. The little champion, wide awake, watched the crew go through a routine change of brake pads, and in less than three minutes from the time Bianchi climbed out Andretti was off, running through the gears as he climbed up the hill and out of sight.

In a minute the yellow light on the side of the track started blinking, and those who were half asleep became alert again. The blinking yellow meant an accident. Passino turned to Chuck Mountain. "You better start counting the cars," he said. It got very quiet, and everyone watched anxiously as lights came up from White House Corner. There was Gurney's car, and McLaren's was still in the pits.

"Has anybody seen three and five?" a mechanic yelled.

"What about six?" somebody else said.

The next voice was one of despair. "That Porsche's been around twice now. If they're still running, they should have been here."

Andretti, doing 150 over the crest of the bill before the Esses, had started to slow down for the corner when suddenly one of the front brakes locked and he went into a wild spin, bouncing off both walls, demolishing the front and back sections of the car, sending the wheels flying and winding up with the battered driver's cabin lying in the middle of the track. Henri Greder, the veteran French rally driver who was right behind him, managed to squeeze past in his GT40, as did Christian Poirot in a Porsche. The next car to come along, a few seconds after Andretti had clambered out, run to the side of the road and collapsed, was driven by McCluskey. Startled by the wreckage, and thinking Andretti was still inside, McCluskey wasn't sure he could make it past so he purposely spun into the wall, knowing if he hit the car Andretti would of a certainty be killed. Seconds after McCluskey's car came to rest Schlesser shot over the hill, running strong in sixth place. Now almost the entire track was blocked. Schlesser saw it and knew he could never stop, so he braked as hard as was safe and attempted to squeeze between the two wrecks. He didn't make it, and within the space of perhaps 30 seconds, three Fords were gone and it was a new race.

They brought Andretti back to the pits on a stretcher, badly shaken and with a suspected cracked rib; the force of the crash had almost torn the safety harness out of its anchorage, and the straps left deep bruises where they cut into Andretti's shoulders. Had he been driving a Ferrari, without either safety belts or roll cage, he would not have gotten off so easily. Schlesser and McCluskey were unhurt and walked back, both of them thoroughly depressed. When McCluskey finally sat down, someone handed him a battery-powered electric razor. Roger put it to his face, pressed the button. And after a few seconds the thing ran out of juice. It had been a bad weekend all around.

That left Gurney in front, Scarfiotti five laps back, Hill and Spence in the Chaparral a lap behind the Ferrari, the Belgian Ferrari another lap astern in fourth and McLaren and Donohue fifth, still another lap in arrears and a total of eight behind the leader. The race was only half over.

About the only thing functioning properly for Ford was the car driven by Gurney and Foyt—that and the clear skies. At least there wouldn't be any rain, but at the moment it was small consolation. Passino ordered the leader slowed to laps of 3:50, and they sat down to have a short conference about the older Mark II driven by Bucknum and Hawkins. After the long pit stop the previous afternoon it had started climbing back through the field, but now it would have to run even harder. It was a calculated risk, but if this car finished fifth or sixth it would mean nothing. In order to act as insurance for the leaders, it had to work its way up to where it could challenge the Ferraris should the necessity arise. Bucknum and Hawkins knew what they had to do, and as the sun came up they were clicking off 3:27 laps with regularity, going hard, trying to move up and knowing their chances were slim. By 5 a.m. they were ninth, by 6 a.m. they had moved up to seventh and an hour later they were sixth and gaining.

In the Ferrari pits there was jubilation when the three Fords crashed. Lini was more convinced than ever the leader couldn't last and was planning his attack when the Parkes-Scarfiotti car came in. It was having brake trouble, and the front discs had to be changed. After the brake problems of the 1965 race Ferrari had installed a quick-change system, but it wasn't nearly as effective as the Ford setup and the car lost eight minutes—more than two laps—while repairs were effected. It was ironic; in previous years it had been Ford with brake troubles and Ferrari taking advantage of them. Now the shoe (or the ventilated disc) was on the other axle. Gurney and Foyt had a seven-lap advantage.

At about the same time, Gurney noticed a red car in his rear-view mirror and thanks to his own reduced pace, the car (he soon saw it was a Ferrari) pulled up behind him and sat there. It was an obvious attempt at harassment, and although Gurney was a veteran of wheel-to-wheel racing, he didn't see any necessity for it now, considering he was more than 50 miles ahead of the second-place car. When he got past Arnage Corner, with the Ferrari still on his tail, he slowed down. The Ferrari did the same. Finally Gurney pulled off on the shoulder and stopped, and the Ferrari went past. Then Dan got moving again and a short time later, running hard, blew past his erstwhile pursuer and saw who was driving. It was Parkes.

Now it was 8 a.m., and all the big Ford had to do was cruise for eight more hours. Lini ordered his lead car to lap at 3:30. It was a move born of desperation, but it was the only thing he could do. Someone had persuaded him the Ford was in trouble, and if his car could catch up, it could win easily. The Ford was all that was left now, as any threat from the Chaparral expired when its transmission did the same shortly after 5 a.m. There was no hope of catching the Ford, there was only the slim chance the Ferrari's speeding up might entice either Gurney or Foyt to do the same and then ... perhaps ...

The morning wore on, with Gurney and Foyt circulating steadily at 3:40, and there was nothing left to do but sit back and worry, sit back and watch the timekeepers watching the cars. At 9:40 there was one less; the Mark II driven by Bucknum and Hawkins had finally blown its engine. It had been a chance worth taking, but it hadn't worked. A few minutes later there was a car—or at least part of one—to watch right in the pits, as McLaren came in with the entire rear body section missing. A latch had come undone and it had blown off while he was doing 200 on Mulsanne. Remington threw McLaren a bunch of straps and sent him back out after the missing body. Regulations forbid the car continuing in this condition, and the only thing to do was see if the body could be rescued. Less than 15 minutes later McLaren was back, with the jury-rigged body hanging on behind, and the mechanics got to work as Foyt pulled in for a routine stop. He eyed the car with relief. "Man, I saw that yellow rear end laying back there and I thought 'My God, where's the rest of that car!' It really shook me up, I'll tell you!" Gurney got in and took off, while the mechanics continued to hustle about the other vehicle. From, the time McLaren came in until the time he was finally ready to run again, 48 minutes passed. Working with a pop-rivet gun, yards of tape and even with belts pulled from their trousers by his fellow mechanics, Bill Eaton, Shelby's sheet-metal man, had wrought some sort of a miracle. The battered Ford was ready to run again and Donohue took off with it, in fifth place and now without a chance of catching anyone. It was, aside from the leader, the only Ford left. The six private entries had long since departed the scene.

The day unfolded, slowly. The stands filled up again, the cars roared by, and the mechanics watched and waited and prayed that Gurney and Foyt would make it to the finish. Every time their big red car shot past, with the number 1 on its nose and flanks being as much a symbol as it was a whim of the organizers, they felt a little better, and the engine never missed a beat. By 11 o'clock the fourth-place Ferrari had gone out with transmission problems and McLaren and Donohue moved up again. It didn't make any difference. The car to worry about was the one driven by Gurney and Foyt, and it was out front.

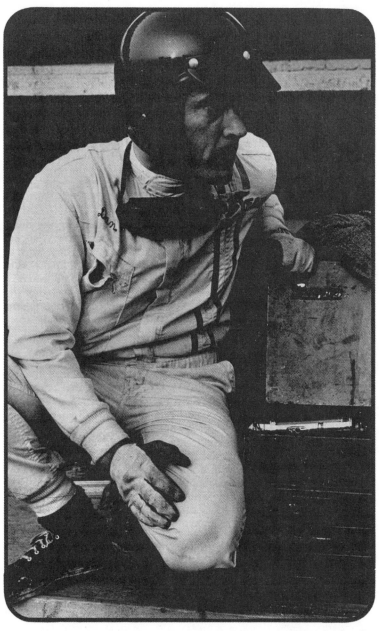

Anxiety: After eight years of trying, and now with a commanding lead and only a few hours to go, Gurney waits in the pits while Foyt brings their car in for refueling and a driver change.

(Top) The winning car after the checker, with Foyt driving and Gurney and the mechanics hanging on as they head for the impound area. (Inset) Phil Remington, who was responsible for so much of the mechanical preparation. (Bottom) The Ferrari driven by Lodovico Scarfiotti and Mike Parkes. It finished second despite breaking all records.

At noon Lini told Scarfiotti to lap faster than 3:30, and the exhausted driver went out to try—and couldn't. The strain had told, and he was no longer in condition to drive that hard. Parkes and Scarfiotti had driven harder and faster for 20 hours than any other men in history—except for the pair in front of them, and the lead was insurmountable.

Just before noon the first chink had appeared in the Ford's armor. During a routine brake pad and tire change, the mechanics noticed one of the front discs, after a day and a night of a record-setting pace, was developing a crack. Should they change it? Remington and Smith took a quick look and made a decision: At the speeds they were running now, it should be good enough to last. If we start to change it, they reasoned, we may make a mistake and that could cost us a half hour. Tell the drivers, and tell no one else; reports of this type have an unpleasant habit of traveling from pit to pit in a hurry. The car went out again, and no one knew the difference. Foyt and Gurney's talents more than made up for the slight weakness in the brakes, and the hands of the clock moved slowly onward.

At 1:55 McLaren was overdue and everyone leaned out of the pits, looking down toward White House for the sight of the big yellow racer. A few minutes later it showed. The coil mounting bracket had broken, and McLaren had stopped and made a temporary repair. While the mechanics fixed it the enormously fast Porsche that had been fifth moved up to fourth, and when McLaren went out again he was three minutes behind the German car. Perry gave him the signal to go faster, and in a half hour he was fourth again.

The race was over, but there were still two hours to go. The last sheet handed down from the timekeeping crew showed the Ferrari had slowed its pace considerably; four laps behind, it had given up the chase, and the only thing left to do was keep rolling to the finish.

At 2:37 Foyt came in and less than two minutes later was out, and the hands of the clock inched forward a bit more. At 3:30 Foyt came in again, this time for a precautionary fuel stop. There was nothing wrong with the car; they were simply making sure. In a minute Foyt went back out, ready for the last half hour, for the eight laps that stood between Ford and victory.

Gurney stood in the pits and watched him pull away. While the car was in, he and A.J. had smiled and made jokes, but now that the car was running again, it was Dan's time to worry. He hadn't won a major European race since 1964, he had been trying to win at Le Mans since 1958, when he made his European debut there. Now it was out of his hands, and he had nothing to do but pace back and forth while Foyt, who had never seen the place before Tuesday evening, clicked off the remaining laps.

The enormous crowd sat there, unusually quiet, jamming into every available space, watching and waiting. The mechanics waited, Remington waited, Passino waited in silence. Every few seconds heads turned to look at the clock hanging near race headquarters. Gurney, pacing up and down on the edge of the track, would snap his head round again and again, almost as if he expected it to reach 4 p.m. in a single bound.

With less than 10 minutes to go, the man with the flag walked past the pits and took up his position on the line. It was getting closer and he watched the timing stand, looking for the signal.

It came. The flag was raised, and in a moment the second-place Ferrari came rolling slowly up from White House to be waved off.

Then there were a few smaller cars, Porsches and Alpines.

And then there was the big red Ford, lights ablaze, growling up the straight and coming sedately across the line, in peculiar contrast to the almost frightening speeds it had displayed through the light and the darkness and through the long morning and even longer afternoon.

The crowd went wild, Foyt and Gurney were swept up to the winner's stand, jeroboams of champagne appeared from somewhere and everyone had a drink. It never tasted better than it did to that unwashed, unshaven crew, standing on the oil-stained asphalt that summer day in western France.

The statistics show that Gurney, Foyt and their Ford covered 3,249.6 miles in the 24 hours for an average of 135.48 mph, shattering the record by the greatest margin in the history of the event. The year before, when two other Fords established the previous mark, their average speed was 125.4. By way of comparison, the average lap time of the winner in 1966 (counting pit stops) was 4:00.1. The average lap time of the 1967 champions was 3:42.7, an unbelievable increase in tempo. The Parkes-Scarfiotti Ferrari, which offered the Fords a sterner test than they had ever dreamed possible, averaged 3:45.0 per lap in being outclassed.

Of the seven Fords entered by the factory, only one retired due to mechanical failure and that one had been sacrificed as part of a scheme that was known to be chancy when it was undertaken. Two finished, and the other four went out because of accidents. The engine in the Gurney-Foyt car, which had produced 494 horsepower when it was built, was up to 499 at the finish, later tests showed.

As a surprise bonus, the lead Ford also won the *Indice au Rendement Energetique,* which is a fuel consumption competition based on such factors as the weight of the car, the size of the engine and the distance it traveled. The winner averaged 5.5 miles per gallon (43.437 liters per 100 kilometers); remarkable in light of its average speed. The car made 17 pit stops, used 20 quarts of oil, changed its front tires and brake pads three times and its rear tires and brake pads twice. The fourth-place Ford, despite spending more than an hour in the pits, covered the same number of laps as did the winner of the previous year, so fast was the pace. Of the 55 cars that started, only 16 managed to make it to the finish.

Those are the bare bones of Le Mans, 1967, as that is all statistics can be. The sound and the fury, the speed and the drama, they are something numbers can never replace.

THE RECORD

GT PROTOTYPE CHRONOLOGICAL SUMMARY
Factory-sponsored Entries

Date	Race	Car-Drivers-Team*	Place (Reason Out)
5/31/64	Nürburg 1,000 Km.	GT40-Hill/McLaren (JW)	Suspension
6/20–21/64	Le Mans 24 Hours	GT40-Hill/McLaren (JW)	Transmission
		GT40-Attwood/Schlesser (JW)	Fire
		GT40-Gregory/Ginther (JW)	Transmission
7/4/64	Rheims 12 Hours	GT40-Hill/McLaren (JW)	Engine
		GT40-Attwood/Schlesser (JW)	Transmission
		GT40-Gregory/Ginther (JW)	Transmission
11/28/64	Nassau	GT40-Hill (JW)	Suspension
		GT40-McLaren (JW)	Suspension

1964 Summary: Started—9 cars. Finished—0.
Nürburg car, plus all three at Le Mans and all except Attwood/ Schlesser car at Rheims were powered by 256 cubic-inch pushrod engines originally developed for Indianapolis and used there in 1963. Other car at Rheims plus two cars at Nassau were powered by Cobra version of 289-inch production engine.

*Initials after drivers' names indicate team responsible for preparing and running the car; JW for John Wyer, SA for Shelby American, HM for Holman-Moody, AM for

Alan Mann and FF for Ford-France. In certain cases the team was not the entrant of record; at Le Mans in 1967 for instance, the Schlesser-Ligier car was entered by Ford-France, but the vehicle was prepared and maintained (to a degree) by Holman-Moody.

2/28/65	Daytona 2,000 Km.	GT40-Miles/Ruby (SA)	1st
		GT40-Ginther/Bondurant (SA)	3rd
3/27/65	Sebring 12 hours	GT40-Miles/McLaren (SA)	2nd
		GT40-Hill/Ginther (SA)	Suspension
4/25/65	Monza 1,000 Km.	GT40-Miles/McLaren (SA)	3rd
		GT40-Maglioli/Amon (SA)	Suspension
5/9/65	Targa Florio	GT40-(open)-Bondurant/ Whitmore (SA)	Accident
6/1/65	Nürburg 1,000 Km.	GT40-Hill/McLaren (SA)	Axle
		GT40-Amon/Bucknum/ Hill/McLaren (SA)	8th
6/19–20/65	Le Mans 24 Hours	GT40-Bondurant/Maglioli	Engine
		GT40-(open)-Trintignant/ Ligier (FF)	Transmission
		GT40-Mueller/Bucknum (SA)	Engine
		GT40-Whitmore/Ireland (JW)	Engine
		Mk. I-Miles/McLaren (SA)	Transmission
		Mk. I-Hill/Amon (SA)	Slave Cylinder

1965 Summary: Started—15 cars. Finished—5.
All GT40s with exception of the Hill/McLaren original car at Nürburg were powered by 289-inch engines. The exception had a 325-inch version of the same engine (Bondurant/Maglioli and Mueller/Bucknum also practiced with the 325 at Le Mans, but raced with the 289). The Mk. IIs were equipped with 427-inch engines (single four-barrel carburetor).

2/5–6/66	Daytona 24 Hours	Mk. II-Miles/Ruby (SA)	1st
		Mk. II-Gurney/Grant (SA)	2nd
		Mk. II-Hansgen/Dono- hue (HM)	3rd
		Mk. II-McLaren/Amon (SA)	5th
		Mk. II-Ginther/Bucknum (HM)	Transmission (automatic)

3/26/66	Sebring 12 Hours	Xl-(open)-Miles/Ruby (SA)	1st
		Mk. II-Hansgen/Donohue (HM)	2nd
		Mk. II-Bucknum/Foyt (HM)	12th
		Mk. II-Gurney/Grant (SA)	Engine
		GT40-G. Hill/Stewart (AM)	Engine
		GT40-Gardner/Whitmore (AM)	Clutch
5/22/66	Spa 1,000 Km.	Mk. II-Gardner /Whitmore (AM)	2nd
6/18–19/66	Le Mans 24 Hours	Mk. II-McLaren/Amon (SA)	1st
		Mk. II-Miles/Hulme (SA)	2nd
		Mk. II-Bucknum/Hutcherson (HM)	3rd
		Mk. II-Gurney/Grant (SA)	Engine
		Mk. II-Hawkins/Donohue (HM)	Transmission
		Mk. II-G Hill/Muir (AM)	Suspension
		Mk. II-Whitmore/Gardner (AM)	Transmission
		Mk. II-Andretti/Bianchi	Engine

1966 Summary: Started—20 cars. Finished—11.

All cars except the two GT40s entered at Sebring were equipped with 427-inch engines (single four-barrel carburetor). The two GT40s had the same 289-inch engine with four double-choke carburetors as employed the previous season and now used by private entrants.

2/4–5/67	Daytona 24 Hours	Mk. II- McLaren/Bianchi (SA)	7th
		Mk. II-Gurney/Foyt (SA)	Engine
		Mk. II-Ruby/Hulme (HM)	Transmission

		Mk. II-Donohue/Revson (HM)	Transmission
		Mk. II-Andretti/Ginther (HM)	Transmission
		Mk. II-Bucknum/Gardner (SA)	Transmission
4/1/67	Sebring 12 Hours	Mk. IV-McLaren/Andretti (SA)	1st
		Mk. II-Foyt/Ruby (HM)	2nd
6/10–11/67	Le Mans 24 Hours	Mk. IV-Gurney/Foyt (SA)	1st
		Mk. IV-McLaren/Donohue (SA)	4th
		Mk. IV-Andretti/ Bianchi (HM)	Accident
		Mk. IV-Ruby/Hulme (HM)	Accident
		Mk. II-Gardner/McCluskey (HM)	Accident
		Mk. II-Schlesser/Ligier (HM)	Accident
		Mk. II-Hawkins/Bucknum (SA)	Engine

1967 Summary: Started—15 cars. Finished—5
All cars were equipped with two-carburetor versions of the 427-inch engine.

Note: The term "factory sponsored entries" in this summary, means cars in which the Ford Motor Company had a prime interest, even though all the races in the table are not necessarily manufacturers championship events (e.g., Rheims and Nassau, 1964). The table does not include any private entries which may have received partial help from the company, nor does it include the Mark II which was turned over to Ford-France after Le Mans 1967 and run by that branch of the company in several European races. Additionally, it should be noted that in the years 1964 and 1965 the Ford Motor Company was one step removed from a direct supervisory interest in the cars. During that period, 24 cars started and five finished. In the years 1966–67, when factory personnel were overseers and all engines were prepared in Dearborn, the record was 35 starts, 16 finishes and five victories in seven races.

GT PROTOTYPE SUMMARY

Four-year Totals: Races entered—17. Wins—6.
Cars entered—59. Cars finished—21.

By Vehicle Type:

	Started	Finished	Wins
GT40	24	5	1
Mk. I	2	0	0
X1	1	1	1
Mk. II	27	12	2
Mk. IV	5	3	2

By Engine Type:

	Started	Finished	Wins
256 cu. in.	6	0	0
289 cu. in.	17	5	1
325 cu. in.	1	0	0
427 cu. in.	35	16	5

Reasons for Retirement:

Transmission	13	(4 Colotti, 1 ZF, 8 Ford)
Engine	10	(1-256 cu. in., 4-289 cu. in., 5-427 cu. in.)
Suspension	6	(5 GT40, 1 Mk. II)
Accident	5	(1 GT40, 2 Mk. II, 2 Mk. IV)
Clutch	1	(GT40)
Slave Cylinder	1	(Mk. I)
Fire	1	(GT40)
Axle	1	(GT40)

TOTAL 38

Note: Reason given for retirement is *final* reason; car may have had difficulty with other components before eventual demise.

By Team:

	Started	Finished	Wins
Shelby American*	28	15	6
Holman-Moody	15	5	0
John Wyer	10	0	0
Alan Mann	5	1	0
Ford-France	1	0	0

*Shelby American was only team to operate both independently and under direct factory supervision; team was 13-5-1 under the first arrangement, and 15-10-5 under the later setup.

GT Prototype Drivers
(Factory Sponsored Entries)

Driver	Races	Finished	Placings
Bruce McLaren	13	8	(1st (2), 2nd, 3rd, 4th, 5th, 7th, 8th)
Ken Miles	7	6	(1st (3), 2nd (2), 3rd)
Lloyd Ruby	6	4	(1st (3), 2nd)
Chris Amon	5	3	(1st, 5th, 8th)
A.J. Foyt	4	3	(1st, 2nd, 12th)
Ronnie Bucknum	7	3	(3rd, 5th, 12th)
Mark Donohue	5	3	(2nd, 3rd, 4th)
Dan Gurney	5	2	(1st, 2nd)
Walt Hansgen	2	2	(2nd, 3rd)
Mario Andretti	4	1	(1st)
Denis Hulme	3	1	(2nd)
Frank Gardner	5	1	(2nd)
John Whitmore	5	1	(2nd)
Jerry Grant	3	1	(2nd)
Richie Ginther	6	1	(3rd)
Bob Bondurant	3	1	(3rd)
Dick Hutcherson	1	1	(3rd)
Lucien Bianchi	3	1	(7th)
Phil Hill	7	1	(8th)

Following drivers failed to finish (number of races entered in parenthesis): Jo Schlesser (3), Dick Attwood (2), Masten Gregory (2), Umberto Maglioli (2), Guy Ligier (2), Graham Hill (2), Paul Hawkins (2), Maurice Trintignant (1), Herbert Mueller (1), Innes Ireland (1), Jackie Stewart (1), Brian Muir (1), Peter Revson (1), Roger McCluskey (1).

Note: McLaren, Phil Hill, Amon and Bucknum, who shared eighth-place car at Nürburgring 1,000 Kilometers 6/1/65, are all given credit for finishing. Amon and Bucknum started in car and were relieved by Hill and McLaren when their original car retired.

U.S. AUTO CLUB—1962 RESULTS
Stock Car Division

Ford—10 Pontiac—10 Mercury—1 Chevrolet—1
a. Ford-Mercury individual winners:

Ford

Norm Nelson—4 (Clermont, Ind., 4/29; Schererville, Ind., 7/7, 8/4; Milwaukee, 9/16).

Don White—2 (Milwaukee, 7/15, 8/16).

Bill Cheesebourg—2 (Clovis, Calif., 3/4; Langhorne, Pa., 5/6).
A.J. Foyt—1 (Gardena, Calif., 2 /25).
Troy Ruttman—1 (Riverside, Calif., 3/18).

Mercury

Troy Ruttman—1 (Schererville, Ind., 9/30).
b. Champion—Paul Goldsmith, Pontiac (entered 20 races, won eight, second three times). Runner-up: Don White, Ford (entered 21 races, won two, second seven times, third five times).
c. Pike's Peak Hillclimb—Curtis Turner (Ford), 14:55.5.

U.S. AUTO CLUB—1963 RESULTS
Stock Car Division

Plymouth—6 Ford—5 Mercury—4 Pontiac—1
a. Ford-Mercury individual winners:

Ford

Curtis Turner—2 (Meadowdale, Ill., 7/28; Springfield, Ill., 8/25).
A.J. Foyt—1 (Indianapolis Fairgrounds, 9/4).
Bill Cheesebourg—1 (Concord, N.C., 3/3).
Don White—1 (Milwaukee, 7/14).

Mercury

Parnelli Jones—3 (Milwaukee, 8/11, 8/15, 9/15).
Elmer Musgrave—1 (Schererville, Ind., 6/23).
b. Champion—Don White, Ford (entered 16 races, won one, placed second in three, fourth in four). Runner-up was A.J. Foyt with four wins (three in Plymouths).
c. Pike's Peak Hillclimb—Parnelli Jones (Mercury), 14:17.4. Runner-up: Curtis Turner (Ford), 14:20.3.

U.S. AUTO CLUB—1964 RESULTS
Stock Car Division

Mercury—7 Dodge—4 Ford—2 Plymouth—2
a. Ford-Mercury individual winners:

Mercury

Parnelli Jones—7 (Castle Rock, Colo., 6/28; Milwaukee, 7/12, 8/16, 8/20—with Rodger Ward, 9/20: Wentzville, Mo., 10/4; Gardena, Calif. 11/14)

Ford

Fred Lorenzen—1 (Clermont, Ind., 5/3).
Bobby Marshman—1 (Springfield, Ill., 8/30).
b. Champion—Parnelli Jones, Mercury (entered 14 races, won seven, placed second in two, fourth in one).
c. Pike's Peak Hillclimb—Parnelli Jones (Mercury), 13:52.2.

U.S. AUTO CLUB—1965 RESULTS
Stock Car Division

Plymouth—11   Ford—2   Dodge—2   Mercury—1
a. Ford-Mercury individual winners:
Ford
A.J. Foyt—1 (Indianapolis Fairgrounds, 9/7).
Don White—1 (Wentzville, Mo., 10/10).
Mercury
Rodger Ward—1 (Gardena, Calif., 12/6/64).
b. Champion—Norm Nelson, Plymouth (entered 16 races, won six, placed second in five).
c. Pike's Peak Hillclimb—Nick Sanborn (Plymouth), 14:17.7. Runner-up: Parnelli Jones (Mercury), 14:19.9.

U.S. AUTO CLUB—1966 RESULTS
Stock Car Division

Plymouth—9   Dodge—8
a. Champions—Norm Nelson, Plymouth (entered 17 races, won seven, placed second in six, third in two, fourth in two).
b. Pike's Peak Hillclimb—Nick Sanborn (Oldsmobile), 14:30.6.

U.S. AUTO CLUB—1967 RESULTS
Stock Car Division

Ford—9   Dodge—9   Plymouth—4
a. Ford individual winners:
   Jack Bowsher—4 (Marne, Mich., 6/9 twice; Chicago, 6/22; Milwaukee, 8/13).
   Parnelli Jones—3(Clermont, Ind., 5/27; Mosport, Canada, 6/29; Milwaukee, 8/17).
   Mario Andretti—1 (Mosport, 6/29).
   A J. Foyt—1 (Milwaukee, 9/17).
b. Champion—Don White, Dodge (entered 22 races, won nine).
c. Pike's Peak Hillclimb—Bill Daniels (Chevrolet), 14:56.0.
d. Seven of the races were held on the three-eighths mile oval at Soldier Field, Chicago. Plymouths and Dodges won eight of these. Of the 15 non-Chicago events, Fords won eight.
e. There were two 125-mile races on 6/29 at Mosport, Jones winning one, Andretti the other.

USAC Winning Drivers, 1956–67
Stock Car Division

Norm Nelson—29	Jack Bowsher—4	Curtis Turner—2
Don White—27	Marshall Teague—3	Bobby Isaac—2
Paul Goldsmith—26	Johnny Mantz—3	Bud Moneymaker—1
Parnelli Jones—13	Jimmy Bryan—3	George Seeger—1
Fred Lorenzen—12	Mike Klapak—3	Jim Rathmann—1
A.J. Foyt—11	Tony Bettenhausen—3	Sherman Utsman—1
Troy Ruttman—7	Bill Cheesebourg—3	Frankie Schneider—1
Les Snow—7	Jim Hurtubise—3	Harold Smith—1
Nelson Stacy—5	Pat Flaherty—2	Bobby Marshman—1
Sam Hanks—5	Elmer Musgrave—2	Joe Leonard—1
Rodger Ward—4	Eddie Sachs—2	Sal Tovella—1
Jerry Unser—4	Len Sutton—2	Mario Andretti—1
Ralph Moody—4	Whitey Gerken—2	

Note—Does not include Pike's Peak.

Ford Motor Company Individual Winners, 1956–1967:
Ford

Fred Lorenzen—12	Jack Bowsher—4	Eddie Sachs—2
DonWhite—10	Mike Klapak—3	Curtis Turner—2
Norm Nelson—9	Tony Bettenhausen—3	George Seeger—1
Troy Ruttman—4	Bill Cheesebourg—3	Sherman Utsman—1
Jerry Unser—4	Parnelli Jones—3	Bobby Marshman—1
Ralph Moody—4	Johnny Mantz—2	Mario Andretti—1
A.J. Foyt—4	Rodger Ward—2	

Mercury

Parnelli Jones—10	Troy Ruttman—2	Elmer Musgrave—1
Sam Hanks—5	Johnny Mantz—1	Rodger Ward—1
Jimmy Bryan—3	Norm Nelson—1	

USAC

STOCK CAR DIVISION RACES WON BY MAKE OF CAR, 1956–1967

	1956	1957	1958	1959	1960	1961	1962	1963	1964	1965	1966	1967	TOTAL
Ford	4	12	6	10	8	7	10	5	2	2	—	9	75
Plymouth	—	—	—	—	—	—	—	6	2	11	9	4	32
Pontiac	—	—	—	2	1	14	10	1	—	—	—	—	28
Mercury	4	4	3	—	—	—	1	4	7	1	—	—	24
Dodge	—	—	—	—	—	—	—	—	4	2	8	9	23
Chevrolet	11	—	3	5	—	1	1	—	—	—	—	—	21
Total Races	19	16	12	17	9	22	22	16	15	16	17	22	203

NASCAR—1962 RESULTS
Grand National Division

Pontiac—22 Chevrolet—14 Plymouth—11 Ford—6
a. Ford individual winners:
   Nelson Stacy—3 (Darlington, 5/12; Charlotte, 5/27; Martinsville, Va., 9/23).
   Fred Lorenzen—2 (Atlanta, 6/10; Augusta, Ga., 9/13).
   Larry Frank—1 (Darlington, 9/3).
b. Grand National champion—Joe Weatherly, Pontiac (nine victories in 52 starts, 39 finishes in top five, 45 in top 10).

NASCAR—1963 RESULTS
Grand National Division

Ford—23 Plymouth—19 Chevrolet—8 Pontiac—4 Mercury—1
a. Ford-Mercury individual winners:
                    Mercury
   Darel Dieringer—1 (Riverside, Calif., 11/3).
                      Ford
   Ned Jarrett—8 (Augusta, Ga., 4/4; Richmond, Va., 5/19, 9/8; Myrtle Beach, S.C., 7/7; Savannah, Ga., 7/10; Asheville, N.C., 7/14; Spartanburg, S.C., 8/14; Moyock, N.C., 9/24).
   Fred Lorenzen—6 (Atlanta, 3/17; Charlotte, 6/2; Bristol, Tenn., 7/28; Weaverville, N.C., 8/11; Huntington, W. Va., 8/18; Martinsville, Va., 9/22).
   Fireball Roberts—4 (Bristol, 3/31; Daytona, 7/4; Old Bridge, N.J., 7/19; Darlington, 9/2).
   Dan Gurney—1 (Riverside, 1/20).
   Tiny Lund—1 (Daytona, 2/24).
   Jimmy Pardue—1 (Moyock, 7/11).
   Glen Wood—1 (Winston-Salem, N.C., 7/13).
   Marvin Panch—1 (N. Wilkesboro, N.C., 9/29).
b. Grand National champion—Joe Weatherly, Pontiac-Mercury (Three victories in 53 starts, 20 finishes in top five, 35 in top 10; drove Mercury at end of season. All wins with Pontiac).
c. Lorenzen became first stock car driver to top $100,000 mark, starting 29 races, winning six, finishing in top five 21 times with his car earning $113,750 in prize money. This was also year a professional golfer first topped $100,000 in prize money, Arnold Palmer receiving $101,555. Roberts, whose car earned $67,320, entered 20 races, won four, finished in top five total of 11 times.
d. Richard Petty won 14 of the 19 Plymouth victories. Lost title to Weatherly on last day; Junior Johnson accounted for seven of the eight Chevrolet wins.
e. Fords earned 51 per cent of the total prize money paid in NASCAR's Grand National Division during the season.

NASCAR—1964 RESULTS
Grand National Division

Ford—30 Dodge—14 Plymouth—12 Mercury—5 Chevrolet—1
a. Ford-Mercury individual winners:

Ford

Ned Jarrett—15 (Concord, N.C., 11/10/63; Spartanburg, S.C., 4/14; Columbia, S.C., 4/16; Hampton, Va., 5/15; Hickory, N.C., 5/16; Asheville, N.C., 5/31; Atlanta, 6/7; Birmingham, 6/21; Manassas, Va., 7/8, 9/18; Weaverville, N.C., 8/9; Moyock, N.C., 8/13; Hillsboro, N.C., 9/20; Savannah, Ga., 10/9; Jacksonville, N.C., 11/8).

Fred Lorenzen—8 (Bristol, Tenn., 3/22, 7/26; Atlanta, 4/5; N. Wilkesboro, 4/19; Martinsville, 4/26, 9/27; Darlington, 5/9, Charlotte, 10/18).

Marvin Panch—3 (Winston-Salem, N.C., 3/30; Weaverville, 4/11; N. Wilkesboro, 10/11).

Junior Johnson—2 (Winston-Salem, 8/22; Roanoke, Va., 8/23).

Fireball Roberts—1 (Augusta, Ga., road course, 11/17/63).

Dan Gurney—1 (Riverside, 1/19).

Mercury

Billy Wade—4 (Old Bridge, N.J., 7/10; Bridgehampton, N.Y., 7/12; Islip, N.Y., 7/15; Watkins Glen, N.Y., 7/19).

Darel Dieringer—1 (Augusta, 11/1).

b. Grand National champion—Richard Petty, Plymouth (nine wins in 61 starts, 37 finishes in top five, 43 in top 10).

c. Petty was biggest individual money winner with his car earning $98,810.
Lorenzen, whose vehicle earned $72,385, started 16 NASCAR events, won eight and finished in top five 10 times. Jarrett won $63,330, winning 15 of 59 starts and placing in top five 40 times.

d. Only non-Ford or Chrysler victory in 1964 season was Wendell Scott's win at Jacksonville, Fla., 12/1/63, in a Chevrolet; this also marked the first NASCAR win for an African-American driver.

e. IMCA and ARCA championships also went to Ford drivers, Dick Hutcherson winning the former (and finishing first in 29 races), Jack Bowsher taking the latter.

f. Lorenzen's victories included three of the nine major races, plus five of the six important races at Bristol, Martinsville and North Wilkesboro. In the one he didn't win, he was second.

NASCAR—1965 RESULTS
Grand National Division

Ford—48 Plymouth—4 Dodge—2 Mercury—1
a. Ford-Mercury individual winners:

Mercury

Darel Dieringer—1 (Daytona, 2/12).

Ford

Junior Johnson—13 (Daytona, 2/12; Richmond, Va., 3/7; N. Wilkesboro, N.C., 4/18, 10/3; Bristol, Tenn., 5/2; Darlington, 5/8; Winston-Salem, N.C., 5/15, 8/28; Hickory, N.C., 5/16; Asheville, N.C., 5/29; Manassas, Va., 7/8; Old Bridge, N.J., 7/9; Martinsville, Va., 9/26).

Ned Jarrett—13 (Spartanburg, S.C., 2/27, 8/14; Weaverville, N.C., 2/28; Hillsborough, N.C., 3/14; Hampton, Va., 5/14; Shelby, N.C., 5/27, 8/5; Harris, N.C., 5/30; Birmingham, 6/6; Bristol, 7/25; Beltsville, Md., 8/25; Darlington, 9/6; Moyock, N.C., 11/7).

Dick Hutcherson—9 (Greenville, S.C., 4/17, 6/19; Nashville, 6/3; Myrtle Beach, S.C., 6/24; Maryville, Tenn., 8/13; Augusta, Ga., 8/15: Moycock, 8/24; New Oxford, Pa., 9/14; Hillsborough, 10/24).

Fred Lorenzen—4 (Daytona, 2/14; Martinsville, 4/25; Charlotte, 5/23, 10/17).

Marvin Panch—4 (Atlanta, 4/11, 6/13; Islip, N.Y., 7/14; Watkins Glen, N.Y., 7/18).

Dan Gurney—1 (Riverside, 1/17).

Tiny Lund—1 (Columbia, S.C., 4/28).

Cale Yarborough—1 (Valdosta, Ga., 6/27).

A.J. Foyt—1 (Daytona, 7/4).

Curtis Turner—1 (Rockingham, N.C., 10/3).

a. Grand National champion—Ned Jarrett (54 starts, 13 victories, 42 finishes in top five. Runner-up was Hutcherson, with 52 starts, nine wins, 32 finishes in top five).

b. Jarrett's car was leading money winner with $77,966, one dollar more than Lorenzen, who started 17 times, won four races, placed in top five a total of five times, and for second straight year won three of the nine major events.

c. Richard Petty was responsible for all four Plymouth wins, David Pearson for both Dodge victories.

d. Hillsborough, N.C., is same town as previous Hillsboro; spelling was changed between 1964 and 1965 seasons.

NASCAR—1966 RESULTS
Grand National Division

Dodge—18 Plymouth—16 Ford—10 Chevrolet—3 Mercury—2
a. Ford-Mercury individual winners:

Ford

Dick Hutcherson—3 (Bristol, Tenn., 3/20; Hillsborough, N.C., 9/18; N. Wilkesboro, N.C., 10/2).

Fred Lorenzen—2 (Martinsville, Va., 9/25; Rockingham, N.C., 10/30).

Elmo Langley—2 (Spartanburg, S.C., 6/4: Manassas, Va., 7/7).

Dan Gurney—1 (Riverside, 1/23).

Darel Dieringer—1 (Monroe, N.C., 5/13).

Tiny Lund—1 (Beltsville, Md., 6/15).

Mercury

Darel Dieringer—2 (Weaverville, N.C., 8/21; Darlington, 9/5).
b. Grand National champion—David Pearson, Dodge (42 starts, 15 wins, 26 finishes in top five). Petty, third in standings, accounted for eight of the Plymouth wins.
c. Ford's total included four of last five races on calendar. Four of the other wins were by 1964-model cars running on minor tracks (scored by independents in mid-season).
d. Dieringer's Comet which won Southern "500" was running as an independent, owner Bud Moore receiving only partial support.

NASCAR—1967 RESULTS
Grand National Division

Plymouth—31   Ford—10   Dodge—5   Chevrolet—3
a. Ford individual winners:
    Dick Hutcherson—2 (Maryville, Tenn., 7/27; Atlanta, 8/6).
    Cale Yarborough—2 (Atlanta, 4/2; Daytona, 7/4).
    Bobby Allison—2 (Rockingham, N.C., 10/29; Weaverville, N.C., 11/5).
    Mario Andretti—1 (Daytona, 2/26).
    Parnelli Jones—1 (Riverside, 1/29).
    Fred Lorenzen—1 (Daytona, 2/24).
    Darel Dieringer—1 (N. Wilkesboro, N.C., 4/16).
b. Grand National champion—Richard Petty (48 starts, 27 wins, 41 finishes in top 10, total earnings of $130,275).
c. Ford victory total included six of the 11 major races.

NASCAR Winners, 1949–1967
Grand National Division

Richard Petty—75	Rex White—26	Bobby Allison—9
Lee Petty—60	Jim Paschal—25	Paul Goldsmith—9
Ned Jarrett—50	Joe Weatherly—24	Cotton Owens—9
Junior Johnson—50	Jack Smith—21	Marshall Teague—7
Herb Thomas—49	Fonty Flock— 19	Bob Welborn—7
Buck Baker—46	Speedy Thompson—20	Jim Reed—7
Tim Flock—40	Curtis Turner—17	Darel Dieringer—7
Fireball Roberts—32	Marvin Panch—17	Ralph Moody—5
David Pearson—30	Dick Hutcherson—14	
Fred Lorenzen—26	Dick Rathmann—13	

Bob Flock, Hershel McGriff, Lloyd Dane, Eddie Pagan, Eddie Gray, Glen Wood, Nelson Stacy, Dan Gurney, Billy Wade, Lee Roy Yarbrough, 4 each.

Dick Linder, Frank Mundy, Bill Blair, Tiny Lund, Parnelli Jones, Cale Yarborough, 3 each.

NASCAR

GRAND NATIONAL DIVISION RACES WON BY MAKE OF CAR, 1949–1967

Cars	'49	'50	'51	'52	'53	'54	'55	'56	'57	'58	'59	'60	'61	'62	'63	'64	'65	'66	'67	Total
Ford	—	1	—	—	—	—	2	14	27	16	10	15	7	6	23	30	48	10	10	219
Plymouth	1	4	2	3	—	—	—	—	—	—	9	8	3	11	19	12	4	16	31	123
Chevrolet	—	—	—	—	—	—	2	3	19	22	13	13	11	14	8	1	—	3	3	112
Oldsmobile	6	10	20	3	9	11	10	1	5	9	5	—	—	—	—	—	—	—	—	89
Hudson	—	—	12	27	22	17	1	—	—	—	—	—	—	—	—	—	—	—	—	79
Pontiac	—	—	—	—	—	—	—	—	2	3	1	7	30	22	4	—	2	—	—	69
Dodge	—	—	—	—	6	1	1	11	—	—	—	1	—	—	—	14	—	18	5	59
Chrysler	—	—	1	1	—	7	27	22	—	—	—	—	1	—	—	—	—	—	—	59
Mercury	—	2	2	—	—	—	—	5	—	—	—	—	—	—	1	5	1	2	—	18
T-Bird	—	—	—	—	—	—	—	—	—	—	6	—	—	—	—	—	—	—	—	6
Lincoln	2	2	—	—	—	—	—	—	—	—	—	—	—	—	—	—	—	—	—	4
Studebaker	—	—	3	—	—	—	—	—	—	—	—	—	—	—	—	—	—	—	—	3
Buick	—	—	—	—	—	—	2	—	—	—	—	—	—	—	—	—	—	—	—	2
Nash	—	—	1	—	—	—	—	—	—	—	—	—	—	—	—	—	—	—	—	1
Total Races	9	19	41	34	37	36	45	56	53	50	44	44	52	53	55	62	55	49	49	843

Red Byron, Gober Sosebee, Danny Letner, Billy Myers, Marvin Porter, Johnny Beauchamp, Tom Pistone, Bobby Johns, Emanuel Zervakis, Jimmy Pardue, A.J. Foyt, Elmo Langley, Gwyn Staley, 2 each.

Jim Roper, Jack White, Harold Kite, Bill Rexford, Johnny Mantz, Leon Sales, Lloyd Moore, Lou Figaro, Jimmy Floria, Tommy Thompson, Neil Cole, M. Burke, Danny Weinberg, Bill Norton, Buddy Shuman, Dick Passwater, Al Keller, John Soares, Chuck Stevenson, Johnny Kieper, Royce Hagerty, Art Watts, Bill Amick, Danny Graves, Frankie Schneider, Shorty Rollins, Joe Eubanks, John Rostek, Joe Lee Johnson, Jim Cook, Bob Burdick, Johnny Allen, Larry Frank, Johnny Rutherford, Wendell Scott, Bobby Isaac, Sam McQuagg, Paul Lewis, Earl Balmer, Jim Hurtubise, Mario Andretti, Buddy Baker, Norm Nelson, Whitey Norman, Harlan Richardson, 1 each.

Ford Motor Company
NASCAR Grand National Division Race Winners, 1949–1967

Ford

Ned Jarrett—43	Eddie Gray—4	A.J. Foyt—1
Fred Lorenzen—26	Eddie Pagan—4	Jimmy Pardue—1
Junior Johnson—26	Paul Goldsmith—4	Larry Frank—1
Fireball Roberts—18	Tiny Lund—3	John Rostek—1
Marvin Panch—14	Cale Yarborough—3	Chuck Stevenson—1
Dick Hutcherson—14	Parnelli Jones—3	Art Watts—1
Ralph Moody—5	Speedy Thompson—3	Bill Amick— 1
Curtis Turner—5	Darel Dieringer—2	Whitey Norman—1
Jim Reed—5	Elmo Langley—2	Shorty Rollins—1
Dan Gurney—4	Bobby Allison—2	Jimmy Floria—1
Glen Wood—4	Marvin Porter—2	Buck Baker—1
Nelson Stacy—4	Lloyd Dane—2	Harlan Richardson—1
Joe Weatherly—4	Mario Andretti—1	

Mercury

Darel Dieringer—5	Tim Flock—1	Marvin Burke—1
Billy Wade—4	Lloyd Dane—1	Bill Norton—1
Billy Myers—2	Bill Blair—1	
Jim Paschal—1	Lloyd Moore—1	

Thunderbird

Curtis Turner—2	Johnny Beauchamp—1
Tom Pistone—2	Cotton Owens—1

Lincoln

Jim Roper—1	Harold Kite—1
Jack White—1	Tim Flock—1

NASCAR MAJOR RACE SUMMARY, 1949–1967
Grand National Division

DAYTONA (1st race 1949; 1st Speedway race 1959)	*Beach Races* (160 miles)	*Daytona "500"*	*Firecracker "400"* (250 until 1963)
	Chrysler 3	Ford 3	Pontiac 4
	Hudson 2	Pontiac 2	Ford 3
	Oldsmobile 2	Plymouth 2	Dodge 2
	Pontiac 2	Oldsmobile 1	
	Lincoln 1	Chevrolet 1	

DARLINGTON (1st race, 1950)		*Southern "500"*	*Rebel "400"* (300 until 1966; 1st race, 1957)
		Ford 5	Ford 7
		Chevrolet 4	Plymouth 2
		Oldsmobile 2	Pontiac 1
		Hudson 2	Chevrolet 1
		Plymouth 2	
		Mercury 1	
		Pontiac 1	
		Dodge 1	

ATLANTA (1st race, 1960)		*Atlanta "500"*	*Dixie "500"* (300 in 1960, then 400 until 1966)
		Ford 5	Ford 4[a]
		Pontiac 2	Pontiac 2
		Plymouth 1	Chevrolet 2
			Plymouth 1

CHARLOTTE (1st race, 1960)		*World "600"*	*National "500"* (400 until 1966)
		Ford 3	Ford 3
		Plymouth 3	Pontiac 2
		Pontiac 1	Dodge 2
		Chevrolet 1	Chevrolet 1

RIVERSIDE (1st race, 1963)		*Riverside "500"*	*Golden State "400"* (1963 only)
		Ford 5	Mercury 1

ROCKINGHAM (1st race, fall 1965)		*Peach Blossom "500"* Plymouth 2	*American "500"* Ford 3

a—Total includes 250-mile race held in 1961 only.

Totals: Seven tracks, 101 races—
Ford—41
Pontiac—17
Plymouth—13
Chevrolet—10
Dodge—5
Oldsmobile—5
Hudson—4
Chrysler—3
Mercury—2
Lincoln—1

Note: Major races are those on the "super speedways" designed and built especially for stock car events at Daytona, Darlington, Atlanta, Charlotte and Rockingham, plus the prestige races on the beach-road course at Daytona and the road circuit at Riverside.

NASCAR Grand National Division
Major Race Winners, 1949–1967

Fred Lorenzen—12 (Ford)

Fireball Roberts—9 (Pontiac 4, Ford 3, Chevrolet 2)

Richard Petty—7 (Plymouth)

Junior Johnson—5 (Chevrolet 3, Ford, Pontiac)

Dan Gurney—4 (Ford)

Marvin Panch—4 (Ford 2, Pontiac, Plymouth)

Nelson Stacy—3 (Ford)

Curtis Turner—3 (Ford)

Herb Thomas—3 (Hudson 2, Chevrolet)

Buck Baker—3 (Oldsmobile, Pontiac, Dodge)

Joe Weatherly—3 (Pontiac 2, Ford)

David Pearson—3 (Pontiac)

Marshall Teague—2 (Hudson)

Lee Petty—2 (Chrysler, Oldsmobile)

Tim Flock—2 (Chrysler)

Paul Goldsmith—2 (Pontiac, Plymouth)

Ned Jarrett—2 (Ford)

A.J. Foyt—2 (Dodge, Ford)

Jim Paschal—2 (Plymouth)

Speedy Thompson—2 (Ford, Chevrolet)

Darel Dieringer—2 (Mercury)

Cale Yarborough—2 (Ford)

Red Byron (Oldsmobile), Harold Kite (Lincoln), Bill Blair (Oldsmobile), Cotton Owens (Pontiac), Bobby Johns (Pontiac), Bob Burdick (Pontiac), Jim Hurtubise (Plymouth), Rex White (Chevrolet), Tiny Lund (Ford), Jack Smith (Pontiac), Sam McQuagg (Dodge), Joe Lee Johnson (Chevrolet), Lee Roy Yarbrough (Dodge), Johnny Mantz (Plymouth), Fonty Flock (Oldsmobile), Jim Reed (Chevrolet), Larry Frank (Ford), Parnelli Jones (Ford), Mario Andretti (Ford), Dick Hutcherson (Ford), Buddy Baker (Dodge), Bobby Allison (Ford), 1 each.

Most Successful Ford Motor Company Drivers, Major NASCAR Races,
1949–1967:

Ford

Fred Lorenzen—12	Ned Jarrett—2	Joe Weatherly—1
Dan Gurney—4	Cale Yarborough—2	Junior Johnson—1
Fireball Roberts—3	Tiny Lund—1	Dick Hutcherson—1
Curtis Turner—3	A.J. Foyt—1	Mario Andretti—1
Nelson Stacy—3	Speedy Thompson—1	Parnelli Jones—1
Marvin Panch—2	Larry Frank—1	Bobby Allison—1

Mercury

Darel Dieringer—2

Lincoln

Harold Kite—1

PHOTO CREDITS

P. 5, Courtesy of the Ford Archives, Henry Ford Museum, Dearborn, Mich. Pp. 8, 14, 15, 16, 17, Ford Archives. P. 19, Museum of Speed, Daytona Beach, Fla. P. 24, Courtesy of NASCAR. Pp. 26, 35, 36, 38, 40, 43, 44, 48, 49, 52, 53, Ford Archives. P. 55, Courtesy of Petersen Publishing Co. Pp. 59, 60, Ford Archives. P. 65, Harrah's Automobile Collection. P. 66, Courtesy of Petersen Publishing Co. Pp. 67, 68, Harrah's Automobile Collection. Pp. 71, 72, Courtesy of Petersen Publishing Co. P. 73, Ford Archives. P. 76 (top), Courtesy of Indianapolis Motor Speedway; (bottom), Courtesy of *The Autocar*. P. 77, Courtesy of *The Motor*. P. 78, Underwood and Underwood. P. 80 (top), Courtesy of Indianapolis Motor Speedway; (middle and bottom), Ford Archives. P. 81, Ford Archives. P. 82, Courtesy of Indianapolis Motor Speedway. P. 83 (top), Courtesy of Indianapolis Motor Speedway; (middle and bottom), Ford Archives. Pp. 86, 87, 89, 93, Courtesy of Indianapolis Motor Speedway. P. 94 (top, middle), Ford Archives; (bottom), Courtesy of Leo Goossen. Pp. 95, 98, 99, 104, Courtesy of Indianapolis Motor Speedway. P. 106 (top), Courtesy of Maurice Gatsonides; (bottom), Courtesy of Rupert Mountain Automotive Research, Ltd. P. 107, Courtesy of Maurice Gatsonides. P. 108, Ford of Britain; P. 112, Courtesy of Petersen Publishing Co. P. 113 (top), Courtesy of Indianapolis Motor Speedway; (middle, bottom), Courtesy of George Rand. P. 114, Courtesy of George Rand; P. 115, Courtesy of Petersen Publishing Co. P. 116 (top, bottom), Courtesy of George Rand; (middle), Courtesy of Petersen Publishing Co. P. 119, Courtesy of Petersen Publishing Co. P. 123, Courtesy of Museum of Speed, Daytona Beach, Fla. Pp. 124, 126, 127, Courtesy of NASCAR. Pp. 133, 134, 135, 139, 142, Courtesy of Federico Kirbus. Pp. 145, 146, 147, 148, 149, 150, 155, 156, Courtesy of Petersen Publishing Co. P. 157, Harrah's Automobile Collection. Pp. 162, 163, Courtesy of Petersen Publishing Co. P. 169 (top), Courtesy of Bill Stroppe; (bottom), Courtesy of Bill France. P. 170 (top), Courtesy of Bill France; (bottom), Ford Photographic/Joe Farkas. P. 175 (top), Daimler-Benz AG; (bottom), Courtesy of Petersen Publishing Co. P. 176 (top), Courtesy of Petersen Publishing Co.; (bottom), Ford Photographic/Joe Farkas. P. 181, Courtesy of Petersen Publishing Co. Pp. 182, 188, Ford Photographic/Joe Farkas. Pp. 193, 197, 204, Courtesy of NASCAR. P. 205 (top), Courtesy of Mrs. E.G. Roberts, Jr.; (bottom), Courtesy of Mrs. John C. Holman. Pp. 220, 221, Courtesy of Bill Stroppe. Pp. 227, 237, 242,

Courtesy of NASCAR. P. 247 (top), Ford Photographic/Joe Farkas; (bottom), Courtesy of Petersen Publishing Co. P. 251, Courtesy of Petersen Publishing Co. P. 262, Courtesy of Fred Lorenzen; P. 263 (top), Courtesy of Fred Lorenzen; (bottom), Courtesy of NASCAR. P. 271 (top), Courtesy of Rupert Mountain Automotive Research, Ltd.; (bottom), Courtesy of NASCAR. Pp. 287, 288, Ford Photographic/Joe Farkas. Pp. 298, 299, Courtesy of All American Racers, Inc.; (inset), Ford Photographic/Joe Farkas. Pp. 304, 305, Courtesy of Indianapolis Motor Speedway. P. 306 (top), Ford Photographic/Joe Farkas; (bottom), Courtesy of Engine and Foundry Division, Ford Motor Company, Pp. 307, 312, 313, Ford Photographic/Joe Farkas. Pp. 314, 315, 316, Courtesy of Indianapolis Motor Speedway. Pp. 317, 322, 323, 324, 325, 326, 327, Ford Photographic/Joe Farkas. Pp. 350, 351, Courtesy of Indianapolis Motor Speedway. Pp. 354, 355, Ford Photographic/Joe Farkas. P. 356, Courtesy of Rupert Mountain Automotive Research, Ltd. P. 357 (top), Courtesy of Rupert Mountain Automotive Research, Ltd.; (bottom), Ford Photographic/Joe Farkas. P. 358, Ford Photographic/Joe Farkas. Pp. 360, 361, Courtesy of Indianapolis Motor Speedway. Pp. 363, 366, 367, Ford Photographic/Joe Farkas. Pp. 368, 369, 370, Courtesy of Indianapolis Motor Speedway. P. 378, Courtesy of Rupert Mountain Automotive Research, Ltd. P. 379 (top, middle), Bernard Cahier; (bottom), Ford Photographic/Joe Farkas. P. 386, Bernard Cahier. P. 387, Ford Photographic/Joe Farkas. P. 391 (top), Courtesy of Rupert Mountain Automotive Research, Ltd.; (middle, bottom), Bernard Cahier. P. 396 (top, bottom), Bernard Cahier; (middle), Ford Photographic/Joe Farkas. P. 397, Bernard Cahier. P. 406 (top, middle), Ford Photographic/Joe Farkas; (bottom), Bernard Cahier. P. 407, Ford Photographic/Joe Farkas. P. 410 (top, bottom), Bernard Cahier; (middle), Ford Photographic/Joe Farkas. P. 411, Bernard Cahier. P. 412 (top), Ford Photographic/Joe Farkas; (bottom), Bernard Cahier. P. 413, Bernard Cahier. P. 424, Courtesy of Petersen Publishing Co. Pp. 425, 432, 433, 437, Ford Photographic/Joe Farkas. P. 443 (top), Bernard Cahier; (middle, bottom), Geoffrey Goddard. P. 444, Bernard Cahier. P. 449 (top), Ford of Britain; (bottom), Bernard Cahier. P. 450 (top, middle), Bernard Cahier; (bottom), Ford of Britain. Pp. 451, 452, 455, 456, 458, 460, 461, Ford of Britain; (inset), Bernard Cahier. P. 462, Bernard Cahier; (inset), Ford of Britain. Pp. 472, 473, 483, 484, 485, 486, 492, 493, 495, Ford Photographic/Joe Farkas. P. 501 (top, bottom), Bernard Cahier; (middle), Ford Photographic/Joe Farkas. P. 502, Ford Photographic/Joe Farkas. P. 508 (top, bottom), Bernard Cahier; (middle), Ford Photographic/Joe Farkas. P. 515 (top), Jean-Pierre Bonnin; (bottom), Ford Photographic/Joe Farkas. Pp. 516, 523, 524, Ford Photographic/Joe Farkas. P. 531 (top, bottom), Ford Photographic/Joe Farkas; (middle), Bernard Cahier. P. 532, Jean-Pierre Bonnin. Pp. 534, 535, Bernard Cahier; (inset), Ford Photographic/Joe Farkas. Pp. 542, 551, Ford Photographic/Joe Farkas. P. 552 (top), Miltos Toscas; (bottom), Ford Photographic/Joe Farkas. P. 559, Miltos Toscas. P. 560, Jean-Pierre Bonnin. P. 561, Miltos Toscas. P. 562 (top, bottom), Ford Photographic/Joe Farkas; (middle), Bernard Cahier. P. 563, Bernard Cahier.

Pp. 575, 576, 585, 586, 587, 588, 589, 590, Ford Photographic/Joe Farkas. P. 599, Courtesy of Engine and Foundry Division, Ford Motor Company. P. 600 (top), Courtesy of Engine and Foundry Division, Ford Motor Company; (bottom), Ford Photographic/Joe Farkas. P. 604, Ford Photographic/Joe Farkas. P. 613 (top), Ford Photographic/Joe Farkas; (bottom), Jean-Pierre Bonnin. P. 614 (top), Miltos Toscas; (bottom), Ford Photographic/Joe Farkas. P. 619, Miltos Toscas. P. 620, Ford Photographic/Joe Farkas. Pp. 622, 623, Miltos Toscas; (inset), Bernard Cahier.

INDEX

Leonard, Joe, 344, 365, 633
Lesovsky, Lujie, 302, 400
Letner, Danny, 640
Lewis, Paul, 640
Ligier, Guy, 529, 607, 626, 627, 630
Lincoln-Mercury, 178, 184, 222, 292, 389, 435
Lindamood, Roger, 428
Linder, Dick, 640
Lindgren, Gerry, 342
Lini, Franco, 606
Littlejohn, Joe, 129, 196
Ljungfeldt, Bo, 377–378, 384, 385–388, 417
Lockhart, Frank, 63, 70, 144, 151
Locomobile, 57
Logghe Stamping, 434
Lolas, 119, 506
Long, Bondy, 480, 569, 584
Long-distance sports car racing, 291
Lorenzen, Fred, 254, 260, 264, 272, 274–275, 280, 281, 289, 466, 469, 478, 487, 489–490, 494, 569, 570, 581, 583, 592, 593, 594, 631, 633, 635, 636, 637, 638, 640, 642, 643
Lorimer, Bert, 30–31
Loste, Jacques, 564
Lotus', 289, 295, 303, 310, 318, 344, 442, 446, 521
Lozano, Roberto, 136
Lund, Tiny, 475, 592, 635, 637, 640, 642, 643
Lundberg, Bjarne, 385
Lunn, Roy, 505, 537
Lurani, Count Giovanni, 441

McAfee, Ernie, 159
McAfee, Jack, 159
McCarver, Jack, 88
McClellan, George, 33
McCluggage, Denise, 385
McCluskey, Roger, 320–328, 607, 627, 630
McCoy, Kid, 30
McCulloch, 231
MacDonald, Arthur, 7, 25

MacDonald, Dave, 177, 335, 336, 401, 409, 479
McElreath, Jim, 318, 320, 328, 346
McEwen, Tom, 436
McFee, Speed, 183
McGrath, Jack, 174, 185, 215
McGriff, Hershel, 172, 173, 640
MacKay, Joe, 216–217, 225, 233, 235, 393
MacKenzie, Doc, 122
McKenzie, Margaret, 377
McKinney, Nile, 70
McLaren, Bruce, 119, 457, 509, 539, 550, 564, 597, 625, 626, 627, 630
McLean, Bob, 544
McLemore, Henry, 122
McNally, Maria, 503
McNamara, Robert, 209, 239–240, 257, 264, 266, 272
MacPherson, E.S., 238
McQuagg, Sam, 640, 642
Macura, Joe, 303, 465, 467
Maglioli, Umberto, 186, 189, 408, 513, 527, 625, 626, 630
Mairesse, Willy, 445, 606
Makinen, Timo, 388
Mann, Alan, 385, 417, 453, 537, 625, 629
Mantz, Johnny, 167, 171, 172–173, 179, 183, 185, 199, 229, 248, 280, 633, 640, 642
Manussis, Johnny, 380
MARC circuit, 232, 274
Marimon, Domingo, 140
Marion, Milt, 21, 122
Mark II, 539, 545, 547, 596
Mark IV, 602
Marriott, Fred, 7, 27
Marshman, Bobby, 296, 320, 328, 331–332, 342, 631, 633
Martin, Ken, 349
Martin, P.E., 101
Martin, Ron, 509
Maseratis, 118
Matthews, Edwin (Banjo), 274, 469, 478
Matthias, Hans, 209, 266, 268, 537
Mays, Rex, 102, 117, 144
Mecke, Ted, 537
Menkel, Tony, 217